W9-BBL-507

READING TO LEARN IN THE CONTENT AREAS

FOURTH EDITION

Judy S. Richardson

Virginia Commonwealth University

Raymond F. Morgan

Old Dominion University

Australia • Canada • Mexico • Singapore • Spain • United Kingdom • United States

Education Editor: Dianne Lindsay
Assistant Editor: Tangelique Williams
Editorial Assistant: Keynia Johnson
Marketing Manager: Becky Tollerson
Project Editor: Trudy Brown
Print Buyer: Barbara Britton

Permissions Editor: Joohee Lee
Production Service: Matrix Productions
Copy Editor: Pat Herbst
Cover Designer: Cassandra Chu
Compositor: G&S Typesetters, Inc.
Printer/Binder: R. R. Donnelley, Crawfordsville

Printed in the United States of America

2 3 4 5 6 03 02 01 00

Library of Congress Cataloging-in-Publication Data

Richardson, Judy S., [date]
Reading to learn in the content areas / Judy S. Richardson, Raymond F. Morgan. — 4th ed.
p. cm.
Includes bibliographical references (p.) and index.
ISBN 0-534-50854-5
1. Content area reading—United States.
I. Morgan, Raymond F. II. Title.
LB1050.455.R53 1999
428'.4'0712—dc21 99-051501

This book is printed on acid-free recycled paper.

For more information, contact
Wadsworth/Thomson Learning
10 Davis Drive
Belmont, CA 94002-3098
USA
www.wadsworth.com

International Headquarters
Thomson Learning
290 Harbor Drive, 2nd Floor
Stamford, CT 06902-7477
USA

UK/Europe/Middle East
Thomson Learning
Berkshire House
168-173 High Holborn
London WC1V 7AA
United Kingdom

Asia
Thomson Learning
60 Albert Street #15-01
Albert Complex
Singapore 189969

Canada
Nelson/Thomson Learning
1120 Birchmount Road
Scarborough, Ontario M1K 5G4
Canada

*To my husband, Terry, who has always loved and supported me,
no matter how busy I tend to be, to my three sons—
Kevin, Darren, and Andrew, and to my wonderful grandchildren—
all of whom have kept me grounded in reality
when I tended to wander too far into the ivory tower.*

—Judy S. Richardson

*To Sue, Jon, and Chris—
know that you are greatly appreciated for your patience
through many writing projects that sometimes
cut short my time with my family.*

—Raymond F. Morgan

CONTENTS

CHAPTER 9 Writing to Learn in the Content Areas 282

CHAPTER 10 Study Skills and Study Systems 323

PREFACE

Who Should Read This Book?

This textbook is for anyone who wants to know how to teach students to learn by using reading and other language arts as tools for acquiring knowledge. Our book is for readers who have never studied about reading, as well as for those who have studied reading methodology but not how to apply that information to subject-area learning. This textbook is not about learning to read. It is a wide-ranging treatise that explains how teachers can use reading and writing as a vehicle for learning in any discipline.

Why Did We Write This Book?

We enjoy reading to learn new material and to augment our knowledge. That is why we have been teachers and college professors for 30-plus years. We believe in what we teach. We have a sense of humor and realize that all serious learning must be put in perspective. We have ideas about how to share the joys of reading, thinking, and learning with students of all ages. We have ideas to share with you.

Teacher preparation has been criticized. Some say teachers are not able to teach students to think critically or to teach students to complete complex tasks required to advance in college or the workplace. Some critics also say teachers learn too much content, not enough methodology. Other critics say the opposite. Many critics say teachers have learned to teach content rather than to teach students the content.

This textbook represents our ongoing effort to find positive solutions to those criticisms. We believe that if teachers learn to follow a simple instructional framework and teach strategically by using activities that demonstrate how reading can be a tool for learning, many classroom problems can be alleviated.

Special Features of This Textbook

1. Reader involvement is important. We believe that readers need to be prepared to read, need some assistance to understand, and need to be guided to reflect on their reading. So we ask readers to engage in all three steps as they read each chapter (we practice what we preach). Our text is reader-friendly: We introduce new terms first with a checklist, then within each chapter in boldface with explanation; and we maintain an informal tone to keep readers comfortable and interested.
2. We take a balanced approach, a realistic and practical treatment of reading and methodology issues, theory, research, and historical perspective. We always try to emphasize the effect of the past on the present.
3. We address teachers of primary through secondary grades. We look at reading in the classroom as a natural tool for learning, no matter what

the grade level or content area. We provide examples that show how an activity can work at different levels and in different contents.

4. We select one instructional framework, one that reflects current thought but is uniquely ours: PAR (preparation/assistance/reflection). We explain it in the first chapter and refer to it throughout the book.
5. Our organization is considerate of our readers. We present a graphic organizer at the beginning, and sometimes at the end, of each chapter. The "Preparing to Read" section, which opens each chapter, builds reader background and provides objectives. A "One-Minute Summary" provides a concise, streamlined overview of each chapter. Assistance and reflection activities provide chapter closure.
6. We use many visuals because visual literacy is the first literacy. One important visual is the "PAR Cross-Reference Guide" at the back of the book. It identifies specific activities for different content areas and grade levels.
7. We believe that reading and the other language arts work together. Just as students listen and discuss to learn, so do they read and write to learn. We integrate the communicative arts. When we describe an activity, we explore with our readers how that activity facilitates and encourages discussion, reading, and writing.
8. Ours is a strategy-based approach. When students learn about a new activity, they should understand that activity as a strategic means to aid learning. We present the activity as a way to enhance instruction and help teachers see how the activity can be both an instructional strategy and a learner strategy.
9. Our book contains several unique chapters. In Chapter 2 we discuss the affective domain of teaching, a crucial topic that often is neglected. Chapter 10 on study skills and Chapter 11 on cooperative study pay more attention to study techniques than many content textbooks do. In Chapter 12 we present ways to help the at-risk reader in the content classroom. All of these chapters offer information on the cutting edge of content-area instruction.

New to This Edition

We updated each chapter. We added new examples of the PAR Lesson Framework to Chapter 1 and present for the first time a lesson from a community college content-area classroom. Chapter 3 (Chapter 12 in the previous edition) discusses the use of multiple resources for teaching and includes a new section on technological resources as well as thematic units, trade books, and literature. Throughout this edition we emphasize the use of technology, and in every chapter a "Technology Box" describes the effective use of the Internet and computer technology.

We extensively revised the chapter (Chapter 12 in this edition) on reading and writing activities for struggling readers, second-language learners, and marginal or poor readers. Also, there is more emphasis on authentic assessment (Chapter 7), plus new coverage of topics such as constructivism, modalities of learning, and conative factors in reading.

Our revision incorporates current research and professional resources. Our goal was to maintain a theory-to-practice balance. Visuals continue to play an important part in expressing our ideas: Cartoons, diagrams, and examples are provided throughout.

Organization of This Book

The first three chapters are foundational. Chapter 1 discusses research on, and principles of, content-area instruction. In it you will discover our philosophy of teaching. Chapter 1 also gives a capsule view of the PAR framework for instruction and describes how it works in three different types of classrooms. Chapter 2 explains how to provide for an affective focus for reading to learn. Chapter 3 presents the importance of learning with multiple resources rather than reliance on only a textbook.

Chapters 4 through 7 are PAR framework chapters. Chapters 4 and 5 are *preparation* chapters, demonstrating how to determine reader background and prepare readers to study content material. Chapter 6 is an *assistance* chapter, demonstrating why and how to provide an appropriate instructional context to develop comprehension. Chapter 7 is a *reflection* chapter. It focuses on why and how to help readers think critically about their reading, extend their reading, and demonstrate knowledge of their reading. Evaluation and assessment are discussed in this chapter.

Chapters 8 through 11 demonstrate how PAR works. We show how vocabulary, writing, study skills, and cooperative learning can be used at all phases of the PAR framework.

Chapter 12 is a special application chapter pertaining to the challenge of working with students who are at risk of failure.

Instructor's Manual

The Instructor's Manual is designed to help instructors teach the class. It summarizes each chapter's main points, theories, and strategies and provides test questions. Using it, instructors will be able to assign group activities for their classes; assign individual activities to students for homework; guide students in analyzing content-area reading material; select test items for multiple-choice, true/false, and essay tests; and display our graphic organizers and vocabulary inventories for each chapter.

Section I explains the features of the Instructor's Manual. Section II contains recommendations about grouping. Section III contains preparation, assistance, and reflection activities; teaching tips on how to use the activities; and other resources that may be used in class, such as quotations, suggestions for further reading, book lists, graphic organizers, vocabulary inventories for each chapter, and test items. In Section IV we provide assignments for the course, such as guides to analyze a chapter in a content-area textbook.

Study Guide

The Study Guide, which students can purchase, presents detailed chapter outlines, extra activities, copies of the vocabulary inventories, and sample test questions.

Acknowledgments

We extend our thanks to our colleagues who encouraged us and aided and abetted us in this endeavor. We appreciate the comments of our students who used the previous edition of the book and provided useful suggestions.

We gratefully acknowledge the contributions of the reviewers, who gave us excellent suggestions throughout the writing of all editions of this text.

The support and kind assistance of our editor, Dianne Lindsay, and our production managers, Trudy Brown and Merrill Peterson, made the writing of this text a pleasant experience.

Reviewers

Larry Andrews, University of Nebraska, Lincoln; Karen Atwood, Southern Utah University; Lois A. Bader, Michigan State University; Ernest Balajthy, SUNY at Geneseo; Shirley A. Biggs, University of Pittsburgh; Timothy Blair, Texas A&M University; Larry Browning, Baylor University; Patricia N. Chrosniak, LeMoyne College; John A. Diehl, Georgia State University; Lisbeth Dixon-Krauss, University of West Florida; Jim Duggins, San Francisco State University; Lois Exendine, Oklahoma Christian College; Pat Gallagher, San Francisco State University; Barbara Guzzetti, Arizona State University; Doris Jakubek, Central Washington University; Karen Kletzing, Aurora University; Bruce Lloyd, Western Michigan University; Hollis Lowery-Moore, Sam Houston State University; James E. McGlinn, University of North Carolina, Asheville; Daniel L. Pearce, Texas A&M at Corpus Christi; T. Gail Pritchard, The University of Alabama; Elaine C. Stephens, Saginaw Valley State University; Roger Steward, University of Wyoming; Katherine Weisendanger, Alfred University; and Terrell A. Young, Washington State University

CHAPTER 1

Processes and Principles of Content-Reading Instruction

To know how to suggest is the art of teaching.

—Anonymous

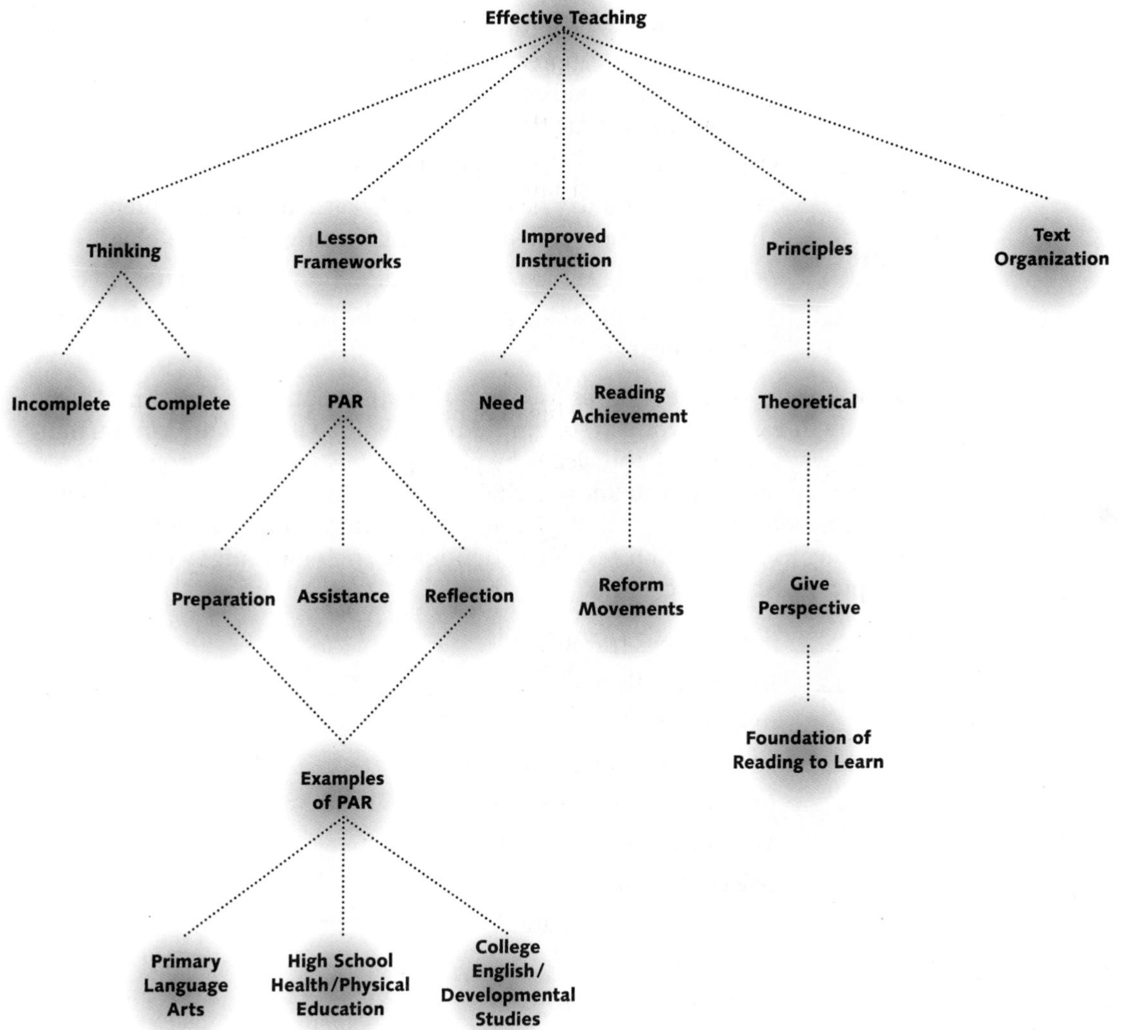

Preparing to Read

1. Check the statements with which you agree. Read the chapter carefully to see which of the statements are true.

   ______ Good students will learn without the benefit of a teacher and sometimes in spite of a teacher.

   ______ Reading after the elementary grades should be taught by English teachers.

   ______ The main goal of education is to guide students to become independent in their learning habits.

   ______ Teachers who can articulate their beliefs are in a good position to improve their instruction.

   ______ Dependent learners are crippled intellectually.

   ______ Most teachers today have a broad background in the content aras and liberal arts, as well as sufficient training in methodology.

   ______ Achievement levels are rising in our nation's public schools.

   ______ Sixty percent of America's high school seniors read at or above the sixth-grade level.

2. Following is a list of terms used in this chapter. Some may be familiar to you in a general context, but in this chapter they may be used in unfamiliar ways. Rate your knowledge by placing a plus sign (+) in front of those you are sure that you know, a check mark (✓) in front of those you have some knowledge about, and a zero (0) in front of those you don't know. Be ready to locate and pay special attention to their meanings when they are presented in the chapter.

   ______ autonomous learners

   ______ incomplete thinking

   ______ fix-up strategies

   ______ PAR Lesson Framework

   ______ preparation step

   ______ assistance step

   ______ reflection step

   ______ family literacy education

   ______ assumptive teaching

   ______ communicative arts

   ______ visual literacy

   ______ technological literacy

______ dependent learners

______ fading

Objectives

As you read this chapter, focus your attention on the following objectives. You will:

1. learn the characteristics of an effective teacher.
2. learn the characteristics of a lesson framework.
3. learn about the PAR Lesson Framework.
4. see examples of the PAR Framework being used at the elementary, high school, and college levels.
5. learn about the need for improving instruction in our nation's schools.
6. become acquainted with eight principles for content-reading instruction, and understand the importance of each.
7. learn how this textbook is organized.

The description of the two teachers in Activity 1.1 is central to understanding the dilemmas that teachers who deal with content at all grade levels face. Everyone wishes to be effective as a teacher, but what makes for effective teaching? And will principals, supervisors, and primarily students value and appreciate the instruction they are receiving? Good teachers like Teacher B are continually exploring and learning in an ongoing effort to facilitate student learning. They make their content areas relevant through absorbing new knowledge in their field and keeping current through their own reading. They provide discussions and activities that link students to the larger outside world.

Effective teachers never use these two classroom strategies: First, they never rely on simply telling students what they need to know in order to be successful in a course. They do not see students as Lockean "little vessels" whom they must fill with knowledge piecemeal every day. Second, effective teachers do not assign new chapters or other readings for homework and discuss them in class the next day.

Good teachers often inspire students to think for themselves in deciding how to solve problems, attack reading selections, and evaluate what they are reading. Inspired instruction helps students to become **autonomous learners**—individuals who are independent in their learning habits. Rosemary Altea in *The Eagle and the Rose* (1995) best encapsuled the role of a teacher:

> Part of his role as my guide is to teach me to teach myself, so when I ask my questions of him, his answer is usually, "What do you think?" He can, and often does, help me discover answers, like all good teachers; and like all good teachers, he is always there to listen, to encourage, and to steer me gently along my path. (p. 74)

ACTIVITY 1.1 A Tale of Two Teachers

Once there were two teachers with very different styles of teaching. Teacher A was very inspiring, a wonderful lecturer who often delivered long orations to interpret the textbook. He rarely worried much about having students read the textbook but rather told his students what they needed to know to pass his course. Students would exit his classes marveling at his in-depth knowledge of the subject matter and his stirring delivery, although few students took notes or worried too much about salient points that were made by this instructor. Everyone agreed that it didn't matter because it was enough for students to listen and absorb wisdom from this interesting man. In short, students related to this teacher.

Many of the same students also had a class with Teacher B. A shy man who usually held a number of books tightly under his right arm as he walked, Teacher B was always disheveled and frumpy. He seemed to have perpetual chalk dust on the back of his clothes from being so shy that he rubbed against the chalkboard as he entered the classroom. He loved books and often told students about the books he was reading. But that was all he ever told them. He taught the poetry class as if he knew nothing. He alternately cajoled and intellectually pushed students to discover the meanings of the poems for themselves. He would call on students to tell what was on their minds after making them read a line or several lines of poetry. As a class moderator he would foster student debate over differences of interpretation. In this way his classroom was always the site of an intellectual debate about possible interpretations of meaning in poetry. Students were very unhappy, to say the least, with this indecisive man as a teacher. Students often implored him to "just tell them what is happening" and interpret the poems for them. But he never would, always preferring to hear what his students had to say and forever happy to coordinate the debate and play the master of ceremonies. Teacher A was revered while Teacher B was often ridiculed.

Unfortunately students did not appreciate or see the true talents of these teachers. Teacher A was an entertainer more than a teacher. He left the school after a few years. Teacher B recently retired after 33 years at the school and finally received the accolades he deserved. Teacher B was the better for many reasons, not the least of which was he always taught thinking along with the reading that he was assigning the class. Whereas Teacher A was more popular, Teacher B was more artful in that he had an uncanny ability to involve students in an efficient and effective discussion. He kept the tone of the class positive and always helped students think critically about the reading material.

How Teachers Can Best Be Effective

Students at all levels need excellent teachers to guide and facilitate their learning. Because the learning process is complex and subtle, at any time a student can lack competence and confidence to learn. At such times a student needs a teacher who is able to impart both content and the desire and willingness to learn. The importance of a good teacher cannot be overstated. As Jonathan Howland (1995) has observed:

> One's world, I would claim, is a collage of texts, and functioning well in this world is a matter of getting a good reading, which is to say an informed and intelligent grasp of the text at hand. An ability to interpret—to stop, to think, to ponder, to wrestle with a book as much as read it—is thus fundamentally useful, for the costs of misinterpretation range from aesthetic gullibility in the classroom to political disaster in the world. (p. 36)

Students, however, do misinterpret text in reading and by doing so are demonstrating **incomplete thinking**. Students manifest incomplete thinking when they skip important steps in the lesson. The student who has trouble identifying all of the steps and who tends to skip steps will have to slow down and rediscover them or else grind to a halt. Such students have no **fix-up strategies** (explained further in Chapter 12)—special intervention strategies students have at their disposal to aid in comprehension when they are confused by the reading material.

This shortcutting of steps has been called two-finger thinking (de Bono, 1976). Two-finger thinking is like two-finger piano playing. A person who plays the piano with only two fingers is using fewer resources than could be used. This is fine for playing chopsticks but not Chopin! In the same way, two-finger thinking uses only part of the brain to perceive and comprehend. Inadequate use of resources can cause trouble when complex learning skills are required. For instance, two-finger thinking might work on an easy math word problem, but a difficult one will stump the reader used to "shortcutting."

Fortunately research has identified reading and writing strategies that are effective in helping students overcome these problems in content-area classrooms (Alvermann & Swafford, 1989; Myers, 1984). In this text we describe many strategies to train students in thinking that is planned and systematic. The initial step for the novice or experienced teacher, however, is acceptance and use of a framework for improving instruction.

Characteristics of a Framework

A framework is the systematic arrangement of the basic parts of something. It is an organized plan condensed to a series of steps, usually represented by key words. The framework becomes, then, a model for completing a task. It must be complete, and all parts of the task need to be clearly explained. A framework for instruction should be an aid to thinking and learning and a way to activate students to learn. An instructional framework that identifies successful components of a content lesson facilitates the relationship among reading, thinking, and learning. These frameworks for content-reading instruction are becoming increasingly popular (Herber, 1978; Singer & Donlan, 1985; Vaughan & Estes, 1986). This is so because frameworks formulate instruction in a complete and flexible way so teachers can implement programs easily. The most popular content-reading frameworks include these three basic assumptions: (1) The learner must be ready to learn; thus, the teacher must prepare the learner beforehand. (2) The learner must be guided through the learning—that is, the teacher must develop comprehension during the lesson. (3) The learner should review what has been learned; to this end, the teacher must provide after-reading opportunities, such as comprehension checks. If these basic steps are repeated consistently in the instructional sequence, the learner begins to use them independently of the teacher, in a self-instructional manner. It does not matter what key words are used in a framework, as long as they stimulate recall of the steps incorporated in the framework.

The PAR Lesson Framework for Instruction

PAR stands for "preparation, assistance, and reflection." The **PAR Lesson Framework** is a framework for content-reading instruction (see Figure 1.1). PAR is similar to other content-instructional frameworks. We coined the acronym *PAR* to develop an association with the golf term *par*, which refers to the completion of a hole or holes by taking the allotted number of strokes but not exceeding the limit. Golfers usually feel very pleased when they achieve par for a course. Likewise teachers who consistently use PAR as the underpinning of their instruction will be pleased because students will be more meaningfully engaged in their learning. As a by-product, discipline problems that grow from inattention and boredom will be greatly reduced. Discipline problems represent probably the main cause of teacher burnout.

In the **preparation step**, as noted in Figure 1.1, teachers need to consider text problems and student background of knowledge. Sometimes students have incorrect or insufficient background knowledge, which makes it difficult for the teacher to have the students begin reading. Instead the teacher needs to choose preparation activities that will build a conceptual base of understanding for students and thereby enable them to be more successful in the reading. The preparation step helps motivate students to want to read. Put another way, the more preparation a teacher does with students, the more motivated they are going to be to study the topic.

Once motivation is heightened in the preparation step, the teacher moves to the **assistance step**, where an instructional context for the lesson is provided. This is the crucial step to help students better comprehend the passage. Teachers many times prepare and motivate students but then tell them to read the passage on their own in class or for homework. Teachers fail to realize that students who are thinking poorly do not have adequate study skills or do not think critically and need assistance as they read to maintain purpose and build comprehension. Comprehension will be improved if strategies are chosen for students to react to as they read. The strategies also help provide a concrete, clear purpose for completing the reading.

In the **reflection step**, teachers use the material that was read to provide extension, enrichment, and critical thinking opportunities. Careful reflection by students is not the same as answering questions either posed by the teacher or listed at the end of the chapter. True reflection occurs when students ask themselves tough questions such as: "What did I learn from this reading?" "Was it appropriate for me?" "Do I believe what the author said?" "Is this reading material worth retaining?" When students truly reflect over a reading, they retain the material longer and at greater depth.

FIGURE 1.1

The PAR Lesson Framework

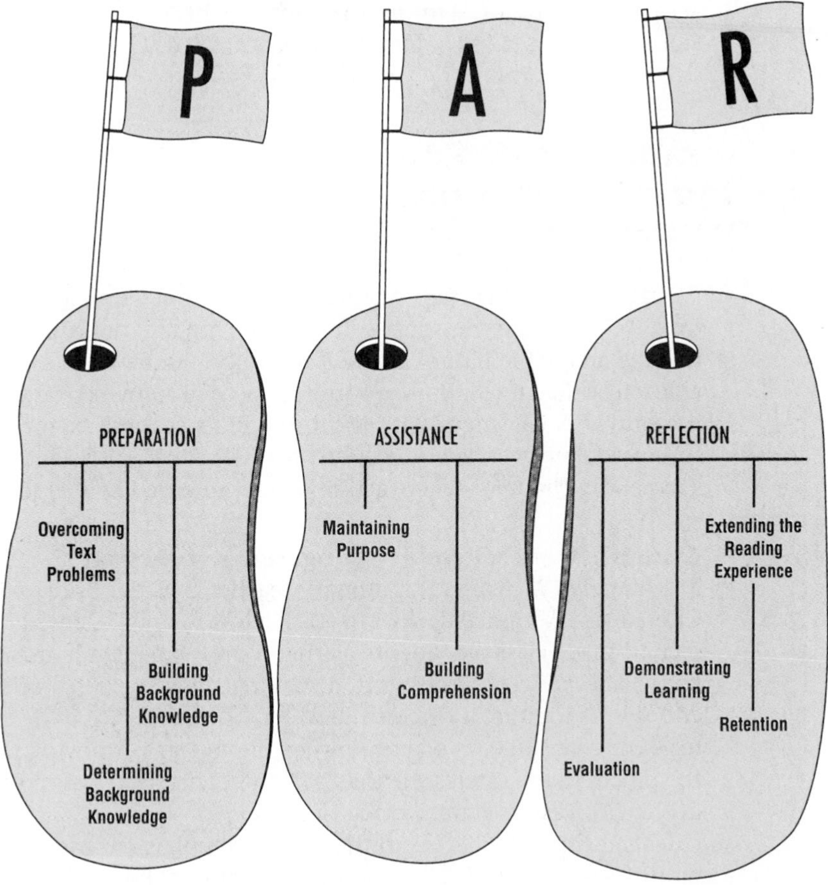

Developed by Dawn Watson and Walter Richards.

At each stage teachers can determine whether students have comprehended the material. Also, using PAR helps to motivate students (motivation is enhanced in the preparation step) and helps students retain the concepts and understanding longer (student retention is especially aided by the reflection step). If teachers consistently model the PAR steps, students will begin to use the steps as they read on their own.

PAR's three steps are applicable in any content area and at any grade level, for both narrative and expository material. Following these instructional steps ensures positive and complete thinking by the learner in the reading experience. The basic terms—*preparation, assistance, reflection*—are already part of the professional language of teachers. We hope that the PAR Lesson Framework will inspire teachers to use preparation, assistance, and reflection to promote solid instruction and learning.

Three examples of content-specific lessons that illustrate use of the PAR Framework are presented next to give the reader a sense of how this simple acronym can be used to improve any teacher's delivery of content. The PAR Framework can help the novice or experienced teacher to become more effective in the classroom.

Three Examples of PAR Being Used to Teach Content

To show that PAR is easily adaptable to any content area at any level of education, we chose three lessons—elementary, high school, and college—to dramatize the adaptable nature of the PAR Lesson Framework. All three teachers are able to use the same framework in leading their learners strategically before, during, and after reading about the subject. Because these examples are meant only to provide an overview, directions for constructing the activities are given in succeeding chapters, where activities are presented in a larger context.

Example from a Primary Language Arts Lesson

Ms. Maureen Moynihan, a primary teacher at Great Bridge Primary School in Chesapeake, Virginia, decides to teach a lesson on "the desert" to her beginning second-grade class of students. Rather than tell her students what they need to know, she prefers to use written materials as the source of information. She chooses to conduct a Directed Reading/Thinking Activity (explained in Chapter 6) to give students practice in reading to learn, knowing that they will find the process more interesting than a lecture. This strategy teaches all three phases of the PAR Lesson Framework.

Ms. Moynihan begins in the *preparation* phase by assessing students' background knowledge. She asks students what they know about the desert and records the following student responses on the chalkboard:

there are cactuses

there are no trees

there are rattlesnakes, scorpions, lizards, owls, birds, and eagles

it is very hot

there is a lot of sand

sometimes you see mirages

there is no water

She next distributes a What-I-Know Activity (WIKA) sheet (explained in Chapter 4) to help preview and ask questions about the upcoming reading (the WIKA sheet is displayed as Activity 1.2). She then begins her preview of the reading called "The Desert" (Scott, Foresman anthology *Happy Faces*, Grade 1, 1993). Ms. Moynihan has the students look at all the pictures in the chapter, study the bold-print words, and review the subtitles. She also reads to the students particular sections or paragraphs that she feels they should think about in greater depth. She points to a picture and asks who they think the roadrunner is run-

ACTIVITY 1.2 What-I-Know Activity Sheet: The Desert

What I Know About the Desert	*What I Know About the Desert After Preview*	*What I Need to Know as I Read*	*What I Know After Reading*	*What I Still Need to Know*
There are cactuses.	The cactuses have flowers.	How do the animals survive?	They rest in the shade to stay cool.	How hot does the desert get?
There are no trees.	There are mountains of sand.	What do desert animals eat?	They eat seeds, plants, snakes, lizards, insects.	How often does it rain? How much?
There are rattlesnakes, scorpions, lizards, owls, birds, and eagles.	There are toads, roadrunners, tigers, and coyotes.	How do the animals get their food?	They hunt at night.	How many different types of animals live in the desert?
It is very hot.	The cactuses have water in them.	Do the animals drink any water?	Yes, they do. Large animals live near a water hole. Small animals get water from their food.	What desert plants have water in them?
There is a lot of sand.		Are there any dangerous desert animals?	Yes, the rattlesnake.	
Sometimes you see mirages.		How do desert animals move?	They move fast over the sand.	
There is barely any water.				

Developed by Maureen Moynihan.

ning from. After the preview the students close their books and relate what they now know about the desert. After listing four new facts they have learned, Ms. Moynihan asks her students to think about additional information they would like or need to know about the desert. On the chalkboard, she writes these six student-generated questions:

How do the animals survive?
What do desert animals eat?
How do the animals get their food?
Do the animals drink any water?
Are there any dangerous desert animals?
How do desert animals move?

Students in the *assistance* phase read individually to find answers to the questions that they themselves asked. Then they discuss their answers in small groups, and, finally, they share their collective answers with the teacher. In this case students were able to answer all of their questions.

As a *reflection* activity the teacher asks the students to again get in groups to generate additional questions to research in the library. The five additional questions that they posed are listed in the "What I Still Need to Know" column of the WIKA sheet in Activity 1.2. In this way students work through all three phases of the PAR Lesson Framework.

Ms. Moynihan decides that students need to complete an additional reflection activity to strengthen vocabulary and ensure learning of the reading material. She decides on a magic-square activity (explained in Chapter 8). In this activity—Activity 1.3—terms from the chapter are placed in the square, and the definitions are numbered and listed below the square. Students read the definitions and match them with the appropriate term by placing the definition number in the square. Then they add the numbers across the rows and down the columns to discover the "magic number."

Example from a High School Health/Physical Education Class

A ninth-grade health and physical education class co-taught by James J. DiNardo III and Yogi Hightower Boothe begins with students taking their seats near other students with whom they have been grouped. The teachers frequently regroup the students heterogeneously based on their reading ability. (The students have been told only that the grouping is "randomly assigned," and they have no reason to question this because they can see no pattern to the groups.)

The *preparation* phase begins immediately as the students enter the room. Students begin the class even before the teachers tell them to, by copying into two-column notes the three objectives for the day, written on the chalkboard. They are accustomed to starting each class this way, and no communication is necessary from the teachers. Once this is done, students are instructed to take a few moments to preview the passage they will be reading today. Each student then peruses the reading, noting features such as title, subtitles, bold-print words and italicized words, pictures and captions, review questions at the end of the reading, and any other clues that might help them to make sense of the text when they later read it.

The teachers then ask all students to close their books. They pass out, one to each student, a single sheet of paper, which they call an anticipation guide (see Activity 1.4). Mr. DiNardo explains to the students, "What good readers do when they read text such as this is that they make predictions about what the text will say. They make such predictions based on prior knowledge. Then when they go into the text, it really does not matter whether they find out that their predictions are true or not. The result of having made the predictions helps them to stay engaged in the text. Today, we help you in this process because *we* have made some predictions for you, on this anticipation guide. All you need to do is, before you read, place a check mark next to the ones you think to be true. Don't be worried at this time about whether or not you are correct. Remember that you are just practicing the habit of predicting prior to reading. In fact, some of these statements you will later find to be correct, some will be incorrect, and some will be arguable. That is, some of you may interpret them to be true, and have evidence to prove it, while others in the room will have evidence that disproves it. We will have to resolve those issues at that time."

Students are then given a few minutes to check the statements on the anticipation guide. Students are told not to open their textbooks, however. Instead,

ACTIVITY 1.3 Magic-Number Squares

NAME ______________________ DATE ____________

Directions: Put the number of the definition listed below into the square with the correct term. Check your answers by adding the numbers across each row and down each column. The MAGIC NUMBER is the total that you get each time.

desert ____	rain ____	water hole ____
hunt ____	scales ____	roadrunner ____
rattlesnake ____	plants / rocks ____	animals ____

1. The desert hardly ever sees this.
2. These need food and water to live.
3. Desert animals do this at night, when it is cool.
4. This may bite, but it will warn you first with the rattle in its tail.
5. These help animals from drying out.
6. Large animals must live near this for survival.
7. This animal has long legs to move fast over the hot ground.
8. This is a dry, hot place.
9. Animals hide under these to stay cool and safe.

THE MAGIC NUMBER IS ____________

Developed by Maureen Moynihan.

they are asked to discuss their selections with the others in their group to compare reasoning and generally to help build each other's background knowledge before engaging in reading.

The teachers move about the room to monitor the discussions, many of which are quite animated because of the nature of the statements and the

ACTIVITY 1.4 Anticipation Guide

NAME ______________________________ DATE ______________

Anticipation Guide: The Digestive System

Instructions: Before reading pages 172 through 176 in your textbook, place a check mark (✓) in the space to the left of each of the statements with which you agree. Then, during or after the reading, cross through statements you wish to change, and check any new ones you find to be true. BE SURE YOU ARE ABLE TO REFER BACK TO THE TEXT TO PROVIDE EVIDENCE FOR OR AGAINST EACH STATEMENT.

____ 1. Saliva is important to digestion.

____ 2. If you ate standing on your head, it would be more difficult for you to swallow, and for the digestive system to function properly.

____ 3. You digest food in your mouth.

____ 4. Your digestive system could still function properly if the middle ten feet of your small intestine were removed.

____ 5. A combination of hydrochloric acid, enzymes, and mucus turns food in your stomach into a thick gooey mush called chyme.

____ 6. If you are preparing to participate in an aerobic sport such as distance running or biking, you should eat a big meal (such as a fast-food hamburger, fries, and shake) at least one hour before you do it.

____ 7. Both the pancreas and the liver produce digestive juices that are stored in the gallbladder.

____ 8. Capillaries and villi play a major role in the digestive process.

____ 9. All remaining undigested food passes through the large intestine, which separates fecal waste from water and prepares it for elimination through the rectum.

____ 10. Diarrhea and constipation are problems of the large intestine.

____ 11. You could die from diarrhea.

____ 12. Ulcers, ulcerative colitis, and heartburn are all caused by the same things.

By Mark A. Forget, Yolanda Hightower Boothe, and James J. DiNardo III.

students' various perceptions and misperceptions. In fact, when Boothe and DiNardo worked with the school's communication skills teacher to construct this anticipation guide, they kept in mind four characteristics that make anticipation guides work well to help students interpret difficult text material:

- They rephrased important concepts in the language of students.
- They included a few statements that are intuitively appealing to students but will be proven to be inaccurate through reading the text.
- They wrote in such a way as to force students to interpret large segments of text such as a paragraph or two. This prevented the experience from turning into a simple "decoding exercise," which is what many textbook-made worksheets are.

- They worded the guide in such a way as to provoke critical thinking about the key concepts. The statements are somewhat vague or subject to interpretation, rather than being true/false statements. Based on their prior knowledge or on the material being presented, students might disagree and provide valid evidence for either side of the argument, both before and after the reading.

Next the *assistance* phase begins. The teachers remind students to begin silent reading without distracting either themselves or others while reading the chapter on nutrition. Students are reminded to note the page, column, and paragraph that they are using to interpret whether a statement is provable.

The room becomes quiet as students engage in reading to find out whether their predictions are correct. Boothe and DiNardo either read at the same time or quietly move around the room to monitor student work with the anticipation guides. One or the other occasionally stops to whisper encouragement to a student, but they are very cautious to avoid any distractions during the reading time.

After about twenty minutes, many of the students are stirring, anticipating the next step: meeting in their groups to attempt to come to a consensus. The teachers instruct them to do just that, reminding the students that to come to consensus is different from attempting to find a majority. They do this to be sure that all voices are heard and that all students participate. Once again, the teachers move around the room to monitor and assist. In addition, they remind students that they must act like "attorneys presenting evidence to support their claims."

This is the *reflection* phase of the lesson. The room is loud, as students argue vociferously over statements such as "You digest food in your mouth." Although few checked that statement before or during the reading, some students found evidence that—because saliva is important to digestion, the mastication process is also important to digestion, and the digestive process at least starts in the mouth—it could be said that digestion occurs in the mouth! Many such arguments occur in the small groups.

The teachers locate the first group to achieve consensus, and they note the statements that group members believe should be checked now that they have read and discussed them. The teachers place a check mark next to those statements on the transparency of the anticipation guide they have on the overhead projector.

The final phase of the discussion occurs when the teachers turn on the overhead projector and ask for the attention of all the students in order to attempt to come to a classroom consensus. Now the students who have had practice in small group discussions sort out their differences over the few statements about which all the class has not yet achieved consensus. This process takes a few more minutes, and students obviously relish their abilities to present their interpretations of the evidence they have found in their textbooks. The discussion is orderly and mature, and all students seem interested in the outcome.

After achieving consensus, the teachers ask the students to report by a show of hands how many felt that using the anticipation guide to make predictions about the reading beforehand had made the passage interesting and desirable to read. All the students raised their hands. In this way the teachers remind the students of the skills they used to engage themselves in the reading.

The class is nearly over. The teachers remind students that they must go back through the reading as a homework assignment to complete their notes based on the objectives that were on the chalkboard at the start of the class, which each student has copied into his or her notebook.

Students usually like the health and physical education classes of Boothe and DiNardo. They say that "We always get to *think* in their class. It's more interesting." The teachers are used to letting the students learn through techniques that encourage them to set their own purposes for reading and then pursue knowledge from the text and reflect on it through discussion or writing. They are able to see the students develop their own understandings of the text. At the same time they know that active pursuit of these understandings will help the students retain the information and apply it in their own lives. They also know that their students have practiced a learning skill that they will be able to use in any class. Boothe and DiNardo are happy to be reading-to-learn teachers.

Example of a College Humanities Lesson

Ms. Ann Woolford-Singh, an assistant professor of English, decides to teach a lesson to her introduction to African-American studies class on the African presence in ancient America. In the *preparation* phase to determine students' prior knowledge, she tries a PreP strategy (Langer, 1981). Through discussion with students she collects on the chalkboard associations they make when seeing the three words *Niña, Pinta,* and *Santa Maria.* The student associations are listed in Activity 1.5. Next, to build on prior knowledge, Ms. Woolford-Singh asks, "How do you feel about the United States celebrating Columbus Day?" The students have mixed reactions, and the discussion is lively. Some students view Columbus as a hero, some as a villain. Her purpose is to get students to think about both the facts and the myths associated with Columbus as a historical figure. At this point she decides the students are ready to read an interesting passage about an African chief named Abukari II, who is discussed in Ivan Van Sertima's *The African Presence in Ancient America: They Came Before Columbus* (1976).

In the *assistance* phase of the lesson, Ms. Woolford-Singh distributes an outline/study guide to help students as they read the passage. Specifically the guide gives major points for the students to be aware of as they read (see Activity 1.6). Students individually react to the guide, then get in small groups to discuss what points from the guide they found in the reading. Students and teacher agree that the PreP strategy and the outline/guide helped them come to a better understanding of the idea that our continent was visited by Africans long before Columbus's voyage.

In the *reflection* phase, Ms. Woolford-Singh presents the following quotation to the students from Van Sertima's book:

> It is harder to believe in Africans crossing the Atlantic, a distance of 1500 miles, than in artists from outer space, etching camels in Marcahuasi. (p. 78)

She asks them to write a letter to the author, Ivan Van Sertima, responding to the treatise that he puts forward and specifically responding to the quotation. Stu-

ACTIVITY 1.5 PreP Strategy

What do you think of when you see these words?

Niña Pinta Santa Maria

Columbus's ships
Crossed the Atlantic
Discovered America
He was lost
Sailors were starving
Ships were strong
Columbus killed off many Indians
He was a hero
Ships were small
Seas were rough
The conditions were bad
Long voyage with lots of storms
They had limited navigational information
He was a bad guy

Developed by Ann Woolford-Singh.

dents work on the letter in class and for homework. The next class period students first share their letters in small groups with classmates. Then they reassemble as a whole class, and volunteers read some letters aloud to the class. The letters allow students to summarize what they have learned and to think critically about the lesson. A student letter is reproduced as Activity 1.7.

Reading Achievement and the Need for Improved Instruction

There is concern in our country about the reading achievement levels of students of all ages and grade levels. Evidence exists that achievement levels are not rising in our nation's schools. Even though the latest 1998 results of the National Assessment of Education Programs (NAEP) showed the first across-the-board rise in reading scores for fourth-, eighth-, and twelfth-grade students in 30 years, reading test gains on the NAEP test over the long term have fluctuated only slightly. The 1998 NAEP results reported that 60 percent of high school seniors can read only at or below the sixth-grade level and that only one-third of all test-takers attained a "proficient" level—a standard that test officials say all students should reach (*National Assessment of Educational Progress*, 1998). Further, published NAEP reports indicate that schools are performing well in teaching the fundamentals of the language arts, but not in teaching advanced reading and expressive skills (Campbell, Donahue, Reese, & Phillips, 1996). Also the

ACTIVITY 1.6 Outline/Study Guide

Check the lines as you find the concepts in the chapter.

____ 1. **Abukari II**
- The Mariner King of Mali
- In 1311 Abukari set sail for a trans-Atlantic voyage

____ 2. **Abukari's Resources**
- Scholars at the University at Timbuktu
- Gold
- Servants
- Established African trade

____ 3. **African Boat Designs**
- Canoe
- Plank
- Papyrus

____ 4. **Heyerdahl's Ra II**
- Proved that the papyrus boats could sail successfully across the Atlantic

____ 5. **Evidence of Pre-Columbian African Presence**
- African artifacts in Olmec Mexico
- Sculptures with Negroid features
- African chieftains in Brazil, Colombia, and Ecuador

____ 6. **Attempts to Recreate History**
- European distortion of African history
- Von Daniken's *Chariot of the Gods*

____ 7. **Rewriting History: A Slow, Painful Process**
- Van Sertima's satirical quote: "It is harder to believe in Africans crossing the Atlantic, a distance of 1500 miles, than in artists from outer space, etching camels in Marcahuasi."

Developed by Ann Woolford-Singh.

recent NAEP report on writing proficiency found that many students at each grade level had difficulty producing effective pieces of writing (Applebee, Langer, Mullis, Latham, & Gentile, 1994).

In addition, a number of recent reports and books have portrayed our nation's schools as being in crisis, questioning the practices and core beliefs of our entire educational system (Hirsch, 1987; Bloom, 1987). William Damon (1995) indicted schools for what he calls the "cult of self-esteem" and the misdirected child-centered approach to education. He called for more intellectual rigor in the schools through presentation of activities that challenge students and capitalize on their spontaneous, natural interests.

Ralph, Keller, and Crouse (1994) hypothesize that achievement levels have not risen because the schools have not been able to raise general intelligence

ACTIVITY 1.7 Letter to an Author

February 4, 1999

Dr. Ivan Van Sertima
Author
The African Presence in Ancient America:
They Came Before Columbus

Dear Dr. Van Sertima:

I am writing you to respond to your satirical statement: "It is harder to believe in Africans crossing the Atlantic, a distance of 1500 miles, than in artists from outer space, etching camels in Marcahuasi" (78). Is it just as hard to believe that man has gone to the moon? It is easier to believe that Elvis is really still alive?

I wholeheartedly agree with your statement. Society in the past and even now does not give the black race credit for much. It is as though any information about black people doing anything before white people must somehow be false and unbelievable. Why does African-American history seem far-fetched to a lot of people, as though we cannot do anything unless white Americans have done it first?

America in general is in denial about the influence of African descendants around the world. We, as you know, were not just house/field slaves, mine laborers, tobacco and cotton pickers, or raisers of white children. We are Jupiter Hammon, who in the early 1700s was a profound poet, and who published a poem, "An Evening Thought," in 1761. We are Martin Delany, who in the mid-1800s wrote eloquently about race relations and slavery. We are Frederick Douglass, who rightly is known as the Great Emancipator. We can no longer be denied. The truth must be told. We have been the backbone of America, and any person who tried to deny our presence must realize that African Americans have made and continue to make tremendous contributions to this country and to the world.

Thank you for all of your research efforts. Your work means a lot, not only to me but to an entire race.

Sincerely,

Student
Introduction to African-American Studies
Tidewater Community College
Virginia Beach Campus

levels. They theorize that NAEP results indicate not only the mathematics, reading, and science abilities of students, but also the level of mental ability and general intelligence of the test-taker. They maintain that until schools emphasize problem solving, critical thinking, and language development in order to raise the levels of intelligence of the student population, achievement scores probably will not climb appreciably. To bolster their findings, they cite reports that show school achievement has not risen beyond the levels reported in the 1970s (National Center for Educational Statistics, 1991; "U.S. Study," 1991; Bracey, 1991).

A number of reports (*Reading Report Card*, 1985; Miklos, 1982; Kirsch & Jungeblut, 1986) published within a few years of each other indicate that students experience difficulty with higher-level reading and writing skills such as critical thinking, drawing inferences, and applying what is read. Applebee, Langer, and Mullis in *Learning to Be Literate in America* (1987), after summarizing several such NAEP studies, maintain that students are having difficulty because schools are not teaching students to learn how to learn. Hynd (1999) recommends, as a result of her study of adolescent reading behaviors when using multiple texts in history, that "students should be taught that texts are to be read critically" (p. 435).

Compounding the issue is the added problem of adult literacy in the United States. In reviewing the National Adult Literacy Survey of 1992, Bowen (1999) concluded:

> although the United States by most measures is the richest and most technologically advanced nation of those surveyed, its adult citizens are more likely to read and use information poorly than are adults in any of the other nations surveyed. (p. 316)

These findings are disheartening when coupled with recent research showing that children of parents with less than a high school education are at a disadvantage in the classroom (National Center for Educational Statistics, 1996). All of this points to the need for **family literacy education**—educators working with the entire family to improve literacy skills—as one way to help solve the literacy problems.

In summary, many current reports indicate that American students

1. are unable to express themselves effectively, either orally or in writing
2. are unable to make inferences from their reading
3. are unable to think critically about what they read
4. cannot process complex written material with facility
5. do not recognize a large body of content knowledge that experts consider essential for informed readers
6. do not prefer reading as a way to learn

Caution is necessary in embracing these conclusions. Many of the reports seem to have design and interpretation problems (Kaestle et al., 1991) and may imply a worse scenario than actually exists. Test scores for children who experience a strong literacy climate at home have remained stable. Westbury (1992) maintains that students are learning what they are taught and that schools may be doing a better job than interpretations of national test results may indicate. Bracey (1991) suggests we need to take a positive approach to working on the problems of those schools truly in crisis, instead of bashing all schools over our current problems. Others, however, such as John Goodlad, feel that the situation has become a crisis for our nation. In *A Place Called School* (1984), Goodlad comments on the "sameness and emotional flatness" (p. 100) of American classrooms. He observed students completing exercise after exercise without active involvement. He saw little opportunity for students to use knowledge in an active, thinking environment. In his best-seller *Cultural Literacy* (1987), Hirsch describes the problem of persons who can "read" but do not understand. He attributes this problem to students' general lack of exposure to "essential" knowledge. Such students, writes Allan Bloom in *The Closing of the American Mind* (1987), are culturally illiterate: "To put the matter at its baldest, we live in a thought-world, and the thinking has gone very bad indeed" (p. 17). Bloom further asserts that students have lost the practice of and the desire for reading. Fredericks (1992) contends that the solution Hirsch and Bloom propose—ensuring that students gain "essential knowledge"—is less effective than teaching students to think about what they read.

Perceived problems in schools have given rise to a number of reform movements to solve the problems discussed above. David Berliner and Bruce Biddle (1995), two prominent psychologists interested in education, are wary of current reform movements and blame them for wasting money, harming already effective school programs, and adding to declining morale among teachers. They view educational reform movements as being spurred by politics to scapegoat educators as a way of "diverting attention from America's deepening social problems" (p. 7). A growing number of researchers (Bracey, 1997; McQuillan, 1998) agree with Berliner and Biddle that children in the United States are reading as well now as they did in past generations, and maybe even better.

Many of the reform movements are top-down directives (from politicians, community leaders, and educational administrators) that emanate from the notion that teachers cannot be trusted to make sound pedagogical decisions (Darling-Hammond, 1993). Though the debate will continue over who wields power in curriculum and pedagogical decision making, many do agree that both prospective and practicing teachers' performance can be improved through more rigorous training. In *A Nation Prepared* (1986), Branscomb and colleagues recommended better training to include a broader background in the content areas and the liberal arts, as well as instruction in methodology. The consensus is that teachers need more exposure to information and training that will enable them to teach higher levels of language and literacy. But often teachers do not have this exposure even though they expect students in their classes to be fluent in processing reading material, making inferences, and reading critically. They assume that students will be able to express their understanding of the material orally and on tests. They expect that students possess a certain amount of knowledge and have a desire to read to learn. This is **assumptive teaching**, described later in this chapter as Principle 7. Such assumptive teaching creates a difficult instructional dilemma (see the Technology Box). Even acknowledging that the schools are doing better than indicated in some interpretations of reports, most educators think that schools should improve a great deal. A Delta Kappa Gamma poll (Day & Anderson, 1992) identified confronting "at risk" issues and advancing literacy as the two leading educational concerns for the foreseeable future. The obvious first step to do as the poll suggests is to encourage teachers to teach language and literacy in content-area instruction. To accomplish this, teachers must have principles to follow. In the next section we present eight guiding principles for facilitating reading to learn.

Eight Principles for Content-Reading Instruction

Teachers who are able to articulate their beliefs about teaching are in a good position to improve their instruction. Like all learners, teachers will alter their approaches if they see a need to do so. We altered our own instruction based on current research. To clarify our own thinking, we encapsulated our approach in eight principles. By sharing these principles with teachers and demonstrating how they relate to content-area teaching, we hope to influence teachers to consider instructional changes in their own classrooms.

These principles are grounded in theory. Many teachers think that theory has nothing to do with the classroom, perhaps because theory has been presented to them in isolation from its application. But we think that when teachers ask for "what works," they are also asking for the reasons why a particular technique works, so they can replicate it in optimal circumstances. Teachers know that imposing an activity on students in the wrong circumstances can produce a teaching disaster. No activity has much merit aside from the construct underlying it (Hayes, Stahl, & Simpson, 1991). Teachers want theory that makes sense because it explains why some activities work well at a particular time in the course of instruction. The eight principles presented here link the theoretical with good practice in content-area instruction.

1. ***Reading is influenced by the reader's personal store of experience and knowledge.***

Successful reading depends on numerous factors. The reader's store of knowledge and experience certainly contributes, as well as the reader's attitude toward reading. Even though many people may share the same experience, read the same book, or hear the same lecture, the thinking and learning that occurs differs from individual to individual because of what each person brings to the experience. Individuals relate to a common body of knowledge in different ways because of what they already know—or don't know. Thus, for example, converting to the metric system will probably be especially difficult for learners who were taught measurements in inches, feet, and miles. Readers unfamiliar with Tennyson's poem "The Charge of the Light Brigade" would probably think the phrase "Charge of the Right Frigate" a strange choice of words for a headline ac-

TECHNOLOGY BOX

Principle 7: Teachers Need to Refrain from Assumptive Teaching: A Computer Example

From Ruth Ellen Sameth, Latin teacher

Some teachers begin to teach their students new information without regard to whether the students have the necessary or prerequisite knowledge in order to learn the new information. Teachers often assume that students learned certain skills or concepts in another discipline in school, in a previous course in that teacher's discipline, or in their "everyday experience." Sometimes we expect that other teachers in other fields have taught students certain skills.

For example, I took students to a computer lab earlier this year in order to do research on the Internet on Roman gods and goddesses. Without even thinking, I told the students to "double-click on the Netscape icon and then enter the website that is written on the board." *I had assumed that my students knew how to identify the Netscape icon, how to use a mouse, and how to put in a new address.* Luckily for me, most of the students actually had the knowledge that I assumed they had. Many of my students, though, were unfamiliar with the concept that when you're entering an address on the World Wide Web, you need to match uppercase and lowercase. So, even students who were very familiar with using computers and the Internet still couldn't actually reach the proper site.

companying an article on naval buildup; they would not see the headline as a play on words. If learners cannot find relevance in a subject, they are likely to ignore it. Teachers, then, must become aware of what previous knowledge and experiences their students possess about a particular concept in content subjects.

2. *The communicative arts foster thinking and learning in content subjects.*

The traditional **communicative or language arts** are listening, speaking, reading, writing, and visual literacy. Kellogg (1972) describes the communicative arts as blocks that build on one another. One cannot use one communicative art without also using another. This integration occurs with greater facility as children practice each literacy skill. Yet school environments are often artificial rather than natural in their application of informative communication. Usually, teachers talk and students listen so much of the time that little response and interaction can take place. In reviewing the 51 articles on content reading published in *The Reading Teacher* from 1969 to 1991, Armbruster (1992) noted the "emphasis on the importance of integrating writing and reading in content instruction." It is our premise that students can learn more if they spend more time practicing all of the language arts in their content subjects. Subject matter and language are inextricably bound.

But the main concern for the subject-matter teacher is teaching content. Nila Banton Smith (1965) reminds readers that the term *primer* did not originally mean "first book to read," as it does today, but referred to the contents of a book as being primary, or foremost. Today, the content of a subject is still primary for teachers, as it should be. But using the communicative arts as a major learning tool creates a very positive combination for enhancing critical thinking and learning. For example, Feathers and Smith (1987) report an observational study of content instruction in elementary and secondary classrooms. Although content predominated in instruction at both levels, content was presented differently in the different grades. Secondary teachers transmitted content mainly through lectures or text reading, whereas elementary teachers infused content with more of the communicative arts. The latter method was seen to be more effective. The communicative arts, then, are essential to teaching content-area subjects, and teachers will want to encourage students' use of all the communicative arts as effective thinking and learning tools. As we present activities in this book, we often identify how they facilitate the use of language to enhance content learning. The role of writing, in particular, is discussed in Chapter 9.

3. ***Literacy includes not only the traditional communicative arts but also visual literacy.***

Sometimes communication occurs most easily through nonverbal, visual literacy. For instance, a picture of a pie divided into pieces may convey the concept of fractions more effectively than a page of explanation. Sinatra (1986) calls **visual literacy** the first and most pervasive literacy. Sinatra's model of literacy development suggests the interactive relationship of visual literacy with the oral and written literacies (see Figure 1.2).

Visual literacy conveys emotion through such means as illustration and art. Visual literacy precedes listening and helps build experiences necessary to thinking and learning. It is action oriented; the scribbles that young children call writing are a manifestation of visual literacy. Teachers know that when they make use of visual aids such as graphs, charts, and pictures, they ensure and reinforce learning for many students. An alternative approach is offered for those who excel in visual but not traditional literacy. Because visual literacy has implications for the affective aspects of instruction, it is discussed further in Chapter 2. Many activities presented in this book capitalize on visual literacy.

Emerging and increasingly sophisticated technologies have become so interwoven with every aspect of our lives that we do not fully comprehend their pervasiveness. Computers are certainly the greatest innovation of technology, but fax machines, cellular phones, ATM machines, voice mail, CD-ROMs, satellite dishes, and microwave ovens also are the new technologies that we now take for granted. Technology also is beginning to play an important role in classrooms. Grabe and Grabe (1998) cite the great need for practical, understandable information about integrating technology in K–12 classroom instruction. By learning such information, teachers can improve the training of students in **technological literacy**—that is, learning to become proficient at using emerging technology. In this text, whenever possible, we show computer applications

FIGURE 1.2

Stage three of literacy development: visual literacy and its interactive relationship with the oral and written languages

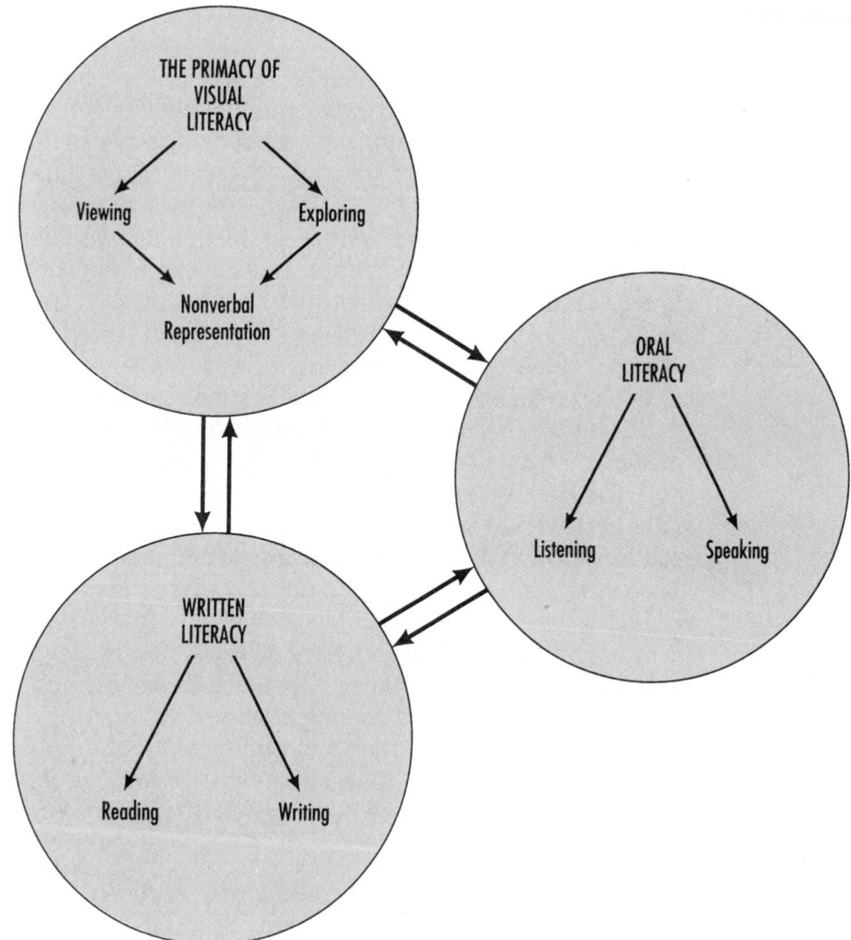

From R. Sinatra, *Visual Literacy Connections to Thinking, Reading and Writing*, 1986. Courtesy of Charles C Thomas, Publisher, Springfield, Illinois.

of objectives and activities learned in content area instruction. Technological literacy and visual literacy are two important and pervasive literacies that teachers need to emphasize to be successful with students. They are discussed further in Chapter 3.

4. ***Reading should be a rewarding experience.***

Reading in content subjects should be satisfying. People avoid doing what is not interesting or rewarding in some personal way. Students avoid reading in content subjects if they find it uninteresting and unrewarding. When left to their own devices, children often select content (nonfiction) books to read just as readily as fiction. We have noticed that younger children are even more likely to read for information than are older ones. If teachers can help by providing a beneficial reading environment in content subjects, learning will improve. Because we think and feel that this principle is so important, we devote an entire chapter—Chapter 2—to the affective dimension of reading in the content areas.

Pleasurable feelings about reading will lead to successful reading and to more reading. Taylor, Frye, and Maruyama (1990) documented that the amount of time students spend reading at school contributes significantly to their level of achievement. The more students observe teachers and parents reading, the more they will want to try it. The more students hear parents and teachers read to them, the more they will want to try it. Teachers would like to teach students who possess good reading habits. This cannot happen simply because teachers tell, or even implore, students to read. However, it will happen through modeling. Morrison and colleagues (1999) documented that teachers who read are better able to motivate students to read. Modeling takes place when teachers share a newspaper article on the content subject or a book they have read that relates to the topic at hand. Modeling is a form of visual literacy. When teachers model reading visually, they are using one communicative art to promote another. We feel teachers need to model use of all of the strategies we describe in this textbook. Morrison and colleagues (1999) found that teachers who read for personal pleasure report using recommended literacy practices in their classrooms significantly more often than do teachers who report less personal reading.

Good readers tend to read because it gives them pleasure and because they do it well; consequently, they get practice in reading and thus get better at it. Poor readers tend to avoid reading because it is not easy, pleasurable, or satisfying. In a series of questionnaires administered over a four-year period to incoming college students, we found a consistent correlation between those who chose not to read and those who perceived that they had poor reading and study habits.

5. ***The practice of critical reading enables better thinking and learning to occur.***

Reading is an active, thinking-related process. As soon as readers can pay more attention to the meaning of words than to their recognition, they can begin to think and learn about the material itself rather than about reading it. Yet students often lack critical thinking skills. It is not that students are incapable of critical thinking; they just have not had the practice. By using tools of literacy and being immersed in a thinking climate, students can practice these skills. Raths, Wassermann, Jones, and Rothstein (1986) believe that teachers who provide students with extensive practice in thinking will train better thinkers. When exercises are provided that ask students only for factual comprehension, thinking deficits will occur (Wassermann, 1987).

Special note: We recognize that literal reading is often a necessary first step toward critical reading. Although we emphasize critical reading, we are not disregarding the importance of factual reading. A reader who already understands material at a factual level and is able to interpret what is read can respond critically with greater success. However, many students who are unable to recall names or dates can predict and infer. It is probably because teachers realize the necessity of literal reading that so much classroom time is spent on literal recall of reading material, to the detriment of higher-level thinking and reading comprehension.

6. ***Meaningful reading should start early and continue throughout life.***

From the first grade on, learning content material is part of most school curricula. Some schools even introduce science, math, and social studies material in kindergarten. The *Weekly Reader*, that ubiquitous early-grades newspaper, contains content material. Because most children are still learning to read in the early grades, reading to learn may not be employed as often as visualizing, listening, and speaking to learn. However, both reading and writing to learn are being advocated more frequently for children in the early grades. By the same reasoning, learning about content subjects continues far beyond high school. Content information bombards learners daily as they listen to radio and watch television, read the newspaper, and surf the Internet on their computers. The basic difference in this learning is that the learner can structure the environment and choose what to learn and what to avoid. The adults whom teachers meet daily will attest that they continue to enjoy and learn about topics that interested them in school. We develop lifelong learners by introducing them to reading for learning's sake at an early age.

7. ***Teachers need to refrain from assumptive teaching.***

Herber (1978) used the term assumptive teaching to describe what teachers do when they unconsciously take for granted that students know how to read and to learn and have the motivation and interest to do so. Teachers may picture all students as having plenty of reading resources and supportive home environments. Unfortunately, these assumptions are not always true.

Some assumptive teaching is necessary. Teachers cannot "start all over again" every year in a content subject. They may need to assume that a particular skill or concept was covered the year before. Yet if a teacher assumes too much about a student's knowledge or frame of mind, the teacher can act as if what is being taught is already known. Finding the point of familiarity with a concept and guiding the students forward is crucial. Content-area teachers should be very certain about what they are assuming their students already know. By learning to determine and build students' background, teachers can avoid assumptive teaching.

8. ***Content-reading instruction enables students to become autonomous learners.***

Dependent learners wait for the teacher to tell them what a word is, what the right answer is, and what to do next. Such learners are crippled intellectually. When they need to function independently, they will not know how. Teachers who abandon the textbook because it seems too hard for their students do their students no favor. Teachers who give students all the answers or hand out the notes already organized in the teacher's style bypass the opportunities for students to learn how to find answers or take notes. High school can become a place where students avoid responsibility. Schools may perpetuate an environment in which students are excused from learning. The goal of teaching is to take students from being dependent on the teacher to being independent in their learning habits. We call this making students autonomous learners. But it is not fair to expect that students can become autonomous in thinking and learning without the benefit of instruction. No matter what the grade level or subject area, teachers can assist students in the transfer to responsibility when they balance the students' level of proficiency and the content to be studied.

One way to describe this change from dependence to independence is **fading** (Moore, Moore, Cunningham, & Cunningham, 1998). Singer and Donlan (1985) have called it "phasing out the teacher and phasing in the student." Armbruster (1992) identified as a trend in content reading the "need to foster independent learners" (p. 166). To become independent learners, students need to practice a study system to make learning easier. The PAR Lesson Framework, explained in this chapter and used as the basis for this textbook, is a system that can enable the teacher to show students how to become autonomous learners. The teacher first models PAR, then gradually weans students to independent use of PAR. The three examples described earlier illustrate such independent learning.

The Organization of This Text

The eight principles presented above are an integral part of the discussion in every chapter. The first two chapters are foundation chapters; they present the basic theory and rationale for the approach used in this text. Chapter 3 deals with how to learn with multiple resources. Chapters 4 and 5 focus on the preparation phase, Chapter 6 on assistance, and Chapter 7 on reflection. Applications for teachers are provided, as well as examples from several content areas and grade levels. Chapters 8 through 11 discuss how PAR works with vocabulary, writing, study skills, and cooperative learning. Chapter 12 is a specialized chapter about at-risk learners and what can be done to support struggling readers in the classroom. Specific strategies and activities are provided.

In each chapter we employ the PAR steps by asking readers to prepare themselves to read, to assist themselves in their reading, and to reflect on their comprehension. We recommend that you, the reader, now select a subject topic to aid you in creating practice activities. The topic should be one that you are currently teaching or may use in the future as you teach. The books you select will be resources for completing some of the assignments given at the end of each chapter. Upon completion of this textbook, you should be able to analyze any resource or textbook for its suitability for learners, its effective qualities, whether it is amenable to the PAR Lesson Framework, its study skills and vocabulary aids, and its attention to different learners. In addition, you should be able to construct activities that help teach content through a reading-to-learn approach.

When teachers use the PAR Lesson Framework, they let students know the plan of the lesson. Teachers can facilitate improvement in students' thinking ability. This type of teacher intervention is a necessary step in improving cognitive ability. Pearson and Tierney (1983) assessed the instructional paradigm most used by teachers at present. It features the use of many practice materials, little explanation of cognitive tasks, little interaction with students about the nature of specific tasks, and strong emphasis on one correct answer, to the extent that teachers supply answers if there is any confusion over a task. Not surprisingly, Pearson and Tierney concluded that such a paradigm is ineffective. Applying the PAR Lesson Framework to teach specific strategies and skills will prove effective in content-area classrooms.

One-Minute Summary

In this chapter we describe the challenge facing teachers in striving for effectiveness in the classroom. We explain why students need excellent and effective teachers to help them overcome the shortcomings in reading, writing, and thinking often evident in the educational setting. We propose instructional frameworks as a way for teachers to become more effective in their teaching. One instructional framework—the PAR Lesson Framework—offers a structured plan for teachers to deliver content in an effective and organized manner. Three examples of PAR Framework lessons are given at the elementary, high school, and college levels, to assist the reader of this text in understanding how PAR works. Also in this chapter we document the need for improved reading instruction as evidenced by failures in reading achievement at all levels of education from kindergarten through adulthood. We summarize our beliefs about reading to learn and lay the foundation for this textbook in the form of eight principles for content-reading instruction. Finally, we discuss how we apply our eight principles and the PAR framework throughout this textbook, and we explain how the textbook is organized.

End-of-Chapter Activities

Assisting Comprehension

1. Were you familiar with all eight of the principles of content-reading instruction described in this chapter? Did you recognize any principles as ones that you use to guide your teaching? Were you not familiar with any of the principles? Were there principles you were aware of but hadn't given much thought to?
2. Return to the anticipation guide (item 1 in "Preparing to Read") and vocabulary list presented at the beginning of this chapter. After reading the chapter, did you change your mind about any statements from the guide? Has your understanding of any of the listed terms altered as a consequence of reading this chapter? In what way?

Reflecting on Your Reading

1. Reflect on any teachers you have encountered that fit the descriptions of Teachers A and B in Activity 1.1. Do you think most persons experience both types of teachers during their school careers?
2. Study the graphic organizer shown here, and fill in the boxes with key concepts taught in this chapter. You may scan the text for answers. When you are finished, think again about all the terms and why they are arranged as they are. Reflect on how the graphic organizer helps clarify your thinking about the chapter.

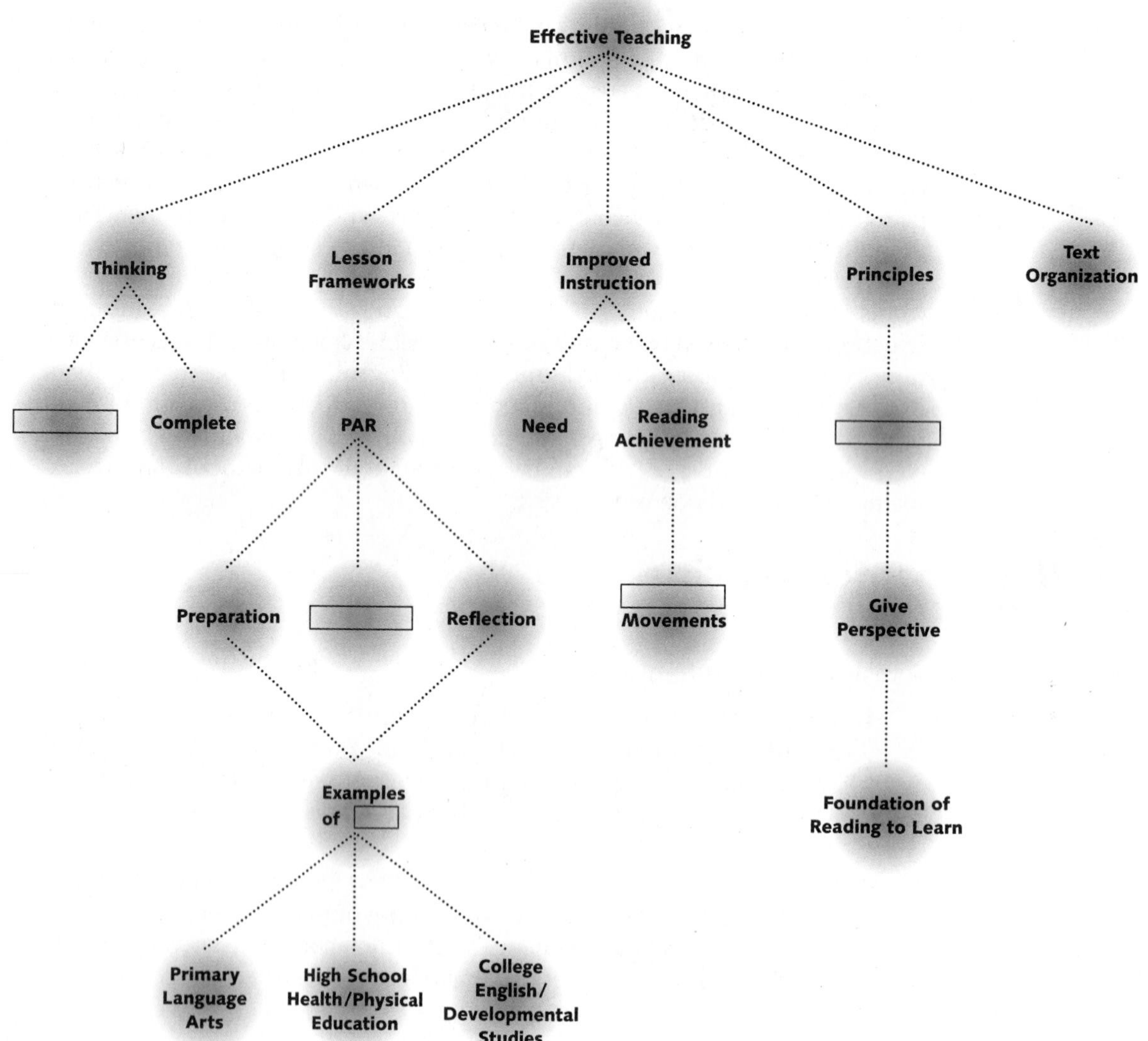

CHAPTER 2

The Affective Domain of Teaching

The three indispensables of genius are understanding, feeling, and perseverance.

—Anonymous

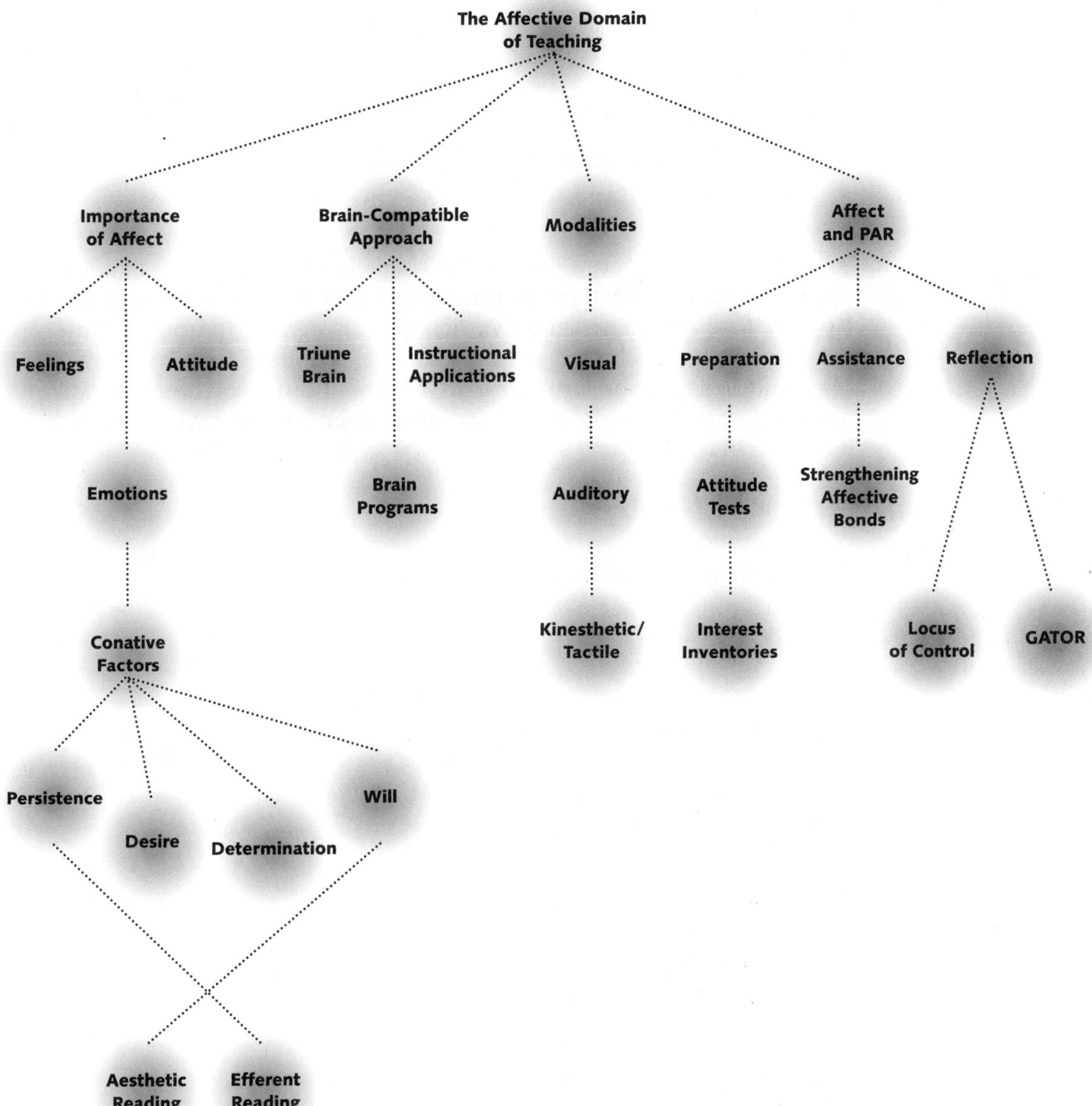

Preparing to Read

1. Before you read Chapter 2, try to answer the following questions to test your background knowledge concerning the affective domain of learning. For any you cannot answer, read the chapter carefully to expand your knowledge.
   a. Why is the affective domain of learning important?
   b. What are conative factors of learning?
   c. How can we use attitude tests and interest inventories to improve instruction?
   d. How can brain function influence students' actions?
   e. What is locus of control? Why is it an important construct for teaching?
2. Following is a list of terms used in this chapter. Some may be familiar to you in a general context, but in this chapter they may be used in unfamiliar ways. Rate your knowledge by placing a plus sign (+) in front of those you are sure that you know, a check mark (✓) in front of those you have some knowledge about, and a zero (0) in front of those you don't know. Be ready to locate and pay special attention to their meanings when they are presented in the chapter.

   ______ affective domain
   ______ attitude
   ______ conative
   ______ aesthetic reading
   ______ efferent reading
   ______ triune-brain theory
   ______ reptilian brain
   ______ old mammalian brain
   ______ new mammalian brain
   ______ downshifting
   ______ program
   ______ visual modality
   ______ auditory modality
   ______ kinesthetic/tactile modality
   ______ constructivist theory
   ______ internal locus of control
   ______ external locus of control

Objectives

As you read this chapter, focus your attention on the following objectives. You will:

1. learn what is meant by *affective domain*.
2. understand why affect is important to reading.
3. learn the importance of attitudes in teaching.
4. learn the importance of conative factors in reading.
5. understand what a brain-compatible approach to teaching is.
6. be able to name the modalities of learning and explain whether they are important in instruction.
7. understand the importance of attitude tests and discuss three attitude tests described in this chapter.
8. learn how to provide assistance in strengthening affective bonds.
9. learn why interest inventories are important.
10. better understand the construct of locus of control and its importance for content-area instruction.
11. be able to incorporate a number of affective strategies into the content-area curriculum.

The Importance of the Affective Domain in Teaching

Any responses to a stimulus that evoke feelings or emotions are said to be part of the **affective domain** of learning. Students in kindergarten through twelfth grade dwell in the affective domain—that is, feelings, emotions, and strong attitudes are very much a part of almost every waking hour. In contrast, teachers often dwell mainly in the cognitive domain, where student achievement is perceived to be the single most important reason for schooling. It is our contention that because of this perceptual mismatch, teachers and students often do not "meet" intellectually in the classroom. To put it another way, their needs are so different—teachers are driven to impart knowledge, students to discover the range of emotions inherent in each new day—that real communication sometimes does not occur in classrooms where the focus of instruction is only on content.

More than six decades ago, Adler (1931) wrote of the importance of self-concept and of children who can learn but won't. Three decades ago, Dechant (1970) cautioned that learning may be motivated not so much by what the teacher does or by after-the-learning events such as rewards and punishments, as by what the learner wants, is interested in, or feels will enhance self-esteem and personal worth. According to Dechant, the motivating condition comes from within and is more psychological than physiological (p. 537).

As we noted in Chapter 1, many reports indicate that students are not reading well. Glasser (1986), in his book *Control Theory in the Classroom*, states that more than half of all students are making little or no effort to learn, mainly because they don't believe that school provides any satisfaction. In a spirited repudiation of stimulus-response theory, Glasser maintains that human behavior is generated by what goes on inside the person. In an interview (Gough, 1987), Glasser spoke of the importance of affect:

> Except for those who live in deepest poverty, the psychological needs—love, power, freedom, and fun—take precedence over the survival needs, which most of us are able to satisfy. All our lives, we search for ways to satisfy our needs for love, belonging, caring, sharing, and cooperation. If a student feels no sense of belonging in school, no sense of being involved in caring and concern, that child will pay little attention to academic subjects. (p. 657)

The most outward manifestation of the affective domain is **attitude**—the mental disposition one exhibits toward others. Educators have known for a long time that student attitude is a crucial variable in reading achievement (Purves & Bech, 1972; Walberg & Tsai, 1985). Frank Smith (1988) notes that the emotional response to reading "is the primary reason most readers read, and probably the primary reason most nonreaders do not read" (p. 177). M. Cecil Smith (1990) found, in a longitudinal study, that reading attitudes tend to be stable over time from childhood through adulthood. It may be true that poor attitudes toward reading (or good attitudes) inculcated early in schooling tend to remain stable throughout one's life. Wolfe and Antinarella (1997) maintain that teachers are still able to win over and inspire students through developing in students attitudes and dispositions for learning that cause them to honor, respect, and value themselves and others.

How Teachers Can Improve Student Attitudes

Research by Heathington and Alexander (1984) indicates that although teachers see attitudes as important, they spend little time trying to change students' poor attitudes. To change student attitudes about reading, teachers first need to listen actively when students are commenting and discussing. Teachers need to concentrate on what students are saying and learn to reply to their comments, not formulate in advance a stock reply. Also, teachers need whenever possible to make reading fun and rewarding. They can do this by encouraging students to read on their own and making certain that reading assignments are not long and overwhelming. Teachers also can have students take part in frequent group sharing experiences. Another element of good teaching is for the teacher always to speak well of reading and be a reader who shares the books she or he is reading.

To promote affect, teachers should bring good literature into the classroom whenever possible, even in content-area classrooms. Bottomley and colleagues (1999) found that a literature-based approach to reading and writing had a greater impact on intermediate-age children's affective orientations toward literacy than did whole-language or basal-reader literacy instruction. In Chapter 3 we show how teachers can augment the textbook curriculum by the use of literature.

If teachers do all of the above, a positive classroom environment will be maintained. Researchers (Brophy, 1982; Fisher & Berliner, 1985) have stressed the importance of creating a positive classroom climate. Teachers should provide a climate that says: "I am never going to give up on you; I believe in you." Many famous people did poorly in school—for example, Albert Einstein, Woodrow Wilson, Thomas Edison, George Bernard Shaw, Pablo Picasso, William Butler Yeats, Henry Ford, and Benjamin Franklin. Paul Harvey, in *Destiny* (Aurandt, 1983), relates how Charles Schultz struggled with rejection in school for years. Schultz was a "loser" in school; no one had faith in him, yet he created *Peanuts*, one of today's most popular comic strips. If we emphasize the positive, each of us someday may play a central role in helping a future genius realize his or her potential. Most important of all, the teacher must value—and we mean truly value—inquiry, problem solving, and reasoning. By keeping an open mind and letting students take part in open-ended discussions, the teacher makes a statement about the true art of teaching that even the most limited students cannot ignore or misinterpret.

Conative Factors in Content-Area Teaching

In *Hooked on Books*, Fader (1976) relates his encounter with remedial students in Los Angeles whom he "catches" reading an article in *Playboy*. They explain to him that they aren't "can't" readers; they are "won't" readers. An aspect that teachers sometimes overlook is students' lack of determination, persistence, and will to gain information through reading. Energy, persistence, desire, determination, and will to learn are defined as **conative** variables (Cooter, 1994). The importance of persistence, determination, and will have been known to educators for a long time. Emerson White wrote in 1886:

> It seems important to note in this connection that the development of the intellectual faculties is conditioned upon the corresponding development of the sensibility and the will. The activity of the mind in knowing depends, among other things, on the acuteness of energy of the senses, the intensity of the emotions and desires, and the energy and constancy of the will. (p. 92)

Almost 100 years later, Paris, Lipson, and Wixson (1983) affirmed the importance of motivation and determination in a student's ability to become an independent learner. They noted that developing independence requires both the skills of reading and the will to learn in increasingly complex environments. Currently researchers like Maurer and Davidson (1999) are calling for teachers not to ignore the affective domain, enthusiasm, and what they call "the power of the heart" in using new technologies in classrooms for the teaching of new skills such as reading and writing.

Recent researchers such as Cooter (1994), Raven (1992), and Berlak (1992) argue for the emergence and realization of the importance of conative components of learning. They see conative factors as separate from but very close to the affective domain of learning. They also maintain that the affective domain and the conative aspects of human behavior are necessary for a student to function cognitively; these domains should not be artificially separated from the cognitive domain.

McDermott (1978) suggests that a child's progress in reading is influenced less by the nature of the reading activity than by the personal relationship the child has developed with the teacher. The argument is that children respond more often to the feelings the teacher displays when asking them to complete an assignment than to the activity itself. Implicit in McDermott's theory is the idea that reading is as much a social event or transaction as an intellectual one.

Two other views include the emotional qualities of reading. First, Barrett (1972) in his taxonomy of reading describes the highest level of comprehension as that of appreciation, which includes emotional response to theme or thesis, identification with characters or incidents, reactions to the author's use of language, and imagery. Second, reading is at least partly an emotional act; according to Rosenblatt (1991):

> We read for information, but we are also conscious of emotions about it and feel pleasure when the words we call up arouse vivid images and are rhythmic to the inner ear. (p. 445)

Rosenblatt categorized reading for pleasure as **aesthetic reading** (from the Greek for "perceiving beauty"), while **efferent reading** (from the Latin for "carry away") helps a reader acquire important information. According to her, the most effective learning takes place when reading is both aesthetic and efferent. The reader interacts more fully with text when both information and reaction to that information are present.

How Affect Is Displayed by Two Students

Let us consider two students to see how persistence, determination, and will can be of paramount importance in a classroom environment. One student, Freddy, has had difficulty in school since the third grade. Now in middle school he finds himself daily moving from classroom to classroom in which little or no talking is allowed among students except during the five minutes between classes. In his science class the typical lesson is going over the questions at the end of the chapter. He is supposed to, but doesn't, read the chapter for homework. The teacher gives a brief lecture about the reading material and addresses a stern lecture to the class about the value of homework and the apparent laziness shown by many students. This lecture is punctuated by the threat of a quiz at the end of the class and the warning that "all this will be on the test on Friday." Students are not allowed to talk to each other (though several write notes). The teacher spends a great deal of time and energy keeping the class "in order," preventing students from talking. Students spend the remainder of the period filling in words in spaces provided on textbook worksheets created by the publisher. To accomplish this task, Freddy does not have to read the text. He simply finds the answers by scanning for bold-print words and other clues that show where he might find the answer that will fill the blank. He seldom does well either on the end-of-class multiple-choice quiz or on the test, but he always acts as though he doesn't care. When the bell rings to change classes, Freddy feels as though he hasn't learned very much. In fact what he is learning is that science is not very interesting and that reading in science is pretty much about filling in spaces on worksheets to keep the teacher happy. In short, his will to be a good student is nonexistent and seems so suppressed that he has no extra energy to enjoy reading books on his own.

Becky is a ninth-grade student who also has had some difficulty since third grade, but her day is different from Freddy's. She starts the day in a 100-minute-long interdisciplinary "Earth class" in which the same teacher teaches both geography and earth science. The class begins with the teacher writing a single word on the chalkboard and then getting all the students involved by writing about what they think they will find about the topic. The anticipation is obvious as the students busily make their predictions. After students make predictions, the teacher asks each student to share aloud as she paraphrases each response on the chalkboard. Students at this point are simultaneously helping the teacher to find out about their prior knowledge and actively building on their own knowledge base through the sharing process. There is an air of importance to what each student has to offer, and the teacher frequently asks the students to explain why they gave certain responses. Both teacher and students respect the background knowledge each person brings to the pursuit of new understandings. The teacher then introduces a skill the students will use to make sense of the reading they are about to do. She points out what "good readers" always do when they read nonfiction text. Then she shows students how they can practice that skill in class today.

She sets up a guided practice in which students are grouped in pairs to read silently and then reflect with one another on what they have read. Students spend about 10 to 15 minutes actively reading a section of text and working with partners to practice recalling in their own words what they have learned. When each partnership has finished the reading, the partners collaborate to create a graphic representation of what they have learned. The teacher moves around the room to keep students on task, clarify important concepts, and answer any questions students might have. When students have finished the reading and shared their graphic representations with other groups in the classroom, the teacher puts six key terms on the chalkboard and asks each student to write a summary of what he or she has learned today, using all of the terms at least once in the summary. The teacher then collects the summaries for evaluation. Throughout the entire process, students in this class are active, engaged, and thoughtful. When Becky leaves her class, she knows she wrote a summary that will demonstrate her successful interpretation of the text. Becky never feels threatened in this class. She knows the teacher is interested not just in the teaching of geography and earth science, but also in sharing important skills that Becky has found out can help her in other subjects as well. Through the purposeful fun she is having in class, Becky is determined to be a better student and a better reader.

These two classroom descriptions illustrate the importance of student satisfaction in the learning process. Even if no more facts and concepts are learned in Becky's class than in Freddy's, Becky has more determination to learn than Freddy because she is learning how to learn in a nonthreatening and enjoyable atmosphere. Becky's teacher is employing strategies and paying attention to conative factors that are compatible with how students best learn new concepts. This technique, called brain-compatible teaching, deserves a close look.

A Brain-Compatible Approach to Teaching

Modern discoveries about how the human brain functions are quite possibly among the most significant scientific events in all of human history. To be able to allow for humans to learn, educators must recognize the dominance of the brain and the way it has evolved. Of particular importance is MacLean's work (1978) on the triune brain, as well as more recent research by Caine and Caine (1991), Healey (1990), Sylwester (1995), Diamond and Hopson (1998), and Jensen (1998), who discuss the evolution of the brain and the roles and functions of the various parts of the brain in teaching and in learning.

Two key concepts on which educators should focus are the role of the affective environment in learning and the importance of language in the physiological and functional development of the brain. To disregard these discoveries and the enormous part they can play in successful learning would be irresponsible, yet most educators either are not aware of these findings or choose to ignore them. Schools continue to teach through the use of segmented concepts reduced to bite-size bits. Such an approach is not inherently interesting because it is not compatible with how the human brain has evolved. In addition, the primary means of controlling students who have difficulty learning in this brain-incompatible system is through the use of threats, either of failure or of disciplinary measures. Since the brain cannot function at its highest level in a threatening environment, the use of threats can only guarantee failure in the learning process.

Sinatra (1986) theorizes that feelings, like language, are linked to brain activity. Debunking the simplistic "left brain/right brain" literature, Sinatra cites a wealth of research, such as Restak's (1982, 1984), to show that most learning tasks require both left-hemisphere and right-hemisphere processing. Cooperation rather than competition between the brain hemispheres is the prevailing mode in most learning. Moreover, Sinatra proposes the importance of the two subcortical brains in the emotional and motivational aspects of learning. He states:

> since the neural pathways between the cortex and the reticular and limbic systems function all the time without our conscious awareness, educators must re-

> alize that curriculum content cannot be approached solely by intellectual reasoning. The systems regulating feeling, emotions, and attentiveness are tied to the very learning of information. (p. 143)

Thus the teacher's attitude toward the reason for learning, and toward the learners themselves, may be a more important factor in how well something is learned than the specific content. In making learning interesting and challenging, teachers are, in reality, activating brain subsystems responsible for alertness and emotional tone. Sinatra criticizes dull worksheet drills as decoding exercises that negate students' eagerness to learn. Berry (1969) agrees that motivation, attention, and memory all operate in an interlocking fashion to enhance learning.

Sinatra's work is compatible with the **triune-brain theory** described by MacLean (1978). This model clarifies how the brain works in general and precisely why affect is so important in reading. MacLean explains that the brain has evolved into three principal parts, each of which handles a different function. The most primitive is the brain stem, often referred to as the **reptilian brain** because reptiles as well as mammals possess this limited brain function. This lowest section of the brain deals with only the most basic needs, such as reaction to immediate threat. This part of the brain holds no memories, which is why when the reptilian brain is in charge, we have no recollection of what occurred.

The middle section of the brain—which MacLean calls the **old mammalian brain** because it is present in all mammals—is a larger and newer portion of the brain. It controls emotions and plays a great role in the learning process by determining whether the newest portion of the brain will be able to fully function. Clark (1983) calls it the "emotional mind." It is the seat of the limbic system, which secretes different chemicals when a mammal is confronted with stimuli. For instance, a negative event may stimulate chemicals that affect the reptilian brain, which may then produce an automatic response to danger, much like freezing or "shutting down."

The upper section of the brain—which MacLean calls the **new mammalian brain**—is the neocortex, the newest and largest portion of the brain. It deals with abilities such as mathematical and verbal acuity and logical reasoning. This is the most complex part of the human brain and, as a result, the one that functions most slowly. The neurological makeup of the neocortex allows learning to take place through associations that can number in the high trillions. Medical researchers know that, through the release of limbic system neurotransmitters, cells of the neocortex are either helped or hindered in their functioning.

Possible applications of the triune-brain theory might include actions such as the following. An animal that encounters a speeding car while crossing a road late at night will most likely seem to freeze, as if it cannot figure out that running would be much safer than not moving. Its instincts tell it to be still until danger passes. If a student perceives an academic climate as threatening, chemicals may very well be secreted to the reptilian brain, telling the brain to, in effect, revert to the instinct of freezing, thereby impeding learning and retention. The primary concern for educators ought to be that the neocortex be allowed to function to its fullest potential by eliminating the possibility of threats. Students such as Becky, described earlier, who feel positive and happy about a learning experience will be better able to process and retain information. Students such as Freddy, who are uncertain and unhappy in a learning situation, either at school or at home, will become emotionally unable to attend to a task for any length of time. Just as the reptilian brain takes over in situations of panic, the limbic system can take over from the highest levels of thinking possible in the neocortex if the emotional climate is threatening or stressful. Hart (1983a) describes the process by which negative messages are sent from the old mammalian to the reptilian brain as **downshifting**.

Research also has shown that brain functioning increases significantly when novelty is present (Restak, 1979) and when subjects experience feelings of pleasure and joy (Sagan, 1977). Conversely, researchers have found that removing touch and movement can result in increases in violent behavior (Penfield, 1975). All of this gives credence to the importance of attitudes, feelings, emotions, motivation, and conative factors in thinking, reading, and learning.

How does the theory of the triune brain apply to reading and thinking about content material? Suppose that Freddy, who dreads science class, did not read the assignment and is confronted with a pop quiz. The old mammalian brain may be activated; a sense of frustration, even panic, may occur. Because the new mammalian brain (neocortex) has little information to contribute, and because hormones associated with anxiety are being generated by the old mammalian brain, the message gets routed or rerouted from the new mammalian brain to the reptilian brain: Shut down and save me! When students say that their minds went blank, they provide an apt description of what literally happened. Similarly, consider the teacher who is struggling to find a way to present content material but cannot seem to get it across to her students. She is using the chapter information, but it just isn't working. She becomes more and more frustrated and less and less effective. Again, a sort of downshifting may be occurring.

The neocortex, according to Leslie Hart (1983b), is what separates humans from most animals. It is in the newest part of the brain, which enables us to make plans and carry them out. Hart suggests that pattern-seeking—efforts to make sense out of complex and often chaotic realities—is the key to human intelligence. Such pattern-seeking can be fostered by what Greenough, Withers, and Anderson (1992) call "enriched environments," where students encounter substantial and varied input, problem-solving efforts, and immediate feedback in the context of real-world problems. The human brain did not develop because of evolutionary needs for rote memory, manipulation of symbols, or dealing with tight, sequential structures or work systems, which today constitute the main concerns of conventional schooling and much training. If a learner already knows at least something about a topic, then a logical, sequential, and fragmented presentation may serve well enough to transfer some new information about that topic to his or her neocortex. But if a learner is not already familiar with the topic, this kind of presentation produces consistently poor learning results.

Hart further suggests that we live by "programs" that we acquire and store for use in the brain. A **program** is a fixed sequence for accomplishing some goal. The goal may be learning a new way of approaching a math problem or something as simple as walking across a room. Human nature makes the working of a program a pleasurable experience; we can rely on its activation to help us achieve a goal. We can use only programs that are built on and stored through experience. Each individual develops his or her own unique programs. Efforts to impose a program on someone who has not developed it on his or her own is a futile endeavor. Yet these brain programs are used to accomplish everything we do. In performing all tasks, we routinely use a three-step cycle: (1) evaluating the situation, (2) selecting the program that seems most appropriate from our store, and (3) implementing it. Fully acquired programs, though laboriously built, have an automatic quality that can easily lead one to forget that other individuals have not already acquired them. For instance, a good reader attempts to read difficult material by using a program developed over the years. Another person might implement a similar program but select a different way of previewing the material. Inefficient readers have not yet developed an effective program for reading difficult material. They don't know what to do and try to keep implementing the program they "know" for reading easy material. Yet most teachers—as good readers—don't even realize that this is the problem; teachers are equipped with programs that have become automatic for them.

Smith (1986) demonstrates that real learning takes place with no effort. He suggests that stress in learning comes only from trying to learn something that seems to have no purpose and that we learn all the time without suspecting that we are doing so. We usually do not try to learn the daily newspaper when we read it, yet hours or days later we can recall many details of what we read. The same phenomenon occurs when a child is able to recall in detail the plot of a movie seen several days earlier. We learn every time we make sense of something; we learn in the act of making sense of the world around us. Thus learning programs acquired are acquired incidentally through the successful creation of meaning in the act of learning. Unfortunately, for many students today the programs acquired are negative. They often are programs of survival resulting from the lack of a brain-compatible environment. They even may be programs of failure and dropping out—a sense that school is "just not for me."

Healey (1990) points out that the neocortex—and especially the prefrontal lobes—foster the ability in humans to stay mentally focused and reflect on meaning. These areas are shaped through the use of language. She further suggests that students' deficiencies in the development of these programs are the result of three factors that contribute to the failure of appropriate language development: (1) insufficient early language development in children, (2) the effects of television, and (3) educational experiences that fail to place stress on language, especially the interactive use of language, both oral and written, to solve real-world problems. According to Healey:

> Language shapes culture, language shapes thinking—and language shapes brains. The verbal bath in which a society soaks its children arranges their synapses and their intellects; it helps them learn to reason, reflect, and respond to the world. . . . The brains of today's children are being structured in language patterns antagonistic to the values and goals of formal education. The culprit is diminished and degraded exposure to the forms of good, meaningful language

> that enables us to converse with others, with the written word, and with our own minds. (p. 86)

She goes on to say that for students to reason effectively and to solve problems, they need to learn to pursue learning through mental thought, uninterrupted by distractions.

Focusing on what the latest brain research is telling us about how students learn (Wolfe & Brandt, 1998; Lowery, 1998; Kotulak, 1996; Diamond & Hopson, 1998), we believe the following are important to teaching:

1. Students remember material best that is structured and meaningful (Jensen, 1998).
2. Because the environment in which a brain operates determines to a large degree the functioning ability of that brain, the classroom should always be a rich environment in which students interact.
3. An enriched environment allows students to make sense of what they are learning.
4. Opportunities to talk and move about are important in allowing for heightening of brain activity.
5. Threats and pressures need to be held to a minimum because they cause the neocortex (the newest and highest level of the brain) to function poorly.
6. Because the brain is essentially curious, learning must be a process of active construction by the learner, whereby students relate what they learn to what they already know.
7. Because learning is strongly influenced by emotion, when emotion is added to learner input, retention is enhanced.
8. Teachers should stress intuitive learning as much as step-by-step logic to allow creative thinking to emerge.

By taking advantage of what we now know about the way the human brain functions, we can create in our classrooms an environment in which all students can perform at their highest potential, developing patterns that will carry them through life as successful learners. In an affective environment that facilitates optimum use of the higher brain functions, students are empowered to become effective, self-motivated learners.

Modalities of Learning

Students learn in different ways (see the Technology Box). Students who learn best through the **visual modality** learn from books, pictures, writing on the board and in notes, and viewing filmstrips, movies, and anything else to be seen. Students who learn primarily through the **auditory modality** respond well to lectures, discussions, and other oral presentations. Some students, espe-

TECHNOLOGY BOX

Example of Finding and Using an Internet Site for Content Area Reading; Internet Site to Celebrate Earth Day

By Jan Stilwell

The site I chose was in the periodical *Web Guide*, found in the school's library/media center. It is an excellent help in finding a variety of interesting and useful Internet sites. I was looking for some new ideas to help my class celebrate Earth Day this year and began my search using this helpful aid. As usual, I was not disappointed! I found a site that I thought might have some current activities and would integrate reading with our celebration of Earth Day.

The site was listed in *Web Guide* under "Education World" on page 31. The site is described as "a comprehensive search engine/directory focusing solely on education" with sites that are current and easy to read and a format that makes finding information "trouble-free." The URL is listed as http://www.education~world.com

I went to the site and found a directory on "Lesson Planning: Celebrate the Year of the Ocean." I clicked once on the title for this site. I found just what I was looking for: "What Are You Doing for Earth Day? 28 Earth Day Activities." I clicked once on this title and began reading the offerings.

A majority of the Earth Day activities integrated reading and writing into the science of conservation and the celebration of Earth Day. The activities were offered on a variety of grade levels with only a few appropriate for kindergarten. However, many of the activities could be adapted to fit any grade level. I found that some of the activities also gave the surfer opportunities to visit other websites that would give further information and links to similar topics. The activities that I found the most interesting, as well as usable for my kindergarten students, included categorizing litter, alphabetizing trash, creating a personal litter bag with an antilittering message, a sequencing activity of planting a tree, and a tasty recipe for Dirt Dessert.

In choosing these activities, I noted that they include the framework for PAR. The *preparation* activities of categorizing and alphabetizing the litter give the young child experiences with the concept of litter and its negative effects while allowing the child to use real reading of materials found in her or his own world. The *assistance* activities of creating the litter bag with slogans and sequencing the planting of a tree support the students as they explore the language of creating slogans and the organization of a task that supports Earth Day to its fullest. The *reflection* activities could include either of the previous activities, but for kindergarten children, creating something to eat serves as an excellent time to reflect on learning as they enjoy what they have made and discuss what they have learned about a topic. The Dirt Dessert (http://www.kab.org/dirt.html) will be used as our reflection activity as we complete our celebration of "Taking Care of Mother Earth" and talk about all that we have learned about litter and our greatest resource: trees.

I hope you find this site useful for your own Earth Day happenings in your classroom. Happy Earth Day, everyone!

cially individuals with severe impairments to auditory and visual processing, learn best through the **kinesthetic/tactile modality**—through muscle movement or through touch. The following list presents characteristics of students who learn through each of these modalities. It is meant not as a checklist of rules of behavior but as a general reminder of behaviors that students who prefer a certain modality of learning often exhibit:

Characteristics of Students Who Learn Through Certain Modalities

The Visual Learner

- Picks up clues to learning by watching
- Likes demonstrations
- Likes descriptions
- Has good imagination
- Remembers faces more often than names
- Takes notes
- Has good handwriting
- Tends to be very deliberate
- When in a new situation is quiet and observant
- Is neat, meticulous
- Prefers art and art museums
- Thinks in pictures and details

The Auditory Learner

- Likes noise and likes to make noise
- Enjoys talking, listening
- When reading, vocalizes and subvocalizes
- Tends to use sound cues to learn words
- Remembers names more often than faces
- Expressive vocabularies are well developed
- Is easily distracted by sound
- Solves problems verbally
- Prefers music, listening to radio

The Kinesthetic/Tactile Learner

- Does not enjoy reading or being read to
- Has spelling problems
- Has poor handwriting
- Does not attend to visual presentations
- Has poor language development
- Is often oblivious to surroundings
- Likes direct involvement in situations

All students have learning strengths. When teachers find out what these are, they are able to include activities in their instruction that use those strengths. For instance, some students learn best by thinking, others by doing, and still others by perception or intuition (Anderson & Adams, 1992). For learners who are intuitive, games, role-plays, peer feedback, and discussion are helpful. Perceptive learners enjoy opportunities to observe, reflect, and listen to lectures. "Thinkers" prefer study time alone and clear, well-structured presentations. "Doers" want to practice and complete projects. Variety in instruction ensures that more students will be accommodated in an effective learning environment.

Samples (1994) encourages teachers to vary instruction so that the learning modalities can be accommodated. Samples has stated:

> Teachers who successfully use diverse learning modes in their instructional approaches accomplish several remarkable things. First, they create a climate where the ways of knowing central to the different modalities are all seen as legitimate, acceptable and desirable. Second, they make sure that each student is encouraged to explore other modalities without threat or penalty. Finally, the teachers synthesize the various contributions of the students' preferences into a comprehensive view of the science that is being studied. (p. 16)

We believe also that teachers have to provide instruction that allows for all the modalities of learning. All students learn by seeing and hearing. Students also need opportunities for movement and to construct and manipulate things with their hands. But even though students need opportunities to learn through different modalities, it is our contention that teachers do not need to separate students or activities according to their preferred modality. In a classroom where a teacher is paying attention to affect and is providing brain-compatible learning, students have ample opportunities to encounter all modalities of learning. An essential by-product of the PAR Lesson Framework, described in Chapter 1, is that students (1) are able by listening to learn from peers in groups and from the teacher in the whole-class discussion, (2) are able to learn visually through constructing graphic organizers and notes and following work the teacher puts on overheads and the chalkboard, and (3) manipulate concrete props such as study guides, What-I-Know Activities, and two-column note-taking worksheets provided by the teacher. In short, using the PAR Lesson Framework provides an avenue for students to learn through differing modalities. Let us now look at each stage of PAR to learn both assessment and teaching strategies for improving instruction related to the affective domain.

Preparation for Affective Teaching

An important part of preparing to teach is to find out what attitudes students exhibit toward school in general and your course in particular. However, we suggest that before doing this, teachers conduct some self-assessment on whether they are exhibiting an enthusiastic and positive attitude about reading in their classroom. One factor found to be positively correlated with both teacher affectivity and attitudinal changes is teacher enthusiasm (Streeter, 1986). According to Collins (1977), teacher enthusiasm affects vocal delivery, eyes, gestures, body movements, facial expressions, word selection, acceptance of ideas and feelings, and overall energy. The teacher attitude survey called *Teacher Inventory of Attitude—Creating a Reading Environment with Feeling* (TIA–CREWF) helps teachers assess whether they are exhibiting an enthusiastic and positive attitude about reading in their classroom (see Activity 2.1). Any K–12 teacher can use this survey for self-assessment.

ACTIVITY 2.1 Teacher Inventory of Attitude—Creating a Reading Environment with Feeling

Directions: Please read each of the following questions, and then circle *often, sometimes, seldom,* or *never* after each question.

1. Do you have patience with those who are having difficulty reading?
   Often Sometimes Seldom Never
2. When you finish explaining the reading assignment, do your students want to find out more about the assignment?
   Often Sometimes Seldom Never
3. Do your students ever get so interested in your reading assignment that they talk about the assignment after it is completed?
   Often Sometimes Seldom Never
4. Do you ask thought-provoking questions about the reading assignments?
   Often Sometimes Seldom Never
5. Do you discuss with your students concepts they might look for before reading their assignments?
   Often Sometimes Seldom Never
6. Do you make difficult material seem easier to read?
   Often Sometimes Seldom Never
7. Do you give students aid in finding resource books for assignments?
   Often Sometimes Seldom Never
8. Do you refrain from giving reading assignments from materials that are often too difficult for students to understand?
   Often Sometimes Seldom Never
9. Do you explain or define the new concepts in reading assignments?
   Often Sometimes Seldom Never
10. Do you tell students when they have done a creditable job on a reading assignment?
    Often Sometimes Seldom Never
11. Do you give reading assignments of appropriate length?
    Often Sometimes Seldom Never
12. When students are reading silently, do you monitor the classroom to make certain the environment is conducive to quiet study?
    Often Sometimes Seldom Never

13. Do you talk to students about the value of reading well in today's society?
    Often Sometimes Seldom Never
14. Do you enlist the help of students in deciding how much reading is needed to complete assignments?
    Often Sometimes Seldom Never
15. After an assignment, do you ask students what they would like to read for further study?
    Often Sometimes Seldom Never
16. Do you know how interested your students are in reading?
    Often Sometimes Seldom Never
17. Are you interested in reading in your daily life?
    Often Sometimes Seldom Never
18. Do you read books for pleasure?
    Often Sometimes Seldom Never
19. Are you flexible in your reading—that is, do you read at different rates for different purposes?
    Often Sometimes Seldom Never
20. Do you find yourself exhibiting more enthusiasm than normal when discussing a certain book?
    Often Sometimes Seldom Never

All 20 items should be answered *often* or *sometimes*.

Scoring key:

15–20 *often* or *sometimes* responses	Very effective
12–14 *often* or *sometimes* responses	Reasonably effective; fair in the affective areas
8–11 *often* or *sometimes* responses	OK; need some improvement
0–7 *often* or *sometimes* responses	Poor; do some rethinking!

Adapted from a questionnaire developed by James Laffey in *Successful Interactions in Reading and Language: A Practical Handbook for Subject Matter Teachers*, by J. Laffey and R. Morgan, 1983, Harrisonburg, VA: Feygan.

Besides using the TIA–CREWF to self-assess their own enthusiasm for reading and proclivity to model affect, teachers also should assess students to determine positive and negative attitudes toward reading. The *Mikulecky Behavioral Reading Attitude Measure* (Mikulecky, Shanklin, & Caverly, 1979) for older students (see Activity 2.2) and the *Elementary Reading Attitude Survey* (McKenna & Kear, 1990) for early-elementary-grade students (see Activity 2.3) were designed to cover a broad range of affective interest and developmental stages. Keys for interpreting these two surveys are provided in Appendix A, along with technical information on their construction and validation. These tests can be given as pretests and again after several months as posttests to determine whether students' attitudes have improved significantly over the period.

Sometimes simply by finding out what students like to do in their spare time, but being aware of their goals and perceived needs, teachers can ensure a more positive atmosphere in the classroom. To this end, teachers can create general-interest inventories such as the one shown in Activity 2.4. One high school English teacher asked her eleventh-graders to indicate what types of writing experiences they liked best. She discovered that they enjoyed writing letters but

ACTIVITY 2.2 Mikulecky Behavioral Reading Attitude Measure

On the following pages are 20 descriptions. You are to respond by indicating how much these descriptions are either unlike you or like you. For *very unlike* you, circle the number 1. For *very like* you, circle the number 5. If you fall somewhere between, circle the appropriate number.

Example:

You receive a book for a Christmas present. You start the book, but decide to stop half-way through.
Very Unlike Me 1 2 3 4 5 Very Like Me

1. You walk into the office of a doctor or dentist and notice that there are magazines set out.
   Very Unlike Me 1 2 3 4 5 Very Like Me
2. People have made jokes about your reading in unusual circumstances or situations.
   Very Unlike Me 1 2 3 4 5 Very Like Me
3. You are in a shopping center you've been to several times when someone asks where books and magazines are sold. You are able to tell the person.
   Very Unlike Me 1 2 3 4 5 Very Like Me
4. You feel very uncomfortable because emergencies have kept you away from reading for a couple of days.
   Very Unlike Me 1 2 3 4 5 Very Like Me
5. You are waiting for a friend in an airport or supermarket and find yourself leafing through the magazines and paperback books.
   Very Unlike Me 1 2 3 4 5 Very Like Me
6. If a group of acquaintances would laugh at you for always being buried in a book, you'd know it's true and wouldn't mind much at all.
   Very Unlike Me 1 2 3 4 5 Very Like Me
7. You are tired of waiting for the dentist, so you start to page through a magazine.
   Very Unlike Me 1 2 3 4 5 Very Like Me
8. People who are regular readers often ask your opinion about new books.
   Very Unlike Me 1 2 3 4 5 Very Like Me
9. One of your first impulses is to "look it up" whenever there is something you don't know or whenever you are going to start something new.
   Very Unlike Me 1 2 3 4 5 Very Like Me
10. Even though you are a very busy person, there is somehow always time for reading.
    Very Unlike Me 1 2 3 4 5 Very Like Me
11. You've finally got some time alone in your favorite chair on a Sunday afternoon. You see something to read and decide to spend a few minutes reading just because you feel like it.
    Very Unlike Me 1 2 3 4 5 Very Like Me
12. You tend to disbelieve and be a little disgusted by people who repeatedly say they don't have time to read.
    Very Unlike Me 1 2 3 4 5 Very Like Me
13. You find yourself giving special books to friends or relatives as gifts.
    Very Unlike Me 1 2 3 4 5 Very Like Me
14. At Christmas time, you look in the display window of a bookstore and find yourself interested in some books and uninterested in others.
    Very Unlike Me 1 2 3 4 5 Very Like Me

15. Sometimes you find yourself so excited by a book you try to get friends to read it.
    Very Unlike Me 1 2 3 4 5 Very Like Me
16. You've just finished reading a story and settled back for a moment to sort of enjoy and remember what you've just read.
    Very Unlike Me 1 2 3 4 5 Very Like Me
17. You choose to read nonrequired books and articles fairly regularly (a few times a week).
    Very Unlike Me 1 2 3 4 5 Very Like Me
18. Your friends would not be at all surprised to see you buying or borrowing a book.
    Very Unlike Me 1 2 3 4 5 Very Like Me
19. You have just gotten comfortably settled in a new city. Among the things you plan to do are check out the library and bookstore.
    Very Unlike Me 1 2 3 4 5 Very Like Me
20. You've just heard about a good book but haven't been able to find it. Even though you've tried, you look for it in one more bookstore.
    Very Unlike Me 1 2 3 4 5 Very Like Me

Reprinted with permission of Larry Mikulecky. Data regarding the construction, validation, and interpretation of this test are contained in Appendix A.

disliked writing essays. The curriculum expectation was that all students would learn and practice writing persuasive essays. While teaching "Sinners in the Hands of an Angry God" by Jonathan Edwards, the teacher talked about this sermon as an example of a persuasive essay. Then she asked the students to relate some of their own experiences in trying to convince someone of something important to them and to estimate how successful their efforts had been. After developing a list of successful persuasion strategies, she told the students to write a persuasive essay in the form of a letter to a real person, trying to persuade that person about an important issue. The assignment was a huge success.

All of the assessment instruments described so far enable teachers to determine what attitudes and interests their students bring to classrooms and thereby to design effective instruction that is sensitive to the students as individuals. When teachers show students that they are interested in them as people, significant changes can occur in student behavior. In the next section we present ways to assist students and use the assessment results.

Assistance by Strengthening Affective Bonds

Affective bonds can be strengthened for students when teachers assist students during the lesson by designing tasks that influence children's motivation. Turner and Paris (1995) explain how the context for literacy includes student choices, a challenge, personal control, collaboration, the construction of meaning, and specific consequences. Choice allows students to select from those areas in

ACTIVITY 2.3 Elementary Reading Attitude Survey

School ______________ Grade ______________ Name ______________

1. How do you feel when you read a book on a rainy Saturday?

2. How do you feel when you read a book in school during free time?
3. How do you feel about reading for fun at home?
4. How do you feel about getting a book as a present?
5. How do you feel about spending free time reading?
6. How do you feel about starting a new book?
7. How do you feel about reading during summer vacation?
8. How do you feel about reading instead of playing?
9. How do you feel about going to a bookstore?
10. How do you feel about reading different kinds of books?
11. How do you feel when the teacher asks you questions about what you read?
12. How do you feel about doing reading workbook pages and worksheets?
13. How do you feel about reading in school?
14. How do you feel about reading your school books?
15. How do you feel about learning from a book?
16. How do you feel when it's time for reading class?
17. How do you feel about the stories you read in reading class?
18. How do you feel when you read out loud in class?
19. How do you feel about using a dictionary?
20. How do you feel about taking a reading test?

From Appendix of McKenna, M. C., & Kear, D. J. (1990, May). Measuring attitude toward reading: A new tool for teachers. *The Reading Teacher, 43*(9), 626–639.

ACTIVITY 2.4 Student Survey

Name ______________ What do you prefer to be called? ______________
Home address ______________ Phone ______________
Name of parent/guardian ______________
Parent's place of employment ______________ Parent's work phone ______________
Your usual grade in Math ______, Social Studies ______, English ______, Science ______. The grade you plan to earn this year in Math ______, Social Studies ______, English ______, Science ______.
What percentage of your grades should come from tests? ______. In what other ways do you want to earn grades? ______________
Complete the following:
My favorite subjects in school are ______________
My least favorite subjects are ______________
Circle all the words that describe you:

healthy	quiet	good sport	friendly
dependable	likable	hard worker	lazy
honest	nervous	cooperative	lonely
worthless	quick-tempered	shy	artistic
sense of humor	cheerful	easily upset	clean, neat appearance
forgetful	easy-going	good leader	easily discouraged

If I could change anything about myself, it would be ______________

If I could change anything about school, it would be ______________

My favorite hobby is ______________
My favorite sport is ______________
At home it is fun to ______________
I like to read about ______________
Ten years from now I would like to be ______________
Things I do well are ______________
What I dislike about classes are ______________
What I dislike about teachers are ______________
Sports I play at school are ______________
Clubs I belong to at school are ______________

---

which they are most interested, thus ensuring greater attention during the task. Challenge keeps students from being bored, as long as the learning tasks are not at the frustration level. Students need to feel that a class is "their class" as much as the teacher's; students are more willing as learners when they feel that they control their own learning. Collaboration or social interaction motivates students to be more curious, confident about, and engaged in learning.

When students can make sense of their learning, developing a knowledge base or constructing their own purposes for reading a selection and developing tasks on their own that demonstrate their learning, they are constructing meaning. The **constructivist theory** of learning emphasizes the important role of the learner in literacy tasks, allowing readers to feel comfortable with learning because they are so fully integrated in putting it all together. Concerning this theory Sparks (1995) has said:

> Constructivists believe that learners build knowledge structures rather than merely receive them from teachers. In this view, knowledge is not simply transmitted from teacher to student, but is instead constructed in the mind of the learner. From a constructivist perspective, it is critical that teachers model appropriate behavior, guide student activities, and provide various forms of examples rather than use common instructional practices that emphasize telling and directing. (p. 5)

If the outcomes of the learning are positive feelings about what is learned and accomplished, then the consequences motivate students to keep learning. If consequences are viewed as outside the student's control, such as teacher judgments, then motivation may be reduced.

Providing Assistance with the Environment

In a recent study of 11,794 school sophomores in 820 schools, achievement gains and engagement were significantly higher in restructured schools (Lee & Smith, 1994). Restructuring efforts included some of the following: school-within-a-school, keeping students in the same homeroom for the four years of high school, cooperative learning foci, teacher teams having common planning time, and flexible time for classes. Smaller schools enjoyed the most gains. Achievement, as tested in math, science, reading, and history, was consistently higher with restructuring. Students became more committed and involved in their learning. Thus both cognitive and affective areas showed improvement.

Individual teachers cannot restructure schools, but they can restructure their classrooms. Forget and Morgan (1995) found that when reading to learn was emphasized in a school-within-a-school setting in working with at-risk youngsters, attitudes and school attendance improved significantly. In addition they found that students' ability to use and think critically about textbook material improved measurably. The way a classroom is arranged, or can be arranged readily, affects the learning and teaching climate. Students who always face forward to the teacher as the main focus in the classroom receive the message that learning takes place through lecture and teacher control. To engage all students in learning, redefinitions of the classroom climate must be made (Kowalski, 1995). A seminar approach, as is used in the Paideia schools (Strong, 1995), calls for long tables with all learners seated facing each other for intensive discussion. If such tables are not available, teachers and students might move several desks together to create the same effect. Group work calls for small clusters of chairs in several parts of a room. Daily (1995) asks teachers to motivate students by modeling the classroom after the workplace. Students are "paid" as a reward for performing well in assignments and completing long-term projects. Activity 2.5 is a teacher's adaptation of Daily's system.

Teachers can also develop thematic units that cross content areas and that are developed around "themes of caring" (Noddings, 1995), such as "caring for strangers and global others by studying war, poverty, and tolerance" (p. 676). When teachers collaborate on such units, students see the value of collaboration more clearly.

Fostering the Habit of Reading

Students learn early that they can avoid reading. Bintz (1993) interviewed many students who were resistant to reading. He found that the majority avoided reading whenever possible, listening instead to the teacher for the basic information to be covered on tests. He concluded that by "resorting to shortcut and survival strategies, students were participating in their own deskilling" (p. 613).

Teachers must be careful to design instruction that includes reading as a crucial component and that ensures the consequences of reading are important as well as interesting. Richardson (1995) shares a personal story of using three techniques to keep her middle-school son reading: reading aloud from democratically chosen selections, reserving a period of time for sustained reading, and respecting her son's choices of reading material. Restrictions were not made, and the new climate of sharing, time, and choice fostered the reading habit. Teachers can implement all three of these techniques in some form in their classrooms. Enlisting parent support and being on the lookout for interesting newspaper articles in your content area are two ways to start.

Reflection Strategies for Affective Teaching

Two strategies will help students become reflective and responsible for their own learning.

Reinforcing Internally Controlled Behaviors

Rotter's (1966) social learning theory suggests that individuals attribute their successes and failures to different sources. People with an **internal locus of control** accept responsibility for the consequences of their behavior. They also perceive the relationship between their conduct and its outcomes. Those with an **external locus of control** blame fate, change, other individuals, or task difficulty for their successes and failures (Chandler, 1975). The concept of locus of control is a legitimate construct for affective teaching because it helps teachers understand certain behaviors in the classroom.

ACTIVITY 2.5 A Version of BrainMakers Incorporated

Materials

- Each student is issued a packet of five checks and one check register. (I go to the bank and beg for donations, but you could make your own for the students.)

Payments

- Each student is paid $50 per day based on a full day's attendance. Sickness and doctors' appointments are not excused. A student who is not there doesn't get paid even if the absence is not his or her fault.
- Paydays are the 15th and 30th of each month.

Deductions (I don't distinguish between types of assignments.)

- Students lose $20 for each missed homework assignment in the 1st nine weeks, $25 in the 2nd nine weeks, $30 in the 3rd nine weeks, $40 in the 4th nine weeks.
- Students lose $10 for a negative phone call home or a scheduled parent conference due to a student's not being responsible.
- Students lose $10 for being tardy.
- When a student is out of checks, he or she will be charged $25 for a new set.
- Students unable to make rent should be charged all that they have in their accounts and then docked a $20 late fee from the next paycheck in addition. (Consider taking away a privilege until enough money is earned to cover rent.)
- No checks or check registers are allowed to go home. Any student losing the checking materials is out of the game for the rest of the year.

Employees' responsibilities

- Students must pay $600 in rent on the 1st of every month for the use of desks, books, cafeteria, playground equipment, computers, etc.
- September rent may be prorated at $15 per day because students won't have any money in their accounts. I actually charged my students rent for September at the end of September and then collected October's rent on the 1st of October. All other rent should be collected on the 1st or the first available school day closest to the 1st of each month.
- Students must endorse their checks when they are paid and then enter the amount correctly in their check registers. (Doing this as a class lesson with an overhead is very important for the first four or five payments until they get the hang of it.) You should have to write rent checks with them for only two months; they should be able to do it by themselves by November.
- Students write a check to you paying for items purchased in the auction (see below).

Auctions

- Auctions are held at the end of each nine-week period, for a total of four auctions. Good marketing in weekly newsletters to parents or sending home flyers can bring in donations to your auction that will save you time and money.
- Have as many parents volunteer for the auctions as you can. They can help move the merchandise to you as you auction it and help the students keep track of how much they are spending so no child spends more than allowed. Also, at the conclusion of the auction the students write you a check for the auction items they just purchased, and parents can help with this and help check the registers for accuracy.

- Allow time before the auction for students to browse and decide what they want to buy. Some will spend all their money on one large item; others will buy several small things.
- Allow time after the auction for students to admire their purchases and, in some instances, trade off with other students for something else.
- Students must always keep a balance in their accounts for emergencies (groceries, medical, bills, etc.); thus they should not be allowed to go below $700 in their accounts. Most times, if rent has been paid, I let them go down to $150 but no lower. They write the amount of money they can spend on a piece of paper before the auction and deduct the amount every time they purchase something so they can keep a running total of what they have left to spend. At the end of the auction, they add up all that they spent and write a check to "BrainMakers, Inc." for the correct amount, putting "auction" on the memo line of the check.

Hints

- Have students (or parent volunteers) cut out the checks, and always keep plenty on hand.
- Have a student fill in the date and the names on the checks so all the teacher has to do is write the amount owed.
- Sign the checks that the teacher uses to pay them before you photocopy them so you won't have to keep signing your signature.
- Consistently check the registers to help students who are having subtraction difficulties, aren't dating the transactions, or are placing their numbers in an incorrect area of the register. Ensuring that students keep accurate records all along is very important and will prevent them from not knowing their account balance because of errors in the register.
- No ink in the registers—pencils only.
- Get auction volunteers to help the students keep track of how much they are spending and to help at the end with check writing. You will be tired after talking the whole auction and trying to keep the students from playing with their new toys. Parents can help with the classroom management.

BrainMakers, Inc. ____________________

Pay to the Order of____________________________________ $__________

____ Dollars

Memo____________________

05100001: 9541 8741 0100

Developed by Chris White, fourth-grade teacher, Shady Grove Elementary, Henrico County, Virginia. This activity was adapted from "A Glimpse of the Real World" by Garrison Daily *Learning Magazine* (September, 1995).

Several studies have specifically tested locus of control and reading achievement (Drummond, Smith, & Pinette, 1975; Culver & Morgan, 1977). These studies support the notion that internally controlled students make greater gains in achievement in general, in reading achievement, and in classroom adjustment. More recent studies have found internally controlled individuals to be more cognitively active in the search and learning activities involved in reading (Creek, McDonald, & Ganley, 1991; DeSanti & Alexander, 1986; Curry, 1990). Recently Chan (1996) found that gifted students in Australia had greater motivation and confidence in their own ability to control successes or failures in school tasks than did a group of average-achieving peers.

Morgan and Culver (1978) have proposed certain guidelines to help teachers select activities that reinforce internally controlled behaviors. Table 2.1 summarizes these guidelines, contrasting activities that reinforce internally controlled behaviors with those that reinforce externally controlled behaviors.

First, teachers need to minimize anxiety over possible failure by building patterns of success for each student in the class. They can accomplish this in several ways. To begin, teachers need to develop a realistic reward system of praise for work completed. The system of rewards can be kept simple if the teacher uses a contractual arrangement that specifies a sequence of graduated tasks, each of which is attainable. The teacher should stress the concept of mastery of the task in grading students, thereby eliminating arbitrary grading, which is a source of agitation to students who are external in their thinking. The teacher can deemphasize the concept of time and thus lessen compulsiveness by allowing students unlimited time to complete and master certain tasks. In addition, teachers should aid school guidance staff in counseling students toward realistic life goals, because externally controlled persons often have unrealistic aspirations or no aspirations at all.

TABLE 2.1 Guidelines for Reinforcing Internally and Externally Controlled Behaviors

Reinforcing Externally Controlled Behaviors	*Reinforcing Internally Controlled Behaviors*
1. Arbitrary grading	1. Using concept of mastery in grading
2. Setting time limits for tasks, which makes students constantly aware of time (compulsiveness)	2. Allowing students enough time to complete and master a task
3. Building anxiety over possible failure	3. Building patterns of success
4. Neglecting to offer rewards for efforts	4. Rewarding students in a controlled manner for effort (praise)
5. No graduated sequencing in learning tasks	5. Developing graduated sequences for the learning tasks
6. Neglecting students' needs for counseling and guidance; students do not develop goals	6. Counseling student toward realistic academic and life goals

Teachers also can adopt strategies that foster self-direction and internal motivation. For instance, they can let students make a set of rules of conduct for the class and start their own class or group traditions, to reinforce the importance of both the group and the individuals in the group. Such an activity, which relies on listening and speaking, can be implemented even in the early grades. Another excellent activity for older students is the "internal-external" journal. Students keep a record of recent events that have happened to them. In the journal they can explain whether the events were orchestrated and controlled by someone other than themselves and, if so, whether these externally controlled events frustrated them. As a variant on the journal idea, students can make a "blame list" to indicate whether positive and negative events that happen to them are their own fault or the fault of others. These activities rely on the use of writing, thus integrating another communicative art into affective education.

One of the most important classroom strategies for helping students develop an internal locus of control is to have them practice decision making whenever possible. Study guides and worksheets described later in this text can be constructed in such a manner that individuals and groups are asked to reason and react to hypothetical situations in which decisions need to be made. Group consensus in decision making about a possible conclusion to a story can be a powerful way to teach self-awareness and self-worth and to teach about relationships with others. The Directed Reading/Thinking Activity (Stauffer, 1969b) is another excellent strategy for teaching group decision making through hypothesizing the outcome of a story. This activity, explained in Chapter 6, enables students to believe in themselves by feeling that what they have to say has dignity and worth.

Questioning

Questions in the affective domain provide linkage among emotions, attitudes, and thoughts or knowledge (Jones, Morgan, & Tonelson, 1992). For example, when students examining the problems faced by Richard Nixon as president of the United States are asked to consider their feelings about these problems, they are connecting knowledge and feelings.

The GATOR (Gaining Acceptance Toward Reading) system can improve instruction by allowing the teacher to ask more reflective questions. To help gain student acceptance of reading, the teacher announces that all questions asked about a lesson, by either the teacher or the students, must be based on "feeling," as must all responses. The entire lesson is taught with questions such as these:

How did that make you feel?

Why is this lesson important?

How did you feel about the main character? Why would you have done or not done what the main character did?

Why is this chapter important?

Tell us why you like what you just read?

GATOR also can be used when students are working in small groups. Students are asked to discuss only emotion-laden questions. As an example, notice these affective questions, which were generated by teachers and students during a brainstorming session after reading "Goodbye, Grandma" by Ray Bradbury (1983):

If you knew that a close relative of yours was about to die, would you treat him or her differently?

How do you think Grandma felt about the beginning and ending of her life?

What if you were given three years to live; how would you do things differently?

There is humor in this story. How do you feel about having humor in a story about death?

Do you feel Grandma is like anyone you know?

What lasting feeling were you left with at the end of the story?

During what parts of this story did you have a warm, happy feeling? Read these parts aloud to the class.

How do you think it will feel to be old?

Do we treat people differently when we know they are dying? Should we?

Using expository materials in a middle-school lesson about seasons and climate from an earth science textbook, a teacher could ask the following affective questions:

How do you feel about today's weather?

Can weather affect your mood and how you feel? Give examples.

How do you feel about the seasons?

What if there were never any change of seasons? Describe what your feelings would be.

One-Minute Summary

Students rarely achieve without having certain concomitant feelings, including a positive attitude and strong emotions of caring for other students, for the subject, and for the teacher. In this chapter we discuss the affective domain—attitudes and interests and conative factors that are important in content-area teaching. We describe a brain-compatible approach to teaching—strategies to heighten students' brain activity and lessen threats and pressures. We also discuss the place in the curriculum of recognizing different modalities of student learning.

We describe preparation, assistance, and reflection strategies to aid teachers in emphasizing the affective domain. Teacher and student attitude tests are presented, as well as general and content-specific interest inventories. Also, ways are shown to assist students in strengthening affective bonds, and two important reflection activities are described to help students achieve better in the classroom.

Throughout the chapter we exhort teachers to bring about lasting achievement by paying attention to not only the cognitive but also the affective domain of learning. Classroom teachers who stress affect to teach cognitive skills and course content will be considerably more successful than those who omit such an emphasis from their classrooms.

End-of-Chapter Activities

Assisting Comprehension

1. Why is it important for teachers to know about the affective domain and to stress affect in their thinking? Why are conative factors important in teaching?
2. Return to the terms listed at the beginning of the chapter. Has your understanding of them altered? In what ways?

Reflecting on Your Reading

Use the GATOR technique to ask yourself several questions about how you feel about this chapter. In asking and answering your own questions, remember that with GATOR no factual comprehension questions can be asked. Try GATOR to have some fun and dwell for a short time in the affective domain!

CHAPTER 3

Learning with Multiple Resources

I have always had a curious nature; I enjoy learning, but I dislike being taught.

—Winston Churchill

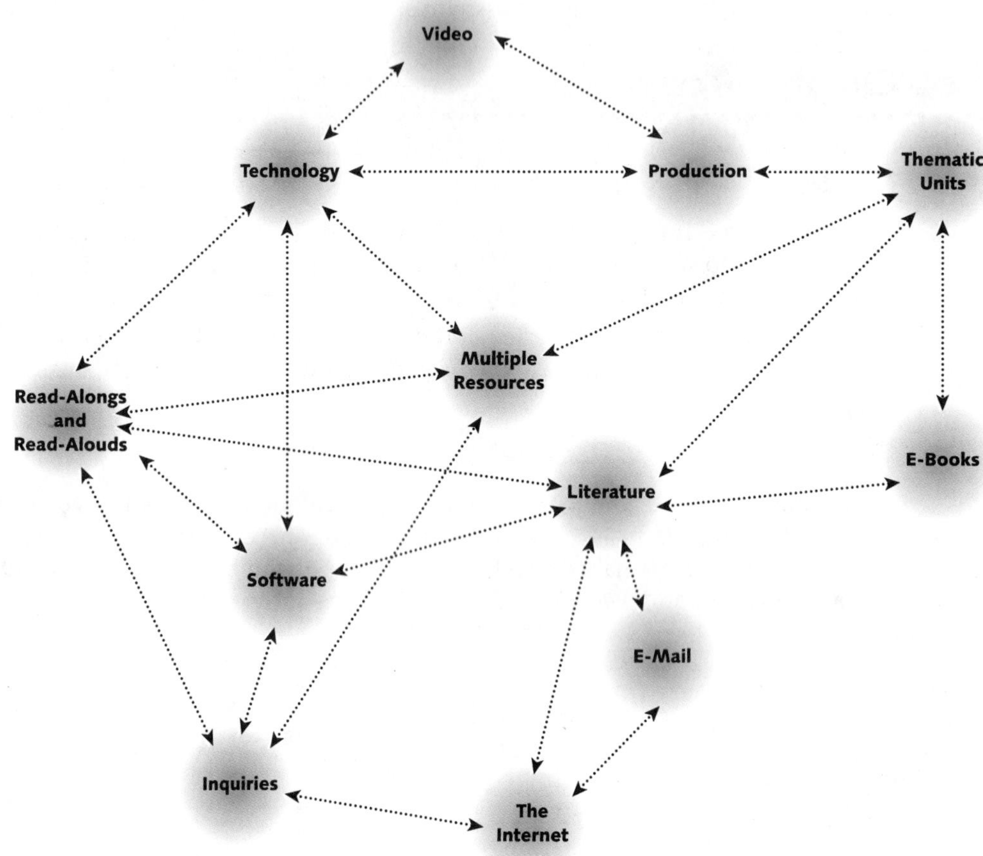

Preparing to Read

1. Think of the last time you wanted to learn about or research a topic of interest to you. Where did you go to find information? What resources did you use?
2. Following is a list of terms used in this chapter. Some may be familiar to you in a general context, but in this chapter they may be used in unfamiliar ways. Rate your knowledge by placing a plus sign (+) in front of those you are sure that you know, a check mark (✓) in front of those you have some knowledge about, and a zero (0) in front of those you don't know. Be ready to locate and pay special attention to their meanings when they are presented in the chapter.

   ______ multitext
   ______ trade book
   ______ reading/writing connection
   ______ literature-rich environment
   ______ electronic text
   ______ hypertext
   ______ electronic book, e-book
   ______ e-classroom
   ______ electronic mail, e-mail
   ______ discussion group
   ______ cyberjournal
   ______ listserv
   ______ read-alongs
   ______ read-alouds
   ______ thematic unit of instruction
   ______ webbing approach
   ______ personal inquiry

Objectives

As you read this chapter, focus your attention on the following objectives. You will:

1. understand the need for complementing content-area instruction with multiple resources, including literature and technology.
2. describe the characteristics of literature-based classrooms.

3. describe several technology resources used in today's classrooms.
4. explain three ways to support literature and technology in the content classroom.
5. identify several techniques and resources for using illustrative excerpts of literature.
6. understand how to plan for thematic units by using both textbooks and literature as a basis for instruction.
7. realize the value of self-generated inquiry learning by using literature and technology.
8. identify ways to teach thinking through literature by having students respond to literature selections.

Why Textbooks Cannot Stand Alone

Textbooks Are Limited by Their Very Purpose

The traditional notion of using one textbook for all classroom assignments is being questioned because this approach limits success. Textbooks are secondary resources. They present condensed information about topics and thus are somewhat like encyclopedias. Textbooks offer an overview of a topic; they do not offer in-depth reporting. Teachers are often frustrated when students submit reports for which the obvious and only source was an encyclopedia. They prefer that students read widely on a topic and read primary sources—those written by the authors who originally considered or researched the topic—rather than secondary sources—materials written to be brief summaries. Secondary sources are, of necessity, brief and condensed. In secondary reports much of the story behind a topic is deleted and the original flavor of the author's enthusiasm and style is necessarily lost.

Because textbooks condense information, their treatment of subject matter can be dry and boring to the reader. Heibert (1999) makes the analogy between a variety of reading resources and a balanced diet. Someone using only one type of reading material may not be receiving all of the nutrients needed to nourish the reading experience—and, we add, balanced knowledge about a content area. Guillaume (1998) proposes complementing the textbook with a multiplicity of resources, including trade books, fiction with content information, magazines, newspapers, and computer software.

Textbooks have been criticized for their conceptual density (Hurd, 1970) and for their doggedly factual presentation of material (Calfee, 1987). They also have been characterized as difficult for students to read and comprehend because the presentation lacks coherence (Armbruster & Anderson, 1984). Too many textbooks are bland collections of facts with not enough emphasis on showing students the relationships among facts or concepts. Textbook writing is often uneven, resulting in some sections that are much harder to read than others. Furthermore, the expository writing found in textbooks is often more difficult—and usually less interesting—for readers than is a narrative or journalistic style. At times teachers use textbooks that are old and outdated and contain numerous errors in light of factual and conceptual changes within a field of study. The textbook used in any given class may not be the one the teacher wants or needs for that particular class but one chosen by a textbook adoption committee or by the teacher who formerly taught the class. We discuss these factors in depth in Chapter 4.

Learners Prefer Other Resources

The modern world provides many resources as learning tools. Technological advances have created choices such as television, video, computer-based instruction, Internet access, and conversations with experts. It is small wonder that students sometimes view a textbook with boredom, skepticism, or distaste. Textbooks as a stand-alone resource simply do not fit today's learner.

To illustrate this point, Thomas Bean (1999) conducted an informal study using his two adolescent daughters as subjects. He asked them to chart their functional uses of literacy for two weeks. Included as literacy tasks were text reading, novel reading, magazine reading, computer use, telephone use, and viewing TV, movies, and videocassettes. The TV/video category accounted for the greatest usage; the telephone was second, the computer third.

Before discounting this study as indicative only of adolescent literacy preferences, take a minute to consider your own habits of learning. For instance, a student of ours recently saw the movie *Elizabeth*, for entertainment but also out of historical curiosity. Elizabeth's love affair with Robert Dudley intrigued her. To find out more, she went to the Internet and read the movie plot at the site www.elizabeth-themovie.com. Then she scanned a historical novel. Although the account was different from the movie's, it did not delve deeply enough to provide answers. Next, the student made a trip to the library and located a biography of Queen Elizabeth I. Intending to read only the part about the relationship with Dudley, she read the entire book. The biographer had used primary sources to document Elizabeth's affair with Dudley—mostly letters written by members of her court. The biographer's account was rather different from the movie's and more likely to be true. In this particular search for facts, the resources that the student used included a movie, an Internet site, a novel, and a biography.

Why do we teach our students to use a textbook as the *main* instructional aid in classrooms? It is the rare classroom—even at the primary level—that does not issue textbooks to students. It is the rare curriculum guide that does not list specific chapters as the way to teach topics in content subjects. Our students know better. They often express an aversion to learning when they think they will need to read a textbook. Bintz (1993) suggested that students "do not lose interest in reading per se" (p. 613) but lose interest in the textbooks as the reading resource.

Learners Struggle with Textbook Readability

Singer and Bean (1988) suggest that "when a heterogeneous group of students progresses through the grades, we can expect its range of reading achievement (in reading age equivalents) to increase from four years at grade one to twelve years at grade twelve" (p. 162). To gauge the range of reading in a heterogeneous class, Singer and Bean advise multiplying the median age of the students by two-thirds. Thus the range in a third-grade class (with a median age of 8) would be about 5 years; in a tenth-grade class (median age 15), the range would be about 10 years. This indication of variation, though not a precise measure, does demonstrate how the same reading material can generate very different reactions from students.

Hill and Erwin (1984) found that more than half of the textbooks they studied were at least one level above their target grade. Some texts for middle-school students were found to be at college level! Other studies suggest that although textbooks are becoming less diffcult for students to read, there is still a problem with material being too difficult for the target audience (Derby, 1987; Morgan, Otto, & Thompson 1976). Looking at readability level, text organization, and cohesion, Kinder, Bursuck, and Epstein (1992) found that social studies textbooks treating the same topic and intended for the same grade varied by as much as six grade levels. In short, although publishers have become more sensitive to producing materials that are both content-rich and readable by the intended audience, many textbooks that teachers are using today are difficult for their students.

Multiple Resources Are the Best Learning Tools

The American student population is growing ever more diverse. It is not unusual for a classroom to include a half-dozen nationalities and cultures or for students to speak several languages. There is growing concern that teachers in all content subjects must be adept at offering reading choices that reflect students' interests, cultures, and customs. A **multitext** approach is necessary. What resources are the best for reading to learn? Literature is a valued resource. In the following section we discuss the benefits of using literature as a learning resource.

Literature in the Content Classroom

In the past decade, the use of trade books has increased dramatically, especially in elementary and middle schools. **Trade books** are books that are considered to be in general use, such as books borrowed from a library or bought at the local bookstore, rather than textbooks bought and studied as a major course resource. Most trade books are written in either a journalistic or a narrative style; they are interesting resources but are not specifically intended as instructional tools. Sloan (1984) summed up the importance of the literature component of a classroom:

> The literate person . . . is not one who knows how to read, but one who reads: fluently, responsively, critically, and because he wants to. . . . Children will become readers only if their emotions have been engaged, their imaginations stirred and stretched by what they find on printed pages. One way—a sure way—to make this happen is through literature.

Because of the numerous limitations inherent in using a single textbook, researchers are calling for the use of "real" literature in all content-area subjects (Wilson, 1988; Allen, Freeman, Lehman, & Scharer, 1995). Reading literature that augments textbook topics also provides necessary practice with enjoyable materials. All readers need practice, but for the struggling learner, practice is crucial. From interviews with 12 successful persons labeled as dyslexic, Fink (1996) found that these persons enjoyed reading challenging books of personal interest, books that took them beyond textbook information.

Calfee (1987) noted that trade books offer causal relationships between concepts and provide a better framework for students to answer their own questions about the reading. Although trade books may have uneven readability, they possess several advantages over textbooks. Guzzetti, Kowalinski, and McGowan (1992) confirmed that using trade books improves the affective domain of learning for students; the researchers were impressed "with students' enthusiasm for self-selection of 'real books'" (p. 115).

Haussamen (1995) stresses the value of reading literature for pleasure and interest versus reading to extract information. Since textbooks do lend themselves to efferent or extraction-type reading, the aesthetic is often lost, and thus any act of reading is devalued (see Chapter 2 for a discussion of aesthetic and efferent reading). Allowing for personal responses to literature can lead students to value reading (Villaune & Hopkins, 1995). Textbooks can be supplemented by fiction—novels and short stories—and nonfiction trade books in psychology, philosophy, religion, technology, history, biography, and autobiography. Also useful in a broad-based literature approach are reference books, magazines, and teacher-created materials from outside sources such as newspapers.

More and more teachers are showing interest in using literature in their curriculum (Allen, Freeman, Lehman, & Scharer, 1995). There are several reasons for such interest. One compelling reason is that when teachers bring complementary reading selections to their students, they can help revitalize instruction by opening new avenues for student and teacher alike. A number of recent research reports call for the use of Asian-American literature (Pang, Colvin, Tran, & Barba, 1992), literature that focuses on minority groups (Bealor, 1992), literature in content areas such as social studies (Guzzetti, Kowalinski, & McGowan, 1992), and literature for special populations such as deaf teenagers (Hartman & Kretschner, 1992). We know of a vocational-education teacher in a shipbuilding class who regularly reads to his students from books about ships, such as "Getting It Right at Swan Hunter," from *The Naval Architect*, and books about the sea, such as *World Beneath the Sea* (National Geographic Society, 1967). He also provides reading lists to supplement each unit of study about shipbuilding. Such a class is intellectually stimulating, and the teacher is constantly modeling his positive feelings for reading with his use of literature.

The most comprehensive motivator to reading and writing is the development of a literacy context (Turner & Paris, 1995). The tasks that teachers assign send messages to students about what is important. Conceptions about what literacy is and involves will influence students' feelings about reading and writing, the roles of literacy, and how much students should integrate such roles in their own lives. In their study, Turner and Paris found that "the most reliable indicator of motivation was the actual daily tasks that teachers provided students in their classrooms" (p. 664). Specifically, they advise teachers to:

1. provide authentic choices and purposes for literacy.
2. allow students to modify tasks so the difficulty and interest levels are challenging.
3. show students how they can control their learning.
4. encourage collaboration.
5. emphasize strategies and metacognition for constructing meaning.
6. use the consequences of tasks to build responsibility, ownership, and self-regulation.

That advice should ring true and seem familiar to readers of this text. Next, we give specific suggestions for how to follow it in order to supplement textbooks with literature.

Characteristics of Effective Literature-Based Classrooms

Through literature I become a thousand [people] and yet remain myself.

—C. S. Lewis

When content-area teachers wish to supplement textbooks with literature-based materials and trade books, the teachers, the classroom curriculum, and the school as a whole should have certain characteristics.

1. **Teachers themselves must be readers.**
Only by reading will teachers model the importance of many resources from which to learn. They cannot model what they do not know and practice. Morrison, Jacobs, and Swinyard (1999) found that teachers who choose reading as a leisure-time activity report using more literacy practices in their classrooms than do teachers who do not read often. Since familiarity with a book influences whether a teacher will use it in the classroom, teachers need to familiarize themselves with a wide variety of literature that reflects the diverse population they serve.

2. **Teachers must be flexible in their work habits.**
To incorporate literature from outside sources in the classroom, teachers must be willing to rearrange topics in the curriculum to take advantage of current articles or stories about a particular topic. Teachers also must be prepared to abandon lesson plans on occasion to follow a gripping news or personal-interest

story. The entertainment value of these stories is fleeting and usually cannot last until some other unit is finished. In other words, teachers must be able to adapt the curriculum to fit the materials available, not vice versa. In addition, teachers need to become adept at saving interesting articles. Students—the teacher's greatest resource—can help as researchers, in finding new material. Students need to be challenged from the beginning of the school year to bring in items of interest or items related to what they are studying. These items can be shared with other classes in an effort to convince others that they too should bring in new materials.

3. Books and resource materials must be everywhere throughout the school.

It is essential that students have access to many books in the classroom, in the school library or media center, and in a nearby public library. In the international study *How in the World do Students Read?* (1992), Elley reports that the countries with the highest literacy scores also had large school and classroom libraries, regular book borrowing, frequent silent reading in class, frequent story reading aloud by teachers, and more hours scheduled for language activities. Teachers and librarians/media-center specialists need to work together to find informational books at a wide range of readability levels and interest levels related to content-area units in both academic and vocational subjects. Teachers in all disciplines within the school need to make up reading lists of acceptable literature and other supplemental books. Reading specialists and librarians/media-center specialists can help compile as many books as possible or borrow from nearby public libraries books not easily located.

4. Teachers must plan how to use literature.

Teachers need to develop the philosophy that literature is an integral part of any content-area curriculum and is an important resource for studying any discipline. In literature-based classrooms, teachers actively plan to use literature and make it as important as the textbook in their teaching. Teachers should plan their instruction to get children interested in these books and in researching the topics in small groups. Teachers also should provide time for students, after they become accustomed to a literature-based environment, to brainstorm and explore their own ideas about topics and how they would like to research them. All of this does not just happen; careful planning by teachers is needed to make such explorative classes work.

5. Students should be given numerous ways to respond to literature.

Students become personally involved in reacting cognitively and affectively to literature. There is additional emphasis on the reflection step of the PAR Lesson Framework to allow students, both orally and in writing, individually and in groups, to respond to the meaning they derive from the reading. Guzzetti (1990) reports on the importance of students responding visually through cognitive maps, charts of character traits (visual illustrations), and written paradigms (creation of a new product based on the author's ideas and students' experiences) to historical fiction and novels. According to Guzzetti, such visual responses help students clarify their thinking and help motivate them through creative activity related to the interpretation of meaning from text.

6. The reading/writing connection must be emphasized in each content-area classroom.
Students learn to write to get ready to read, to read, and then to write about the meaning they derived from reading. This is the **reading/writing connection**, and in this atmosphere writing ability improves dramatically as students read varied literature. Students become used to combining reading and writing in this manner; it happens naturally in the literature-based classroom.

7. The media center should be a hub of learning for the school.
Literature-based programs rely on close cooperation among administrators, teachers, and reading and media specialists to make books a central focus for the school. One vocational-education school that we know about utilizes a research-based curriculum in which the media specialist plays a central role in helping students do research. Teachers in the school stress the use of Directed Reading/Thinking Activities in each vocational and academic class. When students have unanswered questions remaining on their What-I-Know Activity sheets, teachers create a committee and give students on the research committee a number of days to find the answers. The teacher and students sign a special form (see Activity 3.1) and take it to the media specialist. The media specialist, in turn, signs the form to acknowledge the research question and helps the student committee find reference and other material sufficient to answer the students' questions. In this manner the media specialist, teacher, and students team up to find answers to research questions emanating from student inquiry in reading.

8. Reading should be perceived as important.
In many schools, reading is offered as a carrot to those students who finish their regular classroom assignments. This practice lowers the value of reading. Consider the lament of a content-area teacher who said, "You would ask me to have students read in class? My students don't read in class. They go home and read!" When reading is done only as homework, students assign it a lesser value and often do not even bother to do the homework assignment because it has such little value to them. In a **literature-rich environment**, the teacher reads to students daily, students are allowed to read silently on a subject or story of interest, and they read and do research in groups on topics assigned by the teacher or self-selected by the group. Students also keep records and daily logs of reading and writing abilities so that a portfolio is built of their successes in the class.

9. Teachers should model an effective reading process.
Teachers in literature-based classrooms read aloud to students to motivate them to read further on a topic or to complete a story. Teachers also direct students to maturity in reading by modeling correct reading process, using many of the techniques mentioned in this text, such as Directed Reading/Thinking Activities and the question/answer relationship (QAR). When students are reading silently, the teacher also reads silently, to model good reading behavior and show interest in the lesson. Teachers also share what they are reading and writing with the students and generally provide an intellectually stimulating environment.

10. Teachers should stress the affective domain in reading.
Through reading aloud and encouraging the sharing and discussion of books, teachers emphasize the affective domain of reading—how students feel about what they are doing. In our study skills chapter (Chapter 11), we present a study

ACTIVITY 3.1 Research Form

Class: Ship Construction

Research topic: What is the difference between a brittle fracture of a ship's hull and a ductile failure of the hull?

Teacher's signature: Mr. Applegate

Student committee's signatures: Fred Bovine

Susan Henley

Ray Birdsong

Media specialist's signature: Dorothy Sabotka

Beginning date of search: January 3

Search to be completed by: January 10

log for students to keep so that they can self-evaluate how they are doing in the classroom. Through such a device, teachers can allow students to become more internally motivated and to move toward an internal locus of control (discussed in Chapter 2). If students enjoy what they are doing, they tend to feel more "in control" of what is happening in the class. This emphasis on the affective domain is especially evident in the reflection phase of the PAR Lesson Framework. If students are given real opportunities, in an unhurried environment, to think critically and share their thoughts on reading material, their attitude toward class will improve. Allowing more time for sharing and reflection can be done in any grade and in any subject, from kindergarten to the most abstract and difficult twelfth-grade subject.

11. Intellectual curiosity should be encouraged.
In literature-based classrooms, teachers always encourage questions from students about topics related to the subject being studied. Teachers point students in directions to find their own answers rather than simply telling students what they need to know. Teachers also try to get parents involved in stimulating their children's intellectual curiosity. Activity 3.2 shows a letter that a second-grade teacher sent to parents, along with a book list, in an attempt to stimulate reading. The book list includes a brief description of each book, its level of difficulty, topics covered, and whether it is fiction or nonfiction. This is an excellent way to encourage the natural curiosity of a child.

Technology as a Resource

Contemporary professional literature is full of information about using technology in the classroom. Maurer and Davidson (1999) encourage teachers to use technology "to help children become brilliant" (p. 458). They suggest that with technology learning is streamlined and less boring—it is like speed learning.

They say that use of technology "shifts power into the hearts of children" (p. 460). Reinking (1997) suggests that, although technology itself is neutral, the way we use it to learn enables learners to be more creative and engaged. If technological instruction focuses on meaning, stresses comprehension, and allows students to become actively involved with whole texts, then the technology is well used.

Electronic text is beneficial because it is easy to modify with the "delete" or "cut" key. It can be adapted to the reader; you can program electronic text to accept reader responses. Moving from place to place is easy in electronic text. Anderson-Inman (1998) provides a list of several repositories of electronic text, one of which is "The Online Books Page" found at http://www.cs.cmu.edu/books.html. This site is a directory of full-text books available for reading on the Internet.

Wepner, Seminoff, and Blanchard (1995) caution that teachers who understand the goals and are involved in planning for technological innovation will be more successful. They encourage teachers making curricular decisions to ask the following questions:

Where are we?

Where do we want to be?

How do we get there?

How do we know we are there?

Adolescents seem to prefer media such as TV and video, computers, and telephones. Our students generally know more than their teachers about technology and its uses. It is in the area of technology where many teachers become learners themselves, and thus a reciprocal learning environment is created, which facilitates true shared learning.

In the rest of this section we describe several varieties of technological resources. This information may help teachers answer questions and make wise decisions about integrating technology into their classroom instruction. Throughout this text, we present Technology Boxes. Because this field is changing so

ACTIVITY 3.2 Encourage Reading at Home

Dear Parents:

Enclosed is a supplementary reading list for our science textbook, *Discover Science*. Many of your children have expressed an interest in science this year. So, I have created a list of books that can be found at the public library. Our Henrico County Student Outcomes, by which I teach, are divided into headings. These headings are the subjects your children learn about in second-grade science. These subjects include the human body, physical science, earth and space, plants, animals, and dinosaurs. Please encourage your child to read some of these books. With the holidays approaching, they would make great gifts as well as enhance your child's understanding of various science topics.

Sincerely,
Kelly Taylor

Title *Author* *Publisher* *Date*	*Summary of Book*	*Reading Rating*	*Related Science Content*	*Nonfiction/ Fiction*
Shooting Stars Franklyn M. Branley Thomas Y. Crowell 1989	Through beautiful illustrations, this book explains what shooting stars are, what they are made of, and what happens when they land on earth.	Average	Earth and Space (Stars)	Nonfiction
The Magic School Bus Lost in the Solar System Joanna Cole Scholastic, Inc. 1990	The magic school bus turns into a spaceship and takes the students on an exploration of the solar system.	Average	Space	Nonfiction *A combination of fact and fancy
Comets Franklyn M. Branley Harper & Row 1984	This book explains what comets are, how they are formed, and how their unusual orbits bring them into earth's view at predictable intervals, with a special focus on Halley's comet.	Average	Space (Comets)	Nonfiction
The Pumpkin Patch Elizabeth King Dutton 1990	The text and photographs describe the activities in a pumpkin patch as pink-colored seeds become fat pumpkins, ready to be carved into jack-o-lanterns.	Average	Plants	Nonfiction
Discovering Trees Douglas Florian Scribner 1986	This book includes an introduction to trees, their growth, reproduction, usefulness, and facts about specific kinds of trees.	Difficult	Trees	Nonfiction
A Kid's First Book of Gardening Derek Fell Running Press 1989	This book presents information on soil, seeds, easy-to-grow flowers, flowers that keep blooming, bulbs, vegetables, fruits, trees, shrubs, houseplants, gardening in containers, and unusual plants.	Difficult	Plants (Gardening)	Nonfiction

Developed by Kelly Taylor.

rapidly, we invite the reader to visit the Wadsworth website (www.wadsworth.com) and check out the latest information.

TV/Video/Movies

The use of TV, video, and movies as a resource is well established. Video has nearly replaced the film projector and film strips, which became brittle with age. Many studies report that children today watch a great deal more TV than children watched several years ago. Many organizations, including the International Reading Association, sponsor "No TV" days or weeks to highlight the importance of an environment where children can discover resources other than TV. Yet Neuman (1991) comments that just turning off the TV does not lead to more reading. When watching TV is simply a way to pass time, it probably is not stimulating much learning. As Elley (1992) reports in an international literacy study, those who watch TV a lot tend to score at lower levels of literacy than those who watch less TV. However, in some countries with high literacy scores, the average number of hours watched is three or four. In these countries, many foreign films with subtitles and informational films are shown on TV. Unfortunately, the United States fell in the high-hours-of-TV-watching/low-literacy-scores category.

After reviewing 30 years of research, Reinking and Wu (1990) state that the evidence does not clearly show TV as a detriment to literacy. Channel One, controversial as its use is, does provide instant information to schools for a fairly low cost (Johnston, 1995; Celano & Neuman, 1995). It is reasonable to conclude that TV—documentaries, drama, and news shows, for example—can be a vehicle for powerful learning opportunities (Reinking & Pardon, 1995). The United States may need to create opportunities for using TV, video, and movies to better advantage.

What makes these media so popular? They appeal to many of the senses, fostering visual literacy and more. We see, hear, and are entertained by them. Our eyes move from place to place rather than remaining focused on a page. When programs are taped, the video can be used on many different occasions as a learning resource.

Students often prefer to see a video and compare it to the text. For instance, a video can animate a topic that otherwise might be covered in only two or three pages in a textbook chapter. The movie *Pochahontas* was quite disappointing to many teachers because history seemed to suffer for the sake of plot. Yet teachers found that they could start with the movie, guide children to read several resources such as biographies or historical accounts, and then compare the information.

The movie *Clueless* barely credited the novel *Emma* by Jane Austen yet became a start-off point for discussing Austen's novel. *Clueless* can guide students to the movie entitled *Emma* and on to the novel itself. Caution is urged in moving from the movie to literature, however (Baines, 1996). Films often use less sophisticated vocabulary and language and "reduce the complexity of dialogue, plot, characters, and theme" (p. 616). However, video does lure students and can be the springboard to many projects linking the movie and the literature.

A Hypertext Environment

Hypertext allows for the use of a wide variety of resources in content classrooms. Hypertext is especially evident in Internet use. A student can start at one location, click on an icon to find out more about a topic, and immediately be linked to another site where that information is located. Reinking (1997) demonstrated how hypertext works in an online and print-format article as he discussed the possibilities of technology and literacy. That article is located at http://readingonline.org. The learner can go backward, forward, and sideways in several dimensions. Instead of reading each line in order on each page, the learner branches from here to there in a nonlinear fashion. The student can click to view a footnote, then click back to the main article. Readers can check a reference without turning a page.

Hyperlinks are also apparent when one is writing a report, perhaps using an authoring program on a computer. It is possible to have several screens open and available at one time. The writer simply clicks among the screens to navigate from one resource or another.

This environment is similar to that of a learner who leaps from one idea to another. It is a bit like having piles of information on a desk and going from one pile to the other as needed to take care of several tasks. In short, the possibilities that hypertext affords mirror a typical learning environment.

Word Processing and Other Production Applications

Many teachers know that writing is an effective means of learning. Learning logs and journals are two means of enabling students to express what they are learning and clarify difficult concepts. In Chapter 9 we explore the benefits of writing in the content areas more fully. In this chapter we want to point out that writing does not have to be pencil-to-paper; more often in today's world it is fingers-to-keyboard-to-computer. As a matter of fact, to write this edition of our textbook, we used word processing software, whereas the first edition was much more a pencil-and-paper product. Many word processing programs are available. They range from simple ones such as The Writing Center to sophisticated applications such as Microsoft Word. Maurer and Davidson (1999) tell the story of a first-grader who seemed to be "giving up on school." When he realized that he could write on the computer, his whole attitude changed. He had power to accomplish a literacy task in a way that enticed him.

Children's own work can become a learning resource for others. Term papers and reports submitted for only the teacher's eyes can be banished in favor of presentations for all learners to enjoy. Some software applications, such as PowerPoint, let the user create slide shows with text. Audio and animation can be included if the user has reached that level of sophistication. Word processing programs enable users to create, edit, insert pictures and graphics, and make appealing book-like products. Applications such as FrontPage and Dreamweaver enable users to create presentations that can be published on the World Wide Web. Iannone (1998) shows possibilities for using traditional and electronic text in writing instruction. His article shows how teachers can incorporate online student resources in the writing-centered activities. He provides several websites. Alvarez (1998) suggests that students will think differently about their writing and be more enthusiastic as well as careful when they realize that anyone on the Web might access their work. Creating resources that others will read is a great incentive for learners: Literacy becomes very personal and applies the technological features that today's children find so compelling.

We know instructors who have published their textbooks on the World Wide Web with production applications. Their students can read electronic text, see the same illustrations that might be placed in the textbook, but also *hear* the instructor explain points about a graph or lead them through a complicated set of directions. At given points, students can click and soar to other locations (the hypertext feature), escaping the linear nature of a textbook for a nonlinear world. Teachers can create such presentations, or search the World Wide Web for such programs. Although studies have yet to be conducted that prove more learning occurs with such resources, the informal evidence is all around us. Children are intrigued by the multisensual nature of production applications and seem to spend more time on learning when such resources are available.

The addition of graphics to a report enhances student interest and understanding. Using scanners or digital cameras, learners can place graphics in text to create lively visual displays of their learning. Regular photographs can be transferred to computer from a scanner. Digital cameras feed the pictures directly to the computer. Audio can be introduced to a presentation using applications such as SoundEdit or SoundForge, or VisiCam, which enables both sound and audio in a medium-quality but inexpensive form. Imagine how enticing it could be to show what a project looks like to viewers across the country or the world.

Instructional Software

Software is delivered on disk or CD-ROM and usually comes with a manual and supporting materials. Interactive computer books are now available for students to read and respond to on screen (Chu, 1995). Programs like *Oregon Trail* and *Amazon Trail* have been around for some time and have undergone some improvements. *Leonardo the Inventor* takes learners to the Renaissance, where they experience da Vinci's ideas and inventions. Such programs simulate a situation and ask readers to make choices based on information. Careful thinking and interaction and literacy skills are required. Some software features a familiar text but provides for multimedia such as read-alongs and question/answer interaction. Students are expected to respond; their responses are often tracked to provide a "score" for the learner and instructor. This can be a helpful monitoring device for teachers who want to keep a record of which types of resources a student used to learn about a topic and how effective that resource seemed to be.

Instructional software programs can be wonderful learning resources. As with textbooks, some are better than others. Willis, Stephens, and Matthew (1996) encourage teachers to look for attention to the subject matter, efficiency, approach to instruction, appeal, ease of use, and adaptability when they select software. How the software is used makes a difference. Greenlee-Moore and Smith (1996) investigated the effects on reading comprehension when fourth-grade students read shorter and easier or more difficult text using either interactive software or printed text. When reading longer and more difficult narratives, the software group had higher scores. The authors speculate that students paid more attention to the text on computer than to the text in the book.

Instructional software should teach about content as well as stimulate critical thinking rather than skill-and-drill or rote learning of isolated facts. One ma-

TECHNOLOGY BOX

Two Listservs for Content Teachers

Rteacher A listserv about literacy education, especially on the Internet

To subscribe, write to: listserv@listserv.syr.edu

To post a message, write to: rteacher@listserv.syr.edu

Web66 A listserv about the effects of the Web on k–12 instruction

To subscribe, write to: listserv@tc.umn.edu

To post a message, write to: web66@tc.umn.edu

jor advantage of software over Internet resources is that teachers can preview the software and be sure that the content is suitable for the age group. Another advantage is that the teacher does not depend on a connection, which might be expensive, unreliable, or sometimes inaccessible. The Technology Box for Chapter 5 lists some software programs that might help with content instruction.

Electronic Books

An **electronic book**—or **e-book**—is a book presented on a computer. The user's main focus is still on reading text, but the text can be augmented with pictures and hypertext links to create a nonlinear environment. *A Survey of Western Art* enables learners to view and read about art that they otherwise might never see. "Navigating learning" with electronic encyclopedias is an interesting and efficient new way to support textbooks with literature (Wepner, Seminoff, & Blanchard, 1995). *Compton's Interactive Encyclopedia* or *Grolier Multimedia Encyclopedia* are offered on CD-ROM. They rival print versions for number of articles. Ease of navigation from one article to another is good, and readability is fairly simple. *Infopedia* combines the *Funk and Wagnalls Encyclopedia, Roget's Thesaurus, World Almanac*, dictionaries, and an atlas. Sound clips as well as pictures and animation are combined in these electronic books. But be careful! The package is modern, but these are still encyclopedias—which are secondary sources. Consider them as only one condensed source, not an inclusive treatment of any topic.

The Internet

The Internet makes electronic text possible and, some predict, is "the medium of the future" (Anderson-Inman, 1998). The Internet is a collection of many resources—an electronic library of information. Every minute something new is posted for viewers to find. A search engine enables a learner to type in a topic and be presented with many possible resources. Some is trash; much can enhance the learning in content areas. Just as a reader would note the copyright date of a textbook, an Internet user should note when an Internet site was posted and whether it has been revised (Rekrut, 1999). Just as a reader would want to know a text author's credentials, Internet users should be cautious about the source of the information they discover on the Internet; the learner must judge the quality and reliability of the information. Content teachers can help by checking possible sites in advance of sending students to surf the Net.

Leu (1997) says that the Internet is changing what it means to be literate. First, Internet literacy requires new and sophisticated navigational skills. Getting around in the mass of information is a challenge. Second, the learning is endless; just as one masters a new literacy skill on the Net, a new challenge arises. Third, the Internet requires new ways of reasoning and thinking critically. Fourth, content on the Net can be presented with multiple meanings and combinations. These literacy challenges are part of what makes the Internet appealing to students, but the challenge is for teachers to provide guidance so the Internet is used as a tool for effective learning.

A high school math teacher located a site that enlivens the study of the Pythagorean theorem. He found a high school posting about the short story "The Battle of Pythagorus." Here was a wonderful lesson about the theorem using the short story as the lead into the lesson. That site is http://www.fms.k12.nm.us/mesaview/misc/pt.html. Leu (1999) provides numerous lessons in content areas that engage learners on the Internet. For example, he helps learners find out about Japan by visiting "Kid's Web Japan" at http://www.jinjapan.org/kidsweb/. Through a series of steps from this site, students can learn about Japan's climate, culture, and art.

Asking an expert becomes much more possible on the Internet. Rather than traveling to one location, which is expensive and limits the audience, the expert can be available online. We might even see him or her talking to us, listening, and responding. Van Horn (1999) discusses the merits of such a conference, provides tips on setting up a live conference, and explains what equipment might work best in various circumstances. He calls the setting for such conferences the **e-classroom**.

E-Mail / Discussion Groups / Listservs

Electronic mail is sent over the Internet, not unlike a letter except that **e-mail** can be received almost instantaneously. Sending letters by electronic mail enables learners to contact favorite authors or content experts who have made their e-mail addresses available. Many legislators provide their e-mail numbers for constituents, giving students an opportunity to write and receive immediate responses as they study political issues. Several studies have been conducted to determine the impact of e-mail correspondence on literacy skills and learning. Rekrut (1999) believes that e-mail is the best place to start those new to the Internet because it is so simple to learn.

Discussion groups allow many persons to discuss a topic either in real time or over a period of time on a website. Their advantage over e-mail is that they permit more than two people to communicate. A respondent can receive replies from several different people, all of whom can then read each other's responses. Discussion groups are an excellent vehicle for students to learn from each other, to "talk" about a forthcoming test or a point they do not understand. They provide a kind of tutorial online. Stefl-Mabry (1998) describes this type of communication as a **cyberjournal**.

Here is an observation posted by a student commenting on preparation activities:

> These chapters just really emphasized to me the importance of preparing children to read a selection. So many times teachers hurry through the introduction of a book in order to get on with the reading. But children will not be interested or comprehend if we do not take the extra time to introduce the concept properly.

Other students responded to her observation, and the importance of preparation was reinforced by several other students using different examples. This learning took place by electronic discussion with no teacher intervention, although it certainly would be possible for the teacher to intervene if students seemed to misunderstand. The community of learners encouraged by discussion groups makes them an excellent resource for content instruction.

Participation in **listservs** is by subscription. Persons interested in the same topic subscribe to an information source—a listserv—much like subscribing to a magazine. All of the members on the list can read other members' comments. Listservs are a good means of disseminating information quickly to many people who have a common interest. Teachers might subscribe to a listserv where the common topic is lesson plans on teaching grammar. When one subscriber posts his or her plan, all the other members of the listserv receive it. See the Technology Box in Chapter 4 for an example of a listserv communication. The Technology Box for this chapter lists two listservs.

A teacher who is intrigued but does not yet have classroom access to the Internet and the forms of communication described in this section can use floppy disks to create a discussion community (Cole, Raffier, Rogan, & Schleicher, 1998). One student writes a journal entry on disk and then passes the disk to another student, who reacts and passes the disk to another student. The teacher can read the final product.

These resources create a community of learners. Students who might not speak out in class feel freer to communicate via e-mail, discussion groups, and listservs. More perspectives become available in the learning environment (Morrison, 1999).

Using Multiple Resources to Augment Textbook Instruction

Now that we have discussed several resources that might supplant or support the textbook, let us consider how these resources can be put to best use in the content classroom.

Read-Alongs and Read-Alouds

Literature and technology can be easily incorporated into existing instruction with no major restructuring of lessons. The teacher can collect and use excerpts of literature as adjuncts to the content being taught. Two plans of action are read-alongs and read-alouds. Using **read-alongs**, the teacher shares an excerpt with students, who read the piece individually, in small groups, or with the teacher. Using **read-alouds**, the teacher generally reads the excerpt to the entire class.

Teachers need to be on the lookout for passages of literature that illustrate concepts in their field of study. Over time, teachers can compile a collection of examples. Activity 3.3 is a map of possible resources for English, foreign language, mathematics, science, social studies, and art classes. It was generated by a group of teachers who all contributed at least one piece of literature that they found useful for instruction in a content area. For each content area, a resource is listed and a possible use for it is given. For foreign language, the novel *After Long Silence* by Sheri Tepper describes how settlers on a planet learn to communicate with native crystalline structures by unlocking the secret of their language. A bibliography accompanies the map.

Read-alouds are sometimes the better choice, at least initially, because the teacher can stimulate interest and regulate how much attention is given to the excerpt. Read-alouds have been shown to be very effective in engaging students in learning (Erickson, 1996; Richardson, 1995, 2000). However, teachers seem to abandon this practice by the time students start middle school, even though students of all ages enjoy and learn from them (Richardson, 1994).

A social studies teacher tried read-alouds as an assisting activity to help her students understand myths, legends, and fairy tales of different cultures. After listening to read-alouds, students were expected to read stories from Eastern and Western cultures, then write their own myths. These students were ninth-grade honors level, resistant to "baby" activities. Every day during the first unit, on India, and every other day during the second and third units, on China and Japan, the teacher read a myth, a legend, or a fairy tale during the last five to ten minutes of class. The class then discussed the characteristics of these stories, as well as their historical merit. Next came the study of ancient Greece, after which students were to write their own myth, legend, or fairy tale based on one of the civilizations studied.

Students were given two weeks to complete their writing assignment, which was worth a test grade; students also could present their stories orally, for a quiz grade. The products generated were of high quality. Although good work is expected from honors students, the enthusiasm with which these students participated was greater than usual for this unit. They began to remind the teacher when to start the daily read-aloud time. When the teacher asked her students to evaluate the read-alouds, 63 percent responded that they would like them to continue for other units, and this percentage probably understated their enthusiasm. The teacher recalled: "I really believe more students enjoyed this than even said they did, because they kept looking at each other's papers. I had several students talk with me about the survey after we completed it. The comments orally were much more positive."

ACTIVITY 3.3 Map of Literature Resources

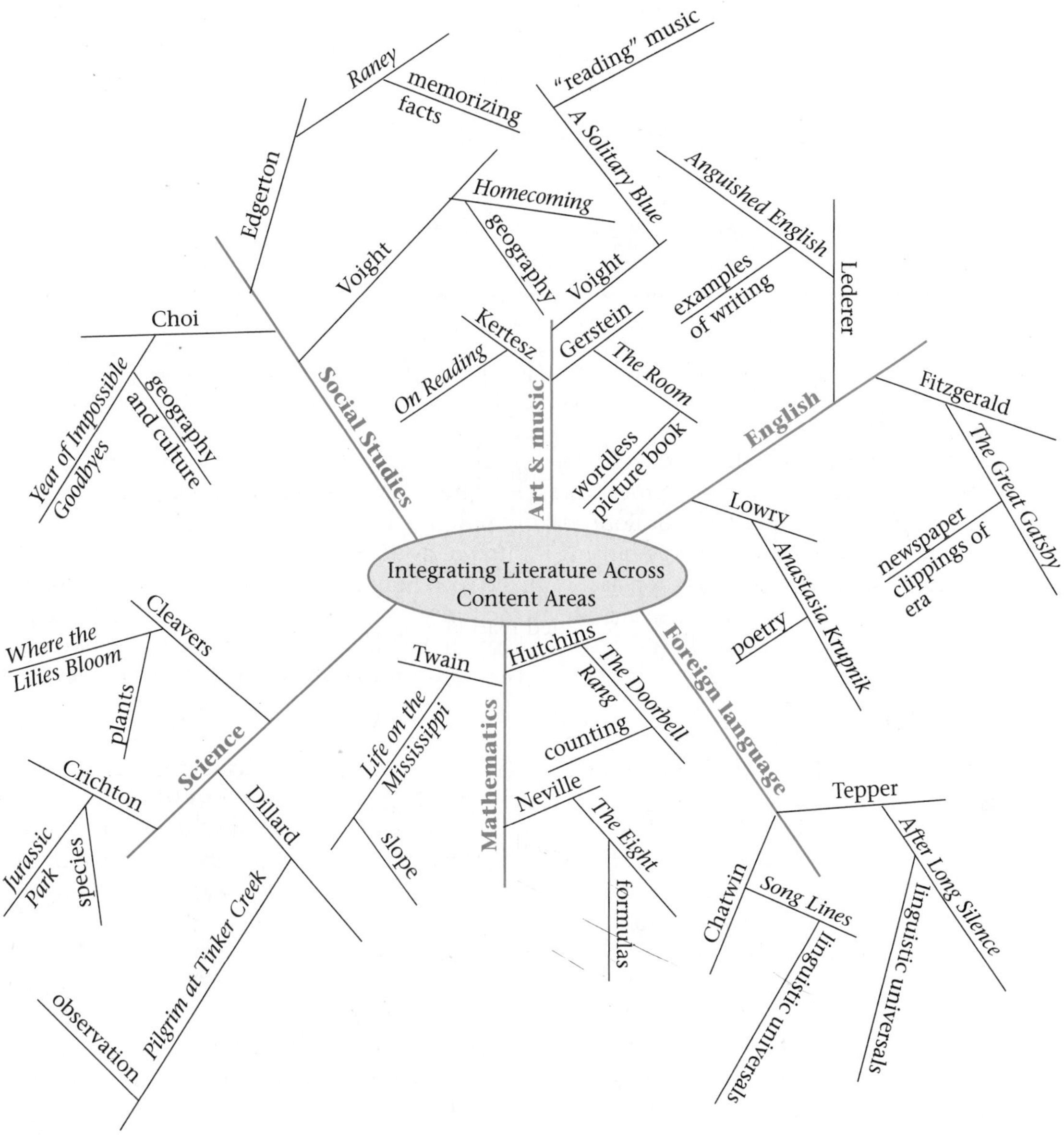

Art
Mordecai Gerstein. (1984). *The Room*. New York: HarperCollins.
Andre Kertesz. (1971). *On Reading*. New York: Grossman.

English
F. Scott Fitzgerald. (1925). *The Great Gatsby*. New York: Scribner.
Richard Lederer. (1987). *Anguished English*. New York: Dell.
Lois Lowry. (1979). *Anastasia Krupnik*. Boston: Houghton Mifflin.

(*continued*) ➤

Foreign Language
Bruce Chatwin. (1987). *Songlines.* New York: Viking Penguin.
Sheri Tepper. (1987). *After Long Silence.* New York: Bantam Books.

Mathematics
Pat Hutchins. (1986). *The Doorbell Rang.* New York: Morrow.
Catherine Neville. (1988). *The Eight.* New York: Ballantine Books.
Mark Twain. (1917). "On Cutoffs and Stephen" from *Life on the Mississippi.* New York: HarperCollins.

Music
Cynthia Voight. (1983). *A Solitary Blue.* New York: Fawcett Juniper/Ballantine.

Science
Vera and Bill Cleaver. (1970). *Where the Lilies Bloom.* Philadelphia: Lippincott.
Michael Crichton. (1990). *Jurassic Park.* New York: Knopf.
Annie Dillard. (1990). *Pilgrim at Tinker Creek.* New York: HarperCollins.

Social Studies
Sook Nyul Choi. (1991). *The Year of Impossible Goodbyes.* Boston: Houghton Mifflin.
Clyde Edgerton. (1985). *Raney.* Chapel Hill, NC: Algonquin.
Cynthia Voight. (1981). *Homecoming.* New York: Atheneum.

In science, brief articles from local newspapers might be used for read-alongs. For example, an article entitled "Lost in the Sauce" relates a food editor's experiences with readers who complain because although they followed a recipe exactly, the product flopped. The editor gives some examples of readers' "exact adaptations" of procedures and ingredients. One erstwhile cook left the cake batter—a mixture of flour, baking powder, and liquid—sitting on the counter for 45 minutes before putting it into the oven. Baking powder begins to give off carbon dioxide as soon as it is mixed with liquid, so the cake batter had no bubbles left to make the cake rise by the time it met the oven! Used as a read-along, this article would illustrate chemistry in practice. Some newspapers include science and food sections once a week whose features can serve as short, relevant read-alongs.

Another science excerpt can be drawn from Robert C. O'Brien's novel *Mrs. Frisby and the Rats of NIMH* (1971), in which a science experiment works better than expected. The scientists divide rats and mice into three groups—control, experimental A, and experimental B—and then inject serums and conduct experiments. The serum works so well for group A that those rats and mice escape and set up their own society. Because this excerpt is several pages long—a whole chapter—it might best be shared through students reading silently and then discussing what constitutes experimental design.

The example of infinity in Norton Juster's *The Phantom Tollbooth* (1961) has captivated mathematics teachers in middle and high schools. The beaver with a 30-foot tail who could build Boulder Dam, also in this novel, provides a humorous look at word problems. This excerpt is only two pages long, so it can be a great read-aloud. Activity 3.4 shows how a mathematics trade book can be combined with a computer activity to explore probability.

Dorothy Giroux, of Loyola University of Chicago, has compiled a comprehensive list of science and mathematics children's trade books, as well as professional teacher resources, for science and mathematics. The list is included in Appendix E. Also included in Appendix E is a chart listing several children's literature books that can be used in science, mathematics, and social studies

ACTIVITY 3.4 Alphabetical Probability

Marilyn Burns in *The I Hate Mathematics! Book* (1975) proposes the "Alphabetical Probability" activity. It combines literature and computer resources and is an enjoyable, concise read-aloud for teachers to stimulate problem solving and simulations. The activity involves math and engages students in the act of reading—a wonderful combination.

> The letter of the alphabet that occurs most often in written English is the letter E. T, A, O, and N are the next most frequent. Letters that are used the least are Q, Z, K, X, and J. Try it for yourself. Make up a chart which has a column for each letter. Then pick a page in this book and tally each time a letter appears. (Burns, 1975, 117)

Before actually completing a tally, students might predict, based on probability, the number of times each of the letters might occur on a page of primary-, middle-, or upper-level material. There might be differences in the frequency of occurrence if the material is from a newspaper, magazine, or novel.

This activity can be done with a computer, once the pages are typed in. The Find feature of a word processing program will calculate the number of times each letter occurs. Then students can chart occurrences and compare them across different reading levels and kinds of material.

---

instruction for early-elementary students; a collection of poems for primary-science students with suggested instructional activities to accompany them; and an annotated list of instructional uses for literature in an earth science classroom. In addition, teachers can find several literature excerpts and many instructional uses for them in the column "Read It Aloud," which appeared in the *Journal of Adolescent and Adult Literacy* four times a year (Richardson, 1994–1997) or in the monograph *Read It Aloud! Using Literature in the Secondary Content Classroom* (Richardson, 2000).

Thematic Units

Teachers who decide to supplement their textbooks with literature and technology will see enough results that they may want to include even more in their instruction. Content-area teachers who move to an integral, saturated use of multiple resources will need to organize classes around units that address particular themes. **Thematic units of instruction** organize instruction around themes rather than solely by topic or content. Shanahan, Robinson, and Schneider (1995) explain that thematic teaching is popular because student knowledge, which tends to be superficial, is enriched when students develop fuller understanding by delving deeply during a thematic unit. Also, thematic units reflect the real world, because learners generally read broadly on a topic rather than confine themselves to one source. Thematic units help teachers become more time-efficient in presenting content. Students taught with themed multiple-resource units have shown higher achievement and better attitudes than those using only a content textbook (Jone, Coombs, & McKinney, 1994).

Shanahan, Robinson, and Schneider caution that thematic units should be developed around themes, not topics. A topical approach can lead to treatment similar to subject treatment, which can lead instruction right back to segmentation. A theme "states a point of view or perspective; it actually takes a position" (p. 718). Thus themes are dynamic and help students think deeply, pull together ideas, make connections among ideas, and blend subjects naturally.

We have seen many teachers construct thematic units with titles such as "The Vietnam Era," "Survival in the World in the 1990s," and "Welcome to Planet Earth." Thematic units, however, can be on a smaller scale, such as the nine-step unit plan developed for a middle-school English class around *The Call of the Wild*, shown in Activity 3.5, the theme for which might be stated as "*The Call of the Wild* is as modern as it is reflective of the past." Or thematic units can be very encompassing, such as the unit on the Chesapeake Bay described later in this chapter. One teacher built a year-long unit by adding poetry to other content lessons throughout the school year (Myers, 1998).

Administrators should encourage teachers to meet in teams to plan activities across the curriculum for interdisciplinary units. Such a breaking down of the traditional disciplines into more favorable climates for interdisciplinary study is a trend that gained momentum in the 1980s and may become a major aspect of all instruction in middle and secondary schools. Even at the elementary level, thematic units can become grade-level or school-level projects rather than simply taught within one self-contained classroom. We know of an ele-

ACTIVITY 3.5 Unit Plan: *The Call of the Wild*

1. Read the novel during the time of the Iditarod Sled Dog Races in Alaska. You will be able to find current pieces on climate, geography, living conditions, and the history of dog races. Use these to compare and contrast with the novel.
2. Read books or articles about gold mining. Help the students identify the physical hardships and dangers of this occupation.
3. Read poetry by Robert Service ("The Cremation of Sam McGee") about Alaska.
4. Read Jack London's short stories about Alaska. Identify and explain the similarities and differences.
5. Discuss types of conflict (man vs. man, man vs. nature, etc.). Read newspaper and magazine articles and ask students to identify the type of conflict; then ask them to do it for key scenes in the novel.
6. Study articles on modern-day sled dogs and their mushers. How are things different today?
7. Write to Alaska's tourist bureau (at least a month before you read the novel) and ask them to send all their brochures. You can also ask for information about a specific topic.
8. Compare the personalities of the main characters (including the dogs) to people prominent in the news. Students will have to read the newspaper and news magazines to make informed comparisons.
9. When bringing outside sources into the classroom, remember to bring ones that are topical and current. A book about a dog written 70 years ago suddenly becomes a modern adventure story if it is coupled with events taking place today. The students instantly see how the novel can relate to their lives. It ceases to be another old and boring book.

Developed by Beth Pallister, Bayside Middle School, Virginia Beach, Virginia.

mentary school where the administrators require grade-level planning by teachers around a theme. Teachers plan together during a Friday afternoon monthly; administrators teach the students while the teachers meet in the library.

If a thematic unit centered on *The Call of the Wild*, the English teacher could work with the social studies/geography teacher to develop collateral activities such as tracing on a map of Alaska the route followed in the novel, identifying landmarks, and discussing Alaska's statehood history. Visiting a site about Alaska on the Internet would help students see what that environment is like and how a person could become isolated and unable to survive. The science teacher could explain Darwinism and account for Buck's regression, describe the stages of hypothermia, and discuss dogs' physical adaptation to the harsh Alaskan environment.

Even in situations where departmentalized classes undermine communication between teachers, coordination can take place if teachers can meet long enough to agree on some books and technological resources to use for a particular unit. For instance, high school history and language arts teachers could coordinate the study of the American Civil War by deciding to read and discuss books such as *Voices from the Civil War* (Metzger, 1989), *Civil War Trivia and Fact Book* (Garrison, 1992), *Touched by Fire: A Photographic Portrait of the Civil War* (W. C. Davis, 1985), *The Long Surrender* (B. Davis, 1985), *A Separate Battle: Women and the Civil War* (Chang, 1991), *Crowns of Thorns and Glory: Mary Todd Lincoln and Varina Howell Davis, the Two First Ladies of the Civil War* (Vander Heuvel, 1988), *Civil War: America Becomes One Nation* (Robertson, 1992), *Blood Brothers: A Short History of the Civil War* (Vandiver, 1992), *Forged in Battle: The Civil War Alliance of Black Soldiers and White Officers* (Glatthaar, 1990), and *Diary of a Confederate Soldier* (W. C. Davis, 1990). Then they could locate and suggest some sites that students might visit. Perhaps they also could use videos, such as the Ken Burns documentary *The Civil War*, as another resource.

Activity 3.6 describes a cross-disciplinary thematic unit—"Cleaning Up the Chesapeake Bay"—developed by a team of teachers working together in staff development sessions. This nine-week unit was developed in Norfolk, Virginia, by Norview High School teachers of math, science, social studies, art, English, business, and vocational education working together over shared planning periods. Notice that many content areas are included in this unit. Planning such units can be time-consuming and difficult, but the benefits of adding new dimensions and vigor to the curricular offerings are certainly worth the effort. Such integrated instruction allows for practice with skills and a focus on instructional unity (Shanahan, 1997).

When developing a unit plan, teachers may need to construct the unit in distinct phases. Moss (1990) lists four:

1. Determining unit objectives and goals
2. Determining the theme or focus of the unit
3. Gathering resources to be used in the unit
4. Deciding student activities for the unit and the sequence of the activities

ACTIVITY 3.6 Thematic Planning Across the Curriculum: Cleaning Up the Chesapeake Bay

Goals: Students will research causes of pollution and develop a plan of action to improve environmental characteristics of the Chesapeake Bay.

Process Objective: Students will integrate information and process skills across the curriculum to produce a plan of action to improve the Chesapeake Bay.

Content Areas

Math	*Earth Science*	*History/Geography*	*Art*
metric system making graphs study wave functions finding parts per million finding rate of increase or decrease of water level, living creatures, area of bay, temperature of water, etc. calculating distance, depth	weather rocks, soil rivers quantitative measurement % of pH phosphates, etc. volume of water transport estuary	laws enacted—federal, state map reading newspaper, magazine articles historical development cultural development time line of development map making	research artwork done in the past: drawings, pictures/photos, sculpture/clay music Indian arts/crafts, tradition produce art of the past: drawing, photo, sculpture, clay interpreting art: practice futuristic art on the bay, paint, sketch, sculpt, music create a model of the bay

English	*Vocational*	*Business*
research techniques proofread, polish final proposal evaluate controversial issues interviews appreciate life on the bay analyze conflict related to life on the bay create poems relevant to subject	take pictures, identify industry on the bay identify new jobs that may be created determine how ships dispose of waste identify manufacturers and processes that produce waste in or near the bay research OSHA laws research EPA guidelines how waste is presently treated	develop an ad campaign develop a budget on clean-up costs—what factors should be in a budget? what are factory cost and consumer cost? projection type proposal

Notes

9-week unit.

Kids selected to participate in program are average / below-average in ability.

Math and science team-teach.

English and history team-teach (research causes).

Two-day field trip at the beginning to Tangier Island:

1. Photos
2. Samples (physical and biological)
3. Interviews, etc.

Take the proposal to an appropriate audience at the end of this project (for example, the General Assembly in Richmond, to a committee on environmental protection, to a congressional committee in Washington, DC).

Divide the units so that all areas have the same focus—for example, Unit 1: Documenting the Problem.

English and history—research background causes and moral dilemma.

Developed by teachers at Norview High School, Norfolk, Virginia.

When determining unit goals, be sure to examine both the curriculum to be taught and the students' backgrounds and abilities. If a unit is to be taught well into the school year, the teacher should know what the students can absorb emotionally and socially, as well as their abilities for reading supplemental literature and using technology. Templeton (1991) advises teachers to wait several weeks before starting a unit at the beginning of the school year, so that students can learn classroom procedures and the teacher can assess their abilities and characteristics.

To begin determining the activities, teachers (either individually or with other teachers) can use the **webbing approach** to brainstorm ideas (Cullinan, Karrer, & Pillar, 1981; Huck, 1979; Huck, Hepler, & Hickman, 1987). The teacher first identifies large categories of information reflecting unit objectives and then narrows the focus to represent smaller concepts with numerous activities. The teacher does not have to use all the activities that are brainstormed, but the brainstorming session provides a springboard for determining how the final unit plan will appear. The teacher can choose themes and activities based on students' needs and interests, current events, and activities that were successful in other thematic units.

Concerning the collection of books, Lynch-Brown and Tomlinson (1993) advise that teachers should let the curriculum drive what books are used, not vice versa. Teachers should avoid including books that are not really relevant, and they should not base the selection of a theme on one or two books that they have on hand. Teachers need to be constantly watching for books and other materials that might be suitable for a particular unit of instruction. Also, whenever possible, they should ask students to help find books about subjects of interest to the class and of importance to class objectives. Students will be eager to help locate Internet resources and are likely to find more than the teacher has time or energy to locate. To find sources of interest, teachers can start with the databases, electronic library catalogs, and periodical indexes in the school library. If resources there are scanty, teachers should check the local public library for resources on a desired topic.

In any search, the school media specialist and reading specialist (if available) should be called upon for valuable assistance. The media specialist can show the teacher how to borrow materials from libraries elsewhere in the state and how to conduct electronic searches of libraries. When choosing literature, teachers may wish to use the SMOG readability formula (found in Appendix B) to obtain a quick estimate of how readable a book may be for students.

Teachers may use any or all of the following supplementary materials in a unit: magazine articles, audiovisuals, artifacts, large-print books, taped books, videotapes, Braille materials, computer software, listservs, and the Internet.

Personal Inquiries

A **personal inquiry** originates from questions that a student asks as a result of exposure to a topic about which she or he wishes to learn more. It is somewhat similar to the old-fashioned term paper traditionally required at the high school level, often in English class. Sometimes students are given a choice of topics to research, or they select their own topics. The emphasis, however, is not so much on what they write about as on their learning to write a research paper. What is important is what students find out from reading supplementary literature—usually primary sources—and using technology. Students are encouraged to develop their own questions. Whereas thematic units are teacher generated, personal inquiries are student generated. Todd (1995) describes the pleasure of independent study that inquiry learning provides.

Emphasis on inquiry learning increased in the 1990s (Rasinski & Padak, 1993). Campbell (1995) declares that lifelong learning and inquiry are the best routes to learning. Examples have been available for many years, especially in literature. Omri, in *The Indian in the Cupboard* (Reid, 1990), finds himself so immersed in reading books about the Iroquois Indian who appears in his cupboard that he doesn't hear the school bell ring. Usually, Omri expresses great dislike for both school and reading. In *Canyons* by Gary Paulsen (1990), Mr. Homesley convinces Brennan to start collecting bugs; they learn about each one together. As a result, Brennan goes to Mr. Homesley when he needs help to find out about the skull he found in the canyon. When materials arrive from Mr. Homesley's friend, Brennan stays up all night reading to unravel his mystery.

Personal inquiry approximates how adults learn. We have a question, and we search for an answer. Our answers are often the result of using literature to learn; most likely we do not use textbooks as our source material. Content teachers who approximate this lifelong learning technique may hook their students on learning in the way that both Omri and Brennan were hooked. Perhaps the best way to begin supplementing content instruction with personal inquiry is to collect questions that students ask, encourage them to find answers, and promote sharing what is learned with all of the students. Teachers who use authentic assessment in the form of portfolios can ask students to demonstrate within a portfolio the results of an inquiry.

What-I-Know Activities work especially well for conducting personal inquiries (see Chapter 4). First, learners complete the section of the sheet on what they already know before reading; then they decide what they would like to know and identify resources that will help them learn. After their reading, they describe what they learned and indicate what they still would like to know.

To fully understand the value of personal inquiries, conduct your own inquiries. Questions can run the gamut. A teacher of drama and literature asked, "Can I make puppets that can be used effectively for telling stories, expressing different personalities in a variety of plots?" A geometry teacher asked, "What geometric properties are exhibited in soap bubbles?" Another physics teacher asked, "What are the areas related to the topic of sound?" Davis (1998) tells how a beehive in a classroom generated questions that students set out to answer: Which one is the queen bee? Where is the queen? What does she look like? How is she different from other bees?

Issues Related to Supporting the Textbook with Multiple Resources

The physical environment of the classroom can facilitate the use of literature and technology to support the textbook because the way a classroom is arranged affects the climate for learning and teaching (Kowalski, 1995). According to Gambrell (1995), the availability of books, opportunities not only to read but to choose what to read, and curiosity appear to motivate both good and poor readers. A classroom arranged to entice readers meets these criteria. When teachers provide bookshelves with literature, folders with newspaper clippings, magazines on racks, and baskets of books on topics being studied, students will be as enticed as any learners who browse in bookstores or libraries and feel the itch to pick up a book! A designated quiet reading spot is a friendly, encouraging touch. If possible, at least three or four computers should be available in the classroom so that students have easy access when they need to practice, write, enter data, send or receive mail, or find information on the Internet.

Locating and obtaining these resources may be less difficult than it first seems. In this textbook we mention several resources located by other teachers. Many parent organizations raise money for purchases. Libraries—either public or school—often loan books for extended classroom use. Students may donate books. Sometimes teachers receive "bonus" books from bookclub orders. If a school cannot afford several computers for each classroom, perhaps a "rolling" computer lab can be established or a stationary lab can be provided.

As teachers integrate more literature into their content teaching, they should remember to include multicultural literature. Bieger (1995) describes a four-level hierarchical framework for teaching multicultural literature: (1) looking at the contributions of people from other cultures; (2) adding information about other cultures to the curriculum; (3) changing the curriculum to help students see different cultures from new perspectives; and (4) identifying as well as proposing solutions to social problems that occur in multicultural environments. In *Reading It Aloud!*, Richardson (2000) presents many pieces of literature and provides instructional possibilities across the content areas.

Supporting the textbook with literature and technology enhances the teacher's ability to distinguish between the relevant information that textbooks offer and any incorrect, outdated, or abbreviated information that they may present. Exemplary programs do this all of the time. For instance, Lafayette Township School in New Jersey was granted the International Reading Association Exemplary Reading Program award (Mahler, 1995). The school integrated instruction in numerous ways—for example, by organizing a Renaissance fair, where middle-school students "read about the Renaissance era, wrote stories, built inventions originally inspired by Leonardo da Vinci, staged a play, and coordinated activities for students in the lower grades to learn more about the Middle Ages" (p. 415). Mahler points out that this school developed a literature-based program for grades 2 through 8. Alvarez and Rodriguez (1995) describe how high school students in an exploratory project called "Explorers of the Universe" learned not only subject matter but also "how to think, learn, and ask questions" (p. 233) as a result of searching in teams for information beyond the classroom textbooks. One group of students began to correspond with two astronomers via telecommunications.

Teaching thinking through personal responses to multitext promotes critical thinking. In using PAR with literature and technology across the curriculum:

P = multitext to prepare readers for forthcoming text content

A = multitext to assist readers in understanding the topic under discussion

R = multitext to reinforce knowledge of a topic or find out more about a topic just studied in the textbook

Teachers need to know ways to encourage students to respond to supplemental literature through writing, discussions in response groups, and even art and drama renderings. In later chapters we describe cooperative-learning response groups (Chapter 11), writing activities and learning logs (Chapter 9), post graphic organizers and other visuals (Chapters 8 and 10), and cooperative drama (Chapter 9), as well as ways to guide students to respond through directed readings (Directed Reading/Thinking Activities, guided-reading procedure, question/answer relationships).

One-Minute Summary

Faced with an ever-expanding amount of content to be digested and learned in every content-area subject, teachers increasingly realize that no one textbook can deliver all the concepts in, and differing viewpoints on, any unit of study. Thus many content-area teachers are turning to resources that complement textbooks. This chapter explores numerous reasons why textbooks need supplementing, the characteristics of effective literature-based instruction, types of technology resources, and three plans of action: read-alongs and read-alouds, thematic units of instruction, and personal inquiries. We also describe how to locate and collect appropriate literature and technological resources, and we discuss ways to get students to make personal responses to resources they read.

End-of-Chapter Activities

Assisting Comprehension

1. Why is there a need to complement textbooks with other resources in a content-area classroom? What elements need to be present for a school or a class to be successful with multitext instruction?
2. Below is a list of the applications and instructional software mentioned in this chapter:

Microsoft Word from Microsoft (see www.microsoft.com)

The Writing Center from The Learning Company

PowerPoint from Microsoft

FrontPage from Microsoft (see www.microsoft.com)

Dreamweaver from Macromedia (see www.dreamweaver.com)

SoundEdit from Macromedia (see www.macromedia.com)

SoundForge from Sonic Foundry

VisiCam from Connectrix (see www.connectrix.com)

Oregon Trail from MECC

Amazon Trail from MECC

Leonardo the Inventor from Softkey, One Athenaeum Street, Cambridge, MA 02142

A Survey of Western Art from Ebook Inc., 32970 Alvarado-Niles, Suite 704, Union City, CA 94587

Compton's Interactive Encyclopedia from Compton's New Media

Grolier Multimedia Encyclopedia from Grolier Publications

Infopedia from Softkey (see www.softkey.com)

Reflecting on Your Reading

1. Choose a topic that you wish to focus on in a future unit of instruction, and make a map of possible activities, as shown in Activity 3.3. Share your rendering with other content-area teachers to get their ideas. Practice in constructing such a map will help you with new topics that you will be teaching.
2. Anderson-Inman wrote a column for the *Journal of Adolescent and Adult Literacy* entitled "Technology Tidbits" from 1994 to 1998. You might want to locate and read some of these columns.

CHAPTER 4

Determining the Reader's Background for Content Material

Material is not inherently meaningful: it is endowed with meaning by a reacting individual, and experiences or previous reaction is a necessary condition.

—James Stroud, *Psychology in Education*

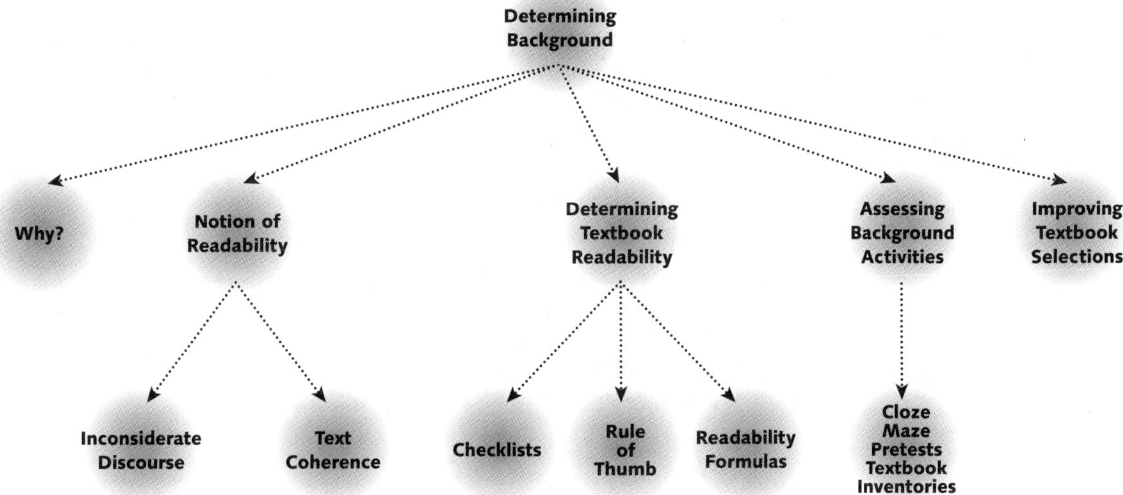

Preparing to Read

1. Did you ever serve on a textbook adoption committee or select material for classroom use? As you read this chapter, think of how you can use the information in it when selecting textbooks and other content material.
2. Following is a list of terms used in this chapter. Some may be familiar to you in a general context, but in this chapter they may be used in unfamiliar ways. Rate your knowledge by placing a plus sign (+) in front of those you are sure that you know, a check mark (✓) in front of those you have some knowledge about, and a zero (0) in front of those you don't know. Be ready to locate and pay special attention to their meanings when they are presented in the chapter.

   ______ readability
   ______ inconsiderate discourse
   ______ textual coherence
   ______ dumbed-down text
   ______ rule of thumb
   ______ readability formulas
   ______ independent-level reading
   ______ refutational texts
   ______ cloze
   ______ maze

Objectives

As you read this chapter, focus your attention on the following objectives. You will:

1. understand how to determine the match between a reader and the material to be read.
2. be able to define the term *readability*.
3. be able to make judgments about the readability of textbook material.
4. become acquainted with situations that may cause readability problems.
5. become acquainted with several activities that can help shape the match between a reader and the material to be read.

6. understand the roles of author, teacher, and student in improving textbook selection.

Why Determining Background Is Important

Most of us prefer to feel comfortable with the material we read. Good readers usually browse before they start to read because they want to see how comfortable they will be with the material. They take note of how much they already know about the topic, how interested they are in the topic, and what strategies they might employ to read the material. They size up the material by asking: Is it easy to follow? Is the content clear? Good readers also assess the relative difficulty of the text. They ask questions such as these: Is it easy to read, like a story (narrative style)? Is it somewhat more difficult, like a newspaper article (journalistic style)? Or is it challenging to read, like many textbooks (expository style with many new facts and concepts)? A reader who knows what lies ahead and can chart a course feels more confident than a reader who opens the book and plunges into the text.

Mature, proficient readers may make this assessment almost automatically and unconsciously. Most students, however, need the teacher's guidance to preview material. It is crucial, then, that teachers carefully study students' reading needs as well as the materials they themselves use as teaching tools. By finding out in advance as much as they can about what readers will encounter on the page, teachers can help students read effectively. Teachers and readers who ignore this step neglect a crucial part of the preparation for reading: Comprehension, not to mention the time spent on instruction, will be lost. Achieving a good match between the reader and the text makes good sense.

Suppose you are assigned to read the following passage on the pathology of viral hepatitis? Unless you are already highly interested in and knowledgeable about the topic, you may feel a little apprehensive. Read the passage now, not to learn the material but to grade it according to the criteria listed after the passage.

> The physical signs and symptoms that the person with hepatitis experiences are reflections of cellular damage in the liver. The hepatocyte has alterations in function resulting from damage caused by the virus and the resultant inflammatory response. The endoplasmic reticulum is the first organelle to undergo change. Since this organelle is responsible for protein and steroid synthesis, glucuronide conjugation, and detoxification, functions that depend on these processes will be altered. The degree of impairment depends on the amount of hepatocellular damage. The mitochondria sustain damage later than the endoplasmic reticulum. The Kupffer cells increase in size and number. The vascular and ductile tissues experience inflammatory changes. In most cases of uncomplicated hepatitis the reticulum framework is not in danger, and excellent healing of the hepatocytes occurs in three to four months.
>
> From Chapter 68, "Disorders of the Liver," in *Medical Surgical Nursing: A Psychological Approach*, by J. Luckmann and K. Sorensen, 1980, Philadelphia, W. B. Saunders Company.

Rate this reading material on each of the following criteria by circling a grade from A to F:

The language and vocabulary are clear to me.
A B C D F
The concepts are well developed.
A B C D F
The paragraph is organized.
A B C D F
The paragraph is well written.
A B C D F
The paragraph is interesting to me.
A B C D F

Now compare your impressions with those of 41 teachers, whose actual ratings were distributed as follows:

The language and vocabulary are clear to me.

A	B	C	D	F
2	0	7	16	16

The concepts are well developed.

A	B	C	D	F
2	3	19	8	9

The paragraph is organized.

A	B	C	D	F
6	12	14	3	6

The paragraph is well written.

A	B	C	D	F
2	9	14	12	4

The paragraph is interesting to me.

A	B	C	D	F
1	1	3	10	26

By considering the ratings—yours and those of 41 others—of that passage, you might gain insight into the problems inherent in reading textbook material. The 41 teachers constitute a fairly homogeneous group: They have a common profession and a recognized level of competence. Thus we might expect their reactions to the passage to be fairly similar. Yet they rated the paragraph differently. Although all 41 of them read the same material, the experiences and interests that each brought to the material, the interaction of each with the material, and the skill of each reader greatly influenced their reactions.

Notice that the first and last ratings that the teachers made about the passage relate to prior knowledge and interest; both are characteristics that reside within the reader. The 41 teachers generally were not confident about the language and vocabulary of the material, nor were they particularly interested in it. Teachers who have background and interest in this field of study probably would give higher ratings.

The middle three ratings relate to the text itself—concept development, organization, and style. These characteristics reside within the text, not the reader. Notice that the 41 teachers rated text characteristics higher. We can conclude that although they did not bring the requisite vocabulary, knowledge, or interest to this material, they recognized that the text was well structured. Reading the complete chapter would be challenging for them because they would be constantly trying to fit new information into a limited background of knowledge, but the text would help them because the writer presents the information well.

The challenge in the classroom is even greater because of the heterogeneity of the students. The experiences, personal interactions, and reading skills of students are likely to be much more varied than those of the 41 teachers.

The Notion of Readability

Chapter 3 stresses the importance of using multiple resources instead of relying entirely on a textbook to convey content information. Unfortunately, some studies indicate that as much as 95 percent of classroom instruction and 90 percent of homework assignments for elementary students are based on textbook materials; the situation is similar at the secondary level (Sosniak & Perlman, 1990). Too often, teachers organize their instruction around the textbook rather than around the topic. Apple (1988) writes, "Whether we like it or not, the curriculum in most American schools is not defined by courses of study or suggested programs, but by one particular artifact, the grade-level-specific text" (p. 85). This is an unfortunate situation because attention to a student's reading level is lacking. And, as we have seen with the hepatitis example, the same material does not impress all readers in the same way. Even if a textbook is enticing, the teacher should use other resources to provide variety and to meet the interests and background needs of all readers in a class. Dove (1998) suggests that "it is no longer unrealistic to consider the textbook as only one of several resources that teachers can use to plan instruction. . . . Given the diversity of students in today's schools, the one-textbook approach is no longer viable" (p. 29).

Teachers need to determine what a textbook and other content material do and do not have to offer. Textbook adoption should be a careful, well-considered process. Applying readability considerations can ensure the selection of material that not only is content-rich but also facilitates reading to learn. The first step is to assess the match between the reader and the material. If the match is not a good one, then the teacher must seriously consider finding materials that better match the readers. To do otherwise handicaps the readers.

What is this notion of readability, and how does the teacher determine the readability match? Dreyer (1984) has written that "the goal of readability research is to match reader and text" (p. 334). Simply stated, **readability** is that match. Readability suggests that content is clear, well expressed, and suited to the reader.

Readability is not a formula. It is an exploration of what characteristics within the reader and within the text will create a successful marriage. By considering readability, teachers are able to prepare readers appropriately to learn. Professional judgment is essential in determining readability; no score or formula can do more than help teachers understand the problems that may arise with reading material. Too many factors are involved for teachers to settle for simple solutions. For instance, careful consideration of grammar and its complexity is necessary when considering why students find written material more difficult than oral discussion of a topic. Unsworth (1999) discusses how English writing "packs" many content words into expository text, many more than in the spoken form. One can determine the lexical or grammatical density of a piece of writing by using Halladay's (1994) formula, which divides the number of lexical items by the number of clauses. Unsworth notes that this technique requires a functional grammatical perspective on English.

Inconsiderate Discourse

"Your ring adjusters will shape to fit you right by following these simple steps." Wait a minute! Are the "ring adjusters" going to follow some simple steps? As written, the subject, *ring adjusters*, is going to follow simple steps. Doesn't the author mean the reader is supposed to follow simple steps? And will the ring adjusters change shape to fit the reader, or fit the ring, or help the ring fit the reader? The author has written an ungrammatical sentence wherein the relationships between subject, verb, and direct object are confused.

Consider another example: "Explain how are certain flowering times adaptive for plant species." A sixth-grader brought his textbook to the science teacher, asking her to explain what this sentence means. No wonder he had problems! By reviewing the chapter, the teacher was able to locate the subheading and text about "flowering times and survival." The question must have been drawn from the material under this subheading, but the wording of the question is confusing.

Readers need to work extra hard to understand the meaning underlying text passages such as those. When confronted with such careless text, the reader must make a decision. Too often students decide that the text is simply not worth the energy. How many readers abandon or postpone the mastery of a new software program because its documentation is poorly written or presented? How many parents become exasperated with the poorly written instructions for assembling a toy? Similarly, some content material, particularly that found in textbooks, may be poorly written and therefore place unnecessary stress on a reader. If such is the case, teachers must identify the difficulties in the material to help the reader expend the least energy for the greatest gain.

Poorly written material is recognizable because of its loose organization, its lack of a discernible style, its incorrect syntax, or its incoherent passages. Armbruster and Anderson (1981) call such material **inconsiderate discourse**. When Olson and Gee (1991) surveyed 47 primary-grade classroom teachers about their impressions of expository text for their students, 23 percent of them identified text characteristics such as "sentence length, page format, inadequate arrangement and unfamiliar presentation of topics, and lack of aids on how to read expository text" as the greatest problems, while another 69 percent cited unfamiliar words. College students indicated in a survey (Smith, 1992) that textbooks are generally boring because passages are too long, the writing style is hard to follow, graphics don't seem to relate to text, and information is either too detailed or repetitive. High school students who were asked to rate their textbooks and indicate how often they read and studied them said that they used mathematics texts most often, followed by social studies, science, and English texts. However, they reported the text they liked *least* was the mathematics text because it was "hard to understand, boring, not specific enough, and poorly arranged" (Lester & Cheek, 1998).

Fortunately, textbooks are changing for the better. Walpole (1999) found that newer science texts are more enticing to readers. She compared science textbooks for third-graders written in 1992 and 1995 and found significant improvements in format, organization, text coherence, and illustrations. These factors all enter the mix that makes text considerate or inconsiderate, coherent or incoherent.

Textual Coherence

For a text to be readable, it must exhibit **textual coherence** (Armbruster, 1984). Textual coherence—the clear presentation of material to facilitate comprehension—can be divided into two categories: global coherence and local coherence.

Global coherence refers to the big picture. Major ideas should span the entire text so that readers are made aware of the global nature of the material and can follow the ideas without becoming confused. The way a text is structured can ensure global coherence. For example, the organization of ideas according to logical patterns, such as clear sequences of cause and effect, aids global comprehension. The style of text is also significant. A narrative style is usually easiest for readers, followed by a more journalistic style. Hardest to read is exposition. It is confusing when a writer mixes exposition and narrative style but doesn't cue the reader. "This is a story about" or "The following description explains" provides clear cues to the style of text to follow. The frequent use of one style also helps the reader understand and effectively follow the structure of the text. Of course, the content of the material and how well the author matches it to the structure are also important for global coherence.

Local coherence involves the many kinds of aids that connect ideas at the more immediate, or local, level. These aids include cues within sentences—phrases or clauses, for example—between sentences, or within paragraphs. When an author clearly identifies the subject and then uses a pronoun to refer to that subject, coherence is much greater than when the pronoun referent is vague and the reader is forced to guess to whom or what the author may be referring. Consider these passages, which Lederer (1987) quotes as an example of text ambiguity:

> Guilt, vengeance, and bitterness can be emotionally destructive to you and your children. You must get rid of them.
>
> After Governor Baldwin watched the lion perform, he was taken to Main Street and fed 25 pounds of raw meat in front of the Cross Keys Theater. (p. 156)

Another type of poorly written text is that in which the author oversimplifies the context. Former Secretary of Education Terrell Bell (Toch, 1984) expressed concern over such textbooks, calling them "dumbed down." In **dumbed-down text**, global coherence may be so simplified that the author can't do justice to the content, and local coherence may be absent because there isn't enough complexity to the text. When important points and intricacies are missing, the reader loses both content and cues.

To determine whether textual coherence is a problem, students are really the best resource. Britton and colleagues (1991) found that college students were able to select with 95 percent accuracy which of two texts on the same topic was easier to learn. Another way is to sample student and teacher opinions. Students and teachers might ask the following types of questions when reviewing text material:

1. Is the text narrative, journalistic, or expository?
2. How clear is this style to the reader? Has the author stated what the style is or cued the reader in any way?
3. Can I identify a clear, major idea that pervades the text, chapter, section, lesson, paragraph?
4. Are the ideas arranged in a clear, logical organizational pattern? How clearly is this pattern revealed to the reader?
5. Does the content match the structure and organization?
6. Are aids available to help the reader, such as
   - **a.** headings and subheadings
   - **b.** topic sentence
   - **c.** lively presentation of information
   - **d.** explicit statements to guide the reader
   - **e.** logical ordering
   - **f.** consistency
   - **g.** clarity of references, such as pronoun to antecedent
   - **h.** questions asked often of the reader, not saved until the end
   - **i.** enough, but not too many, details

Determining the Readability of Textbooks

Checklists

One way to determine the readability of text material is to use a checklist to aid in judging the overall strengths and weaknesses of the text. Creating an evaluative checklist, which the teacher can then use as a guide, ensures both "readability and relevance" (Danielson, 1987, p. 185). One fairly extensive checklist to help teachers consider readability carefully and efficiently is Bader's (1987) textbook analysis chart (see Figure 4.1). The chart identifies several areas of concern and lists specific items for teacher evaluation. The user is encouraged to summarize the textbook's strengths and weaknesses after completing the checklist and then to decide the implications of the summary for teaching the material evaluated.

The Bader analysis encourages teachers to consider several factors that contribute to readability. The category "Linguistic Factors," for example, describes word difficulty in six ways, whereas a readability formula considers only the length of a word. The "Writing Style" category considers four measures of style, whereas a readability formula considers only sentence length. The four other categories are not considered at all in a formula. "Conceptual Factors" and "Organizational Factors" include criteria that many authors identify as having a crucial effect on text difficulty. In addition, the teacher is asked to think

FIGURE 4.1 Bader's textbook analysis chart

Book Title ______
Publisher ______
Grade Level ______
Content Area ______

+ Excellent/ Evident Throughout	✓ Average/ Somewhat Evident	– Poor/ Not Evident		Comments
LINGUISTIC FACTORS:				
______	______	______	Generally appropriate to intended grade level(s) according to ______ formula	______
______	______	______	Linguistic patterns suitable to most populations and fit intended level(s)	______
______	______	______	Vocabulary choice and control suitable	______
______	______	______	New vocabulary highlighted, italicized, in boldface, or underlined	______
______	______	______	New vocabulary defined in context	______
______	______	______	New vocabulary defined in margin guides, glossary, beginning or end of chapter	______

(*continued*) ➤

continued

+ Excellent/ Evident Throughout	✓ Average/ Somewhat Evident	– Poor/ Not Evident		*Comments*
CONCEPTUAL FACTORS:				
			Conceptual level generally appropriate to intended grade level(s)	
			Concepts presented deductively	
			Concepts presented inductively	
			Major ideas are highlighted, italicized, in boldface type, or underlined	
			Appropriate assumptions made regarding prior level of concepts	
			Sufficient development of new concepts through examples, illustrations, analogies, redundancy	
			No evidence of sexual, racial, economic, cultural, or political bias	
ORGANIZATIONAL FACTORS:				
			Units, chapters, table of contents, index present clear, logical development of subject	
			Chapters of instructional segments contain headings and subheadings that aid comprehension of subject	
			Introductory, definitional, illustrative, summary paragraphs/sections used as necessary	
			Topic sentences of paragraphs clearly identifiable or easily inferred	
			Each chapter/section/unit contains a well-written summary and/or overview	
WRITING STYLE:				
			Ideas are expressed clearly and directly	
			Word choice is appropriate	
			Tone and manner of expression are appealing to intended readers	
			Mechanics are correct	
LEARNING AIDS:				
			Questions/tasks appropriate to conceptual development of intended age/grade level(s)	
			Questions/tasks span levels of reasoning: literal, interpretive, critical, values clarification, problem-solving	
			Questions/tasks can be used as reading guides	
			Suitable supplementary readings suggested	

+ Excellent/ Evident Throughout	✓ Average/ Somewhat Evident	– Poor/ Not Evident		Comments
TEACHING AIDS:				
______	______	______	Clear, convenient to use	______
______	______	______	Helpful ideas for conceptual development	______
______	______	______	Alternative instructional suggestions given for poor readers, slow learning students, advanced students	______
______	______	______	Contains objectives, management plans, evaluation guidelines, tests of satisfactory quality	______
______	______	______	Supplementary aids available	______
BINDING/PRINTING/FORMAT/ILLUSTRATIONS:				
______	______	______	Size of book is appropriate	______
______	______	______	Cover, binding, and paper are appropriate	______
______	______	______	Typeface is appropriate	______
______	______	______	Format is appropriate	______
______	______	______	Pictures, charts, graphs are appealing	______
______	______	______	Illustrations aid comprehension of text	______
______	______	______	Illustrations are free of sexual, social, cultural bias	______
SUMMARY:				
______	______	______	Totals	______

The strengths are:

The weaknesses are:

As a teacher, I will need to:

Original text analysis chart by Dr. Lois Bader, Michigan State University. Used with permission of Lois Bader.

about "Learning Aids," because such aids will make otherwise difficult material easier for students to handle. The "Teaching Aids" category also gives teachers direction in how to guide the reading of otherwise difficult material. As Sinatra (1986) has noted, visual aids often make difficult material readable. Because features such as typography, format, illustrations, and book appearance can enhance meaning in a text, Bader includes these items in her last category.

However, the promotion of checklists to determine whether material is poorly written or difficult must be qualified:

- No one checklist can cover all the factors important to teachers.

- Checklists must be general; only teachers can make them specific—by adding their own items reflecting their own needs for teaching the instructional material.
- Most checklists cover instructional design but not instructional content (Moore & Murphy, 1987).

But, armed with tools such as those presented in this chapter and with some knowledge of why determining the difficulty of reading material is important, we believe that teachers can proceed wisely.

Special note: What makes mathematics textbooks easier or harder to read? Here, the reading rules are a bit different. Examples often require bottom-to-top, circular, diagonal, or backward reading rather than more conventional directionality. A mathematics text should include specific explanations and directions for students (Georgia Department of Education, 1975). These directions should make clear to students that the reading of mathematics materials may employ different rules. Also, readability formulas, explained later in this chapter, may be more difficult to administer with mathematics textbooks.

The Rule of Thumb

A quick and reader-centered way to determine readability is to teach students to use the **rule of thumb** (Veatch, 1968). Younger students are told to select a book they want to read and to open to a middle page. If they spot an unknown word while reading that page, they press a thumb on the table. For each hard word, they press down another finger. If they press down five or more fingers by the time they finish the page, the book may be too hard. Three or fewer fingers indicates a more reasonable challenge. No fingers means the book might be very easy. Older students can determine readability by using two hands and closing their fingers into fists. One closed fist indicates that the book is just right, two closed fists may indicate difficulty, and only one or two closed fingers may indicate easy material.

Of course, students should read the chosen book even if it appears to be too easy or too hard, if that is their wish. The rule of thumb is not scientific and is only intended to help readers make decisions. It is not intended to discourage a reader from trying any book. Its value is that it encourages the reader to be responsible for determining difficulty. This involvement of the reader promotes independence.

Readability Formulas

Readability formulas are a major resource for determining the difficulty of material. Fry, a noted expert on readability formulas, quotes Farr as estimating that "over 40 percent of the state and local school districts in the United States use readability formulas as one criterion in textbook selection" (Fry, 1987, p. 339). Readability formulas are fairly reliable measures—if not always the most effective ones—for making instructional decisions about texts.

TECHNOLOGY BOX

Example of Useful Information from a Listserv

Subject: [CRALIST: 257] Date: Wed, 25 Mar 98 12:49:46 EST From: cralist@archon.educ.kent.edu To: "Multiple recipients of list" <cralist@archon.educ.kent.edu

A week or so ago the legislative committee emailed the cra Listserv with information about checkpoints for progress, a.k.a. America Reads. We are adding to this information today by listing excerpts from children's books that represent what children in the 1st, 2nd, and 3rd grade should be able to read and understand.

1st grade
Franklin Is Bossy, by Paulette Bourgeois
In his room, Franklin built a castle. He made a cape to be brave in. He made shields and swords and suits of armor. He drew pictures. He played house. He read stories. He played by himself for one whole hour, and then he didn't know what to do. So, Franklin went looking for company. His friends were in the river, cooling off.

2nd grade
Curious George, by H. A. Rey
The hat had been on the man's head. George thought it would be nice to have it on his own head. He picked it up and put it on. The hat covered George's head. He couldn't see. The man picked him up quickly and popped him into a bag. George was caught. The man with the big yellow hat put George into a little boat, and a sailor rowed them both across the water to a big ship.

3rd grade
Sarah, Plain and Tall, by Patricia MacLaclan
I held my breath and floated at last, looking up into the sky, afraid to speak. Crows flew over, three in a row. And I could hear a killdeer in the field. We climbed the bank and dried ourselves and lay in the grass again. The cows watched, their eyes sad in their dinner-plate faces. And I slept, dreaming a perfect dream. The fields had turned into a sea that gleamed like sun on glass. And Sarah was happy.

Books to read at 1st, 2nd, and 3rd grade levels

1st
Amelia Bedelia
Clifford the Big Red Dog
Freight Train
The Very Hungry Caterpillar
Frog and Toad Are Friends
There's an Alligator Under My Bed
Bedtime for Francis
Freckle Juice

2nd
Corduroy
Ira Sleeps Over
Bony-Legs
Where Is Cuddly Cat

3rd
Encyclopedia Brown, Boy Detective
The Fantastic Mr. Fox
The Boxcar Children
There's a Boy in the Girl's Bathroom

For complete information about America Reads: http://www.ed.gov/inits/americareads/arc

A quick first look at material to spot potential problems with difficulty can be accomplished by using a readability formula. Because formulas identify a certain grade level of difficulty, they are used most often to report information about textbook difficulty in terms of reading-level scores. A formula can be very helpful when a prediction of difficulty is necessary, such as when a textbook adoption committee considers several texts but cannot try out the book on real students. Similarly, a formula may be useful and efficient when a teacher wants to assess the difficulty of several materials that students are to read on their own in the library. A readability formula offers a fairly quick measure and can be used independently of student interaction. However, the teacher must not rely on the grade level obtained as an exact measure; it is only a predictor.

How Readability Formulas Work

Klare (1974–1975) reviewed the development and uses of readability formulas from 1960 to the mid-1970s and explained their basic components. Over the years, reading researchers have developed and statistically validated many readability formulas. Some are cumbersome in that they necessitate checking long lists of words. Both the Dale and Chall (1948) and the Spache (1953) measure "word familiarity"—that is, whether students should be expected to know a word within a given passage—by relying on lengthy word lists. The Lexile Framework developed in the mid-1980s is based on the words found in textbooks. Mosenthal and Kirsch (1998) developed a comprehensive measure that focuses on the structure and density that create complexity. Their measure demonstrates that difficulty in reading a document may be due more to the document's complexity than to the reader's abilities.

Essentially, two measurements are used in the majority of formulas: sentence difficulty and word difficulty. The underlying assumption is that the longer sentences and words are, the harder the material will be. Usually, this assumption holds true; sometimes, however, it is questionable. For instance, in William Faulkner's novel *The Sound and the Fury*, several sentences are as much as one and one-half pages long, and most readers would agree that the length of Faulkner's sentences makes for challenging reading. But could one say that because Ernest Hemingway's sentences are shorter, his material is easy to read? In these cases, one reads to understand style and theme, and sentence length is of little importance. These two sentences better illustrate the point:

> The children played on the playground with the elephant.
>
> We reneged on all prior briefs.

A readability formula would score the first sentence as the more difficult, but would it be the more difficult for children to comprehend?

The syntactical structure of sentences probably deserves more attention than it receives in readability formulas (Richardson, 1975; Singh, 1995). For example, sentences in the active voice may be easier to understand than those in the passive voice. Readability formulas do not measure with such sensitivity.

Also, word length may be a fairly accurate indicator of difficulty. Just as short sentences seem to be easier to read, the assumption that short words are easier on a reader also seems generally true. First-graders recognize a lot of one-syllable words. But *elephant* might be an easier word for young readers than *the*. *Elephant* may be longer, but it's a lot easier to picture an *elephant* than to picture *the*! Because seeing words in the mind's eye facilitates comprehension, the longer word is easier in this case. Few readers wish to encounter a lot of long words all at once, but they will be very bored by too many short ones. Given these qualifiers, the way most readability formulas measure reading material is common, if not commonsense.

A few formulas remain popular because they are easy to apply and seem reliable. We describe the Fry readability formula here and the SMOG formula in Appendix B. Hill and Erwin (1984) found that most teachers in their study preferred the Fry formula, but both are simple to calculate and are accepted favorably by many teachers.

The Fry Readability Graph

The Fry readability graph (see Figure 4.2) was developed by Edward Fry in the 1960s for African teachers who taught English as a second language. In 1977, Fry revised the graph to include explanations, directions, and an extension to the 17th-grade level. The Fry graph offers a quantifiable, efficient way to measure text difficulty.

To use this graph, teachers select at least three 100-word passages from different parts of the material (see Figure 4.2, direction 1). For each 100-word passage, two counts are made: the number of syllables and the number of sentences (directions 2 and 3). The three counts of syllables are added, then averaged; the three counts of sentences are added, then averaged (direction 4). The teacher then locates the average for the number of syllables across the top of the graph and the average for the number of sentences along the side of the graph. The point at which these two averages intersect is the readability score. The point will fall within a fanlike, numbered segment on the graph; this number corresponds to the grade-level score. Fry says to count all words, including proper nouns, initials, and numerals (direction 1), and he defines *word* as well as *syllable* (directions 6 and 7). If a point falls in a gray area, the score is unreliable and should be recalculated by using additional 100-word passages. The worksheet shown in Figure 4.3 is intended to help the reader remember and apply Fry's directions.

The Fry formula is more usable for upper-elementary and higher-level materials than for lower-level material because at least 100 words are needed for computation. Forgan and Mangrum (1985) developed a way to adapt the Fry for shorter materials, and their procedure is described and illustrated in Appendix B.

For **independent-level reading**—materials that students will read on their own—the SMOG formula of McLaughlin (1969) may be used. Directions for using it are presented in Appendix B. In choosing between the Fry and the SMOG, it is important to remember that these two formulas are used for different

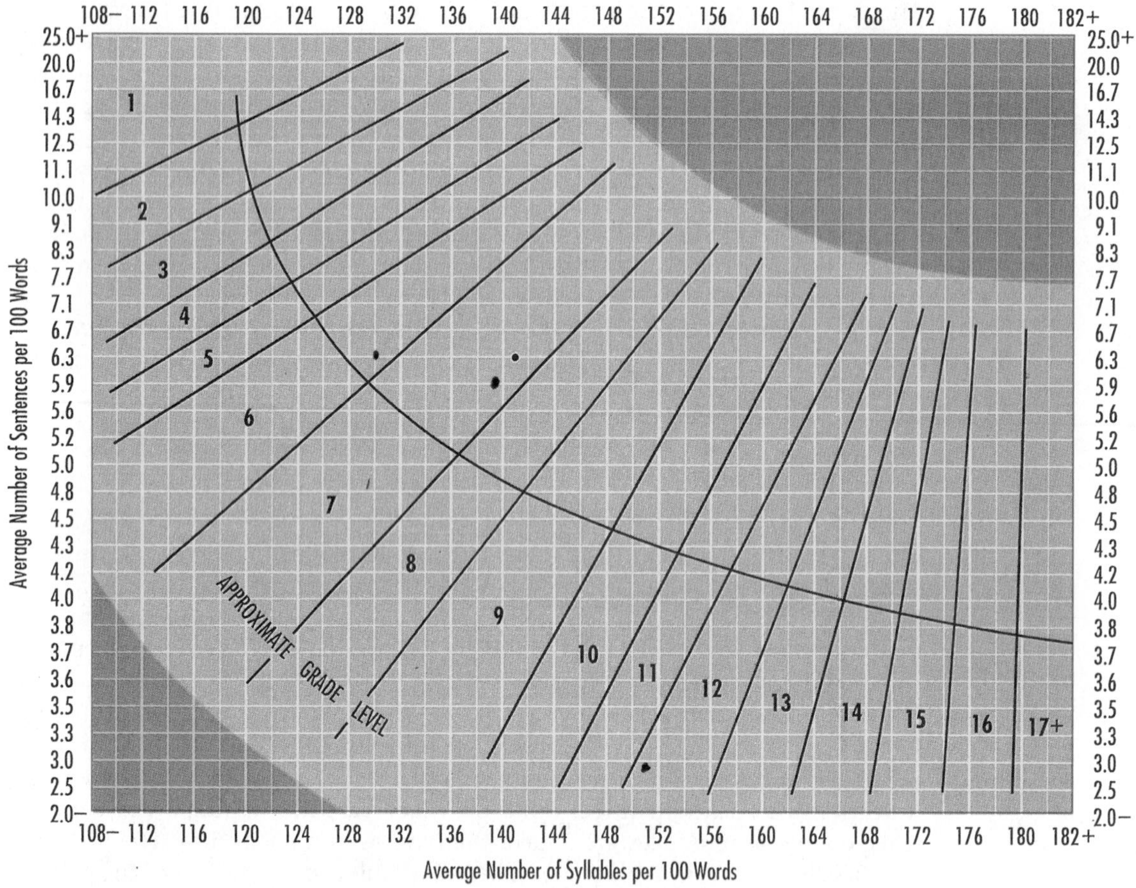

FIGURE 4.2 The Fry readability graph. From *Journal of Reading, 21*, 242–252.

Expanded Directions for Working Fry Readability Graph

1. Randomly select three (3) sample passages and count out exactly 100 words each, beginning with the beginning of a sentence. Do count proper nouns, initializations, and numerals.
2. Count the number of sentences in the hundred words, estimating length of the fraction of the last sentence to the nearest one-tenth.
3. Count the total number of syllables in the 100-word passage. If you don't have a hand counter available, an easy way is to simply put a mark above every syllable over one in each word, then when you get to the end of the passage, count the number of marks and add 100. Small calculators can also be used as counters by pushing numeral 1, then push the + sign for each word or syllable when counting.
4. Enter graph with *average* sentence length and *average* number of syllables; plot dot where the two lines intersect. Area where dot is plotted will give you the approximate grade level.
5. If a great deal of variability is found in syllable count or sentence count, putting more samples into the average is desirable.
6. A word is defined as a group of symbols with a space on either side; thus, *Joe, IRA, 1945,* and & are each one word.
7. A syllable is defined as a phonetic syllable. Generally, there are as many syllables as vowel sounds. For example, *stopped* is one syllable and *wanted* is two syllables. When counting syllables for numerals and initializations, count one syllable for each symbol. For example, *1945* is four syllables, *IRA* is three syllables, and & is one syllable.

Plot the averages found on the Fry graph.				
	1st 100 Words	2nd 100 Words	3rd 100 Words	Average
Page #				
# Syllables				
# Sentences				

FIGURE 4.3

purposes and that the readability scores they yield are read differently. The Fry formula measures the readability of material used in an instructional setting. Because the teacher will explain difficult words and sentences, the Fry score is based on students' understanding 65 to 75 percent of the material at a given grade level. The SMOG formula is intended to measure the readability of material that a teacher will *not* be teaching, such as material that the teacher has suggested a student use independently. Because the teacher will *not* be explaining the difficult words and sentences, the SMOG score is based on students' understanding 90 to 100 percent of the material. If a Fry and a SMOG were calculated on the same material, the Fry score probably would be lower.

Readability Statistics from Your Word Processor

Word processing programs such as WordPerfect and Microsoft Word provide readability statistics for any document being processed. In WordPerfect they can be found under "Grammatik" on the toolbar. In Microsoft Word they can be found by clicking on "Tools" and then clicking on "Grammar." Both provide the Flesch-Kincaid grade level, which measures readability based on the average number of syllables per word and the average number of words per sentence. The score is reported as a grade level similar to the Fry grade-level score. Some programs provide various measures with which to compare the Flesch-Kincaid grade-level scores. Simply by typing a few passages into the computer and using the readability measures the program provides, you can get a feel for the readability of text without counting words and syllables.

Some Cautions About Readability Formulas

In recent literature, professionals warn teachers to be aware of the limitations of readability formulas. They are not precise determiners of the difficulty of material; they are only predictors of how difficult the material might be for readers.

1. A readability formula gives a grade-level score, which is not a very specific measure of difficulty because grade level can be so ambiguous. Cadenhead (1987) describes this ambiguity as the "metaphor of reading level" and claims that it is a major problem of readability formulas. What does 17th-grade level mean when applied to a topic such as "electrical attraction of dielectric insulation" without consideration of the reader's interests, background, and knowledge? A grade-level readability score gives teachers a start in their considerations of text difficulty, not a complete picture.

2. The lengths of sentences and words are convenient and credible indicators of readability and fit neatly into a formula but are not comprehensive measures.
The various factors that make a text coherent are difficult to quantify. One cannot "compute" such factors in a simple readability formula.

3. Measures of word and sentence length are sometimes not the most accurate indicators of difficulty.
In one study (Carson, Chase, Gibson, & Hargrove, 1992), college students read texts measured by a formula as being at their level; however, the texts were not equally readable because of the conceptual difficulty of the material. To further illustrate this point, we refer readers to noted author E. B. White's (1951) essay "Calculating Machine," which recounts White's reaction when he received a "reading-ease calculator" developed by General Motors and based on the Flesch Reading Ease Formula. "Communication by the written word," writes White, "is a subtler (and more beautiful) thing than Dr. Flesch and General Motors imagine" (p. 166). His point—that it is dangerous to reduce language to such simplistic evaluation—is well taken. (For further information about the Flesch formula, refer to the references.)

4. The fewer sections of material measured, the less consistent and reliable the resulting score is likely to be.
Even three sections may be too few. If three or fewer sections are measured, the teacher should be cautious about accepting the results. We include the Fry Short Formula in Appendix B, but ask the reader to realize that it is already a shortcut! The Fry Short Formula should be used only when the material contains less than 100 words, such as in textbooks for young readers. However, almost always in such a case, the teacher can assess readability efficiently by relying on checklists and professional judgment.

There is more to readability than readability formulas. Much research has been conducted about texts and text-related matters since readability formulas were developed in the 1920s (Davison, 1984). We know enough to move beyond rigid adherence to mathematical formulas. Although formulas can tell us some things—they yield levels based on the percentage of readers who have performed well at those levels—they tell us a lot less than we want to know. Fry (1989) argues that some reading professionals may not like formulas because they are "so objective." When others argue that readability formulas are not comprehensive enough, his response is: "Readability formulas do not deny all this, they simply state that in general, on the average, the two inputs of sentence length and word difficulty accurately predict how easily a given passage will be understood by the average reader" (p. 295).

A report by Guzzetti and colleagues (1995) recommends that students themselves give considerable input about the readability of texts. The researchers found that a broad sample of students in science classes prefer **refutational texts**, in which both sides of an argument are presented and debated. Also, they found that students prefer expository texts over narrative ones. The students gave researchers specific ideas about how the sample text material they were reading could be improved. The researchers recommend that teachers send students' critiques and suggestions to publishers in order to make textbooks more interesting and comprehensible.

The concept of readability and the efficacy of readability formulas stir much controversy. We maintain that formulas provide only one measure and should be used with checklists and commonsense criteria to judge the readability of a text for a group of students.

Assessing Background Activities

Several activities can aid teachers in assessing students' background. As teachers model them, students will begin to understand the importance of assessing their own backgrounds. Cloze procedure, the maze, pretests and self-inventories are usually constructed by the teacher. As students understand their own role in the process, they will discover that they can factstorm and create WIKAs by themselves.

Cloze Procedure

Cloze procedure offers an interactive way to assess the match between the reader and the text. The term **cloze**, first used by Wilson Taylor in 1953, reflects the Gestalt principle of closure, or "the tendency to perceive things as wholes, even if parts are missing" (Harris & Hodges, 1995, p. 33). In the cloze procedure, a passage is cut up so that students can fill it in. The premise is that readers rely on prior knowledge and use of context as they close, or complete, the cut-up passage. This technique relies heavily on the Gestalt concept of perceiving the whole of things. Ebbinghaus (1908), in the late 1800s, used a modified form of closure when he conducted his verbal-learning and retention studies (described in Chapter 10).

When Taylor designed the cloze procedure, as we now use it, his purpose was to determine the readability of material for different readers. In the strict format that Taylor designed, a passage of 250 words or more is chosen and words are deleted at regular intervals—every 5th, 10th, or *n*th (any predetermined number) word. The beginning and ending sentences remain intact. Blanks replace the deleted words, and no clues other than the context of the material are provided to the reader, who must fill in those blanks. In a review of the research, Jongsma (1980) found that the cloze procedure is useful at any grade level if the pattern of deletions is sensitive to the students' familiarity with language. We recommend that, generally, every 10th word be deleted for primary students, because young students need more clues than older, more proficient readers with greater reading experience. Every 5th word should be deleted for older students (fourth grade and above) because they have had more experience with reading and using context.

Using Cloze to Determine Prior Knowledge

By using a cloze test, a teacher can find out whether students have prior knowledge about upcoming material and are able to adapt to the author's style. The readers are able to demonstrate their prior knowledge because they have to apply it when choosing the best words to insert in a cut-up passage. Their background knowledge helps them fill in gaps; their prior knowledge of language also helps them make good choices. If students complete the cloze with ease, they achieve an *independent-level score,* indicating that they can read the material on their own. If they can adapt when the teacher provides instruction about the material, they achieve an *instructional-level score.* A *frustration-level score* indicates that the material is difficult for readers to understand even with instruction.

Because the purpose of cloze procedure is to help a teacher quickly see whether students have adequate background knowledge and understand the language clues used in the material in question, scoring should be rapid and efficient. When cloze is used to determine prior knowledge, students are not expected to see the cloze exercise again, nor will the teacher be using it as a teaching tool. When cloze is used in this way, exact word replacement is the most efficient scoring procedure. In Taylor's presentation of cloze, only the exact word that was deleted is counted as a correct answer, and research (Bormouth, 1969) indicates that the exact word score is the most valid. When synonyms are accepted, the scoring criteria must be raised and the cloze must be modified, usually for instructional rather than readability purposes. Although scoring seems stringent, the criteria for achieving an instructional level of readability are quite relaxed to compensate for inadequate prior knowledge and the synonym factor. A score of 40 to 60 percent correct is acceptable.

Here are directions for constructing a cloze test to ascertain a reader's prior knowledge in kindergarten through third grade:

1. Select a passage of about 125 words.
2. Leave the first sentence intact.
3. Delete consistently every 10th word thereafter until a total of 10 deletions occurs. Make all blanks uniform in length.
4. Leave the last sentence intact, or include the remainder of the paragraph to give the passage continuity.
5. Make a key of the exact words that have been deleted.
6. Write directions for your students that stress the purpose of the activity—to determine prior knowledge, not to test them. Explain that they are to fill each blank with the word they think the author might have used.
7. For each student, count the number of correct responses and multiply by 10 (if 10 blanks were used) to express a percentage.
8. Use these scores to determine whether students will (a) be independent in reading the passage, (b) simply be able to understand the passage, or (c) be frustrated in their reading. A score of 60 percent or higher indicates the independent level; a score between 40 and 60 percent indicates the instructional level. The material is suitable for teaching students with those scores. A score of less than 40 percent indicates the frustration level; the material may be too hard for students achieving

such a low score. It may be helpful to list your students under each of these three levels, as follows:

Independent	*Instructional*	*Frustration*
(scores above 60%) Material is easy (list students)	(scores 40% to 60%) Material is suitable (list students)	(scores below 40%) Material is too difficult (list students)

Here are directions for constructing a cloze test for use with students in the fourth through twelfth grades:

1. Select a passage of 250 to 300 words.
2. Leave the first sentence intact.
3. Delete consistently every 5th word thereafter until a total of 50 deletions occurs. Make all blanks uniform in length.
4. Leave the last sentence intact, or include the remainder of the paragraph to give the passage continuity.
5. Make a key of the exact words that have been deleted.
6. Write directions for your students.
7. For each student, count the number of correct responses and multiply by 2 (if 50 blanks were used) to express a percentage.
8. Use these scores to determine whether students will (a) be independent in reading the passage, (b) simply be able to understand the passage, or (c) be frustrated in their reading. A score of 60 percent or higher indicates the independent level; a score between 40 and 60 percent indicates the instructional level. The material is suitable for teaching students with those scores. A score of less than 40 percent indicates the frustration level; the material may be too hard for students achieving such a low score. It may be helpful to list your students under each of these three levels, as follows:

Independent	*Instructional*	*Frustration*
(scores above 60%) Material is easy (list students)	(scores 40% to 60%) Material is suitable (list students)	(scores below 40%) Material is too difficult (list students)

Examples of Cloze to Determine Prior Knowledge

An English teacher faced with a new textbook and eleventh-graders in a school new to her wondered how the students might perform with the textbook and what accommodations she might need to make. These students had been labeled "high ability," but she knew that labels often do not indicate true performance. So she developed a cloze on a 300-word passage from the introduction to the textbook. The passage compared the origins of early American literature to men landing on the moon: Both were adventures and initial explorations of a new era. Would her students have sufficient background to understand this analogy? Would they have enough language skill to read this and ensuing passages with facility?

She administered the cloze during the first week of school, before issuing textbooks, so that she could anticipate difficulties before starting the year. Students were instructed to do their best to fill in the words they thought would fit, as a way to help the teacher get to know them better; the teacher assured them that they would not be graded. She never returned the cloze to the students; the exercise was for diagnosis, not instruction. She scored it using the exact-word criterion. In this way, she was able to develop a quick profile for 55 students in two sections. One student scored at the independent level; 2 scored at the frustration level. She decided that with proper guidance the majority of students would bring adequate knowledge to the textbook. She made a note to watch the two students who scored poorly, as well as the high scorer.

As the first weeks passed, she learned that one of the low-scoring students came from an abusive home and could not concentrate on academics even though he was capable. The other low scorer was very unhappy to have been placed in a high-ability class because all she wanted to do was play in the band and coast through school. The teacher was able to find some appropriate help for each of them. The high scorer continued to perform almost flawlessly on the assignments during the beginning weeks of school. The teacher discovered that this student was new to the school but had been in advanced classes in her previous school. Within the first three weeks, the teacher was able to recommend that the student be placed in an advanced class; the cloze results provided supporting documentation.

The teacher might have missed an opportunity to help these three students had she not administered the cloze. Helpful diagnostic information was learned from an activity that took little time; it was administered to 55 students in one 15-minute period.

Activity 4.1 is a cloze for an elementary-grade-level social studies chapter about St. Petersburg, Russia. Activity 4.2 is an example of a cloze for high school reading from a technology textbook on the construction of the small gasoline engine.

A note of caution is in order. A cloze procedure can reveal what students already know about a subject and can indicate whether the material is appropriate. The better students do, the more they probably know about the topic. If most students fall in the frustration level, the material is inappropriate because they may not bring enough background to it. Ashby-Davis (1985) cautions, however, that cloze procedure is not like the usual reading that students do. Reading speed, eye movements, and use of context are likely to be different when reading a cloze. Therefore, although a cloze may be a helpful indicator of a student's background in a particular topic, it should not be relied on to tell a teacher about a student's general reading skills.

ACTIVITY 4.1 Cloze for Elementary Social Studies

A Visit to St. Petersburg, Russia

St. Petersburg was first called Lovingood. It is on the delta of the Neva River. ___1___ is at the eastern end of the Gulf of ___2___. The city is built on both bodies of the ___3___ and on islands in the river. It is the ___4___ largest city in Russia. The city is a major ___5___. St. Petersburg is famous for its elaborate palaces and ___6___. One of the city's most visited attractions is the ___7___ Palace. It was the winter home of the Czars ___8___ the 1917 Russian Revolution. The Hermitage is a museum. ___9___ has a great art collection. Visitors to St. Petersburg ___10___ its beauty and history. It is a majestic city.

Answer Key:

1. it
2. Finland
3. Neva
4. second
5. seaport
6. churches
7. Winter
8. before
9. It
10. love

Using Cloze to Build on Prior Knowledge

When a cloze is used for instructional purposes instead of for assessing the match between the reader and the material, the range of possible cloze constructions increases. Instead of exact replacement of vocabulary, synonyms can be considered. In constructing an instructional cloze, the teacher leaves beginning and ending sentences intact, but the deletions can serve different instructional purposes. For example, the teacher may delete all of the nouns and then ask students to predict what part of speech the words to replace deleted words must be. Such a cloze activity builds awareness of nouns and helps students become proficient readers of their grammar books. An instructional cloze can also include clues. For example, in Activity 4.3 the teacher deleted important terms about the making of the cell and provided a diagram of an animal cell. Clues from the reading help provide a student with the answers. At the same time the student is given visual clues on the drawing to help in decision making.

Whatever the design, the instructional cloze can be used to help teachers learn what their students already know and, along with discussion of the choices made, build their knowledge of the material. Discussion also should whet readers' appetites for the reading material that follows, thus giving students a purpose for reading and assisting their comprehension of the material. Since discussing the students' choices is an obvious part of the activity when it is used for instruction, cloze also fosters listening and speaking opportunities. Although word choice is limited to single-word entries, some writing is occurring as well. Some teachers find cloze useful as a technique for reflection. Such an activity, the interactive cloze procedure, is explained in Chapter 8, on vocabulary.

ACTIVITY 4.2 Cloze for Secondary Vocational Education

Student Directions: Below is a passage taken from your technology textbook. Some of the words the author wrote have been deleted. Your job is to write in the blank the word that you *think* the author might have used in the same space. Your choices will help me get to know you as readers of this textbook. Good luck and do your best!

Construction of the Small Gasoline Engine

The internal combustion engine is classified as a *heat* engine; its power is produced by burning a fuel. The energy stored in ___1___ fuel is released when ___2___ is burned. *Internal combustion* ___3___ that the fuel is ___4___ inside the engine itself. ___5___ most common fuel is ___6___. If gasoline is to ___7___ inside the engine, there ___8___ be oxygen present to ___9___ the combustion. Therefore, the ___10___ needs to be a ___11___ of gasoline and air. ___12___ ignited, a fuel mixture ___13___ gasoline and air burns ___14___; it almost explodes. The ___15___ is designed to harness ___16___ energy.

The engine contains ___17___ cylindrical area commonly called ___18___ *cylinder* that is open ___19___ both ends. The top ___20___ the cylinder is covered ___21___ a tightly bolted-down plate ___22___ the *cylinder head.* The ___23___ contains a *piston,* which ___24___ a cylindrical part that ___25___ the cylinder with little ___26___. The piston is free ___27___ slide up and down ___28___ the cylinder. The air/fuel ___29___ is brought into the ___30___, then the piston moves ___31___ and compresses it into ___32___ small space called the ___33___ chamber. The *combustion chamber* is ___34___ area where the fuel ___35___ burned; it usually consists ___36___ a cavity in the ___37___ head and perhaps the ___38___ part of the cylinder. ___39___ the fuel is ignited ___40___ burns, tremendous pressure builds ___41___. This pressure forces the ___42___ back down the cylinder; ___43___ the untamed energy of ___44___ is harnessed to become ___45___ mechanical energy. The basic ___46___ within the engine is ___47___ of the piston sliding ___48___ and down the cylinder, ___49___ *reciprocating* motion.

There are ___50___ many problems, however. How can the up-and-down motion of the piston be converted into useful rotary motion? How can exhaust gases be removed? How can new fuel mixture be brought into the combustion chamber? Studying the engine's basic parts can help answer these questions.

Answers:

1. the
2. it
3. means
4. burned
5. The
6. gasoline
7. burn
8. must
9. support
10. fuel
11. mixture
12. When
13. of
14. rapidly
15. engine
16. this
17. a
18. the
19. at
20. of
21. with
22. called
23. cylinder
24. is
25. fits
26. clearance
27. to
28. within
29. mixture
30. cylinder
31. up
32. a
33. combustion
34. the
35. is
36. of
37. cylinder
38. uppermost
39. When
40. and
41. up
42. piston
43. thus
44. combustion
45. useful
46. motion
47. that
48. up
49. a
50. still

ACTIVITY 4.3 Cloze for Building on Prior Knowledge

Cloze Activity on Identity

Cells are made of smaller parts that do certain jobs. Look at the animal cell on the next page. It is about 1,600 times larger than the actual size of the cell. Notice the cell has a large (1) __________ floating in cytoplasm.

The cell has an outer covering called the (2) __________ __________. The cell membrane lets nutrients, water, and other materials in and out of the cell. The inside of the cell is filled with cytoplasm—a clear, jellylike material. Cytoplasm is mostly water, but it also contains dissolved nutrients and cell parts called (3) __________.

The organelles in the cytoplasm have different jobs. Some organelles help make proteins in the cell. Others release energy from nutrients. The saclike organelles in the picture—called (4) __________ —store nutrients, water, and wastes.

Find the nucleus in the cell. The nucleus is a large organelle. It has a membrane that surrounds a mesh of structures called chromosomes. The chromosomes are made of (5) __________ —deoxyribonucleic acid. The chromosomes contain instructions that control all the cell's activities. For example, chromosomes control how fast the cell grows and when the cell reproduces.

Different kinds of organisms have different numbers of chromosomes in their cells. Most of your cells have 46 chromosomes. A crayfish has 200 chromosomes in most of its cells, while a sunflower has 17 chromosomes in most of its cells.

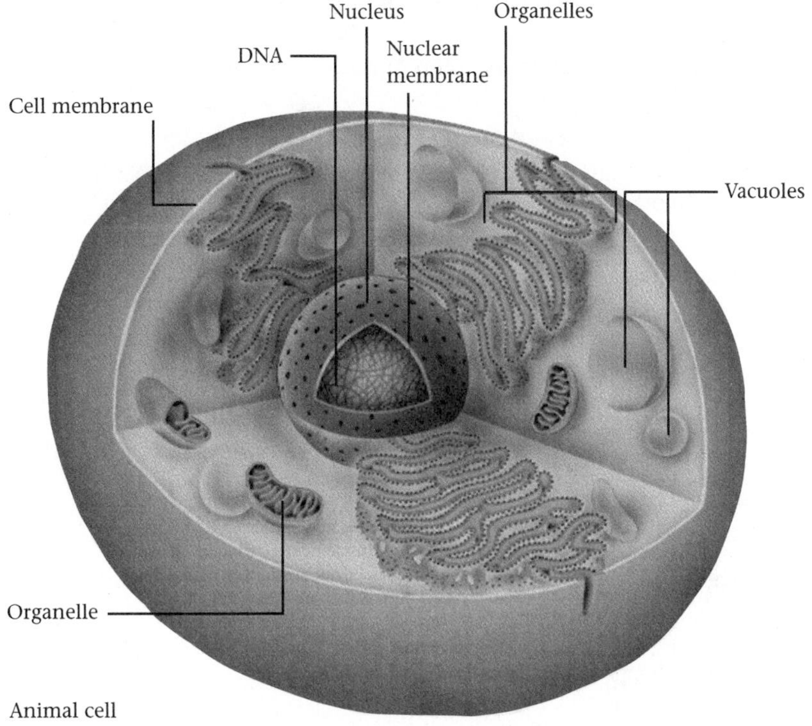

Animal cell

The Maze

A predeterminer similar to cloze but easier for students to respond to is a **maze** (Guthrie, Burnam, Caplan, & Seifert, 1974), which is especially useful for ascertaining students' prior knowledge and understanding of a subject. The teacher selects a passage of 100 to 120 words from a representative part of the textbook and deletes every 5th or 10th word. The students are then given three choices: (1) the correct word, (2) a grammatically similar but incorrect word, and (3) a distracter, which is a grammatically different and incorrect word. Because a maze is easier for students to complete than a cloze, the scoring criteria are more stringent. A maze is a bit harder to construct than a cloze because the teacher must provide three choices for each deleted word; nevertheless, many teachers prefer it. Activity 4.4 shows a maze for primary science material.

Like cloze, a maze builds background as it reveals it. Because choices are given, students who lack prior knowledge have some material to react to. This

ACTIVITY 4.4 A Maze for Primary Science Students

What Can Make Things Move?

Air can make things move. It can make a toy frog jump. Squeezing pushes { art / are / air } through a tube.

Air fills the legs under the { frog. / fig. / from. } The legs push the frog to make it jump. { And / Air / At } can make a horn blow.

Squeezing pushes air through { the / them / tug } horn. Then the horn makes a sound.

Moving air { also / as / ago } makes this party blower work. Moving air is a { poor. / push. / pin. }

Wind is moving air. Wind can fill the sails { of / on / or } a boat and push it across the water.

Wind { cane / coat / can } push a pinwheel and turn a windmill. Water can { made / make / mask } things move, too.

Water can make a water wheel { turn. / torn. / told. } It can also push people and things.

Developed by Marvette Darby.

interaction promotes the use of partial associations. Many teachers prefer maze to cloze for building background because it is less threatening to students and promotes discussion successfully. From the maze, students can move right into reading the whole material, practicing the use of context clues.

Pretests of Knowledge

Pretests of knowledge are quick, sensible ways to discover students' background knowledge. Teachers construct the tests for students to take before they begin reading. The tests are not graded; the teacher and students use them to see what students already know and what they should learn. Pretests can be developed in various ways.

Recognition Pretests

Recognition pretests provide a good way to find out what students know about the content to be taught. Holmes and Roser (1987) recommend the recognition technique as an informal pretest. Teachers can use the subheadings in a chapter as stems for a multiple-choice format; alternatives are derived from chapter content. Sometimes a teacher designs a pretest from the important points to be learned in a text. One high school drama teacher wrote questions about 10 major ideas in a chapter on the origins of the theater (see Activity 4.5). Student answers helped him see what points needed the most emphasis in the lesson.

Self-Inventories

A discriminative self-inventory (Dale, O'Rourke, & Bamman, 1971) helps the teacher identify which words in the text the students know and do not know. The teacher chooses the important words and presents them along with a symbol system, such as check marks for older students or faces for younger students. Students then react to each word. The self-inventory in Activity 4.6 was developed by a teacher to determine background for reading an eighth-grade mathematics text. The self-inventory in Activity 4.7 was developed by a teacher to determine background for reading a third-grade health text. After students judge for themselves whether they know the words and rate each word, both teacher and students will be ready to focus attention when they meet those words in the material to be read. Students appreciate such an activity because they feel in charge of what they already know and are well primed to concentrate on finding out what they themselves have realized that they do not know. Self-inventories are also discussed in Chapter 8.

Factstorming

Factstorming is another form of pretest that teachers can conduct easily. Factstorming is useful for assessing reader background. A whole class can participate at once, informally, with no paperwork. The activity proceeds from a single, generative question. Factstorming is similar to brainstorming but focuses

ACTIVITY 4.5 Recognition Pretest for High School Drama Class

What I Know About the Origins of Theatre; or, It's All Greek to Me!

Directions: Circle the answers you think are correct.

1. The Great Dionysia was:
   a. a famous Las Vegas magician
   b. Celine Dion's first stage name
   c. a Greek celebration with play competitions
2. "Komos" is:
   a. Kramer's last name on *Seinfeld*
   b. a Japanese robe
   c. the root of the word "comedy"
3. The "skene" was used for:
   a. making skinny Greek actors look good on stage
   b. Greek acne medication
   c. scene-building
4. Thespis was:
   a. the first Greek scholar to write a thesis
   b. Memphis's original name before Elvis
   c. the first actor
5. The "chorus" was:
   a. that awful group of singers before the Show Choir
   b. a virus during Greek times
   c. an important element in Aeschylus' plays
6. The "deus ex machina" was used to lift a
   a. rude and self-centered actor off the stage
   b. rude and self-centered director off the stage
   c. "god" from backstage and plop him in the middle of the action
7. Greek audiences loved to:
   a. pay attention and absorb the whole theatrical experience
   b. go to Augustus Starbucks after the play
   c. applaud, hiss, cheer, and even get into fights over the action on stage
8. True or False:
   Women sat alone and in the back of Greek audiences.
9. True or False:
   The altar was always in the center of the stage.
10. Euripides' play *Medea* was:
    a. about the media
    b. about medical miracles of the time
    c. the Greek equivalent of *The Young and the Restless*

Developed by Stephen D. Rudlin.

ACTIVITY 4.6 Self-Inventory: Eighth-Grade Math

Below is a list of terms and symbols that we will use while working in Chapter 14. This exercise will not be graded; it will help you and me to know what you already know.

Place a + beside the ones you know; place a ✓ beside the ones you know something about; place a 0 beside the ones you don't know.

_______ range
_______ mode
_______ outcomes
_______ probability
_______ compound probability
_______ $\cap$
_______ $\subset$

_______ median
_______ mean
_______ favorable outcomes
_______ sample space
_______ $\cup$
_______ $\supset$

Developed by Sherry Gott.

ACTIVITY 4.7 Self-Inventory: Third-Grade Health

Use the following symbols to tell how well you know these words. Remember: You won't be graded and you aren't expected to know all the words.

I know it!

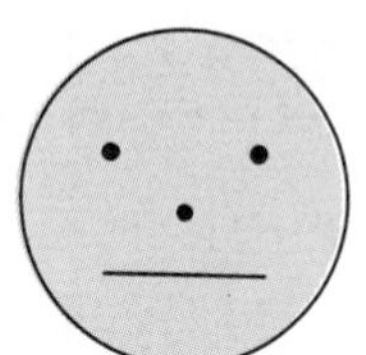

So-so

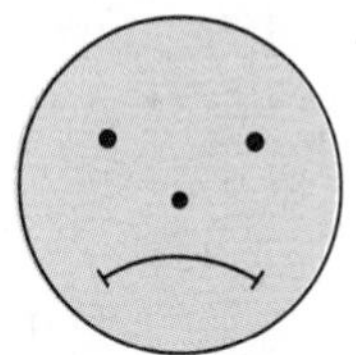

I don't know it.

_______ 1. FATS
_______ 2. CARBOHYDRATES
_______ 3. OXYGEN
_______ 4. WATER

_______ 5. VITAMINS
_______ 6. AMINO ACIDS
_______ 7. MINERALS
_______ 8. PROTEIN

_______ 9. CARBON
_______ 10. HYDROGEN
_______ 11. FOOD
_______ 12. MARROW

Developed by Kathy Feltus.

on facts and associations pertinent to the topic, whereas brainstorming focuses on problem solving. The teacher asks students to tell anything they can think of about the topic to be read—for instance, "Tell anything you know about the internal combustion engine." Responses are written on the chalkboard or on a transparency and discussed as they are entered.

PreP Strategy

A sophisticated version of factstorming is PreP, a prereading plan (Langer, 1981). PreP has three phases: (1) initial associations with the concept, as in factstorming; (2) reflections on the initial concept, when students are asked to explain why they thought of a particular response, thus building an awareness of their prior knowledge and associations; and (3) reformulation of knowledge, when new ideas learned during the first two phases are articulated. PreP helps ascertain prior knowledge and also builds background. The steps encourage the reader to use whatever prior knowledge is available by listening carefully to the opinions of others. Misperceptions can be corrected in a nonthreatening way, with whole-group discussion as a supportive environment for expression. Listening, speaking, and reading are all taking place in a PreP activity. In Activity 4.8 students categorize the words they have generated during the PreP and use the categories to guide their reading.

KWL Activity

Another activity designed to find out what students already know about the content to be studied is KWL (Ogle, 1986, 1992; Heller, 1986; Carr & Ogle, 1987). The *K* stands for what students know before they begin to read. The teacher asks students to state facts they know in the first of three columns. The *W* stands for

ACTIVITY 4.8 PreP with Categorization

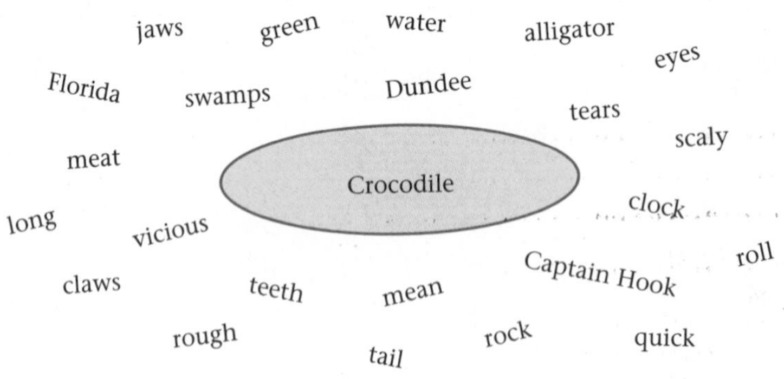

Categories:

Characteristics *Habitat/Environment* *Associations*

what students want to know. When students tell the teacher this information, the teacher can determine what they think is important about the material. These responses are recorded in the middle column. The *L* stands for what was learned. After reading, the students consider the third column and match what they knew in advance and what they wanted to learn with what they did learn. This activity not only helps the teacher and students determine prior knowledge, it also models an appropriate reflection strategy after reading has occurred.

What-I-Know Activity

An alternative to KWL is the What-I-Know Activity (WIKA). The steps that students employ better reflect the terminology and steps of the PAR Lesson Framework. To use this activity (see Activity 4.9), students, prior to reading, factstorm what they already know about the topic in the first column. In the second column they formulate questions about what they would like to learn from the reading. During reading, they jot down information as they read it. After the reading they record, in the fourth column, the answers to the questions. If they can't find an answer to a question, the question gets shifted to the fifth column, "What I'd Still Like to Know."

ACTIVITY 4.9 What I Know Activity

Before Reading		**During Reading**	**After Reading**	
What I Already Know	*What I'd Like to Know*	*Interesting or Important Concepts from My Reading*	*What I Know Now*	*What I'd Still Like to Know*
The telephone works by electricity	How does electricity make the phone work?	Electricity circuits	A circuit is completed	I need a simpler book about this topic!
You shouldn't use the phone in a lightning storm	Why shouldn't you use the phone in a storm?	Electricity travels and current jumps	The current might jump—electricity might be conducted beyond the normal current by lightning	A clearer explanation about telephones and lightning
I can hear another voice and speak in return	What is the role of vibration in carrying sound from one place to another?	There is a diaphragm in my telephone!	Sound vibrates and causes changes in air pressure. When air pressure hits the diaphragm, it vibrates again, reconstructing the original sound	I need to be able to explain about the diaphragm

When students fill in the column labeled "What I Already Know," they are giving the teacher information about their prior knowledge. If students are encouraged to add to their own list after listening to and learning from class discussion, they are building background by using other students' knowledge. This information can be placed in the "What I'd Like to Know" column. Another way to complete this column is to make questions of the subheadings in the material. "What I Know Now" is the column in which information learned from the text is recorded. Completing the "What I'd Still Like to Know" column will encourage development of comprehension and reflective thinking. The class discussion and recording of associations integrate the communicative arts.

Activity 4.9 represents the results of a What-I-Know Activity produced by a reader of a chapter about the basic telephone system. The reader already knows a bit, then creates questions based on the subheadings to complete the second column. In the third column, she jots down interesting concepts as she reads about them. In the fourth column, she answers the questions posed in column two. In the fifth column, she indicates the gaps in her knowledge.

Teacher-Constructed Textbook Inventories

At the beginning of a school year, content teachers might use a textbook inventory as a class activity to help them learn about their students' proficiency in using textbooks. This activity assesses students' knowledge of the parts of a book and can be effective at any grade level—K through 12. Activity 4.10 is based on the "Textbook Treasure Hunt" (Bryant, 1984) and could be used with the textbook you are reading now. Activity 4.11 is a parts-of-the-book search developed to help students in a computer class become familiar with a word processing manual.

Improving Textbook Selection

Textbook authors, teachers, and students have responsibility for improving the quality of textbooks. Some authors are inconsiderate of their readers. Authors need to keep their readers in mind as they write. If a passage includes many concepts, its organization should be made very clear. Such clarity enables teachers to develop instructional activities that can help students learn the important concepts. Authors should include important terms in the material, but if the author suspects that these terms will be new to the reader, then meaning and pronunciation keys should be provided. In his foreword to Allan Bloom's *The Closing of the American Mind*, Saul Bellow (1987), a noted novelist, admits that "it is never easy to take the mental measure of your readers." Although textbook writers cannot know the individual literacy levels of prospective readers, nor their interests and attitudes, they can be sensitive to the general needs of a group of readers. Authors should take into account what readers should be expected to

ACTIVITY 4.10 Teacher-Constructed Textbook Inventory

Textbook Treasure Hunt

There are many hidden treasures in your textbook. After you have completed the path below, you will have discovered some interesting facts! Write your answers and the page number(s) on which you found the information on a clean sheet of notebook paper.

1. Locate the example of a Textbook Treasure Hunt in your text. What kind of book was used in this hunt?
2. The PAR framework in Chapter 1 is a framework for ____ instruction.
3. How many chapters are in your text?
4. In the Elementary Reading Attitude Survey, feelings are noted by the expressions of ________.
5. Give the names of the authors. Where do they teach?
6. How many appendixes does this book contain? Name the topics of each.
7. DRTA stands for ________.
8. Each chapter ends with a One-Minute Summary and ________.
9. The 6 sides of a cube in a cubing exercise are:
10. Activity 4.3 is a ________ procedure about ________.
11. Name and describe at least one reading procedure developed by A.V. Manzo.
12. How many lines are in a cinquain?
13. What does a Bader Textbook Analysis Chart help you do?
14. Find the PAR Cross-Reference Guide to classroom activities at the back of your textbook. What activities would be suitable for a middle-school math class?

ACTIVITY 4.11 Parts-of-the-Book Search for WordPerfect 6.0 Intermediate Manual

Becoming Familiar and Comfortable with the Manual

1. What are the titles of the three people named in the acknowledgments section of the book?

   a. ____________ b. ____________ c. ____________

2. On what page do you find the explanation of the special symbols used in the table of contents? How many special symbols are used in the manual?

   Page ________ Number of special symbols ________

3. How many appendixes does the manual contain? ____________ Which appendix explains the features bars? ____________

4. On what page does the manual begin talking about using columns, and how many different types of column does WordPerfect allow you to choose from?

   Page ________ ________ Types of Column

5. What two things do you find at the end of each section?

   a. ____________ b. ____________

6. What are the two types of "objectives" found in the manual? Explain the difference.

   a. ____________________________

   b. ____________________________

7. On what page will you find an explanation of the icons for drawing tools used in WP Draw? Page ________

8. On what page will you find an explanation of how to insert columns or rows into a table? Page ________

9. Where did you look to find the page number to answer the previous question—the table of contents or the index? ____________ Would either one work? Yes ________ No ________

10. On what page would you find a table listing the different custom box types? Page ________ How many types are available to you? ____________

11. Name the three major topics covered in the manual. a. ____________

    b. ____________ c. ____________

12. Where do you find an explanation of the keyboard shortcuts? ____________

Developed by Mary L. Seward.

---

know and what they will need an author's help to learn. In this way, authors can become more considerate of their readers.

Certainly, teachers play a very important role in identifying text-based problems and finding solutions. Shanker (1984) discussed the importance of evaluating textbooks and laid the responsibility for doing so on the teacher. He called for training in education courses to enable teachers to evaluate textbooks. Teachers must understand that text coherence comprises many factors. A readability formula does not provide enough information on which to base a judgment about text-based problems. Teachers can determine a great deal about readability, but they also need help from other educational personnel. For example, Speigel and Wright (1983), reporting on a study of biology teachers' impressions of the readability of the text materials they used, comment that teachers were aware of many readability factors. Teachers, they write, should be encouraged to apply this intuitive understanding in their selection of text materials. Such encouragement must come from administrators and textbook selection committees.

The ultimate consumer of the content material is the student. Students need to move toward independence in assessing their own background for reading as soon as possible in their school careers. They must begin to ask questions about their reading material by applying the factors discussed in this chapter: Is this material too difficult for me? Is it poorly written? What do I already know about this topic? What aids in this textbook will make my reading easier? Questions such as these will not occur to many students until teachers model their importance by helping students understand why they should be asked. Even first-graders are capable of discovering the difficulty of a book by using the rule of thumb. A fifth-grader can ask, "What do I already know about fractions?" A tenth-grader can assess whether poetry causes her difficulty. Ultimately, the buck stops with the students. But too great a burden is placed on students if authors and teachers offer them little help in assuming responsibility in reading.

Wray (1994) describes the roles of text author, student, teacher as interactive. He encourages students to consider the author's role in clarifying meaning through text. This can be done only when teachers support students in becoming critics rather than remaining passive recipients. When asked to provide an example of dumbed-down text, one graduate student stated that he could not think of an example because he wouldn't read a book like that. We wish that all students were so empowered.

One-Minute Summary

In this chapter we explain the importance of assessing students' background for reading textbook materials. We present the concept of readability and explain its importance for successful instruction in content areas. We show how, through a series of activities, teachers can determine the suitability of material for students. We discuss how textbooks can be improved when authors, teachers, and students are aware of readability issues and assume responsibility for improving the reading material.

End-of-Chapter Activities

Assisting Comprehension

1. Practice assessing the readability of a textbook from which you will teach by using the Bader textbook analysis chart. Then select a passage and follow the formula procedures to obtain a Fry rating. What do you think about these ratings? Do you feel that they are accurate and informative?

2. Read *Anguished English* by Richard Lederer (1987). Besides laughing a lot, you will enjoy learning about textual coherence from his many examples.

Reflecting on Your Reading

Study Table 4.1. We have rated each activity. See how the activity ratings compare with each other. Do you agree with our rating? Use the space provided to fill in your own ratings.

TABLE 4.1

Activity	*Materials Needed*	*Authors' Rating*	*Your Rating*
Text coherence questions	Teacher, text	*****	
Checklists	Teacher, text	****	
Readability formulas	Teacher, text	**	
Rule of thumb	Material, text	***	
Cloze	Teacher, text, students	****	
Maze	Teacher, text, students	****	
Pretests	Teacher, text, students	****	
Factstorming, PreP	Teacher, students	*****	
KWL/WIKA	Teacher, text, students	*****	
Parts-of-book search	Teacher, text, students	*****	

CHAPTER 5

Building the Reader's Background for Content Material

The only man who can change his mind is the man who's got one.

—Wescott

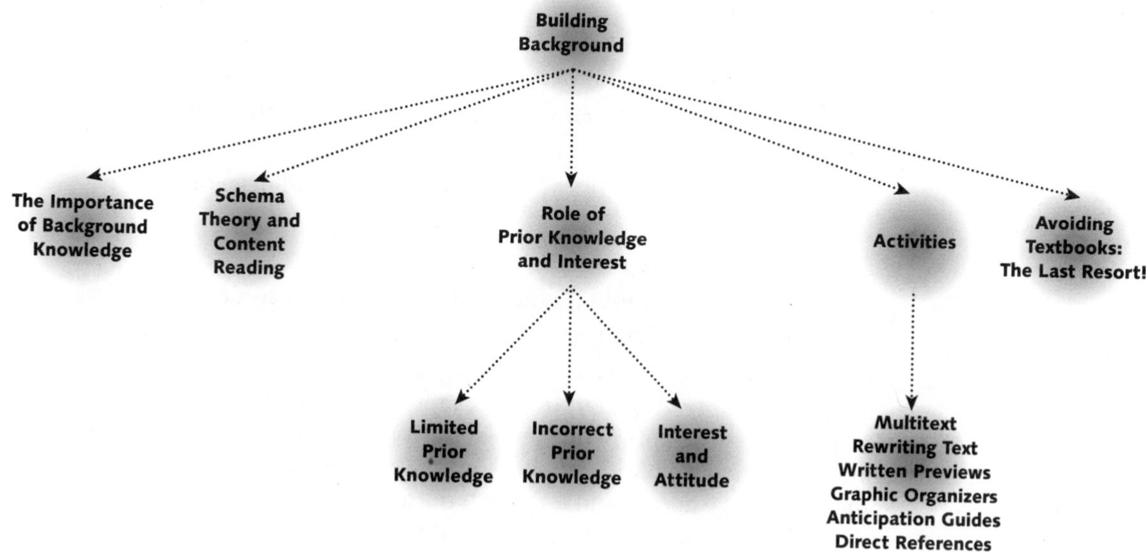

Preparing to Read

1. Read and consider each of these statements. If you agree with the statement, place a 1 beside it; if you disagree, place a 2 beside it. Be ready to explain your reasoning.

   ______ Learners retrieve information from cognitively organized links.

   ______ What the learner already knows is the most important factor in future learning.

   ______ A student who tells the teacher "I like mathematics" but never reads the material is demonstrating cognitive dissonance.

   ______ Reading and writing instruction are integrated through the use of anticipation guides.

   ______ There is no perfectly "right" way to create and develop an activity.

   ______ Analogies have limited influence in instruction.

   ______ The teacher should ignore the textbook when students have difficulty reading it.

2. Following is a list of terms used in this chapter. Some may be familiar to you in a general context, but in this chapter they may be used in unfamiliar ways. Rate your knowledge by placing a plus sign (+) in front of those you are sure that you know, a check mark (✓) in front of those you have some knowledge about, and a zero (0) in front of those you don't know. Be ready to locate and pay special attention to their meanings when they are presented in the chapter.

   ______ prior knowledge

   ______ schema

   ______ schemata

   ______ cognitive dissonance

   ______ multitext strategy

   ______ graphic organizer

   ______ anticipation guides

   ______ direct reference

Objectives

As you read this chapter, focus your attention on the following objectives. You will:

1. be able to identify pertinent research that supports the concepts of schema theory and prior knowledge.
2. understand the importance of building background.
3. become acquainted with several activities that help build the match between the reader and the material to be read.
4. understand the decisions that teachers must make in building background for text material and guiding readers appropriately.

The Importance of Background Knowledge

Green Eggs and Ham by Dr. Seuss (1960) is a favorite children's story. What a lot of time Sam-I-am spends arguing with his friend to try the delectable concoction that gives the book its name! The friend assumes that he won't like green eggs and ham, probably because green is not usually associated with eggs—unless they are rotten. His background—limited to the color rather than the taste of green eggs—interferes. Sam-I-am's only strategy is to nag. Finally the friend tries this dish, likes it, and vows to eat it in any number of creative ways in the future. The ending of this delightful story is happy, and the repetitive, though nagging, dialogue is fun for young readers.

In real life, convincing someone to try anything as seemingly revolting as green eggs and ham will require more than nagging. Teachers often may feel like Sam-I-am, pestering students to read the content material, insisting that the reading is interesting and informative. Sometimes, however, students' background knowledge is as limited as that of Sam-I-am's reluctant friend. An unpleasant experience with any aspect of reading or with a subject can cause students to be almost as stubborn about reading an assignment as Sam-I-am's friend is about eating green eggs and ham. For example, some research indicates that students do not like to read textbooks (Maria & Junge, 1993; McKewon, Bede, & Worthy, 1992). One obvious solution to this dilemma is to use multiple resources in the classroom, as discussed in Chapter 3. However, when a textbook must be the major resource, both research and practice confirm that strategies to build reader background do work. Such strategies entice students to try the reading and give readers the connection points to understand what they read. In this chapter we discuss several strategies that encourage students to read.

TECHNOLOGY BOX

Software Programs with Content-Instructional Uses

Personal Filing System
Source: Software Publishing Corporation
Price: @ $80.00
Grade level: Elementary +
Description: This information management software package allows users to create databases. Files can be designed, edited, and updated to reflect current classroom needs. Students may store facts about a topic and then sort to find patterns.

Crossword Magic
Source: L & S Computerware
Price: @ $50.00
Grade level: 4–adult
Description: This is a utility program to create crossword puzzles, which can be used to build background knowledge. Crossword puzzles can also be used to reinforce vocabulary in content instruction.

The Geometric Golfer
Source: Mecc
Price: @ $50.00
Grade level: 7–12
Description: This program is an educational game with ten different golf courses. The object is to improve golf scores; because the "ball" and hole are polygons and moving the "ball" must be done by sliding, flipping, turning, shrinking, and enlarging, the game is geometric in nature. Students develop spatial sense, problem-solving, and visualization skills.

Easy Book Deluxe
Source: Sunburst Communications
Price: @ $70.00
Grade level: 3–8
Description: This program allows students to write, illustrate, and print their work in book form. It is easy to use and very motivating. Content reports can be produced.

Schema Theory and Content Reading

Prior knowledge is the knowledge a reader already has and brings to a reading experience. It greatly influences new learning. Psychologists Combs and Snygg (1959) maintain that learning takes place when the "perceptual field" is organized in a meaningful pattern. They define the perceptual field as a fluid organization of meanings existing for an individual at any instant. It is the basis for a person's reactions to any new event. The learner attempts to relate new information to already known information in order to make sense of the world. When doing this, the learner is drawing a **schema** (plural, **schemata**), or mental blueprint, of the way in which reality is constructed.

Schema theory offers a way of explaining how prior knowledge is stored in memory. The information a learner acquires about a topic is organized cognitively into a framework, or schema. The framework grows to include other topics, thus creating larger and larger schemata, arranged in a hierarchy. Learners retrieve information by understanding how newly encountered material links to what they already have organized cognitively. Interrelationships among schemata aid understanding. Psychologists stress that learning new information depends on relating the new to something already known. Rumelhart (1980) stresses that schemata, which may be likened to diagrams or drawings stored in the brain, are fundamental to all processing of information. Often the diagrams are incomplete, but they create a fuller picture as more information is found to complete them.

Learning occurs by a process of planning and building information in the brain. Frank Smith (1994) explains the process this way: Just seeing words (page-to-eye) or even saying words (page-to-eye-to-mouth) is fairly superficial. Connecting the intent of the words to what is already stored in one's schemata (eye-to-brain) is real reading. Thus, what learners already know helps them to read more effectively. Smith concludes that the eye-to-brain connection is far more complex than the mere intake of information.

Gestalt psychologists probably introduced the term *schema* in the 1930s (Anderson & Pearson, 1984). Bartlett (1932) used the term to explain how information that has been learned is stored in the brain and, with repeated use, becomes part of a system of integrated knowledge. Anderson and Pearson speculate that the term became popular because Piaget used it extensively. Piaget (1952) believed that children form a mental image of previous experiences, which in turn contributes to new experiences. Miller (1956) discussed the relationship of short-term to long-term memory in a similar way. Learners chunk knowledge in an organized fashion by connecting a new segment to what they already know. Only by so doing can a learner move the new chunk of information from short-term memory to long-term memory.

Anderson (1985) is credited with introducing schema theory to the field of reading, although the concept, if not the term, had been applied in reading research previously. When Chall (1947) tested sixth- and eighth-graders on their knowledge of tuberculosis and then tested their reading of a passage on the same topic, she found that those with the highest knowledge scores also had the highest reading-comprehension scores. She concluded that previous knowledge heavily influences reading. Rumelhart (1980) also has written extensively about how learners comprehend by building "blocks of cognition" as they fill in a partially completed schema during reading. Hirsch (1987) writes that schemata are essential to literacy in two major ways: Information is stored so that it can be retrieved, and it is organized so that it can be used quickly and efficiently by the reader.

Content teachers will find schema theory useful as they prepare their students to read an assignment. One middle-school mathematics teacher created a "discovery activity" designed to build her students' background by helping them see relationships between what they already knew and what they were about to learn. She was preparing them for a unit on the properties of quadrilaterals, showing them how to use what they already knew about parallel lines, perpendicular lines, and angles. This activity (see Activity 5.1) exemplifies the concept of building background by connecting the known to the new while making the content interesting.

The Role of the Reader's Prior Knowledge and Interest

The protagonist in the comic reads the first direction for making an angel food cake. She expects the verb *separate* to mean "set or keep apart." In her schema, the verb *separate* does not include a picture for "detach," so she puts each egg in a different location, rather than detaching the egg whites from the yolks. Fortunately, she seems intent and interested in what she is doing. If she were in a home economics class, the teacher would need to help her build a more sophisticated schema.

Drum (1985) found that fourth-grade science and social studies texts that were equal in vocabulary frequency, syntactic complexity, and overall structure

ACTIVITY 5.1 Activity to Discover Prior Knowledge

What's in a Shape? The Properties of Quadrilaterals

The procedures were:

1. Introduce students to a new chapter by having them read only one page of that chapter.
2. Ask students to point out examples of the different types of quadrilaterals using pictures on pages in the chapter—squares, rectangles, parallelograms, trapezoids, rhombuses.
3. Have students put their desks together with a partner; then provide them with a compass, protractor, ruler, and worksheet.
4. Read the worksheet directions aloud: "Find as many true properties about quadrilaterals as possible. Draw lines, measure with a ruler and a protractor, and use a compass to assist in making conjectures. List at least four conjectures for each type of quadrilateral."
5. After group work, discuss the conjectures. Create a master list and have the class agree or disagree with each conjecture.
6. State that conjectures will be verified by information in the chapter.

Developed by Jeannette Rosenberg.

B.C. Reprinted with permission of Johnny Hart and Creators Syndicate, Inc.

were not equally easy for the fourth-graders in her study to read. Prior knowledge seemed to play a significant part in making the social studies texts easy for these students. In other words, no matter how well written material is, if readers do not possess background knowledge or interest in reading the material, students will find it hard to read.

If learners cannot find relevance in a selection, they are likely to ignore it. Thus teachers must become aware of their students' knowledge and experiences about a particular topic and build on that knowledge. Discovering whether students have developed any schemata can help the teacher generate content-reading lessons that are directed, meaningful, and highly personal. Teachers need to help students build programs for learning.

For example, going from an easy text to a more difficult one can build and strengthen schemata. Gallagher (1995) had much success pairing adolescent literature with adult literature by "bridging" (Brown & Stephens, 1995). Studying the theme of the power of love in Harper Lee's novel *To Kill a Mockingbird* made it easier for students to grasp that same theme in Nathaniel Hawthorne's *The House of the Seven Gables*.

Prior knowledge and interest are reader-based concepts: The possible problems they pose reside primarily with the reader and only secondarily in the material. As we saw in the teachers' ratings of the hepatitis passage in Chapter 4, the text is only one part of the necessary interaction. Even though readers thought that text was well written, they did not rate it highly in the categories relating to themselves as readers. In the same way, we cannot hold the author of the angel food cake recipe at fault because the protagonist in the comic does not know the meaning of the verb *separate*. The responsibility falls on the teacher and the learner.

Limited Prior Knowledge

It is conceivable—though not likely—that readers have absolutely no background for a topic they are to study. More likely, readers have some related experience, limited information, or even incorrect information. Most of the time readers have some knowledge about the topic to be studied. Even if they know little about the specific content, they may understand a related concept. For instance, fifth-graders may not know much about the Pilgrims, but they may know what it's like to be uprooted and have to relocate to a strange place. These students, then, would have some background that the teacher could use in introducing the reading.

The following dialogue illustrates how difficult it is to understand material when one has limited prior background.

> "Do I deserve a mulligan?" asked Bob.
>
> "No, but don't take a drop," said Al. "Use a hand-mashie, then fly the bogey high to the carpet and maybe you'll get a gimme within the leather."
>
> "You're right," said Bob. "I'll cover the flag for a birdie and at least get a ginsberg if I'm not stymied."
>
> (Morgan, Meeks, Schollaert, & Paul, 1986, pp. 2–3)

Unless you are a golfer, reading this dialogue might be more an exercise in pronouncing the words than in understanding the text. Try to answer the following questions about the passage:

1. Does Bob deserve a mulligan?
   (a) yes; (b) no; (c) maybe
2. What does Al think Bob should do?
   (a) catch a gimme; (b) take a drop; (c) use a hand-mashie; (d) fly a kite
3. What does Bob decide to do?
   (a) cover the flag; (b) take a drop; (c) birdie-up
4. How can Bob get a birdie?
   (a) by getting stymied; (b) by getting a ginsberg; (c) by covering the flag
5. If Bob is not stymied, what will he get?
   (a) a hickie; (b) a birdie; (c) a mulligan; (d) a ginsberg

The answers are b, c, a, c, and d. The test was factual in nature. You probably scored 100 percent because you were able to look back at the passage and find the facts. But do you know what this passage is about? To comprehend it fully, you need broad prior knowledge about golf.

What is a mulligan? What is a birdie? Readers who don't know golf may try to create meaning for these words by calling on their store of information. Likewise, many students are able to answer rote questions after a reading without really understanding the passage. The following translation shows how paraphrasing by using more familiar language—more likely to be present in one's background—makes the passage meaningful:

1. **"Do I deserve a mulligan?" asked Bob.**

Bob asks if he deserves a second shot without a penalty.

2. **"No, but don't take a drop," said Al. "Use a hand-mashie, then fly the bogey high to the carpet and maybe you'll get a gimme within the leather."**

Al says no but warns Bob not to take the option of moving his ball from a difficult location and dropping it at a better spot, which may cost him a penalty stroke. Another (but illegal) move is to kick the ball out of trouble with his foot (a "hand-mashie"). He then can hit the ball with a high trajectory to the green, or "carpet" (where the hole is). If Bob gets the ball within 18 inches of the hole, or cup ("leather"), he can pick up his ball and give himself one stroke (a "gimme") rather than having to take several strokes (the more strokes or hits one has, the worse one's score in golf).

3. "You're right," said Bob. "I'll cover the flag for a birdie and at least get a ginsberg if I'm not stymied."

Bob will attempt to hit the ball close to the hole so that he has a chance for a "birdie" (one stroke under par). If he gets on the green, he can lay up his putt to the hole ("get a ginsberg"). In earlier days, golfers did not mark their balls, so they could get stymied by another ball—that is, have to shoot around the ball of another player. Bob is being facetious here. In modern golf a player cannot get stymied on the green.

Incorrect Prior Knowledge

Sometimes, readers have incorrect knowledge about material to be studied. Grace Hamlin, a teacher, wrote this "telegram" to illustrate how incorrect knowledge can influence one's reading: WON TRIP FOR TWO ST. MATTHEW'S ISLAND PACK SMALL BAG MEET AT AIRPORT 9 AM TOMORROW. Readers who "know" that islands are tropical, have a warm climate, and are surrounded by beaches for swimming and sunbathing will pack a suitcase with sunglasses, shorts, bathing suits, and suntan lotion. St. Matthew's Island, however, is off the coast of Alaska, where the average temperature is 37 degrees. Incorrect knowledge in this case will impede comprehension. Similarly, readers who "know" that the dinosaurs were destroyed by other animals will have difficulty reading and understanding a theory proposing that dinosaurs were destroyed by the consequences of a giant meteor.

Maria and MacGinitie (1987) discuss the difference between having correct, though insufficient, prior knowledge and having incorrect prior knowledge. They conclude that students are less likely to overcome a problem of incorrect knowledge, because the new information conflicts with their prior "knowledge." In this situation, building students' knowledge is essential because material will be most "unreadable" to the students who try to refute the material as they read.

Interest and Attitude

Even the most proficient reader experiences difficulty in understanding and thinking about a subject that he or she is not interested in. Remember that a majority (26) of the 41 teachers who graded the paragraph in Chapter 4 gave it an F for interest! Yet these were good readers. We might speculate that their lack of interest in viral hepatitis negatively influenced a good match with this material. Some recent studies indicate that interest in a topic plays a very important role in students' comprehension (Lin, Zabrucky, & Moore, 1997; Schumm, Mangrum, Gordon, & Doucette, 1992; Wade & Adams, 1990). When asked to address textbook issues, 41 percent of teenage respondents commented that they would "include topics in their textbooks that would interest them" (Lester & Cheek, 1998).

If teachers recognize that their students bring little interest or negative attitudes to the content material, they can use many activities to stimulate interest, a positive attitude, and some appreciation for the subject. A teacher who simply assumes that students are interested in and positive toward the subject is likely to be disappointed, and the students probably will not understand the reading. This situation can be seen as a form of **cognitive dissonance**, defined in *A Dictionary of Reading* (Harris & Hodges, 1995) as "a motivational state of tension resulting from an inconsistency in one's attitudes, beliefs, perceived behaviors, etc." (p. 34). In short, students' reading proficiency may conflict with their lack of interest to create a conflict that blocks learning.

We are reminded of an old story, told by one of our reading professors, about a little girl who goes to the library and asks for a book about penguins. Excited that this small child is requesting information, the librarian selects a large volume on penguins and offers it to her. The child takes the book, almost staggering under its weight, and trudges home. The next day she returns it. "How did you like that book about penguins?" the librarian eagerly asks. "To tell you the truth," the girl replies, "this book tells more about penguins than I care to know." A similar situation occurs when teachers misinterpret a little interest as a lot and thus do not match the reader with a suitable text. In Chapter 2 we covered this situation in depth and offered several means to determine students' interests and attitudes, as well as activities to stimulate positive feelings. The activities we offer in this chapter can also help determine interests and attitudes if teachers are sensitive to students' responses.

Some Activities for Building Background

In Chapter 4 we discussed the role that textbook authors play in facilitating reading. Here we feature the roles of the teacher and student. The major factor in improving the quality of interaction with the text is preparation. Many activities can help the teacher and students prepare for the text. In the rest of this chapter we describe tried-and-true activities that prepare readers by building their backgrounds. The activities represent possibilities but are not an exhaustive list. By considering why an activity could help build background, teachers will build their own backgrounds for creating other activities.

Multitext Strategies

By enlisting the help of a media specialist or reading specialist, the teacher may discover several trade books that treat the topic to be studied. The teacher should study those books to ascertain whether they match the reading levels and backgrounds of students. The teacher may use checklists and readability formulas (see Chapter 4). The newly selected trade books can be assigned as preparation for the regularly assigned textbooks. Students can read books matched to their own levels and thus build background about a topic before reading textbook material.

This **multitext strategy** offers versatility: Different reading levels within a classroom can be accommodated when many books are used. The lists of books can be expanded over the years with the help of professional journals. However, teachers must know thoroughly the content of the required material and then familiarize themselves with each new book that might be included on the multiple-text list. In addition, most teachers will want to consider a readability match for each book to ensure a good reading match. This activity requires extra planning time.

We like multitext strategies at the preparation stage because we want our students to experience not only the required text but also varied resources that build background. At times, however, the teacher will decide to substitute multiple texts for the original textbook. In that case, the strategy can be classified as one to assist comprehension.

Another popular way to use multiple texts is in a reflection activity, when the teacher gives students a list of books from which to do independent reading. The teacher can assemble all the books she or he can find that seem suitable as background material, make them available, but leave the responsibility of selection to the readers. Ammons (1987) demonstrates such a procedure with a class of fifth-graders preparing to learn about dinosaurs. First, the students pose questions to which they want to find answers. Next, Ammons introduces several trade books that might give them answers. Then the students select their own books and read to find the answers. They can use the rule of thumb to help them in their selections. In this way, students build their background knowledge by using a multitext strategy.

Adapting Text: Rewriting Text

One form of adaptation involves rewriting the material. Rewriting can be used to prepare students before introducing them to the original material. By using rewritten material as an introduction to the original text, teachers can simplify writing styles and clarify concepts that students may have difficulty understanding. However, in returning to the original text, teachers will still be using required materials, and students will receive the message that the text material is important.

Siedow and Hasselbring (1984) found that when eighth-grade social studies material was rewritten to a lower readability level, the comprehension of poor readers improved. Currie (1990) rewrote text by shortening sentences, replacing unfamiliar words, changing metaphors to more literal phrases, and clarifying. Teachers using these materials reported that students, whether high or low achievers, significantly improved their grades. Beck, McKeown, Sinatra, and Loxterman (1991) revised a fifth-grade social studies text to create a more casual and explanatory style, then compared students who read the original and revised versions. Students who read the revised version recalled and explained the events better and answered more questions correctly.

The assignment to revise Virginia Woolf's essay "Professions for Women" (1966) illustrates rewriting (see Activity 5.2). Rewriting this essay was a desperate move. The teacher had assigned the essay to stimulate the writing of a freshman college English class. The students interpreted Woolf's metaphoric angel literally and thought that Woolf had a ghost looking over her shoulder. They also could not understand why Woolf mentioned buying an expensive cat. Woolf's writing was not at fault; the readers did not possess the appropriate background for the essay. Their backgrounds apparently did not include the metaphors or experiences that Woolf had selected, and they did not know how to relate to the allusions in her essay. Rewriting was chosen because the essay was required reading for the course: No other could be substituted for it even though it was clearly difficult for the readers.

Students read the rewrite first, as an introduction; then they read the original essay and compared the two versions. The results were very satisfactory. Students understood clearly the concepts that Woolf was conveying, and, as an unexpected bonus, they realized how much better written Woolf's essay was than the rewrite. As a preparation strategy, rewriting in this case proved very successful.

ACTIVITY 5.2 A Rewrite of "Professions for Women" (Excerpt)

I was asked to speak to you about women as professionals and tell you about what has happened to me. This is difficult because my experiences in my job as a writer may not be that outstanding. There have been many famous women writers before me who have learned and shown me the best way to succeed at writing. Because of their reputations, families today accept women who become writers. They know that they won't have to pay a lot of money for writing equipment or courses!

My story is this. I wrote regularly every day, then submitted an article to a newspaper. The article was accepted, I got paid; I became a journalist. However, I did not act like a struggling writer who spends her hard-earned money on household needs; I bought a Persian cat.

My article was a book review. I had trouble writing it and other reviews because something nagged at me. I felt that because I am a woman, I should be "feminine": have sympathy, be charming, unselfish, keep the family peaceful, sacrifice, and be very pure. When I began to write, this is what women were supposed to be like, and every family taught its girls to be this way. So when I started to write criticisms of a famous man's novel, all of the things I had learned about being a woman got in the way of my writing critically instead of writing just nice things. This problem was like a ghost whispering in my ear. I called this problem ghost "The Angel in the House" because it was always there, in my "house," telling me to be nice rather than truthful.

I got rid of this problem. I realized that being nice is not always the most important thing. Also, I had inherited some money, so I felt I didn't have to do what others expected of me in order to earn a living! I had to get rid of this obsession with being feminine rather than being truthful in order to write clearly. I killed my problem ghost before it could kill my true thoughts and reactions. This is really hard to do because "feminine" ideas creep up on you before you realize that what you're writing is not a true criticism but something you were raised to believe. It took a long time to realize what was my idea and what was society's idea about what I should write.

Readability as measured by the Fry formula:
Original passage = 9th grade
Rewritten passage = 7th grade

Rewriting can bring down the readability level, as measured by a readability formula, sometimes to a significant degree. In the case of Woolf's essay, the original was found to be at ninth-grade level and the rewrite at seventh-grade level (according to the Fry graph). Sometimes a revision does not lower the readability level but does clarify difficult material. The goal should be to present necessary material in an understandable form, as a prelude to reading the original, not to show a change in a readability formula.

Like so many other activities, rewriting can be used at every step of the PAR Lesson Framework. If a rewrite is used in place of the original material, then it is no longer being used to prepare the reader; in that case, rewriting assists comprehension. One teacher once rewrote portions of the Georgia Juvenile Court Code because the code was too hard for tenth-graders to understand in its legal form (measured at the 14th-grade level). The rewrite, to seventh-grade level, enabled students to read with attention to the main points. Rewriting also can be used as a reflective-reading technique. A teacher might ask students to think about the material and try to rewrite it for younger students. In this way, students gain writing practice and demonstrate their learning, and an integration of the communicative arts takes place. Rewriting also can be a useful tool for the at-risk reader who needs to learn the same content as classmates but has difficulty reading at their level.

The biggest drawback to rewriting is the time that it takes. On one rewrite of a 15-page social studies selection, one teacher spent four hours. The Woolf rewrite consumed two hours. Because a teacher's time is precious, teachers will want to weigh their options carefully in attempting to overcome text-based problems. If rewriting is the best choice, we suggest these six steps:

1. Read and restate the ideas in your own words.
2. Identify the concepts that are especially important for students to know.
3. Keep rewrites short and to the point.
4. Explain difficult concepts in the rewrite. Reformulate particularly difficult words into words that you think students already know.
5. Make sentences short, and use the active voice whenever possible.
6. Underline specialized vocabulary to make it easier to note difficult words.

Previewing Text: Written Previews

Teachers can use written previews and graphic organizers to preview textbooks. Graves, Prenn, and Cooke (1985) suggest that teachers write brief previews of the material to be read by students. These previews—especially valuable for difficult material—provide a reference point and offer students a way to organize new information. The written preview should be fairly short and usually is read aloud to the class before silent reading of the original material is done. Teachers can use the information gained from their own previewing of the material to write the preview. In writing previews, a teacher can follow these steps:

1. Select a situation familiar to the students and relevant to the topic. Describe the situation and pose questions that will enhance interest in the topic.
2. If the material demands background knowledge that students do not have, include a brief section providing the necessary information.
3. Provide a synopsis of the material.
4. Provide directions for reading the material to facilitate comprehension.

After a teacher reads the first few sentences of the preview, time should be allotted to discuss the questions posed therein. After the teacher reads the remainder of the preview, the students should begin reading the text material right away. Activity 5.3 is a preview of "Two Kinds," by Amy Tan (1993), written for ninth-grade students in an English class.

Written previews are less time-consuming than rewrites, and they accomplish similar purposes. They build the reader's background and help the reader organize the forthcoming text material. If a teacher writes previews carefully, the structure of the text will be more apparent to its readers.

Structuring Text by Using Graphic Organizers

Like written previews, **graphic organizers** help the reader prepare for reading by presenting, so to speak, a road map of the text. A graphic organizer is a visual overview that demonstrates how the important concepts, as represented by the vocabulary in a reading selection, fit together. Promoting *visual literacy*—the ability to interpret visual and hierarchical information—a graphic organizer is effective because readers are asked to interpret a concise, comprehensive, and compact visual aid. At the beginning of each chapter in this book we present a graphic organizer to help readers see the relationships among the concepts and the key terms in the chapter through a visual representation of its content.

ACTIVITY 5.3 A Written Preview of "Two Kinds" by Amy Tan

Have you ever had a conflict with your parents or guardian about their expectations of you? How about when you were moving to a new school or area? For example, I remember when my family and I moved into our new house. Everybody in the neighborhood knew one another and thus expected us to join this community family too. But my mother made it known to all the neighbors that we were different. We couldn't play with the other children in the neighborhood. As far as she was concerned, her daughters were not going to join the other teen mothers. She had high expectations of her children. Sometimes I thought she was totally ridiculous. She was suspicious of every male. As a result, we sometimes got into arguments.

How did you handle your conflicts with your parents, such as what they expected from you? How did you react when you were not in agreement with them? How did you resolve the conflict?

Activity by Etta Malcolm.

A structured overview (Earle & Barron, 1973) is one type of graphic organizer that is normally used in the preparation phase before reading. This type of visual aid is in the form of a hierarchical diagram of words, sometimes described as a *tree diagram*. Structured overviews are constructed by teachers, whereas other types of graphic organizers may be constructed by students (or by teachers and students together) in the postreading phase of reflection over the lesson. Activity 5.4 represents a structured overview of brands in a vocational-education marketing text.

Rakes, Rakes, and Smith (1995) comment that research on prior knowledge supports the use of overviews as aids in organizing students' thoughts. When readers understand the relationships among concepts in a selection, they can begin to connect the new relationships to their previous knowledge. Robinson's (1998) megastudy of 16 studies on graphic organizers indicates that graphic organizers facilitate memory for text. This outcome is most likely because they

ACTIVITY 5.4 Structured Overview for a Vocational-Education Marketing Text

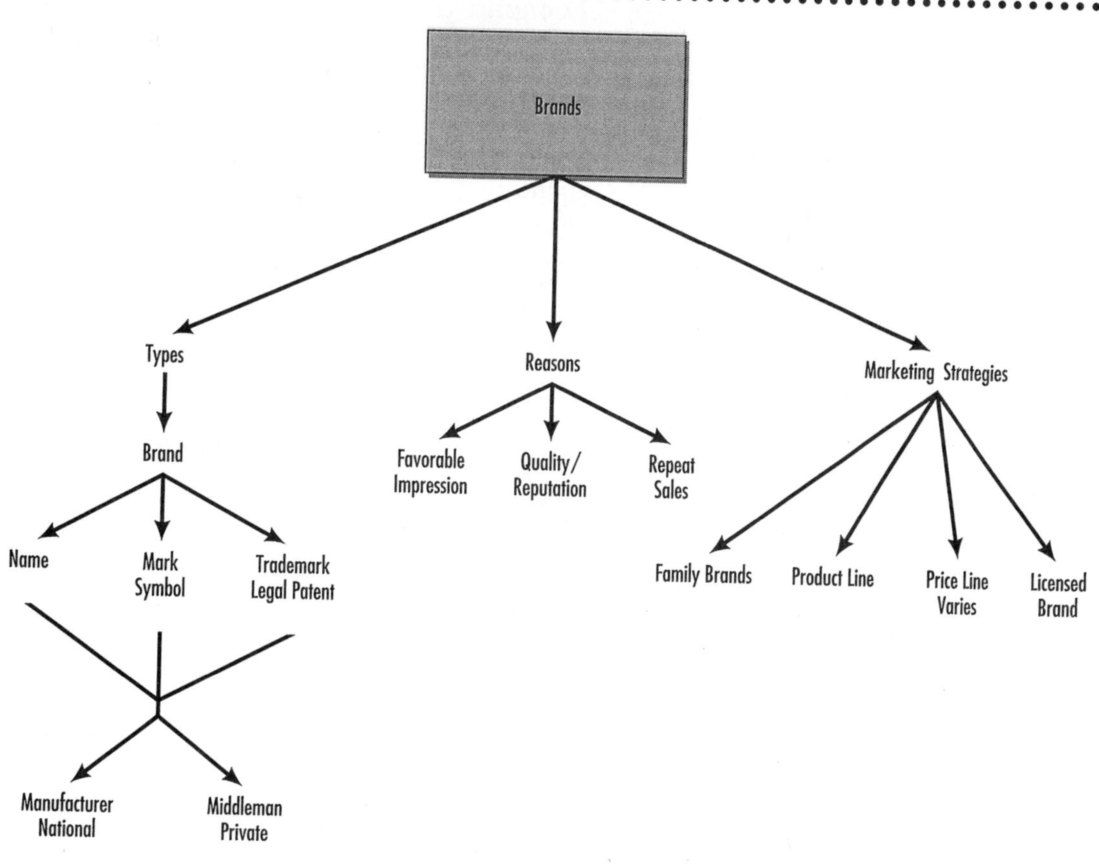

connect schema and help students see connections between the new and the known.

Teachers usually find graphic organizers challenging to prepare but very much worth the effort. To construct one, a teacher should follow these steps:

1. Identify the superordinate, or major, concept; then identify all supporting concepts in the material.
2. List all key terms from the material that reflect the identified concepts.
3. Connect the terms to show the relationships among concepts.
4. To show relationships between new concepts and already-learned ones, add any terms that are from the previous lesson or that you feel are part of students' background knowledge.
5. Construct a diagram based on these connections, and use it to introduce the reading material.

When developing a graphic organizer, it is not necessary to use every word that might be new to readers. Some new words may not contribute to the diagram. Including words already known to the students is useful when these words represent key concepts, because familiarity will aid understanding.

We find that when graphic organizers are pictorial, students enjoy and remember them better. Teachers should explain to students why they prepared the graphic organizer as they did, noting the relationships. This presentation should include a discussion to which students can contribute what they know about the terms as well as what they predict they will be learning, based on the chart. Students should keep the organizer available for reference while they are reading, so they can occasionally check back to see the relationships as they encounter the terms.

After reading, students can use the graphic organizer as an aid for refocusing and reflecting on the learning. It can even be used as a check of comprehension. Thus the graphic organizer can be useful at each of the PAR steps and promote integration of the communicative arts. Activities 5.5 and 5.6 provide examples of graphic organizers prepared by teachers in different content areas. The organizer for primary science (Activity 5.5) uses circles, rectangles, and arrows to show relationships. The organizer for middle-school science (Activity 5.6) uses students' prior knowledge about animal kingdoms and begins to link that knowledge to new information.

Anticipation Guides

Anticipation guides, sometimes called *reaction* or *prediction guides*, prepare readers by asking them to react to a series of statements that are related to the content of the material. In reacting to these statements, students anticipate, or predict, what the content will be. We use an anticipation guide at the beginning of this chapter (see item 1 in "Preparing to Read"): We ask our readers whether they agree or disagree with a number of statements and why. Erickson, Huber, Bea, Smith, and McKenzie (1987) cite three reasons why anticipation guides are valuable:

ACTIVITY 5.5 Graphic Organizer for Primary Science

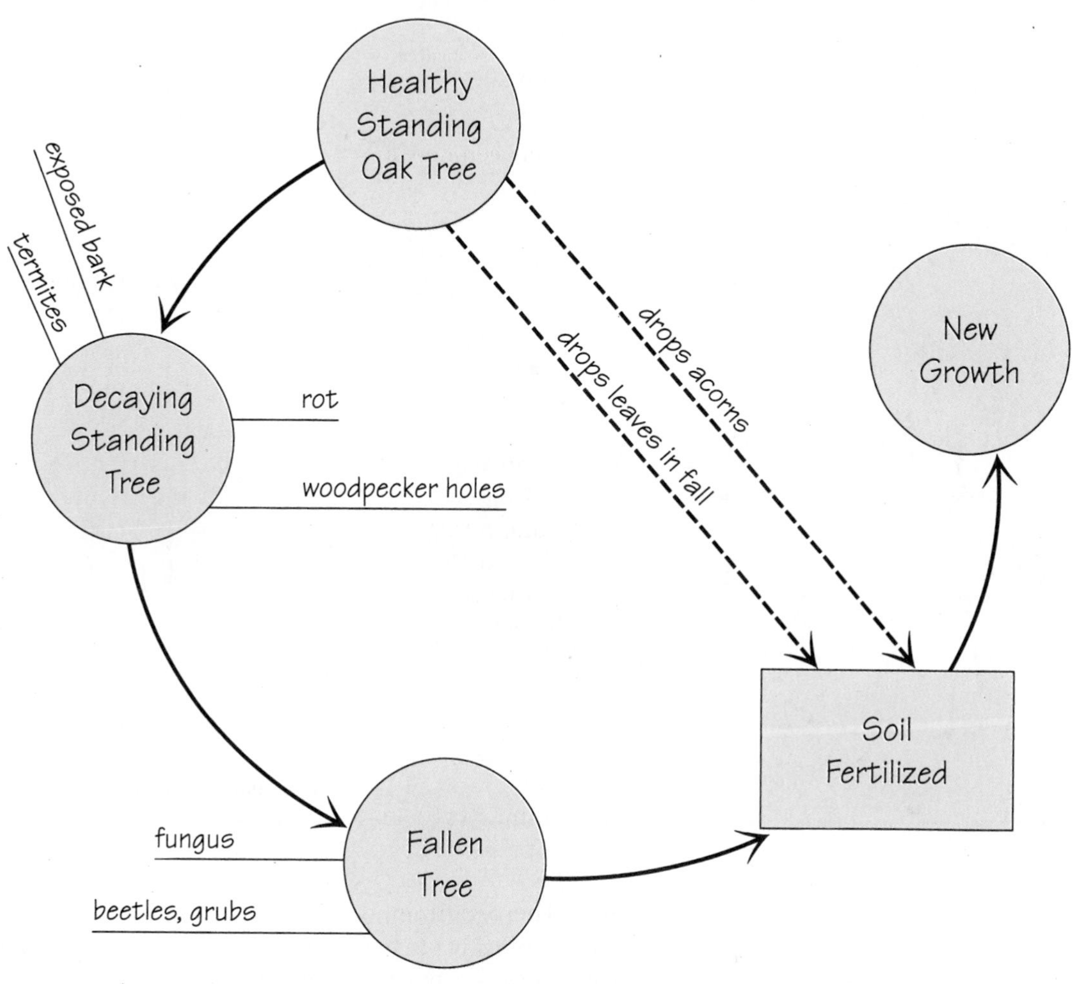

Developed by Kathryn Davis.

1. Students need to (a) connect what they already know with new information and (b) realize that they do already know something that will help them comprehend better.
2. Students exposed to anticipation guides tend to become interested and participate in lively discussion, which motivates reading.
3. Reading and writing instruction are easily integrated when anticipation guides are used.

ACTIVITY 5.6 Graphic Organizer for Middle-School Science

Directions: Chapters 10–14 in our textbook are about animals. Using these chapters, you will fill in the chart below. This chart will then be kept in your notebook.

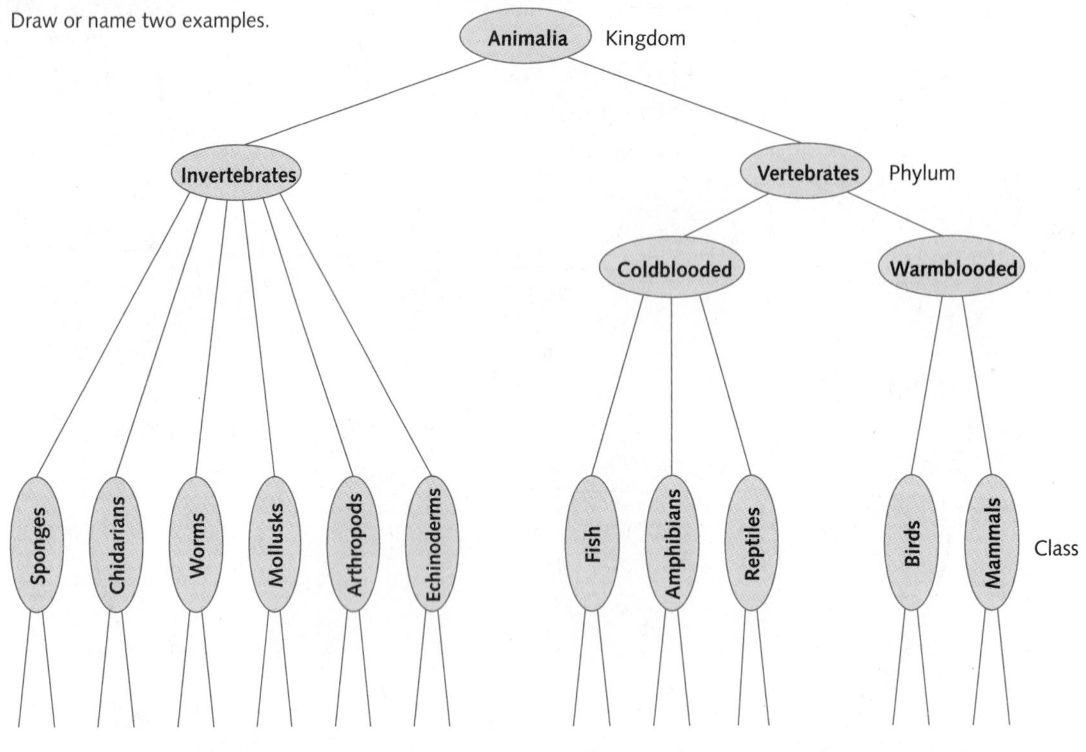

Developed by Laurie A. Schofield.

Suppose that fifth-graders in a rural community are about to study ballet in their music class. The teacher is sensitive to her students' misconceptions about ballet. She determines that their schema for ballet includes incorrect prior knowledge such as "Ballet is something girls do, not strong men; it's boring." If the teacher ignores this misconception, the students will likely reject any new information about ballet and hold fast to their previously formulated picture. Instead, the teacher uses the children's schema as a base for expanding knowledge and develops an anticipation guide. By presenting the statements shown in Activity 5.7, she gets students to verbalize their prior knowledge. Then she presents new experiences and information by showing a videotape of a performance of *The Nutcracker*. The students reformulate their knowledge after discovering new information. They change their opinions for all four statements listed in the activity. A different schema is created.

ACTIVITY 5.7 The Anticipation of Ballet

Before we begin our lesson today, read each of the following statements carefully and circle *Agree* or *Disagree* to show what you think. Be ready to discuss your opinions with the class. Do not talk with anyone else *yet* about your answers. Remember . . . this is *your opinion* and it will not be graded!

Agree	Disagree	**1.** Ballet is only for girls.
Agree	Disagree	**2.** Ballet music is always slow and soft.
Agree	Disagree	**3.** Ballet dancers are strong, muscular, and in very good physical condition.
Agree	Disagree	**4.** Russia is one country that has produced many very good ballet dancers.

Developed by Todd Barnes.

Anticipation guides involve students in discussion and reading and also can include writing if students are asked to respond in writing to the statements. Many teachers have students refer to the guide as they read, which enhances comprehension. If students return to the guide after reading, to clarify or rethink previous positions, PAR is applied throughout the administration of the guide. Conley (1985) argues that such guides are excellent tools for developing critical thinking and promoting cross-cultural understanding. Truly eclectic, anticipation guides are very well received by both teachers and students.

Making an anticipation guide takes some thought but becomes easier with practice. The basic steps for constructing an anticipation guide are as follows:

1. Read the content passage, and identify the major concepts.
2. Decide which concepts are most important to stimulate student background and beliefs.
3. Write three to five statements on the concepts. The statements should reflect the students' background and be thought provoking. General statements, rather than statements that are too specific, work best. Well-known quotations and idioms are successful.
4. Display the guide on the chalkboard, with an overhead projector, or on worksheets. Give clear directions. (These will vary depending on the age group and variations in the guide.) Leave space for responses.
5. Conduct class discussion based on your concept statements. Students must support their responses; "yes" and "no" are not acceptable answers. Students should argue from their past experiences and explain their decisions. (After the guide has been used a few times, small groups can conduct discussions simultaneously, or individuals can complete the guide independently and then reconvene.)
6. It is best to return to the anticipation guide after the material has been read. In this way, students can compare their first responses to the information they have gained.

Duffelmeyer (1994) cautions that anticipation guides are likely to fail if teachers write flawed statements—statements that do not elicit students' prior knowledge, that are based on very broad common knowledge and do not relate effectively to the specific topic, or that are based on subordinate rather than superordinate ideas.

Activities 5.8, 5.9, and 5.10 are anticipation guides constructed by teachers of primary science, high school geography, and vocational-education welding classes, respectively. There is no "right" way to create a guide. Anticipation guides that reflect sound instructional principles and research are developed every day by enterprising teachers. Notice that in Activity 5.9 some statements are quite creative in that students might be quick to agree with them if they do not think carefully. Such statements are designed to make students think more critically about reading material.

ACTIVITY 5.8 Anticipation / Prediction Guide: Primary Science

Directions: Read these statements to yourself as I read them aloud. If you agree with a statement, be ready to explain why. We will check all statements we agree with in the prereading column. Then we will read to see if we should change our minds.

Prediction Guide for Mammals

Before		After
______	 [bird] are mammals.	______
______	 [butterfly] are mammals.	______
______	All mammals have 4  [leg].	______
______	 [whale] are mammals.	______
______	Some mammals can  [fly].	______

ACTIVITY 5.9 Anticipation / Prediction Guide: High School Geography

NAME ______________________________ DATE ______________

Antarctic Ice Video

Before viewing: In the space to the left of each statement, place a check mark (✓) if you agree or think the statement is true.

During or after viewing: Add new check marks or cross through those marks about which you have changed your mind. Keep in mind that this is not like a traditional "worksheet." You may have to put on your thinking-caps and "read between the lines." Use the space under each statement to note a detail or two to support your thinking.

___ 1. McMurdo Station is the scientific "headquarters" of the continent of Antarctica.

___ 2. Satellite images show that Antarctica doubles in size each winter.

___ 3. Not one woman survived the Shackleton expedition to Antarctica.

___ 4. Most people who live in Antarctica are scientists.

___ 5. Ice ages occur regularly, and we are currently in an "interglacial period," a brief period between two ice ages.

___ 6. If the western ice shelf melts, Virginia Beach will no longer exist.

___ 7. The one good thing about living in Antarctica is that it is a fairly safe place to be.

___ 8. The movement of ice occurs at different speeds at different places.

___ 9. There is more than one way to investigate what exists under the ice.

___ 10. Fossils prove that the ice was not always there.

___ 11. One reason for rapid ice movement is convection.

___ 12. If the ice starts to move faster, we are in trouble.

___ 13. One thing that has been learned through studying Greenland ice cores is that past ice ages occurred very suddenly.

___ 14. The earth's climate of the last 10,000 years is mild compared to its climate of the previous 40,000 years.

___ 15. If the average temperature of the earth went either up or down by only a few degrees, it could lead to a world disaster, and it could happen within the next 10 years.

Developed by Mark Forget.

ACTIVITY 5.10 Anticipation/Prediction Guide: Shielded Metal-Arc Welding

Directions: Read each statement below carefully. Check either *agree* or *disagree* to show what you think. Do this both before and after reading. You should be able to defend your answers.

Prereading			Postreading	
Agree	Disagree	STATEMENTS	Agree	Disagree
______	______	1. Skill in performing welding operations requires practice.	______	______
______	______	2. The first basic operation is learning to strike an arc and run a curved bead.	______	______
______	______	3. The current used in a welding operation depends only on the size and type of electrode used.	______	______
______	______	4. A proper arc length between the electrode and the work is required to generate the heat needed for welding.	______	______
______	______	5. Using the correct electrode angle will ensure proper penetration and bead formation.	______	______
______	______	6. It is safe to touch the welding bench with an uninsulated holder.	______	______
______	______	7. It is important to have correct welding heat to make a sound weld.	______	______

Analogies

Analogies present comparisons between known and unknown concepts. Analogies are like previews in that both begin with a connection point to the reader's background. However, analogies carry out a comparison, whereas previews focus more directly on the material to be read.

Analogies are excellent tools for content-reading teachers because they are simple to create and highly relevant for students. They can be presented in oral or written form, as an informal introduction to content material. They also promote listening and speaking, and if students are encouraged to write their own analogies after reading certain material, then analogies become useful reflection and writing activities as well. The example shown in Activity 5.11 was developed by a third-grade teacher.

ACTIVITY 5.11 Analogy

Goal: To enable students to connect new knowledge with existing knowledge.

Directions: Read the following paragraphs as a primer for small-group discussion comparing cars with bodies.

Materials: Paper
Pencils

Your body is very similar to a car in the way that it acts. You may have been told to "rev up your engine" one time. When a car revs up, it begins to go.

A car needs many different substances to keep it running well. It might need oil for the parts and air for the filters, as you would need oil for your joints or air for your lungs.

Actually, there are many other things that a car and your body have in common. A car needs gasoline to make it go. What do you need? (food)

Now divide the students into small groups and let them list on paper the ways that cars and bodies are similar. Some suggestions that you will be looking for are:

Fats/oil
Protein/gasoline
Carbohydrates/spark plugs
Vitamins/fuel additives, super power gasoline
Minerals/paint, rustproofers
Air/air conditioning
muscles/wheels
heart/engine

Return to the class in 15 or 20 minutes and share the group information. Write the analogies on the board. Ask for comments or changes.

Developed by Kathy Feltus.

We can liken practicing for a basketball game to preparation for reading by relating a familiar concept to a less familiar one. Playing the game actually takes up the smallest amount of time; the greatest amount of time is spent in workouts, strategy sessions, viewing game films, and concentrated practice—all intended to ensure success in the game itself. After the game, more time is spent analyzing what occurred on the court, and then preparation for the next game begins. The question is asked, "Why did we do well in this game," or "Why didn't we do well?" So it is with reading. A proficient reader spends time getting ready to read by determining and building background. Instead of plunging into the reading, the reader must prepare. Good comprehension is a natural result, just as playing a game successfully is the natural result of hard work in practice. Teachers who are aware of this phenomenon and aid students in the preparation stage of reading are like good coaches. The coach is there at every step to help and encourage the students as they take responsibility and work through the lesson. Students who realize that preparation for reading is like court practice will reap benefits in higher achievement and better grades.

When a high school junior resisted reading a history chapter that explained the circumstances leading to the American Revolution, his parent (a reading specialist, of course!) tried this preparation strategy:

"Suppose," the parent suggested, "that your parents decided to go to Europe for six months, leaving you on your own at home. You would have the car and access to money; you would be able to make all of your own decisions. What would your reaction be?" As you might imagine, the high school junior thought this would be an excellent arrangement. "However," the parent continued, "we would arrive home again and take charge once more. We would want our car back, and you would have to ask for permission to do the things you'd been doing freely. Now, how would you feel?" The junior did not like the turn of events. "Would you still love us?" the parent inquired, assuming, of course, that teenagers do love their parents even though they have funny ways of showing it!

"Well, yes," the junior reluctantly agreed. "But I'd be insulted, and family life wouldn't be the same."

"Exactly," agreed the parent. "That's the way it was with the British and their American colonies. The British had to attend to problems in Europe and in their own government. They let the American colonists have free rein for a while. Then they turned their attention back to the Americans. But the Americans didn't appreciate the intervention after this period of time. Many of them still 'loved' the British, but they deeply resented the renewed control. While you're reading this chapter, you might want to keep in mind your own reactions to this hypothetical situation and compare those feelings to the reactions of the colonists." Much later in the month, this junior grudgingly reported to his parent that the chapter had turned out to be "pretty easy to read" because he understood the circumstances better than for most of the other chapters in the book.

This on-the-spot analogy was simple enough to construct. The teacher/parent understood several characteristics of 16-year-olds and applied them to building an analogy that would hook the reader to the content material. The informal analogy was a simple preparation strategy. It worked because the reading took on new meaning for the student. His comprehension was enhanced, enough so that he admitted it to a parent!

Direct References and Simple Discussion

Sometimes teachers find that students have incorrect knowledge. What is the best way to build prior knowledge for readers with misconceptions? When Dole, Valencia, Greer, and Wardrop (1991) compared the use of interactive and teacher-directed strategies, they found that teacher direction increased students' comprehension of a passage. In this regard, **direct references** and discussion can be used as an effective strategy.

Maria and MacGinitie (1987) conducted a study in which they asked students in the fifth and sixth grades to read two types of materials. The first made specific reference to the misconceptions that the researchers had identified during a pretest and contrasted those misconceptions with correct information. The second was written with the correct information but no direct refutation of predetermined misconceptions. The researchers found that student recall was significantly better on the text that confronted the misconceptions.

Guzzetti, Snyder, and Glass (1992) conducted a meta-analysis of studies about children's misconceptions. They found that some type of intervention was enough to establish for students a degree of discomfort with their prior beliefs (p. 648). Three strategies were found to be effective means of intervention: (1) Using refutational text, a teacher provides a passage directly refuting the misconception; this is similar to the preview activity. (2) Augmented activation activities use learners' prior knowledge first to activate discussion and then to supplement the material generated with the correct information; this is similar to what might occur with factstorming and PreP or anticipation guides. (3) Also effective is the discussion web (Alvermann, 1991) (see Chapter 7), because students must articulate and defend their positions by referring to text and discussing with peers. Guzzetti, Snyder, and Glass (1992) conclude that, regardless of which specific activity is used, dissatisfaction with incorrect prior knowledge must be created before the misconception will be altered.

Avoiding Textbooks: A Teacher's Last Resort

Teachers sometimes avoid textbooks, perhaps because they are uncertain about their effectiveness (Hinchman, 1987). Teachers may not know what else to do when they see that a textbook is difficult for their students, and they may resort to avoidance tactics in desperation. Some teachers read the textbook aloud to their students; others tell students the information and require no reading; still others have students take notes from the teacher's synopsis of the material. Some findings indicate that teachers rely on textbooks for very little of their instruction because they realize that there is a mismatch between the text and the students. Davey (1988) found that several teachers used the textbook only as a supplement to their instruction, not as a basis for it. The teachers in this study indicated that they avoided textbooks because of the differences among their students and because they lacked the time to cover the whole text.

We think that avoiding textbooks is a poor response and sends students an undesirable message. Students may inadvertently learn that it is not necessary to read a textbook at all because teachers will tell them what they need to know. Teachers in fact do students a disservice when they avoid textbook material. Such messages to students are powerful deterrents to future reading for knowledge. First, important information may be overlooked by the teacher and missed entirely by the students when a teacher avoids textbook material. Second, students need to read and see teachers valuing reading material if they are to become informed and avid readers themselves. The less practice students receive in reading to learn, the weaker their reading will be. The more students receive the message that they can skip the reading material and just listen to the teacher, the more ambivalent they will be about reading to learn. Third, and most crucial, when teachers avoid textbook material, they may be contributing to the literacy problem described in a number of NAEP reports: Students who have the basic skills to read but read little are ill equipped to live in a literate America.

A longitudinal study compared Asian—Taiwanese, Japanese, Chinese—students to American students of comparable ages, school and city sizes, and socioeconomic backgrounds (Stevenson, 1992). Among the results were these findings:

1. Although reading abilities were comparable, American students spent less time reading for pleasure in grades K through 12.
2. American children completed far less homework—a quarter as much as the Taiwanese and half as much as the Japanese children.
3. When asked to make a wish, 70 percent of the Chinese students made a wish related to education; less than 10 percent of the Americans did so.
4. Asian systems stress effort. Parents, children, and teachers are expected to exert the effort needed to enable students to succeed. If a student is not learning, more effort is expected, not less.

From the study, Stevenson concluded that American students are passive learners who are not motivated to read. By avoiding textbooks, teachers may be contributing to the very problem that their profession is supposed to be solving. A better solution is to create appropriate activities to determine and build background so that students are prepared to read and learn from multiple resources, including textbooks. When students are prepared, even difficult resources are easier to read. Students are more interested in and willing to read when they feel confident that they will understand.

One-Minute Summary

In this chapter we discuss the importance of students' prior knowledge in reading. Understanding the role of student background and interest is very important in preparing effective lessons. Careful preparation by the teacher may help to overcome students' limited or incorrect prior knowledge about a topic. We include many activities—some developed by classroom teachers—for building background. We suggest that textbook material sometimes needs adaptation but should not be eliminated from the curriculum. We demonstrate how preparation activities can promote reading, writing, speaking, and listening and can incorporate all the steps of PAR. We emphasize that the way a teacher uses an activity is more important than rigorous adherence to prescribed steps. We include variations of activities that demonstrate the creativity of the teachers who constructed them.

End-of-Chapter Activities

Assisting Comprehension

Select a chapter from a content-area textbook. Using the following questions as a guide, reflect on what your text offers to help you as a teacher build your students' background for reading the text:

a. What aids are provided in the text chapter to help you build on students' prior knowledge?

b. Is there a chapter preview or summary that could be used to build on it?

c. Are there any statements, such as those identifying objectives, that could be used in an anticipation guide?

d. Is there a graphic organizer?

e. Are these aids suitable for your students?

f. Are these aids sufficient for your students?

g. As a teacher, should you construct some aids to help yourself build on student prior knowledge? If so, what will you construct?

Reflecting on Your Reading

1. Table 5.1 provides an overview of the activities presented in this chapter. We have rated each activity. Do you agree with our ratings? Fill in your own ratings in the column provided.
2. Refer to the statements in item 1 of the "Preparing to Read" section of this chapter. Would you answer any differently after having read this chapter? Or would all your answers remain the same? Reflect over the seven statements to gain a further understanding of this chapter.

TABLE 5.1

Activity	*Materials Needed*	*Authors' Rating*	*Your Rating*
Multitext	Teacher, text	*****	
Rewriting text	Teacher, text	***	
Written previews	Teacher, text	****	
Graphic organizers	Material, text	*****	
Anticipation guides	Teacher, text, students	*****	
Analogies	Teacher, text, students	*****	
Direct reference	Teacher, text, students	****	

CHAPTER 6

Assisting Comprehension

No man really becomes a fool until he stops asking questions.

—Steinmetz

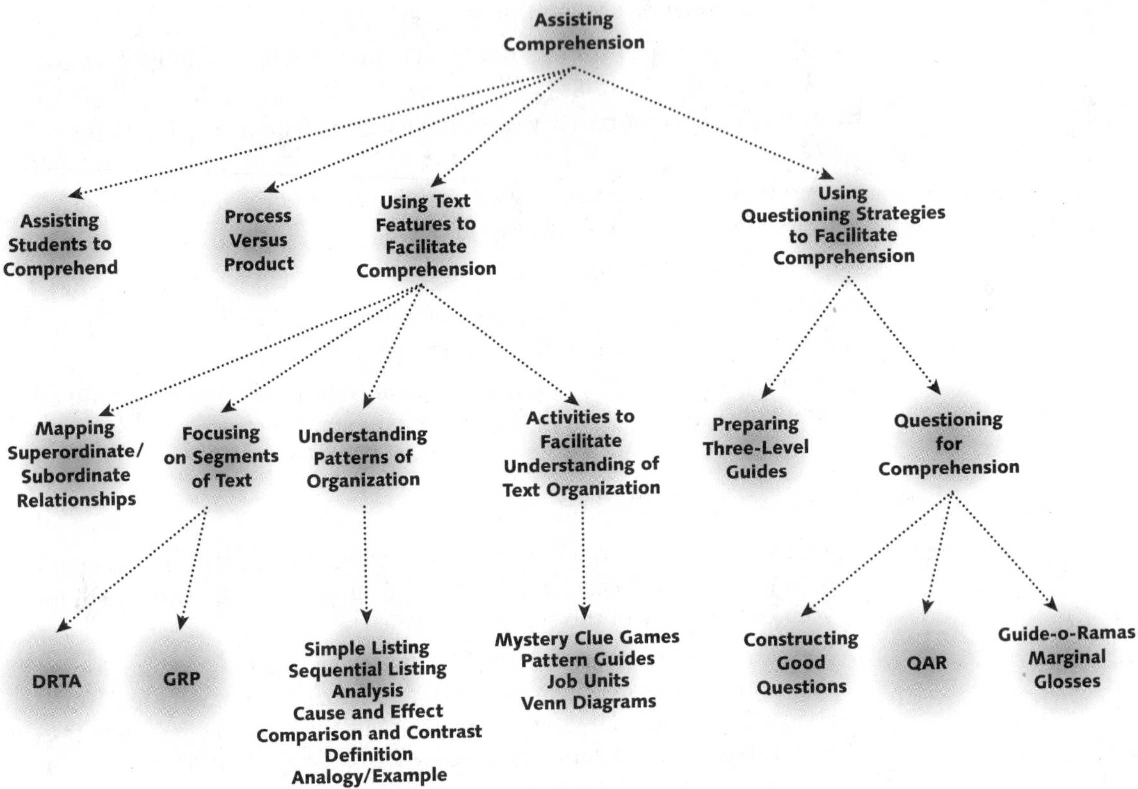

Preparing to Read

1. Think about the last time you read a challenging text. What strategies did you use to understand it? Did you organize the information? Did you ask yourself questions?
2. Following is a list of terms used in this chapter. Some may be familiar to you in a general context, but in this chapter they may be used in unfamiliar ways. Rate your knowledge by placing a plus sign (+) in front of those you are sure that you know, a check mark (✓) in front of those you have some knowledge about, and a zero (0) in front of those you don't know. Be ready to locate and pay special attention to their meanings when they are presented in the chapter.

_______ adjunct strategies
_______ situated cognition
_______ product
_______ process
_______ constructivism
_______ superordinate
_______ subordinate
_______ segments
_______ chunks
_______ DRTA
_______ patterns of organization
_______ discourse analysis
_______ jot charts
_______ taxonomy
_______ metacognition
_______ QAR

Objectives

As you read this chapter, focus your attention on the following objectives. You will:

1. be able to define *reading comprehension*, using a historical perspective when forming your definition.
2. understand the difference between process and product as they relate to reading comprehension.

3. learn to define *constructivism.*
4. identify several text features that can facilitate comprehension.
5. describe effective questioning strategies.
6. describe a number of activities that assist and guide students to better understanding of text.

Assisting Students to Comprehend

In Chapters 4 and 5 you learned how to prepare your students to read content material. The next step in the PAR Lesson Framework is to assist students to read with understanding. The environment that teachers foster is important in facilitating comprehension. Teachers must consider the contexts that facilitate comprehension and then provide appropriate strategies and activities. Students often do not realize that the complexities of text can facilitate or impede their understanding, nor do they realize that skillful questioning—on their part and on their teacher's—can lead to greater understanding. Teachers assist most effectively when they model consistently how to determine and build background, and how to think through material to deepen understanding.

What is comprehension? William S. Gray (1941/1984) wrote that comprehension "assumes that the reader not only apprehends the author's meaning but also reflects on the significance of the ideas presented, evaluates them critically, and makes application of them in the solutions of problems" (p. 18). Forty-four years later, in *The Reading Report Card* (1985), reading is described as analytic, interactive, constructive, and strategic. This definition—like Gray's—implies that apprehension and reflection are requisites of comprehension. A reader must grab hold of—apprehend—and ponder the significance of the content. This analysis must be active (principle 8 in Chapter 1), generating strategies that aid the reader now and in future reading.

Garner (1985a) provides evidence that specific instructional assistance can guide students from a stage of strategic deficiency to a stage of strategic efficiency. It is the teacher's role to teach students about comprehension as well as text information (Fielding & Pearson, 1994). Unfortunately, some teachers do not provide instructional assistance. The sobering news from Garner's review is that teachers too often assume that students automatically comprehend what they read. Comprehension is not that easy. By using adjunct strategies, teachers provide strategic help at the assistance stage. **Adjunct strategies** are ways of learning modeled alongside the actual encounter with reading matter rather than before or after the reading is done. Brown, Collins, and Duguid (1989) call this **situated cognition**, whereby students learn about comprehension strategies embedded in discussion about texts.

Teachers use adjunct strategies more often than pre- or postreading strategies (Rakes & Chance, 1990). Of the students polled by Rakes and Chance, 78 percent (of 182) at the secondary level and 59 percent (of 156) in the elementary grades said that teachers had taught them strategies to use as they are reading. Recent reviews of research show that with careful and directed instruction, students can acquire effective strategies for reading comprehension (Fielding & Pearson, 1994). How the teacher presents the content material, complemented by adjunct strategies, will make the difference in how well the students learn the material. In this chapter we focus on ways to assist students to comprehend as they read content material.

Process Versus Product

Although historically the study of reading comprehension has reflected different schools of thought at different times, the changes in definition over time exhibit more continuity than contrast. Huey (1908/1968) and then Thorndike (1917) defined *reading* as a thinking process, implying that comprehension is not only recognizing letters and words but also thinking about what those symbols mean. Sixty years later, Hillerich (1979) drew the same conclusion when he identified reading comprehension as "nothing more than thinking as applied to reading" (p. 3). A little earlier, Frank Smith (1971), drawing from his study of communication systems, argued for a definition of *comprehension* as "the reduction of uncertainty" (p. 17). Smith explained that as readers gain information by reading, they rely on what they know to "reduce the number of alternative possibilities" (p. 17). Pearson and Johnson (1978) picture reading comprehension as the building of bridges between the new and the known. The continuity among these definitions, which span 70 years, is apparent.

The definition of *comprehension* has not changed substantially, but the way we study comprehension has changed. New interest in how to teach reading comprehension has been generated by the recognition that comprehension is not a passive, receptive process but an active, constructive, reader-based process. In the past, reading researchers studied measurable results of reading comprehension to help them explain how comprehension occurs. They expected that, after reading, readers would be able to answer questions of varying difficulty, organize information, and explain its implications. The answers, which demonstrated whether the reader had learned the content, were the **products** of comprehension.

The **process** of learning, in contrast, refers to the mental activity that goes on as the reader is reading and thinking about the material. While this mental activity is occurring, the reader is seeking assistance in understanding the material. The reader wants to sort facts from implications, identify the organization of the material, and use picture clues and text aids to help with this understanding. **Constructivism** is a term used by reading experts of this era to explain what happens as a reader processes text (Pearson & Stephens, 1994). Fosnot (1996) called constructivism "the most current psychology of learning." In a constructivist model, teachers are not transmitting knowledge to passive learners;

instead, learners are building information from the assistance that teachers provide (Weaver, 1994). The reader must actively construct meaning by relating new material to the known, using reasoning and developing concepts. The process is not only individual but also social, because "by articulating ideas and experience through writing, speaking, and/or visually representing, students deepen their thinking and construct and organize their understanding of new material" (Gill & Dupree, 1998, p. 95). The teacher's role is to employ teaching strategies that assist this understanding, including those that integrate listening, speaking, reading, and writing.

By discovering what readers do as they read, we can design strategies for assistance that enhance their learning. Goodman and Burke (1972) use a tape of a child reading a story and reflecting on his reading to illustrate this relationship. The story is about an oxygen failure on a spaceship. A canary is kept on board as a warning device. The child reads aloud but consistently skips the word *oxygen* because, he says, he doesn't know it. At the end of the story, while trying to retell the events to the teacher, he comments that they should have put an oxygen mask on the canary. After this comment, he says with excitement: "Oxygen! That was the word I couldn't get!" This child was thinking as he read, trying to put together the clues. He was processing what he thought of as "unknown data." When he reached the stage of retelling the story, he realized that he did know; he had put the clues together. If the teacher had interpreted as a final product his failure to pronounce the word while he was reading, she would have thought he did not know the word. In fact, all along he was still constructing meaning. Ultimately, his processing led to a correct understanding. As this experience illustrates, we must give our students every chance to process information, thus discovering meaning as they read, before we measure their understanding. Figure 6.1 illustrates this distinction between process and product in reading comprehension.

Using Text Features to Facilitate Comprehension

Comprehension is influenced by how a text is organized and by how much teachers help students to understand that organization. Gordon (1990) compared sixth-graders' awareness of text characteristics from the beginning to the end of a school year. She found that one major change was greater understanding of both narrative and expository text structure. Williams, Taylor, and Ganger (1981) found that a typical instructional task of "finding the main idea" can be very difficult for students through the middle grade levels, particularly when the text is vague. Brown and Day (1983) found that the ability to construct main-idea statements develops later than other summarization skills. Although summarizing is difficult for many poor comprehenders, Hare and Borchardt (1984) trained students to summarize effectively by demonstrating how to use many parts of a text. Meyer, Brandt, and Bluth (1980) tested children at both

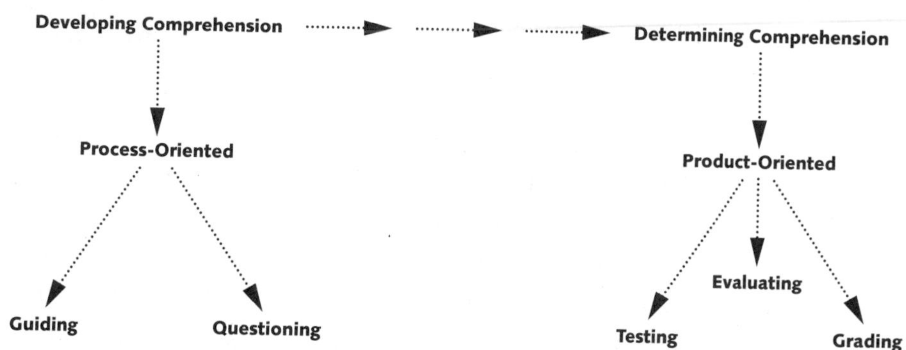

FIGURE 6.1 Process versus product in reading comprehension

the third- and ninth-grade levels and found that both groups were deficient in their understanding of superordination and subordination of information.

Mapping Superordinate/Subordinate Relationships

As Armbruster (1984) points out, expository text should contain **superordinate** ideas, which span whole sections of material, and, within those sections, **subordinate** information, which clarifies the superordinate. Readers need to keep in mind the major thrust of the material in order to understand the relationship between superordinate ideas and subordinate information. For instance, in this textbook, the major—superordinate—theme is the PAR Lesson Framework. Each chapter explains aspects of the framework—subordinate information.

Mapping is one activity that demonstrates the adjunct strategy of organizing information into major and subordinate ideas. The activity can assist readers in understanding concept relationships. Mapping (Heimlich & Pittleman, 1985) has in fact become a very popular activity for helping readers develop comprehension. Just as travelers use a map to help them find their way, readers can use a diagram that shows the route to understanding a passage, and they themselves can make maps to show their understanding.

The primary purpose of mapping is to portray the relationship of major and supporting ideas visually. Because maps encourage students to refer to the reading material and engage in interactive learning, reading educators recognize their value in assisting comprehension. Mapping can be used to teach vocabulary and to introduce outlining and note taking, and as a study aid. In Chapter 8, we discuss concept, semantic, and word mapping as ways to help learners with vocabulary. Mapping can be used to introduce a topic before any reading takes place. In this case, the teacher probably has already made the map or is relying on students' prior knowledge to construct the map; thus the strategy is to use prior knowledge to prepare the reader. Mapping also can be used to aid reading reflections, because after the map is made it becomes a study aid. The following are suggestions for developing a map (based on Santeusanio, 1983):

1. Identify the main idea of the content passage. (Sometimes just the topic or a question may stimulate map generation.) Write the main

idea anywhere on the page, leaving room for other information to be written around it.

2. Circle the main idea.
3. Identify secondary categories, which may be chapter subheadings.
4. Connect the secondary categories to the main idea.
5. Find supporting details.
6. Connect supporting details to the idea or category that they support.
7. Connect all notes to other notes in a way that makes sense.

Although mapping a whole chapter may be time-consuming, we recommend it for portions of a chapter that a teacher identifies as very important, to help readers understand the superordinate/subordinate relationship.

Maps engage readers as they read, reread, and study, and they demonstrate the hierarchical nature of exposition. Muth (1987) reports that mapping, because it is a hierarchical strategy, has been found to be highly successful in aiding students to understand expository text. Once teachers have mapped several times with students, students will become proficient at making their own maps. Since a map is a diagram of information, it is a visual learning aid. Often, especially for younger readers, drawings added to the map will stimulate learning. Such visual reinforcement capitalizes on visual literacy and right-brain functions. Activity 6.1 shows how a technology teacher used mapping to show the parts of a computer. (See also the Technology Box.)

Integration of all the communicative arts occurs when mapping is used. Class discussion must take place for the map to be developed. This requires students to listen to each other and speak on the topic. Reading is the source of the information mapped, and writing can be incorporated if the teacher asks students to use the map as a frame of reference for writing about the reading topic. For instance, students could be assigned to write a six-paragraph essay about the parts of the computer, as generated from the map. A science teacher who wants students to write reports about planets could have students map the information on a planet provided in an encyclopedia. Then students might refer to primary sources to find out more about each portion of the map. Finally, the map could be transformed into the table of contents for the report (see Activity 6.2). The map in Activity 6.3 was constructed by fifth-graders as they read about and discussed the five kingdoms of living things. Students were able to refer to the text material and worked in groups.

Focusing on Segments of Text

Authors usually organize text by dividing it into meaningful sections, or **segments**, signified by subheadings. Readers must learn to pay attention to subheadings as a way to focus on important information. Readers who attend to one segment, or **chunk** of material, at a time make their reading more manageable. Casteel (1990) found that chunking material helped the students in his study, particularly low-ability students, to score higher on tests (chunking is also discussed as a memory-enhancing strategy in Chapter 10, on study skills).

ACTIVITY 6.1 Computer Map

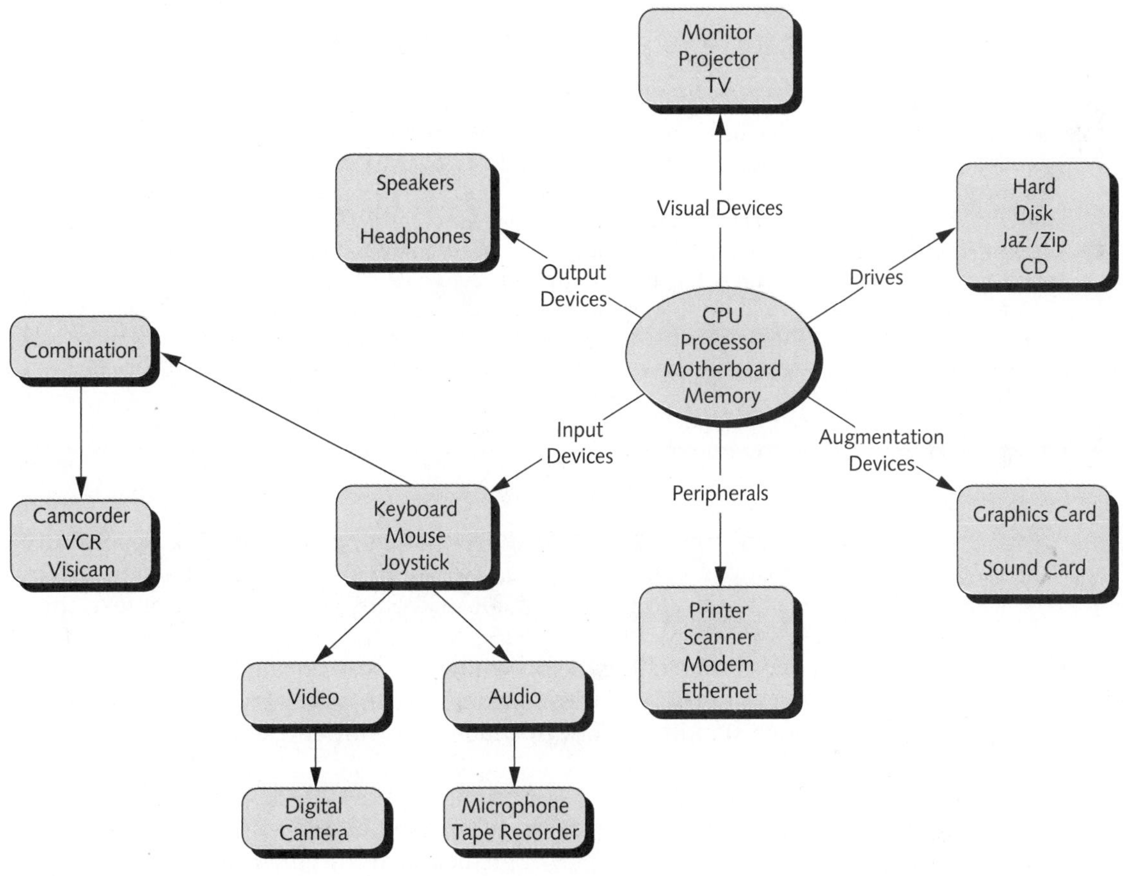

Teachers can help students read and understand by encouraging them to turn subheadings into questions or purpose statements, then reading to answer the question or fulfill the purpose. Such activities model the strategy of using segments of text to gain understanding.

Directed Reading/Thinking Activity

The **Directed Reading/Thinking Activity (DRTA)** helps students to understand that each segment of text can help them figure out the next segment. As advocated by Stauffer (1969a), the DRTA has three basic steps: predicting, reading, and proving. Predicting involves asking readers to use not only what they already know but also whatever they can learn from a quick preview of the material to predict what the material is going to be about. Predicting prepares the reader for comprehension. It is an extremely important DRTA step, but it cannot stand alone. Because students are encouraged to predict aloud, and to justify

TECHNOLOGY BOX

Software for Creating Maps and Graphic Organizers

Maps and graphic organizers help learners construct knowledge because they show connections between concepts. A software program that helps students make their own diagrams is a useful technology tool. Computer-based mapping allows students to envision how a knowledge domain is structured and to make changes as they learn more. One such program is *Inspiration*. With this software, students start by making a premap of a major idea and several terms. This process utilizes their previous background knowledge. Next, they create an expanded map that is more complex. After class work and text reading, the map may be revised to reflect more complete learning.

Inspiration is available from Inspiration Software, Inc., 7412 SW Beaverton Hillsdale Highway, Suite 102, Portland, OR 97225. See also "Computer-Based Concept Mapping: Active Studying for Active Learners," by L. Anderson-Inman and L. Zeitz, 1993, August–September, *The Computing Teacher*, 21, pp. 6–10.

their predictions, the DRTA offers a lively listening and speaking opportunity within a social context. Although an overall prediction may be made, teachers encourage readers to make predictions about specific portions of text, then read the appropriate portion to confirm or alter the predictions. Students reflect aloud on those predictions before going on to read another segment. The teacher guides the DRTA process, making sure that each student is actively involved in understanding each segment before continuing to the next. The DRTA involves all three stages of PAR; hence it is a versatile activity. WIKA and KWL activities, discussed in Chapter 4, are similar to the DRTA in promoting the strategy of involving the reader before, during, and after reading. With the DRTA, learners also apply the strategies of prediction and segmenting text.

Figures 6.2 and 6.3 outline the DRTA steps to apply to fiction and nonfiction material, respectively. Notice that step 2 in the fiction DRTA requests that readers read to find out whether the predictions they made were accurate. Step 4 in the nonfiction DRTA requests that readers read to find the answers to questions they have generated, and step 5 calls on students to think deeply by defending responses. These steps focus on purposeful reading; they are the foundation for a successful DRTA. A teacher must decide in advance how to segment the material for a DRTA. The organization of the material is the key factor affecting this segmentation.

The predicting steps of the DRTA build purpose for reading. When readers are asked what they think might happen next and then read to verify their prediction, they are being encouraged to read purposefully. Readers become very excited about this predictive involvement in their own reading. Often they share their predictions orally before the individual reading occurs. This activity incorporates listening and speaking. If students are asked to write down what they predict during various portions of the reading and then review those written

ACTIVITY 6.2 A Map Becomes a Table of Contents

Brief Survey
Moons
JUPITER
Composition
Rings

Table of Contents

Brief survey of Jupiter	p. 1
Composition of Jupiter	p. 2
Moons of Jupiter	p. 4
Rings of Jupiter	p. 5

ACTIVITY 6.3 Five Kingdoms Graphic Organizer, Fifth-Grade Science

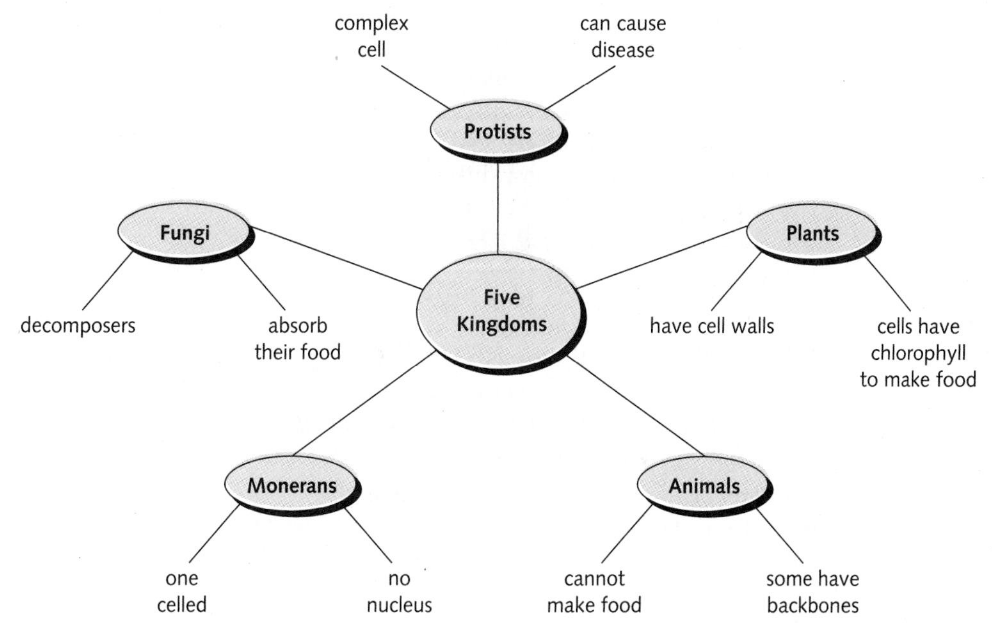

Developed by Jacqueline T. McDonnough.

FIGURE 6.2

DRTA for fiction

1. Previewing
   Preread: Title
   Pictures
   Subtitles
   Introduction (if story is long enough)
   Close book and make hypotheses: What do you think will happen?
   Why do you think that? (What gives you the clue?)
2. Verifying
   Read: To find whether or not predictions were right
3. Reflecting on Reading
   Developing comprehension by:
   Checking on individual and group hypotheses
   Staying with or redefining hypotheses

FIGURE 6.3

DRTA for nonfiction

1. Previewing
   Study: Title
   Introduction
   Subtitles
   Pictures
   Charts
   Maps
   Graphs
   Summary or conclusion
   End-of-chapter questions
2. Decision Making
   What is known after previewing?
   What do we need to learn?
3. Writing
   Writing specific questions students need to learn
4. Reading
   Finding the answers to students' written questions
5. Reflect on the reading by:
   Determining answers to students' questions
   Having students defend their inferences by referring to text
   Finding out what we still need to know

predictions at the end of the DRTA, writing is used as a way to determine purpose within the DRTA.

Our experience with the DRTA shows that students are quite imaginative when formulating predictions about fiction but can be dreadfully boring when trying to do the same for nonfiction. The reason for the difference may lie in the fact that they are not predicting the nonfiction outcome in the same sense as they do for fiction. The procedure for nonfiction DRTAs is to survey, question, and then read for answers. The result, without proper preparation, can be similar to just "doing the questions at the end of the chapter." This defeats the purpose of the DRTA, which is to allow students to create their own purpose in reading. Therefore, step 5 in the nonfiction DRTA is crucial and should not be neglected. The predicting process itself is sufficient for fictional readings.

The dialogue in Activity 6.4, transcribed from a seventh-grade social studies teacher's DRTA lesson on the caste system in India, shows how well PAR is incorporated in a DRTA. The purpose-setting statements, which are based on segments of the material to be read, are italicized.

DRTA lessons help teachers to model the reading process at its best. What good readers do as they read is predict and speculate; read to confirm; and stop reading and carry on a mental discussion of what they understand. The material is divided into manageable units. DRTAs provide a vehicle for figuring out content as the reading occurs; they emphasize reading as a constructive process rather than a measurement of comprehension. DRTAs also build readers' self-concepts. When readers see that what they predict helps them to understand better, and that everyone's speculations are important whether or not they are proven to be what the author concluded, they feel more confident about their reading. At the elementary level, teachers can encourage readers to become "reading detectives." Playing a game of detection motivates students to read and to take charge of their own reading. We cannot stress enough the pervasive benefits of using DRTAs to teach content subjects.

Guided-Reading Procedure

The guided-reading procedure (GRP) (Manzo, 1975) offers an excellent way to teach students to gather and organize information around main ideas. GRP uses brainstorming to collect information as accurately as possible and then rereading to correct misinformation and fill in conceptual gaps. The second reading is very important because students must prove that their statements are correct or disprove fellow students' statements. In conducting GRPs, we have noted the students' intensity of purpose and focus during the second reading of the text segment. According to researchers Colwell, Mangano, Childs, and Case (1986), GRP is a very effective teacher-directed technique. It can be used to aid students in becoming more independent in their thinking and studying. Following are the steps teachers use when applying the guided-reading procedure:

1. Prepare the students for the lesson by clarifying key concepts about the reading; assess students' background knowledge. The teacher may ask students to clarify vocabulary terms or make predictions concerning concepts inherent to the reading.
2. Assign a selection of appropriate length, and ask students to remember all they can about the reading. Manzo (1975) gives these general guidelines for passage length: primary students—90 words, 3 minutes; intermediate students—500 words, 5 minutes; junior high school students—900 words, 7 minutes; high school students—2,000 words, 10 minutes.

ACTIVITY 6.4 DRTA Transcript: Seventh-Grade Social Studies

Material Used: "A Coward"
Objective: Students will describe the role of persons or groups in India's society.

Teacher: We have been learning about the caste system in India and how parents arrange their children's marriages. Today we are going to read another story about the caste system and marriages in India. What is the title of this story?
Student: "A Coward."
Teacher: What do you think that has to do with marriage?
Student: He must be afraid to get married.
Teacher: *Read the first paragraph and see if you get any clues.*
Teacher: Was he afraid to get married?
Student: No, SHE's the coward!
Teacher: What do you think will happen?
Student: Maybe he will talk to her parents. He's in a higher caste, so they should like that. He doesn't care about his parents, so he will marry her anyway.
Teacher: *Read the next part and see if he does talk to her parents.*
Teacher: Did he ask her parents?
Student: No, she asked them. So she's gotten braver, but she got into more trouble.
Teacher: How?
Student: They made her quit college.
Teacher: Do you think Reshav will still talk to her parents?
Student: He might. When she doesn't come back to college, he might come to see what is wrong.
Teacher: Do you think Prema's parents will let her marry Reshav if they meet him?
Student: Probably not. They don't want to be disgraced.
Teacher: What do you think will happen next?
Student: I think that Reshav will come to talk to the parents. If they say no, they could run away to another town. If he can talk Prema into leaving her parents.
Teacher: *Read the next section to see if that happens.*
Teacher: Did Reshav come to talk to Prema's parents?
Student: No, her father is going to talk to Reshav. He's afraid that she might kill herself. She's weird!
Teacher: How do you think the meeting with Reshav will go?
Student: They will probably start to like him. He goes to college, so he must be smart. They will probably let him marry her because her father doesn't want her to kill herself.
Teacher: *Read the next section and see what happens.*
Teacher: Did Reshav meet her parents?
Student: No, the two fathers met and Reshav's father got really mad.
Teacher: What about Reshav?
Student: He wants to marry Prema in secret, but he's afraid of his father. Maybe he's going to wait until his father dies, and then marry her.
Teacher: *Finish the story and see if they do get married.*
Teacher: What happened?
Student: Gosh! *He* was the coward! He's going to feel rotten when he finds out what she did. He might even kill himself. Then the parents would really feel bad.

Developed by Faye Freeman.

3. After the students have completed the assignment, have them close the book and relate everything they know about the material they just read. Then list statements on the board without editing, whenever possible assigning two students to act as class recorders. Using student recorders makes it easier for the teacher to monitor and guide the class discussion.
4. Direct students to look for inconsistencies and misinformation, first through discussion and then through reading the material.
5. Add new information. If reading a narrative, help students organize and categorize concepts into a loose outline. For nonfiction material, students can put information into two, three, or four categories and title each category.
6. Have students reread the selection to determine whether the information they listed is accurate.
7. To strengthen short-term recall, test students on the reading.

Part I of Activity 6.5 lists the statements that students made in the first phase of a GRP. Listed in Part II of the activity are the categories in which students chose to group the facts that they listed.

Understanding Patterns of Organization

As many as 17 **patterns of organization**—ways in which segments of language can be ordered—have been identified in good writing. A few of them predominate in textbooks. The study and identification of patterns of organization in written material is called **discourse analysis**. When readers learn to recognize organizational patterns and the relationship between superordinate ideas and subordinate information, they take a giant step toward independence in reading.

We have combined research identifying several basic patterns (Kolozow & Lehmann, 1982) to target seven that often are recognizable in content textbooks: simple listing, sequential listing, analysis, cause and effect, comparison and contrast, definition, and analogy/example. We describe and illustrate each one in turn.

Simple Listing

A simple listing is an enumeration of facts or events in no special order. The superordinate information is the topic or event; the facts or traits that follow are the subordinate or supporting information. Some words that may signal this pattern are *also*, *another*, and *several*.

Example: "We presented several principles in Chapter 1. For the most part, each can be considered independently of the others. The first one stresses the relationship of the communicative arts to content-reading instruction. Another states that reading should be a pleasurable experience."

Sequential Listing

In a sequential listing, chronological or some other logical order of presentation is important. The superordinate information is the topic or event; the facts or traits then presented in appropriate order are the subordinate information. Henk

ACTIVITY 6.5 Guided-Reading Procedure: Earth Science

Part I

Statements from ninth-grade earth science students after the first reading:

1. The word *planet* comes from the Greek word for wanderer.
2. 11 kilometers per second is escape velocity.
3. Newton's third law of motion is that every action has an equal and opposite reaction.
4. Inertia is a little thing that doesn't let a planet travel in a straight line in space travel.
5. Newton has a theory of universal gravitation.
6. A reflecting telescope uses mirrors instead of a lens.
7. Heliocentric is a model of the solar system.
8. Astronomers used to think the sun and other planets revolved around the earth.
9. The earth's inertia combines with the sun's gravity to make us orbit around the sun.
10. Inertia is an object that keeps moving in one direction.
11. Refracting telescopes are tubes with lenses that bend the light from the stars.
12. Reflecting and refracting telescopes can only be used at night, so you have to use radio-telescopes during the day.
13. A satellite is an object in orbit around another large body.
14. Probes travel out to the other parts of the solar system.
15. In 1610, an Italian noble named Galileo was the first to use a telescope.
16. Isaac Newton was from England.
17. Sputnik was the first orbiter in 1957.
18. Nine planets orbit around the sun.
19. Reflecting telescopes use two or more mirrors to reflect stars' light.

Part II

Categories:

Celestial Bodies　　Celestial Mechanics　　Measuring Instruments

Recorded and developed by Brian Alexander.

and Helfeldt (1987) explain that even capable readers need assistance in applying the sequence patterns used in directions. Some words that signal this pattern are *first, second, next, before, during, then,* and *finally.*

Example: "Gray's may be the simplest and friendliest of the taxonomies. Gray said that one must first read the lines and then read between the lines; then one can read beyond the lines."

Analysis

Analysis takes an important idea (superordinate information) and investigates the relationships of the parts of that idea (subordinate information) to the whole. Some words and phrases that signal this pattern are *consider, analyze, investigate, the first part suggests,* and *this element means.*

Example: "Consider how the child concluded that the word he had been unable to pronounce was *oxygen*. The first portion of his behavior, when he skipped the word, indicated that he did not know the word at all. Yet he was able to recognize it when he had a context for it during the recall stage. This means that he was processing information all along."

Cause and Effect

The pattern of cause and effect takes an event or effect (the superordinate information) and presents discourse in terms of the causes (subordinate information) of that event. The effect is thus shown to be a result of causes. Some words and phrases that signal this pattern are *because, hence, therefore, as a result,* and *this led to.*

Example: "When teachers prepare students to read content material, they help students understand better. As a result of such preparation, teachers will see that students are more interested, pay more attention, and comprehend better."

Comparison and Contrast

Sometimes a writer seeks to highlight similarities and differences between facts, events, or authors. The basic comparison or contrast is the superordinate information, and the specific similarities and differences are the subordinate information. Some words and phrases that signal this pattern are *in contrast, in the same way, on the other hand, either . . . or,* and *similarly.*

Example: "A checklist offers less mathematical precision; on the other hand, it provides more qualitative information."

Definition

A definition provides an explanation of a concept or topic (superordinate information) by using synonyms to describe it (subordinate information). Some words and phrases that signal this pattern are *described as, synonymous with, is,* and *equals.*

Example: "Reading can be described as analytic, interactive, constructive, and strategic. The active, integrated thinking that leads to a conclusion as a result of reading is comprehension."

Analogy/Example

Analogies were introduced in Chapter 5 as a way to prepare readers. Sometimes a writer uses an example—a specific instance or a similar situation (subordinate information)—to explain a topic or concept (superordinate information). Analogies are a type of example. Some words and phrases that signal this pattern are *for example, for instance, likened to, analogous to,* and *is like.*

Example: "Reading is like a game of basketball. To play one's best game, lots of preparation and practice are necessary. In reading, this is analogous to preparing by determining and building background for the material to be read."

Often, more than one pattern is apparent in a single section of text. A writer may analyze by means of a comparison/contrast. Definition is often accompanied by example. Some patterns appear frequently in particular content subjects.

Table 6.1 suggests some possible matchings, but it is only a guide. Also, teachers need to consider the grade level they teach and the specific materials they use, because different patterns may dominate at different grade levels and in different subjects.

Strategic instruction will show readers how to identify patterns of organization. General or global comprehension of the material—understanding the text overall—is enhanced for the reader. One simple activity to raise awareness of organization is to have students peruse the table of contents of a textbook and ask, "How did the author organize this writing? What overall patterns of organization do you see in the table of contents?" Also, a teacher may simply ask students to identify the pattern of organization in a chapter, a subchapter, or even a paragraph. Teachers also can devise activities to assist readers in identifying patterns, as we explain in the next section.

Activities to Facilitate Understanding of Text Organization

When the teacher uses activities to assist understanding of text organization, reading to learn is much easier. Activities assist students and create an interesting learning environment. Here we present some of our favorites.

Mystery Clue Game

The group mystery clue game is designed to help readers understand sequence. It works very well when it is important for students to understand a sequence of events. The idea for this activity comes from *Turn-ons* (Smuin, 1978); we have adapted it to fit content materials.

1. To construct a mystery clue game, the teacher first studies the sequence of events in the material and writes clear, specific clue cards for each event. More than one card may be made for each clue.
2. The teacher divides the class into small groups and gives each group member at least one clue card. Each group can have one complete set of cards, but each group member is responsible for his or her own cards within that set.
3. No student may show a card to another in the group, but cards can be

TABLE 6.1 Some Patterns of Organization Used Frequently in Content Textbooks

Science	*Math*	*Social Studies*	*English*	*Health*
Sequential listing	Sequential listing	Cause/effect	Cause/effect	Comparison/contrast
Cause/effect	Simple listing	Simple listing	Comparison/contrast	Simple listing
Definition	Analysis	Example	Example	Definition
	Definition	Analysis		

read aloud or paraphrased so that all group members know what is on each card. In this way, students who are poor readers will still be encouraged to try to read and to participate.

4. Each group of students must use the clues the teacher gives them to solve the mystery. For example, they must find the murderer, the weapon, the time and place of the murder, the motive, and the victim. Or they must find the equation that will solve a problem, or the formula that will make a chemical.
5. A time limit is usually given.
6. A group scribe reports the group's solution to the whole class.
7. Students are instructed to read the material to find out which group came closest to solving the mystery.

This cooperative activity promotes oral language as well as reading, and it works well in most content areas. For instance, science teachers can write clues to performing an experiment, mathematics teachers can write clues to deriving a formula, and social studies teachers can write clues to sequencing historical events. The goal of the activity is for students to approximate the sequence of events before reading and then read with the purpose of checking their predictions. It is not necessary for students to memorize specific details. As they read, they will think back to their clues and construct meaning.

Activity 6.6 is a mystery clue game for a French lesson to assist students in mastering the Paris Metro. Students in small groups have to read (translate) the ten clue cards (without referring to their textbooks) and put the cards in the correct chronological order. In doing so, students learn the logical steps in taking the Paris Metro and grasp the relationship between the Metro, the grammar, and the vocabulary presented in the French textbook. In Chapter 12 we present a mystery clue game for at-risk first-graders.

Pattern Guides

Pattern guides (Herber, 1978; Vacca & Vacca, 1999) will be most useful in helping students recognize a predominant pattern such as cause and effect or comparison and contrast. To construct them, the teacher locates the pattern, decides on the major ideas to be stressed, and designs the pattern-oriented guide.

Pattern guides can help students see causal relationships. Students need to learn to distinguish cause and effect when reading text materials, especially in social studies, science, and vocational education. Simply asking students to search for causes is often not successful; students tend to neglect—or worse, misunderstand and misuse—this pattern without the teacher's intervention, support, and patience. Moreover, finding causal relationships is difficult because the cause of an event or situation may not be known or may be not traceable. Even so, students should endeavor to distinguish cause and effect for practice in the thinking it affords. Activity 6.7 provides an example of a cause-and-effect guide at middle-school level. A compare/contrast pattern guide in intermediate social studies appears as Activity 6.8.

ACTIVITY 6.6 Mystery Clue Game for a French Lesson

Luc et Jérome veulent aller au Louvre pour apprendre quelque chose pour leur classe d'art.

A la bouche du métro ils regardent le plan et ils comprennent qu'il faut prendre une correspondance.

Ils prennent la direction Porte de Clignancourt et ils prennent une autre correspondance aux Halles.

Bon! Ils sont là!

Après le musée, ils font des achats.

Ils n'ont pas de voiture. C'est trop loin—ils ne peuvent pas aller à pied ou prendre leurs vélos. Le taxi est trop cher, ainsi ils veulent prendre le métro.

Ils vont au métro—c'est la station Maubert-Mutalité. Ils achètent deux billets de seconde.

D'abord, ils prennent la direction Boulogne–Point de St Cloud, et ils changent à Odéon.

Ils prennent la direction Pont de Neuilly. Ils descendent à Louvre.

Ils entrent dans le Louvre où ils voient la Joconde (Mona Lisa) et la Vénus de Milo.

ENGLISH TRANSLATION IN CHRONOLOGICAL ORDER

1. Luke and Jeremy want to go to the Louvre in order to learn something for their art class.
2. They don't have a car. It is too far—they can't walk or take their bikes. A taxi costs too much, so they want to take the Metro.
3. At the Metro entrance, they look at the map and they understand that they will have to transfer to another line on the Metro.
4. They go into the Metro station "Maubert-Mutalité." They buy two second-class tickets.
5. First, they take "Boulogne–Point de Saint Cloud" direction, and they change at "Odéon."
6. They take "Porte de Clignancourt" direction, and they make another change at "Les Halles."
7. They take the "Pont de Neuilly" direction. They get off at "Louvre."
8. Good! They are there.
9. They enter the Louvre, where they see the *Mona Lisa* and the *Venus de Milo*.
10. After the museum, they run errands.

Developed by Laura Clevinger.

Organizational (Jot) Charts

Jot charts organize text information by showing comparisons and contrasts. Students complete a matrix as a way to see how ideas are alike and different. Jot charts are relatively simple to construct and can be used at any grade level and in any content area. The teacher usually sets up the matrix and encourages students to fill it in as they read. In this way, students understand the relationships and build meaning as they read. When completed, jot charts become a good study aid. If they are filled in by groups of students, the social aspects of learning are also included in the activity.

We present three examples of jot charts to demonstrate their diversity in activating comprehension. The chart in Activity 6.9 was developed for an elementary-science unit. Activity 6.10 shows a chart developed for a middle-school drama class. Activity 6.11 depicts a chart of mathematical formulas.

ACTIVITY 6.7 Cause-and-Effect Pattern Guide: Back Bay and False Cape State Parks

Name ______________________________

Based on information from the reading selection, match the effects listed in the second column to the causes listed in the first column. Be prepared to explain your choices.

CAUSES

___ 1. Inland, away from the ocean, the influence of salt spray decreases.

___ 2. Grasses disappeared in the bay waters around 1980.

___ 3. There was a great amount of dredging and development along the northern part of the bay.

___ 4. Residential subdivisions, a golf course, and farms use chemicals to eliminate weeds and fertilize land.

___ 5. The Civilian Conservation Corps built dunes up along the seashore.

___ 6. In the absence of grasses, algae feed on the nutrients.

___ 7. Currituck Inlet closed naturally, and the Knotts Island Causeway was built in 1890.

___ 8. Eurasian milfoil grass was planted and spread to cover 88% of the bay floor.

___ 9. Marsh grass is abundant in the tidal flatlands.

___ 10. City officials commissioned a study of Back Bay.

EFFECTS

a. Maritime forests and inland marshes are protected from the ocean.

b. Water circulation was cut down, and the salinity (saltiness) of the water in the bay decreased.

c. Stormwater management regulations were made to control runoff from new development, and new development was limited upstream from Back Bay.

d. Low shrubs and trees are able to grow, forming the maritime forest habitat.

e. The bay water gets cloudy and blocks the sunlight needed to grow grasses.

f. Food depended on by the waterfowl disappeared, sediment at the bottom of the bay was free to erode, and fish lost their cover.

g. 40% of the citation largemouth bass caught in Virginia came out of Back Bay by 1978.

h. Erosion is reduced, nutrients are recycled, and habitats for many species of fish and other wildlife are created.

i. Nitrogen and phosphorus levels in the bay water exceed state reference levels and pose a serious water quality problem.

j. Sediment flooded into the bay from streams and tributaries, causing loss of sunlight reaching the grasses.

Developed by Mark Forget.

Venn Diagrams

Venn diagrams provide another way to demonstrate similarities and differences. Facts or ideas about the topic from two different perspectives or eras are listed in two different columns. Then similarities are listed in a third, central column. The differences and similarities are enclosed in two circles that overlap, with the overlapping portion listing the similarities and the nonoverlapping portions listing the differences. This graphic depiction helps readers see, understand, and

ACTIVITY 6.8 Pattern Guide: Communities Everywhere Have Needs

Thesis: Communities everywhere have needs. Some communities are alike and some are different.

Directions:
1. Read each sentence.
2. Decide if the sentence tells how communities are alike or how they are different.
3. Place an *A* beside the sentence if it shows how communities are *alike*.
4. Place a *D* beside the sentence if it shows how communities are *different*.

When everyone is finished, we will discuss our answers.

_____ 1. Communities everywhere have a need to communicate.
_____ 2. The people of China speak many different dialects.
_____ 3. The people of Africa speak many different dialects. One language spoken is Swahili.
_____ 4. People everywhere live and work together.
_____ 5. People everywhere need food and shelter.
_____ 6. The people of China use chopsticks when eating.
_____ 7. The people of Quebec speak French.
_____ 8. The people in Canada enjoy going to concerts, just like the people in America.
_____ 9. The people of Africa enjoy listening to and watching a storyteller.
_____ 10. The people in Dakar enjoy watching television.
_____ 11. An abacus is used for counting in China.
_____ 12. People everywhere need transportation.
_____ 13. People everywhere need to communicate in writing.
_____ 14. The Chinese language has characters instead of letters.
_____ 15. Rice is an important grain in China.

Developed by Vicki Douglas.

---

remember the patterns. Activity 6.12 is a Venn diagram for comparing and contrasting education now with education in the 1800s. It is designed for a fourth-grade history class.

Using Questioning Strategies to Facilitate Comprehension

Experts have described many levels of comprehension, but it is useful to condense our initial discussion to three: (1) understanding the facts, (2) seeing the implications of the reading, and (3) applying this understanding to other topics or areas. Fact, implication, and application are the three levels that classroom content teachers will employ when assisting their students' comprehension. They represent a way to facilitate comprehension, not to simplify or isolate information.

ACTIVITY 6.9 Jot Chart: Third-Grade Science

Nutrient	*How this nutrient helps your body*	*Examples of foods that contain this nutrient*
Protein	Helps your body make new cells	peanuts, eggs, beans, fish, peanut butter
Carbohydrate	Gives you quick energy	pineapples, bananas, rice, pasta, strawberries, green beans, corn, potatoes
Fats	Give your body energy to store	bacon, peanuts, cheese, steak, butter, walnuts
Vitamins and minerals	Help your body use proteins, carbohydrates, and fats	bananas, milk, orange juice, whole wheat bread, whole grain cereal
Water	Makes up half of your body weight	Almost all foods and liquids contain some water.

Developed by Mendy Mathena.

Understanding at all levels must be connected to be effective. Teachers will want their students to read the material carefully for a literal understanding of the facts, to see the connection between the facts and the entire subject, and to apply what they have learned to other situations. Consider the following as an example of these three basic levels of comprehension. To understand the significance of the Alamo in American history, students must comprehend the following: (1) *facts*—what the Alamo is, where it is located, and what happened there; (2) *implications*—why the Battle of the Alamo is considered so important even though it involved very few people; (3) *application*—why expressions such as "Remember the Alamo" might inspire soldiers going to battle.

Preparing Three-Level Guides

Readers must grasp the facts before they can interpret and apply them. Usually, comprehension at the literal level precedes comprehension at the implication level, which in turn precedes comprehension at the application level. This hierarchical relationship is called a **taxonomy**. Many reading professionals have developed guides to comprehension based on this three-level taxonomy. Gray's (1960) may be the simplest and friendliest. Gray said that one must first read the lines and then read between the lines before one can read beyond the lines. Herber (1978) called the three levels of comprehension *literal*, *interpretive*, and *applied*.

Three-level guides (Herber, 1978) connect and integrate the three levels of comprehension with a series of statements to which students react. Because

ACTIVITY 6.10 Character Clue Chart: "Trifles" by Susan Glaspell

Name	*Physical*	*Mental/Emotional*	*Environmental*	*Background*
Sheriff Peters	mid-life heavily dressed against the cold	businesslike, practical	cold, spends most of time investigating upstairs	came to arrest Mrs. Wright last night
County Attorney Henderson	young man note-taker heavy clothes for the cold	impatient, bossy, suspicious, condescending, critical, sarcastic, facetious	cold, notices messy threadbare house, keeps looking for clues, motive	here to investigate and accuse Mrs. Wright
Mr. Hale	mid-life heavy clothes for the cold	neighborly, helpful	cold, most of the time upstairs	farmer, on the farm nearby, found the dead body
Mrs. Peters	slight, wiry, thin nervous face frightened voice heavy clothes for the cold	nervous, browbeaten, frightened, apologetic, believes in the law and punishment	cold, in the kitchen	sheriff's wife, coming to get a few things to take to Mrs. Wright in jail, not raised in this area, bad experience as a child, also her 2-yr.-old died
Mrs. Hale	large, "comfortable" heavy clothes for the cold	disturbed, fearful, defensive, protective, loyal, resentful, compassionate, hard-working	cold, familiar in the kitchen and on a farm	friend to Mrs. Wright when they were young, hadn't visited for a year, a hard-working farm wife, knew Mr. Wright and didn't like him.

Who are the people in your play? What are they like? As you read your script, watch for clues about the characters. In the appropriate squares, list the facts you find.

Developed by Candace Wyngaard.

three-level guides demonstrate the hierarchical nature of comprehension and call for student reaction to a series of statements, they provide a comprehensive activity for assisting comprehension. Such guides should not be used every day. But when used occasionally to help readers see the interconnectedness of literal, inferential, and applied learning, the three-level guide is an excellent activity. Activities 6.13, 6.14, and 6.15 are examples of three-level guides from classes in business management, English, and mathematics. They offer some variety in the use of directions and distracters and in consideration of age and content.

Three-level guides need follow no exact or specific requirements, but certain guidelines are helpful in their construction. The following are based on

ACTIVITY 6.11 Jot Chart: Formulas

	Shape	Picture	Perimeter/Surface Area	Area/ Volume
2-dimensional	Circle	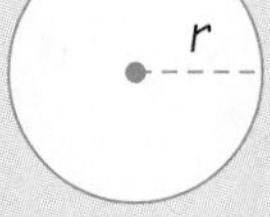 r	$2\pi r$	πr^2
	Triangle	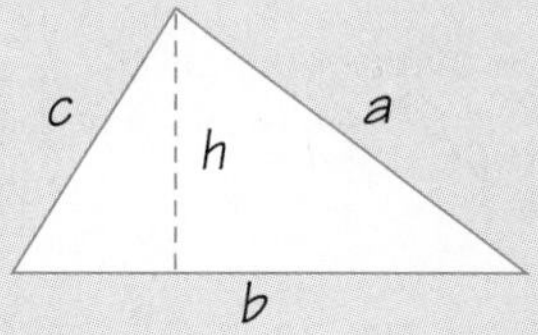 c, h, a, b	$a + b + c$	$\frac{1}{2} bh$
	Square	 x	$4x$	x^2
	Rectangle	 w, l	$2l + 2w$	lw
3-dimensional			Surface Area	Volume
	Cone	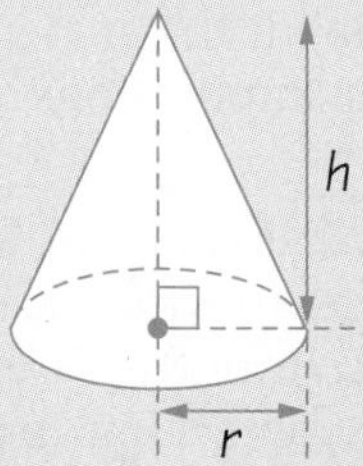 h, r	$\pi rh + \pi r^2$	$\frac{1}{3}\pi r^2 h$
	Rectangular Box	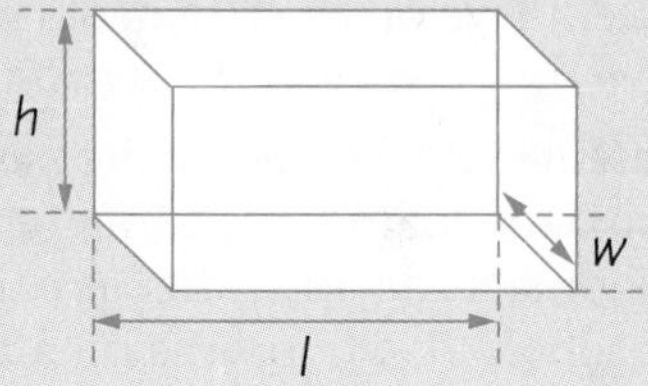 h, w, l	$2(lw) +$ $2(lw) +$ $2(hw) =$ surface area	lwh

Developed by Serena Marshall.

ACTIVITY 6.12 Venn Diagram of History Lesson, Fourth Grade

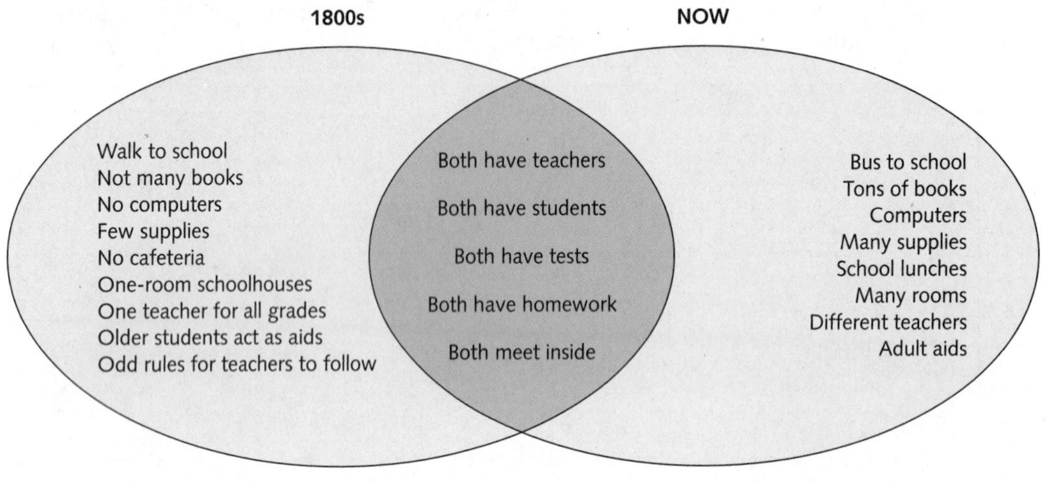

Developed by Heather L. Brown.

suggestions by Herber (1978) and Vacca and Vacca (1999) and our own trial-and-error experiences:

1. Determine whether the text material requires students to (a) understand a superordinate concept, (b) identify subordinate details, and (c) understand applications of the concept. If it does, a three-level guide will be an appropriate activity.
2. Determine the content objectives. What specifically do you want the students to know about this material? This specific content should be the major ideas, the implications, or the interpretation that you want students to learn.
3. Take these content ideas and create a series of statements from them. (Some teachers prefer to write main ideas as questions, then rephrase them as statements, until they are comfortable with the generation of statements. Other teachers like to insert a mental "The author means" in front of each statement to ensure that the statements match the interpretation level.) Five or six statements will be ideal. Edit them for clarity. You have now designed the second level of your guide.
4. Study these statements and refer to the passage to identify the major facts that support the main ideas contained in your level 2 statements. Write these major facts down, either as paraphrases or as exact replications. (Some teachers like to insert a mental "The author says" in front of these statements to ensure that the statements match the literal

ACTIVITY 6.13 Three-Level Study Guide in Business Management

Determining Credit Standing
From: *Business, Principles and Management*

I. Check what the author said. Check three.

_____ 1. Businesses often apply for the "4 c's" of credit.

_____ 2. *Capacity* refers to technical know-how and sound performance.

_____ 3. *Conditions* deals with an applicant's financial worth.

_____ 4. *Character* relates to the economic conditions of the economy.

_____ 5. A credit check is needed for a trade credit application.

II. What did the author mean? Check three.

_____ 1. Retaining credit is more difficult to get than trade credit.

_____ 2. Having capital is an important factor for credit after someone has lost a job.

_____ 3. Paying one's debts in a steady and timely fashion is important for keeping a good credit rating.

_____ 4. The most important factor in getting credit is one's earning power and potential for earning money.

_____ 5. The stability of the local economy may be a factor in a person obtaining credit.

III. What can we take from this reading as being important in our own lives? Check any.

_____ 1. Our past can come home to haunt us.

_____ 2. Live for today — spend all you want and have fun.

_____ 3. Reputation is built slowly over time and must be carefully guarded.

_____ 4. Nothing succeeds like success.

_____ 5. You are the master of your ship.

_____ 6. Time is the school in which we learn, and time is the fire in which we burn.

ACTIVITY 6.14 Three-Level Guide for Thoreau's *Walden*, Chapter 1, "Economy"

Henry's House Rules

Directions: This is a worksheet to help ensure that we are all on the "same page" in *Walden*. Working in pairs and thinking about what we've just read, read the statements in each of the three sections. **Circle the letters** of the statements that you think **do not apply** to this chapter. At least one statement at each level is **not** an accurate reflection of what Thoreau said or meant.

The **Level One** instruction means "Does Thoreau say this plainly?" The sentence may be word for word from your text, or I may have put it in my own words.

Level Two is **not asking** for Thoreau's exact words or the face value of the statement. It is asking for the **meaning** that you think Thoreau wants to get across to the reader.

Level Three contains statements that Thoreau might—or might not—say to you today if he were in our classroom. These statements apply to modern life. Be sure you can explain why you believe he would—or would not—say these statements in Level Three.

Level One: What did Thoreau say? Choose one statement that does **not** fit.

1. The mass of men lead lives of quiet desperation.
2. If I repent anything, it is very likely my good behavior.
3. Shelter is so necessary that it is very important to own your own house.
4. Living well is living simply and wisely.
5. It is not necessary that a man should earn his living by the sweat of his brow.

Level Two: What did Thoreau mean? Choose two statements that **don't** fit.

1. Most people today are not really happy with the life they lead; life is more of a struggle than a joy.
2. Following society's mores is the way to become your very best "self" and will lead to a satisfying life.
3. It is worth whatever amount of work it takes to own your house.
4. We get so caught up in materialism and striving for things we don't really need that it complicates our lives.
5. The work we do should not drain us of energy and joy.

Level Three: How would Thoreau's thoughts or philosophies apply to modern life? Choose one statement that does **not** fit.

1. In order to live life fully, we need to be able to enjoy and appreciate what we are doing at the moment; if we wish we could do something else, we need to figure out why we feel this way and what we might do to correct the situation.
2. We need to examine our personal reasons for the things we do, say, and think; simply conforming to the status quo diminishes our personality and our capacity to live our own lives.
3. You cannot live your own life fully until you own your own place and are then able to do whatever you want.
4. We work so hard to get things that it seems as though our possessions own us; our "stuff" (or what we want to get) rules the way we live.
5. The work we choose should not be drudgery to us.

Developed by Margaret M. Brulatour.

ACTIVITY 6.15 A Three-Level Guide for Math

I. Below are eight sentences. Read each one and check the ones that you think say what your author says on pages 1–3. If you have trouble, read the section referred to in parentheses.

_____ Statements made in mathematics have to be true or false. (page 1, paragraph 1)
_____ Statements made in mathematics have to be true. (p. 1, par. 1)
_____ It is possible to make false statements true by using negation. (p. 3)
_____ A value can have more than one expression. (p. 1, par. 2)
_____ A value is defined as a numerical expression. (p. 1, par. 2)
_____ Equations indicate that a numerical expression either equals or does not equal a specified value. (p. 2)
_____ Equations have to contain two expressions of equal value. (p. 2)
_____ Conjunctions and disjunctions are statements using *and, but,* or *or* to link numerical expressions about a value. (p. 2)

II. Place the following number sentences under the correct column. Sentences may be used more than once or not at all! Portions of sentences can be used in some columns.

$4 + 3 \neq 7$
$2 + 2 = 4$ or $2/2 = 4$
$4 + 1$ and $3 + 2$ and $5 = 5$
$6 + 1 = 8$
Divide 9 by 3.
It is not true that $6 + 1 = 8$.

Numerical Expression	Statement	Value	Equation	Conjunction	Disjunction	Negation

III. Consider each assertion below. Check it if you agree with it. Star it if you think it can be supported by information on pages 1–4, and tell why.

_____ Statements are more than assertions.
_____ Values can be expressed in different ways but still be the same values.
_____ Symbols often convey meaning more efficiently than words.
_____ It is important to think carefully about what a statement means.

Developed from information on pages 1–4 of Chapter 1, "Mathematical Statements and Proofs," of *Modern School Mathematics*, 1971, Boston: Houghton Mifflin.

level.) You should have about two literal statements to support each major inference. These statements constitute level 1 of the guide.

5. Now you are ready to design the third level. Statements at level 3 should apply the major ideas but also should capitalize on students' previous knowledge. These statements often look like those developed for an anticipation guide; the difference is that statements constructed for a three-level guide are directly connected to the passage content. (Some teachers like to insert a mental "We can use" in front of these statements to ensure that the statements match the applied level.) Probably four or more of these statements will round out the guide.

6. Devise your directions and decide whether you want to add some distracters, particularly at level 1. Both of these tasks will depend very much on your students' ages, abilities, and appreciation of the content. Make certain that directions are complete and clear. If distracters are added, make certain that your students are ready for them.

When introducing three-level guides for the first few times, teachers should use them as a whole-class activity. All students should have individual copies or be able to view the guide on a chalkboard or overhead projector. In this way, all students experience the new activity at once, discussion is promoted in a non-threatening environment, and students become acclimated to the new activity. Since the value of three-level guides lies in understanding at three levels and in articulating that understanding, oral communication is an important part of the activity. By discussing reactions with each other, students begin to realize the interdependence of facts, implications, and applications in understanding a topic. Three-level guides promote constructive comprehension at its best. The teacher's problem will be to cut off the discussion at an appropriate time. What a wonderful problem to have!

After gaining some experience with guides, students can use them in small groups or independently with homework assignments. At this point, if students are sophisticated enough to be discerning, distracters are a desirable addition. If too many distracters are used initially at levels 2 and 3, they can give a hidden message to students that there really are right and wrong responses to these statements. Used later, they can give the message that it is important to be a discriminating reader.

Like anticipation guides, three-level guides offer plentiful writing opportunities. Because the statements require students to connect their prior knowledge with new information, particularly at level 3, teachers can ask students to write explanations of why they responded in a certain way to a statement. To encourage reflection, teachers might ask students to write their own statements for each level.

Three-level guides are not necessarily easy to construct. Teachers need to practice making and using them. It might be wise to ask a teacher who is familiar with guides to look at yours before you try it in a class. Once you have tried three-level guides, you will receive student feedback about your construction efforts. Since the assistance that three-level guides provide to readers is immediately discernible, you probably will be as enthusiastic about them as most teachers are.

Questioning for Comprehension

Durkin (1979) found that teachers rely on questioning more than on any other comprehension technique. When it works, it works very well. Questions can help teachers to know whether students understand text and can guide readers to consider many aspects of material. Question-generated discussions lead to the creation of meaning for readers (Alvermann, O'Brien, & Dillon, 1990; Barton,

1995). Questions are excellent probes. Robert Sternberg (1994) argues that the ability to ask good questions and to know how to answer them is the most essential part of intelligence. Well-considered questions are essential to guide students' thinking and reasoning abilities (Marashio, 1995; LeNoir, 1993). Often, however, questioning does not work very well because teachers fall into some common traps.

As we pointed out earlier, a major reason why questioning is not successful is that teachers confuse the *product* of comprehension with the *process* of learning when they question. A teacher who requires students to close their books and recite information before they have a chance to assimilate that information is testing a product rather than assisting the process of constructing meaning. Furthermore, recitation relies on the literal level and does not encourage higher-level thinking.

A second trap is to write questions that focus on literal comprehension. Gusak (1967) reported that 78 percent of the questions asked in second grade were literal, 65 percent in fourth grade were literal, and 58 percent in sixth grade were literal. Observing at the upper-elementary level, Durkin (1979) found that teachers asked mostly literal questions, expecting a specific response. Durkin (1981) then studied teachers' manuals for basal reading instruction and discovered that low-level literal questions with one correct response were the major instructional strategy provided for teachers. Newer research shows the emphasis hasn't changed. Armbruster and colleagues (1991) studied science and social studies lessons for fourth-graders and found that 90 percent of the questions were teacher generated and explicit. In a study of two American history classes, Sturtevant (1992) found that teachers stressed textbook reading and factual information. Reutzel and Daines (1987) reached the same conclusion after a study of seven major basal readers. When Young and Daines (1992) looked at the types of questions that students and their teachers asked, they found that students were more likely to ask interpretive questions and teachers asked literal questions about the same material.

Getting little practice in answering higher-level questions, students are ill equipped to think critically. Elementary students are trapped into expecting only literal questions; secondary students will remain in the trap because the literal question has been their previous experience. Research shows, however, that when instructional strategies are altered so that the focus is on inferences and main ideas, students respond with improved recall and greater understanding (Hansen, 1981; Hansen & Pearson, 1983; Raphael, 1984). Cooter, Joseph, and Flynt (1986) were able to show that third- and fourth-graders who were asked no literal questions in a five-month period performed significantly better than a control group on inferential comprehension and just as well on literal comprehension. Menke and Pressley (1994) encourage teachers and their students to use *why* questions because their use greatly increases factual memory.

When students are encouraged to develop their own questions, they develop higher-level understanding. Ciardello (1998) argues that the process of asking questions helps students to focus on and learn content, as well as develop cognitive strategies that will help them understand new and challenging material. Ciardello describes a technique called TeachQuest, in which the teacher guides students through a series of steps to identify and classify divergent-thinking questions. The goal is for students to generate their own divergent-thinking questions. Crapse (1995) reports that "through the experience of honest questioning, I have observed students celebrating their own insights and solutions to problems posed" (p. 390).

Providing students with a prompt for generating their own questions of many varieties and on many levels can also be helpful. A social studies teacher adapted the "Question Mark: Questioning for Quality Thinking," Activity 6.16, from a bookmark format developed by the Maryland State Department of Education. The bookmark uses Bloom's (1956) six-level taxonomy of questions: knowledge, comprehension, application, analysis, synthesis, and evaluation. Reminders of what each level means and stimulus questions are written on the bookmark. This bookmark works especially well for students when doing a Directed Reading/Thinking Activity (explained earlier in this chapter) by helping them generate questions beyond the factual level. It will eliminate boredom often associated with answering textbook questions that too often are low level. This technique also gives students opportunities to use inference, because many of the questions they ask will not be answered directly in the text.

Another trap that teachers sometimes fall into is misjudging the difficulty of the questions they are asking or failing to match the questions to the students' ability. Generally, questions are simplest when students are to recognize and locate answers in the text rather than close their books and try to recall the same information. Easy questions also include those asked during reading or shortly after reading, questions that have only one or two parts, oral questions rather than written ones, and those that allow students to choose an answer from among several alternatives. We are not suggesting that all questions should be asked in the simplest manner; we are cautioning that many times teachers do not consider the difficulty of their questions and their students' ability to answer them.

A final trap that often snares teachers is focusing more on the questions asked and the responses expected than on the students' actual responses. Recall that Durkin's research cited earlier in this discussion found that teachers too often expect one response and do not consider an alternative. As Dillon (1983) remarks, we should "stress the nature of questions rather than their frequency and pace, and the type of student response rather than the type of teacher question" (p. 8). Students' answers can tell a lot about their understanding of the topic. We need to listen for answers that let us know how well we are assisting the development of comprehension.

Constructing Good Questions

We have learned much about how to question from the extensive studies of reading comprehension conducted over the past few decades. Although much of this research has been conducted with elementary students, the implications are relevant for secondary instruction as well. Students who have not received a firm foundation in reading comprehension in elementary school will

ACTIVITY 6.16 Higher-Level Questioning Bookmark

Question Mark: Questioning for Quality Thinking

Knowledge: Identification and recall of information
Who, what, when, where, how ___________?
Describe ___________.

Comprehension: Organization and selection of facts and ideas
Retell ___________ in your own words. What is the main idea of ___________?

Application: Use of facts, rules, principles
How is ___________ an example of ___________?
How is ___________ related to ___________?
Why is ___________ significant?

Analysis: Separation of a whole into component parts
What are the parts or features of ___________?
Classify ___________ according to ___________.
Outline/diagram/web ___________.
How does ___________ compare/contrast with ___________?
What evidence can you list for ___________?

Synthesis: Combination of ideas to form a new whole
What would you predict/infer from ___________?
What ideas can you add to ___________?
How would you create/design a new ___________?
What might happen if you combined ___________ with ___________?
What solutions would you suggest for ___________?

Evaluation: Development of opinions, judgments, or decisions
Do you agree ___________?
What do you think about ___________?
What is the most important ___________?
Prioritize ___________.
How would you decide about ___________?
What criteria would you use to assess ___________?

Maryland State Department of Education; adapted by Mark Forget.

not be well equipped in secondary school. To help teachers construct good questions, we summarize here what we consider the most important research considerations:

1. Simplify your questions! Although teachers want to challenge their students, they should challenge within a range that allows students to succeed. Consider using these guidelines:

a. Identify the purpose of the questions. (Will it measure fact, implication, or applied levels of comprehension? A particular organizational pattern? A superordinate or subordinate idea?) Is this purpose justified? Does it contribute to a balance of comprehension levels within the lesson?

b. Identify the type of response demanded by the question (recognition, recall, production, or generation of a new idea from the information). Is this expectation justified, given the age and ability of the group? Have you provided an example of what you want? If you wish students to produce a modern dialogue for a character in *Hamlet*, can you give them an example first?

c. Might the question elicit more than one reasonable response? If this is a possibility, will you be able to accept different responses and use them to assist instruction?

d. Does this question contain several parts? Will these parts be clear to the students, and can they remember all of the parts as they respond?

e. Write the question clearly and concisely. Then decide whether to pose it orally or in writing.

2. Share with students the reasons for your questions. Let them know the process you use to develop questions and the process you would use to answer them. This knowledge helps them to see what types of questions are important to you in this area (Pearson, 1985). It also helps them to understand how they should be thinking when they respond and what you are thinking when you question. This process—thinking about thinking—is called **metacognition** (Babbs & Moe, 1983). Helping students think about your reasoning and about their own reading processes eventually will produce independent readers. This sharing is a form of think-aloud (Davey, 1983), discussed in Chapter 11, and think-along (Ehlinger & Pritchard, 1994).

3. Encourage students to ask questions about your questions and to ask their own questions. Goodlad (1984) suggests that students will thrive when they can participate in classroom questioning more directly than they do in most classrooms today. Beyer (1984) says that teacher-dominated questioning inhibits student independence and limits thinking. "Instruction that leads to systematic question-asking by students would be more appropriate, but such an approach is rare indeed" (p. 489).

4. Provide plenty of practice in answering questions at different levels of comprehension. Check yourself occasionally to make sure that you are not leaning on the literal level too heavily. Training and practice result in learning the material (Brown, Campione, & Day, 1981; Paris, Cross, & Lipson, 1984) and in learning how to understand material in sophisticated ways. Wassermann (1987) argues that students' depth and breadth

of understanding improve when they are asked challenging questions. Also, students who learn to take another's perspective may become better readers as a result (Gardner & Smith, 1987). But students must have opportunities for practice to master this ability.

5. Allow discussions, which give students practice in asking and answering questions (Perez & Strickland, 1987; Alvermann, 1987a; Alvermann et al., 1996). Chapter 7 contains many suggestions for generating student discussions to facilitate critical thinking.
6. Ask students the types of questions you know they are able to answer. Try not to expect too much too soon, but do expect as much as students can do. For example, research indicates that students can identify main-idea statements earlier than they can make such statements (Afflerbach, 1987). If students seem consistently unable to answer a certain type of comprehension question even after you have followed these suggestions, we suggest that you review the most recent findings in the research literature for clues.

The Question/Answer Relationship

Raphael (1984, 1986) has studied and applied the **question/answer relationship (QAR)**. QAR is a four-level taxonomy: (1) right there, (2) think and search, (3) the author and you, and (4) on your own. The best way to introduce QAR is with a visual aid showing the QAR relationship. Figure 6.4 shows one teacher's illustrated introduction to QAR.

After introducing QAR, the teacher uses a short passage to demonstrate how QAR is applied. To model the use of QAR, the teacher provides, labels, and answers at least one question at each QAR level. The teacher then moves gradually to having students answer questions and identifying the QAR for themselves. At various times throughout the school year, the teacher should refer to QAR. Activity 6.17 lists QAR questions that a primary-mathematics teacher used.

Because QAR is a straightforward procedure, easily implemented, quickly beneficial to students, and useful at any grade and in any content area, we encourage content teachers to use it in their instruction. QAR has been proven to increase students' comprehension more than several other questioning strategies have (Jenkins & Lawler, 1990). Research (Ezell, H. K. and colleagues, 1996) shows that students who used QAR maintain good comprehension skills during their next school year. They show the most proficiency with text-explicit questions; they do not perform quite as well with implicit questioning. QAR fosters listening, speaking, and reading, and if students write their own questions, it also offers opportunities for writing.

Guide-o-Ramas and Marginal Glosses

A guide-o-rama (Cunningham & Shablak, 1975) alerts the reader to notice certain information in a reading passage. The teacher creates directions for these passages and encourages the students to use the directions as they read. For instance, if the teacher sees that the word *perverse* is used in an unusual way, he

QAR

I. Where is the answer?

Right there!

Words are right there in the text.

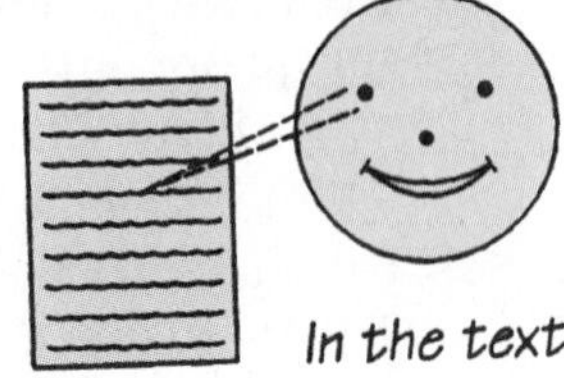

II. Where is the answer?

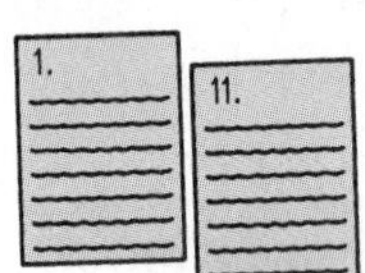

Think and search!

Words are in the text but not spelled out for you. Think about what the author is saying.

Hmm! Gotta think about this.

III. Where is the answer?

What I know

You and the author!

Think about what you have learned and what is in the text.

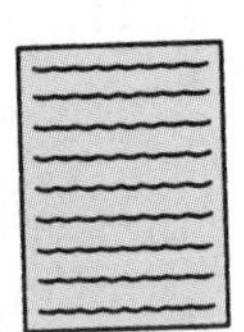

What the author says

IV. Where is the answer?

On your own!

Answer is in your head!

FIGURE 6.4

Introduction to QAR

ACTIVITY 6.17 QAR Questions in Primary-Level Math

These QAR questions are used with *Alexander, Who Used to Be Rich Last Sunday*, by Judith Viorst (1978). Alexander receives a dollar from his grandparents. Where did the money go? The book tells about how Alexander spent the money and what he has left—bus tokens.

Right There: How much money did Alexander receive from his grandparents?

Think and Search: How did Alexander spend his money?

Author and You: Do you think Alexander spent his money wisely?

On My Own: If you had a dollar, how would you spend it?

---

might write this: "On page 13, second paragraph, third line, the word *perverse* is used a little differently from what you'd expect. Pay attention to the meaning." When a teacher prepares several directions such as this and gives them to readers to refer to while reading, readers have a panoramic view of the reading—hence the name *guide-o-rama*.

Marginal glosses (Singer & Donlan, 1985) are often found in content textbooks. Glosses are comments that authors make to their readers as asides, sometimes in the margin of the page. Because the comments are intended to help the reader understand the passage, they assist the reader in developing comprehension. Teachers can write their own marginal glosses if texts do not include them or if additional ones are needed. Also, a guide-o-rama can be designed as a gloss.

Singer and Donlan (1985) suggest that teachers make marginal glosses as follows:

1. Fold a ditto master against the margin of a text.
2. Identify the book page at the top of the master, and line up numbers beside the teacher directives.
3. Write the marginal notes on the ditto master.
4. Duplicate and give students copies of these notes to match to text pages and lines as they read.

Marginal glosses and guide-o-ramas are like having the teacher go home with the students and look over their shoulders as they read, guiding their reading attention. These strategies can help students use features of text as well as help teachers facilitate comprehension by questioning. We suggest that the teacher select either very difficult portions of text to gloss or beginning portions, when the reading may be tougher. Making guide-o-ramas or glosses for use throughout a text would be very time-consuming. However, to provide assistance in developing comprehension of challenging reading, they are worth the time. Activity 6.18 is a marginal gloss for high school mathematics; Activity 6.19 is one for high school earth science.

ACTIVITY 6.18 Marginal Gloss for High School Mathematics

5–1 Compound
Sentences

pg 246

Objectives:

① Graph compound sentences in one variable on the # line.

② Solve systems of inequalities by graphing

Key Concept:

A ∩ B

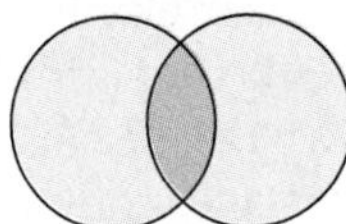

Set A Set B

Key Concept:

A ∪ B

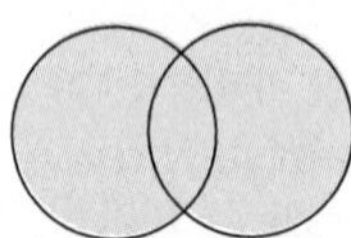

Set A Set B

Tip:

To help to distinguish between ∩ & ∪, think of a labor union for "∪" and think of street intersections for "∩". Why are these analogies helpful?

Developed by Suzanna Hintz.

ACTIVITY 6.19 Marginal Gloss for High School Earth Science

How can I use this information?

1. Vocabulary Word ________________
   Definition in your own words:
   (Use the picture for help, if needed.)

2. What do you think *mass* is?

3. Why do you think ice floats in water?

4. Why do you think the average Earth density is greater than the average density of the Earth's crust?

5. Given a rock with a mass of 550g and a density of 2.75 g/cm^3, calculate the volume of the rock.

6. BRING A ROCK TO CLASS TOMORROW—no larger than an egg!

7. What brand-name product has used density of the product in its advertising?

Place on top edge at p. ___ in binding.

Complete this side first.

Part I: What Do I Know?

Topic Heading:

Vocabulary Word:

Using words, give the density formula:

Recall: Volume = length × width × height

Average Earth density (include units):

Average density of Earth's crust (include units):

Recall from Chapter 1 two (2) materials found in the Earth's core:

1.

2.

One-Minute Summary

This chapter contains assistance activities to be used in the assistance phase of the PAR Lesson Framework for improving comprehension. The activities shift the focus from the product to the process of comprehension. To truly comprehend, readers must "build bridges" and construct an understanding based on what they already know and can add to that knowledge with newly presented information.

We consider two factors that facilitate comprehension: text features and questioning strategies. Comprehension is enhanced when readers attend to text features such as superordinate and subordinate relationships, significant chunks, and patterns of organization. Comprehension can be divided into at least three levels: literal, interpretive, and application. A taxonomic approach balances the attention paid to each level. We discuss the role of questioning in facilitating comprehension. We introduce several activities to show how text features and questioning strategies can lead students to effective cognitive strategies to apprehend deep meaning.

End-of-Chapter Activities

Assisting Comprehension

1. See how many of the seven patterns of organization described in this chapter you can locate in a content-area textbook. Are they easy to find?
2. Review some questions that you recently constructed for students to answer. Do they focus equally on each of the three levels of comprehension explained in this chapter? If they do not, what level of comprehension is predominant?
3. Having read this chapter, what ideas for appropriate activities to assist your students' comprehension do you now have?

Reflecting on Your Reading

Think about changes that you can make in your instruction to assist your students in understanding textbook material. Choose several of the strategies and activities discussed in this chapter and begin using them as soon as possible in your classroom.

CHAPTER 7

Reflection in Reading: Autonomy, Critical Thinking, Evaluation

Educate yourself, do not let me educate you—use me, do not be used by me.

—Robert Henri

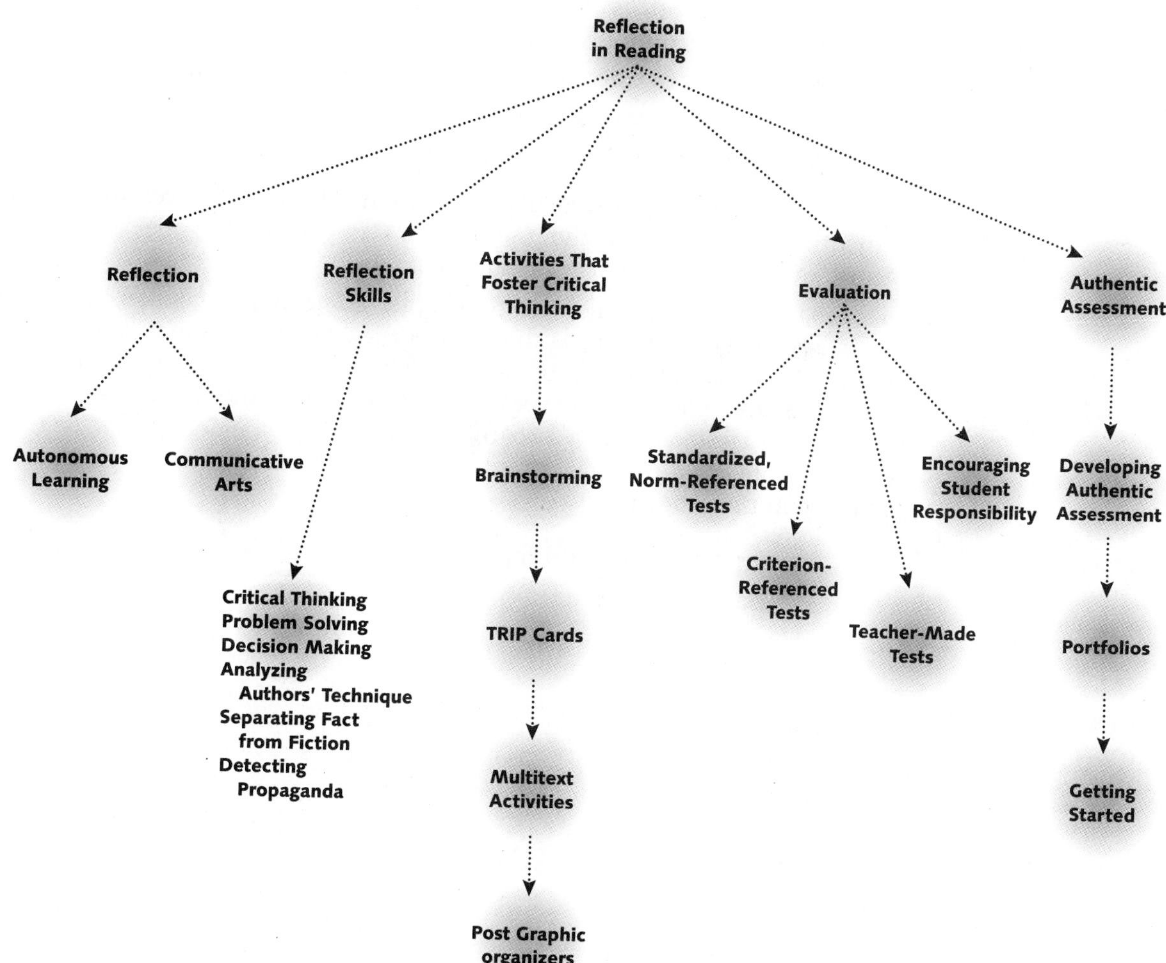

Preparing to Read

1. Before reading this chapter, check any of the following statements that you agree with. After reading the chapter, see whether you have changed your mind.

   ______ Critical thinking takes place only after reading, when the reader decides on the validity of what has been read.

   ______ Critical thinking is an all-encompassing construct that can take place before, during, and after reading.

   ______ There is no agreement on the exact nature of critical thinking.

   ______ There are systematic steps one has to take to solve a problem.

   ______ Critical thinking is one aspect of effective thinking.

2. How do you evaluate your students? Do you rely on tests? Have you tried authentic assessment? How about portfolios? Can you describe one "authentic" measure that you use in your classroom?

3. Following is a list of terms used in this chapter. Some may be familiar to you in a general context, but in this chapter they may be used in unfamiliar ways. Rate your knowledge by placing a plus sign (+) in front of those you are sure that you know, a check mark (✓) in front of those you have some knowledge about, and a zero (0) in front of those you don't know. Be ready to locate and pay special attention to their meanings when they are presented in the chapter.

   ______ comprehension monitoring
   ______ free rides
   ______ informative communication
   ______ textual evidence
   ______ effective thinking
   ______ propaganda
   ______ brainstorming
   ______ literary gift exchange
   ______ assessment
   ______ evaluation
   ______ norm-referenced tests
   ______ validity
   ______ reliability
   ______ criterion-referenced tests
   ______ nontraditional tests

______ factstorming
______ SCORER
______ test-wise
______ authentic assessment
______ portfolio

Objectives

As you read this chapter, focus your attention on the following objectives. You will:

1. understand the central role that students play during the reflection phase of learning.
2. recognize the important role of the communicative arts in content-area reading instruction.
3. understand the nature of critical thinking, from its narrowest to its broadest sense.
4. be able to use activities described in this chapter to teach important reflection skills.
5. define the term *evaluation* and describe its influence on reflection.
6. understand how to apply PAR in designing classroom tests.
7. describe traditional tests, including standardized, criterion-referenced, and teacher-made tests.
8. understand the problems of traditional tests and learn some suggestions for improving them.
9. understand the importance of nontraditional testing.
10. understand how being test-wise affects student performance on tests.
11. learn about practical forms of authentic assessment for the content classroom.

Shoe. Reprinted with permission of Tribune Media Services.

Reflection

A reporter once asked Coach John McKay, "What do you think about the execution of your team?" After very little reflection, the coach replied, "I'm all for it." We are not certain that Coach McKay reflected sufficiently before answering, but we do know that reflective thinking is very important in life.

The third step in the PAR Lesson Framework is reflection, which takes place after reading has been completed. Whereas the preparation phase of the lesson helps in motivation of students and the assistance phase aids in building comprehension, the reflection phase helps students clarify thinking and focus understanding. Full understanding cannot be achieved until reflection occurs. Although the teacher may guide students by providing instructional support, the student's role is crucial at this stage.

There are also several important by-products of this third phase. One is that it helps students think critically about what they have learned and have yet to learn about the lesson. Such critical thinking is necessary if students are going to become mature readers. A second by-product is that true reflection on the reading helps students retain understanding for a longer period of time. The more we reflect on reading material or on the lesson at hand, the longer we will remember it and the more likely we will be to use the knowledge we retain. In this manner knowledge is related in a meaningful way to what is already known so that it will be retained and become the basis for further learning. William S. Gray (1960) described this process as "reading beyond the lines." A third by-product is demonstration of one's learning through some system of evaluation. In this chapter we discuss all of these aspects of reflection.

The Move Toward Autonomous Learning

Although teachers must initially prepare and assist readers, readers must take charge of their own learning as soon as possible. The goal is to help students become autonomous learners. Hawkes and Schell (1987) caution that teacher-set reasons to read may encourage dependence and a passive approach to reading. Self-set reasons to read promote reading that is active and ultimately independent.

"By teaching us how to read, they had taught us how to get away," observe the rats in Robert O'Brien's *Mrs. Frisby and the Rats of NIMH* (1971). In this children's novel, scientists conduct experiments to teach rats to read. Because the rats are fed a superdrug to make them smart, the scientists anticipate that the rats will learn some letter-sound and word-picture relationships. They do not expect that the rats will actually ever understand and apply what they read. They underestimate what reading is all about. These rats want to escape from the lab, and their goal is vital: They are willing to work at reading so they can use this new skill to escape. The rats use all of their communication skills. They study pictures presented to them, they listen to clues to the meaning of the pictures, and they consult with each other about what they are learning—the connections between letters and sounds, pictures and words. And then they read! Later, in their new home, they even begin to keep a written record of their progress.

The story of the rats of NIMH demonstrates how cooperative study and the communicative arts can produce reflective readers who think critically, enrich their environment, and use reading as a lifelong process. The key to the rats' success is that they became autonomous learners, and no test of their success could demonstrate their learning better than the self-supporting community the rats built. The rats had a great desire to escape NIMH and plenty of opportunities for practice as well as plenty of clues in their environment. The natural result was comprehension and escape. The scientists, to their misfortune, did not realize the important role of the learner in the success of their experiment.

Principle 8 in Chapter 1 states: "Content-reading instruction enables students to become autonomous learners." Teachers help students achieve this independence by allowing students, as soon as possible, to take active, responsible roles. However, students may be left stranded unless teachers guide them toward independence by showing them how to use their own communication skills. Kletzein (1991) investigated adolescents' use of strategies for reading. She found that students used many strategies when they were reading independently but students with poor comprehension were less flexible. Good readers are able to pause and demonstrate their comprehension by retelling and analyzing what they have read and by using certain strategies consistently. They are practicing **comprehension monitoring**. In contrast, poor readers seem to lose track of their reading and to have no particular strategies for comprehending. In other words, poor readers do not seem to function independently. Kletzein recommended that students "need to be given more control over the strategies so that they can use them independently" (p. 83).

Although teachers can point out what is important about content material, students must ultimately evaluate its worth for themselves (Cioffi, 1992). Thus, for example, Angeletti (1991) used question cards with her second-graders to encourage them to express opinions about content they had read.

Bohan and Bass (1991) helped students in a fourth-grade math class become independent by taking **free rides** in solving problems about fractions. "After the teacher covered multiplication of two fractions, the class was told the next type of problem, multiplying mixed numbers, was a free ride—a situation in which they were solving a seemingly new type of problem, but one that was not really new because they had previously acquired the knowledge needed to find the product" (p. 4). The next day, a student volunteered another case in which free rides could apply. This situation exemplifies the elements of reflection: The teacher provides a context and encourages students to manage their own learning at the application level. In this way students become self-managed and acquire skills to enhance their own attending, learning, and thinking.

The Role of the Communicative Arts

We believe, as stated in principle 2, that "The communicative arts foster thinking and learning in content subjects." As Alvermann (1987a) puts it: "Writers, speakers, readers, and listeners all engage in reciprocal processes aimed at creating understanding through shared responsibilities of communication" (p. 112). Allen, Brown, and Yatvin (1986) use the term **informative communication** to describe ways that children—through listening, speaking, reading, and writing—acquire knowledge of the world around them and learn to use knowledge productively. Just as students read to learn, they listen to learn, speak to learn, and write to learn.

More than at any other stage, reflective learning depends on informative communication. A 15-year-old high school student recently said, "We need more class discussion. You can read stuff out of the book and answer questions, but you never really learn it unless you talk about it. We need more time to ask questions." Teachers have to let go, learn not to talk, but encourage students to ask their own questions and cooperate with each other in their learning (Barton, 1995) (see the Technology Box). Alvermann (1987a) contends that one of the easiest things a teacher can do to limit the amount of teacher talk and increase the amount of student talk is to discontinue the use of teacher questions. Counselors practice such a philosophy when they avoid too many questions or suggestions and guide their clients by listening attentively.

The discussion web (Alvermann, 1991) is an activity in which teachers first prepare students to read, asking them to think of a question they would like to have answered, and then assign the reading. Students discuss the reading in pairs. Next, two pairs of readers meet together to discuss their information and reach a consensus. A recorder from this group reports to the whole class. The final step is for each student to write an answer to the question that was asked before the reading began. This activity also models the before, during, and after steps (PAR) of reading; puts the student first; employs all of the language arts as well as cooperative grouping; and leads to reflection.

Listening and speaking reflectively about reading reinforce learning in a social context. Such discussion reflects students' thinking. By listening to and considering the viewpoints of other participants, students may gain different and deeper insights about a topic. Other examples surface. New connections are made. Most important, students gain control of their own learning. Richardson (1999b) reports that students prefer discussion to lecture as a means of deep learning, although many students she interviewed reported that few discussions occurred in their classes. Students are aware of how discussions help them understand what they read. Alvermann and colleagues (1996) recommend that productive small-group discussions be fostered by

> Providing students with frequent opportunities to discuss what they read; developing a sense of community in the classroom; attending to group dynamics; and building on students' keen sense of conditions that foster good discussion. (p. 264)

They further caution that teachers should take care to moderate rather than dominate a discussion and find topics that engage students.

Socratic discussions (Adler, 1994) lead to "enlarged understanding of ideas and values by means of Socratic questioning and active participation in the discussion of books and other works" (p. 8). Socrates wanted answers from his pu-

TECHNOLOGY BOX

A Cooperative Review Activity for Geometry Students

Developed by Lindsay E. Bruce, Jr.

Use the website: Math for Morons Like Us—Geometry
http://library.advanced.org/20991/geo/index.html
@ 1998 *ThinkQuest Team 20991*
Rob Andrus, John Pruess, Garrett Stettler

Pairs of students select a topic from the website, with teacher approval, from among the following general topics:

- Parallel lines
- Congruent triangles
- Isosceles and equilateral triangles
- Quadrilaterals
- Parallelograms
- Ratios
- Similar polygons
- Special triangles
- Circles
- Area
- Coordinate geometry
- Triangle inequality
- Solids

Students gather information from the website, with the goal of creating a 5-to-10-minute lesson on their topic. They rely on the tutorial at the website.
Students make an appointment with the teacher for consultation. When ready, they present a lesson and then give a preapproved quiz on their lesson.

pils that clarified ideas. Adler (1984) explains this type of discussion as conversation about a material, in which a facilitator—the teacher or someone else—asks questions that encourage thought, not right or wrong responses. To conduct a Socratic discussion, it is best to designate a specific amount of time, perhaps 50 minutes for older students and less for younger students. All discussants read a common text and respond to a question that jump-starts the discussion. After that, the teacher (or facilitator) moderates to make sure everyone who wishes to discuss gets a chance. The discussion should not wander and should refer to relevant text, called **textual evidence** (Tredway, 1995), as a means of supporting the comments made.

Discussions work best with 25 or fewer participants. Students learn to respect other views, take turns, and paraphrase. Discussions also improve vocabulary and provide practice at higher levels of comprehension, and explore relationships between ideas. Even young children can conduct a version of the Socratic discussion. We have witnessed first-graders discussing their impressions of Picasso's blue and rose periods.

We presented various ways to enhance discussions in Chapter 5 as effective means of confronting misconceptions about prior knowledge. As we present information about critical thinking later in this chapter, remember that activities promoting a cooperative, communicative arts approach and placing the student in the role of independent learner will work best to promote reflection.

Important Reflection Skills

Critical Thinking

Oliver Wendell Holmes once said, "Every now and then a man's mind is stretched by a new idea and never shrinks back to its former dimensions." One of the most important ways to have students reflect on reading is to ask them to think critically about what they read. Postreading activities designed to improve critical thinking are a crucial part of learning in content-area subjects. However, recent studies and national reports indicate that such activities are also a neglected part of instruction. Kirsch and Jungeblut (1986) report that today's young adults are literate but have difficulty with the more complex and challenging reading that is required in their adult life. The study notes the inability of young people to analyze and understand complicated material. Sternberg (1994) laments the lack of correspondence between what is required for critical thinking in adulthood and what is being taught in schools today. Hynd (1999) encourages teachers to expose middle and high school students to historical documents and multiple texts. In this way, they will read different or even opposing views and begin to think like historians. As students experience the process that historians use in researching and writing about history, they may be able to apply the thinking process to other subjects as well. Thinking like a researcher enables students to think critically. By reinforcing the reading experience through critical thinking, teachers can challenge students to think about content material in new ways.

Too often, however, classroom teachers, especially at the elementary level, shy away from teaching critical thinking. One reason for this is that there is no clear definition of the construct. Another reason is that teachers mistakenly believe that *critical* means to find fault and emphasize the negative. Also, critical thinking is a difficult construct to measure through teacher-made tests, and critical thinking skills are not mandated for minimum competency in many subjects. In addition, some teachers have the notion that at-risk learners are not capable of critical thinking. Finally, teachers often say that they do not have adequate time to plan instruction in critical thinking and lack appropriate materials and books to teach it properly. Despite these perceived obstacles, the teaching of critical thinking should not be neglected at any K through 12 grade level. This important ability leads to greater success in academic subjects and will be of use to students after graduation. In short, critical thinking is a skill that will aid students in all facets of life, during and beyond the school day.

Critical thinking as an important dimension of learning is emphasized in textbooks, in the research literature, and in published programs. Unks (1985) said that the ability to think critically is one of the most agreed-upon educational objectives. But even though almost everyone agrees that some elements of critical thinking need to be taught across the curriculum, the concept remains so vague that educators are not certain about its meaning, about the best ways for classroom teachers to teach it, or even about whether it can be taught. After examining a textbook that contained practice examples in teaching critical thinking, a reviewer once remarked: "It was a good book but it really didn't contain much critical thinking." This comment underscores the subjective nature of the concept.

The literature, in fact, supports two interpretations of critical thinking. One is a narrow definition of critical thinking as the mastery and use of certain skills necessary for the assessment of statements (Beyer, 1983). These skills take the same form as logic or deduction and may include judging the acceptability of authority statements, judging contradictory statements, and judging whether a conclusion follows necessarily from its premises. A more-encompassing definition includes these skills as well as inductive types of skills, such as hypothesis testing, proposition generation, and creative argument (Facione, 1984; Sternberg & Baron, 1985). We agree with the latter definition and emphasize critical thinking in this broader sense throughout this text.

We can clarify our view of critical thinking by studying what happens when the skill is put to use. McPeck (1981, p. 13) identified 10 features of critical thinking:

1. Critical thinking cannot be taught in the abstract, in isolation. It is not a distinct subject but is taught in content disciplines. It is critical thinking "about something."
2. Although the term may have one correct meaning, the criteria for its correct application vary from discipline to discipline.
3. Critical thinking does not necessarily mean disagreement with, or rejection of, accepted norms.
4. Critical thinking deals with the student's skills to think in such a way as to suspend or temporarily reject evidence from a discipline when the student feels there is insufficient data to establish the truth of some proposition.
5. Critical thinking includes the thought process involved in problem solving and active thinking.
6. Formal and informal logic is not sufficient for thinking critically.
7. Because critical thinking involves knowledge and skill, a critical thinker in one discipline may not be a critical thinker in another discipline.
8. Critical thinking has both a "task" and an "achievement" phase. It does not necessarily imply success.
9. Critical thinking may include the use of methods and strategies as exemplars.
10. Critical thinking does not have the same scope or boundaries as rationality, but it is a dimension of rational thought.

McPeck suggests that at the core of critical thinking is practicing the skill of reflective skepticism. In our complex and rapidly changing society, the ability to be reflective and to be skeptical when weighing evidence before making decisions is of great importance. More than 60 years ago John Dewey (1933) spoke of the importance of reflective thinking:

> When a situation arises containing a difficulty or perplexity, the person who finds himself in it may take one of a number of courses. He may dodge it, dropping the activity that brought it about, turning to something else. He may indulge in a flight of fancy, imagining himself powerful or wealthy, or in some other way in possession of the means that would enable him to deal with the difficulty. Or, finally, he may face the situation. In this case, he begins to reflect. (p. 102)

Students in kindergarten through twelfth grade are seldom taught to reflect, to solve problems by "facing the situation," except in published programs on thinking or in "critical thinking" sections of basal reading materials. The first of McPeck's features calls into question the effectiveness of any published program that teaches critical thinking as a skill, isolated from content. Reyes (1986), in a review of a social studies series, found that publishers did not deliver material that developed strong critical thinking, even though they promised it. In another study, researchers (Woodward, Elliott, & Nagel, 1986) found that the critical thinking skills emphasized in elementary basal materials were those that could be most readily tested, such as map and globe skills.

Evidence indicates that teachers do not need published "thinking" programs and that they cannot depend on basal reading materials to teach critical thinking skills. However, they do need to integrate their own critical thinking lessons with those of the textbook they are using. For example, to teach critical thinking, teachers might present study guides that emphasize critical thinking, then have small groups of students practice a problem-solving exercise. In this manner, students are taught critical thinking in a concrete context of carefully guided thinking. Studies indicate that, especially in early adolescence, formal reasoning and thinking can best be taught through the teacher's use of guided prompts such as graphic overviews and study guides, which enable students to structure their thinking more easily (Arlin, 1984; Strahan, 1983).

In addition to asking teachers to emphasize critical thinking, noted educator Art Costa has called for a school environment in which principals and other school leaders encourage teachers "to look carefully at the intelligent behavior of their own students" (Brandt, 1988, p. 13). Further, Costa calls for administrators to model intelligent behavior themselves by spending more time discussing thinking, encouraging teachers themselves to engage in critical thinking, and purchasing materials to support the teaching of critical thinking.

We agree with McPeck (1981) that critical thinking is a multifaceted and complex process that enables students to gather data, test hypotheses, and reflect in a skeptical and disciplined manner. The eventual products of this process are life decisions made by persons under pressure to think. Critical thinking, then, is what Moore, McCann, and McCann (1981) call **effective thinking**.

Problem Solving and Decision Making

Critical thinking leads to effective decision making. Figure 7.1 presents a model that illustrates steps in problem solving, all of which lead to effective decision making. Students who use such a model will be more effective thinkers; both their creative and contemplative abilities will improve (Parnes & Noller, 1973). We offer the following steps in problem solving:

1. *Gathering ideas and information.* Students brainstorm to generate enough information to begin defining the problem. They can play a "reading detective" game or do research to gather information from all possible sources.
2. *Defining the problem.* Students recognize the need to resolve a situation that has no apparent solution. They should be asked to clarify the nature of the task and completely describe the situation in writing.
3. *Forming tentative conclusions.* This is a creative phase in which students suggest possible solutions from available data.
4. *Testing conclusions.* Students discuss in groups which conclusions work best as solutions to the problem. Poor choices are eliminated until workable solutions remain. Students also may establish criteria for evaluating outcomes.
5. *Making a decision.* Students select one of the remaining solutions and give reasons for their choice.

Study guides, such as the one in Activity 7.1, can be constructed by teachers as cognitive maps to assist students in using the problem-solving steps detailed in Figure 7.1. Activity 7.2 contains a guide that students can complete to discover the analogies between two stories. It is especially important to start this type of activity in early-elementary classrooms because unsophisticated

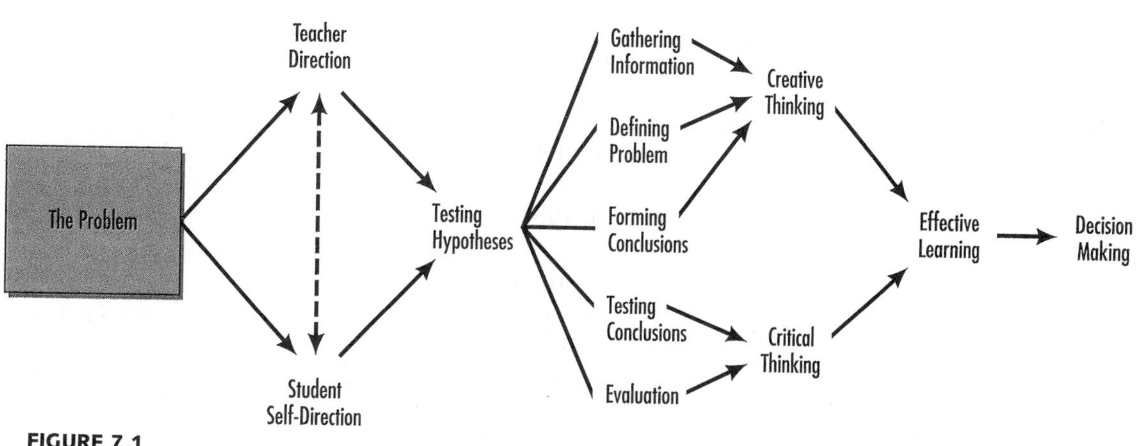

FIGURE 7.1

ACTIVITY 7.1 Critical Thinking Guide: Problem Solving

Problem

Why do we need to solve problem?

Ways to Solving Problem	Reasons for Choosing Method
Method 1	Positive outcomes Negative outcomes
Method 2	Positive outcomes Negative outcomes
Method 3	Positive outcomes Negative outcomes
Best Way to Solve Problem	Reasons for Choosing to Solve Problem in this Manner

Adapted from a decision-making model by J. McTighe and F. T. Ryman, Jr. (1988), Cueing Thinking in the Classroom: The Promise of Theory-Embedded Tools, *Educational Leadership*, *45*(7), 18–24.

ACTIVITY 7.2 Critical Thinking Guide: Similarity in the Themes of Two Stories

Story Reflection

Story 1		Story 2
Theme: Event Event Event	How themes are similar	Theme: Event Event Event

learners seldom let their minds journey across stories to think about possible similarities.

Group decision making can also be taught through the use of a group-and-label technique. The teacher begins by writing the topic on the board and telling students that they will be reviewing important terminology. Then students volunteer any terms they can think of that fall under the topic heading. The teacher may ask leading questions or even eliminate this step by preparing the list in advance on the board or on a worksheet. Students reorganize the list into smaller lists of items that have something in common. Each of these sublists is then given a label. Students may work individually or in small groups to reorga-

ACTIVITY 7.3 Group-and-Label Technique: Consumer Mathematics

unit price
sales slip
regular time
cash
checking account
straight time
estimate
overtime
FICA
outstanding check
reconciliation statement
income
wage

check stub
deposit slip
gross pay
sales tax
time card
withdraw
net pay
average price
canceled check
piece rate
endorsed
withholding tax

take-home pay
balance
checkbook
fractional price
social security
commission
bank statement
overdrawn
salary plus commission
certified check
deposit

Product Purchasing	*Money Records/Banking*	*Wages*
unit price	cash	regular time
sales slip	reconciliation statement	straight time
estimate	outstanding check	overtime
sales tax	certified check	income
average price	endorsed	wage
fractional price	checking account	gross pay
	checkbook	net pay
	deposit slip	take-home pay
	deposit	withholding tax
	withdraw	FICA
	check stub	social security
	balance	piece rate
	bank statement	commission
	overdrawn	salary plus commission
	canceled check	time card

nize and label the words. Activity 7.3 provides an example of a group-and-label technique for consumer mathematics. Activity 7.4 shows how grouping and labeling might work for a first-grade social studies unit on communities.

Analyzing Authors' Techniques

Rarely are students asked to examine an author's background to determine whether the author is noted for a particular bias. However, as students evaluate content information, they should note the source of that information. Most important, they should ask who the writer is and what his or her qualifications are. This analysis is especially important when reading from the World Wide Web.

ACTIVITY 7.4 Group-and-Label Technique: First-Grade Social Studies

From a jumbled list of words, the students will be asked to divide the words into four groups, according to their similarities. The teacher will write these four groups of words on the chalkboard. The students will label these groups. These labels will be written by the teacher on the board as titles for the groups of words.

GETTING TO SCHOOL

school bus "The bus driver brings me to school."
walking "I walk to school with my sister."
Mom's station wagon "My mom drives me to school in her station wagon."
Daddy's pickup truck "My daddy drives me to school in his pickup truck."
Bicycle "I ride my bicycle to school."

THINGS USED AT SCHOOL

ruler
books "I learn to read in first grade."
writing tablet "I write in my tablet."
pencils "My teacher sharpens my pencil every day."
crayons "I like to color pictures with my crayons."
glue
scissors "I cut the paper with my scissors."

ROOMS AT SCHOOL

office "I'm scared to go to the principal's office."
classroom
library "I like to check out books at the library."
cafeteria "We eat in the cafeteria."
nurse's clinic
auditorium
gymnasium "I play in the gym."

PEOPLE AT SCHOOL

teacher "My teacher helps me to read."
coach "The coach is my friend."
librarian "The librarian always reads us a story."
principal
secretary
nurse "The nurse is nice."
bus driver
cafeteria workers
janitors and cleaning workers
guidance counselor

Developed by Gail Perrer.

Anyone can post a website, but the discriminating reader must decide whether the author is really qualified to do so. Baumann and Johnson (1984, p. 78) ask that students read with these questions in mind:

1. What is the source? Is anything known about the author's qualifications, the reputation of the publisher, and the date of publication?
2. What is the author's primary aim—information, instruction, or persuasion?
3. Are the statements primarily facts, inferences, or opinions?
4. Does the author rely heavily on connotative words that may indicate a bias?
5. Does the author use negative propaganda techniques?

Students can think about and discuss these questions in groups after they read a narrative or expository selection. Also, students can be supplied with multiple-choice items, such as those in Activity 7.5, to assist them in learning to ascertain an author's qualifications for writing accurate and unbiased statements on a subject. Such an activity can be used to begin class discussion on a reading or to initiate debate after reading.

Separating Fact from Opinion

Separating fact from opinion is another higher-level thinking skill that can be taught to students starting in the early-elementary years. To do so, teachers must train students to see relationships between and among facts, to distinguish fact from opinion, to grasp subtle implications, and to interpret the deeper meanings an author has in mind. Often the reader must bring to bear past experiences and background to derive accurate interpretations. With frequent practice, students can become adept at interpreting an author's point of view and detecting biases. Activities 7.6 and 7.7 present ideas for constructing guides and worksheets to illustrate fact and opinion, to help students distinguish one from the other, and to give students practice in writing facts and opinions.

Detecting Propaganda

Skilled readers know how to absorb important information and throw away what is of no use. They are especially adept at recognizing **propaganda**—persuasive, one-sided statements designed to change beliefs or sway opinion. Propaganda can be glaring or extremely subtle, and students need to be made aware, even in the elementary years, of the effects propaganda can have, particularly in the marketplace. The following are the most often used forms of propaganda:

1. Appeal to the bandwagon—aimed at the "masses"—to join a large group that is satisfied with an idea or product. Readers of this kind of propaganda are made to feel left out if they don't go along with the crowd.

ACTIVITY 7.5 Evaluating the Reliability of Sources

Supply students with multiple-choice items like the following. The student checks the source that is the most reliable of the three suggested.

1. Japan has the highest per capita income of any country in the world.
   —— a. Joan Armentrag, salesperson at Bloomingdale's
   —— b. Bob Hoskins, star golfer
   —— c. Dr. Alice MacKenzie, economic analyst, the Ford Foundation
2. Mathematics is of no use to anyone.
   —— a. Bob Brotig, high school dropout
   —— b. Bill Johnson, editor, *The Mathematics Teacher*
   —— c. Susan Winnifred, personnel, the Rand Corporation
3. We have proved that honey bees communicate with each other.
   —— a. John Bowyer, salesman, Sue Ann Honey Co.
   —— b. Jane Maupin, high school biology teacher
   —— c. Martha Daughtry, bank teller
4. Forty-six percent of all married women with children now work outside the home.
   —— a. Sue Ann Begley, electrician
   —— b. Carol Radziwell, professional pollster
   —— c. Joe Blotnik, marriage counselor
5. We must stop polluting our bays and oceans.
   —— a. Clinton Weststock, president, Save the Bay Foundation
   —— b. Marjorie Seldon, engineer, Olin Oil Refinery, Gulfport, MI
   —— c. Carl Kanipe, free-lance writer of human-interest stories

---

2. **2.** Emotional language, which plays on the subtle connotations of words carefully chosen to evoke strong feelings.
3. **3.** Appeal to prestige—associating a person, product, or concept with something deemed to be important or prestigious by the reader or viewer.
4. **4.** Plain-folks appeal—the use of persons in an advertisement who seem typical, average, or ordinary (sometimes even dull). The idea is to build trust by depicting people as "regular" folks.
5. **5.** Testimonial—the use of a famous person to give heightened credibility to a concept, idea, or product.

Teachers at all grade levels need to prepare students to recognize propaganda techniques. After the basic techniques have been explained, students can be asked to bring in examples of advertisements from newspapers and magazines. In literature classes, students can be asked to discover examples in plays,

ACTIVITY 7.6 Energy: Fact or Opinion?

Directions: Place an *F* by the statements of facts and an *O* by the statements of opinions.

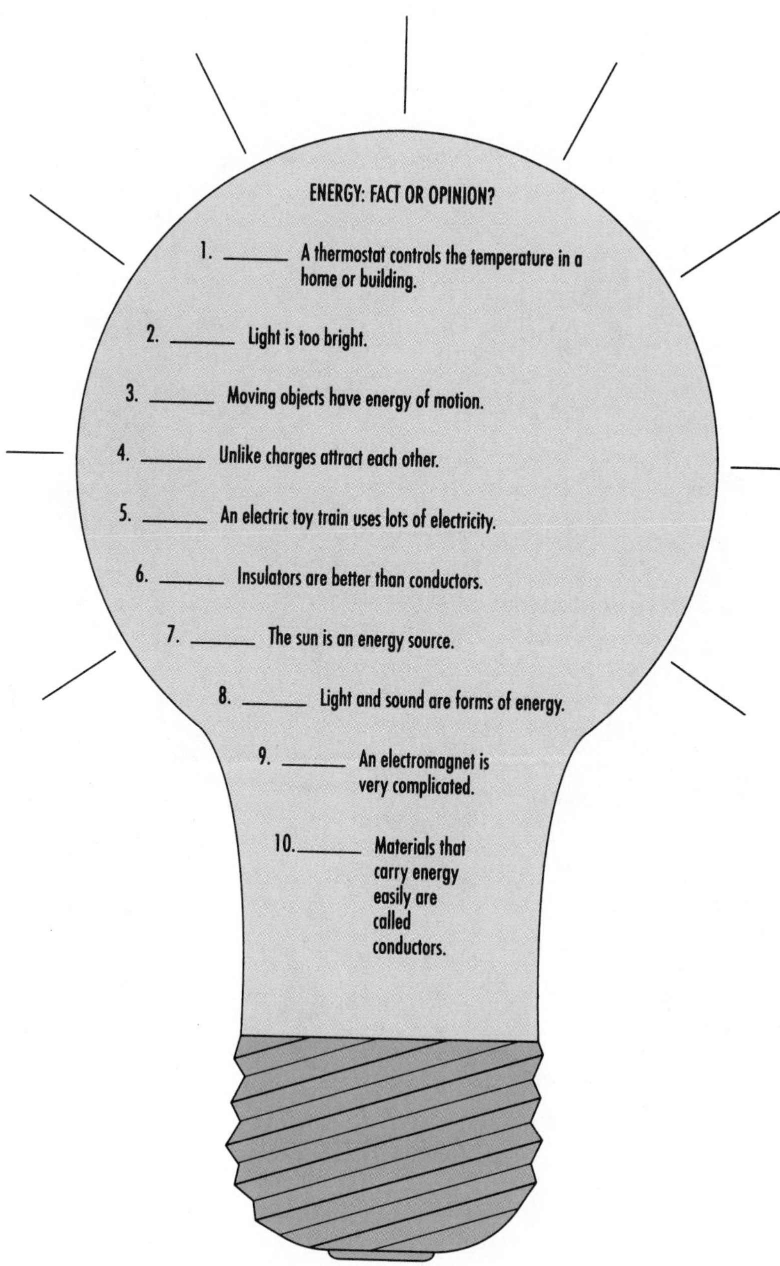

ENERGY: FACT OR OPINION?
1. ______ A thermostat controls the temperature in a home or building.
2. ______ Light is too bright.
3. ______ Moving objects have energy of motion.
4. ______ Unlike charges attract each other.
5. ______ An electric toy train uses lots of electricity.
6. ______ Insulators are better than conductors.
7. ______ The sun is an energy source.
8. ______ Light and sound are forms of energy.
9. ______ An electromagnet is very complicated.
10.______ Materials that carry energy easily are called conductors.

Developed by Laura Allin.

ACTIVITY 7.7 Fact or Opinion: Fifth-Grade Level

O Abraham Lincoln was the best president of our country.

F In 1862, President Lincoln wrote the Emancipation Proclamation.

F The "War Between the States" was another name for the Civil War.

F Sometimes Union and Confederate soldiers who fought each other in battle were from the same family.

O General Ulysses S. Grant was a better officer than General Robert E. Lee.

F The Emancipation Proclamation was written to free all slaves on January 1, 1863.

O Confederate troops should have pursued Union troops right after winning the battle of Bull Run; instead, they stopped to picnic.

F General Lee and the Confederate army surrendered to General Grant and the Union at Appomattox Court House, Virginia.

President Lincoln

Gen. Grant Gen. Lee

The Civil War: Fact or Opinion

DIRECTIONS: Place an F by statements that you think are "Facts" and an O by the statements that seem to be "Opinions."

Developed by Sue Meador.

short stories, and novels. *A Tale of Two Cities*, for example, contains examples of each of these propaganda techniques. Master storytellers like Charles Dickens know how to use such techniques deftly to develop complicated plots.

When discussing environmental issues in a science class, would proponents of industry be likely to take a different position from Greenpeace? How might this difference be manifested in propaganda techniques? Activity 7.8 provides a sample activity for teaching students to recognize propaganda. Students are asked to match statements to the propaganda technique they employ.

Activities That Foster Reflective Thinking

Brainstorming

Brainstorming—whole-class or group discussion of a topic in order to reach consensus or solve a problem—enhances reflective thinking and is appropriate to any grade level. Brainstorming is reflective and creative in nature. Brainstorming sessions can last from 10 minutes to an hour and can be designed to teach any of the skills discussed in this chapter. An especially productive brainstorming session is one in which small groups of students list as many possible alternative solutions to a problem as they can. Group captains are chosen to report findings to the entire class. The teacher lists on the chalkboard alternatives that the students deem worthy. Discussion then centers on how to narrow the choices to one or two and why the final choices are the best ones. An important consideration is the size of the brainstorming group. Five-person groups seem to work best; however, three- and four-person groups are also suitable. The most vocal students tend to dominate groups of six students or more.

The "Ready Reading Reference Bookmark" (see Figure 7.2) developed by Kapinus (1986) can be used to get students ready to brainstorm after reading a passage. In the section "After you read," students can use brainstorming to perform the five thinking operations called for: retelling, summarizing, asking, picturing, and deciding. Students also can brainstorm the "While you read" and "If you don't understand" operations at other points in the lesson—before reading, for example, or after reading specific sections.

TRIP Cards

Another activity that uses cooperative groups and student discussion to build reflection skills is TRIP (Think/Reflect in Pairs). For this activity, the teacher divides students into pairs. Students share information on TRIP cards, which list propaganda techniques or situational problems. Answers are printed on the back of the cards for immediate reinforcement. Points may be assigned for correct answers, with a designated number of points needed for a good grade in the class.

In a different TRIP activity, students are presented problems from a textbook. They first solve the problem in pairs, then write the problem on the front and

ACTIVITY 7.8 Spotting Propaganda

Match each statement with the propaganda technique used.

a. appeal to bandwagon
b. emotional language
c. appeal to prestige
d. plain-folks appeal
e. testimonial

____ 1. Come on down to Charlie Winkler's Auto before every one of these beauties is sold.
____ 2. Michael Jordan, former Chicago Bulls star, thinks Nike shoes are the best.
____ 3. You'll be glowing all over in your new Evening Time gown.
____ 4. Why, people in every walk of life buy our product.
____ 5. Join the American Dining Club today, a way of life for those who enjoy the good life.
____ 6. Already, over 85% of our workers have given to this worthy cause.
____ 7. I'll stack our doughnut makers up against any others, as the best in the business!
____ 8. Even butcher Fred Jones likes our new frozen yogurt coolers.
____ 9. One must drink our wine to appreciate the truly fine things in life.
____ 10. Lift the weights that Arnold Schwarzenegger lifts—a sure way to a better body.

---

the answer on the back of a card. In this manner, students create their own TRIP files for reinforcement or future use. Activity 7.9 shows eight TRIP cards made by an algebra class.

Multitext Activities

Many teachers' manuals suggest multitext activities as a way to encourage reflective thinking. Often teachers feel too rushed to cover curriculum and skip this enriching resource, although research supports the use of many reading materials to solidify learning about a topic. In Chapter 5, we described multitext activities in the preparation stage of PAR. A multitext approach also helps readers reflect by extending their knowledge of a topic after study. In Chapter 3 we explored in depth the use of literature in content-area study.

Literary Gift Exchanges

Schadt (1989) describes the **literary gift exchange** as a way to enrich readers. Each student brings to class an object reminiscent of a character or action from literature read about in the content area and exchanges it with a designated partner. Students must be able to explain their gifts. Schadt noticed that students began to reread material after he initiated the exchange procedure.

FIGURE 7.2

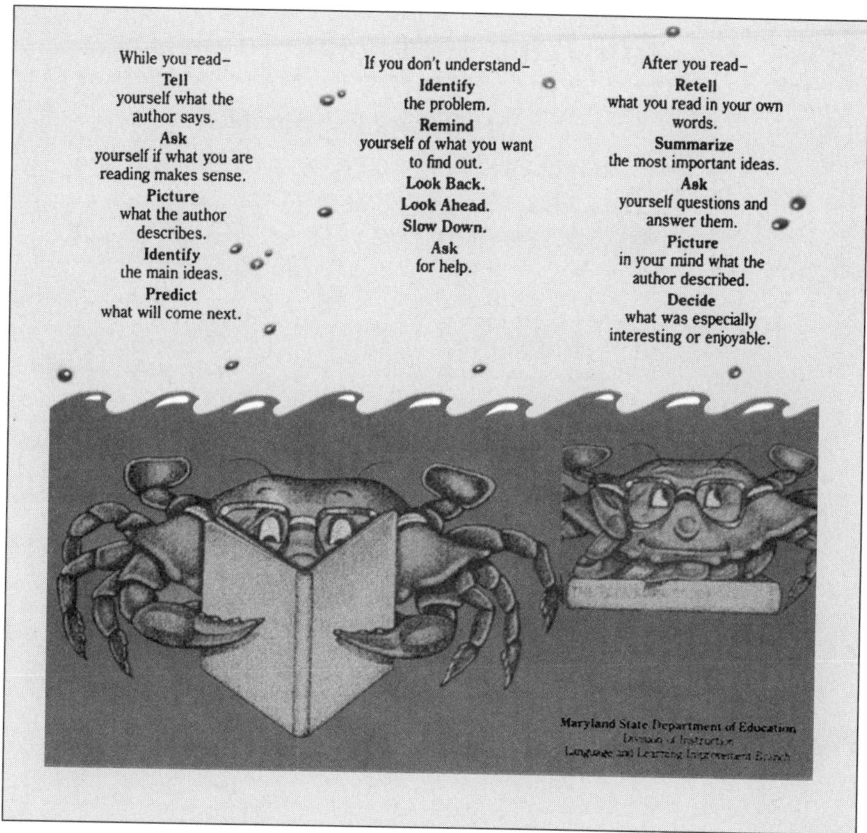

Post Graphic Organizers

Designing post graphic organizers is another reflection activity that students of all ages enjoy. After reading is completed, students form groups. Each group selects a theme for the material studied and designs a way to present the material visually to the rest of the class. A group of secondary advanced-placement chemistry students created the post graphic organizer shown in Activity 7.10. They titled the post graphic organizer "Fluids in a Nutshell." In Activity 7.11, a middle-school mathematics teacher has students sort eight geometric situations and create an organizer to which they add a reflective statement.

Evaluation

The term **assessment** generally refers to any observations—informal and performance-related—that teachers use to determine students' background, motivation, interests, strategies, and prior skills (Flippo, 1997). Assessment is an

ACTIVITY 7.9 TRIP Cards for Algebra I

Factoring Polynomials

Front of Card	Back of Card
$(x + 2)(x + 9)$	$x^2 + 11x + 18$
$(x + 1)(5x + 3)$	$5x^2 + 8x + 3$
$(2x + 5)(2x + 1)$	$4x^2 + 12x + 5$
$(x + 7)(x - 7)$	$x^2 - 49$
$(5x + 2y)(x - 2y)$	$5x^2 - 8xy - 4y^2$
Prime	$x^2 - 12x - 30$
$(x - 2)(x + 5)$	$x^2 + 3x - 10$
$(x + 2)(x - 6)$	$x^2 - 4x - 12$

Developed by Ronda Clancy.

ongoing process; each time a teacher begins a new unit of instruction, assessment should occur. We prefer to call this process "determining background," which we described in Chapters 4 and 5, along with several assessment procedures. **Evaluation** is a term usually reserved for making judgments about students' performance. Reflection often involves evaluation, testing what was learned. This is the time when the product of comprehension is demonstrated, whether through formal tests or other means of assigning grades that represent a measure of learning. In this section, we explore several ways that evaluations of students' content knowledge can be made, from traditional and standardized measures to informal and nontraditional measures.

ACTIVITY 7.10 Post Graphic Organizer: Chemistry

Fluids in a Nutshell

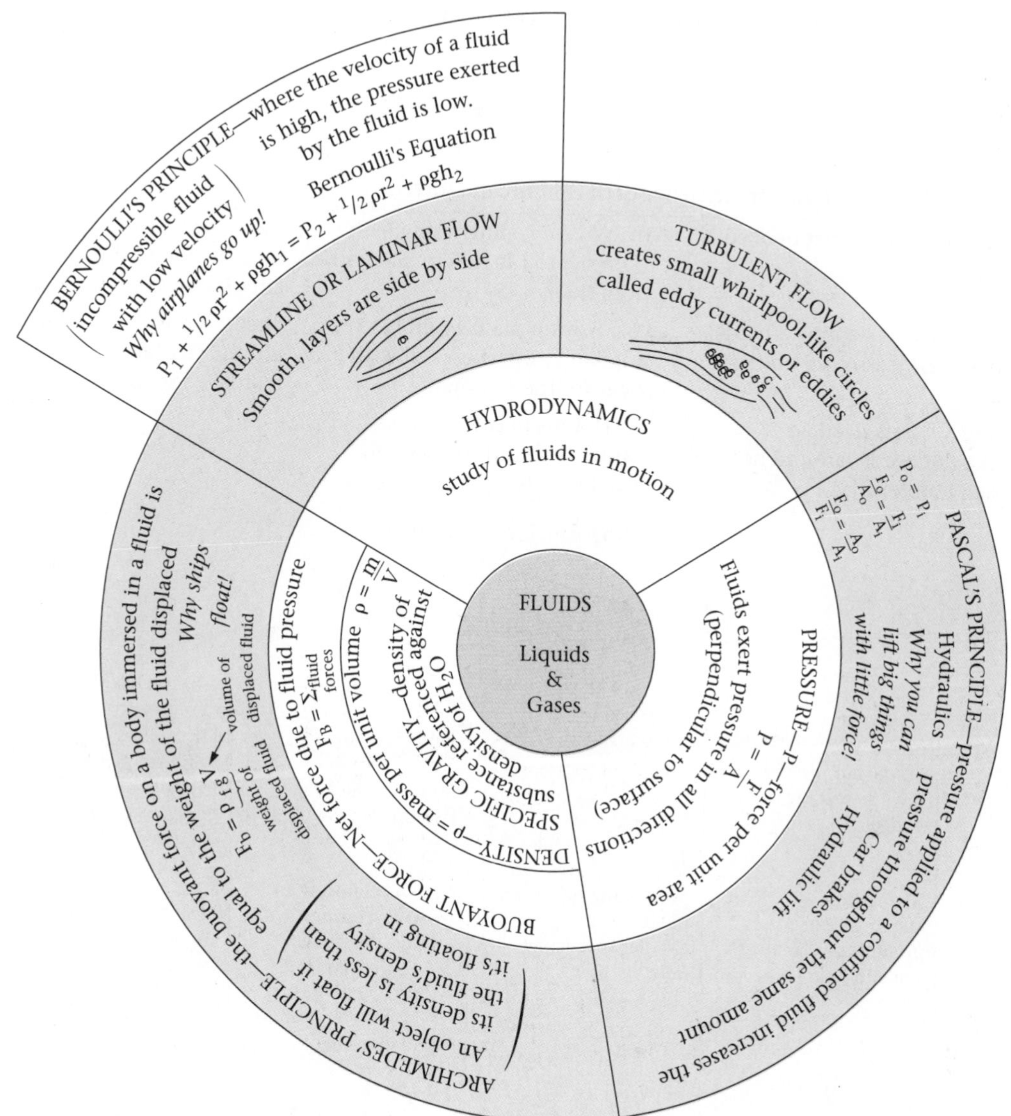

BERNOULLI'S PRINCIPLE—where the velocity of a fluid is high, the pressure exerted by the fluid is low.
incompressible fluid with low velocity
Why airplanes go up!
Bernoulli's Equation
$P_1 + 1/2\,\rho r^2 + \rho g h_1 = P_2 + 1/2\,\rho r^2 + \rho g h_2$
STREAMLINE OR LAMINAR FLOW
Smooth, layers are side by side
TURBULENT FLOW
creates small whirlpool-like circles called eddy currents or eddies
HYDRODYNAMICS
study of fluids in motion
FLUIDS
Liquids & Gases
PASCAL'S PRINCIPLE—pressure applied to a confined fluid increases the pressure throughout the same amount
Hydraulics
Why you can lift big things with little force!
Car brakes
Hydraulic lift
$P_o = P_i$
$\frac{F_o}{A_o} = \frac{F_i}{A_i}$
$\frac{F_o}{F_i} = \frac{A_o}{A_i}$
PRESSURE—P—force per unit area
$P = \frac{F}{A}$
Fluids exert pressure in all directions (perpendicular to surface)
DENSITY—ρ = mass per unit volume $\rho = \frac{m}{V}$
SPECIFIC GRAVITY—density of substance referenced against density of H_2O
BUOYANT FORCE—Net force due to fluid pressure
$F_B = \Sigma_{fluid\ forces}$
displaced fluid
ARCHIMEDES' PRINCIPLE—the buoyant force on a body immersed in a fluid is equal to the weight of the fluid displaced
Why ships float!
$F_b = \rho f g V$
weight of displaced fluid
volume of displaced fluid
An object will float if its density is less than the fluid's density it's floating in

Developed by Scot M. Paterson.

ACTIVITY 7.11 Post Graphic Organizer: Geometry

Sorting the Situations

What is being described? Written below are situations that involve either perimeter, area, circumference, or volume.

Step 1: Please cut out each sentence and paste it in the correct column in the graphic organizer on the next page.

Step 2: Create your own sentence for each column and include it in the graphic organizer.

Missy wants to carpet her bedroom floor.	Mr. Wilson is purchasing bathroom tile to tile his circular bathroom floor.	Carly is planning to plant rosebushes around the border of her circular swimming pool.
Ms. Yesbeck is stapling a border around the classroom bulletin board.	Mrs. Ashton plans to fill her rectangular swimming pool with water for the summer.	Shelly is sewing a lace border around her favorite rectangular blanket.
Jennifer wants to add a polka-dot border around her beach umbrella.	Mr. Hollins needs to fill his planter with dirt to plant his prize begonia.	

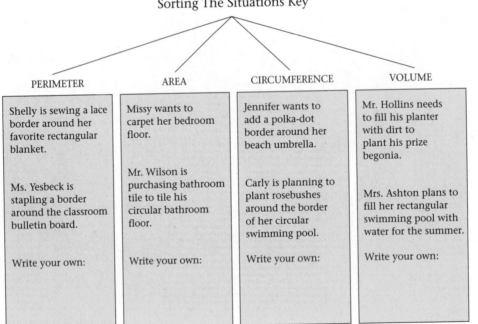

Sorting The Situations Key

PERIMETER	AREA	CIRCUMFERENCE	VOLUME
Shelly is sewing a lace border around her favorite rectangular blanket.	Missy wants to carpet her bedroom floor.	Jennifer wants to add a polka-dot border around her beach umbrella.	Mr. Hollins needs to fill his planter with dirt to plant his prize begonia.
Ms. Yesbeck is stapling a border around the classroom bulletin board.	Mr. Wilson is purchasing bathroom tile to tile his circular bathroom floor.	Carly is planning to plant rosebushes around the border of her circular swimming pool.	Mrs. Ashton plans to fill her rectangular swimming pool with water for the summer.
Write your own:	Write your own:	Write your own:	Write your own:

Developed by Diana Yesbeck.

Standardized, Norm-Referenced Tests

The major purpose of standardized, norm-referenced tests is to evaluate the amount of information that students know about a subject. These tests usually consist of multiple-choice or closure questions, which are readily and quickly scored by scan sheets or sometimes by hand. One correct answer is expected per item. Many classroom teachers follow standardized test formats as they construct classroom tests.

Standardized tests are used to compare the performance of groups, such as the results from one school compared to those of a school system, or a system to the state, or the state to the nation. The tests are designed with care by a group of experts and are pilot-tested on a representative sample of students. The results are studied, the test is modified, and a set of norms is developed. These norms become the basis for comparing results; hence the term **norm-referenced test** is often used to describe standardized tests. Scores on a standardized test are given in percentiles, stanines, standard-score equivalents, grade equivalents, or normal-curve equivalents.

Not all standardized tests are equally satisfactory to all users. Perhaps the norming groups are not representative of the particular population to be tested. Perhaps the items on the test do not reflect the content taught to the students tested. Perhaps the test purports to test content that, in fact, it does not really test. Standardized tests, however, are subject to a system of checks that help users make appropriate selections. These measurement concepts include validity and reliability. **Validity** is the "truthfulness" of the test—a check of whether the standardized test actually measures what it claims to measure. **Reliability** is the "consistency" of the test—whether it will produce roughly the same results if administered more than once to the same group in the same time period. Reliability is a check of how dependable the test is.

Because the main purpose of a standardized test is to compare the performance of groups rather than to provide a measure of individual student performance and a grade, teachers usually do not rely on these tests for their classroom evaluation. A school system should select the standardized test best suited to its system by asking these questions:

1. Does this test measure what has been taught?
2. Can we depend on it to give about the same results if we administer it today and tomorrow?
3. Is the norming group similar to our group of students?

Often such questions do not yield satisfactory answers but, nevertheless, school systems use them as a measure of performance. They do so because comparisons can be made across schools, divisions, states, and nations.

Standardized tests have an important place in the evaluation process. However, they should not be the only means of evaluation or the one means by which decisions are made about students' classroom performance. "High stakes" are associated with the use of standardized tests. Calkins, Montgomery, and Santman (1998) explain that standardized tests are not necessarily the "enemy" but they warn that teachers must learn how to understand what they reveal and cannot reveal about individual performance. For instance, Bardovi-Harlig and Dornyei (1998) refer to the "washback" effect of tests. Because of constant exposure, students and teachers become very familiar with the language of standardized tests; this familiarity itself can influence test results. By consistently raising questions and balancing test results with authentic assessment (discussed later in this chapter) when test scores are used to make judgments about students and schools, teachers can keep the role of standardized tests in perspective for themselves—and, we hope—for administrators and the community.

Criterion-Referenced Tests

Criterion-referenced tests are less formal than standardized tests, although their format is much like that of standardized tests—usually multiple-choice or closure questions. Criterion-referenced tests can be standardized, but their major purpose is not comparison, so they usually are not normed. Because they are less formal, short-answer, true/false, and other objective-type items might be included. The purpose of criterion-referenced tests is to measure whether a student can perform a specific task or knows a specific body of knowledge. Thus their purpose resembles that of classroom tests.

The criterion is the level of performance necessary to indicate that a student "knows" the task. The clients decide this criterion. Thus two schools could use the same test but set a different criterion. One school might set 85 percent as a passing score, and the other might set 90 percent as passing. The level of performance on the task is the score: A score of 85 percent means that the student responded correctly to 85 percent of the items. No grade-equivalent score, stanines, or other scores are provided.

Because criterion-referenced tests indicate mastery of a task, they should be based on specific objectives. For example, the objective might be stated: "The student will demonstrate mastery by correctly identifying 48 of 50 states and their capitals." A student who has been taught 50 states and capitals and can identify 48 on the test has demonstrated mastery of the criterion. A school system that elects to use a criterion-referenced test developed by an outside source can select an appropriate test by asking these questions:

1. Do the objectives and criteria match our objectives in this content?
2. Are there enough items included to give us a good indication that our students have met the criteria?
3. Do the test items reflect the way in which we taught the information?

Criterion-referenced tests are not new, but their evolution into more uniform, formalized tests is. In fact, the concept of criterion mastery is what individual teachers rely on as they design classroom tests that are criterion-referenced but are for individual classroom use.

Teacher-Made Tests

A product results from understanding. Tests offer a way to measure this product. There comes a time when the readers have read and thought about the material, the words have been learned, the relationships have been built, patterns of organization have been identified, and activities have facilitated satisfactory understanding. In short, comprehension has been developed, and the time has come to measure the learning achieved by evaluating the level of learning.

Tests are the culmination of periods of study about a content topic. Tests come in many forms, from informal observations of student learning to formal final exams. Students' ages and the topics covered influence the type of evaluation to be made. Teachers do need to test in some way; that is part of their instruction.

Tests should match the learning, not vice versa. Beyer (1984) writes: "Much so-called teaching of thinking skills consists largely of giving students practice in answering old test questions, a procedure that probably focuses students' attention more on question-answering techniques than on the specific cognitive skills that are the intended outcomes of such activities" (p. 486). Rather than giving practice with stale questions, teachers will want to discover ways to improve their tests, thereby eliciting the cognitive skills that are the ultimate goal of instruction.

A teacher's main purpose for giving a test is to evaluate student-generated products that demonstrate learning. Traditionally, teachers ask questions about what they have taught, and students answer them. Teachers then evaluate the answers as a gauge of how well students have learned the material. A secondary purpose is to provide test grades as one sign of progress in a report to students, parents, and administrators.

In addition, students' performance on a test should provide teachers with information about how well the teachers presented content material. Overlooked in the past, this purpose for testing has the greatest potential for creating an optimal learning environment in classrooms. If students can produce fine responses to questions, teachers may conclude not only that students are confident with the topic but also that they as teachers are presenting the content in ways that assist comprehension effectively. If students cannot produce satisfactory answers, the material may need to be retaught with different instructional strategies. Teachers who consider tests as a way to evaluate their own instruction, as well as to evaluate students' knowledge and to assign grades, often alter their instruction and revise their tests. The result is that both teachers and students begin to improve at their respective jobs.

The Role of Pop Quizzes

The use of pop quizzes can blur the distinction between tests aimed at assisting versus measuring comprehension. Teachers usually give pop quizzes to find out whether students have read an assignment. But suppose students attempted to read the assignment and experienced difficulty? A pop quiz may penalize students for not understanding rather than for not reading the material. Students may require assistance before they will be able to demonstrate learning.

Nessel (1987) comments that question-and-answer sessions that do not develop understanding "amount to a thinly disguised test, not a true exchange of ideas" (p. 443). When question-and-answer sessions become drills, teachers will not be able to determine whether a question has been misunderstood or poorly phrased or whether the student has difficulty constructing a response. Unless teachers use pop quizzes for instruction rather than for grading, they will defeat their own purposes and send an incorrect message to students: It's not important to understand the material, just to recount it!

Instead, pop quizzes should be used to evaluate what teachers can be reasonably sure has been achieved. For instance, rather than "popping" questions for a grade, a teacher could check to see whether students followed instructions for reading an assignment. A teacher could also use a writing activity (such as the activities described in Chapter 9) to make certain that homework was attempted. If understanding the homework was the problem, the students' written comments will show the teacher that the attempt was made. If students do this, they demonstrate that they tried to read for the assigned purpose. This demonstration will accomplish the same purpose as a pop quiz.

One middle-school mathematics teacher, Mary Broussard, allows students to accumulate points toward their final grade by doing homework. The students are also tested, and the homework points do not outweigh the test grade. This teacher encourages students to try, knowing that they can get some credit for doing so, and she uses the class review to clear up confusions.

Activity 7.12 shows a homework comprehension sheet designed by a middle-school social studies teacher to indicate whether students attempted their homework and also to help the teacher focus the lesson. Before assigning the reading as homework, the teacher asked the students to survey the reading and write three questions that they expected to answer from it. When they arrived in class the next day, the teacher distributed this exercise. The teacher could rapidly review the responses to the homework comprehension sheet to find out who had completed the assignment. Areas of student confusion as well as student interests could be ascertained. This activity serves as a check of homework and also as a way to determine student background for the rest of the lesson.

We encourage teachers to think carefully about why they plan to administer a pop quiz, then design the quiz to achieve their objectives. If the objective is to promote student independence and responsibility, then the social studies teacher's solution works very well. If it is to "catch" students, we ask teachers to please think again about assisting versus evaluating comprehension.

Traditional Evaluation

Traditional test items include objective questions, essay questions, or a combination. Objective tests include multiple-choice, true/false, matching, and completion questions. Teachers find such items easy to grade but difficult to phrase. Students sometimes label objective items as "tricky," "confusing," or even "too easy." Essay tests require students to write about a given topic. Students some-

ACTIVITY 7.12 Homework Comprehension Sheet

On this paper (front and back) I want you to answer the following questions as completely as you can.

1. How did you study pages 192–194 in Social Studies?
2. What did you learn from these pages?
3. Do you see any similarities between your life and the life of the people mentioned?
4. Were there any passages, terms, or concepts you found difficult to understand?
5. What part of this reading did you find most interesting?
6. How do you feel you answered these questions?
7. Why do you feel the way you do?

Developed by Charles Carroll.

---

times label essay questions as "confusing," "too hard," or "not fair." Essay formats are also labeled "subjective" because teachers must spend time considering responses carefully when grading. However, essay questions are not subjective or difficult to grade when questions are written clearly and carefully. Furthermore, essay questions offer a viable way to evaluate critical thinking and the applied level of comprehension.

Problems with Traditional Tests The single greatest problem with traditional tests is that the grades students receive are very often disappointing to teachers. We think that the single best solution to this problem is for teachers to stop giving tests before students experience the preparation and assistance phases of the PAR Lesson Framework. Yet, even allowing for this solution, many other problems with traditional tests have been identified.

Captrends ("Window on the classroom," 1984) reports a study of 342 teacher-made tests in a Cleveland, Ohio, school district. Administrators, supervisors, and teachers representing all subject areas reviewed tests from all grade levels. The format that these reviewers found throughout the tests was similar to the format that we described: objective, short-answer questions. Only 2 percent of all items in the 342 tests were of the essay type.

The researchers found many problems with the presentation of the test items. Directions were often unclear, sometimes nonexistent. Poor legibility, incorrect grammar, and weak writing skills made some items difficult to read. Point values for test items and sections were noticeably absent. Ambiguity in questions led to the possibility of more than one correct response or student confusion about choices to make in responding to items. In addition, the types of questions asked were predominantly literal. Almost 80 percent of all the items concentrated on knowledge of facts, terms, and rules. The middle-school tests used literal questions even more than the elementary or high school tests did. Questions at the application level of comprehension accounted for only

3 percent of all the questions asked. Hathaway (1983) provides a more complete description of this project.

One eighth-grade English teacher took a "hard look" at her test and found that

> the primary comprehension focus was a mixture of all three levels, but more literal and inferential than application. . . . comprehension was dependent on recall more than real learning. . . . the test was too long and looked hard. . . . I neglected to give point values or the weight of the test in the final grade. (Baxter, 1985)

This teacher revised her test and summarized her satisfaction with the new version:

> All in all, I feel that the best feature of my redesigned test is that it captures many concepts and is a more appealing form. In relation to the original test, I feel this test allows the students to demonstrate more of his/her knowledge of the material covered in the unit by giving specific responses, especially in the discussion section. I feel this test will net better student response because it appears shorter, looks more appealing, and is different from usual tests I would have given in similar teaching situations before. (Baxter, 1985)

We see five problems as characteristic of teacher-designed classroom tests. First, students today are "overstuffed and undernourished" (Dempster, 1993, p. 434) as they read to learn from textbooks. Textbooks tend to bombard the learner with an abundance of facts without incorporating enough in-depth explanation. Students are left with many details and only superficial understanding of a topic. Tests based on such textbooks focus on details rather than on major ideas.

Second, teachers seem to rely on the objective format, and factual questions dominate their tests. We infer that teachers find such items relatively easy to construct. Perhaps they think knowledge of facts is especially important to test. Certainly, if an excessive amount of detailed material on a topic is presented in a textbook, teachers are likely to consider factual questioning a logical choice. Whatever the underlying reasons, a major problem with this format is that students learn what we model. If we send the message through our tests that the factual level is much more important than the interpretive or applied level, then that is what students will learn; and even if our instruction emphasizes interpretation and application of content, the message inherent in the test questions will supersede the instructional intent. Students won't learn how to think critically if we don't require that they demonstrate such thinking on tests. Notice how Activity 7.13 provides a check on whether students understand a third-grade mathematics lesson by asking students to demonstrate learning through interpretation and application.

Third, teachers seem to have difficulty expressing themselves clearly when they write questions and construct tests. Perhaps they need more practice in writing and in expressing themselves. However, the problem may indicate more specifically that teachers need practice in constructing good questions.

ACTIVITY 7.13 Demonstrating Learning Through Interpretation and Application, Third-Grade Math

Summing Up Your Measurements

These activities are designed to determine how well you have understood the chapter on measurements. You will demonstrate your knowledge and understanding by performing the following activities.

The first activity will be done with your assigned group. The next three will be performed on your own. Be careful and have fun!

1. Read the recipe first. Make the individual assignments. With your group, make a vanilla pudding.
   - Who will read the recipe?
   - Who will assemble the cooking utensils and cups?
   - Who will mix the ingredients?
   - Who will pour the "hot" mixture into the cups? (Use pot holders!)
   - Who will place the cups in the pan and take them to the refrigerator?
2. Read the outdoor thermometer at three different periods of the day (morning, midday, afternoon). Record the temperature at each period.
3. Use the scales to weigh your empty lunch box, your mathematics book, and your wallet/purse. Record each weight.
4. Measure the perimeter of your desktop, your closet cubbyholes, and any other item on the classroom floor. Record each.

Developed by Bessie Haskins.

Fourth, students may not be ready for a test because they have not developed enough understanding of a topic. This problem might occur because teachers need to provide more assistance or because students have not assumed enough responsibility for their own learning.

Fifth, students must be responsible for demonstrating their learning. They need to take an active role in designing assessments that help them demonstrate what they know in relation to real-life situations. If teachers are always the ones designing tests, then students have a very limited role—regurgitating information for the teacher. This is why so many students tend to quit rather than study; they don't see any point to a test that doesn't seem "real" to them.

How to Improve the Design of Tests Many teachers like to use traditional tests. There is great value in what is known and experienced. By reviewing the flaws discovered in many tests, teachers can improve traditional tests immensely. When constructing traditional tests, keep in mind these general guidelines:

1. Questions on a test should reflect a balance among the three basic comprehension levels.

2. The difficulty of questions should be related to the task required. Recall is harder than recognition; production is harder than recall. Questions with several parts are more difficult than questions with one part. Selecting is easier than generating. Teachers should try to vary their use of difficult and easy questions within a test.
3. Sometimes the answer that a student gives is unanticipated but better than the expected response. Teachers will want to write questions carefully to avoid ambiguity but still encourage spontaneous critical thinking.
4. The best-worded test items do not provide secondary clues to the correct answer. Carter (1986) found that teachers often give inadvertent clues to students, who are very facile at discerning this giveaway. For instance, students learn that correct answers on a multiple-choice test are often keyed to choice c and that the longest choice is most likely to be the correct answer. Also, the stem often signals one obvious match among the multiple choices. Students realize that for both multiple-choice and true/false items, positive statements are more likely than negative statements to be correct choices. Teachers sometimes give answers away with grammatical clues. With Carter's study in mind, teachers will want to express themselves very carefully!
5. When wording test items, teachers need to consider their students' language proficiency. A well-worded test that does not match the students' knowledge of language will result in poor comprehension even though the students' learning may be excellent. Drum, Calfee, and Cook (1981, pp. 488–489) caution that the abilities needed for successful test performance on a comprehension test include the following:

   Accurate and fluent word recognition

   Knowledge of specific word meanings

   Knowledge of syntactic/semantic clause and sentence relationships

   Recognition of the superordinate/subordinate idea structure of passages

   Identification of the specific information requested in questions

   Evaluation of the alternate choices in order to select the one that fits

Preparing and Assisting Students for Traditional Tests By using the PAR Lesson Framework, teachers can fulfill much of their instructional role in readying students to take tests. We find that some other techniques also prepare and assist students in test performance.

Using Study Questions. Teachers who encourage students to use study questions find this technique very helpful. Study questions can be used in a variety of ways. The teacher can prepare a list of questions to be included on the test and distribute the list at the beginning of a unit so students can refer to it throughout the unit. Or the teacher can suggest possible test questions as instruction proceeds and then review all of the questions after completing the unit. This list can become the pool for essay-test items. The teacher might tell students that the test will include only questions from this list. Such a technique has merit for two reasons: A test bank is acquired as the unit progresses, thus eliminating last-minute test construction; and students have a study guide that is familiar, thorough, and not intimidating. If the teacher creates questions that follow the question-construction guidelines and covers representative content with these questions, the technique works well.

Some teachers advise students before testing about what the specific test questions will be. This technique works better with essay questions than with objective questions. Although many teachers are hesitant about providing questions in advance, fearing that students will not study everything, this can be a wise way to prepare and assist students. The fact is that students cannot study everything anyhow, and they certainly cannot remember everything for a long period of time. If the essential information is covered in the proposed questions, then a question list can be very effective.

Having students themselves create the questions for a test is sometimes a good technique. This option requires that students understand the content thoroughly and also understand how to write good questions. An alternative for younger students and those not proficient at question construction is to have students use brainstorming to predict possible test topics and then informally generate questions. A first-grader could speculate: "I think you might ask me to explain about how fish breathe." Students can construct possible items for an objective as well as an essay test, or they can review items from sample tests that the teacher provides. Teachers who encourage students to create possible test questions should be sure to include some version of the students' questions on the actual test.

Any variation on student construction of the test questions will provide students with practice in questioning and answering, provoke critical thinking, and promote the students' responsibility for their own learning. Another bonus is that students who are familiar with the teacher's way of designing a test will be less anxious about being tested. Test anxiety accounts for much poor test response.

Using Open Books or Notes. Teachers find that allowing students to use open books or open notes—or both—enables students to concentrate on producing the best response on a test and assists them in the actual test-taking process. This technique encourages good note-taking strategies and clear organization of information by promoting recognition and production rather than recall.

Nontraditional Tests

Everyone appreciates variety. Teachers may be pleasantly surprised to find that students increase productivity when an evaluation device looks more like the strategies that have been used to instruct than the same old test format. "Conventional policy-based testing . . . is the wrong kind of tool for thoughtfulness. It makes people accountable only for the development of very low levels of knowledge and skill" (Brown, 1987, p. 5). Although Brown's comments refer specifically to standardized tests, we think they are applicable to teacher-made, nontraditional tests as well. We encourage teachers to use new strategies for testing, arguing that even when poorly made objective tests are redesigned, they do not correlate with the type of achievement required in a world where concepts are more important than facts. We must alter our testing procedures if we want to produce critical, thoughtful readers. Creative thinkers often perform much better on tests that are nontraditional and reflect nontraditional instructional activities.

By employing some of the strategies that we present in this book, teachers can construct tests that contain few traditional items. The most **nontraditional test** would eliminate questioning altogether. Although teachers may not wish to design an entire test with no questions, some nontraditional items might spark interest. Primary teachers are especially attracted by nontraditional tests, and intermediate and secondary teachers may prefer adding some nontraditional items to a more traditional test. The possibilities are as numerous as the types of activities presented in this text.

The following activities can be used as nontraditional test items. Teachers who have designed tests using such items report that they elicit more critical thinking from their students. We are sure that teachers will see the possibilities for designing many activities as nontraditional test items.

Graphic Organizers Chapters in this book begin with graphic organizers. At the end of some chapters, the organizer is repeated, but with gaps; the reader is asked to identify what is missing and recall where it should be placed within the organizer. This activity encourages readers to remember what they have read. Similarly, a teacher can instruct by using a graphic organizer, map, structured overview, jot chart, or any such visual aid and then present the organizer with blanks on a test, where it becomes a nontraditional test item for eliciting responses that demonstrate knowledge of facts. Such is the case with the example in Activity 7.14, designed by an eleventh-grade teacher. If the teacher provides a list of terms that could complete the organizer, then recognition of facts is tested. Such is the case in the example in Activity 7.15, designed for an elementary social studies class.

If the teacher asks students to explain why they positioned words at certain points on the organizer, then the interpretive level of comprehension is being tested. If the teacher asks students to create an organizer using terms they learned during the lesson, the applied level of comprehension is demonstrated. No traditional questions are asked, yet comprehension can be evaluated and graded. The test item might read as follows:

> Study the organizer I have drawn for you. It is like the one we studied in class, but in this one there are several blank spaces. Using the list of terms attached, fill in the term that fits best in each space (1 point each). Then write one sentence beside each term listed; this sentence should explain why you think the term belongs where you put it in the organizer (2 points each). Next, write an essay that includes the information in this organizer. Your first paragraph should

provide four (4) details. Your last paragraph should summarize by telling what new information you have learned by reading this chapter (25 points).

Notice that the directions are specific and that point values are given for each procedure. Factual knowledge is tested, but some interpretation and application are also required. Writing an essay is also part of this question. Because the components of the essay are defined, grading it should be simple. It is also possible to prepare a rubric for this essay:

> An A essay will contain 3 or 4 paragraphs that explain fully all of the information on the organizer. Students not only will demonstrate factual knowledge but also will show inferences and applications. The entire list of terms will be appropriately placed and thoroughly defined. The essay will have a clear beginning and end.
>
> A B essay will contain 2 or 3 paragraphs that explain the information on the organizer. Students will demonstrate factual and interpretive knowledge. The entire list of terms will be appropriately placed and adequately explained. The essay will have a clear beginning and end.

ACTIVITY 7.14 Geometry Organizer

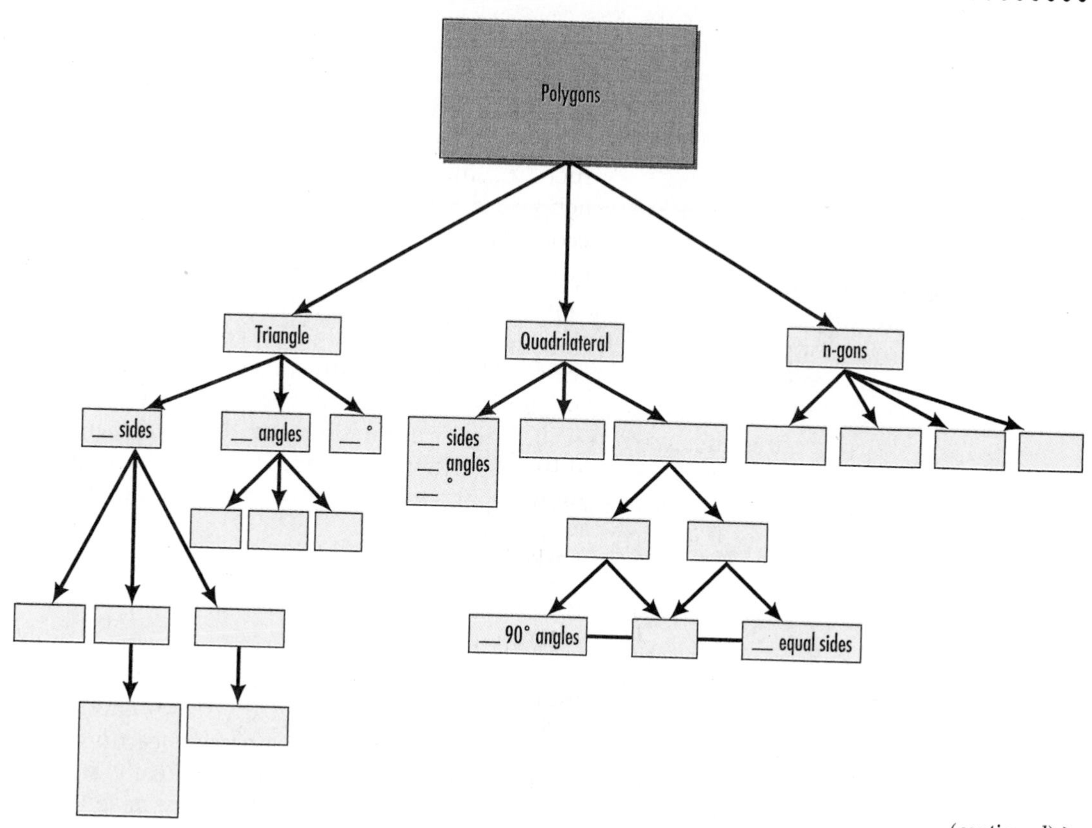

(continued) ➤

continued

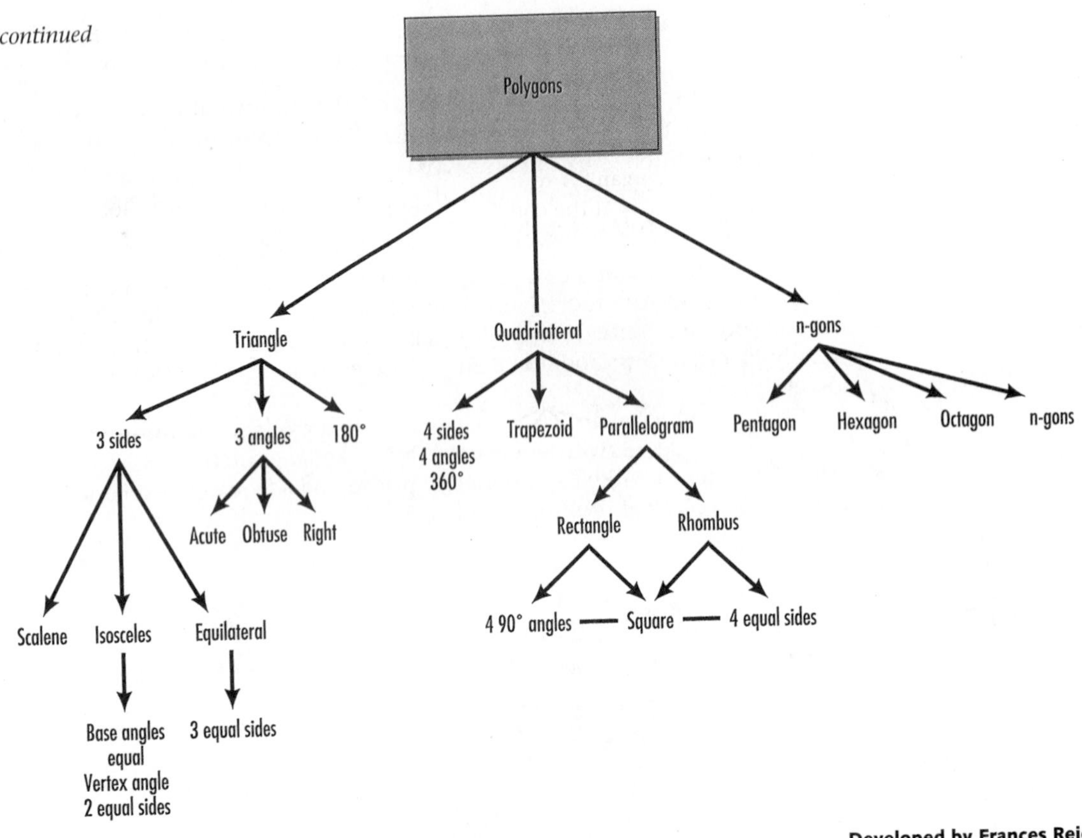

Developed by Frances Reid.

Factstorming **Factstorming** is a good preparation activity because students identify familiar terms about a topic before they study further. Students can add to the list produced by factstorming after their studying is completed; the additions become an evaluation of new learning. If students are asked to explain each addition, they are demonstrating interpretation of information. If students categorize the already-known and new information and then write an essay about this categorization, application is demonstrated. The use of factstorming as a test item is similar to the last step in either a KWL or a What-I-Know Activity (WIKA), but it is graded.

Encouraging Student Responsibility

Teachers can design evaluation that encourages students to take responsibility for their own learning. Coleman and colleagues (1969) stated that students need to perceive that they have a significant influence over their own educational destinies. Negative perceptions are often the result of a passive learning situation in which children accept control by others as their fate. Ideally, students should view evaluation as an opportunity to express what they have learned

ACTIVITY 7.15 Social Studies Organizer

Description of Activity: The students fill in a graphic organizer to determine comprehension. The overview was previously introduced on an overhead projector to help build background of key concepts in the unit. The students received a copy of the organizer to take home and study. The graphic organizer is presented to the Chapter 1 students as a posttest at the conclusion of the unit. Since Chapter 1 students may have a difficult time remembering the concept names, an answer key has to be included with the organizer.

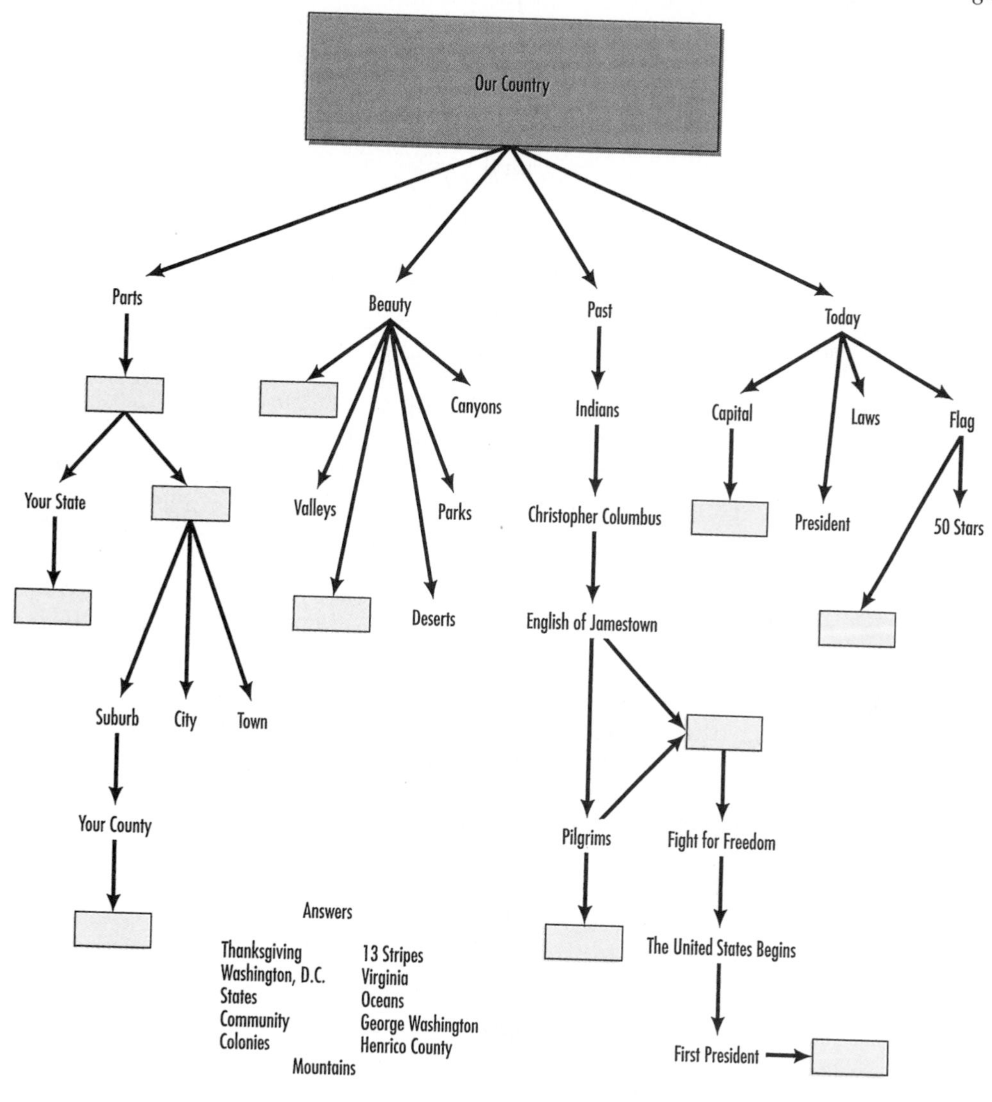

Developed by Sandra Zeller and Brenda Winston.

rather than as an exercise in futility. How can such an active view of evaluation be implemented? First we provide some ideas specific to traditional and non-traditional test formats. Then we suggest an approach to evaluation more encompassing than specific testing.

A Test PAR

Teachers can design tests with a self-rating included on the test. Hoffman (1983) originated this rating technique to be used in journal entries, and Richardson (1992b) created a version for tests. The first questions on a test might be: How did you study for this test? How much did you study? How well do you think you will do? The answers show how the students prepared. Before the test is returned, a second set of questions should be asked: Now that you have taken the test, and before it is returned, was this test what you expected and prepared for? What grade do you think you will receive? These questions can assist the student in taking responsibility for studying and producing a good test response. The third set of questions promotes reflection. It is answered after the teacher returns and reviews the test with the students: Now that you have gone over your test, would you say that you studied adequately? Was your grade representative of your learning? Why or why not? What have you learned about taking tests?

Such a three-step process built into the testing procedure will send the message that the student is ultimately responsible for demonstrating learning. If teachers use the procedure often on tests, the student should begin to take a more active role. Teachers will also be enlightened by students' views of studying and taking tests and can apply this information in their instruction and when constructing tests. Students' responses to such questions also foster writing opportunities. For this test PAR to work, teachers should grade and return tests promptly. The answers should be reviewed—through written comments on the tests, in-class discussion, or both—so that students can use the test as a learning experience for the next test. Only under these conditions can an environment for reflection be assured.

One of the requirements for designing good tests is to use previous tests as the basis for constructing new ones. Students learn how to take an individual teacher's tests by learning that teacher's style. Teachers should learn how to design tests based on students' styles of learning as well. Did students need clearer directions? Did they use appropriate study procedures? Do they need reminders about certain test procedures?

Helping Students Become Test-Wise

The acronym **SCORER** (Carmen & Adams, 1972; Lee & Allen, 1981) refers to a test-taking strategy. High SCORERs **s**chedule their time; identify **c**lue words to help answer the questions (the directions should contain them); **o**mit the hardest items, at least at first; **r**ead carefully to be sure they understand and fully answer the question; **e**stimate what to include in the response, perhaps by jotting down some notes or an outline; and **r**eview their responses before turning in the test. Teachers might teach SCORER to students and then insert the acronym into test directions or include it as a reminder on tests. Students even could be asked to account for how they used SCORER while completing the test. This strategy places responsibility on students to take a test wisely, in an organized and comprehensive manner. SCORER can be used as part of any test design.

There are other ways to make certain students become **test-wise**—that is, able to use a plan of attack regardless of the specific test content. Students become used to taking tests. They become confident because they understand how tests are designed and can capitalize on that knowledge to demonstrate their learning. Being test-wise is knowing the program, to use Hart's (1983a) terminology—or, in other words, the system. When students know how to take a test, they can concentrate their energy on answering the items. Being test-wise helps alleviate test anxiety. Panic—the "blank mind" syndrome—can be avoided. The older mammalian brain can send encouraging messages to the newer mammalian brain, and the student can then apply thinking skills to show knowledge.

Carter's (1986) study, cited earlier, indicated that students discern the inadvertent clues teachers give in test items; this is a test-wise ability. Many teachers provide a bit of information in one question that can help students answer another question. Students who watch for these clues are SCORERs. Studies (Scruggs, White, & Bennion, 1986; Ritter & Idol-Mastas, 1986) indicate that instruction in test-wise skills can help students perform better on tests. An instructional session that reviews a list of test-taking tips is helpful, particularly with older students, in improving results on standardized tests. When a teacher wants students to improve performance on classroom tests, such test-wise instruction is best done in the content teacher's classrooms with application to a particular test. The following list of test-taking tips indicates the kinds of suggestions that teachers can give to help students become proficient test-takers:

1. Be calm.
2. Read through the entire test before answering any items. Look for questions that might provide clues to other answers.
3. Plan your time. If one question is worth several points and others are worth much less, spend the majority of the time on the question or questions where the greatest number of points can be made.
4. Answer first the questions for which you are most confident about your answers.
5. On objective tests, remember to be logical and reasonable. Consider your possible answers carefully. Look for "giveaway" words that indicate extremes: *all, none, never, always*. They probably should be avoided when you select the correct answer. On multiple-choice items, think what the answer should be; then look at the choices. Also, eliminate implausible responses by thinking carefully about each choice.
6. For essays, jot down an outline of what you intend to write before you start writing. Be sure you understand the teacher's terms: *List* means to state a series, but *describe* means to explain the items. *Compare* means to show similarities; *contrast* means to show differences. Make sure you answer all the parts of a question.

A Checklist for Designing a Test

The following questions constitute a checklist for test construction. The checklist is useful for teachers who want to review previously designed tests that have produced unsatisfactory results.

1. How did you prepare the class to study for this test? If you suggested certain study strategies, are you asking questions that will capitalize on these strategies? For instance, if you suggested that students study causes and effects by using a pattern guide, are you designing test items that will call for a demonstration of causes and effects?
2. Are you including SCORER, a self-evaluation of test preparedness, or some other way of reminding students about their responsibilities as test-takers?
3. Do the items on your test reflect your goals and objectives in teaching the content? Test items should test what was taught. If a major objective is that students be able to name states and their capitals, how can this test measure that objective?
4. What is your main comprehension focus? Why? If you think that factual knowledge is more important on this test than interpretation or application, can you justify this emphasis? Remember that many tests rely too much on factual questions at the expense of other levels of comprehension. Be sure that the factual level is the most important for this test.
5. Do you require comprehension at each of the three levels? What proportion of your questions addresses each level? What is your reasoning for this division? Remember that tests imply the kind of thinking that teachers expect of their students. Have you asked your students to think broadly and deeply?
6. What types of responses are you asking of students? Will they need to recognize, recall, or produce information? A good balance of responses is usually preferable to only recognition, recall, or production. More thinking is required of students when production is requested.
7. Did you phrase your test items so that comprehension is dependent on the learned material rather than on experience or verbatim recall? Remember that although the preparation stage often calls for students to identify what they already know before a topic is taught, your test should find out what they have learned since then.
8. Is the weight of the test in the final grade clear to students? Is the weight of each item on the test clear? Is the weight of parts of an item clear within the item?
9. Did you consider alternatives to traditional test items, such as statements (instead of questions) or graphic organizers? Is writing an important part of your test? Why or why not?
10. For objective tests, what format have you selected and why (multiple-

choice, true/false, incomplete sentences, short answers)? How many of each type did you include? Why?

11. For essay tests, have you carefully asked for all of the aspects of the answer that you are looking for? Are descriptive words (such as *describe* or *compare*) clear?
12. Is the wording on this test clear? Is the test uncluttered, with items well spaced? Does the test look appealing?
13. Have you been considerate of the needs of mainstreamed students in your test design?

Authentic Assessment

We have already pointed out that students are often stuffed with literal information but not often encouraged to think about how such information can be relevant to them. **Authentic assessment** offers a viable solution. This term often refers to evaluation that takes place in naturalistic situations that resemble the settings where a skill or knowledge is actually used or applied. While the term "assessment" implies finding out what students already know, authentic assessment is broader in application, including informal evaluation procedures as well as determination of prior knowledge. In this section we describe ways to use authentic assessment as a means of evaluating what students have learned.

When teachers employ some nontraditional test items, they are moving toward authentic assessment, which is alternative, performance based, and process oriented. Traditional tests are specific measures given at specified times. Authentic assessment measures or samples student performance over time to see how student learning develops, matures, and ultimately reflects knowledge of the concepts learned in a real context. Brady (1993) suggests that authentic assessment builds relationships among the physical environment, the people who live in that environment, the reasons for or beliefs about completing activities in that environment, and the manifestation of these beliefs in human behavior. In short, authentic assessment is a means of showing students why they are learning, as well as a means of showing educators what students have learned.

Authentic assessment emphasizes realistic and challenging material used over time (Biggs, 1992) as evaluation and can be a link between previously taught material and current instruction. As Hager and Gable (1993) indicate, the increased use of observational and performance-based measures and process instruments, as well as content- or course-specific instruction, is essential to authentic assessment. Students can help decide what should be assessed, thus gaining an important role in demonstrating their own learning. Students enjoy creating authentic projects. In 1995, a group of middle-school students wrote a script for and produced a video about the hazards of drugs. As they graduated from high school in 1999, these students were still talking about the fun they had making the video. It is doubtful that they would have remembered the information learned about drug hazards so well if a test or paper assignment had been the measure of evaluation.

The contexts for authentic assessment might include observing a performance or simulation, or completing a task in a real-world situation. Students will want to do well because the real-world consequences are clear. For instance, actually driving a car yields a more authentic assessment than taking a paper-and-pencil test in a driver education course. Or, encouraging the student to show what steps were followed to complete a math problem is a way of demonstrating the logical processing of information. The process of completing the task reveals as much about the student's learning—maybe more—than the product recorded as a test grade.

Developing Authentic Assessments

Tierney (1998) writes about the reform in assessment practices. He points out that developing better evaluation means more than just creating a new test. He argues that, if the point of literacy is to become immersed in text rather than to "be subjugated by it" (p. 375), then we must be thoughtful about how we incorporate authentic assessment into our evaluation procedures. Because learning is a complicated process, evaluation must consider many complex ways to represent itself. Should observation be an assessment component? How? For how long? Under what conditions? Should learners select for themselves what will illustrate their learning? Worthen (1993) suggests that activities based on learning logs, double-entry journals (both explained in Chapter 9), and observation notes can reveal much about student performance over time. In Chapter 9 we describe a process activity called C3B4Me that clearly shows how students improve their writing over time. We know teachers who keep gummed labels on a clipboard; as they walk around the classroom, they make notes on these labels, which they later stick into a student's folder. These notes often reveal important learning patterns. Such notes can be kept in any content classroom; they could be particularly useful during science labs, reading or writing workshops, cooperative group work, or library work. Performance measures might include oral debates, post graphic organizers, or even presentations developed using the computer program Power Point (see Chapter 3). Wiggins (1990) suggests that a hands-on science test may be more logical than a paper-and-pencil test.

Rhodes and Shanklin (1993) suggest three ways to increase the authenticity of assessment in the classroom from the very start:

1. Provide students with opportunities that let them use language in natural social contexts.
2. Give students choices in materials and activities to ensure they will discover genuine purposes for reading and writing.
3. Follow students' natural leads to focus on communication through interaction with others.

Portfolios as a Means of Authentic Assessment

Many educators advocate the use of portfolios in which students can keep their best work. A **portfolio** is a representative sampling of artifacts that demonstrate a feature or specialty about a person. It is not simply a collection but a showcase. A student might collect many samples of work, but only one artifact might be selected for inclusion in the portfolio because it demonstrates best what the student is showing about herself or himself. Unlike traditional tests, many portfolios demonstrate growth over time.

Portfolios can be used at any grade level. Wagner, Brock, and Agnew (1994) advocate the use of portfolios in teacher education courses, to help students develop a greater understanding of themselves as readers and language users. Here are some general guidelines for portfolio selections in graduate education:

Required Contents

Introduction: Write a basic statement comparing your teaching abilities and the goals you had when you entered the program with your exiting abilities and goals.

Statement of purpose for portfolio: Explain how you will use this portfolio in the future.

Videotape of teaching: Include a tape at least 20 minutes long, to demonstrate your teaching of reading.

Position paper: Explain your position about the teaching of reading and the models that have influenced this position. Include your view of diagnosis, evaluation, authentic assessment, and continuing assessment.

Lesson plans: Include a short sequence with an annotation to explain what you and your students learned over the period of time selected.

Selected entries from a teaching journal: Annotate the entries to indicate what you think they reflect about your view of reading instruction.

Evidence of technological competence: Explain the software that you use, your Internet teaching experiences, and so on.

Scholarly paper: Choose a paper from any of your courses, and explain how this paper reflects your learning experience and knowledge.

Outline of courses taken: For each course include an annotation indicating what was most significant about the course from your perspective.

Summary: Retrospectively analyze what you learned in the program, and indicate how you intend to apply this knowledge in your career.

Suggested Contents

An order for reading materials with rationale for purchase

Photographs of different teaching products, such as bulletin boards and student projects

Critiques of research

Signature activities (those that show your unique strengths)

Portfolios also work well with elementary and secondary students (Cleland, 1999; Abruscato, 1993). Activity 7.16 is an artifact selected by a third-grader to show the many facts he learned over 12 weeks while he studied animals. Activity 7.17 is a list of history trade books that a fourth-grader included in his portfolio to show how he much he had read in 4 weeks.

When students are involved in an authentic assessment plan from the start of the grading period, they become more active participants in the learning

ACTIVITY 7.16 A Page from a Third-Grader's Portfolio

My
Fantastic
Animals

Did you know that snakes eat bats?

Did you know that the Indian Python is one of the largest snakes in the world?

The smallest snakes can fit in your hand.

Hummingbirds can fly backwards and hover motionless.

This is my mini-page about animals. I wanted to include this page in my portfolio to show what I learned about animals.

This page was created with *The Writing Center*, from The Learning Company, 6943 Kaiser Drive, Fremont, CA 94555.

ACTIVITY 7.17 A Page from a Fourth-Grader's Portfolio

Books I read in History:

Meet Martin Luther King, Jr.
Meet Maya Angelou
The Story of Harriet Tubman, Conductor of the Underground Railroad
The Story of George Washington Carver
If You Traveled on the Underground Railroad

I chose this list of books I read to put in my portfolio because I never liked to read before. I did not know very much about history, but now I have practiced reading and learned a lot too! I like to read about real people and find out about real things.

---

process. Students should be encouraged to develop goals for their progress during the period and indicate possible ways in which they can demonstrate their growth at the end of the period. Teachers in consultation with their students can guide students toward realistic and reasonable goals. Students then collect their own evidence of their learning from the very beginning of a grading period. Teachers should supply each student with a folder, and then teacher and students decide together what types of work will be kept in it. At the end of a specified period of time, students designate which pieces of work in the folder show progress or demonstrate a particular accomplishment. It is a good idea to keep the portfolio folders in the classroom in a storage file at all times. This ensures that papers will not be lost and provides easy access for students wishing to peruse or upgrade their portfolios. Products they select may reflect their learning much more fully over a long time than a traditional test—which captures only one moment in time—could do.

What types of samples should be collected during weeks one, two, three, and so on? What types of samples should be collected to demonstrate the achievement of course goals? Some measures of prior knowledge of the topic, such as recognition pretests or anticipation guides, would provide a baseline measure (see Chapters 4 and 5). For instance, preattitude and postattitude surveys might be the first and last pieces collected. Work samples, such as jot charts (explained in Chapter 6), two-column notes (explained in Chapter 10), and graphic organizers, might be included. Quizzes, tests, and corrections could be saved. At grading time, the most representative piece and a "best" piece could be selected. Both process activities and products can be collected.

Abruscato (1993) describes Vermont's adoption of writing and math portfolios as a major means of statewide assessment. The assessment includes evidence of problem-solving and communication skills. Samples included in the writing portfolio are a table of contents, a "best piece," a letter, creative writing, a personal response, a prose piece from a content area, and an on-the-spot writing sample. Samples included in the math portfolio are five to seven "best pieces," such as puzzles, a letter to the evaluator, and a collection of math work.

Results so far indicate that the students who score highest on their writing read at least once a week for pleasure. The greatest problem discovered by studying the math portfolios is that students have trouble presenting their results clearly and lack variety in their approaches to solving problems. Such findings will help educators build a more effective curriculum and enhance learning.

Here are some general guidelines for assembling a portfolio:

1. Organize with a table of contents and section divisions. Select categories to best represent your progress, such as "favorite activities," "activities I did not like," and "what I am most proud of."
2. Include representative samples of your work over time. Be sure to date the samples and make clear why you included them.
3. Annotate each sample to explain why it is included. The focus here is on individual samples, not the total progression.
4. Conclude with a reflective but brief summary that explains your progress in relation to the portfolio contents: What were your goals? What was learned? How, *overall*, do these artifacts demonstrate this?
5. Make sure that the number of samples is reasonable and representative of the depth and breadth of your learning (at least one sample per week during a 10- or 12-week grading period).

Teachers need to establish what they expect their students to demonstrate in the portfolios. Will specific knowledge be expected? Will some example of weekly progress be necessary? How will the portfolios be graded, if at all? Will they constitute the total grade or a portion of the grade? Who will read the portfolios—just the teacher and student, the parent, the principal, other students? After making the expectations clear to students, teachers need to encourage students to take ownership and make their own choices within the established parameters. It is a good idea to hold at least a midpoint conference so that students can practice articulating their choices and the teacher can guide the process. Activity 7.18 is an example of a portfolio guideline for high school English students.

Getting Started with Authentic Assessment

In the classroom, content-area teachers can begin focusing on authentic assessment by keeping a checklist of essential developments that they want students to demonstrate. The checklists presented in Activity 7.19 can be modified as new criteria are added and then removed as students' developmental needs are met. Such a checklist can help teachers keep an ongoing record of subtle developments in the students' reading, writing, and thinking abilities.

A small start such as using a checklist is the easiest way to begin authentic assessment. At this level the students' development—trial and error, dialogue, self-criticism—can be assessed most readily. Samples can be taken over time, and students can be involved in designing the assessment and collecting the samples. Also, the teacher can make certain that both process and product are measured

ACTIVITY 7.18 Portfolio Requirements for English 11/ First Grading Period

This portfolio will count as 25% of your grade. Include pieces that YOU think best represent your learning about Early American History and Literature.

You should have at least eight pieces, one per week. Each should be annotated to explain why it represents your learning for this marking period. You may include more than one piece of the same type (2–3 maps), but there should be some variety also.

You should write a summary of no more than 2 pages that explains how you met the objectives for this unit.

SUGGESTIONS FOR SELECTIONS:

Completed jot chart of Early American authors: their work, language style, and representative vocabulary
Quizzes taken
Essays written—this can include any drafts that you think show your progress in writing and thinking about the topic
Three-level guides completed and annotated
Notes from any day's discussions
Post graphic organizer of *The Crucible*
Favorite quotes from *The Crucible*
Maps of *The Crucible*: acts, characters

ACTIVITY 7.19 Checklist for Assessment Observed over the Month of ______________

★ Excellent √ Good × Average ♦ Lacking—needs to improve

Name	Student Self-Evaluation	Decision Making	Questioning	Problem Solving	Attitude & Motivation	Inferential Thinking	Clarity of Writing
Bobby	√	★	★	√	★	√	×
Sue	×	√	×	♦	√	×	×
Beverly	★	√	★	★	√	√	★
Joan	♦	♦	×	♦	√	√	×
Jim	×	√	×	×	√	√	♦

and that audiences—such as the students, their parents, and administrators—will be able to understand the samples and how they demonstrate progress in learning. Authentic assessment is the ultimate nontraditional evaluation. It is a challenge that can bring new enthusiasm to learning in every content area.

One-Minute Summary

Teachers must foster learning by developing reading comprehension and providing adequate classroom time after the reading for students to reflect on what they have learned. In this chapter we provide a rationale for the importance of the third phase of the PAR Lesson Framework—reflection—and we present strategies for teaching important reflection skills such as critical thinking, problem solving, decision making, analyzing an author's techniques, separating fact from opinion, detecting propaganda, and test taking. We demonstrate the need to help students go from dependence to independence in reading—to make students autonomous learners. We make the case that student reflection aids in comprehension and retention of reading. We present activities that foster reflection in reading and writing, such as brainstorming, TRIP cards, and post graphic organizers.

Evaluation is a large component of the reflection phase. We describe tests and authentic assessment as ways to measure whether desired learning outcomes are taking place. We explain ways to evaluate both traditionally and in a more authentic manner, especially by introducing portfolios in classrooms.

All of the strategies discussed in this chapter direct students toward independence. Educators of adults write about lifelong learners. Surely the ultimate goal of content reading is to produce lifelong learners. Adults prefer to learn independently. Although they may study in formal courses, they identify their own areas of concentration and structure their learning accordingly. By introducing new activities, allowing plenty of practice, and then directing students to apply the strategies learned from those activities as they read on their own, teachers enable their students to become independent learners. This independence goes a long way toward ensuring that students will still be learning about your subject long after they have graduated.

End-of-Chapter Activities

Assisting Comprehension

1. If you would like a "primer" on putting standardized tests in perspective, read *A Teacher's Guide to Standardized Reading Tests* by Calkins, Montgomery, and Santman (1998). This book might be called a "survival guide" for teachers who feel overwhelmed by the emphasis on standardized tests in today's teaching world.

2. Study the graphic organizer that follows. Can you fill in the blanks without looking at the complete version at the beginning of the chapter?

Reflecting on Your Reading

Identify the three most significant things you learned in this chapter. Jot them down; then draft an explanation of why these three items are important to you. Give specific examples of how you can use this new information in your own teaching. Keep this draft for reference in the next few months.

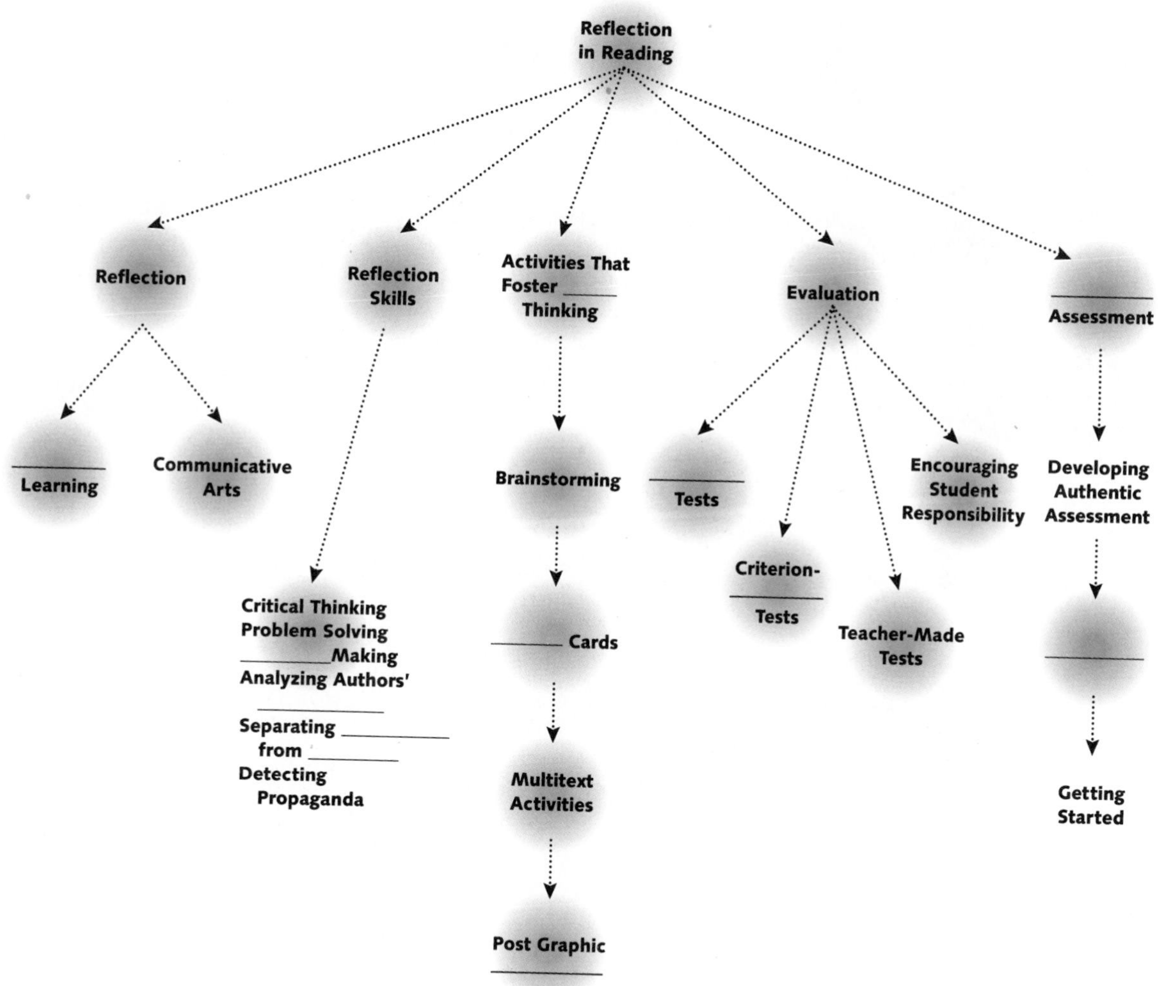

CHAPTER 8

Teaching Vocabulary

Words are things; and a small drop of ink, falling like dew upon a thought, produces that which makes thousands, perhaps millions, think.

—Lord Byron

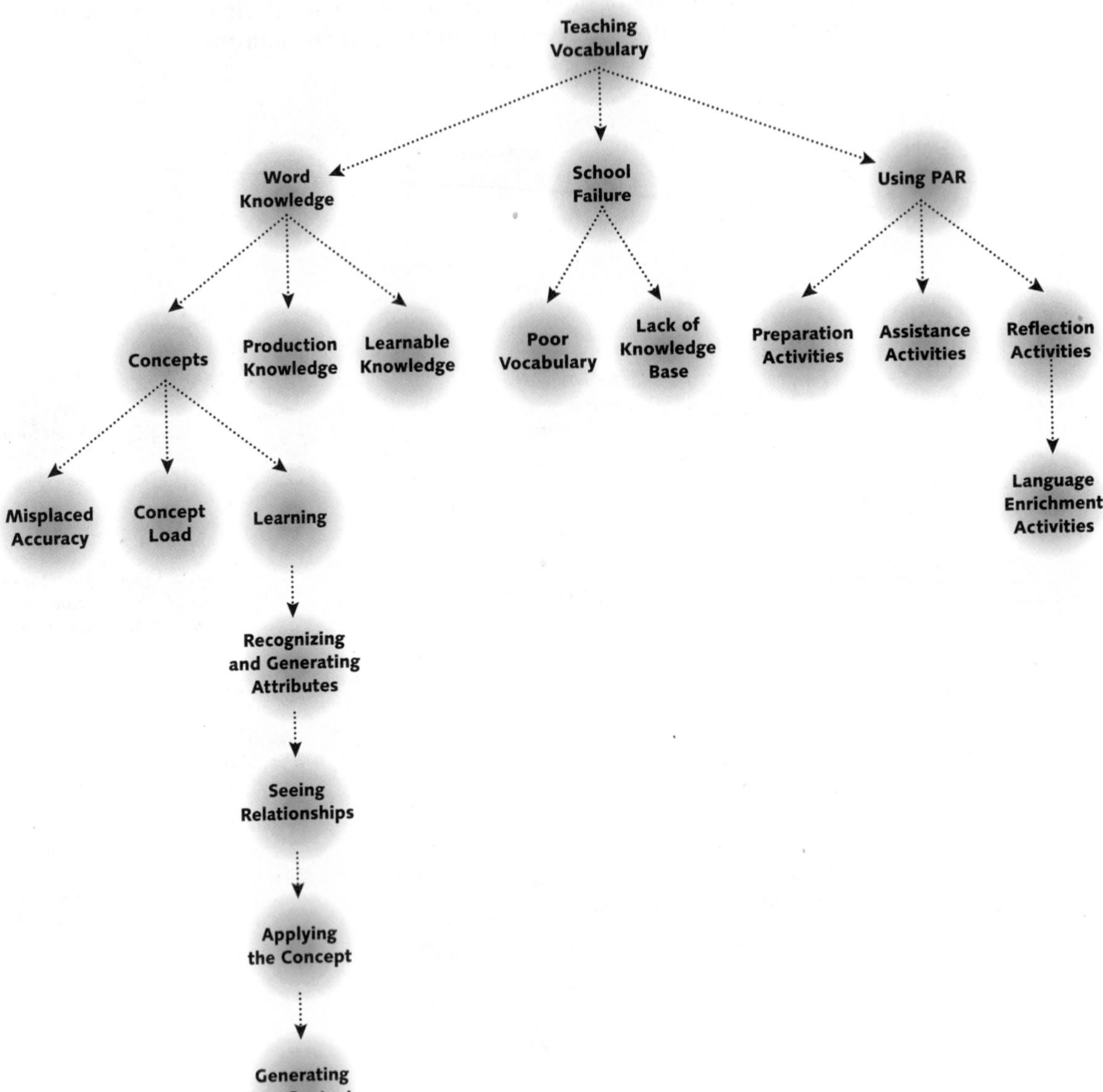

Preparing to Read

1. Before beginning this chapter, list some ways in which you think content-area teachers can generate enthusiasm for word study. How can we get students more interested in finding out the meanings of unfamiliar words? As you read the chapter, see whether any of your ideas coincide with those presented in the chapter.
2. Following is a list of terms used in this chapter. Some may be familiar to you in a general context, but in this chapter they may be used in unfamiliar ways. Rate your knowledge by placing a plus sign (+) in front of those you are sure you know, a check mark (✓) in front of those you have some knowledge about, and a zero (0) in front of those you don't know. Be ready to locate and pay special attention to their meanings when they are presented in the chapter.

_____ misplaced accuracy
_____ production knowledge
_____ learnable knowledge
_____ contextual knowledge
_____ conceptual base
_____ categorization
_____ closed sort
_____ open sort
_____ TOAST
_____ magic squares

Objectives

As you read this chapter, focus your attention on the following objectives. You will:

1. understand the relationship of vocabulary knowledge to reading comprehension.
2. understand the four necessary mental operations for mastering new vocabulary.
3. realize that a student's lack of understanding of concepts and vocabulary can contribute significantly to failure in school.
4. use teaching strategies to increase a student's conceptual understanding of words.

5. identify strategies and activities for teaching vocabulary before, during, and after reading.
6. learn about some enrichment activities for teaching vocabulary.

Understanding Words as Concepts

It has been said that war is too important to leave to the generals. Likewise, vocabulary development is too important to leave to the English and reading teachers. Vocabulary development needs to take place in all content classrooms. Each content field has unique terms and specialized vocabulary whose meanings, if known, lead the reader to the core of conceptual understanding of the text. For instance, in a mathematics lesson on addition and subtraction of fractions, consider the importance of the term *common denominator*. Little else can make sense to the student who does not know this important concept. If teachers in all content areas concentrate on effectively teaching the understanding of terms and concepts within a unit of instruction, students will develop better speaking, listening, reading, and writing vocabularies.

Research has documented the importance of understanding nuances, or shades of meaning. Important concepts are often conveyed through subtle distinctions in meaning. Columnist George Will once wrote that anyone who does not know the difference between *disinterested* (impartial) and *uninterested* (not interested) should be tried in court by an uninterested judge. As another example, consider these three examples:

The man stuffed the basket.

The man wove the basket.

The man emptied the basket.

Describe the mental image you have of the action that each sentence is describing. Would differences in background experiences create different mental images? Can you describe a second mental image for each sentence?

Students' comprehension is greatly influenced by their vocabulary knowledge, which is greatly influenced by their reading. Booth and Hall (1994) found that older students (16 years) used many more sophisticated words than younger students (13 years), most probably because of greater exposure to text reading. They speculate that skilled reading comprehension is reliant on sophisticated word knowledge. A clear indication for teachers is that we must teach directly the many meanings of important words.

Misplaced accuracy often undermines vocabulary knowledge. In practice, teachers limit the study of vocabulary to cursory exercise. This situation is analogous to that of car owners who regularly take their cars to the local car wash but forget to take them to a mechanic for important maintenance, such as lubrication, oil and filter changes, and tune-ups. In short, they take more care with the cosmetics than with the substance of the automobile—the engine, drive train, and chassis. Similarly, teachers who always have students read blithely through chapters without concentrating on the vocabulary—especially the vocabulary that carries the major concept load of the chapter—are guilty of emphasizing form over substance. Meaning in a reading passage is conveyed in words, which are the essence of the chapter, much as the engine and chassis are the underpinnings or the foundation of the automobile. Attention to detail is the foundation of understanding. Words, technical vocabulary, and key concepts are the details of a chapter or passage that students must understand for the big picture of the chapter to come into focus.

A Closer Look at Word Knowledge

A half-century ago, Davis (1944) and Thurstone (1946) wrote that knowledge of word meanings is one of the most important factors in reading comprehension. More recent research attests to the correlation between vocabulary knowledge and unit test scores, oral-reading rates, and teacher judgment (Lovitt, Horton & Bergerud, 1987) as well as comprehension. It is generally agreed that readers can "know" a word but each person may relate it to a different experience. The sentence "John took a plane," for example, could be interpreted in different ways. A young child reading it might imagine playing with a toy; a high school student would imagine a scene in an airport; and an adult who is a carpenter might imagine a carpenter's tool. Simpson (1987) notes that "word knowledge is not a static product but a fluid quality that takes on additional characteristics and attributes as the learner experiences more" (p. 21).

Kibby (1995) proposes a continuum of word knowledge progressing from **production knowledge** to potentially **learnable knowledge**. Production knowledge is evident when a student knows a word so well that she or he can use it with facility in speech and writing. A student does not have learnable knowledge until background knowledge and pertinent information are provided concerning a concept about which students are unclear. Figure 8.1 shows this model.

When an association or concept is known only vaguely or is not known at all, teachers need either to provide learning opportunities or to postpone instruction until students learn prerequisite knowledge. Teachers need ways to determine when to spend time on vocabulary. If they find that students already know a concept and words associated with it, time spent on vocabulary will be wasted. If they assume that students know something that they do not know, the time not spent on vocabulary will cripple the lesson. Groff (1981) argues that direct instruction of reading vocabulary is needed and appropriate for most students.

Generally, concepts and words associated with them are best learned by starting with concrete experiences. Consider this story:

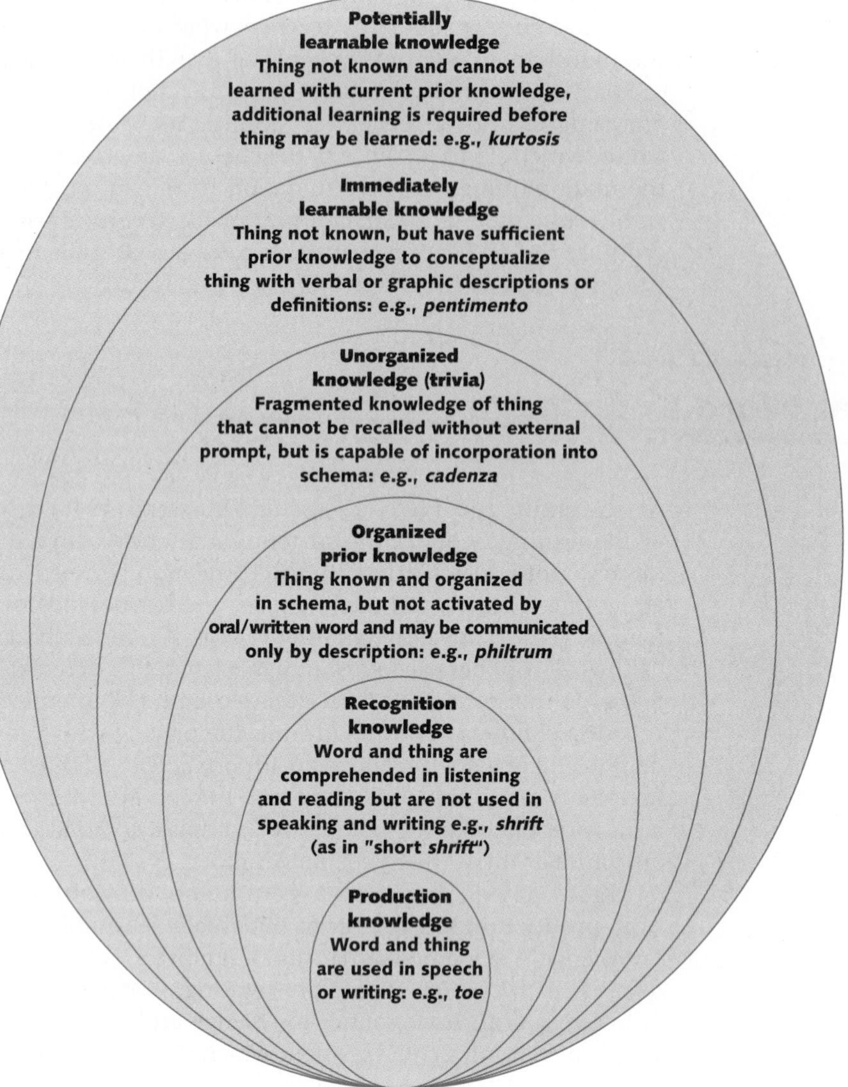

Potentially learnable knowledge
Thing not known and cannot be learned with current prior knowledge, additional learning is required before thing may be learned: e.g., *kurtosis*
Immediately learnable knowledge
Thing not known, but have sufficient prior knowledge to conceptualize thing with verbal or graphic descriptions or definitions: e.g., *pentimento*
Unorganized knowledge (trivia)
Fragmented knowledge of thing that cannot be recalled without external prompt, but is capable of incorporation into schema: e.g., *cadenza*
Organized prior knowledge
Thing known and organized in schema, but not activated by oral/written word and may be communicated only by description: e.g., *philtrum*
Recognition knowledge
Word and thing are comprehended in listening and reading but are not used in speaking and writing e.g., *shrift* (as in "short *shrift*")
Production knowledge
Word and thing are used in speech or writing: e.g., *toe*

FIGURE 8.1

A model of the relation of things and words in an individual's lexicon. *Note*: A "thing" is any real or imaginable object, feeling, action, or idea. (From Kibby, M. W. (1995, November). The organization and teaching of things and the words that signify them. *Journal of Adolescent & Adult Literacy*, *39*(3), 208–223. Reprinted by permission of the International Reading Assoc. and Michael W. Kibby.)

A nine-year-old was visiting a theme park with his parents. They walked past a ride named "Ribbault's Adventure." Although the father pronounced the ride's name to the boy, he kept asking when they would get a chance to ride "Rabbit's Adventure." In exasperation, the father turned to the mother and asked, "Why can't he remember the name of the ride?"

The mother pointed out that the boy had read *Alice in Wonderland* and *Peter Rabbit* and had picked a name that was close in looks and sounds to "Ribbault's Adventure." "Perhaps," she suggested, "when he gets on the ride, he will call it what it is."

> Sure enough, the guide on Ribbault's Adventure explained who Ribbault was. And when the boy exited the ride, he remarked, "That was fun. I'd like to ride Ribbault's Adventure again before we go home."

This child was probably at what Kibby calls the stage of "immediately learnable knowledge." He did not know about Ribbault's adventure but had enough prior knowledge about adventures to "get it" once he received more information and an experience to link with the words.

Full concept learning of vocabulary, according to Simpson (1987), requires four mental operations: (1) recognizing and generating critical attributes—both examples and nonexamples—of a concept; (2) seeing relationships between the concept to be learned and what is already known; (3) applying the concept to a variety of contexts, and (4) generating new contexts for the learned concept. The first of these operations can be developed by asking students to exclude a concept from a list in which it does not belong, as in the following:

muezzin mosque minaret *mangrove*

Also, students can brainstorm attributes and nonattributes of a given concept, as shown in Activity 8.1.

Students can better understand relationships (operation 2) by brainstorming about targeted vocabulary concepts, then writing possible definitions. For mental operation 3, students can apply what they know about a vocabulary concept by being exposed to the word in different contexts. Stahl (1983) calls this teaching comprehension through developing **contextual knowledge**.

Students can learn how to generate new contexts for a learned vocabulary term (operation 4) by creating new sentences using previously learned concepts. To encourage frequent practice at this task, Simpson (1987) recommends a technique called paired-word sentence generation: Two words are given, and

ACTIVITY 8.1 Concept Learning: World History

Use the textbook to brainstorm attributes and nonattributes of *nationalism*.

ATTRIBUTES	NONATTRIBUTES
honor	maturity
pride	democracy
superiority	cooperation
wealth	isolationism
power	equality
imperialism	
prestige	
force	
fascism	

students are asked to write a sentence demonstrating the relationships between them. Possible examples are *method-analysis, genes-environment, graph-plot,* and *juvenile delinquency–recession*. A sentence for *juvenile delinquency–recession* might be: "Incidents of juvenile delinquency occur more frequently during a recession."

Vocabulary and School Failure

Many times there is a mismatch between school expectations and students' achievement, especially in the case of at-risk students (discussed more fully in Chapter 12). This is true despite a plethora of compensatory educational programs designed to reduce the conceptual and language deficits of culturally disadvantaged and minority children (Lindfors, 1980). These children are often taught vocabulary through rote exercises that require dictionary definitions of extensive numbers of technical and specialized terms. In a typical exercise, the teacher informs students that before reading the chapter they must find, look up in the dictionary, and define 30 words found in the chapter. No wonder reading is often thought of as decidedly dull by students who have to perform such rote tasks. This method of teaching vocabulary and concepts is product oriented; the rote production of the written word is the product. Such vocabulary exercises are used despite the fact that most disadvantaged students, at-risk populations, and generally poor readers use action words in much of their communication ("he gone," for example); they use process to facilitate information rather than memorization of an extensive written vocabulary. Because rote vocabulary exercises present words and terms in the abstract, these students seem unable to grasp either their surface or their underlying meaning.

To help these students, and all students learning words for which they seem to have no prior experiences or concepts, teachers need to present concepts in a very concrete manner, through direct and purposeful experiences (Piaget & Inhelder, 1969). When hands-on experiences are not possible, students need "activities of observation," such as field trips, demonstrations, graphics, and visuals, to build a knowledge base for learning.

Remember that a reader's background knowledge is very important in determining how much of the vocabulary she or he will understand and absorb. Students with broad background and understanding of the world will have an easier time learning vocabulary because of their broader background experience. This view has been substantiated in the research literature for decades (Ausubel, 1968; Henry, 1974; Graves, 1985; Carr & Wixson, 1986). For instance, those students who have toured historic Philadelphia can relate to a passage about the influence of the Constitution more easily than can those lacking such firsthand experience. Teachers who follow this view emphasize building on background knowledge in all phases of the PAR Lesson Framework. For example, a teacher might ask students what they know about small-loan agencies in a business mathematics lesson on small loans. She might carefully present new vocabulary such as *collateral, passbook savings, debt,* and *consolidation loans*. At each phase of the lesson, she would try to identify how much students already know about the topic. In this manner, the teacher is helping build students' general background knowledge.

Much of the discussion in this chapter so far deals with ways to help students to establish a **conceptual base** of understanding—an underlying knowledge of the subject matter—with which to grow in knowledge of vocabulary. We feel that vocabulary instruction can be beneficial in increasing the base of knowledge at any phase of a lesson. Teachers need to make their own vocabulary lessons that will aid students prior to, during, and after reading. They cannot always rely on basal reading series or textbook manuals' vocabulary exercises, because they mostly stress teaching vocabulary before the reading, and recent research (Ryder & Graves, 1994) shows that much of this type of vocabulary instruction is not sufficient to improve student comprehension. Carver (1994) argues also that simply letting students read freely in class or at home does not guarantee large vocabulary growth.

At times, students need preparation (P) in vocabulary before reading a chapter or lesson; often, students need assistance (A) with vocabulary during or immediately after the reading; and on occasion, students need longer periods of reflection (R) on vocabulary, to understand how terms convey meaning and relationships. Research by Memory (1990) suggests that vocabulary development can be effective when taught at any of these stages—before, during, or after the reading assignment.

In the remainder of this chapter we describe several strategies for developing vocabulary. They can be used before reading, during reading, or shortly after reading. They also can be used as follow-up activities (usually the next day) to reading. We describe how teachers can use these strategies to teach vocabulary through understandable activities that are meaningful to students.

Teaching Vocabulary in Preparation for Reading

Research by Medo and Ryder (1993) shows that vocabulary instruction prior to reading improves student comprehension regardless of students' reading ability. Teaching vocabulary before reading involves not so much the teacher "teaching" the terms as the student exploring and attempting to make sense of them before beginning the reading. As strategic learners, students need to recognize whether a link exists between words in the content material and their own knowledge. Douglas Barnes (1976) speaks to the matter in this way:

> Children are not "little vessels . . . ready to have imperial gallons of facts poured into them until they were full to the brim," as Dickens put it. They have a personal history outside the school and its curriculum. In order to arrive at school they have mastered many complex systems of knowledge; otherwise they could not cope with everyday life. School for every child is a confrontation between

> what he "knows" already and what the school offers; this is true both of social learning and of the kinds of learning which constitute the manifest curriculum. Whenever school learning has gone beyond meaningless rote, we can take it that a child has made some kind of relationship between what he knows already and what the school has presented. (p. 22)

Several activities—word inventories, graphic organizers, mapping, modified cloze, possible sentences, vocabulary connections, and capsule vocabulary—can be used before reading to strengthen the relationship between what the student already knows and what is provided in the text.

Word Inventories

Introduced in Chapter 4 as self-inventories, word inventories are used consistently in this text at the start of each chapter. This activity encourages readers to assess their own prior knowledge and rate themselves. Although teachers can use the ratings to instruct, readers are in charge of their own assessment of conceptual knowledge. Activity 8.2 is an example of a word inventory developed for elementary school students.

Graphic Organizers

Recent reviews of graphic organizer research (Dunston, 1992; Rice, 1992; Swafford & Alvermann, 1989) conclude that graphic organizers significantly aid stu-

ACTIVITY 8.2 Word Inventory in Elementary English

Directions: Use the happy faces to tell how well you know these words. This isn't a test and you won't be graded. Remember: You aren't supposed to know all the words.

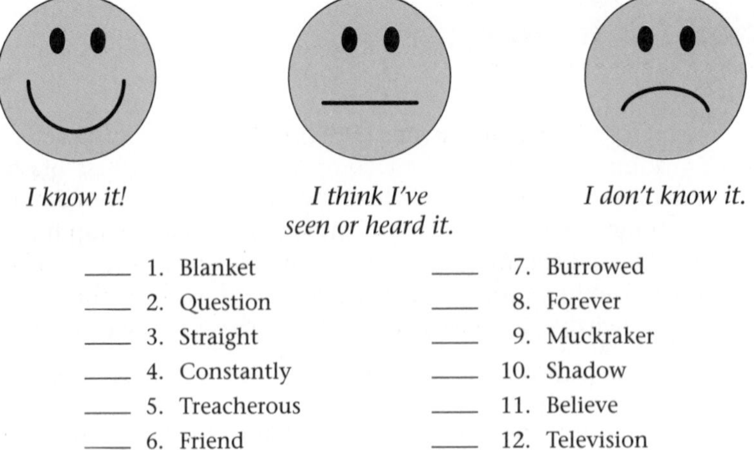
I know it!
I think I've seen or heard it.
I don't know it.

____	1. Blanket	____	7. Burrowed
____	2. Question	____	8. Forever
____	3. Straight	____	9. Muckraker
____	4. Constantly	____	10. Shadow
____	5. Treacherous	____	11. Believe
____	6. Friend	____	12. Television

Developed by Terry Bryce.

dents in remembering text. Graphic organizers can be an effective strategy for getting students on the same wavelength as the teacher in understanding the direction a lesson is taking. The teacher interacts with students by displaying the diagram and discussing why it is arranged in a particular way.

A semantic map (Johnson & Pearson, 1984) is one of the most popular types of graphic organizers because it is excellent at depicting the interrelationships and hierarchies of concepts in a lesson. Research (Bos & Anders, 1990) demonstrates the effectiveness of semantic mapping for increasing reading comprehension and vocabulary learning. Mapping was introduced in Chapter 6 as a way to develop comprehension. A semantic map can be used as a prereading or postreading exercise. To use semantic mapping before reading, follow these steps:

1. Select an important word from the reading assignment.
2. Ask students to think of as many related words and key concepts as possible that will help in understanding the key word.
3. List these words on the board as they are identified.
4. As an extension of this activity, have students rank the words or categorize them as "most important" and "least important." This activity may help students begin to see that all words in the lesson are not equally important and that information needs to be categorized.
5. Organize the words into a diagram similar to the one in Activity 8.3 in elementary language arts.

Activity 8.4 shows a variation of a semantic map. In this activity the Spanish teacher helped students to learn about types of chili peppers.

Using the semantic map as their base, Schwartz and Raphael (1985) designed a word map. Directly under the key word, which is circled or boxed, examples that remind students of that word are placed. To the right of the key word, properties are written. The teacher might ask, "What is it like?" Directly above the key word, the concept of the word is represented as a definition or description. In this way students are led in their understanding from concrete examples to abstract definitions and concepts. Activity 8.5 is a word map for the key word *metaphor*. Novak and Gowin (1984) describe a similar technique, which they call concept mapping (see Activity 8.6 on floral arrangement). The biggest difference between Novak and Gowin's concept map and Johnson and Pearson's word map is the heavy emphasis on linking words in the concept map. Both semantic maps and concept maps provide excellent ways of getting students to clarify their thinking before reading the assignment.

Modified Cloze Procedures

Cloze as a means of determining reader background was introduced in Chapter 4. Cloze passages can also be constructed to teach technical or general vocabulary. Passages used in this manner are modified for instructional purposes. Instead of deleting words at predetermined intervals, as when measuring readability and checking students' reading ability, teachers select an important passage from the text and delete key words. Teachers may also create their own

ACTIVITY 8.3 Semantic Map in Elementary Language Arts

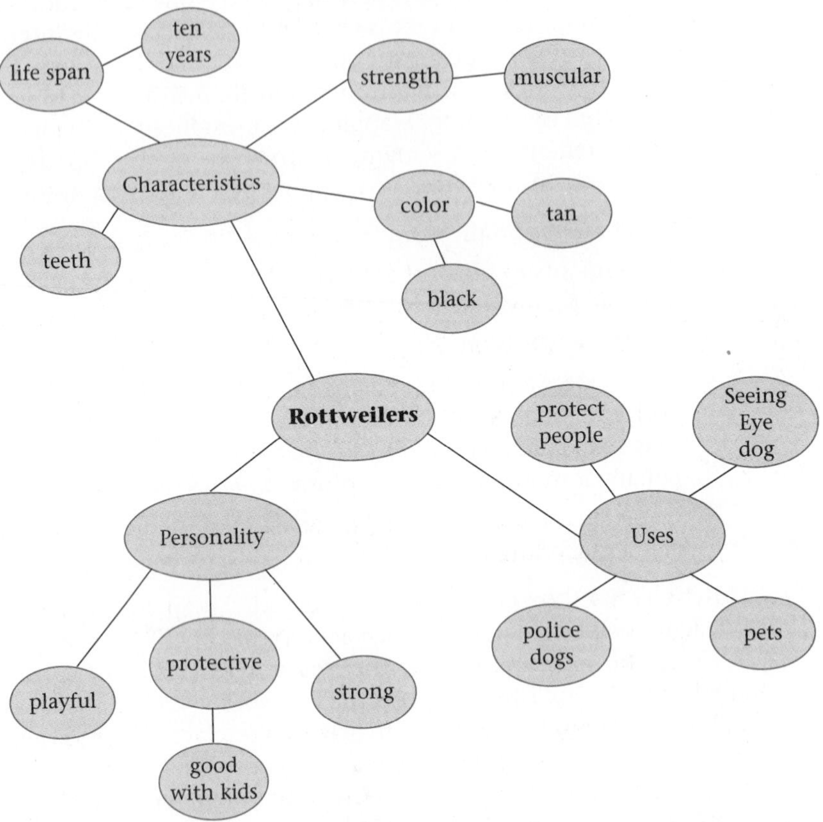

cloze passage of 50 to 100 words to assess students' knowledge of vocabulary and concepts on a certain topic. Activity 8.7 presents a passage of approximately 100 words constructed by a teacher to assess students' knowledge of the first settlers in North America. Students can fill in the blanks individually, then discuss their answers in small groups. The best, or most unusual, answers can eventually be shared with the entire class.

Possible Sentences

Possible Sentences (Moore & Arthur, 1981) is an activity that combines vocabulary and prediction. It is designed to acquaint students with new vocabulary that they will encounter in their reading and guide them as they attempt to verify the accuracy of the statements they generate. Additionally, it arouses curios-

ACTIVITY 8.4 Semantic Map in Spanish

Developed by Brian Littman.

ity concerning the passage to be read. This activity is best used when unfamiliar vocabulary is mixed with familiar terminology. When using this technique, the teacher might give students a worksheet such as the one shown in Activity 8.8. Teachers pick between five and eight vocabulary terms, such as those from elementary science in Activity 8.8.

For each term, students write a possible sentence on the left side of the worksheet. Then, during reading, they look for the real meaning of the term and write this meaning in a sentence. In doing so, students create a mnemonic, with the possible sentence cueing them to the real meaning of the word. This is a simple but powerful strategy for learning words. Recent research attests to the advantage of using such mnemonic devices to learn vocabulary (Levin, Levin, Glassman, & Nordwall, 1992; Moore & Surber, 1992; Scruggs, Mastropier, Brigham, & Sullivan, 1992). Mnemonic devices are discussed in detail in Chapter 10.

ACTIVITY 8.5 Word Map for the Key Word *Metaphor*

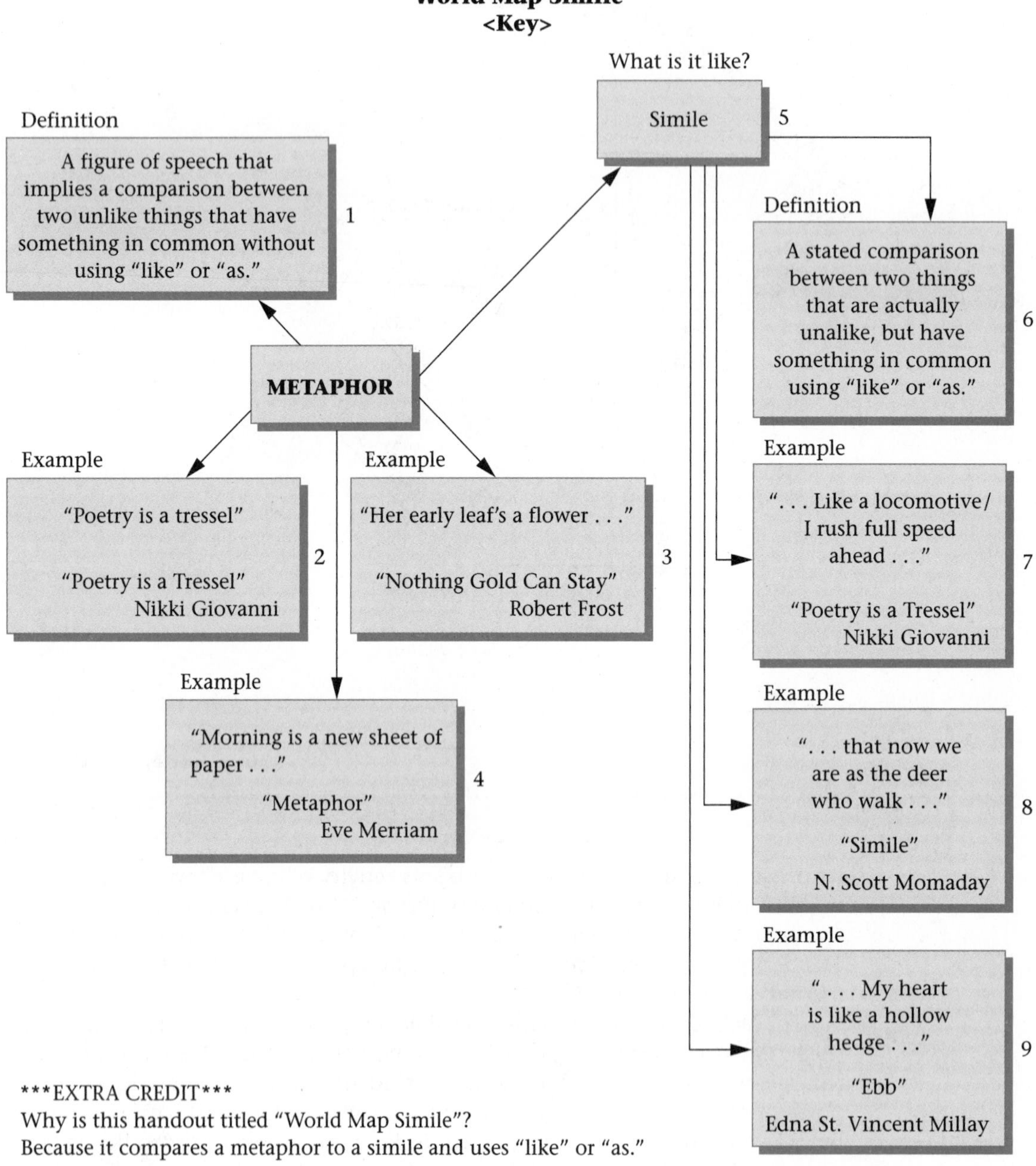
World Map Simile
<Key>
What is it like?
Simile
5
Definition
A figure of speech that implies a comparison between two unlike things that have something in common without using "like" or "as."
1
METAPHOR
Definition
A stated comparison between two things that are actually unalike, but have something in common using "like" or "as."
6
Example
"Poetry is a tressel"
"Poetry is a Tressel"
Nikki Giovanni
2
Example
"Her early leaf's a flower . . ."
"Nothing Gold Can Stay"
Robert Frost
3
Example
". . . Like a locomotive/
I rush full speed
ahead . . ."
"Poetry is a Tressel"
Nikki Giovanni
7
Example
"Morning is a new sheet of paper . . ."
"Metaphor"
Eve Merriam
4
Example
". . . that now we
are as the deer
who walk . . ."
"Simile"
N. Scott Momaday
8
Example
" . . . My heart
is like a hollow
hedge . . ."
"Ebb"
Edna St. Vincent Millay
9

EXTRA CREDIT
Why is this handout titled "World Map Simile"?
Because it compares a metaphor to a simile and uses "like" or "as."

Developed by Tara Furges.

ACTIVITY 8.6 Concept Map: Horticulture

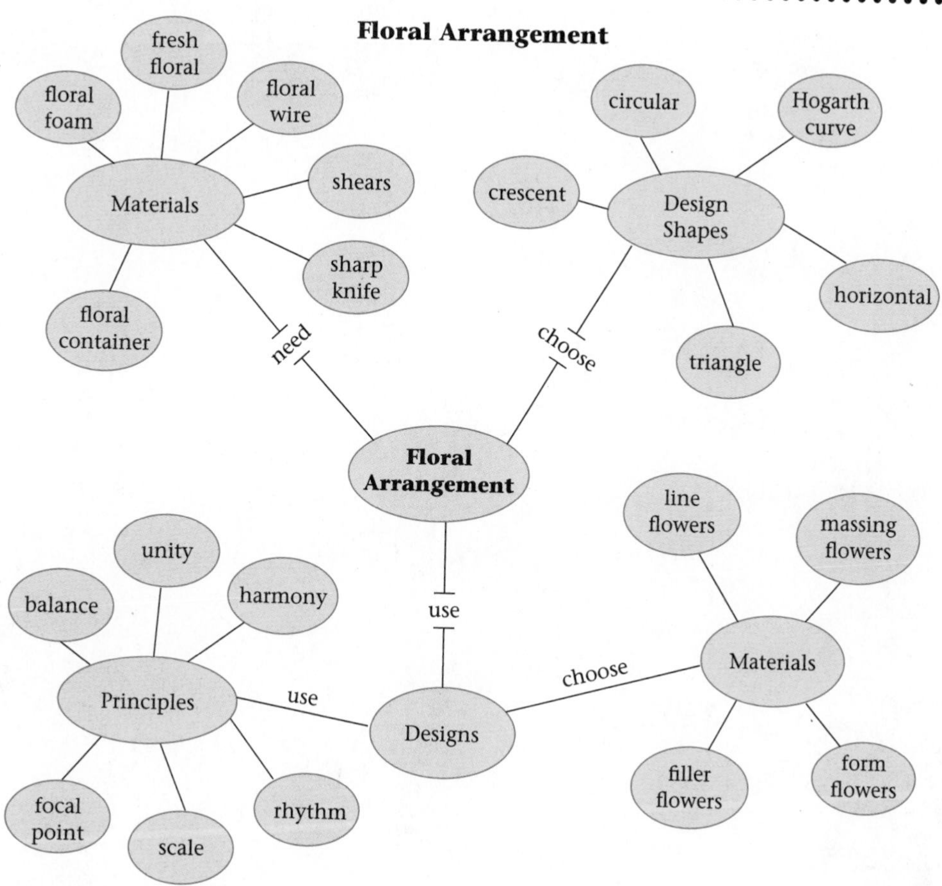

ACTIVITY 8.7 Modified Cloze Procedure: Exploring the New Land

The United States of America is a young country. It is only about ____________ years old. North America had been explored for more than ____________ years before any settlers came to live here. After the first settlement at ____________ in 1607, many more European settlers came to North America. Some wanted to find ____________ freedom. Others came for the chance to own ____________. Still others came to teach ____________ to American Indians. At first, it was ____________ for the colonists. Many did not know how to ____________ the land and were not used to wild ____________. As a result, many colonists ____________.

ACTIVITY 8.8 Possible Sentences: Elementary Science

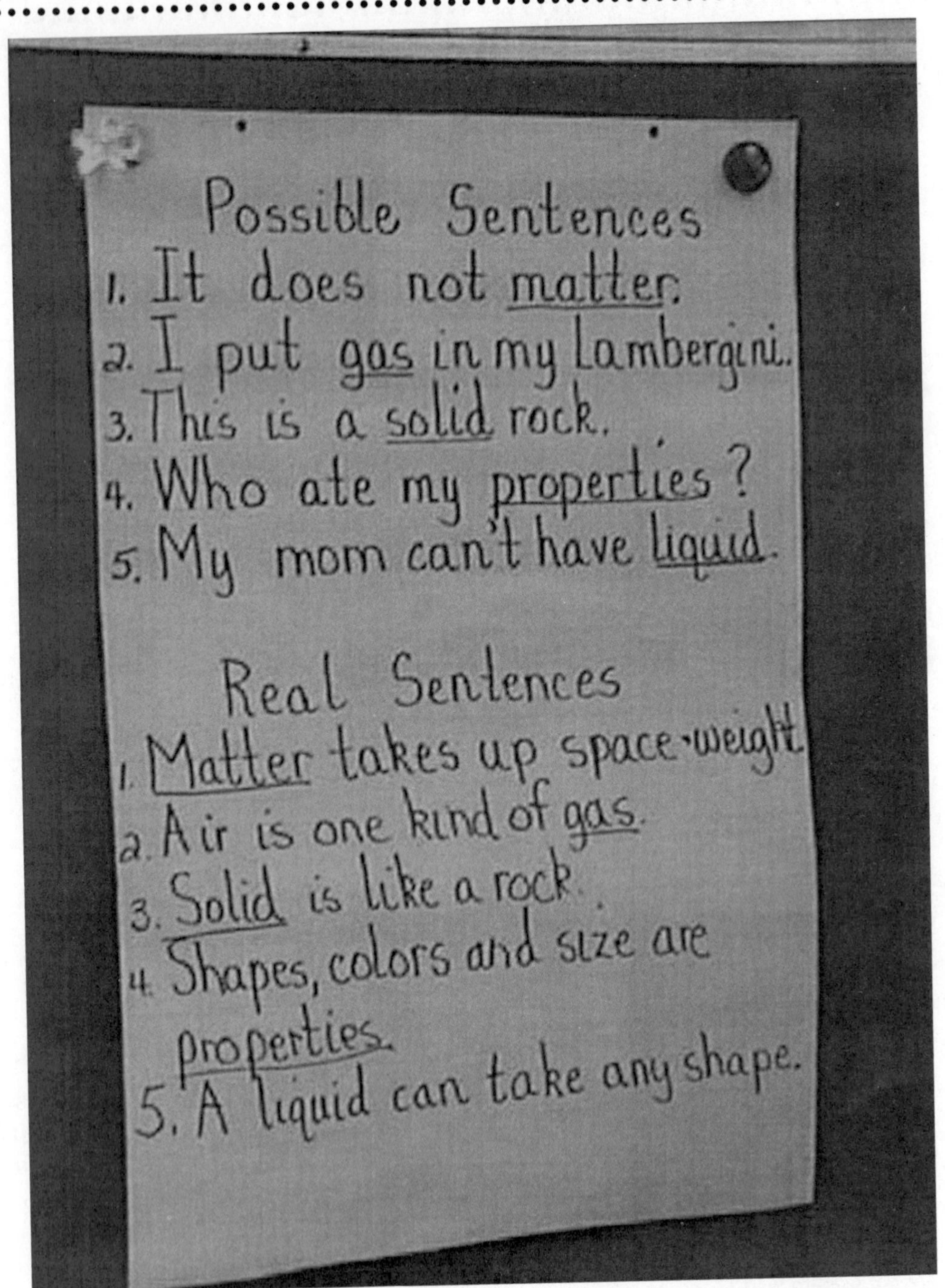

Possible Sentences
1. It does not matter.
2. I put gas in my Lambergini.
3. This is a solid rock.
4. Who ate my properties?
5. My mom can't have liquid.
Real Sentences
1. Matter takes up space-weight
2. Air is one kind of gas.
3. Solid is like a rock.
4. Shapes, colors and size are properties.
5. A liquid can take any shape.

Developed by Suzanne McDaniel.

Vocabulary Connections

Iwicki (1992) describes a strategy whereby students use a term from a previous book in shared literature study to describe a situation in a book currently being studied. In this way, connections are made between old vocabulary and the new book. For example, the word *pandemonium*, found in *Welcome Home, Jelly Bean* (Shyer, 1988), can be related to events in *The Black Stallion* (Farley, 1941). In other content areas, words from a previous chapter can be used to see relationships in a new one. In occupational mathematics, for example, the term *conversion* may be used with *product volumes* in one chapter and again in a chapter on the use of mathematics in leisure-time activities (converting international track-and-field times from English measurements to metrics). Iwicki reports that Vocabulary Connections is an activity that retains its appeal to students throughout schooling. It is an excellent way for students to use higher-level thinking skills in comparing vocabulary from one content-area subject to another.

Capsule Vocabulary

Capsule Vocabulary (Crist, 1975) is an activity that helps readers explore meaning relationships among words and helps students develop a connection between those relationships and what the students already know. The teacher selects a list or capsule of several words either found in the text or useful for understanding the text material. After the teacher briefly defines each word and uses it in a sentence, students work in pairs to use the terms in sentences. Next, students write sentences or a summary using the words. Then they check their sentences against the text material.

Here is an example of the use of Capsule Vocabulary in an English as a second language class. Students worked in pairs to write sentences about new words they had encountered. Eighteen students from Cambodia, Vietnam, Korea, and Russia with widely different levels of English proficiency participated. Some had been in the United States for three years, some for less than two weeks. The teacher, Barbara Ingber, prepared a list of numbered words pertaining to shopping in a supermarket: *supermarket, cashier, coupons, groceries, food, detergent, diapers, bag, shopping cart, money*, and *change*. She dictated these words, and students wrote them in their notebooks using temporary spellings. Then the teacher asked for students to call the words back to her as she wrote each one on the chalkboard using the correct spelling. Students tried to define words as they were written on the board. For those they could not define, the teacher provided a definition with a sentence or an action (she pretended to push a shopping cart). Next the students worked in pairs, orally making sentences for each word. She was careful to pair students from different countries so that each had to communicate in English, the common language. Students then wrote their sentences on the board. The group studied each sentence and made corrections for standard English, with the teacher's help. Students then copied the corrected sentences and read them aloud to their partners. This activity utilized paired learning, as well as listening, speaking, reading, and writing.

Assisting Students to Learn Vocabulary

Mealey and Konopak (1990), in an excellent review of the research on preteaching content-area vocabulary, questioned the value of solely preteaching content terms. Like these researchers, we maintain that students need to be assisted in all content areas and at every grade level in interpreting unfamiliar words. Teachers cannot "protect" students from words by teaching prior to reading every difficult term that they will encounter. McMurray, Laffey, and Morgan (1979) found that students skipped over unfamiliar words when they had no strategy for learning vocabulary. Hynd, McNish, Lay, and Fowler (1995) report that students tend to skip over text that does not confirm their prior knowledge, unless their attention is directed specifically to it. Teachers need to assist students in understanding words that clarify text for the reader. Five excellent techniques for assisting readers are context clue discovery, structural analysis, word attack paradigms, vocabulary lists, and quadrant cards. Also, activities already introduced in this text, such as organizational (jot) charts, can be adapted to assist readers.

Context Clue Discovery

To begin to understand the importance of "concepts in context," think of any word in isolation; then try to define it. Take, for example, the word *run*. It is not difficult to give a synonym for the word, but it does not have a clear meaning until it is placed in a context. You may have thought immediately of the most common definition, "to move with haste," but "to be or campaign as a candidate for election," "to publish, print or make copies," or even "to cause the stitches in a garment to unravel" would have been equally accurate. A precise meaning cannot be determined until *run* is seen in context.

Students often use context clues to help determine the meaning of a word (Konopak, 1988). Sometimes, however, students are not successful at making use of context clues because they lack a systematic strategy for figuring out the unknown word (Hafner, 1967). To help students develop the ability to use context to discover the meaning of unfamiliar words, teachers can discuss specific clues that they should look for in the text.

Definitions

Authors often define a word in the sentence in which it first appears. This technique is used frequently in textbooks when an author introduces terminology. Note the following examples:

> The *marginal revenue product* of the input is the change in total revenue associated with using one more unit of the variable input.
>
> The *peltier effect* is the production of heat at the junction of two metals on the passage of a current.

Signal Words

Certain words or phrases may be used to signal the reader that a word or term is about to be explained or that an example will be presented. Some of the most frequently used signal words are listed below, followed by two sentences using signal words.

for example	these (synonym)	in the way that
this way	especially	such
such as		like

Martin Luther King was more than just a leader in America, *in that* he was recognized worldwide.

The man lost the sympathy of the judge, *especially* when he was found in a drunken stupor shortly after being let out of jail.

Direct Explanations

Often authors provide an explanation of an unfamiliar term that is being introduced. This technique is used frequently in difficult technical writing.

Joe was a *social being,* whose thoughts and behaviors were strongly influenced by the people and things around him and whose thoughts and behaviors strongly influenced the people he was around.

Mead emphasized that the mind is a social product; indeed, one of the most important achievements of socialization is the development of *cognitive abilities*—intellectual capacities such as perceiving, remembering, reasoning, calculating, believing.

Synonyms

A complex term may be followed by a simpler, more commonly understood word, even though the words may not be perfect synonyms. Again, the author is attempting to provide the reader with an explanation or definition—in this instance, by using a comparison. In the following example, *obscure* is explained by comparison to the word *unintelligible*. In the second sentence, *attacks* helps explain *audacious comments*.

The lecture was so *obscure* that the students labeled it *unintelligible*.

There were *audacious comments* and *attacks* on prominent leaders of the opposition.

Antonyms

An author may define or explain a term by contrasting it with words of opposite meaning:

The young swimmer did not have the *perseverance* of her older teammates and *quit* at the halfway point in the race.

All this is rather *optimistic*, though it is better to err on the side of hope than in favor of *despair*.

Inferences

Students can often infer the meaning of an unfamiliar word from the mood and tone of the selection. In this case, meaning must be deduced through a combination of the author's use of mood, tone, and imagery and the reader's background knowledge and experience. The author thus paints a picture of meaning rather than concretely defining or explaining the word within the text. In the passage that follows, the meaning of *opaque* is not made clear. The reader must infer the meaning from the mood and tone of the paragraph and from personal experience with a substance such as black asphalt.

> This is it, this is it, right now, the present, this empty gas station, here, this western wind, this tang of coffee on the tongue, and I am patting the puppy, I am watching the mountain. And the second I verbalize this awareness in my brain, I cease to see the mountain or feel the puppy. I am *opaque*, so much black asphalt. But at the same second, the second I know I've lost it, I also realize that the puppy is still squirming on his back under my hand. Nothing has changed for him. He draws his legs down to stretch the skin out so he feels every fingertip's stroke along his furred and arching side, his flank, his flung-back throat. (From *Pilgrim at Tinker Creek*, by Annie Dillard, New York: Harper's Magazine Press, 1975)

Research suggests that students can use context clue strategies to unlock the meaning of unfamiliar terms (Stahl, 1986). Therefore, it is a good idea to have these six clues (with explanations and sample sentences) posted at points around the classroom or on a handout to be kept in the student's work folder.

Structural Analysis

Even if students practice and remember the strategy, context clues sometimes are not going to be of much help in decoding unfamiliar words (Schatz, 1984). For example, readers probably would have trouble guessing the meaning of the following italicized terms from clues in the context:

> Nations impose burdens that violate the laws of *equity*.
>
> A very important finding about the effects of mass media relates to *latency*.
>
> They put a *lien* on our house.

Using context clues in these sentences would probably give readers a vague idea of the meaning or no idea at all. In these cases, it may be faster to use structural analysis to derive the meaning.

Consider the following passage concerning sexual dimorphism:

> An interesting relationship between sexual dimorphism and domestic duties exists among some species. Consider an example from birds. The sexes of song sparrows look very much alike. The males have no conspicuous qualities which immediately serve to release reproductive behavior in females. Thus courtship in this species may be a rather extended process as pair-bonding (mating) is estab-

lished. Once a pair has formed, both sexes enter into the nest building, feeding and defense of the young. The male may only mate once in a season but he helps to maximize the number of young which reach adulthood carrying his genes. He is rather inconspicuous, so whereas he doesn't turn on females very easily, he also doesn't attract predators to the nest.

The peacock, on the other hand, is raucous and garish. When he displays to a drab peahen, he must present a veritable barrage of releasers to her reproductive IRMs. In any case, he displays madly and frequently and is successful indeed. Once having seduced an awed peahen, he doesn't stay to help with the mundane chores of child rearing, but instead disappears into the sunset looking for new conquests.

(From R. A. Wallace, *Biology: The World of Life*. Copyright 1975 by Goodyear Publishing Co., Santa Monica, California)

After reading this passage we know the following:

A relationship exists between sexual dimorphism and some species.

Sparrows share domestic duties.

Peafowl do not share domestic duties.

Mating and pair-bonding are different for sparrows and peafowl.

What is the cause of the difference? Your response should be "sexual dimorphism." If you know that *di* mean "two" and *morph* means "form or shape," then you can figure out the term *sexual dimorphism*. (See Appendix C for a list of prefixes, suffixes, and roots of words, with their meanings and examples.)

Word Attack Paradigms

Aguiar and Brady (1991) suggest that vocabulary deficits of less-skilled readers stem from difficulty in establishing accurate phonological representations for new words. Their research points to the importance of structural analysis and the following strategy, called a word attack paradigm, to help students with the recognition of words.

In this activity, students are given a card with a series of steps to aid them in deciphering new words when they encounter them in reading. Such a paradigm might look like this:

1. Figure out the word from the meaning of the sentence. The word must make sense in the sentence.
2. Take off the ending of the word. Certain endings, such as *s, d, r, es, ed, er, est, al, ing,* may be enough to make the word look "new."
3. Break the word into syllables. Don't be afraid to try two or three ways to break the word. Look for prefixes, suffixes, and root words that are familiar.
4. Sound the word out. Try to break the word into syllables several times, sounding it out each time. Do you know a word that begins with the same letters? Do you know a word that ends the same? Put them together.

5. Look in the glossary if the book has one.
6. Ask a friend in class or the teacher, or, as a last resort, find the definition of the word in a dictionary.

A word attack paradigm gives students a way to attempt newfound words without resorting first to a dictionary. Students should keep the paradigm in their folder, or a large one should be posted on the wall by the teacher.

Vocabulary Lists

Students can be encouraged to make vocabulary lists of new terms they have mastered, whether by context clue discovery, structural analysis, or word attack paradigm. Students may keep such lists in notebooks or on file cards. If they use cards, they can write the word and its dictionary pronunciation on the front side, and on the back they can write the sentence in which the word was found and the dictionary definition. Periodically, students can exchange their notebooks or file cards and call out vocabulary terms to each other, as they often do with spelling words: One student calls out the term, and the other gives the definition and uses the word in a sentence. In this manner, students can make a habit of working daily and weekly with words to expand their content vocabulary. Activity 8.9 is an example of a vocabulary list with several words recorded.

Quadrant Cards

Quadrant cards (Frager, 1991) are a variation on a list or word card. Students use 4-by-6-inch cards or half sheets of paper divided into four parts. In the top left quadrant of the card, the word to be learned is listed. A synonym or definition goes in the top right quadrant. Associations for the word go in the bottom left quadrant, and antonyms are placed in the bottom right quadrant.

Organizational (Jot) Charts

Students can compare and contrast words using organizational (jot) charts, as described in Chapter 6. For instance, a Spanish teacher had third-year students

ACTIVITY 8.9 Beginning Vocabulary List

Word	*Page #*	*Possible Definition*	*Verified Definition*
Dwelling	132	Living area	A place where people live
Fossil	133	To harden or make like stone	The remains, trace, or impression of an animal or plant that lived long ago

ACTIVITY 8.10 Los Mandatos Regulares

Key	*Tú*		*Ud.*		*Uds.*	
afirmativo hablar comer escribir	**-ar** **-er, ir**	habla- come escribe	**-ar** **-er, ir**	hable coma escriba	**-ar** **-er, ir**	hablen coman escriban
irregulares	decir-di hacer-haz ir-ve poner-pon	salir-sal ser-sé tener-ten venir-ven	dar-dé estar-esté ir-vaya saber-sepa	ser-sea	dar-den estar-estén ir-vayan saber-sepan	ser-sean
escribir **negativo** hablar comer	**-ar** **-er, ir**	no hables no comas no escribas	**-ar** **-er, ir**	no hable no coma no escriba	**-ar** **-er, ir**	no hablen no coman no escriban
irregulares	**dar-** **ir-** **estar-** **ser-**	no des no vayas no estés no seas	dar- estar- ir- saber- ser-	no dé no esté no vaya no sepa no sea	dar- estar- ir- saber- ser-	no den no estén no vayan no sepan no sean

Developed by Heather Hemstreet.

chart the command words so they could see at a glance on one simple chart the relationship of the three types of commands in negative and affirmative statements. Activity 8.10 shows the chart.

Reflecting on Vocabulary for Comprehension and Retention

An intriguing finding consistently emerging from reading research is that it can be as beneficial—or more so—to teach vocabulary after reading or during reading, as before the reading (Memory, 1990; Mealey & Konopak, 1990). For years the conventional wisdom has been that vocabulary is best taught before reading. In fact, however, the more students are asked to discuss, brainstorm, and think about what they have learned, the more they comprehend and retain the material. Thus the reflection phase of vocabulary development holds much promise in helping students thoroughly grasp the meaning of difficult terms in their reading. In this section, we offer a number of strategies for reflection; these are best carried out by students working in small groups.

Interactive Cloze Procedure

Meeks and Morgan (1978) describe a strategy called the interactive cloze procedure, which was designed to encourage students to pay close attention to words in print and to actively seek the meaning of passages by studying vocabulary terms. They offer the following paradigm for using the interactive cloze:

1. Select a passage of 100 to 150 words from a textbook. It should be a passage that students have had difficulty comprehending or one that the instructor feels is important for them to comprehend fully.
2. Make appropriate deletions of nouns, verbs, adjectives, or adverbs. The teacher can vary the form and number of deletions depending on the purpose of the exercise.
3. Have students complete the cloze passage individually, filling in as many blanks as possible. Set a time limit based on the difficulty of the passage.
4. Divide students into small groups, three to four students per group. Instruct them to compare answers and come to a joint decision about the best response for each blank.
5. Reassemble the class as a whole. Read the selection intact from the text. Give students opportunities to express opinions on the suitability of the author's choice of terms compared to their choices.
6. Strengthen short-term recall by testing using the cloze passage.

Meeks and Morgan described using the technique to teach imagery by omitting words that produce vivid images. Activity 8.11 is such a cloze, based on a passage from H. G. Wells's *The Red Room* (1896).

ACTIVITY 8.11 Interactive Cloze: H. G. Wells

I saw the candle in the right sconce of one of the mirrors ________________ and go right out, and almost immediately its companion followed it. There was no mistake about it. The flame vanished, as if the wicks had been suddenly ________________ between a ________________ and a thumb, leaving the wick neither ________________ nor smoking, but ________________. While I stood ________________, the candle at the ________________ of the bed went out, and the ________________ seemed to take another step towards me.

Vocabulary words:

finger	gaping	wink	black
shadows	foot	glowing	nipped

Semantic Feature Analysis

Semantic feature analysis (Baldwin, Ford, & Readance, 1981; Johnson & Pearson, 1984) is a technique for helping students understand deeper meanings and nuances of language. To accomplish the analysis, first the teacher lists terms vertically on the chalkboard and asks students to help choose the features that will be written across the top of the chalkboard. (Teachers can also choose the features beforehand.) Students then complete the matrix by marking a plus sign (+) for features that apply to each word. In certain situations, students can be asked to make finer discriminations: always (A), sometimes (S), or never (N). We recommend students do this analysis after reading the lesson, using a technique such as the guided-reading procedure or the Directed Reading/Thinking Activity (see Chapter 6). Activity 8.12 shows a semantic feature analysis used in a science class on energy.

Word Puzzles

Almost all students enjoy word puzzles, and computer programs now make them easier to construct. The teacher enters the vocabulary terms and definitions, and the computer program constructs the puzzle. If a computer is unavailable, teachers can construct their own puzzles by graphically displaying the terms across and down and drawing boxes around the words. The boxes are numbered both across and down, and definitions are placed beside the grid. Activity 8.13 is a word puzzle in geography made for second grade.

Post Graphic Organizers

Earlier in this chapter, we discussed how students could help construct their own graphic organizers before reading to learn new vocabulary terms and to attempt to construct a hierarchical pattern of organization. To enhance concept development, students can return to the organizers after reading. Post graphic organizers for use in the reflection phase of learning were described in Chapter 7. Here we present a variation specifically for vocabulary. Students can construct a post graphic organizer directly after the reading. Activity 8.14 shows a post graphic organizer completed by several college students on the subject of how best to construct graphic representations.

Categorization

One of the best ways for students to learn relationships of concepts after a reading is through a categorization activity. **Categorization** is the act of assigning something to a class, group, or division. Categorization can be accomplished through a word relationship activity that begins with the teacher suggesting a topic and asking students to supply words that describe the topic. The teacher may supplement the words given by the students or skim the text to find more

ACTIVITY 8.12 Grid for Semantic Feature Analysis

Topic: Energy (Chapter 11)
Directions: Mark those features that apply to each vocabulary term.

A = the vocabulary term always applies to the feature
S = the vocabulary term sometimes applies to the feature
N = the vocabulary term never applies to the feature

FEATURES

VOCABULARY TERMS	Renewable Resource	Nonrenewable Resource	Fossil Fuels—(Direct use)	Nuclear material	Naturally occurs	Man-made materials	Conservable	Pro-environment	Pollutant
Uranium^{235}									
Hydrogen									
Biomass									
Geothermal energy									
Hydroelectricity									
Wind energy									
Passive solar heating									
Active solar heating									
Deuterium + Tritium									
Oil									
Coal									
Natural gas									

Developed by Wendy Barcroft.

words. If students' abilities or backgrounds are limited, the teacher can provide the list. The list shown in Activity 8.15 from a chapter on the body systems in science was developed by a teacher.

Students organize the list of words into smaller lists of items that have something in common (see Activity 8.15). It is best during this phase for students to

ACTIVITY 8.13 Geographic Terms Word Puzzle

NAME ______________________________

					3 I											
					S					5 M						
					L					6 O	C	E	A	N		
			1 V		A					U						
	2 P	L	A	I	N					N						
			L		4 D	E	S	E	R	T					8 H	
			L							A					I	
9 R	I	V	E	R						I					L	
			Y					7 P	E	N	I	N	S	U	L	A

DOWN

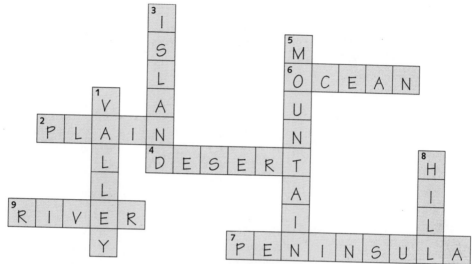

1. Low land between hills or mountains.
3. Land that has water all around it.
5. The highest kind of land.
8. Land that rises above the land around it.

ACROSS

2. Flat land.
4. A dry place with little rain.
6. A very large body of salt water.
7. Land that has water on three sides.
9. A long body of water that flows across the land.

Developed by Laurie Smith.

work in small groups to categorize and label the words. The groups explain their categories and labels to the entire class; then the whole class tries to reach a consensus on what the correct labels are and where the particular words belong. During this final phase, the teacher needs to act as a guide to make certain that discussion and labeling are being channeled in the proper direction. It is also essential that students be allowed to provide a rationale for their decisions.

The focus on explanation and discussion in this activity makes it an excellent strategy for teaching difficult vocabulary, concept development, and critical thinking, especially since all learning depends on students' ability to create meaningful categories of information. Practiced in a relaxed and purposeful atmosphere, this activity can be a powerful tool for helping students develop concepts, improve comprehension, and retain information.

ACTIVITY 8.14 Post Graphic Organizer on Creating Graphic Representations

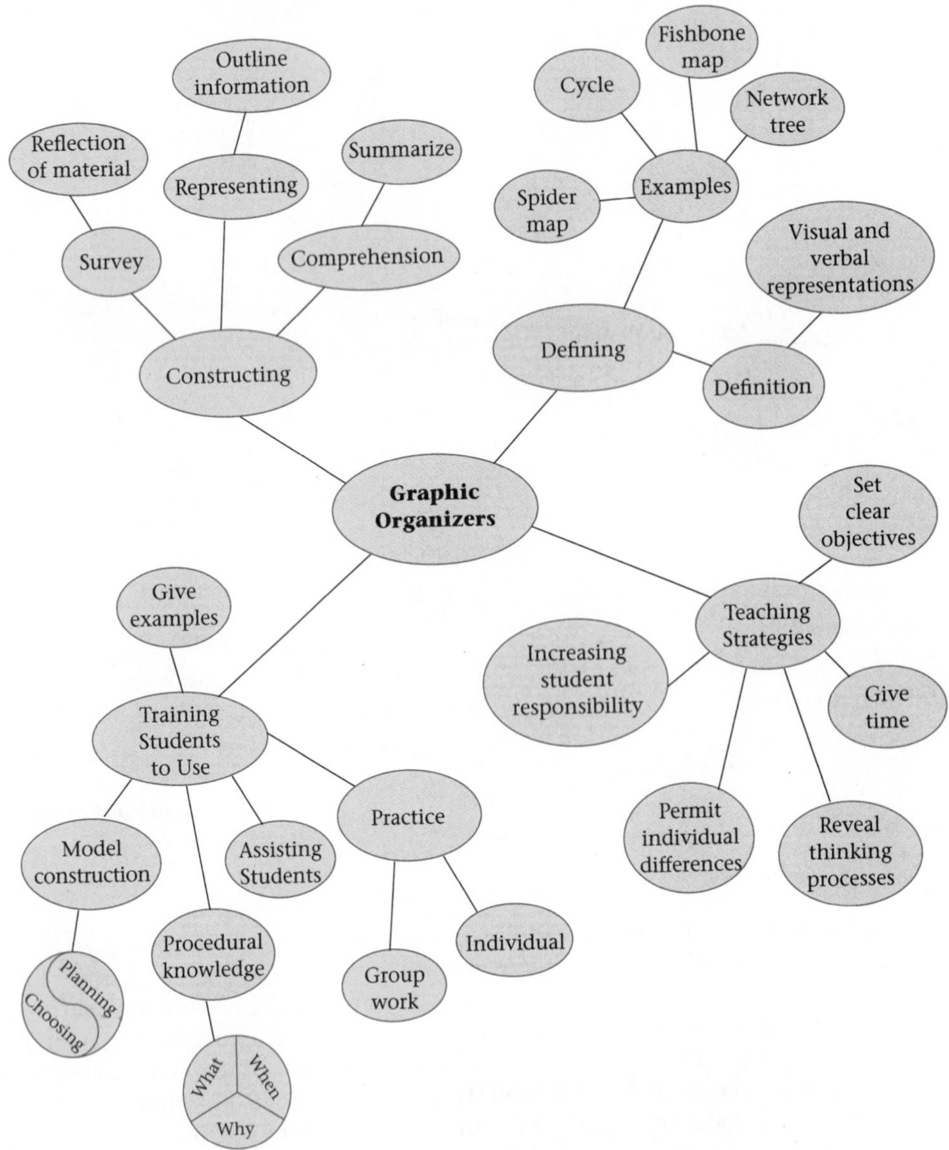

Created by Jackie Meccariello, Terry Bryce, and Racheal Curry.

ACTIVITY 8.15 Categorization Exercise: Body Systems

Below are three categories that describe functioning systems in the human body—the digestive, respiratory, and circulatory systems.

DIGESTIVE	RESPIRATORY	CIRCULATORY

Place each of the following vocabulary terms in the correct category.

aorta	gastric juice	trachea
esophagus	diaphragm	flatus
ulcer	lung	artery
atrium	salivary gland	asthma
pneumonia	angina pectoris	hypertension
bronchi	ventricle	peristaltic waves

ANSWERS:

DIGESTIVE	RESPIRATORY	CIRCULATORY
ulcer	asthma	aorta
gastric juice	pneumonia	atrium
salivary glands	bronchi	angina pectoris
flatus	diaphragm	ventricle
peristaltic waves	lung	artery
esophagus	trachea	hypertension

Developed by Kim Blowe.

Word Sorts

Another type of categorization strategy is a word sort as described by Gillett and Temple (1983). In this activity, students individually or in small groups sort out technical terms that are written on cards, on the chalkboard, or on a worksheet. They categorize like words and title the categories. In a **closed sort**, students are given the categories in advance. This teaches classification and deductive reasoning. In an **open sort**, students have to group words as concepts and title the relationship. This teaches inference, or reading between the lines, as discussed in Chapter 6.

DRTA Vocabulary Search

When doing a Directed Reading/Thinking Activity in a content-area classroom, the teacher can ask students to jot down difficult vocabulary terms. The student lists are given to the teacher without student names, and these terms become the words to be studied after the DRTA or at the beginning of the next class period.

The teacher first teaches word recognition by using a "word families" phonics approach to sound out the word. If the word is *expressive,* for example, the teacher asks for other words in the same word family:

express
expression
press
pressure

Students work through the word family to sound out the word, thereby achieving word recognition.

Next comes a skimming and scanning exercise. The teacher begins by asking "Who can find *expressive* first in the story? Give me the page, column, and paragraph number, and then read the paragraph the word is found in." After the word search, the paragraph is read, and students with the aid of the teacher try to figure out the meaning of the word in the context of the story or chapter. Here the teacher can ask students to use the context clue discovery strategy explained earlier in this chapter. This word search approach teaches word recognition, speed-reading, and comprehension through the use of context clues. Keep in mind that the words to be studied are the ones with which students are actually having difficulty, not the ones a manual says are going to give them difficulty.

A Vocabulary Study System

Dana and Rodriguez (1992) proposed a vocabulary study system using the acronym **TOAST**. In a study they found the system to be more effective for learning vocabulary than other selected study methods. The steps in this vocabulary study technique are as follows:

T: Test. Students self-test to determine which vocabulary terms they cannot spell, define, or use in sentences.

O: Organize. Students organize these words into semantically related groups; arrange words into categories by structure or function, such as words that sound alike or are the same part of speech; categorize words as somewhat familiar or completely unfamiliar.

A: Anchor. Students "anchor" the words in memory by using a key-word method (assigning a picture and caption to a vocabulary term), tape-recording definitions, creating a mnemonic device, or mixing the words on cards and ordering them from difficult to easy.

S: Say. Students review the words by calling the spellings, definitions, and uses in sentences to another student. The first review session begins 5 to 10 minutes after initial study and is followed at intervals by several more.

T: Test. Immediately after each review, students self-administer a posttest in which they spell, define, and use in context all the vocabulary terms with which they originally had difficulty. The response mode may be oral, written, or silent thought.

We recommend this vocabulary study system from early elementary grades through high school as a good method for getting students actively involved in the study of words. Keep in mind that TOAST encompasses all aspects of PAR.

Vocabulary Self-Collection Strategy

Another good strategy for use after reading is the vocabulary self-collection strategy (VSS) (Haggard, 1986). VSS is a cooperative vocabulary activity that allows both teachers and students to share words that they wish to learn and remember. The strategy begins after students read an assignment. Each member of the class, including the teacher, is asked to bring a word that is perceived as important for the class to learn. Words usually come from the content-area textbook but also may come from what students have heard within or outside the classroom. Students share their words in class, defining and elaborating on the presented words as the teacher writes them on the chalkboard. Then as a whole class, students decide which words are most important and should be learned by the class. The students then record the chosen words in vocabulary notebooks. Class discussions ensue in which students use the words in purposeful sentences.

VSS can also be used as a cooperative assignment for groups. Each group member is expected to bring a word, and the groups decide what the words mean and which words are important enough for the entire class to learn. After working at length with their words, groups present their chosen words to the class. Words can be used for review and later study.

A nice feature of VSS is that the set of vocabulary terms generated by this activity (with the exception of the one or two words suggested by the teacher) emanate from the students and are words for which they have shown interest.

Additional Reflection Activities for Enriching Language

Students find many of the activities described in this chapter so enjoyable that their interest in words is heightened. In this section, emphasizing word play, we offer additional techniques that will help students experience the pleasure of working with words. Specifically, we present five techniques: word analogies, magic squares, vocabulary illustrations, vocabulary bingo, and word bubbles.

Word Analogies

Word analogies are enjoyable activities that are excellent for teaching higher-level thinking. To do word analogies, students must be able to perceive relationships between what amounts to two sides of an equation. This may be critical thinking at its best, in that the student is often forced to attempt various combinations of possible answers in solving the problem. At first, students may have difficulty with this concept; therefore, the teacher should practice with students and explain the equation used in analogies:

__________ is to __________ as __________ is to __________ .

or

__________ : __________ :: __________ : __________ .

For elementary students, teachers first spell out "is to . . . as" rather than use symbols. In addition, students say that analogies are easiest when the blank is in the fourth position, as in terms 1 and 2 in Activity 8.16, an early-elementary activity in language arts. More difficult analogies can be constructed by varying the position of the blank, as in items 3 through 6. Analogies can also present a sophisticated challenge for older students, as illustrated in Activity 8.17, a high school Spanish I activity.

Magic Squares

Any vocabulary activity can come alive through the use of magic squares, a technique that can be used at all levels—elementary, junior high, and high school. **Magic squares** are special arrangements of numbers that when added across, down, or diagonally always equal the same sum. Teachers can construct these

ACTIVITY 8.16 Word Analogies: Language Arts

1. Hot is to cold as day is to __________ .
   up night long
2. Dog is to cat as small is to __________ .
   little big short
3. Puppy is to __________ as young is to old.
   playful dog kitten
4. __________ is to white as on is to off.
   Red Black Door
5. Happy is to __________ as stop is to go.
   glad sad frown
6. Slow is to __________ as long is to short.
   silly happy fast

Developed by Colleen Kean.

ACTIVITY 8.17 Word Analogies: Spanish I

Directions: Choose the answer that best completes the analogy.

Model:	hot : cold :: up down	over wet down under
1.	él : ella :: ellos : ______	Juan son las ellas
2.	mira : televisión :: gana : ______	poco dinero mucho ganar
3.	viajar : nadar :: viajo : ______	viajan nadan nado Mexíco
4.	Juan : él :: Pablo y Sara : ______	ellos los ellas las
5.	mal : bien :: un poco : ______	ahora mucho dinero siempre
6.	invierno: ______ :: primavera : llueve	frío viento nieva verano
7.	toco : ______ :: escucho : discos	canto ahora tocar guitarra
8.	cantan : canto :: ______ : hablo	hablan cantar hablar música
9.	como : estás :: ______ : tardes	buenos días noches bueñas
10.	______ : Srta. :: señor : Sr.	señora usted hola señorita

Developed by William Cathell.

vocabulary exercises by having students match a lettered column of words to a numbered column of definitions. Letters on each square of the grid match the lettered words. Students try to find the magic number by matching the correct word and definition and entering the number in the appropriate square or grid. Activity 8.18 gives explicit instructions in how to construct magic squares. Activity 8.19 gives various magic-square combinations, and Activity 8.20 is an example of a magic square in elementary mathematics.

Vocabulary Illustrations

Joe Antinarella, an English teacher at Tidewater Community College in Chesapeake, Virginia, developed a creative way to enrich students' study of vocabulary that he calls vocabulary illustrations. He has students first define a word on a piece of drawing paper, then find a picture or make an original drawing that illustrates the concept. Below the picture, students use the term in a sentence that clarifies or goes along with what is happening in the picture or drawing. Activity 8.21 is a vocabulary illustration completed by a student in an early-elementary language arts classroom. Activity 8.22 shows an example created by a student in a seventh-grade English class.

Vocabulary Bingo

Bingo is one of the most popular of all games. Playing vocabulary bingo lets teachers work with words in a relaxed atmosphere. Steps in playing vocabulary bingo are as follows:

ACTIVITY 8.18 Instructions for Making Magic Squares

1. Start with a range of numbers, such as 1 to 9 or 4 to 12, to fill 9 squares in a 3×3 magic square.
2. Add the first and last numbers: $1 + 9 = 10$; $4 + 12 = 16$.
3. Determine the midpoint and put that number in the middle of the square: Between 1 and 9, put 5; between 4 and 12, put 8.
4. Add the first and last numbers: $1 + 5 + 9 = 15$.
5. Make combinations that add up to this magic-square number and fill in the square.

8	1	6
3	5	7
4	9	2

As a shortcut to step 5, take the first number in your sequence, such as number 1; counting from that number, follow the directions below. In the diagram below, 1 is used as the first number.

1. Put the 1st number in the center of the top row.
2. Put the 2nd number diagonally to the right; then place it in the corresponding position in the magic square.
3. Put the 3rd number diagonally to the right; then place it in the corresponding position. Since you can't put the 4th number on the diagonal, you drop it below the 3rd number.
4. Place the 5th number and then the 6th number on the diagonal.
5. You can't put the 7th number on the diagonal, so drop the 7th number down below the 6th.
6. Put the 8th number diagonally to the right, and move to the corresponding position.
7. Put the 9th number diagonally to the right; then move it to the corresponding position below.

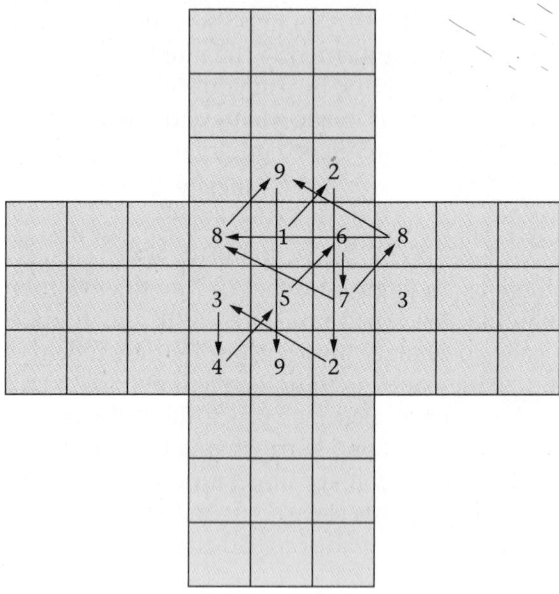

Variations on combinations:

672	294	438	618	492	834	276
159	753	951	753	357	159	951
834	618	276	294	816	672	438

ACTIVITY 8.19 Magic-Square Combinations

9	2	7
4	6	8
5	10	3

18

16	2	3	13
5	11	10	8
9	7	6	12
4	14	15	1

34

19	2	15	23	6
25	8	16	4	12
1	14	22	10	18
7	20	3	11	24
13	21	9	17	5

65

1. Students make a "bingo" card from a list of vocabulary items. (The game works best with at least 20 words.) Students should be encouraged to select words at random to fill each square.
2. The teacher (or student reader) reads definitions of the words aloud, and the students cover the word that they believe matches the definition. (It's handy to have the definitions on 3-by-5-inch cards and to shuffle the cards between games.) The winner is the first person to cover a vertical, horizontal, or diagonal row.
3. Check the winner by rereading the definitions used. This step not only keeps everyone honest but serves as reinforcement and provides an opportunity for students to ask questions.

A sample bingo game in mathematics is shown in Activity 8.23.

Bingo is an excellent game to play as a review. Most students enjoy the competition and participate enthusiastically. The constant repetition of the definitions is a good reinforcer for the aural learner. Bingo can be played in any content area. For instance, in chemistry students can make bingo cards with symbols of elements, and the names of the elements are called out. For a higher level of difficulty, the caller can use other characteristics of elements such as atomic number or a description—for example, "a silvery liquid at room temperature" or "used to fill balloons." As a variation on Activity 8.23 in mathematics, the bingo cards contain the pictures of the shapes, and the caller names the shapes.

Word Bubbles

The word bubble provides a good review of vocabulary. Students are given one clue to the word's meanings on a line below the bubble. Using this clue and the list of words to be reviewed, they fill in the bubble and list other clues on the lines. Activity 8.24 is an example word bubble for a third-grade mathematics class.

ACTIVITY 8.20 Magic Squares: Two-Digit Subtraction

NAME ________________________ DATE ____________

Directions: Put the number of the answer that best completes the statement listed in ABC order. Then place the number in the matching block. Check your answers to see if the sums of all rows, both across and down, add up to the magic number.

A. 56 minus 13 is	1. 57
B. 72 minus 15 is	2. 78 − 17 =
C. 40 subtract 10 is	3. 30 apples
D. 25	4. 33
E. 68 − 24 =	5. 44
F. 75 apples less 45 apples is	6. 43
G. 61	7. 100 − 75 =
H. 80 apples less 22 apples is	8. 30
I. 99 − 66 =	9. 58 apples
	10. 32 apples

A. 6	B. 1	C. 8	15
D. 7	E. 5	F. 3	15
G. 2	H. 9	I. 4	15
15	15	15	

The magic number is 15

Developed by Laurie Smith.

One-Minute Summary

The main reason for vocabulary study is to develop concepts and help students see relationships inherent in the reading. Teachers need to take sufficient time to prepare for the reading lesson by sometimes having students study difficult

Goalie
A goalkeeper

by Michael

If I played socer I would be a goalie.

ACTIVITY 8.22 Vocabulary Illustration: Seventh-Grade English

Opulence

Definition- excessive wealth, grandeur

These four pictures are a good example of opulence because these things are things people with excessive wealth could afford to have.

ACTIVITY 8.23 Shapes and Solids Bingo

Clues (also write on index cards):

Square—a shape with four equal sides and four right angles
Rectangle—a shape with four sides, two of them longer than the other two; and four right angles
Triangle—a shape with three sides
Circle—a round shape with no angles
Pentagon—a shape with five sides and five angles
Octagon—a shape with eight sides and eight angles
Trapezoid—a shape with four sides and four angles, which are not right angles
Cube—a solid with six equal square sides
Cylinder—a solid shaped like a can
Sphere—a solid shaped like a ball
Rectangular prism—a solid shaped like a box
Pyramid—a solid with sides shaped like triangles

Directions: Each student should prepare a bingo card with 25 spaces. Write each term twice to fill up 24 boxes. The extra box can be a "free" box in the middle. The teacher shuffles the index cards and reads the *clues only*. The students decide which term matches the clue and cover one space with a chip. If all the clues are read without reaching a "Bingo," the cards can be reshuffled before continuing.

Square	Rectangle	Octagon	Trapezoid	Pentagon
Triangle	Circle	Cube	Cylinder	Sphere
Cylinder	Sphere	FREE	Rectangle	Rectangular Prism
Circle	Octagon	Square	Triangle	Trapezoid
Cube	Pentagon	Pyramid	Rectangular Prism	Pyramid

Developed by Mary Fagerland.

ACTIVITY 8.24 Word Bubble, Third-Grade Mathematics

Measure Your Words

Directions: Use the measurement word clue under each bubble to help you place the correct word from the word column in a bubble (in the example, "inch" is the word in the bubble). Then look at the word column again to add two more clue words on the blank lines extending below each bubble.

Example:

Words
inch
benchmark
foot
yard
mile
perimeter
ounce
pound
temperature
cup
pint
quart
gallon

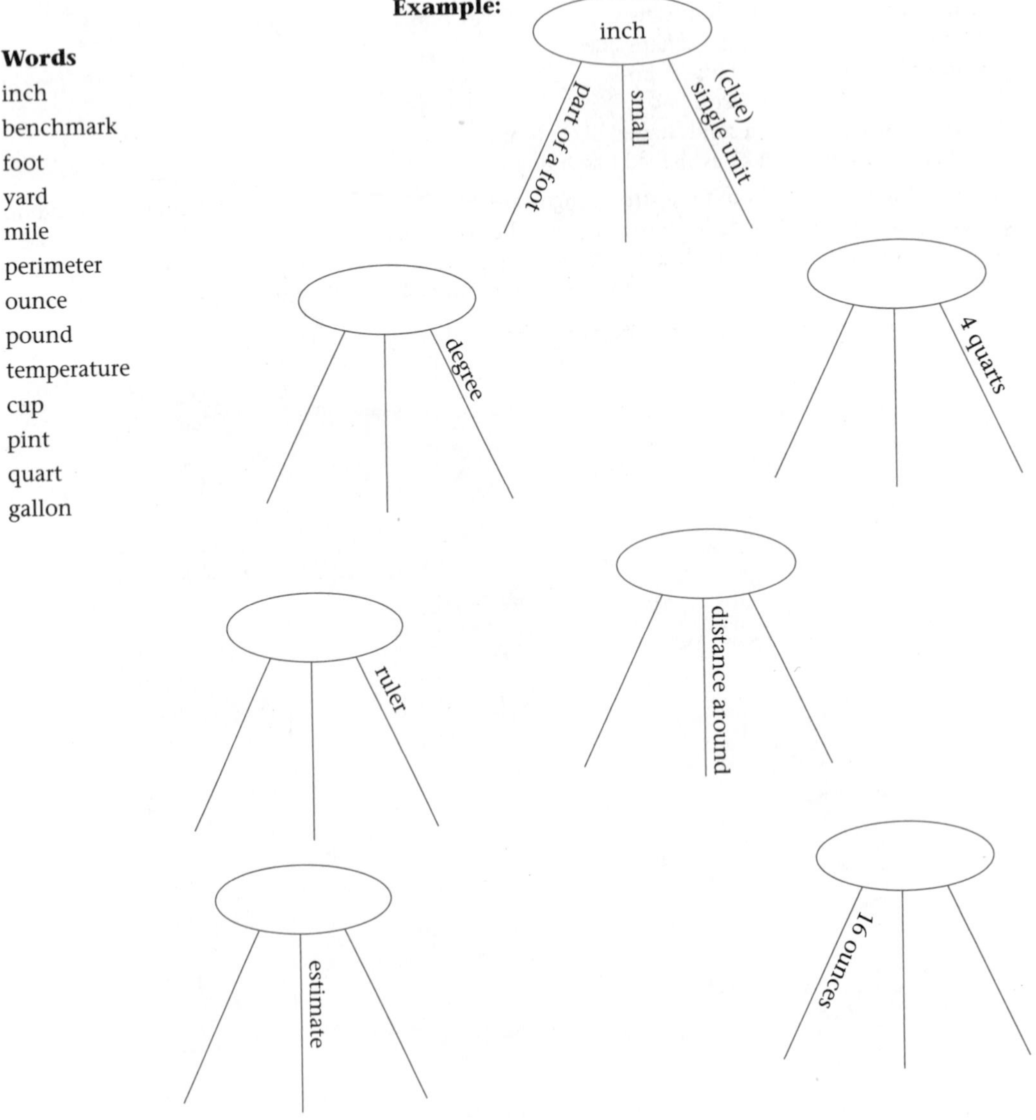

For extra credit, make your own word bubble game using the words not found in this exercise.

Developed by Bessie Haskins.

vocabulary terms before the reading. Also, teachers need to assist students with certain long-term aids and strategies to help them grasp the meaning of unfamiliar words. Often, however, it may be best to have students reflect on difficult vocabulary after the reading, when they have established a conceptual base with which to learn. Numerous vocabulary strategies are presented with the idea that students learn and grow intellectually when teachers spend more time teaching vocabulary. Research is cited throughout the chapter in support of the idea that increasing vocabulary knowledge is central to producing richer, deeper reading experiences for students.

End-of-Chapter Activities

Assisting Comprehension

See how well you remember the strategies listed below by placing them in the correct category on this organizational chart.

Activity Name	*Preparation*	*Assistance*	*Reflection*

Semantic map
Structural analysis
Context clue discovery
Word analogies
Semantic feature analysis
Vocabulary lists
Post graphic organizers
Word inventories
Categorization
Vocabulary bingo
Graphic organizers
Quadrant cards
Concept mapping
Magic squares
Word puzzles
Vocabulary self-collection strategy
Possible Sentences
Organizational (jot) charts
Word bubbles
Vocabulary illustrations
Modified cloze
Interactive cloze procedure
Vocabulary Connections
Capsule Vocabulary
Word attack paradigms
TOAST
DRTA vocabulary search
Word sorts

Reflecting on Your Reading

1. Return to the first item in the "Preparing to Read" section at the beginning of this chapter. How many ideas did you have that were similar to ones covered in the chapter? Now reflect on ways in which your ideas about vocabulary instruction have been expanded through reading this chapter. Also, begin to think about how you will incorporate these strategies into your own teaching.
2. See whether you can complete the magic square in Activity 8.25.

ACTIVITY 8.25 Magic Square, End-of-Chapter Review

Directions: Put the number of the definition from below into the square with the appropriate term. Check your answers by adding the numbers to see if the sums of all rows, both across and down, add up to the magic number.

Comprehension ______	Reading to learn ______	Prior knowledge ______
Preparation ______	Assistance ______	Reflection ______
Anticipation guide ______	PAR framework for Instruction ______	Cooperative learning (pairs, groups) ______

The Magic Number is ________________

1. Bringing meaning to the written word.
2. A strategy designed to get students thinking about what you will be teaching before the content is actually introduced.
3. That stage of the PAR Lesson Framework that provides students with the opportunity to think about what has been learned, making new information their own.
4. "None of us is as smart as all of us" is a good argument for this strategy.
5. That stage of the PAR Lesson Framework in which the student is reading and making sense of new information.
6. After learning to read, the emphasis will be on ________________.
7. That stage of the PAR Lesson Framework that builds background and determines experience before reading occurs.
8. The knowledge that one already possesses before beginning to read new material.
9. The mnemonic used in this textbook to indicate before-during-after reading steps.

CHAPTER 9

Writing to Learn in the Content Areas

The problems of the human heart in conflict with itself . . . alone can make good writing because only that is worth writing about, worth the agony and the sweat.

—William Faulkner

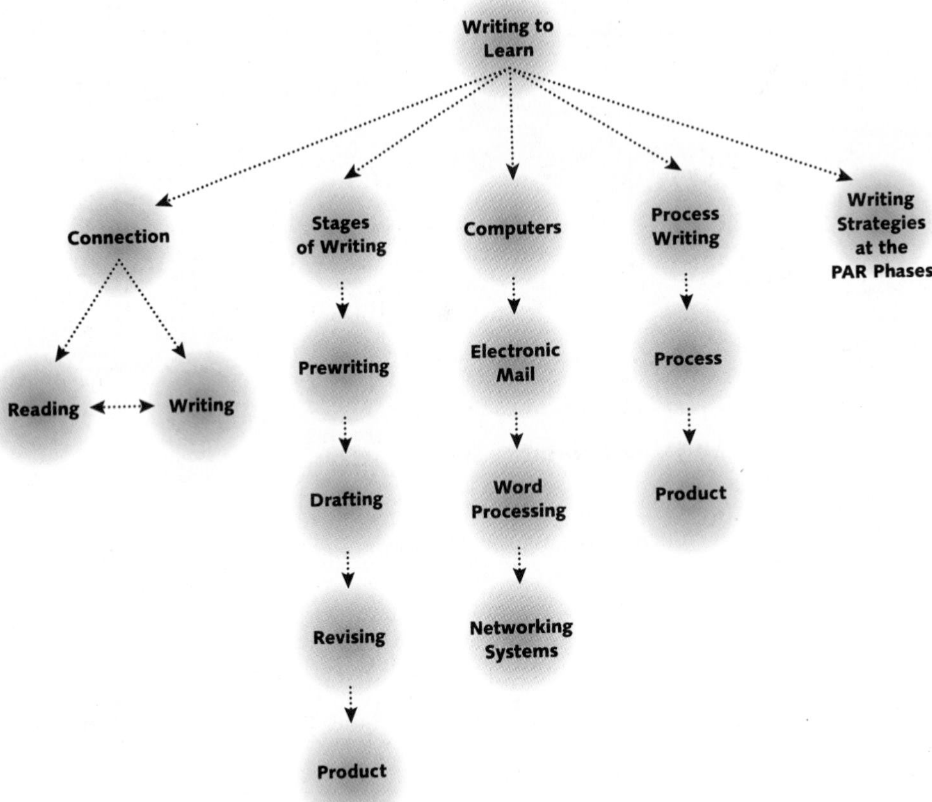

Preparing to Read

1. Anticipate what you will learn in this chapter by checking any of the statements with which you agree. Be ready to explain your choices. After reading the chapter, return to decide whether you wish to reconsider any of your selections.

   ______ Writing is the most complex of the communicative arts.

   ______ Writing is often taught as a way of learning in the content areas.

   ______ Writing should not be taught to young children in early elementary grades.

   ______ All writing should lead to a formal product, or publication of the writing.

   ______ Computers can provide an exciting way to help students improve their writing skills.

   ______ Writers may make major changes in their material during what is called the revising stage.

2. Following is a list of terms used in this chapter. Some may be familiar to you in a general context, but in this chapter they may be used in unfamiliar ways. Rate your knowledge by placing a plus sign (+) in front of those you are sure that you know, a check mark (✓) in front of those you have some knowledge about, and a zero (0) in front of those you don't know. Be ready to locate and pay special attention to their meanings when they are presented in the chapter.

   ______ reading-writing connection

   ______ emergent literacy

   ______ process writing

   ______ prewriting stage

   ______ drafting stage

   ______ revising stage

   ______ producing stage

   ______ product

   ______ zero draft

   ______ cubing

   ______ perspective cubing

   ______ brain writing

   ______ quick-write

   ______ free-write

   ______ student-generated questions

_____ learning log
_____ double-entry journal
_____ content journal
_____ annotating
_____ REAP
_____ biopoem
_____ cinquain
_____ first-person summary
_____ RAFT
_____ guided-writing procedure
_____ collaborative writing
_____ C3B4Me
_____ GIST
_____ rubric

Objectives

As you read this chapter, focus your attention on the following objectives. You will:

1. learn about the connection between reading to learn and writing to learn.
2. learn to distinguish between the process of writing and the products of writing.
3. see ways in which computers can aid students in learning to write.
4. identify the stages of writing, from prewriting through revision and publishing strategies.
5. learn strategies for preparing, assisting, and reflecting over writing.
6. see how writing can complement reading as a way to learn in the content areas.
7. learn ways to grade students' writing.

The quotation at the beginning of this chapter by William Faulkner attests to the private and personal nature of writing, what Faulkner calls "the agony and the sweat" of the process. Few ventures that students undertake can compare with the exhilarating but often exasperating process of creating ideas on a page. Writing may be the most complex communication process within the communicative arts. Writing challenges the learner to communicate not only with others but also with herself or himself. One can progress from a blank sheet to a page filled with statements about content learned, revelations about thoughts, discoveries about self. Writing is active involvement. Writing allows students to explore subject matter. Writing can challenge and enhance thinking skills more than any of the other communicative arts if it is viewed as a way of discovering, rather than solely as a means of testing knowledge.

Writing is the true complement to reading because it enables students to clarify and think critically about concepts that they encounter in reading. Reading and writing are often taught as separate enterprises even though research has found that writing can be used in every content area as an effective means of learning (Brown, Phillips, & Stephens, 1992). Unfortunately, writing is not used often enough as a way of learning in the content areas. A number of reports (National Center for Educational Statistics, 1991; U.S. Department of Education, 1993) have declared that teachers do not provide enough writing opportunities for students. Donald Graves (1994) points out also that there is not enough in-service and preservice training for teachers in how to effectively teach writing. Probably as a direct result, students' writing skills have been declining for several years. Teachers have been missing out on a valuable way to teach students in the content areas.

The Importance of the Reading-Writing Connection

Students need to write about what they are going to read about and after the reading use writing again as a culminating activity for clarification of what was read. This write-read-write model is sometimes referred to as the **reading-writing connection**. As students embrace this model, they are using writing as a tool for learning content. Content teachers, then, need to emphasize writing as a way to learn.

We know now that writing can be taught to children at a younger age than was previously thought. Research on writing indicates that very young children can create forms of writing that they can explain to adults (Teale & Sulzby, 1986). This writing includes pictures, which Vygotsky (1978b) describes as gestures that represent the child's thought. Figure 9.1 shows kindergartners' writing about and pictures of a bicycle and a bus.

Children in the early grades are capable of writing reports about content subjects (Calkins, 1986). Although these reports may contain inventive spelling and pictures that one might not expect to find in an older student's report, they reflect learning through language. Teachers are now encouraged to recognize this early reading and writing as **emergent literacy** and to foster children's use of all of the communicative arts as early as possible in content subjects. Figure 9.2 contains two writing samples from a first-grader. Both demonstrate learning about science through writing. The teacher made comments about the content of the writing, not about the "invented" or "temporary" spellings.

FIGURE 9.1

Writing to learn in kindergarten

DaRius
Ride off Tow find
I can not help
I see WhaT I like Tow do
I See a bicycle

The Process and Products of Writing

Readers process information and think it through while reading to learn, developing ideas, and relying on assistance from teachers or their own metacognitive resources to gain understanding. In the same way, writers think, prewrite, and draft while engaged in the process of writing. Gone are the days when teachers maintained that one draft was all that the student needed to produce. Many teachers now stress **process writing**, whereby the student goes through many distinct phases in writing—from initial brainstorming of ideas, researching the topic, and organizing information and ideas into a coherent piece of writing. The student working through this process may produce several drafts until the message to be conveyed becomes clear. An important part of the process is to have peers and others read drafts to help improve the writing.

Teachers often use the products of writing as a form of evaluation, such as evaluating a test essay or research report. But teachers need to see products of writing not only as a versatile way of evaluating a student but also as a unique way to develop comprehension. For instance, many fiction writers confess that they did not know what a particular fictional character was going to do until they

started writing. Their preparation gave them a direction but not exact knowledge of how the writing would turn out. Only by creating did they discover. The same held true for us as textbook writers. We learned more about our field of knowledge as we wrote this book. We discovered ways to express the information that we wanted to share with readers; before we drafted this text, we did not know all that we would write. In a similar way, readers learn as they read. Since both reading and writing can assist comprehension, it seems logical to use them in tandem when assisting readers. Unfortunately, writing is not used very often as an activity to help students understand content material (Pearce & Bader, 1984; Bader & Pearce, 1983).

Teachers like Miss K in *Ralph S. Mouse* by Beverly Cleary (1982) would turn anything into a writing project. When Miss K and her class discover that Ralph the mouse came to school with Ryan, she inspires the students to write about mice and, later, to write rejoinders to a newspaper article that contained misinformation about their projects. Many teachers, in contrast, seem to use writing activities that are mainly product oriented and graded. Research shows, however, that writing can be a powerful tool to assist comprehension. Jacobs (1987) noted that writing can be compared to the ordering of thought. It is the formation of an idea, or a cluster of ideas, from the writer's experiences and imagination. It is a conscious shaping of the materials selected by the writer to be included in composition. In selecting what to put in and leave out, the child is using the elements of writing draftsmanship that he or she can manage.

There is a relationship between the process of writing and the products of writing. Much process-oriented writing results in a formal product. The best products are generated when students are given opportunities for prewriting, writing, and revising. Not all writing leads to a formal product, but all writing can be a means of learning.

FIGURE 9.2

Writing to learn in first grade

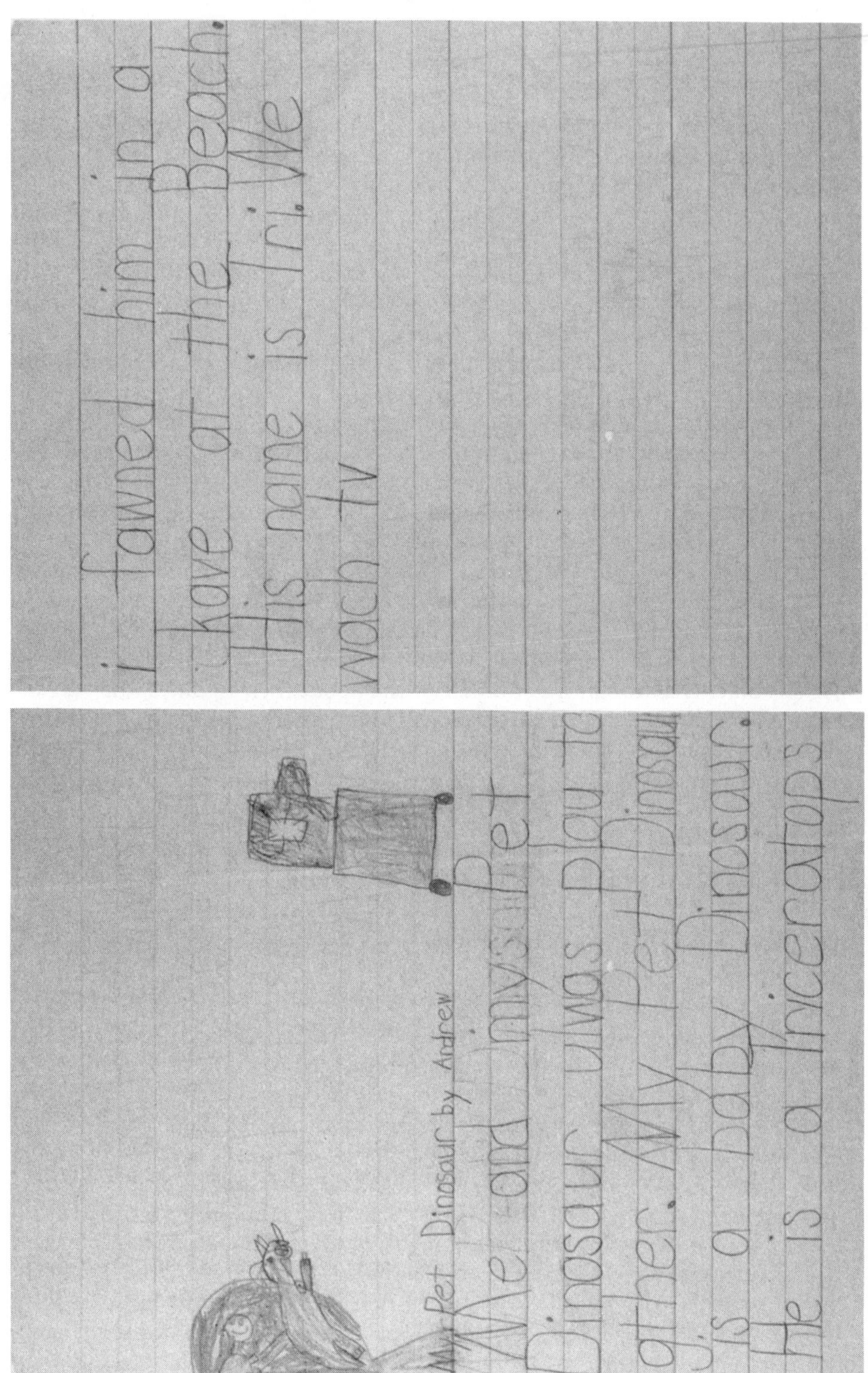
My Pet Dinosaur by Andrew
Me and my Pet
Dinosaur alwas plau to
gather. My Pet Dinosaur
is a baby Dinosaur.
He is a Triceratops
I fawned him in a
cave at the Beach.
His name is Tri. We
woch tv

The Computer and Writing

The personal computer provides an exciting venue for students to improve their writing skills. A number of studies (Silva, Meagher, Valenzuela, & Crenshaw, 1996; Rekrut, 1999) recommend that students begin using the Internet by attempting electronic mail (e-mail) exchanges. Students can exchange e-mail with other students and even with authors and experts. Silva and colleagues (1996) found that students using such telecommunications progressed more quickly than students who were asked to use the more traditional practice of grammar and textbook readings. Wagner (1995) describes how vocational students used Internet Relay Chat (IRC) to talk with other students and learn about other cultures and lifestyles. The Technology Box in this chapter shows an example of an e-mail exchange used for collecting and learning new information.

Word processing on the computer gives students an opportunity to greatly improve their writing skills. Students can write drafts quickly, revise, and save anything they have written. Most word processing programs can help students check for errors before making final copies.

Certainly a third area for growth is the networking systems and databases available to students to perform the research necessary for their writing. As Rekrut (1999) observed: "The depth and breadth of information available is virtually incomprehensible; the World Wide Web is indeed aptly named" (p. 546). When students assess information and write about their findings, they are using real-world practice that can only increase overall competence in writing. Teachers need to encourage students both at home and at school to use this tool when it is available.

Stages of Writing

Teachers need to be aware that the writing process occurs in stages. Brown, Phillips, and Stephens (1992) suggest four stages: In the **prewriting stage**, writers prepare by identifying what they already know about the topic, selecting ideas to write about, and establishing a purpose for their writing. This stage, which might include putting rough thoughts on paper, focusing on one idea, or deciding on a certain approach to the topic, is very much like determining background and then setting a purpose for reading. In the **drafting stage**—where some researchers also include revising—writers create a draft by writing to get the ideas down and to carry out their purposes. They are thinking, changing direction, organizing, and reorganizing purposes. Although they are writing with a finished product in mind, at this point they are not focusing on functional writing concerns. In the **revising stage**—which some researchers call evaluating and publishing—writers reflect on what they have written, and they rewrite for some form of publication. Their efforts can include major reorganization of the material, additions and deletions, and editorial changes. Only at the final stages do writers pay a lot of attention to the format of their writing. Up to this point, they are

TECHNOLOGY BOX

An E-Mail Conversation to Collect Information

Subject: Re: Help!
Date: Thu, 18 Jun 1998 11:40:53 +0000 From: jrichard@saturn.vcu.edu To: A W←–
@hotmail.com>

> Dear Dr. Richardson,

> I really hate to bother you, but I have been looking for something you talked about in class one night last semester. I have flipped through every page in the book and in my notes, and I can't find it to save my life. There is a really neat way of giving students roles during the writing process. I think one is a mad man and an architect, What are the rest? Please let me know whenever you get a chance. I may be blind, but if it is not in the book, you may want to consider putting it in there. I think it is such a good idea. Thanks so much for your help.
Fondly,
A W

Dear A W, You are right—this is a great way to remember the roles of a writer. I told you all in oral form because I had just learned about it from attending the Virginia English Second Language conference. I do have the information at home for inclusion in the fourth edition of our text.

Here are the roles:

Madman = write like a madman

Architect = give thought to what you wrote

Carpenter = construct your sentences and put them in order

Judge/evaluate = critique your work

Remember that the domains tested in writing on the Virginia SOLs are composing (madman & architect); style/expression (carpenter); and mechanics (judge).
Best wishes.
JSR

more concerned with setting down the content; writing at the beginning stages is a way of thinking. The fourth stage of writing is called the **producing stage**. It represents the culmination of thinking in a **product** to be shared with a particular audience. It is important to understand that some writing never reaches the fourth stage because the writer never intended to share it with an audience.

The prewriting stage matches well what happens before reading, which corresponds to what we call *preparation*. The drafting and revising stages match what happens during reading, or what we call *assistance*. The production stage can be likened to the *reflection* phase, which occurs after reading. Breaking down the writing process into several phases is advisable, because this process is new to many students. Activity 9.1 was developed by a primary-science teacher to direct her students through the various stages of writing. Though not exactly the same as the Brown, Phillips, and Stevens model, it does present roughly the same stages.

Wolfe and Reising, in their book *Writing for Learning in the Content Areas* (1983), describe a number of stages in the writing process. They maintain that students must have a prevision experience, in which they reflect on what they will write about and then select a topic. In this manner students build a **zero draft**—a collection bank of new data for the first draft. After this there are both first-draft and revision phases, in which students make changes, revise, and edit. In the teacher inquiry stage, the teacher reads not as a grader but as a reviewer of the student's work. The teacher gives as much feedback as possible about ways to improve the draft. The students make a final revision based on all the learning that has preceded in the earlier stages, and finally there is an attempt to evaluate and publish the final product. The distinct stages of the process-writing approach allow teacher and student to work together toward a final product that is well written and meaningful.

The Preparation Phase of Writing

Pearce and Davison (1988) conducted a study to see how often junior high school mathematics teachers used writing activities with their students. They found that writing was seldom used to guide thinking and learning, especially in the preparation phase of learning. In a follow-up study, Davison and Pearce (1988b) looked at five mathematics textbook series to determine whether these texts included suggestions for writing activities. Not surprisingly, they found few suggestions, and almost none were suggestions for writing before reading. Teachers in various content areas confirm that they find few suggestions in their textbooks for using writing as a preparation activity. Because teachers rely on textbooks and teachers' manuals for the majority of their instruction, they may be missing a rich source of preparation through writing activities.

Preparing students to read through writing can be a powerful way for students to learn in the content areas. Davis and Winek (1989) noted that students who know little about a topic may have considerable difficulty even beginning to write. By providing their students with carefully directed lessons with plenty of opportunities to read, think, and write before reading, these authors found that their seventh-grade social studies students produced some publishable articles.

In this text, in earlier chapters, we presented a number of activities that pertain to writing in preparation for reading. Anticipation guides (Chapter 5) and

ACTIVITY 9.1 Stages in the Writing Process: Primary Science

I. Prewriting

The teacher will show the book *Desert Voices*, written by Byrd Baylor and Peter Parnall, to the class, and she will mention that these authors have worked together on three Caldecott Honor Books. (It may be necessary to refresh their minds about the annual Caldecott and Newbery Awards.)

"Byrd Baylor, who writes the words of the book, lives in the Southwest. I don't know which *particular* state in the southwestern portion of the United States. The title of this book has the word *desert* in it, and she has written another book called *The Desert Is Theirs*. If she lives in the Southwest and likes to write about deserts, could you guess a state where she *might* live?" (The students will remember, hopefully, that Arizona has desert land.)

"Peter Parnall illustrates the book. He lives on a farm in Maine with his wife and two children."

"If the title of the book is *Desert Voices*, who might be speaking? Who are the voices in the desert?" (Wait for responses.) "Byrd Baylor has written the words for ten desert creatures as they tell us what it is like for the desert to be their home. I will read you what the jackrabbit and the rattlesnake have to say." (Teacher reads aloud.)

A. *Factstorming*

The teacher will divide the class into small groups of four or five students. She lists on the chalkboard the names of the other creatures who "speak" in *Desert Voices*: pack rat, spadefoot toad, cactus wren, desert tortoise, buzzard, lizard, coyote. (The tenth voice is entitled "Desert Person.")

B. *The Assignment*

"Each group must select one of these creatures or any other desert animal or plant that has been mentioned in our unit. Each group member should jot down on a piece of paper any ideas he or she has about this creature's feelings relating to living in the desert. You may want to think about the appearance of this creature or thing. Does it have any body parts or habitat specifically suited to the desert's environment? After you jot down your ideas, place your paper in the center of the table and choose another member's paper. Add some of your ideas to his or her paper. After you have written something on every other group member's page, your group as a whole should compile the *best* list of ideas. Then we will begin to write our individual drafts."

II. Writing

III. Rewriting

Students may work in pairs to edit and proofread each other's work. The child's partner would be from another "creature's" group.

IV. Postwriting

Oral presentations
Room displays
Compilation of compositions dealing with the same "voice" into book form

Note: Naturally this project would continue for several days. Even the group factstorming might require more than one day, especially if some reference work were necessary.

Developed by Kathryn Davis.

factstorming, PreP, and What-I-Know activities (Chapter 4) all utilize writing to prepare students to read. In this section we present additional writing activities to use before reading, to clarify students' thinking and spark interest in the material to be read.

Cubing

Cubing is an activity that can prepare students as both writers and readers by having them think on six levels of cognition. Cowan and Cowan (1980) originated cubing as a way to stimulate writing, especially when writers have a block and can't think of anything to write. The writer imagines a cube, puts one of the six tasks on each of the six sides, and considers each task for no more than five minutes. Because all six sides are considered, the writer has to look at a subject from a number of perspectives. When applied to reading (Vaughan & Estes, 1986), cubing can lead to purposeful reading and help to develop reading comprehension. Activity 9.2 shows the use of cubing in a mathematics class on linear equations.

The teacher may begin cubing by modeling the strategy on a simple construct such as a pencil. Then the teacher has students practice cubing on a concept that is in their sphere of prior knowledge. Finally, students practice cubing on difficult concepts to clarify thinking.

When a teacher actually constructs a cube and uses it as a visual prop, students can gain a rapid understanding of the reading material. Making the cube is simple. Cover a square tissue box with construction paper, and label each side; or use the outline that we provide in Figure 9.3 to construct a cube from a strong material, such as cardboard. Most teachers, no matter what grade level they teach, find that the cube is an enticing prop for their students to manipulate. One teacher brought a cube to the classroom but did not have time to use it for several days. Left casually on her desk, the cube generated so much curiosity that the teacher was forced to use the activity.

A variation called **perspective cubing** (Whitehead, 1994) helps students consider concepts from perspectives other than their own. A number of teachers report excellent success with it. Students select a chart, map, graph, or picture in a textbook, and then study and write about it from these six viewpoints:

1. **Face One: Space**
   What would it look like up close?
   What would it look like from a distance?
2. **Face Two: Time**
   What do we think about it today?
   What will people think about it in 100 years?
   What did people think about it 100 years ago?
3. **Face Three: Location**
   What does it look like from above?
   What does it look like from the side?
   What does it look like from below?

ACTIVITY 9.2 High School Mathematics: Cubing the Slope-Intercept Form of Linear Equations

Describe: It is the equation of a line, and it has two variables. It is written with the y-variable all by itself on one side.

Compare: Compared to the standard form, $Ax + By = C$, it is easier to use to find the line.

Associate: It makes me think of the coordinate plane with the X and Y axis.

Analyze: It is $y = mx + b$. The y is a variable, and so is the x. The m tells the slope of the line (how steep it is). The slope, m, is the rise over run, the change in y over the change in x. The b tells where the line crosses the y-axis. It is called the y-intercept.

Apply: For the line written $y = mx + b$, which has a slope of m and a y-intercept at b, there are an infinite number of solutions for x and y. For each x, there is a y, and vice versa. An example is $y = 2x + 3$. The slope is 2, which means the rise in the y-value is 2 for every increase in the run of the x-value. The line crosses the y-axis at 3. So it looks like this:

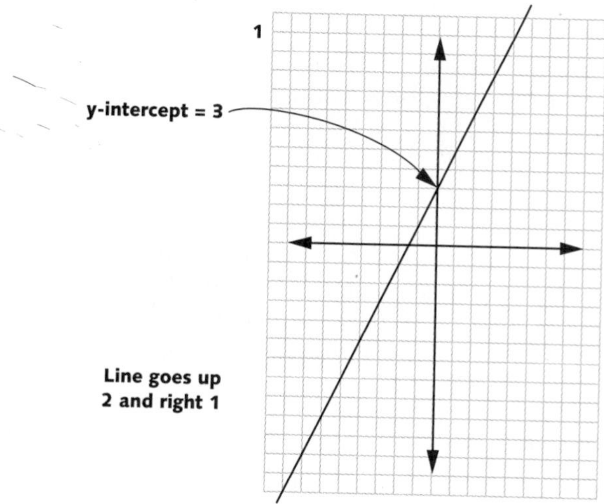

Argue: The slope-intercept form of writing linear equations is the easiest one to be able to see the line quickly. It is better than the standard form because you don't need to change the signs or anything to calculate the slope or intercept. I can just look at the equation and picture the line in my head.

Developed by Mark Forget.

4. **Face Four: Culture**
   What would the indigenous people (first settlers of this land) think about it?
   What would visitors from another country think about it?
5. **Face Five: Talk**
   If it could talk, what might it say?

FIGURE 9.3

Cubing: Making the cube (Brown, Phillips, & Stephens, 1992)

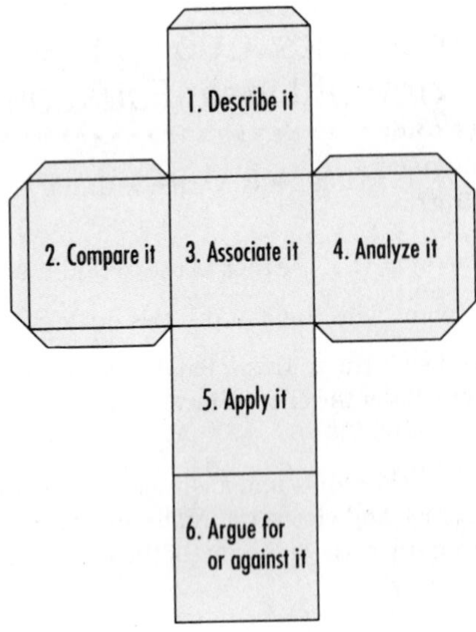

6. **Face Six: Size**
   If it changed size, how would that change affect the way we might think about it?

Brain Writing

A variation of factstorming called **brain writing** (Brown, Phillips, & Stephens, 1992) can help students generate ideas. Small groups of students respond to a topic, write down their ideas, and then exchange and add to each other's lists. While working in the brain-writing groups, students could do any of the following:

1. Predict and write down the definition of a new word in the chapter.
2. Write what they think a visual aid is illustrating or could have to do with the topic.
3. Write how the new topic might fit with the previous topics studied.
4. For mathematics, students could write out what they think a particular symbol might mean, what the possible steps for solving a problem could be, or why a particular unit of study is presented at a particular place in the text. For example, a fourth-grade mathematics textbook starts the chapter on fractions with a picture of a sectioned pizza, but no explanation is given. Elementary students could be asked to write why they think this illustration has been selected.
5. For science, students could write what they anticipate to be the steps in an experiment, what a formula will produce, what the composition of a substance is, or why certain conditions facilitate certain results.

6. For social studies, students could write about problems people might face when they move from one place to another or after they have settled in a new place (Pearce, 1987).
7. For English, students could write why they think a particular punctuation rule might be necessary: What would happen if we didn't use commas in our writing?

Three Warm-up Writing Activities

When students first enter the classroom, teachers can direct them to write as a warm-up to the intended instruction for the day. One activity is called a **quick-write** because teachers ask students to jot down ideas and write for one or two minutes on the topic to be studied. Also, the students can be asked to complete a **free-write**, writing that takes somewhat longer to complete, usually from three to five minutes. A free-write is an attempt to motivate students by getting them to write their perceptions of certain events or classroom operations. Students are encouraged to think and write without the encumbrance of worry over mechanics and correctness. The only rule is that once students put pencil to paper, they cannot stop until they are completely out of ideas or until the teacher calls an end to the free-write. In this way, the student is guaranteed to exhibit a free association of ideas. If, however, students cannot sustain a free-write over five minutes, teachers can start with the easier quick-write for shorter practice and less frustration. Pope and Praeter (1990) found students preferred free-writing and brain writing over other writing to learn strategies in content areas.

A third writing activity to begin a class is **student-generated questions**. Students can be asked in small groups to write questions that they would like answered about the topic to be studied. As a variation, the questions can be about anything the students have studied about which they are unsure, so that concepts learned in the past few classes can be clarified. Activity 9.3 presents a quick-write from an English class. Activity 9.4 presents a free-write from a high school geography class. Activity 9.5 presents student-generated questions from a chemistry class.

The Assistance Phase of Writing

The drafting stage of writing is much like the assistance phase in reading. Process is emphasized, and writers begin to realize what they have to say and what they understand about a topic. The flow of thought is represented in the writer's draft as it is in the reader's discussion. According to Self (1987), using writing to assist in teaching content material fulfills the following purposes:

1. Focusing students' attention
2. Engaging students actively
3. Arousing students' curiosity

ACTIVITY 9.3 Quick-Write on Mark Twain's *Huckleberry Finn*

I believe that Mark Twain is one of the better writers of American literature. I actually read this book for my 11th grade It. English class (which is a surprise because I rarely read the books we're assigned in English). I can see how the book was so controversial, being that the best character (I think) is black. He is very real and down to earth. The book is very easy to read and hard to put down. My only problem with it is when the character of Tom Sawyer comes in. I'm not very fond of this character. In fact I hate him. He just makes the story drag on, making me think "UGH! When is this going to end?!" Although I realize that he is only trying to make things more adventurous but I still find it very stupid. I was very angry in the end when Tom explains that Jim had been set free by Miss Watson and the whole escape plan was unnecessary. So much time wasted! I could have gone out with my friends instead of reading that crap! Anyway, I think the book was done very well overall despite the Tom Sawyer character.

Dave N. Aznar

---

4. Helping students discover disparate elements in the material
5. Helping students make connections between the material and themselves
6. Helping students "make their own meaning" from the material
7. Helping students think out loud
8. Helping students find what they do and do not know
9. Helping teachers diagnose the students' successes and problems
10. Preparing students to discuss material

Gebhard (1983) suggests four principles for developing writing activities that assist in comprehension. First, students need an audience other than the teacher. Peers are a fine resource because they can provide supportive comments and suggestions. Often, students become much more active and committed to writing when the audience is someone other than the teacher. The use of peers as an audience conveys the message that the process of writing is more important than the final product, which is the case when writing is an activity to assist comprehension. Writing for peers may alleviate the teacher's need to "grade" the writing at all. If the teacher does decide to grade, then the revision and editing of the paper mean that the teacher will see a polished product. Correction will take second place to content.

A project at Tidewater Community College in Virginia Beach, Virginia, provides an interesting example of writing that is shared by peers. Students from nearby Salem High School share their thoughts on poems and other readings with students in an English class at the college. Student at both schools use the correspondence to clarify ideas and concepts while simultaneously improving their writing skills. Activity 9.6 is a letter from a student at Salem High School to a college student on interpreting the poem "Poetry" by Nikki Giovanni.

ACTIVITY 9.4 Free-Writes in Geography

Students in a ninth-grade geography class have been studying northern Eurasia (the former USSR). The teacher writes the following on the chalkboard

communism v. market economy
autocracy v. democracy

and asks students to discuss these terms in their own groups of three. After a few minutes of small-group discussion, the teacher informs students that they will perform a free-write as a prereading activity to prepare for the day's reading, the second chapter on northern Eurasia. The teacher reinforces the rules of free-write, stating to students that once they begin writing, they may not stop during the five minutes. Rather, they should rewrite the last phrase or sentence if they confront writer's block. The following are a few of the results. (They are reproduced with original student spelling and grammar.)

> Democracy is what we have in our country where the people have rights and freedoms. Autocracy is led by a couple of leaders and they own all the land. With a communist there is no freedom. The government does what it wants and there is no incentive to do well in life. The government gets the profits. Unlike with a democracy where the people keep the money that they make. So they want to do well in life and will work harder to make money and start new businesses. In communist countries the people must do what ever their government tells them to do and are not have the freedoms of other countries such as speech and religion. Russia was once communist and after they were no longer comunist they became poor because they people weren't use to it and wanted a leader. They had the freedoms but didn't know what to do with it.

> I know that capitalism is when you have ownership and it is not shared with the government. You are able to be richer or poorer than other people. Comunism is the complete opposite. Everything is owned and controlled by the government and you don't own anything you have. If you won a million dollars, you'd own 0% of it. Or if you've been working in a factory for 40 years you can never buy it. That's just the way it goes!!!!!!!!!!!!!!!!!!!!!!
>
> ¡Yep!

> Capitalism is a government that is more right wing and comunism is far left wing because of its government trying to take care of the people too much which causes no insentive for the people, but under capitalism people have different wages and therefore have an incentive to work hard.

> Capitalism is when the businesses are owned by people. It is also called a market economy. Communist is when the government makes people work and get all the money. Democracy is when the people of a country get to select a leader. Autocracy is when a person is put into power without an election. In my view capitalism and democracy are the 2 top keys to true power of the people.

Developed by Mark Forget.

ACTIVITY 9.5 Student-Generated Questions in Chemistry

What are mole ratios?

What are the mass and mole relationships in a chemical reaction?

What is stoichiometry?

Chris Morgan

ACTIVITY 9.6 Letter from One Student to Another Concerning a Poem

March 25, 1999

Dear Jason,

I, also must admit that I had to read "Poetry" by Nikki Giovanni, more than once to understand the poem secure enough to analyze it. Reading your letter and the verses in which you sighted, made me look at the poem in a different light. I didn't notice the "dark touch" it had.

My interpretation was much different. In lines 14-20 I understood it to say that poets, in general, are overwhelmed in their thoughts. They write what comes to mind, they understand it, but it really doesn't matter if we do. In lines 21-26 it sounds as if the writer is putting poets on a pedistool, that they are better than the average individual and their thoughts. The last three lines sum up the entire poem. I think the poem is not about poetry necessarily, but about the poets. There is a constant reinforcement of loniless, which you pointed out in your letter.

I enjoyed the poem and your letter. Please take in consideration my out look.

Sincerely,

Second, the writing task needs to be of some importance to the student. Simply because the teacher may grade a piece of writing does not mean the student is motivated. Students need to be able to write about topics that interest them. The Foxfire books illustrate this principle of consequential writing very well. Eliot Wigginton (1986) inspired his English students in Rabun Gap, Georgia, to write about the crafts and habits of their own community. In this way he combined the subjects of English and social studies, using writing as the medium of instruction. This assignment itself was much more inspiring to students than receiving a grade. The audience consisted of their fellow students and their community. The work was collaborative, with many students planning and writing together. The collaboration assisted students in creating a cultural history of their community. The result of their writing is the Foxfire books, the success of which has been phenomenal.

Third, writing assignments should be varied. No one wants to do the same old thing again and again. Copying definitions quickly gets very monotonous. Later in this section, we provide several teacher-tried ideas to vary writing assignments. Several publications also help content teachers find innovative and varied ways to introduce writing across the curriculum. Some are listed in the "Reflecting on Your Reading" section at the end of this chapter.

Fourth, writing activities should connect prior knowledge to new information, providing students with a creative challenge. As we have shown, cubing does this well. Another excellent activity to encourage this connection is the jot chart, introduced in Chapter 6 as a way to promote comprehension; obviously jot charts can have more than one purpose. Jot charts provide a matrix for learning by providing students with an organizational guide, a series of boxes in which they can enter their jottings about the content areas as they read and thereby see the connections between what they already knew, what they need to find out, and—when the chart is completed—what they have learned.

Davison and Pearce (1988a, pp. 10–11), by modifying Applebee's (1981) classification system, divide writing activities into five types:

1. Direct use of language—copying and transcribing information, such as copying from the board or glossary
2. Linguistic translation—translation of words or other symbols, such as writing the meaning of a formula
3. Summarizing/interpreting—paraphrasing, making notes about material, such as explaining in one's own words or keeping a journal
4. Applied use of language—a new idea is implied in written form, such as writing possible test questions
5. Creative use of language—using writing to explore and convey related information, such as writing a report

Davison and Pearce found that the copying tasks were those predominantly used by the junior high school mathematics teachers in their study. Creative activities were seldom used, group writing opportunities were scarce, and the audience for the writing was usually the teacher. In practice, then, teachers do not seem to be following Gebhard's (1983) suggestions, probably because they do not realize how helpful writing activities can be in assisting students' comprehension. Yet the possibilities are great. Following are a number of ideas for content teachers, beginning with learning logs and annotations.

Learning Logs

Request that students write regularly in a journal called a **learning log**, under headings such as "Two new ideas I learned this week in science and how I can apply them to my life" or "How I felt about my progress in math class this week." These entries can be read by other students or by the teacher, but they should be valued for their introspective qualities and not graded. Richardson (1992a) found that such journal writing helps students to work through problems they are having in learning material and to verbalize concerns that the reader can respond to individually, also in written form. Sheryl Lam, a vocational education teacher, discovered that journal writing enabled her to better monitor the progress of her cooperative education students as they worked in their placements: "Since I have 13 students in five different concentration areas, it is not always easy to deal with all of their problems at once. For me as the teacher, I can focus on each student's problems or successes one at a time; no one gets left out. For the student it's a catharsis."

Learning logs are a relatively simple yet effective way to get all students to write in content-area classes. They stimulate thinking. Normally students write in their logs every day, as either an in-class or an out-of-class activity. Students can be asked to write entries that persuade, that describe personal experiences and responses to stimuli, that give information, or that are creative and spontaneous. Activity 9.7, a learning log from a high school science class, demonstrates how a log can be used to document students' problem-solving abilities.

Once students have practice in keeping a log, the teacher can ask them to respond in a more open-ended, less structured fashion. For instance, Page (1987) got the following response from a student, Carla, in exploring *Antigone* in a high school English class:

> I get Sophocles and Socrates mixed up. Socrates is a philosopher. Athena is talked about a great deal in mythology. Wow, they had dramatic competitions. I wonder if he had the record for the most wins at a competition. I bet if Polynices were alive, he would be very proud of his sister. I would! The chorus seems similar to today's narrator.

Page notes also that students are more motivated to learn when they keep a journal, or log. She cites the positive comments of three students about such writing:

> I love the writing journals. Having to keep a writing journal is the extra push I need to expand my ideas, when otherwise I would not. My journal has brought to life to many ideas that may have died if I had not been required to keep a journal. I am somewhat proud of it. —Carla

> Writing journals are my favorite. I like having a place to write down important events in my life, and literary ideas, poems, stories, etc. —Allison

> I feel that the writing journal by far is the most expressive and open writing that we have done in class. I always try to come up with original and creative entries. I feel that the journal has sparked some new creativity in me—and my essays (product paper) reflect it. They seem to be more imaginative than before. —Betsy

Another journal activity, the **double-entry journal** (Vaughan, 1990), is a log in which students write on the left side of the page about their prior knowledge of a topic. After reading, they enter comments about what they learned on the right side of the page. These comments might include drawings or questions. A class log, or class notebook (Richardson, 1992a), is a combined writing and note-taking activity that encourages students to take responsibility for writing about class content. Sometimes called **content journals**, they provide a way for students to review and interpret information to be discussed in class (Anderson,

ACTIVITY 9.7 Hank's Learning Log Entry Documented His Thinking Process with Bulbs and Batteries

The only preknowledge I brought to this activity was how to put batteries in a flashlight. Using that knowledge, I immediately put the two batteries together like this:

Then, I ignored the wires to see what would happen if I just placed the bulb on top of the battery, because that is how a flashlight seems to work. It didn't work.

One person in my group said, "Remember, it's a circuit." So I held the wires to either end of both batteries and twisted them together and touched the bottom of the bulb. That did not work either, so I untwisted the wire ends and touched the bottom of the bulb with them separate from each other, but simultaneously. However, the bulb would not light.

I had a lot of trouble holding everything together, so I reasoned that I probably only had to use one battery since a positive charge from one end and a negative charge at the other end was all that two (or more) batteries really amounted to. I thought that maybe the problem was that the circuit was broken because of all my fumbling around. I retried touching the ends of the wires to the bulb, but it still would not light.

Then I remembered when I installed a new phone last year, I had to wrap the end of a wire around something that looked like a screw. So I tried wrapping the wire ends around the bulb. The bulb still would not light.

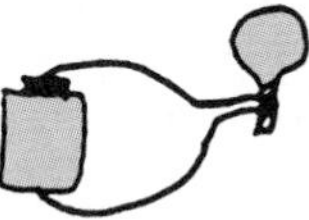

I unwrapped one of the wires from around the bulb, intending to try twisting it again with the end of the other wire and then wrapping that whole thing around the neck of the bulb. However, before I did that, I accidentally touched the end of that wire on the bottom of the bulb and I saw a very quick flicker. For a moment, I wasn't sure what I had done to make it work. Then I deliberately touched the bottom of the bulb again and got the bulb to light.

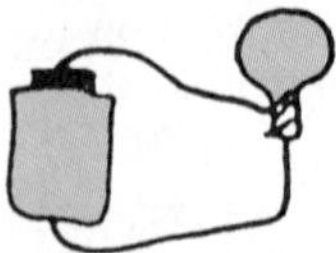

Next, I wondered if I could reverse the wrapping wire and the bottom-touching wire to make the bulb light up. The bulb lit up this way as well.

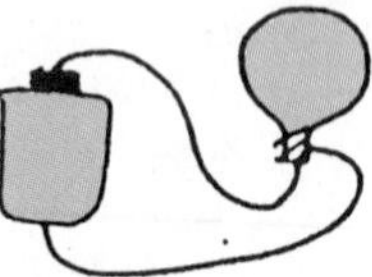

Next, I realized that my original "flashlight model" would work if I added a wire to complete the circuit, when working with my partner.

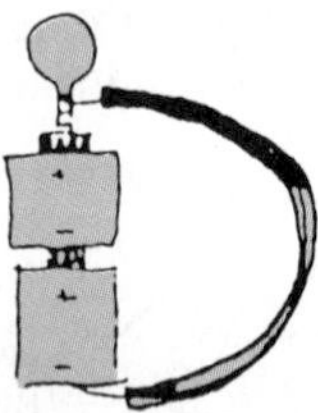

From Debby Deal (1998). "Portfolios, Learning Logs, and Eulogies: Using expressive writing in a science methods class." In Sturtevant, E. G., Dugan, J. A., Linder, P., and Linek, W. M. *Literacy and Community: The Twentieth Yearbook of the College Reading Association.* Used with permission.

1993). Students can write in the journals during class—for instance, during the reading of a passage or text. Students also can write in journals at home as a way to clarify their thinking. Activity 9.8 is an example of a content journal developed by a student in a college course on the teaching of reading.

Annotations

Students need frequent chances to practice critical thinking in their reading and writing. One way of providing these opportunities for older students—middle and secondary level—is through a system of annotation. **Annotating**, making notes about a reading, will help students think about their understanding of the material and enable them to get their reflections down in writing.

One such system is **REAP** (read, encode, annotate, ponder), developed by Eanet and Manzo (1976). This procedure is designed to improve comprehension skills by helping students summarize material in their own words and develop writing as well as reading ability. The four steps in REAP are as follows:

R—Reading to discover the author's ideas

E—Encoding into your own language

ACTIVITY 9.8 Reading Response Journal

Quote or Point Made by the Author	*Response*
Failure to recognize and account for individual differences is a major failing of all the specialized approaches.	Teachers should vary instruction according to individual differences. Children have to master prerequisite skills.
It is true that seatwork in the form of workbook exercise can deteriorate into nothing more than busywork. Yet, with proper teacher-directed instruction, children can become actively engaged in meaningful practice.	The key word here is *meaningful.* Only workbook pages that are meaningful to children should be assigned.
Although current educational trends emphasize basic skills and the passing of tests to show that a person is literate, greater emphasis should be placed on skills that enable learners to acquire information on their own.	The authors are saying that the basic skills taught are not the ones children need to acquire information on their own. Are the authors referring to higher-level thinking skills?

A—Annotating your interpretation of the author's ideas

P—Pondering whether the text information is significant

Creating annotations will help students increase their maturity and independence in reading. Although annotations may be submitted for grading—perhaps as homework or class grades—they are probably more valuable as written notes to facilitate understanding. Below we describe seven different annotation styles, which students can use singly or in combination.

1. The *heuristic* annotation is a statement, usually in the author's words, that has two purposes: to suggest the ideas of the reading selection and to provoke a response. To write the statement, the annotator needs to find the essence in a stimulating manner. The quotation selected must represent the theme or main idea of the selection.
2. The *summary* annotation condenses the selection into a concise form. It should be brief, clear, and to the point. It includes no more or less than is necessary to convey adequately the development and relationship of the author's main ideas. In the case of a story, the summary annotation is a synopsis—the main events of the plot.
3. The *thesis* annotation is an incisive statement of the author's proposition. As the word *incisive* implies, it cuts directly to the heart of the matter. With fiction, it can substitute for a statement of theme. One approach is to ask oneself, "What is the author saying? What one idea or point is being made?" The thesis annotation is best written in precise wording; unnecessary connectives are removed to produce a telegram-like but unambiguous statement.
4. The *question* annotation directs attention to the ideas the annotator considers most germane; the question may or may not be the same as

the author's thesis. The annotator must first determine the most significant issue at hand and then express this notation in question form. This annotation answers the question "What questions are the authors answering with the narrative?"

5. The *critical* annotation is the annotator's response to the author's thesis. In general, a reader may have one of three responses: agreement, disagreement, or a combination of the two. The first sentence in the annotation should state the author's thesis. The next sentence should state the position taken with respect to the thesis. The remaining sentences are devoted to defending this position.
6. The *intention* annotation is a statement of the author's intention, plan, or purpose—as the student perceives it—in writing the selection. This type of annotation is particularly useful with material of a persuasive, ironic, or satirical nature. Determining intention requires that the annotator bring to bear all available clues—both intrinsic, such as tone and use of language, and extrinsic, such as background knowledge about the author.
7. The *motivation* annotation is a statement that attempts to speculate about the probable motive behind the author's writing. It is an attempt to find the source of the author's belief system and perceptions. The motivation annotation is a high form of criticism, often requiring penetrating psychological insight.

Other Assisting Activities

Many writing activities can be practiced with students at the assistance phase of learning. Students can write out the steps they would follow to solve a math problem or complete an experiment. The teacher can ask them to speculate on what would happen if they altered one step. Students also can practice writing about mathematics problems through being asked to write questions about them: What is the sum of 15 and 30? The questions should reflect students' knowledge of the vocabulary and the correct operations.

In a history class students can be asked to rewrite a historic event by altering one cause or one effect. Then students can contrast the way the event really happened with their invented version. In the same way, students in an English class can choose a topic that they are studying and write about it from the perspective of the subject. For instance, one might become an author and, through the author's words, explain word choice or style or plot choices. In science, one might become a blood cell and describe a journey through the body. Activity 9.9 presents a story by a child writing as a blood cell.

Biopoems

Another helpful writing activity is the modified **biopoem**, a poem whose subject is the writer himself or herself. Gere (1985, p. 222) provides the following pattern for writing biopoems:

ACTIVITY 9.9 A Day in the Life of a Blood Cell

There I was, stuck on a boring day doing absolutely nothing. It was 1:32 in the afternoon. Agent 002 was in hot pursuit of the gangster known as Ned the Nucleus. Agent 0012 called me for backup because there was a shootout at the Cell Bank on 112 Membrane Street. I rode out there, but there was a backup in the bloodstream so I rode down the back way. Ned the Nucleus was threatening to blow the cell bank sky high. I snuck up and over the cell wall. I climbed up the cell bank with the help of Don the DNA. I went in and brought out Bob the Brain Cell. How could I be that stupid; now Ned the Nucleus had a gun. He was shooting at the cops. What could we do?

I went back to the station and figured out a plan. I'd go in the bank disguised as a customer! He'd hold me hostage, then I'd hit him with my elbow and put him under arrest! I got into the building okay. Then I went up to the top floor. He had two other hostages. Their names were Rick the Red Blood Cell and Wally the White Blood Cell. He was arrested on the spot. I got promoted to Chief Lieutenant. Ned the Nucleus got 15–20 years and $500,000 cell bail. A very good lesson was learned today. Killing cells doesn't pay.

Headlines!
Ned the Nucleus Breaks Out of Jail!!

So now I had to get him back in jail. I went to headquarters so I could get all of the information. Then it hit me like a Mike Tyson jab. Where else would he be than Ned's Night Club in downtown Los Nucleus? So I took the bloodstream down there. He wasn't there, but I got some useful information. They told me he was at the dock. On San Fran Cellular's finest dock, Cells Wharf. I pulled up in the bad neighborhood. I wasn't alone, though. I had the help of Carl the Blood Clot, and Priscilla the Spore. Ned the Nucleus was not alone; in fact, he had his whole gang there! I recognized some of their faces; they were Beau the Bruise, Cad the Cut, Rick the Red Blood Cell, and Wally the White Blood Cell, who had faked being a hostage at the bank. We called for backup and got out of there.

We missed the bullets shot at us and met the other cops at my house, where we had told them to go. We went back to the wharf with the SWAT team and the rest of the police squad. We had a stakeout. People shot at us from the water with their stun guns. Our snipers from the roof shot them. Then we had a shootout. But we had them surrounded, so they just gave up. I got a medal of honor and became head of the SWAT team and the police. But to me it was just another day in the life of a detective.

Written by Jon Morgan.

Line 1: First name
Line 2: Four traits that describe the author
Line 3: Relative of ("brother," "sister," "daughter," etc.)
Line 4: Lover of (list three things or people)
Line 5: Who feels (three items)
Line 7: Who fears (three items)
Line 8: Who gives (three items)
Line 9: Who would like to see (three items)
Line 10: Resident of
Line 11: Last name

A biopoem can also be adapted to different subject matter, as illustrated in Activity 9.10. In this modified version, written by an elementary social studies teacher, the subject is the state of Virginia, and the poem is condensed to seven lines. An example of a biopoem written by an early elementary student is provided in Activity 9.11.

Cinquains

Another writing strategy similar to the biopeom is a **cinquain**. A cinquain (pronounced sin-kán) is a five-line poem with the following pattern: The first line is a noun or the subject of the poem; the second line consists of two words

ACTIVITY 9.10 Modified Biopoem

Virginia
Coastal, warm, fertile
Land, missionary, adventure
Planter, slave, farmer
First, tobacco, General Assembly
Smith, Rolfe, Pocahontas
Southern Colony

Written by M. J. Weatherford. Used with permission.

ACTIVITY 9.11 Biopoem

Note from the teacher: At the elementary grade levels I thought it was easier for the students to include what each line was trying to express. Upper elementary and above are capable of understanding the poem without the "clue words."

Andrea

who is blue-eyed, brown-haired and nice
relative of Aunt Kathy
lover of Mom, Aunt Kathy, and Louie (my dog)
who feels good, happy and tired
who needs more chapter books, friends, and long nails
who fears snakes, mom dying, mom's lupus
who give clothes, toys, and money
who would like to see Spice Girls, 'N Sync and Backstreet Boys
resident of Virginia Beach

Mathopoulos

Developed by Terry Bryce.

that describe the first line (adjectives); the third line is three action words (verbs); the fourth line contains four words that convey a feeling; and the fifth line is a single word that refers back to the first line. Students at all educational levels will be pleased to participate in this language enrichment activity. Cinquains require thought and concentration and can be tried in any content area. Activities 9.12 and 9.13 contain examples written by students in middle and high school.

ACTIVITY 9.12 Cinquains: Junior High School

(After reading *Johnny Tremain*)

The Sons of Liberty
brave, aggressive
daring, risk-taking, rebelling
they detested British taxes
Whigs

Johnny Tremain
apprentice, brave
hardworking, riding, daring
true to the Whigs
silversmith

Developed in Anne Forrester's class.

ACTIVITY 9.13 Cinquains: High School

viruses
subcellular, deadly
invading, threatening, killing
can attack almost anybody
poison

(On composer Richard Wagner)

monster
conceited, talented
haranguing, groveling, unloving
unscrupulous in every way
genius

Developed in Sharon Gray's class.

First-Person Summary

A **first-person summary** is an excellent writing activity in which students write about something in the first person, as if they were part of the enterprise or the action. Often students read an assignment or memorize information without a true understanding of the material. First-person summaries allow them to process information by writing in their own words about a topic. Using the first person encourages them to become personally involved in the material. Teachers may be able to recognize and correct any deficiencies in students' understanding by reading their summaries. For instance, when studying photosynthesis in science, students might write a first-person essay in which they take the part of a water molecule. They must explain how they get into a plant, where they journey in the plant, what happens once they reach the chloroplast, and so on. In this way, students gain a deeper understanding of the photosynthesis process, and teachers can identify problems students are encountering. This type of assignment can work with a topic such as "A Day in the Life of a New Irish Immigrant in 1835" or "A Day in the Life of a Blood Cell," as already demonstrated in Activity 9.9.

Triangle Truths and Smart Remarks

Two other activities described by Morgan, Forget, and Antinarella (1996) are triangle truths and smart remarks. Triangle truths can be described by students as they read or directly after they read a passage. In a log or notebook, the student draws a triangle that contains four important pieces of information. One piece of information goes at each angle of the triangle (the clues), and one piece (the response that the reader must supply) goes in the center of the triangle. All the bits of information are connected to define, describe, or highlight a particular idea, person, or fact from the reading. The goal of the activity is to supply the correct response in the center of the triangle. A finished triangle could look like this:

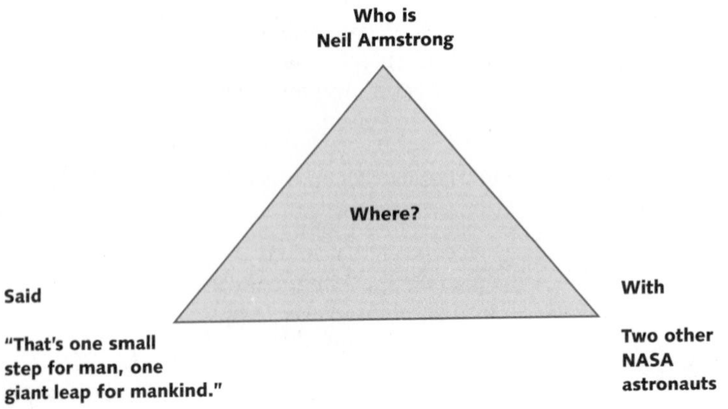

Some words posing questions to be answered in the center of the triangle are *who, what, where, when, how, why, tried, wanted, made,* and *found.*

Smart remarks are comments or questions that enable students to see in writing what they believe or need to know. The remarks are personal comments about what the reading says to the reader and how it makes the reader feel. The comments, when studied later by the students, show what was gained from the reading. After reading a passage in "Energy and Catalysts," a student might make the following remarks:

> What is a catalyst? Look up or ask. Adding salt to water should be a chemical change. Heat must be energy released. *Exothermic* and *endothermic*—these words remind me of a "thermos" bottle. Energy must *exit* in exothermic reactions. Remember the prefix "ex." How do rechargeable batteries fit into this? Ask! I'm not sure how you can *add* energy.

The goal of smart remarks is to write to clarify thinking as one reads and to think deeply about what has been read.

The Reflection Phase of Writing

A number of researchers (Atwell, 1987; Sanacore, 1998) maintain that the "publication" of writing is a natural way for motivation in writing to occur. Atwell believes that teachers should support student publication efforts because students write better when they know someone will read their writing.

When writing is to be published or finished as a product, writers should be concerned not only with content but also with form. After the writing has been revised, an audience will read it and react in a formal way. During revision, writers are still learning to express what they understand about the information, but they also are learning to be considerate of their audience by putting the writing in a consistent, organized format. During revision, writers should be concerned with correct spelling, grammar, and organization. Often, teachers confuse the evaluation stage with the drafting stage and expect students to produce writing that meets format considerations before or while they are writing to express content. This is a difficult chore even for the most experienced writers. Here is a rule of thumb to use when analyzing a student's piece of writing:

Fluency → Clarity → Correctness → Eloquence & Style

Many students have poor handwriting, spelling, and grammar skills. In analyzing student writing, teachers first need to put much stock on the sincerity and fluency of the effort. Later, they can ask for more clarity. Finally, the goal is to produce students who write correctly and with some style. Remember that, for the student, motivation to write may come from the teacher, who follows this progression in grading and analyzing student writing.

RAFT (Vanderventer, 1979) offers one way for writers and their teachers to keep the appropriate audience in focus. *R* stands for the role of the writer: What is the writer's role—reporter, observer, eyewitness? *A* stands for audience: Who will be reading this writing—the teacher, other students, a parent, people in the community, an editor? *F* stands for format: What is the best way to present this writing—in a letter, as an article, a report, a poem? *T* stands for the topic: What is the subject of this writing—a famous mathematician, prehistoric cave dwellers, a reaction to a specific event? When teachers are clear about the purpose of the writing and students keep RAFT in mind, the product will be clearer and more focused.

Whenever possible, as with RAFT, students should write for an audience, even if "publishing" means merely taking completed writing products home to parents or other family. As students' writing skills develop, it becomes very important to get them to write with attention to the finished product.

Activities for Reflective Writing

A number of activities are well suited to helping students write reflectively with a goal of building a product.

Guided-Writing Procedure

The **guided-writing procedure** (Smith & Bean, 1980) is a strategy that uses writing specifically to enhance comprehension. Because guided writing leads to a graded product, we classify it as a reflection activity; however, guided writing also involves the preparation and assistance steps. Smith and Bean give seven steps for its implementation, to be completed in two days. On the first day, the teacher (1) activates students' prior knowledge to facilitate prewriting, (2) has students factstorm and categorize their facts, (3) has students write two paragraphs using this organized list, and (4) has students read about the topic. On the second day, the teacher (5) has students check their drafts for functional writing concerns, (6) assigns rewriting based on functional needs and revision to incorporate the information from the reading, and (7) gives a quiz. Alternatives to giving a quiz include submitting the rewritten paragraphs, which we think is just as appropriate.

Activity 9.14 is an example of a modified guided-writing procedure used by a middle-school English teacher to help her students write limericks.

Book Diary

A book diary (Steen, 1991) is an exercise in which students respond in writing to the supplementary reading they have done. The teacher designs a form on which students write responses to specific questions about the material. For example: "This is what I already know about ________________." "I liked this part of the book because ________________." "The most important facts I learned were ________________." Steen saw much progress in students' maturity as writers as a result of using book diaries. Teachers will be able to see immediately the learning that is taking place. Depending on how the teacher phrases the questions and designs the format, book diaries could be used

ACTIVITY 9.14 Guided Writing: Limericks

Strategy: The purpose of this activity is to extend the students' abilities to compose a poem. They will achieve this purpose in a guided-writing exercise. I have students write poetry because they will understand poetry better after they have become poets. The exercise will begin with clustering, and from there the students will be guided through their first and final drafts. Because this is a guided exercise, I will first determine the students' background, build on that background, direct the study, and finally determine their comprehension. The final extension of this activity is publishing these poems.

First step: Prewriting (determining background)

The teacher writes the word *limerick* on the board and then draws a circle around it. He/She then asks the students to think about the characteristics of that word. As they give answers, the teacher writes them on lines extended from the main word. Then the teacher directs them to look at some limericks in the text.

Second step: Prewriting (building background)

The limericks are read and studied for rhyme scheme and rhythm. The characteristics are listed as further subtopics of the main topic, "limericks."

Third step: Guiding the first draft (developing comprehension)

1. Tell the students that instead of writing limericks, they will be writing pigericks.
2. Pigericks are like limericks, except they are always about pigs. They are short, have lines that rhyme, and contain a definite rhythm. Furthermore, they are humorous.
3. Pass out handouts on pigericks and show Arnold Lobel's book title *The Book of Pigericks*. Go over the poems, noticing the similarities between limericks and pigericks.
4. On the board or overhead, begin a line for a pigerick. Have the students continue brainstorming the remainder of the poem.
5. Assign the writing of a pigerick. Monitor.

Fourth step: Revising (reflection)

6. Have students exchange their poems and share suggestions.
7. Students then revise and rewrite onto large index cards. Next, they illustrate.
8. Post the finished products on the bulletin board.

(*continued*) ➤

equally well for younger students, as were Steen's, or for older students. At-risk learners may find them less threatening than assignments that start with a blank page.

Content-Focused Drama

Cooter and Chilcoat (1991) describe how high school students can cooperatively study and perform content-focused melodramas to stimulate connections between what they know and what historical texts describe. Students pick a topic of interest within a unit of study and, in groups of five or six, develop a melodrama by writing the plot, developing characters, and making scenery. Students draft the writing in several stages: (1) the prewriting stage, in which they research

Clustering

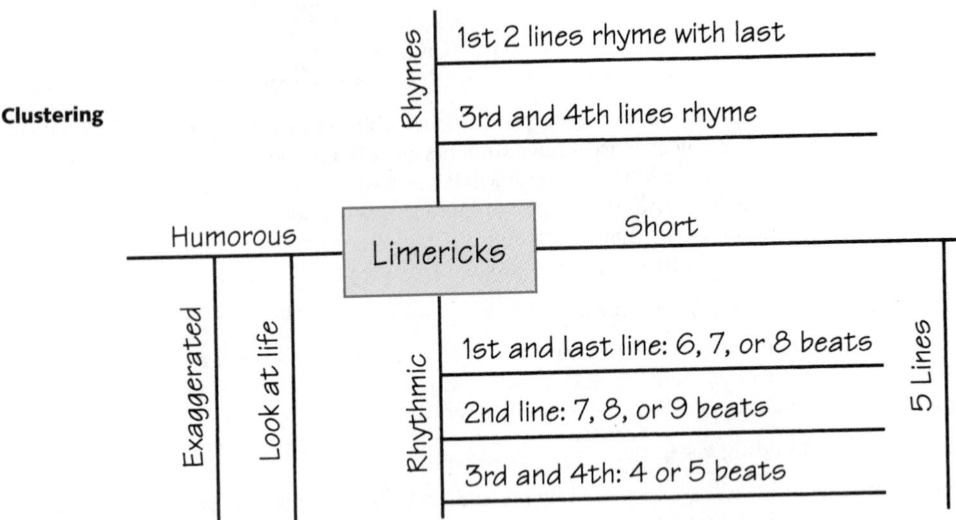

Students' Limericks:

There was a giant pig named Moe Cork
Who acted on a stage in New York
Said he, "Of we three
I am the greatest of thee
Because my head is made of more pork."

There once was a piggy named Lance,
Who wanted to do nothing but dance.
He danced every day,
In a very awkward way.
But that was okay for dancing Lance.

Developed by Frances Lively.

---

the topic, organize facts, and develop characters, composing the (2) initial draft of the script, and (3) conferencing with the teacher to revise, edit, and polish the final script. Cooter and Chilcoat advise that the teacher work with students on grasping the elements of melodrama: stereotyped characters, superheroes, archvillains as ruffians and cads, romantic loves, excessive acting, overblown conflict, plenty of action. The authors list a number of benefits of such drama: development of cultural literacy, student collaboration and responsibility training, teacher support, teaching of creativity, and the teaching of reading/writing connections.

Collaborative Writing

We mentioned **collaborative writing** in connection with the Foxfire books, cited earlier as an example of making writing relevant and relating it to students' backgrounds. Collaborative writing is most effective in demonstrating to students the necessity of finished products that reflect consideration for the intended reader. When students work together, they are less intimidated by what they see as the immensity of the tasks involved in thinking, drafting, revising, and evaluating. Brunwin (1989) organized the students in an entire elementary school to produce a historical account of their neighborhood. They developed questions, targeted the best persons to ask, conducted and transcribed interviews, organized their material, and wrote a book to report their findings.

Collaborative writing need not involve such large groups. One teacher divided her class into several groups. Each individual read an article and reacted to it independently. Then individuals brought their reactions to their assigned group. Within the group, a common draft was produced, using the individual reactions. Each group member then revised the draft and brought suggestions back to the group. Last, the group evaluated and rewrote the paper, which the teacher then graded. She discovered that students were able to demonstrate their knowledge of the content very well while practicing good writing skills—and, as a bonus, she received fewer papers to grade. Activity 9.15 presents a jot chart for peer editing of writing. While working collaboratively in teams like those mentioned above, students can edit each other's papers using such a jot chart to help improve the final product of the writing.

C3B4Me

Yeager (1991) introduced **C3B4Me** (See Three Before Me) to remind students that writing that is to be turned in for a grade must be carefully reviewed and revised. Students should remember to see three other helpers before submitting the work to the teacher. First, the writer should confer with himself or herself. Next, the writer should confer with a peer, asking for specific advice about designated portions of the writing—not just "Do you like my work?" but "Do you think I have been clear enough in this section?" Last, the writer should be able to consult a "reading associate." Teachers can facilitate the revising/evaluating process by organizing the class into three types of associates. One type is students who have volunteered to be editors for other class members; they and the teacher agree that they have this skill. A second type is a student who has volunteered to illustrate others' written work. A third type of associate can be designated to help a writer find an available editor or illustrator. In the C3B4Me process, students or "associates" may find a jot chart (as in Activity 9.15) helpful during the peer review process.

GIST

A number of strategies for teaching students to summarize text effectively have been developed and explored. A strategy called **GIST** (Cunningham, 1982)—"generating interactions between schemata and text"—has been found to effectively improve students' reading comprehension and summary writing (Bean & Steenwyk, 1984). With GIST teachers must model and guide after the reading stage of a lesson. The reader is interrupted and directed to record a summary of the material just read. Cunningham recommends the following steps:

ACTIVITY 9.15 Jot Chart for Peer Editing: Process

Name: ______________________ Date: ______________

Topic: ______________________

Controlling Idea: ______________________

Audience: ______________________

Major Points	*Supporting Details*	*Transitions*

1. Select a short passage in a chapter that has an important main idea. A passage containing from three to five paragraphs works best. Type the paragraphs on an overhead transparency.
2. Place the transparency on the projector, but display only the first paragraph (cover the others). Put 20 blanks on the chalkboard. Have students read the paragraph, and instruct them to write a 20-word (or less) summary in their own words.
3. Have students generate a class summary on the board in 30 or fewer words. Their individual summaries will function as guides for this process.
4. Reveal the next paragraph of the text, and have students generate a summary of 30 or fewer words that encompasses both of the first two paragraphs.
5. Continue this procedure paragraph by paragraph until students have produced a GIST statement for the entire passage being taught. In time, they will be able to generate GIST statements for segments of text in a single step.

By restricting the length of students' GIST summaries, the teacher compels the students to use the three major strategies necessary for comprehension and retention of key ideas in any text. They must delete trivial information, select key ideas, and generalize in their own words (Kintch & Van Dijk, 1978). In this manner, GIST is beneficial for teaching reading and writing. Eventually the GIST can be constructed after the reading as an excellent reflective activity, although it is important first to practice with the strategy at both the assistance and the reflection phases of the lesson. Activity 9.16 presents a GIST done cooperatively by teacher and students in a high school class. Changes in word selection are noted to show how students attempted to arrive at a better GIST.

Grading Reflective Writing

Teachers sometimes question whether they should accept writing from students when it contains grammatical errors, misspellings, and other errors. "Surely seventh-graders can write better than this!" they admonish. However, teachers must allow students to start where they are and to focus on one stage of writing at a time.

Errors are a normal part of learning, and they will occur in student writing. The amount and types of writing practice that students have had will determine their level of sophistication. If the pressure to focus on errors is eliminated during the prewriting and drafting stages, when the focus should be on the content, then attention to errors can be greater during the revision stage. If students have had prewriting and drafting opportunities, their revised writing will reflect both improved content and improved form.

Teachers can guide students in their writing activities by making clear their expectations for the final product. Students should understand exactly what will

ACTIVITY 9.16 GIST from Chapter 23, Section 1, of *World Geography*, Baerwald and Fraser (1992)

The section was entitled "Creating the Modern Middle East." Students were limited to 30-word summaries.

After reading pages 449–450, "Regions Uniting Peoples":

> Under the Ottomans, ethnically diverse "rayahs" with different languages and cultures populated the Middle East. Conflict and discontent led to desires to establish independent homelands. Europeans also wanted influence there.

After reading pages 449–451, adding the subtitle "The Impact of World War I":

> Many ethnically diverse cultures desired homelands. Allies in World War I tricked Arabs into fighting Ottomans to achieve independence. The unfortunate result was French and British control instead of Ottoman.

After reading pages 449–454 (the total section), including the subtitle "Struggle Between Arabs and Jews":

> Palestine was a British "mandate" claimed by Arabs and Zionists. 1930s holocaust led to increased Jewish population. UN-sponsored partition into Arab/Jewish state resulted in Arab/Jewish hatred and war.

Developed by Mark Forget.

---

be evaluated. Of course, the content of the writing is most important. But, "content" is a vague criterion. To clarify expectations and grading criteria for students, Pearce (1983) suggests that teachers use a checklist or a rubric. A **rubric** is an expectation guide that lists the qualities of a range of papers—from the strongest to the weakest (see Activity 9.17). A rubric aids the students, who can refer to it as they revise, and the teacher, who can refer to it during grading. Similarly, checklists are useful because they list the features the teacher expects to find in the writing (see Activity 9.18). Teachers can use a checklist to quickly rate the features of a written assignment, and students can check their papers against this list during revision. Teachers might even provide their point scale for checklists or criteria for grading as in Activity 9.19. Also, they can hand out the rubric or checklist when giving the assignment. In this way, students know in advance what factors will be considered in their grade, and they have a chance to organize their writing accordingly.

As with reflective reading, students should be very involved at the evaluation and publishing stage of writing. Even if the teacher gives the final grade—as the teacher does if students take a test to demonstrate learning after reading—students should have every opportunity to evaluate their own writing before giving it to the teacher. Only when students know that their own analysis is a crucial part of the process will they take responsibility for it.

Another way to facilitate such realization and responsibility is to allow prevision and revision opportunities. Teachers can give students the option of turn-

ACTIVITY 9.17 A Rubric for Grading

Paper topic: 1960s approaches to civil rights in the U.S.

High-quality papers contain:

An overview of civil rights or their lack during the 1960s, with 3 specific examples.
A statement defining civil disobedience, with 3 examples of how it was used and Martin Luther King's role.
At least one other approach to civil rights, with specific examples, and a comparison of this approach with King's civil disobedience that illustrates differences or similarities in at least 2 ways.
Good organization, well-developed arguments, few mechanical errors (sentence fragments, grammatical errors, spelling errors).

Medium-quality papers contain:

An overview of civil rights during the 1960s, with 2 specific examples.
A statement defining civil disobedience, with 2 examples of its use and Martin Luther King's involvement.
One other approach to civil rights, with examples, and a comparison of it with King's civil disobedience by their differences.
Good organization, few mechanical errors, moderately developed arguments.

Lower-quality papers contain:

A general statement defining civil disobedience with reference to Martin Luther King's involvement and at least 1 example.
One other approach to civil rights and how it differed from civil disobedience.
Fair organization, some mechanical errors.

Lowest-quality papers contain:

A general statement on who Martin Luther King was or a general statement on civil disobedience.
A general statement that not all Blacks agreed with civil disobedience.
A list of points, poor organization, many mechanical errors.

From Pearce, D. L. (1983, December). Guidelines for the use and evaluation of writing in content classrooms. *Journal of Reading, 27*(3), 212–218. Reprinted with permission of Daniel L. Pearce and the International Reading Association.

ing in drafts of assigned writing early, for prevision review at "no cost" to the grade. After receiving a graded writing assignment, students can be encouraged to rewrite the paper and receive an average of the first grade and a second grade. Using a computer and word processing program helps students become more receptive to polishing their writing (Brown, Phillips, & Stephens, 1992). Writing a draft and then returning to it with a critical eye is much easier when the major work does not have to be recopied. Cronin, Meadows, and Sinatra (1990) found that secondary students who used the computer for writing assignments across the curriculum increased in writing ability, attaining 100 percent success on a standard written essay test.

ACTIVITY 9.18 Writing Assignment Checklist

Content	Weak	Average	Strong
1. Clear and interesting topic or main idea.			
2. Topic appropriate to the assignment.			
3. Ideas and details support and develop the topic.			
4. Ideas stated clearly and developed fully.			
5. Good use of language.			
Form			
6. Introduction, body, and conclusion.			
7. Details arranged logically; appropriate to the topic.			
8. Coherent; paragraphs constructed well.			
Mechanics			
9. Grammar and usage.			
10. Spelling, capitalization, punctuation.			

Comments:

Key:
Strong—10 points
Average/Strong—7 points
Average—5 points
Weak—3 points

Developed by Dianne Duncan.

One-Minute Summary

In this chapter we describe how to teach, emphasize, and apply writing across the content areas and at different grade levels. The connection between reading and writing is discussed, as well as the importance of teaching writing in the earliest elementary grades. We differentiate between processes and products of writing and describe several stages of writing across the curriculum. Computer applications of writing are explained, and we give examples of how writing can be improved through using this new and valuable tool. Activities to promote

ACTIVITY 9.19 Criteria for Grading

Names: ______________________________

____

Used at least 5 facts ________

Beginning ________

Middle ________

End ________

Bat has a name ________

Story has title ________

Illustration(s) ________

This is the evaluation form the teacher constructs for evaluating the students' performance. After the teacher completes this evaluation, it is kept and attached to the students' writing sample. These stories will be placed in a portfolio and made accessible to parents during visitation.

Developed by Polly Gilbert.

writing at each phase of the PAR Lesson Framework are explained to demonstrate how easily writing to learn can be incorporated into content instruction. Real classroom applications are included to show teachers how content writing works in action. A section on grading students' reflective writing demonstrates how important it is to be concise in grading writing through the use of rubrics, checklists, and set criteria.

End-of-Chapter Activities

1. Try keeping your own learning log to record your reactions as you use the writing strategies described in this chapter. Assess how each activity helps you teach the writing process. Learn to practice writing in your log every day. Share the writing in your log with your students.
2. Try cubing. Write a short paragraph about this chapter on each of the following six levels of the cube:

   How would you describe this chapter?

   To what would you compare this chapter?

   What does this chapter make you think of?

   How would you analyze this chapter?

Apply this chapter to your own life.

Do you agree with the tenets of this chapter? Argue for or against writing to learn in the content areas.

Reflecting on Your Reading

These textbooks are excellent extension reading resources for finding out more about writing to learn in the content classrooms:

Brown, J., Phillips, L., & Stephens, E. (1992). *Toward literacy: Theory and applications for teaching writing in the content areas*. Belmont, CA: Wadsworth.

Wolfe, D., & Reising, R. (1983). *Writing for learning in the content areas*. Portland, ME: J. Weston Walch.

Graves, D. (1994). *A fresh look at writing*. Portsmouth, NH: Heinemann.

Atwell, N. (1989). *Coming to know: Writing to learn in the intermediate grades*. Portsmouth, NH: Heinemann.

Bright, R. (1995). *Writing instruction in the intermediate grades: What is said, what is done, what is understood*. Newark, DE: International Reading Association.

Bromley, K. (1993). *Journaling: Engagements in reading, writing, and thinking*. New York: Scholastic.

Fulwiler, T. (1987). *Teaching with writing*. Portsmouth, NH: Boynton/Cook.

Gere, A. R. (Ed.). (1985). *Roots in the sawdust: Writing to learn across the curriculum*. Urbana, IL: National Council of Teachers of English.

Martin, N., D'Arcy, P., Newton, B., & Parker, R. (1976). *Writing and learning across the curriculum*. Montclair, NJ: Boynton/Cook.

Maxwell, R. (1996). *Writing across the curriculum in the middle and high schools*. Boston: Allyn and Bacon.

Murray, D. (1982). *Learning by teaching*. Montclair, NJ: Boynton/Cook.

Wollman-Bonilla, J. (1991). *Response journals*. New York: Scholastic.

CHAPTER 10

Study Skills and Study Systems

Order and simplification are the first steps toward the mastery of a subject—the actual enemy is the unknown.

—Thomas Mann, *Buddenbrooks*

The art of remembering is the art of thinking.

—William James, *Talks to Teachers on Psychology*

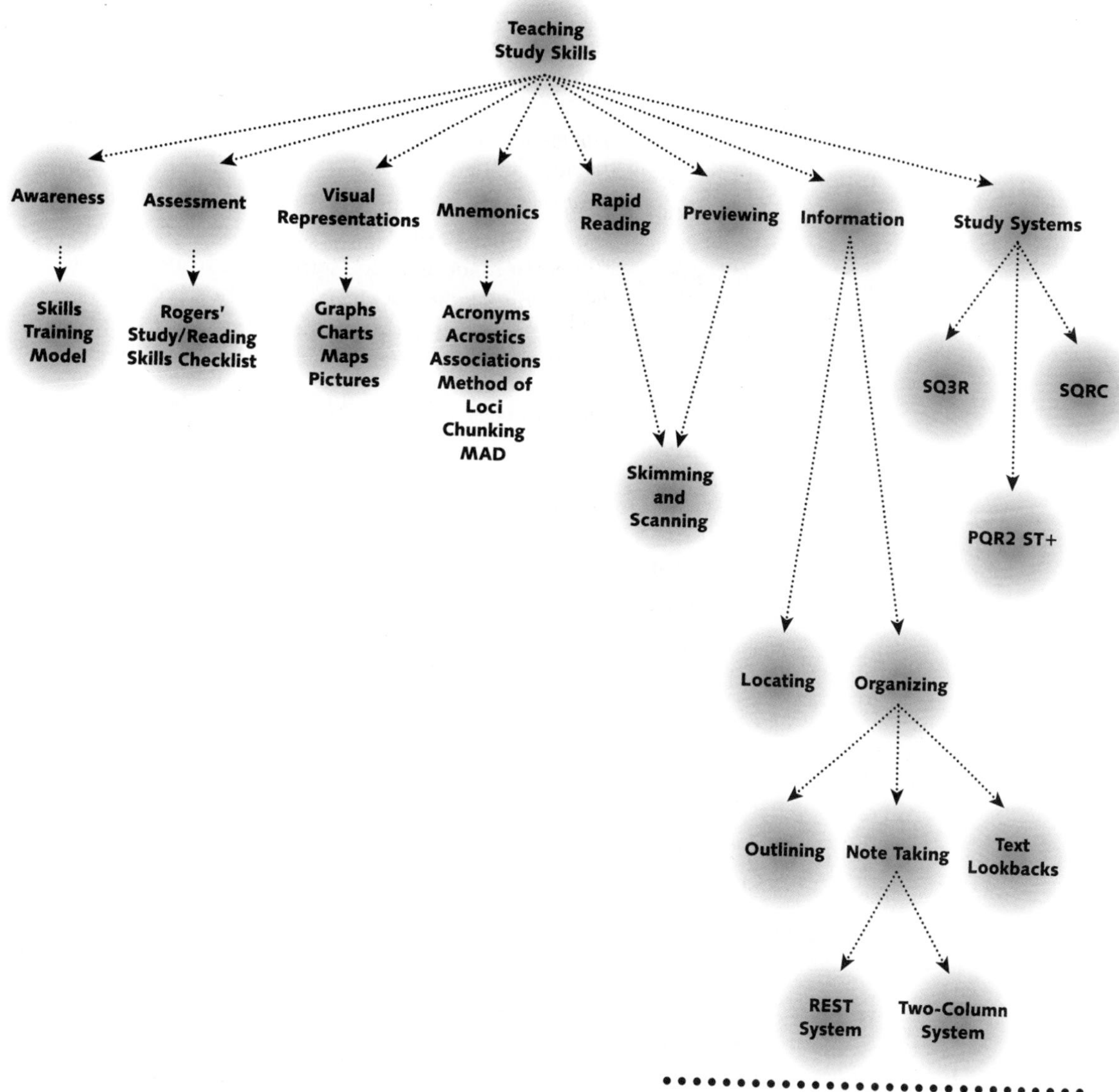

Preparing to Read

1. How many of these study skills do you make your students aware of as you teach your subject?

   ______ previewing
   ______ skimming
   ______ using a system of study
   ______ note taking
   ______ rapid reading
   ______ studying charts, maps, and graphs
   ______ remembering and using mnemonics

   Did you check most or few? In this chapter we explain why all of them are important study skills that need to be taught.

2. Following is a list of terms used in this chapter. Some may be familiar to you in a general context, but in this chapter they may be used in unfamiliar ways. Rate your knowledge by placing a plus sign (+) in front of those you are sure that you know, a check mark (✓) in front of those you have some knowledge about, and a zero (0) in front of those you don't know. Be ready to locate and pay special attention to their meanings when they are presented in the chapter.

   ______ skills training model
   ______ external distracters
   ______ internal distracters
   ______ physical distracters
   ______ visual representations
   ______ massed study
   ______ mnemonics
   ______ acronym
   ______ acrostic
   ______ MAD
   ______ saccadic eye movements
   ______ fixations
   ______ rauding
   ______ mental push-ups
   ______ rapid-reading drills
   ______ preview and rapid-reading drill
   ______ previewing

______ skimming
______ scanning
______ outlining
______ text lookback
______ study system

Objectives

As you read this chapter, focus your attention on the following objectives. You will:

1. understand the importance of developing students' ability to use study skills at all grade levels.
2. learn the importance of the skills training model.
3. be able to assess students at all grade levels in their use of study skills.
4. learn about teaching visual representations and other visual aids.
5. understand study strategies such as mnemonics and associational learning.
6. understand and be able to use rapid reading and previewing.
7. be able to teach students how to gather and locate information in textbooks.
8. be able to instruct students in how to organize materials through underlining, note taking, and outlining.
9. understand systems of study described in this chapter and be able to use them in your own classroom.

Alfred North Whitehead once said, "We think in generalities, we live in detail." Many K–12 students are not good at the detailed thinking that Whitehead alluded to. Study and disciplined inquiry of all kinds are, in actuality, attention to detail. Many students refuse to study when the details seem, to them, overwhelming and confusing. Yet these same students can describe in great detail events such as a trip to the mall: They can provide details about what they spent, what they did, whom they saw, and how each person was dressed. By contrast, our posturing, lecturing, and badgering is ineffective in getting children to enjoy learning and to study efficiently. Being told to study is not enough. Providing opportunities whereby study leads to interesting information, where the payoff is worth the effort expended, is the most effective way to convince students to study.

In fact, students have indicated that they do want to be taught study skills (Hornberger & Whitford, 1983). But unfortunately, most teachers do not seem to know about or to value study strategies and are unsure how to integrate study skills with content (Jackson & Cunningham, 1994). In this chapter we explain the importance of study, types of study strategies, and study systems. The strategies emphasize the importance of the reflection phase of the PAR Lesson Framework, whereby greater retention of the reading matter is brought about. The best place to teach students how to be reflective in studying is in the classroom. Because teachers have little control over study behaviors outside class, they must provide careful guidance and practice that will carry over to independent study.

Making Students Aware of Study Skills

The most important first step in teaching students study skills is to make them aware that they are learning a new study skill. To make students aware of the learning strategies they are employing, teachers should use a **skills training model**. To employ such a model, follow these steps:

1. *Explain the skill being taught.* Explain to your students that they will be asked to think in a certain way, to make judgments, and to practice effective thinking.
2. *Introduce the lesson.* When introducing the content lesson, make certain that new information is related to the students' prior knowledge.
3. *Develop structured practice using the skill.* Explain how the students are to use the skill appropriately. Have them practice using the skill for 20 to 30 minutes.
4. *Summarize how the skill was used in the content lesson.* Explain again why the skill is important for the students to master and how it helped them understand the lesson better.
5. *Continue practice with the skill.* It is advisable to go through steps 1 through 4 in at least five additional lessons. For elementary and middle-school students, this practice should be with different content lessons, to ensure transfer of the skill to other disciplines.

At any of the five steps listed above, the teacher can reference the skill that is being learned in the lesson. For instance, an anticipation guide (explained in Chapter 5) or previewing will teach the skill of predicting outcomes from printed material. When teachers use this paradigm they will be providing guided practice and direct teaching to help students to acquire skills, internalize skills by repeated practice, and transfer skills to other learning contexts. When students know the plan of the lesson and the skill being taught, teachers can facilitate improvement in students' thinking ability. This type of teacher intervention is a necessary step in improving cognitive ability. Pearson and Tierney (1983), however, assessed the instructional paradigm most used by teachers at present—which features the use of many practice materials, little explanation of cognitive tasks, little interaction with students about the nature of specific tasks, and strong emphasis on one correct answer—to determine the extent to which teachers supply answers if there is any confusion over a task. Not surprisingly, Pearson and Tierney concluded that such a paradigm is ineffective. The skills training model creates an opportunity for students to assess, regulate, and evaluate their own comprehension, a crucial component of the complex process of reading (Meeks, 1991). Every study skill that we describe in this chapter can be introduced to students through the skills training model.

The Importance of Study Skills

In 1917 Thorndike described the process of reading a paragraph. Educators today can still profit from studying his interpretation for its remarkable clarity about the nature of the reading process:

> Understanding a paragraph is like solving a problem in mathematics. It consists in selecting the right elements of the situation and putting them together in the right relations, and also with the right amount of weight or influence or force for each. The mind is assailed as it were by every word in the paragraph. It must select, repress, soften, emphasize, correlate and organize, all under the influence of the right mental set or purpose or demand. (p. 329)

As Thorndike suggests, reading can be seen as a problem-solving task. This task can be difficult because it requires readers to have a positive attitude toward the purpose for reading, the demands of the text, and their own background experience. Most important, the reader must be in a good frame of mind—have a good mental set—and must have clarity of thought before beginning to read. Reading for study cannot occur unless these conditions are met. In short, the combination of reading and study is a disciplined inquiry that demands training over many years of schooling.

Although children are taught to read at an early age, often there is no concomitant emphasis on study or study skills (Durkin, 1979; Wertsch, 1978; Schallert & Kleiman, 1979). In middle school—or even high school—a teacher may announce that for a period of time students will be trained in how to study and better retain the information they read. We find two problems with this approach: (1) It is isolated from the reading process and transmits the message that study isn't really connected to reading. (2) This focus on study skills in middle school or high school transmits the message that study skills are pertinent and applicable only late in one's education.

We believe that it is because of this hit-or-miss approach to teaching study and retention strategies that so many studies and reports suggest that training in these skills does not guarantee a high level of comprehension (Armbruster & Anderson, 1981; J. Britton et al., 1975). This is particularly unfortunate, since Elliott and Wendling (1966) substantiated over three decades ago that 75 percent of academic failure is caused by poor study and examination strategies, and Brown and Peterson (1969) found that dropouts often are unable to memorize and retain information. For over three decades researchers (Elliott & Wendling, 1966; Weinstein & Mayer, 1986; Borkowski, Johnston, & Reid, 1987; Borkowski,

Estrada, Milstead, & Hale, 1989; Salembier, 1999) have reported that these are teachable skills that enhance achievement and performance, and that by means of these skills a high percentage of high school students could learn and do passing work. There also is growing evidence (Schunk & Rice, 1992; Borkowski, Weyhing, & Carr, 1988) that convincing students of the value of study strategies will both promote student achievement and ensure that student use of such strategies is maintained. Making information relevant to students increases their motivation to study (Frymier & Schulman, 1995). When teaching study skills, teachers should remember that what is needed is a student-centered approach, based on constructivist theory (discussed in Chapter 6). Kauchak and Eggen (1998) list four key components to learning that we feel teachers should keep in mind when teaching study skills:

1. Learners construct knowledge for themselves rather than waiting for the teacher to give them knowledge piecemeal.
2. New learning builds on prior knowledge.
3. Learning is enhanced by social interaction.
4. Authentic learning promotes meaningful learning.

Assessing Study Skills

Most standardized achievement tests include subtests of study skills. However, these subtests are usually limited in scope, measuring the students' knowledge of "standard" items such as reference skills, alphabetization, and the ability to read maps, charts, and graphs. Often neglected are important skills such as following directions, presenting a report, test taking, note taking, and memory training. To address the need for a broader assessment of study skills, Rogers (1984) divides them into three broad categories: (1) special study/reading comprehension skills, (2) information-location skills, and (3) study and retention strategies. His "study/reading skills checklist," reproduced as Activity 10.1, is thorough. By reviewing his checklist, teachers can see how many study skills are related to reading, and how easy it is to assume what students "ought to know," until we realize how much there is to know. Content-area teachers could design tests for each of the areas on this checklist or have a reading specialist help question children, individually or in small groups, on how often and how well they use the skills listed. However, such a formal level of assessment is usually not necessary. Discussion and observation, combined with a briefer survey, will most likely provide enough information for teachers to realize what study skills their students really know about, and use. Or, Davis (1990) has designed a "self-report survey on the reading process" that asks students to answer honestly 15 questions about their study/reading habits. By responding on a Likert scale, both students and teachers can see in which areas students need the most help.

ACTIVITY 10.1 Study/Reading Skills Checklist

	Degree of skill		
	Absent	Low	High
I. Special study-reading comprehension skills			
A. Ability to interpret graphic aids			
Can the student interpret these graphic aids?			
1. maps			
2. globes			
3. graphs			
4. charts			
5. tables			
6. cartoons			
7. pictures			
8. diagrams			
9. other organizing or iconic aids			
B. Ability to follow directions			
Can the student follow . . .			
1. simple directions?			
2. a more complex set of directions?			
II. Information location skills			
A. Ability to vary rate of reading			
Can the student do the following?			
1. scan			
2. skim			
3. read at slow rate for difficult materials			
4. read at average rate for reading level			
B. Ability to locate information by use of book parts			
Can the student use book parts to identify the following information?			
1. title			
2. author or editor			
3. publisher			
4. city of publication			
5. name of series			
6. edition			
7. copyright date			
8. date of publication			
Can the student quickly locate and understand the function of the following parts of a book?			
1. preface			
2. foreword			
3. introduction			
4. table of contents			

(continued) ➤

continued

	Degree of skill		
	Absent	Low	High
5. list of figures			
6. chapter headings			
7. subtitles			
8. footnotes			
9. bibliography			
10. glossary			
11. index			
12. appendix			
C. Ability to locate information in reference works Can the student do the following?			
1. locate information in a dictionary			
a. using the guide words			
b. using a thumb index			
c. locating root word			
d. locating derivations of root word			
e. using the pronunciation key			
f. selecting word meaning appropriate to passage under study			
g. noting word origin			
2. locate information in an encyclopedia			
a. using information on spine to locate appropriate volume			
b. using guide words to locate section			
c. using index volume			
3. use other reference works such as:			
a. telephone directory			
b. newspapers			
c. magazines			
d. atlases			
e. television listings			
f. schedules			
g. various periodical literature indices			
h. others ( )			
D. Ability to locate information in the library Can the student do the following?			
1. locate material by using the card catalog			
a. by subject			
b. by author			
c. by title			
2. find the materials organized in the library			
a. fiction section			
b. reference section			
c. periodical section			
d. vertical file			
e. others ( )			

	Degree of skill		
	Absent	Low	High
III. Study and retention strategies			
A. Ability to study information and remember it			
Can the student do the following?			
1. highlight important information			
2. underline important information			
3. use oral repetition to increase retention			
4. ask and answer questions to increase retention			
5. employ a systematic study procedure			
(such as SQ3R)			
6. demonstrate effective study habits			
a. set a regular study time			
b. leave adequate time for test or project preparation			
c. recognize importance of self-motivation in learning			
B. Ability to organize information			
Can the student do the following?			
1. take notes			
2. note source of information			
3. write a summary for a paragraph			
4. write a summary for a short selection			
5. write a summary integrating information from more than one source			
6. write a summary for a longer selection			
7. make graphic aids to summarize information			
8. write an outline of a paragraph			
9. write an outline of a short selection			
10. write an outline for longer selections			
11. write an outline integrating information from more than one source			
12. use the outline to write a report or to make an oral report			

From Rogers, D. B. (1984, January). Assessing study skills. *Journal of Reading, 27*(4), 346–354.

Because much study is done independently, in the home, teachers also may want to design an assessment of what parents do to help students study and how students evaluate their own study habits. Activity 10.2 provides examples of these kinds of assessment for kindergartners and first-graders. The survey can be adapted for any grade level. Teachers who have compared parents' to students' responses have discovered discrepancies in what each group perceives is true. For instance, parents indicate that students do have a special place to study (see "Survey of Parents," item 1), but students indicate that they do not ("Survey of Students," item 6). Discussing such findings early in the school year, perhaps at a back-to-school meeting, can help establish positive study environments from the beginning of the school year.

ACTIVITY 10.2 Study Skills for Kindergarten and First-Grade Students

SURVEY OF PARENTS

Please circle YES or NO in front of each statement.

YES	NO	1. My child has a special place to study. Where?____________
YES	NO	2. My child has an independent reading time each night. When?____________
YES	NO	3. My child watches television while completing homework.
YES	NO	4. I always supervise my child's homework period.
YES	NO	5. I sometimes help my child with homework.
YES	NO	6. I listen to my child read.
YES	NO	7. My child has a set bedtime. When?____________
YES	NO	8. I check over my child's homework.
YES	NO	9. My child has a place to put materials that must be returned to school.
YES	NO	10. My child eats breakfast daily.
YES	NO	11. I discuss with my child how he or she does in school each day.
YES	NO	12. I read to my child often.

SURVEY OF STUDENTS

Circle the true sentences as I read them.

1. I bring my books to school each day.
2. I listen in class.
3. I read the directions when I begin my work.
4. I ask questions when I don't know what to do.
5. I do my homework every night.
6. I have a special place to do my homework.
7. No one helps me with my homework.
8. I watch TV when I do my homework.
9. I bring my homework to school.
10. I am a good student.

These two surveys were adapted with permission from surveys done by Cornelia Hill.

The surveys in Activity 10.2 also provide several indicators about environments conducive to studying. Three types of distracters lead to poor study habits. **External distracters** include too many stimuli at the study area, such as a television, a telephone, or visitors; lack of proper equipment so that the student must constantly interrupt study to find a pencil, dictionary, and so on; and poor lighting or uncomfortable surroundings. **Internal distracters** include daydreaming, lack of organized study plans, unrealistic goals ("I will study five chapters in 30 minutes"), and unresolved personal problems. **Physical distracters** include lack of sleep, poor diet, mental fatigue, and over- or understimulation.

Teachers can help students experiment to eliminate study distracters. One way is to challenge students to study in their usual way for a block of time (dependent on the age of the students) and then in the teacher's way for the same amount of time. While studying, students note how much they accomplish. Usually they discover by experimenting that at least some of the teacher's tips about a study environment really do help them study.

For many students, changing the study environment at home might be difficult. We work with children in inner cities who have witnessed murders, dodged bullets, and gone to bed hungry on numerous occasions. Experimenting with study environments at home will not work under such conditions. In such cases, arranging for the school or community to provide a study environment in another location will help, such as in the school after hours or in a local community center or church.

Without a good study environment, study strategies will not be very effective. The only environment over which the teacher has control is his or her classroom. Modeling the following strategies in that classroom will be the first step.

Learning from Visual Representations

Visual representations are visual aids and graph clues designed to help readers comprehend a content textbook. Yet one of the most common responses of students when questioned about such aids is that they "skip over them" (Gillespie, 1993). Worse yet, the only time many students get instruction in how to read charts, maps, and graphs is during the infamous "chart, map, and graph week" instituted by many well-meaning but misdirected schools and school systems. Because these skills are taught in isolation, there is little transfer by students into everyday instruction. Teachers need to teach these specialized reading procedures during day-to-day instruction, not just during special weeks.

Reading Graphic Information

If students are having particular difficulty reading graphic information, teachers can use a modified cloze procedure to teach the skill. Activity 10.3 shows how a modified cloze procedure can be used to help students read an air-pressure map. So often, readers incorrectly assume that the graph is a "free page"! Richardson and Forget (1995) illustrated the calculations that Mark Twain used in "proving" that the Mississippi River would be shortened to a mile and three-quarters in length 742 years from the time he wrote *Life on the Mississippi*. By reading a graph that applies the formula for slope, readers can see how slope always reflects the relationship of one variable to another. Both Twain's humorous essay and the formula for slope are more interesting and clear when the graphic information is available.

Reading Pictures and Maps

Pictures make a textbook interesting and vital. Teachers should frequently ask students to "read" the pictures in an effort to clarify thinking about concepts in the chapter. Cartoons are specialized pictures that carry significant messages or

ACTIVITY 10.3 Visual Representation: Reading an Air-Pressure Map

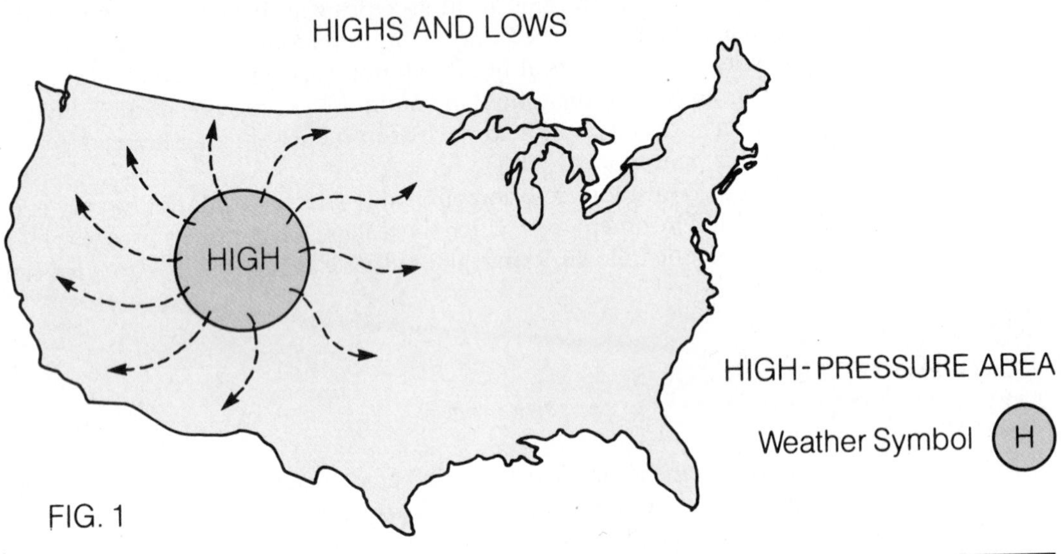

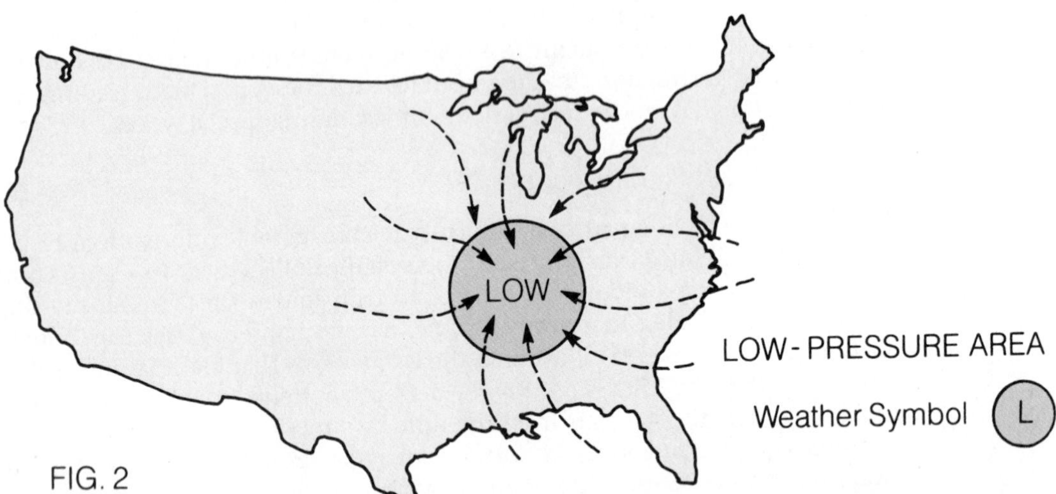

Directions: In Fig. 1, draw and label a low-pressure area and show its air direction. In Fig. 2, draw and label a high-pressure area and show its air direction. Answer the following on the back of the paper: The air in a high-pressure area is spiraling ______ in a ______ direction, with the highest pressure at its ______ . The air in a low-pressure area is spiraling ______ in a ______ direction, with the lowest air pressure at its ______ .

propaganda. What meaning does the cartoon on page 338 convey to you? Does it convey irony? Pessimism? Is it a satire on the world of education? Although you have wide-ranging background experiences to help you interpret the cartoon, students sometimes lack such experience. Thus teachers need to question students about the perceptual content of cartoons, as demonstrated in Activity 10.4.

Activity 10.5 demonstrates how teachers can teach students to label maps. Labeling may be done either after students memorize a map or as they consult maps in their textbook. We recommend map labeling as the primary way to get students to learn to use maps and to better remember certain important locations on a map.

Making Mnemonic Associations

Students need to know that learning is difficult but always rewarding. Sternberg (1991) noted that learning and retention are enhanced when students study in fairly equal distributions over time rather than in what he calls **massed study**—last-minute cramming before a test or exam. Many students cram because it is human nature to put off study to the last minute. Also students form this habit because teachers do not explain to them how distributed study enhances retention. The famous Ebbinghaus (1908) studies around the turn of the twentieth century described the difficulty of learning. Ebbinghaus postulated that tremendous amounts of information are forgotten in a short period of time—up to 60 or 70 percent in only a few days. He also made these important discoveries, which still seem to hold true:

1. Fatigue is a factor affecting one's ability to remember.
2. Earlier study and learning tends to get buried by later learning.
3. Learned images may decay over time and end up changed in meaning from what was originally perceived.
4. Memories erode, and most information (an estimated 90 percent) is forgotten over prolonged periods of time.

In short, forgetting is natural and remembering is difficult.

Fortunately the use of **mnemonics**—devices and techniques to improve memory—can help students in what Ebbinghaus describes as the difficult task of learning. Peters and Levin (1986) found that mnemonics benefited both above- and below-average readers when they read short fictional passages as well as longer content passages. Students instructed in mnemonic strategies remembered significantly more information on names and accomplishments than did those in the control group. Similarly, Levin, Morrison, and McGivern (1986) found that students given instruction in mnemonic techniques scored significantly higher on tests of immediate recall and on recall tests administered three days later than did either a group taught to memorize material or group members who were given motivational talks and then used their usual methods of

ACTIVITY 10.4 Interpreting a Cartoon

1. Describe what is happening in this cartoon.
2. Explain the meaning of each of the three figures.
3. Explain the significance of the decoy, labeled "INF." What is the INF treaty?
4. From your reading of this cartoon, do you feel we should trust the Russians and enter into more and bigger disarmament treaties with them? Why or why not?

Cartoon by Roberto Lianez, Norview High School, Norfolk, VA. Used with permission.

---

study. Mnemonics instruction also has been found to be effective for learning new words in foreign-language classes (Cohen, 1987). Studies (Levin, Levin, Glassman, & Nordwall, 1992; Scruggs, Mastropier, Brigham, & Sullivan, 1992) have found that key-word mnemonics significantly affected retention of text material, attesting to the benefits of mnemonic techniques.

Despite these favorable studies, teachers do little memory training with their students, even though it takes only a small effort to get students to try mnemonics. For example, a teacher can give vocabulary or chapter terms that need

ACTIVITY 10.5 Developing Map Skills

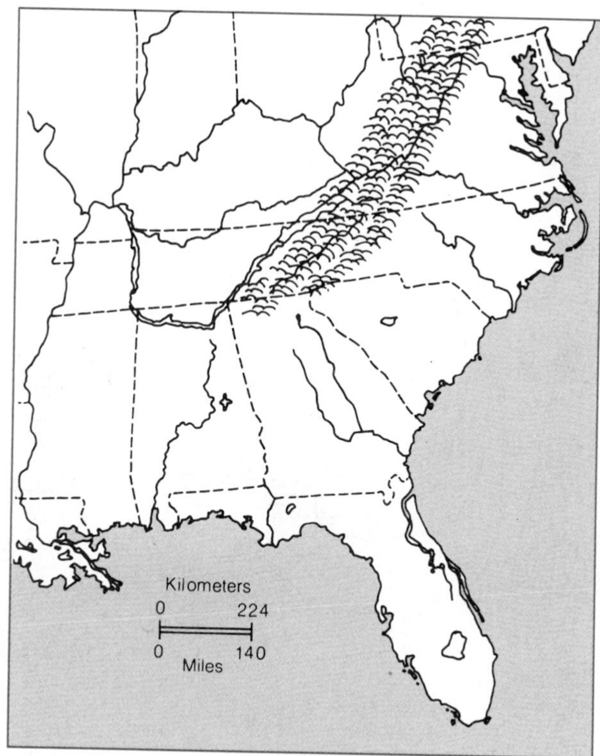

Complete this map. Use the map of the Colonial Southeast on page 210 to help you complete this activity.

1. Color the water area BLUE.
2. Color the area covered by the eleven states of the Southeast LIGHT YELLOW.
3. Print the names of the states in the proper places on the map.
4. Print these names in the proper places:
   Mountains: Appalachians, Blue Ridge
   Plains: Atlantic Coastal, Gulf Coastal
   Rivers: Potomac, James, Savannah, Mississippi, St. Johns
   Bays: Chesapeake, Delaware
5. Print these names of early settlements in the proper places on the map:
   Jamestown St. Mary's
   Charleston Williamsburg
   Savannah
6. With a BLUE crayon trace over each of the rivers listed above.

Reprinted by permission of H. L. Schwadron.

to be memorized and ask students to form groups in which they create their own mnemonics and share them with the class. The teacher can give rewards for the ones judged to be the best. Through such practice, students form the habit of creating mnemonics for themselves.

In the remainder of this section we describe acronyms, acrostics, and other mnemonic learning techniques. These can be a welcome learning aid, especially for poor readers who find that they forget material too quickly (remember Ebbinghaus's studies showing that forgetting is natural). If we could help students to remember from 10 to 30 items with ease, think how their self-concepts and self-images might be affected. With practice, there seems to be almost no limit to improvement in long-term memory skill. We recommend familiarizing children in primary grades with these memory-enhancing techniques. Then they will possess a skill useful for the rest of their education.

Acronyms

The most time-honored of mnemonics, an **acronym** is a word or phrase composed entirely of letters that are cues to the words we want to remember. PAR is an acronym for the instructional framework that we explain in this book. For another example, suppose that you are reviewing musculoskeletal systems for a test, and among the things you want to remember are the six boundaries of the axilla: apex, base, anterior wall, posterior wall, medial wall, and lateral wall. The initial letters are A, B, A, P, M, and L. You could rearrange these letters to form the acronym A.B. PALM. Or consider the following list of the six branches of the axillary artery: supreme thoraces, thoracromial, lateral thoracic, anterior humeral circumflex, posterior humeral circumflex, and subscapular. You could use the initial letters S, T, L, A, P, and S to form the name of a fictitious patron saint of arteries: ST. LAPS. Here are a few examples of commonly used acronyms:

HOMES The Great Lakes: Huron, Ontario, Michigan, Erie, Superior

ROY G BIV The colors of the spectrum: red, orange, yellow, green, blue, indigo, violet

FACE The notes represented by the spaces of the G clef

Acrostics

An **acrostic** is a phrase or sentence in which the first letter of each word is a cue. For example, another way of remembering the boundaries of the axilla—initial letters **A**, **B**, **A**, **P**, **M**, and **L**—would be to create a phrase such as "**A**bove, **B**elow, **A**nd **P**retty **M**uch **L**ost."

To remember the names of the planets—**M**ercury, **V**enus, **E**arth, **M**ars, **J**upiter, **S**aturn, **U**ranus, **N**eptune, **P**luto—you might use the following acrostic: **M**y **V**ery **E**ducated **M**other **J**ust **S**erved **U**s **N**ine **P**izzas.

Acrostics can be made for any area. To improve reading-study skills, ask students to **relax** by doing the following:

Rest plenty.

Exude enthusiasm.

Laugh often.

Anticipate what's coming.

Xcite yourself about the reading.

Suppose you had to remember these nautical terms: **B**ow, **S**tern, **C**abin, **T**raveler. You could use this acrostic: **B**ig **S**torms **C**ause **T**rouble.

Associations

Students can be taught to memorize words by associating the words to be learned with outrageous images. For instance, to memorize the words in the left column, students can imagine the images in the right column:

Word	*Image*
sweater	. . . sweater
horse	. . . a gigantic horse wearing a gigantic sweater
surf	. . . a huge horse surfing

iron gate ... a surfer on a high surfboard flying over an iron gate
typewriter ... tiny iron gates spewing out of a typewriter

In this manner, one word leads to the next to make a long list of associations.

Another means of associational learning is a peg-word system. Peg-word systems associate a target word with a numbered peg word. Listed below are ten peg words that name familiar places found at many schools:

1. Computer Center
2. Guidance Office
3. Cafeteria
4. Auditorium
5. Library
6. Classroom
7. Hallway
8. Principal's Office
9. Nurse's Clinic
10. Gymnasium

The words to be memorized—*plot, setting,* and *character*—are linked to the peg words through outrageous images. You can remember the words *plot, setting,* and *character* by associating each with one of the numbered peg words:

1. A criminal with a *plot* to blow up the *library*
2. Someone *setting* a tray down in the *cafeteria*
3. A drunken *character* sitting in the back of a *classroom* filled with disbelieving students

The peg words do not have to name places. They can be words that sound similar or rhyme with the words to be learned. An example would be the peg word *commotion* for *commodities* in an economics class or *this criminal* for *discrimination.*

Method of Loci

The method of loci (Latin for "places") improves students' ability to remember lists of unrelated objects. It also can be a sequencing task, enabling a student to remember items in a definite order. In this ancient method, used by Roman orators, a person mentally walks through a house that has very familiar surroundings. Cicero and other classical orators constructed "memory places" and linked sections of their speeches to architectural features. Then, as they spoke, they imagined the place where they had established the link. This process enabled them to remember huge amounts of information.

By choosing from 15 to 20 distinct loci—for example, the stove, the closet, the desk, the kitchen sink—students can mentally place objects to be learned in strategic spots throughout the house. In a variation, students memorize words by placing them in strategic places in each of the six or seven rooms where they have classes each day or in various places around the school.

Chunking

The chunking of large amounts of information into categories can help students remember information more readily and retrieve information faster. Suppose you have to learn these 15 items in a language arts unit on puppetry:

director	equipment	props	create	purchase
lights	story development	size of puppets	analysis	microphone
copyright	budget	sound	stories	spotlight

Chunking information into categories makes learning the 15 items much easier:

Scripts	**Technical**
director	lights
copyright	equipment
story development	props
budget	size of puppets
create	sound
analysis	microphone
stories	spotlight
purchase	

Chunking information through categorization exercises (which can be used to review for tests) is an excellent way to help poor readers understand text material. Chunking capitalizes on connecting prior knowledge to new knowledge, thus enhancing learning. Once students become more practiced at chunking, they can construct hierarchies of mnemonics to learn 15 to 50 items. Activity 10.6 provides an example from a "Teen Living" class in home economics, where the total number of items to be learned is 17.

Remember that complicated hierarchies of mnemonics are best constructed by middle-school and high school students who have considerable experience with using simple acronyms and acrostics. This level of chunking is the most difficult mnemonic to construct, but it allows students considerable leeway in memorizing prodigious amounts of information.

Go MAD

One way to familiarize primary and upper-elementary children with mnemonics is to go **MAD**—use the Mnemonic-A-Day technique. Have students work in groups to make a mnemonic a day for 10 days. The only stipulation is that each new mnemonic has to be in a different content area than the one created the day before. Children keep MAD logs and periodically refer to the logs to make certain they remember all accumulated mnemonics. By making a game of it,

ACTIVITY 10.6 Chunking through Categorization

Being a Successful Babysitter

Acronym = JOG

(J)ob acceptance		(O)n the job		(G)etting started	
P	Parents' permission	N	No TV	P	Prompt for arrival
A	Address of family	A	Attend to task	A	Address where couple will be
D	Day and time	M	Make file of family after job	R	Reaching doctors, firefighters, etc.
M	Meet children	E	Exploring in house is out		
O	Offer fee	S	Stay awake		
M	Meet family				

teachers can reward individuals or groups who can create a MAD example for the most days consecutively. This can be an enjoyable yet purposeful activity.

Rapid Reading

One of Edmund Burke Huey's tenets in *The Psychology and Pedagogy of Reading* (1908/1968) was that children should be taught, from the first reading instruction, to read as fast as the nature of the reading materials and their purpose will allow. Huey recommended speed drills to help students get information efficiently and effectively. Unfortunately, many professionals have forgotten Huey's work, and rapid reading has fallen into disfavor as a bona fide reading skill that students should be acquiring.

After Huey, William S. Gray, in a 1925 review of the literature on speed of reading, endorsed speed-reading by concluding that such training could result in increased speed without a concurrent drop in comprehension. Many studies followed that addressed the value of speed-reading, yet more than 90 years after Huey's pronouncement, probably no area of reading is as controversial as speed-reading (Carver, 1992). The very mention of speed-reading carries with it a negative connotation for many teachers at all levels of education. In recent studies of adult readers, Carver (1985, 1992) concluded that the speed-readers he tested comprehended less than 75 percent of eighth-grade material when reading faster than 600 words per minute. He also found that much of what passes as speed-reading is really skimming—glossing material at between 600 and 1,000 words per minute at fairly low comprehension levels. Other studies question the quality of speed-reading research (Collins, 1979; Fleisher, Jenkins, & Pany, 1979), the limited utility of eye-movement training (McConkie & Rayner, 1976; Rayner, 1978), and the limits to speed in the act of reading (Carver, 1985; Spache, 1976). Yet much more research on speed-reading is needed, as evidenced in a study by Just, Carpenter, and Masson (1982), which found fairly positive results for speed-readers when they answered higher-level comprehension questions.

Perhaps one problem with speed-reading is the misconception that one can read faster simply by accelerating a physical activity. Simply stated, the physical process of reading requires the eyes to move in a jerky pattern over the page, stopping to let the brain take in information, then moving again. These **saccadic eye movements** and **fixations** constitute the physical process of reading. A reader could get quite a headache by trying to accelerate this physical process too much. What is important is how readers manipulate the information taken in with a fixation or, as Frank Smith (1988) puts it, what goes on "between the eye and the brain" rather than from the page to the eye. This mental process requires the chunking of information into the largest meaningful units that one can assimilate and relating those chunks to an existing schema. We described this type of brain activity in the preceding section, on mnemonic associations.

We do not recommend speed-reading per se, but we do advocate rapid reading or speeding up one's reading along with an emphasis on previewing the material. Previewing (explained later in the chapter) brings purpose to the reading by letting the reader decide what he or she needs and wants to know.

We maintain that students can find answers to their questions quickly by reading more rapidly after the previewing stage. We also suggest that it is better to read a chapter several times rapidly than it is to read the chapter one time at a laboriously slow rate. Providing verification for several rapid readings, Samuels (1979) found that repeated reading enhanced reader fluency and comprehension. We are not advocating reading 1,000 words or more a minute, but we do believe that some study reading should be done at rates above 300 words per minute. In fact, Bill Cosby (1986), the comedian with a Ph.D. in education, advocates three steps to faster reading: previewing, skimming, and clustering, which is grouping several words together as they connect meaningfully.

Shifting Gears While Reading

Carver (1992) described five basic reading processes—scanning, skimming, rauding, learning, and memorizing—that bring the nature of speed-reading into better focus. Table 10.1 summarizes these five processes in terms of their goals and culminating components and lists typical reading rates of college students using each process. According to Carver, **rauding** is the bringing together of reading (looking and understanding) and "auding" (listening and understanding) into "ordinary reading." Carver states that the typical seventh-grader has a rauding rate of 190 words per minute but a below-average student may raud at 140 words per minute. The large variability in rauding rates means that poor readers will be left far behind in the volume of reading they can accomplish, unless teachers intervene to show them that they can read at different rates depending on the purpose for reading. Specifically, students can learn to "shift gears" to scan and skim material during the previewing stage. Students may then raud at 200 to 300 words per minute for better comprehension. When studying for a test or attempting to memorize large amounts of material, students may need to shift to gear 2 or gear 1 (see Table 10.1) and reread material at a much slower rate. A frequent problem is that, without training, students do not change their reading speed when they encounter difficult or easy material (Carver, 1983; Miller & Coleman, 1971; Zuber & Wetzel, 1981); instead, they use their rauding speed for all reading.

Rapid-Reading Exercises

There are three reasonably easy exercises that teachers can ask students to practice in order to increase their reading speed. The first of these, **mental push-ups**, consists of rate and comprehension drills. At the beginning of class, the teacher asks students to use a 3-by-5-inch card to "mentally push" themselves down one page of a content chapter or story so quickly that they cannot absorb all the information on the page. (Older students who have had practice in the technique and who have better fine-motor control can use a finger to pace themselves.) Then students close the book and write down what they learned. After the first reading, the amount retained is usually two or three words. The students

TABLE 10.1 Summary of the Relationships Among Gears, Basic Reading Processes, Goals, Culminating Components, and Rates

Reading Gear	*Five Basic Reading Processes*	*Goals of Model Process*	*Culminating Component of the Model Processes*	*Typical College Rates for Model Processes*
5	Scanning	Find target word	Lexical access	600 wpm
4	Skimming	Find transposed words	Semantic encoding	450 wpm
3	Rauding	Comprehend complete thoughts in sentences	Sentential integration	300 wpm
2	Learning	Pass multiple-choice test	Idea remembering	200 wpm
1	Memorizing	Recall, orally or in writing	Fact rehearsal	138 wpm

From Carver, R. P. (1992, October). Reading rate: Theory, research, and practical applications. *Journal of Reading, 36*(2), 84–95. Reprinted with permission of Ronald P. Carver and the International Reading Association.

repeat the procedure as many times as needed (usually two to four) until there is a "rush" of information—that is, until they comprehend and can write out or verbalize most of what is on the page. With extended practice, students will need fewer readings to comprehend the material. This technique can be used to clarify cognitive structure and increase student attention at the beginning of a class period. With practice, it will help make students more facile and mentally alert when reading short passages.

Another rapid-reading activity is a variation on mental push-ups. Teachers can conduct three-minute **rapid-reading drills** at the beginning of classes. In a straightforward rapid-reading drill, students are asked to read as fast as possible. Again, young children can use a 3-by-5-inch card as a pacer; later they can use the finger-pacing technique. The teacher can conduct one or two three-minute drills without taking away too much time from the day's lesson. Students taking rapid-reading drills are not asked to write out what they learned. As a variation, however, they could be asked to form groups in which each person discusses what she or he remembers from the reading.

A third exercise, the **preview and rapid-reading drill**, can be used when the teacher is directing the reading of a content chapter. The teacher monitors the previewing phase, culminating with students' writing specific questions that they wish to have answered in the reading. The previewing phase can be done by the whole class, in groups, or by individuals working on their own. The teacher asks the students to read more rapidly than usual to find the answers to their preview questions.

Those three activities can be accomplished in any content area and can be started with better readers at the second-grade level. Students generally express interest in such activities. They can see fairly immediate results and appreciate being able to improve their own reading rate.

Previewing

Chapter 6 describes the Directed Reading/Thinking Activity (DRTA) (Stauffer, 1969a), which is a technique that teachers can use to model correct reading process. Fundamental to the DRTA is **previewing**, a process that is important for clarifying "cognitive structure" (Ausubel, 1968), or the clarity of student thinking, before students read textbook material. In the previewing stage, students select strategies appropriate to the depth and duration of study needed.

To select proper strategies—whether note taking, underlining, or rapid reading—students must spend time clarifying their thinking about the topic. Then they need to ask themselves questions such as the following:

How interested am I in this section?

How deeply do I need to think and concentrate to learn this material?

How fast can I read this material?

What do I still need to learn about this topic?

Teachers might take students step-by-step through the previewing phase, then ask them to write down how they will study the material.

Just as one might size up a piece of clothing and decide whether it is too big and needs altering, a reader can size up a reading selection and realize that "mental alterations" are needed. Such assessment is the purpose of previewing. Sometimes the preview yields all the information the reader needs, so the material need not be read. In many instances, however, the preview builds anticipation for material that is not familiar to the reader. If teachers model previewing from elementary school onward, students' comprehension of expository and narrative material should be enhanced.

Learning to Preview

Previewing in order to clarify thinking reduces uncertainty about the reading assignment, allowing students to gain confidence, read in a more relaxed manner, gain interest, and improve their attitude toward the material. In addition, previewing strategies enable students to decide how much of the material is in their own background of experience. As a result of the previewing strategy, learners are clearer about what they know and what they need to know. In effect, they set a purpose for reading before they begin.

When previewing a technical chapter or a report, students should examine and think about the following:

1. Title and subtitle—to discover the overall topic of the chapter or article
2. Author's name—to see whether the author is a recognized authority
3. Copyright—to see whether the material is current
4. Introduction—to learn what the author intends to talk about
5. Headings and subheadings—to identify the topic of the sections that follow (Forming these headings into questions gives purpose to the reading.)
6. Graphs, charts, maps, tables, pictures—to aid in understanding specific aspects of the chapter or article
7. Summary—to get an overview of the reading
8. Questions—to review important topics covered in the chapter

In practicing with a group or class, the teacher assists students in deciding what they already know about the material and what they need to learn. The reader turns those things that are not known into questions, which provide a purpose for reading.

Students reading fiction need to preview the title, illustrations, and introduction in order to make hypotheses about the outcome of the story. This preview heightens suspense and aids in maintaining interest. Most important, predicting of story structure gives the reader a purpose for reading—namely, to find out whether the predictions are correct.

Whether students are reading fiction or expository or informational material, a very important reason for previewing is that it forces them to do the sophisticated kind of thinking required for drawing inferences and developing interpretations. Thus students think critically about the chapter or story before the reading, operating at times on those higher levels of cognition described by Adler and Van Doren (1972), Bloom (1956), Herber (1978), and Barrett (1972).

We find that students on any level generally will not preview material on their own unless teachers model and provide practice in this important skill. First, teachers should make students aware that they are teaching both content and the strategy of previewing. Students can be made aware by following the skills training model described earlier in this chapter. Second, teachers need to review with students the table of contents of a textbook to aid them in discovering the theme or structure of the course material. In this way, students will get the gist or overall idea of what the author is attempting to teach in the textbook. The teacher might ask, for example, why the author chose to organize the table of contents in a particular manner.

For each new reading or unit of instruction, the teacher can ask students to return to the table of contents to see how this particular segment of learning fits into the overall textbook scheme or pattern. Teachers with a class of poor readers can model the previewing strategy by using preview questions they have constructed and annotated.

Skimming and Scanning

Skimming is rapid glancing through text to find out generally what the reading is about (Jacobson, 1998). **Scanning** is rapid reading for some specific purpose—for instance, to find out where, when, or how something happened. When scanning, the reader may read an introduction or opening paragraph, a summary, and the first and last sentences of each paragraph, note material in bold print, and glance at visual aids. Unlike skimming, in which the reader glances at the whole text to get a general sense of the piece, scanning is searching for specific information, such as a word or detail. Researchers have reported on the importance of skimming content materials for organizing details and making inferences (Sherer, 1975). Carver, as noted earlier, mentions the importance of scanning to find particular target words.

Skills in skimming and scanning allow students to preview information. Students need to be reminded that previewing helps to clarify thinking and set a purpose for reading and that they will learn further details in the full reading. Students need much practice (beginning at an early age) to acquire these skills. We recommend scanning drills, in which teachers ask students to scan rapidly, looking for answers to *who, what, when,* and *where* questions in the chapter. Students need to be reminded to skim one or two sentences in each paragraph in addition to the title, author, headings, and so on, as described earlier. Scanning can be practiced as students demonstrate how they confirmed predictions, or found a word's meaning, by returning to that place in the material.

Locating Information

Eighteenth-century chronicler James Boswell, in his life of Samuel Johnson, wrote, "Knowledge is of two kinds. We know a subject ourselves, or we know where we can find information upon it." As students progress in school, this second kind of knowledge becomes increasingly important. They need to know how to find information in textbooks, dictionaries, encyclopedias, and trade books. If teachers are unsure how adept their students are at finding information, an activity such as the "Textbook Treasure Hunt" (see Activity 4.10) can help.

Instruction in locating information should begin as soon as reading instruction starts. Picture dictionaries, such as *My Little Dictionary* (Scott, Foresman, 1964) and *The Storybook Dictionary* (Golden Press, 1966), can provide an introduction to this reference skill. In addition, teachers can create their own picture dictionaries from file cards of words and pictures that students match to each other. As children mature, teachers can introduce alphabetizing through handmade picture books, or they can emphasize alphabetizing by using the published picture dictionaries. In primary grades students can be taught how to file pictures and materials alphabetically according to key index words, such as *farm, city, animal,* and *house*. Because many young children are acquainted with computer technology, they should be shown how to use e-book (electronic book) dictionaries and encyclopedias. After using e-books, children can produce their own version by using a word processing program and importing graphics to illustrate their computer pages, which can then be printed. Activity 7.17 is an example of such a page, placed in a child's portfolio.

From the primary grades on, children can be shown how to use tables of contents and how to scan a textbook for its overall organization. In content-reading classes, teachers can discuss tables of contents, glossaries, indexes, headings, picture clues, charts, maps, and graphs. The teacher can introduce all of these skills by asking children first to find the reference (glossary, table of contents) and then to locate particular information (a definition in the glossary, a section in the table of contents). Teachers should train students to locate information as they complete daily lessons in their basal readers and content textbooks. In this manner, students at an early age will see the usefulness of this skill.

In the intermediate grades, students read well enough to gain from systematic instruction in how to locate information. A trip to the school or public library today is quite different from a trip in the 1970s. Gone are the card files. In their place are computer catalogs (com cats). Students learn to enter a topic and ask the computer to scan a database for resources on that topic. Reading material might still be in book or magazine form, but just as often students are directed to film, microfiche, or microfilm, on which material can be stored more efficiently and then retrieved and read by means of a projection device.

Information housed in ERIC resources is now available not only in libraries but also on the Internet. Students can link directly to ERIC sites such as "ERIC via the Web" and "ERIC Search Wizard." By typing in a search word, students can access an abstract and the publication information about any ERIC document. The material can then be purchased online, and the copy is sent to the student.

Often students bypass a computer catalog search altogether and search via the Internet for information. Search engines such as Yahoo! and Excite enable learners to type in a search word and locate any materials matching that search entry in the vast World Wide Web storehouse. Usually, students specify how many matches they wish to see, because it is possible that hundreds could be located. Some middle-school students became so sophisticated in using the Internet for research that they developed their own site to explain the Dewey decimal system, "Do We Really Know Dewey?" The site was located at *http://tqjunior.advanced.org/5002/* at the time of press for this book.

Libraries, especially university libraries, are designing customized search tools for their patrons. A library user can customize a page with the search tools that he or she prefers to use. For instance, Virginia Commonwealth University offers a feature called "My Library" that lets users specify their favorite resources to conduct searches. The customized page is accessible from any computer as long as the user enters a password.

Another type of customized page is for an online newspaper. When the reader selects the types of news articles and features she or he prefers, it is possible to customize a page with the day's news stories, favorite chat groups, horoscope, stock portfolio quotes, and so on. The Technology Box lists some of these, as well as some personalized webpage services where people can create their own newspapers online.

Teachers should caution their students that research on the Internet is sometimes risky. Regulations about what can be posted and by whom are sparse. It is very possible that an attractive, well-designed website has posted incorrect, misleading, or out-of-date information. Students need to check when the site was posted, when it was last updated, who posted the information, and what the credentials of the poster are.

Organizing Information

Outlining and note taking are the study strategies that students use most frequently (Annis & Davis, 1978, 1982). There is no agreement, however, on the best way to teach these skills. Underlining is often cited in the literature as a way to help students organize their thinking enough to begin an outline. Underlining, then, can be a first step to outlining.

McAndrew (1983), in a review of the literature on underlining, made several suggestions for teaching this skill if students own their textbooks. To begin, teachers should create "pre-underlining" reading assignments in handout materials that coincide with the textbook. Teachers need to show students how to underline relevant material. Students need to learn how to underline superordinate statements rather than subordinate details. When they learn this, students

TECHNOLOGY BOX

Creating a Customized News Page

Customize a page that contains your favorite news, chat group, and search tools at

My Yahoo! *http://my.yahoo.com*
My Excite *http://my.excite.com*

Create your own newspaper at

CRAYON *http://www.crayon.net* (good for younger users)
NEWSPAGE *http://www.newspage.com* (good for older users)

To view some sites where customized libraries are offered (usually requires membership), go to

My Library at Virginia Commonwealth University
http://www.library.vcu.edu/mylibrary
My Gateway at University of Washington
http://www.lib.washington.edu/resource/hlepMyGateway.html
My Library at North Carolina State University
http://www.mylib.ncsu.edu
My UCLA at University of California Los Angeles
http://www.my.ucla.edu

To search ERIC online, go to

ERIC via web *http://ericae.net/asesearch.htm*

Or

ERIC Search Wizard *http://ericae.net/scripts/ewiz/amain2.asp*

Ask the ERIC experts (reply within 48 hours) at

http://www.askeric.org/Qa

will underline relatively little, but what they underline will be important. McAndrew notes that teachers should remind students that with underlining, less is more, and that any time they save by underlining can be put to good use in further study of the material.

Teachers also need to teach students when to use techniques other than underlining. McAndrew cites research (Fowler & Baker, 1974; Rickards & August, 1975; Cashen & Leicht, 1970) showing that when these suggestions are followed, significant learning occurs. Even when underlining in textbooks is not possible, pre-underlining is an important study strategy for students to learn.

Outlining

Outlining is an organizational tool that allows readers to create for themselves a condensed presentation of the chapter that they want to understand. Outlining is particularly useful because it actively involves the reader and because the notes are made on a separate sheet of paper, not in the textbook, which the student might not own. A well-made outline shows the relationship of main ideas, supporting details, definitions of terms, and other data to the overall topic. Mapping can be an early and unstructured form of outlining. Outlines are valuable because they help students understand difficult texts, take notes, write papers, and give oral presentations.

When students first begin to practice outlining, they should not concentrate on form (no need for a B for every A). Teachers can help students learn to outline by preparing outlines with key words missing. By replacing missing words or terms, even very young children can begin to learn outlining. Teachers can give students partially completed outlines to complete as they read a chapter—for example,

Time of Wars

I. Charlemagne
- **A.** King of ____________________
- **B.** Crowned head of the ____________________ Empire
- **C.** Set up ____________________
- **D.** Ruled fairly

II. Vikings
- **A.** Fierce ____________________
- **B.** Interested in ____________________
- **C.** Traders

The following are some features of successful outlines:

1. The material itself determines the number of headings and subheadings.
2. Each heading expresses one main idea.
3. Ideas are parallel. All ideas recorded with Roman numerals are equally important.
4. All subheadings relate to the major heading above them.
5. In a formal outline, each category has more than one heading.
6. Each new level of heading is indented under the heading above it.
7. The first letter of the first word in each heading and subheading is capitalized.

An outline enables students to organize material in a hierarchical fashion. This can be accomplished by using a graphic pattern as well as in traditional ways. Activity 10.7 shows a graphic representation of material that follows a cause-and-effect pattern of organization.

ACTIVITY 10.7 Note Taking: Cause-Effect Pattern Guide

After the Industrial Revolution, the United States emerged as the world's greatest industrial power.

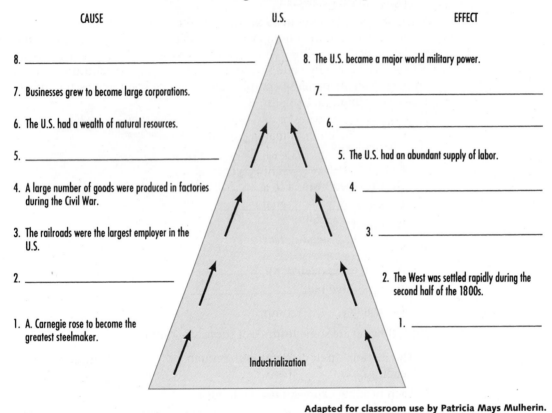

CAUSE	U.S.	EFFECT
8. ______		8. The U.S. became a major world military power.
7. Businesses grew to become large corporations.		7. ______
6. The U.S. had a wealth of natural resources.		6. ______
5. ______		5. The U.S. had an abundant supply of labor.
4. A large number of goods were produced in factories during the Civil War.		4. ______
3. The railroads were the largest employer in the U.S.		3. ______
2. ______		2. The West was settled rapidly during the second half of the 1800s.
1. A. Carnegie rose to become the greatest steelmaker.	Industrialization	1. ______

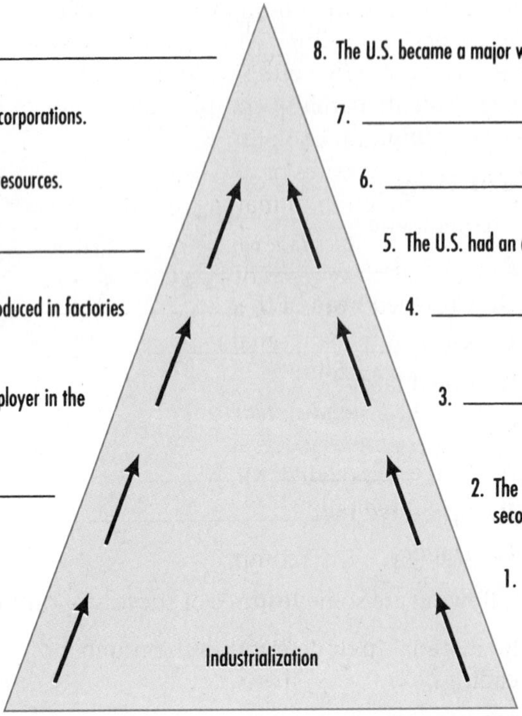

Adapted for classroom use by Patricia Mays Mulherin.

Note Taking

Note taking, an often-used study skill, produces good study results. Research focusing on the time students spent on study procedures (isolated from actual study time) showed that note taking is more effective than underlining (McAndrew, 1983). McAndrew offers teachers these suggestions to help their students become effective note takers (p. 107):

1. Be certain students realize that the use of notes to store information is more important than the act of taking the notes.
2. Try to use a spaced lecture format.
3. Insert questions, verbal cues, and nonverbal cues into lectures to highlight structure.

4. Write material on the board to be sure students will record it.
5. When using transparencies or slides, compensate for possible overload of information.
6. Tell students what type of test to expect.
7. Use handouts, especially with poor note takers.
8. Give students handouts that provide space for student notes.

To the students who are taking notes, Morgan, Meeks, Schollaert, and Paul (1986) offer some practical advice:

1. *Do not use a spiral notebook (contrary to what is often advocated).* A two- or three-ring notebook filled with loose-leaf paper enables students to rearrange their notes or any other material and permits the easy addition or subtraction of material.
2. *Write on every other line whenever possible or when it seems logical to separate topics.* By leaving a lot of white space, students give themselves room to correct errors or add points they missed. In addition, every-other-line note taking makes for easier reading when students review or study for an exam.
3. *Develop a shorthand system.* Students should reduce frequently used words to a symbol, such as "w" for *with*. Other commonly used words should be abbreviated. Morgan and colleagues (1986) offer examples of such abbreviations:

compare	comp.	data bank	d.b.
important	imp.	evaluation	eval.
advantage	advan.	developed	dev.
introduction	intro.	literature	lit.
continued	cont.	definition	def.
organization	org.	individual	ind.
information	info.	psychology	psych.
example	ex.		

   Content words should be recorded in full and spellings checked with a dictionary or textbook.
4. *Underline, star, or record the teacher's pet theories or concepts.* Listen for key statements such as "I particularly agree with this theory" or "You'll probably be seeing this information again." Statements like those might mean that the material will appear on an exam. If the teacher writes terminology or math examples on the board, always record them word for word (or figure by figure). If the teacher lists or numbers remarks, such as "three significant facts stand out," those should be numbered and indented in the notes.
5. *Do not try to outline notes according to a Roman numeral system with main ideas and supporting details.* No one thinks in Roman numerals.

Important points may be missed if students worry too much about how they are taking the notes. Until notes are organized at a later time, students should not worry about the main idea of the lecture.

6. *Do not disregard related discussions.* Teachers frequently use questions as a teaching tool. Students should write down questions that are introduced for discussion purposes. Often, such discussions stray from the subject, but the teacher always has a reason for asking the question.
7. *Ask questions when there is misunderstanding.* If any student is confused by a concept or misses a point in the lecture, usually other students have missed it too. Students should not be embarrassed to ask for clarification.
8. *Review often and with different purposes in mind.* When rereading textbook assignments, students should coordinate the chapter with their notes. Make certain main ideas from the chapter are included directly into the lecture notes. For some students, rewriting notes is a helpful memory device. Even though this process is time-consuming, it may be worth the effort if it helps students retain the material.

Richardson (1996) offers a tip for teachers. When teachers allow students to use notes during a test, they will see a great improvement over time in students' use of note taking. Of course, students should not be able to find the answers to test questions directly in the notes, but should be required to use inference and application skills when forming their answers.

REST System of Note Taking

The REST system (Morgan, Meeks, Schollaert, & Paul, 1986) has been proposed as a way to prepare for note taking before a lecture. This system takes into account the importance of note taking to help integrate the lecture with the textbook. In using the REST system, students should follow these steps:

1. Record. Write down as much of what the teacher says as possible, excluding repetitions and digressions.
2. Edit. Condense notes, editing out irrelevant material.
3. Synthesize. Compare condensed notes with related material in textbook, and jot down important points stressed in both the lecture and the textbook.
4. Think. Think and study to ensure retention.

To help students practice REST, teachers should distribute handouts for note taking that include space for writing notes on the lecture, for making notes to oneself, and for summarizing main ideas. An example of such a handout completed by a high school student in art history is shown in Activity 10.8.

Two-Column Note Taking

The Cornell system (Pauk, 1974), a practical approach to taking notes, is an alternative to the REST system. Pauk's two-column note-taking system, or "5r's,"

ACTIVITY 10.8 Art History Note-Taking Handout

Topics and Notes to Yourself	Lecture Notes
Purpose →	Make public understand what is the purpose of the art
1) Slides	Liz Taylor } everybody recognizes
(Mona Lisa)	Marilyn Monroe } everybody recognizes
2) History	
1st & 2nd A.D.	Ginger Rogers — almost forgotten
☆ Learn for test	Greeks — naturalists
term imp. → barbaric p. 327 "barbe"	Romans — hedonists
Assignment →	Think about Andy Warhol's soup can

Summarization and Main Ideas

Art is a reflection of history.
Need to study both the purpose
and the style.

has an advantage over REST in that it can be used with younger children. To use this system, students divide the page in the following way:

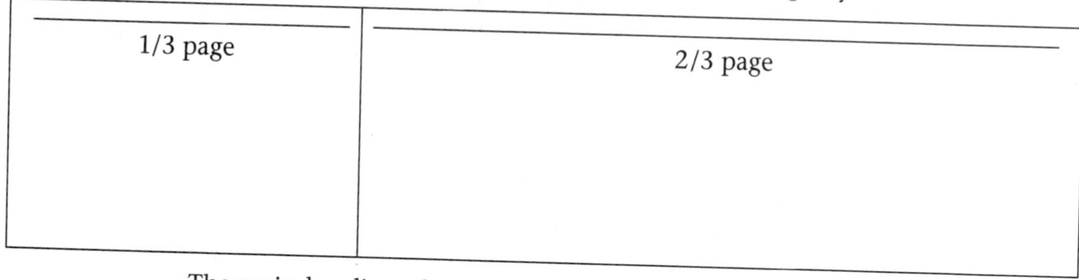

The main heading, the notes students make for themselves, and key words all go in the narrow left column. The students also may use the left side as their side to record topics, questions, key phrases, definitions, comments, and summaries of information from the lecturer or textbook. The wider right column is for information from the lecturer or textbook.

The key to two-column note taking is space. Just as adolescents and even younger students need physical space, they also need intellectual space—that is, space to think. The left column provides space for students to question themselves about the big picture of the lesson and the major concepts to be learned. The system is based on the sound theory of categorization, with subordinate concepts consolidated and organized under superordinate headings.

Students practice these steps (the 5r's):

Step 1: They *record* the information as they hear it or read it.

Step 2: They *reduce* the information by putting their abbreviated notes about it in the narrow left column.

Step 3: They *recite* the information by using their reduction notes with the recorded notes in the wider right column.

Steps 4 and 5: They *reflect on* and *review* the notes over time.

The two-column system allows much flexibility of studying for students. Pairs of students can "call" the notes to each other, covering either column and questioning each other as to what belongs in that column. Teachers can ask students to get into groups at the beginning or end of class and brainstorm two or three recently covered major topics (to go in the left column). In this manner note taking is made an integral part of all the operations of the class.

When this system is used effectively, students improve markedly. However, new studies (Spor & Schneider, 1999) show that only 30 percent of teachers work with students on any outlining or note-taking procedure at all. And many simply tell students to "put a line down the page about one-third of the way across the page, creating two columns, and take notes like this from now on." Students do not continue (or even start) to use the method because they have no practice in using it.

Activity 10.9 is an example of a note-taking handout from a middle-school science class. Teachers can prepare such handouts and give them to students before a lecture or before students read a chapter, so that they can practice the two-column method. This handout employs a modified cloze procedure: Students fill in gaps as they listen to the lecture or read the chapter. In subsequent lessons, more and more notes are omitted (more blanks are used) until eventually students complete all the note taking themselves.

Text Lookbacks

Garner (1985b) discusses the importance of reexamining text—backtracking, or **text lookback**—in overcoming memory difficulties. There is evidence that both children and adults fail to use this strategy (Garner, Macready, & Wagoner, 1985; Alexander, Hare, & Garner, 1984), even though research (Amlund, Kardash, & Kulhavy, 1986; Samuels, 1979) shows that repeated readings and reinspection of text make a significant difference in recall.

Ruth Strang, the great reading educator, once remarked that she was disappointed when she entered a school library and found students reading for long periods of time without looking up to reflect on what they were reading and not glancing back over material during their study. We recommend that teachers ask students to use the lookback strategy after a reading by working in groups to clarify confusing points. For instance, students in a social studies class can be asked to reinspect a chapter on economic interdependence to find why credit and credit buying are so important to the American economy and to economic

ACTIVITY 10.9 Two-Column Note Taking

Chapter 3: The Chemistry of Living Things

I. Matter.

1. Anything that takes up ______________ and has ______________.
2. Made up of ______________ ______________.
3. They gain energy; they ______________.

II. Physical properties of matter.

1. Examples of ______________ of matter—color, texture, shape, hardness, mass, volume, density.
2. Physical properties help ______________ kinds of matter.

III. Particle theory of matter.

1. It helps to explain the difference among the ______________ of ______________.
   - A. All ______________ made up of very tiny ______________.
   - B. There are ______________ between ______________.
   - C. All the ______________ in a substance are the ______________; different substances are made of ______________.
   - D. ______________ ______________ draw particles together; the attractions may be ______________ or weak.
   - E. The ______________ move at all ______________; as particles gain ______________, they move ______________.

IV. Phase is a ______________ used to ______________ matter.

1. ______________ phases of matter.
   - A. Solids have a ______________ and ______________. Particles very ______________ together. Gives solids their ______________.
   - B. Liquids have a definite ______________ but no definite ______________. Particles move ______________.
   - C. Gases have no definite ______________ or ______________.

(continued) ➤

V. Elements exist in nature as ______________, ______________, or ______________.

1. All matter made up of ______________ or more ______________.
2. ______________ known elements.
3. Exists as ______________, ______________, or gases.
4. Most are ______________ at room temperature.
5. Oxygen, hydrogen, and nitrogen exist as ______________.
6. Two elements exist as ______________ at room temperature—mercury and bromine.
7. Each element is made up of only one kind of ______________.
8. Elements are a form of ______________ that cannot be ______________ into simpler substances by any ______________ or by ______________.

VI. Atoms are the ______________ of an ______________.

1. Made up of ______________.
   A. ______________ have a plus (+) charge.
   B. ______________ have a minus (−) charge.
   C. ______________ have 0 charge.
2. ______________ and ______________ are found in the nucleus of an atom.
3. ______________ found outside nucleus in ______________.
4. ______________ and ______________ can create ______________ of ______________ or ______________ of ______________.

   Ex:

VII. Compounds are substances made of more than ______________ kind of ______________.

1. A compound is formed when ______________ are ______________.

   Ex: Oxygen and hydrogen are ______________. They combine to form ______________.
2. Water is a compound, H_2O.
3. Most ______________ made of ______________.
4. A compound cannot be separated into the ______________ that form it except through a ______________.

VIII. Molecule is made of ______ or more ______ chemically bonded.	1. A molecule of water is H_2O: 2 ______ of ______ and 1 ______ of ______. 2. A molecule of carbon dioxide is 1 ______ of ______ and 2 ______ of ______.
IX. Chemical symbol consists of a ______ letters or a ______ and ______ letters.	1. It is the shorthand name of a ______. 2. Example C is a ______ for the element carbon.
X. Chemical formula is a combination of ______ that represent a ______.	1. Example of a ______ for carbon dioxide is CO. 2. Subscripts are ______ written below line in a chemical formula. They tell the ______ of ______ in the molecule. Ex: H_2O is ______ atom of ______.

Developed by Brenda Hamilton.

growth. Students can then be asked to write a group summary of what the text says about the important concept of credit.

For both summaries and text lookback, Garner (1985b) stresses the following:

1. Some ideas are more important than others.
2. Some ideas can (and must) be ignored.
3. Students need to be taught how to use titles and topic sentences.
4. Students need to learn that ideas cross boundaries of sentences.
5. "Piecemeal" reading that focuses on comprehending one sentence at a time is not conducive to summarizing or gaining ideas from text.
6. Rules of summarization need to be learned and practiced.
7. Students must be taught how and when to apply both summarization and lookback strategies.
8. These strategies cannot be adequately accomplished in a hurried classroom atmosphere and environment.
9. Students need to practice these strategies in a number of content areas to effect transfer.

Garner and associates (Garner, Hare, Alexander, Haynes, & Winograd, 1984) also maintain that readers should be taught the following: why to use lookbacks (because readers can't remember everything); when to use them (when the question calls for information from the text); and where to use them (where skimming or scanning will help one to find the portion of the text that should be read carefully). Next, readers should practice looking back for answers to questions asked after the reading is completed. Lookbacks are necessary when readers realize that they didn't understand all of what they read. Good readers evaluate their reading and make decisions on whether to look back. But poor readers rarely have this skill, so text lookbacks will give them much-needed practice in this aspect of critical thinking.

Study Systems

As soon as children in the first grade are ready, they should begin reading stories under the teacher's direction using the DRTA technique (Stauffer, 1969b). If such guided practice continues, teachers gradually give more and more responsibility for learning to students, as illustrated in Pearson's (1985) model (see Figure 10.1). If practice in using the DRTA is schoolwide and responsibility is taught, students will receive a firm foundation in study reading. Then by fifth or sixth grade, students can be taught a **study system**, a systematic way of studying text. Study systems are a natural outgrowth of previewing, skimming, and teacher-modeled reading lessons such as the DRTA. In this section we examine three study systems.

SQ3R

SQ3R (Robinson, 1961)—which stands for Survey, Question, Read, Recite, Review—is a study system that has been practiced for many years. Table 10.2 summarizes the SQ3R steps.

Tadlock's (1978) explanation of the success of SQ3R is based on information-processing theory (Neisser, 1967; Hunt, 1971; Newell & Simon, 1972). According to Tadlock, we naturally try to reduce uncertainty by (1) processing information through sensory organs; (2) sending information through memory systems; (3) structuring and categorizing information in the most meaningful manner, in order to see conceptual relationships; and (4) storing information for recall at a future time (p. 111). She postulates that SQ3R compensates for any deficiencies in our information-processing system through the use of a highly structured study and memory technique. It is important to note that other study systems similar to SQ3R—such as PQ4R (Preview, Question, Read, Recite, Review, Rewrite), SQ4R (Survey, Question, Read, Recite, Review, Rewrite), and SRR (Survey, Read, Review)—can work equally well because all rest on the same premise. Students should be encouraged to try a study system and adapt it to their own needs. Strict adherence to the steps is less important than applying a study strategy that is based on the four criteria that Tadlock describes.

An alternative to SQ3R is REAP, described in Chapter 9 as a writing-to-learn activity. REAP is also useful for improving study skills because when students

FIGURE 10.1

The gradual release of responsibility of instruction

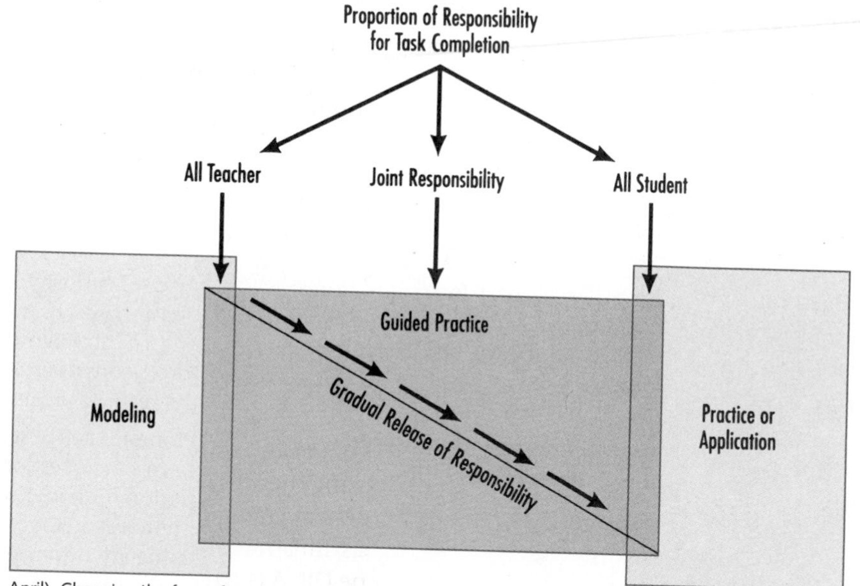

From Pearson, P. D. (1985, April). Changing the face of reading comprehension instruction. *The Reading Teacher*, *38*(8), 724–738. Reprinted with permission of P. David Pearson and the International Reading Association.

annotate, they pay attention and reinforce their reading by writing. In Chapter 11 we present a REAP activity completed in cooperative groups.

Study systems such as these have not really permeated schools across the country. Spor and Schneider (1999) found in a sampling of teachers that 44 percent had heard about the SQ3R method but of those only 17 percent had used it with students. There are probably three reasons for this low percentage. First, teachers themselves did not learn through such a study system; thus they often give only lip service to the techniques described. Second, teachers may have been required to use a study system imposed by their own teachers, but they did not understand the underlying reasons for the system. Teachers themselves need to practice previewing and study systems before they can believe in and teach such systems to others. Third, study strategies are not systematically introduced throughout educational systems from the early elementary years.

PQR2 ST+

The PQR2 ST+ study system developed by Morgan, Forget, and Antinarella (1996) is a complete study system. It has the following steps:

Preview: This is a very important step that good readers always do. Students take a quick overview of the material to be read before they start reading. Here is what to look for in the preview:

- title
- introduction

TABLE 10.2 SQ3R

Technique	*Procedure*	*Values*
Survey	Read questions and summary at end of the chapter. Skim-read divisions of material, which usually are in boldface type. Read captions under pictures and graphs.	Highlights major ideas and emphases of chapter; helps organize ideas for better understanding later.
Question	Turn each heading into a question. (Practice will make this skill automatic.) Write questions in outline form.	Arouses curiosity; increases comprehension; recalls information already known; highlights major points; forces conscious effort in applying the reading process.
Read	Read each section of the material to answer questions from headings.	Promotes active search for answers to specific questions; forces concentration for better comprehension; improves memory; aids in lengthening attention span.
Recite	After reading entire section, close book and write the answer to your question plus any significant cues; use your own words; write key examples; make notes brief.	Encourages students to use their own words and not simply copy from book; improves memory and ensures greater understanding.
Review	Study the topical outline and notes; try to see relationships; check memory by trying to recall main points; cover subpoints and try to recall them from seeing main points.	Clarifies relationships; checks short-term recall; prepares students for class.

- subtitles
- pictures
- charts, maps, graphs
- bold print and italicized words
- summary
- review questions

Question: In the left column of a page formatted for two-column notes, students write the question or objective to be achieved. A good way to do this is to turn the heading that introduces a passage into a question.

Read: Students read the subsection silently, thinking about how to express the information in *personal terms*.

Remember: In the right column of the notes, *with the book closed*, students write down the details of what they read. These notes must be in the student's own words! The students recall as much as possible but do not worry about missing some details.

Scan: Students rapidly scan the same subsection of the text to see whether they missed any details that are important or got anything wrong in their notes.

Touch Up: Students add any important details to their notes.

+ (Plus): The last step should be done within the first 24 hours after the reading. Students return to study from the notes by folding the page so that only the question shows. Students see whether they can remember the details noted on the right side. Because of the way the notes are taken, students are able to recall important details. Students go over the notes one more time before the test.

SQRC

Sakta (1999) proposed another study system similar to SQ3R. The SQRC procedure, which works best with expository readings, has four steps: State, Question, Read, and Conclude. It is carried out in three phases of the reading process: before, during, and after reading. First, students are given a general statement that they must support or refute based on what they find in the reading. Here are the phases of the strategy:

- *Phase 1: Before reading*
  The teacher introduces the topic and activates prior knowledge. Students then get a guide sheet (see Activity 10.10), on which they write whether they are for or against the position statement given by the teacher, and why. Next students rewrite their position statement in question form.
- *Phase 2: During reading*
  Students read the text to find information that supports their position. They also are instructed to take notes of salient points while reading. Immediately after reading, students review their notes and write a brief conclusion.
- *Phase 3: After reading*
  The class is divided into two groups, each group representing a position. With several students from each side acting as judges, students representing each position present arguments. The teacher serves as a consultant but does not offer opinions. After debate, the judges render a decision as to which side presented the stronger case.

Sakta (1999) presents results of a study she conducted that points to the effectiveness of the SQRC strategy for systematic study. The strategy is beneficial because, like SQ3R and PQR2 ST+, it combines key elements of cognitive learning theory and constructivist approaches.

ACTIVITY 10.10 The SQRC Reading/Thinking Guide Sheet

NAME ______________________________ CLASS ______________

Title of reading assignment: ______________________________

Directions: Before reading the assignment, state your belief or position about the topic by selecting one of the two statements supplied by the teacher, or write your own position statement. Restate your position in the form of a question and write it in the space labeled "Question." As you read, use this question to guide your reading and thinking about the topic. Take notes on (1) facts that support your position and (2) facts that refute, or do not support, your position. When you are finished reading, review your notes and write your conclusion. The conclusion may or may not support your original position statement.

Statement: ______________________________

Question: ______________________________

Facts that support my position statement:

____

____

____

____

____

Facts that refute my position statement:

____

____

____

____

____

Conclusion:

____

____

____

____

____

From Sakta, C. G. (Dec. 98/Jan. 99). SQRC: A strategy for guiding reading and higher level thinking. *Journal of Adolescent and Adult Literacy*, *42*(4), 265–269. Reprinted with permission of Cathy G. Sakta and the International Reading Association.

One-Minute Summary

Study skills need to be taught systematically, and emphasized in early elementary grades through high school. As students mature and progress through school, the skills that are taught may include locating information, previewing materials, organizing material for study, and using study systems. In this chapter we describe an assessment technique designed to find out whether students use adequate study skills. The teaching of study skills cannot be left to chance. Students at all levels need to be made aware of good study practices through the use of a skills training model.

Students must be convinced that study practices really will be more a help than a hindrance and that the hard work involved will pay off. Teacher modeling and involving students in trying out study skills is the most effective way to impart this message. Table 10.3 summarizes the strategies discussed in this chapter and indicates where each can be introduced in the school continuum.

TABLE 10.3 Introducing and Teaching Reading-Study Skills: A Kindergarten Through Grade 12 Timetable

	K	*1*	*2*	*3*	*4*	*5*	*6*	*7*	*8*	*9*	*10*	*11*	*12*
Skills training model	—	—	—	—	—	—	—	—	—	—	—	—	—
Locating information				—	—	—	—	—	—	—	—	—	—
Interpreting charts and graphs			—	—	—	—	—	—	—	—	—	—	—
Analyzing pictures	—	—	—	—	—	—	—	—	—	—	—	—	—
Reading maps			—	—	—	—	—	—	—	—	—	—	—
Mnemonics			—	—	—	—	—	—	—	—	—	—	—
Previewing		—	—	—	—	—	—	—	—	—	—	—	—
Rapid reading					—	—	—	—	—	—	—	—	—
Outlining					—	—	—	—	—	—	—	—	—
Note Taking					—	—	—	—	—	—	—	—	—
Text Lookbacks					—	—	—	—	—	—	—	—	—
SQ3R				—	—	—	—	—	—	—	—	—	—
PQR2 ST+			—	—	—	—	—	—	—	—	—	—	—
SQRC		—	—	—	—	—	—	—	—	—	—	—	—

End-of-Chapter Activities

Assisting Comprehension

1. Either use the two-column system to take notes in a class that you are presently attending, or practice the REST system or PQR2 ST+. If you feel the system is a good aid to learning, use it with your students in a forthcoming lesson. Ask students whether they enjoyed the activity.
2. Choose a book that is fairly easy to read, and try the "mental push-up" rapid-reading exercise described in this chapter. Does your reading speed increase as your comprehension increases? Try this and the other two rapid-reading exercises to get in the habit of reading faster.

Reflecting on Your Reading

1. Identify the most important things you learned in this chapter.
2. List ways in which you might change the day-to-day operations of your class to incorporate some or all of the techniques described in this chapter.

CHAPTER 11

Cooperative Study for Communication and Collaboration

The attainment of knowledge does not comprise all which is contained in the larger term of education.

—Webster

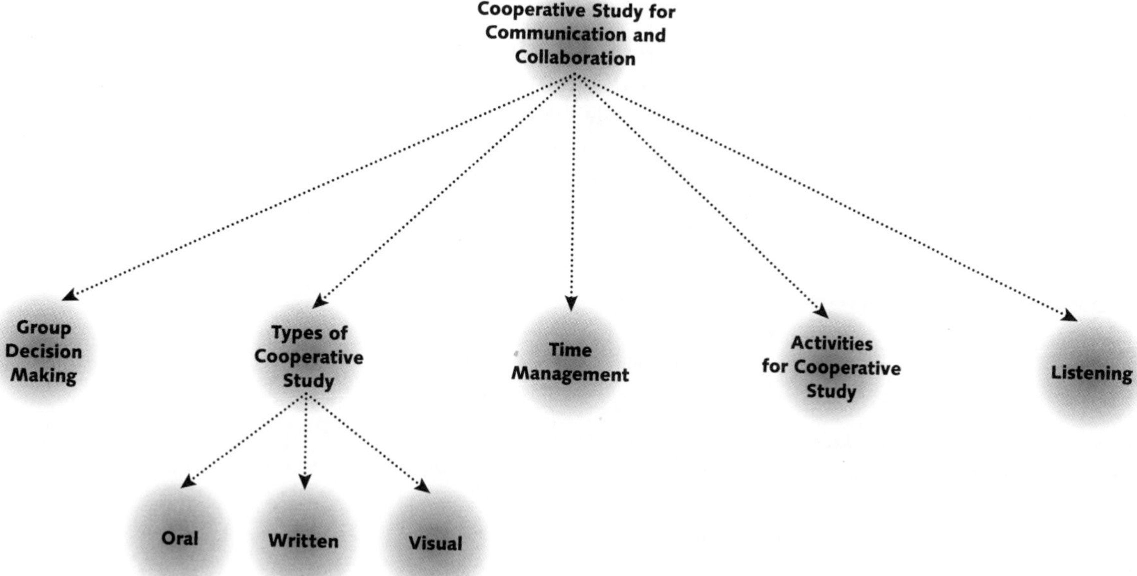

Preparing to Read

1. Do an assessment of your own study habits. Are you a "loner" or a "groupie"? If you like to study alone, list some of the benefits of individual study from your perspective. If you like to study in a group, list some benefits you derive from such study. Whatever your preference, as you read this chapter, keep an open mind concerning the flexibility of using both types of study behavior—quiet, individual study and group study.
2. Following is a list of terms used in this chapter. Some may be familiar to you in a general context, but in this chapter they may be used in unfamiliar ways. Rate your knowledge by placing a plus sign (+) in front of those you are sure that you know, a check mark (✓) in front of those you have some knowledge about, and a zero (0) in front of those you don't know. Be ready to locate and pay special attention to their meanings when they are presented in the chapter.

   ______ individual phase

   ______ consensus

   ______ arbitration

   ______ time management

   ______ ABOUT/POINT

   ______ student-generated questions

   ______ summarization

   ______ jigsaw

   ______ think-aloud

Objectives

As you read this chapter, focus your attention on the following objectives. You will:

1. understand the term *cooperative study*.
2. understand the group decision-making process.
3. understand the various categories of cooperative study.
4. be aware of why cooperative study is effective.
5. be able to use cooperative study techniques explained in this chapter.
6. understand the importance of cooperative learning through writing.
7. learn the importance of listening to students' achievement in all content classes.

The Importance of Cooperative Study

A growing body of research indicates that giving students opportunities to study cooperatively in the classroom can enhance learning (Johnson & Johnson, 1987; Abrami, Chambers, d'Apollonia, Farrell, & DeSimone, 1992; Alexander & DeAlba, 1997; Leinhardt, Stainton, & Bausmith, 1998; Rekrut, 1997). New research by Wiegel (1998) suggests that even kindergarten students can achieve more when they work for sustained periods in cooperative groups. A positive aspect of cooperative learning is that it may lessen stress reactions such as self-deprecation, lack of clear goals, disparagement, immature relationships with teachers, and pervasive depression (Gentile & McMillan, 1987).

It especially enables low achievers to gain success without the feelings of failure and isolation that often accompany more traditional learning (Coleman, 1994; Kirkland, 1993). Most important, students learn the skill of working together as they discuss what and how material can best be learned. Students who work together also appear to have a higher regard for school and for the subjects they are studying and are more confident and self-assured. Rasinski and Nathenson-Mejia (1987) note that the cooperative classroom environment fosters social development and teaches students social responsibility and concern for one another. Fogarty (1998) calls for small-group cooperative tasks as a means to challenge students "through the experience of doing" (p. 657). Vaughan and Estes (1986), in discussing cooperative learning, observed that

> An advantage is an increase in the amount of understanding of ideas; with two people studying a text, the chances are that one of them will understand something that confuses the other. Hence, we find again . . . that the object of study is understanding. Rarely, outside of school settings, does one find solitary attempts at understanding; usually people invite others to share in their discoveries and to engage in cooperative learning activities. This is true for erudite scientists and casual readers alike. (p. 147)

Slavin (1991) conducted a review of the literature on 60 studies that contrasted the achievement outcomes of cooperative learning and traditional methods in elementary and secondary schools. His conclusions were as follows:

1. Cooperative learning has positive effects on student achievement. The groups must have two important features: group goals and individual accountability.
2. When students of different racial or ethnic backgrounds work together toward a common goal, they gain liking and respect for one another. Cooperative learning improves social acceptance of mainstreamed students by their classmates and increases friendships among students in general.
3. Other outcomes include gains in self-esteem, time on task, attendance, and ability to work effectively with others.

TECHNOLOGY BOX

Some Technology Terms

ASCII stands for American Standard Code for Information Interchange. This usually means that the message will be sent in plain text, without the "fancy" codes a word processing program would use.

Asynchronous communication is communication that can occur over the Internet, but the sender and receiver may respond at different times; the message waits for the recipient to read and respond to it. Discussion groups and listservs (see Chapter 3) are examples of asynchronous communication.

CD-ROM stands for Compact Disc Read Only Memory, meaning that data is stored on a disk in digital form and can be read but not altered.

Clipboards hold images and text in a buffer for exchange between different documents or programs on a computer.

Copy and Paste commands allow a person to type one text, then place it in other locations. The computer holds the information in memory when the Copy command is used; it places the information where a user indicates when the Paste command is used.

Database is an application program where information can be stored in an organized manner and searched by categories.

FAQs are frequently asked questions. When visiting many websites, one will see FAQs listed in the site's table of contents. Viewers visit this area to see whether the questions they have about the issue or product have been asked by others and what response they have been given. Reading FAQs and their answers may save time.

Fonts are standardized designs of characters, which determine the look of text (Geneva, New York, etc.).

Hypertext is text that can be examined in a nonlinear manner (see Chapter 3).

HTML stands for Hypertext Markup Language, which are special codes inserted into text so it can be displayed by a browser.

Icons are images used to represent an action or category of information.

Internet is the international web of computer networks.

LAN is a Local Access Network, or computers that are interconnected in one location, such as in a school.

Modem is a computer peripheral device used to connect, through telephone wires, a computer to other computers for information exchange.

Piracy is the illegal copying of software.

Public domain is free-use software, with no copyright restrictions.

Synchronous communication is communication that can occur over the Internet, but both the sender and the recipient respond to each other within the same time frame. Conversations occur in "real time." Chat rooms are examples of synchronous discussion.

URLs are the "uniform resource locator" numbers that are addresses to a location on the Internet. They usually start with "http://www"

Virus is a program that causes damage to a computer; it is usually "uninvited" by the recipient, via disk or e-mail.

World Wide Web is a system of Internet resources linking hypertext-like documents.

Another reason for the use of cooperative study is that it helps students set purposes for their reading and monitor whether those purposes are being met. Although at first teachers must help readers set purposes, readers must begin to set their own purposes for reading as soon as possible. Hawkes and Schell (1987) caution that teacher-set reasons to read may encourage dependence and a passive approach to reading. Self-set reasons to read promote the development of readers who are active and ultimately independent. To wean readers from dependence, teachers can use many of the activities mentioned in this chapter until students are familiar with them and understand what purpose setting involves—that is, until students are able to perform alone what initially they could accomplish only with the aid of the teacher (Gavelek, 1986).

Researchers note that cooperative learning enables students to display more positive attitudes and helps them increase intrinsic motivation to learn (Wood, 1987). We tend to think of cooperative learning taking place mainly at the upper-elementary and middle-school levels. But cooperative learning can take place at the kindergarten level (Vermette, 1994). When students work in small groups on an assigned task that has been clearly explained to them, they often prosper in their learning environment. But cooperative learning and study means more than telling students to get together in groups and work. Rather, it is a structured experience in which students, preferably in groups of two, three, or four, practice learning content by using study skills emphasized by the teacher for a particular lesson. Glasser (1986, p. 75) gives eight reasons why "small learning teams" will motivate almost all students. According to Glasser, these teams do the following:

1. Create a sense of belonging.
2. Provide initial motivation for students who have not worked previously.
3. Provide ego fulfillment for stronger students to help weaker ones.
4. Provide continued motivation for weaker students, who see that team effort brings rewards, whereas their individual efforts were usually not good enough to get rewarded.
5. Free students from dependence on the teacher.
6. Enable students to get past superficiality to learn in-depth and vital knowledge.
7. Teach students how to convince others that they have learned the material (communication skills).
8. Keep students interested and achieving by having teachers change the teams on a regular basis. There is always the chance that a student who is not doing well with one team will be more successful as a member of another cooperative learning team.

Group Decision Making

One of the main goals in teaching is to help students become autonomous learners. Research has shown that students may not exhibit independent learning habits even when they know and use certain cognitive strategies (Borkowski, Carr, Rellinger, & Pressley, 1990; Paris & Winograd, 1990). Teachers need to help students become independent by encouraging group decision making and having students work in teams or small groups whenever possible. Learning is enhanced when such cooperative learning teams are emphasized in content teaching (Meloth & Deering, 1992; Johnson & Johnson, 1987; Abrami et al., 1992).

In having students work in groups, we recommend a stylized three-step process analogous to the steps in the PAR Lesson Framework described in Chapter 1. In the preparation phase, it is important for individual students to commit to something, usually written, to be shared later with the group. In this **individual phase**, the teacher is attempting to get a commitment from the student. This can be difficult because students today often do not wish to commit to anything; their cop-out is not to get involved in classroom activities. This sense of involvement is crucial to successful group interaction, however. Lack of commitment is the reason so much group work degenerates, with students getting away from the subject to be discussed or the problem to be solved.

The second phase is the actual work to be done in groups. The key word here is **consensus**. In the group phase the students should share what they have done individually and arrive at a consensus, whenever possible, on the best possible answer. The teacher provides much assistance in this phase by moving from group to group to help students with areas of difficulty and to make certain groups are staying on topic.

In the third phase, involving reflection, the teacher may lead a discussion with the groups, an exercise in **arbitration**. The teacher acts as an arbiter to resolve difficult points of the lesson on which students could not come to consensus. Also, in this phase groups may give reports to the whole class on their group findings.

To recap, here are the three phases of good group process:

Phase I: Individual Phase.	Key concept: commitment.
Phase II: Group Work.	Key concept: consensus.
Phase III: Teacher-Led Discussion.	Key concept: arbitration.

Teachers often express frustration with the results of group work. One solution is to have students role-play different scenarios in which certain members of the groups might sabotage the group effort. When students consider for themselves what a possible obstacle to the success of their group work could be and how they might confront that difficulty before it escalates out of control, they become more productive in groups. Swafford (1995) describes a technique she uses with college students. Groups are given one of three scenarios in which one person in a group is not participating at all, underparticipating, or overparticipating. By discussing these problems and acting out a solution for the rest of the class, everyone experiences the process of commitment, consensus, and arbitration in a friendly atmosphere.

The technique that Swafford (1995) used with her students could help students move toward successful cooperative group work. However, group work can cause significant problems in how students view themselves or are viewed by their peers (Alvermann, 1996). Some students feel left out; others feel unable to contribute. Alvermann cautions that just creating groups is not enough; the teacher must monitor progress and discuss with individual students their perceptions of group work. By considering the real problems that can occur, and devising solutions themselves, students come to understand that they can succeed in cooperative groups. The goal is that the teacher gradually releases purpose-setting responsibility to the students, enabling them to become independent learners. This goal is especially difficult to meet with at-risk students, but it is equally as important.

Types of Cooperative Study

Oral Cooperative Study

Wood (1987), in a comprehensive review of cooperative learning approaches, maintains that verbalizing newly acquired information is the most powerful study technique. Following are some of Wood's suggestions for combining oral and cooperative study:

- *Group recalling*: Content teachers provide groups of two or three students with different reading material about the same topic. Students read material silently and retell, in their own words, what they have learned to their group. Group members may add to any retelling by sharing similar information from their reading or from their own experiences.
- *Associational dialogue*: Students work in pairs from an assigned vocabulary list to discuss each word on the list. In this manner, students learn by interacting with others.
- *Needs grouping*: To determine students' conceptual knowledge of a subject, teachers give pretests. Students who do not do well on particular areas of the pretest can be grouped together for reflective study over that part of the unit.
- *Buddy system*: Teachers pair weaker students with stronger ones. In this ability grouping, each student is asked to take responsibility for the other's learning. Daniel Fader describes this process in *Hooked on Books* (1966).
- *Cybernetic sessions*: Wood cites Masztal's (1986) work in describing a technique to summarize lessons through group interaction. After reading a selection, groups brainstorm answers to thought-provoking questions posed by the teacher. Answers are shared in the group and with the whole class.
- *Research grouping*: During a unit of study, students work in groups to research a topic in the classroom or in the library.

Written Cooperative Study

Writing can be incorporated into cooperative study in several ways. Davey (1987), for example, recommends the following steps as effective in guiding students' writing of research reports:

1. *Topic selection*: Students use factstorming to select a topic or subtopic. (See Chapter 4 for examples of factstorming.)
2. *Planning*: Teams need to establish a research plan. They generate questions to be answered and a schedule for study.
3. *Researching the topic*: Teams divide questions to be answered and begin taking notes, working in class and in the library. The teacher may help with a library search guide (explained in Chapter 10).
4. *Organizing*: Teams meet to share information, organize material in outline form, and decide what information to delete and which questions to research further.
5. *Writing*: Team members work individually or in pairs to write the first draft, check initial drafts, and revise and edit the final report.

In Chapter 9, REAP (Eanet & Manzo, 1976) was described as a writing activity. One English teacher combined REAP with cooperative grouping to teach students the important study skills of organizing information, reflecting on their reading, thinking critically, and reaching a deeper level of comprehension. After each student read an assigned article, "The Whiny Generation," she divided them into seven groups. Each group received an annotation card with one of the seven types of annotation written on it (to review the seven styles of annotation, see Chapter 9). The group then wrote an annotation to match the type for this article. The results are given in Activity 11.1.

Visual Cooperative Study

Students at any grade level can make and produce postreading concept maps and post graphic organizers, both valuable aids for cooperative study and learning. Bean, Singer, Sorter, and Frazee (1986) found that a group given instruction in summarizing, generating questions, and creating graphic organizers scored significantly better on text recall than did either a group instructed in graphic organizers only or a group instructed in outlining.

Graphic organizers allow students to display graphically and visually what they comprehend in a particular reading selection. They also encourage class participation and enable students to interact with each other while involved in the learning process. Students can take part in a group process to create graphic organizers such as the one in Activity 11.2, which is the product of students' brainstorming after reading a volleyball rulebook in physical education class.

Spanish I students from an at-risk school illustrated in cooperative groups some conversations from their textbook. For the conversation illustrated in Ac-

ACTIVITY 11.1 Written Cooperative Study: REAP Note-Taking Practice

Following are examples of the kind of notes that an eleventh-grade class produced after reading the assigned essay, "The Whiny Generation."

Heuristic annotation: Provocation: intended primarily to stimulate response. Usually employs the author's own words.

This baby boomer is "fed up" with "the handful of spoiled, self-indulgent, overgrown adolescents" called "Generation X."

Summary annotation: A general sense of the piece, its style and scope; most objective and informative in a nonarousing way.

Martin asserts that people in their twenties should not blame boomers for their problems, but should be patient, look at the mistakes they have made in their own lives, and educate themselves to prepare for the opportunities that exist for them in such fields as computers, telecommunications, and health care.

Thesis annotation: An incisive statement of the basic thesis of the work.

People in their twenties should stop complaining and work hard to achieve realistic goals.

Question annotation: Provides explicit focus to the notion that the annotation writer thought to be most germane.

Do twentysomethings have anything to whine about? Absolutely not, claims Martin.

Critical annotation: An informative critical response to a thesis or supporting premise.

Martin labels a whole generation as spoiled, naive whiners who squandered their opportunities. Blaming the problems of Generation X totally on their own behavior and values, is not right! It's just as bad as the twentysomethings blaming all their problems on the fortysomethings. He ignores the plight of those who made what he would call the right decisions, such as majoring in computer science, and who still are struggling. He also does not admit that the baby boomers dominate in most fields and that they made some rotten decisions that will hurt generations to come.

Intention annotation: Statement of the author's intention as students might see it.

The author intends to show that the twentysomething generation has nothing to complain about and has only itself to blame for missed economic opportunities.

Motivation annotation: Why the author wrote the passage.

The author wanted to defend his generation against the criticism of the twentysomething generation.

Developed by Jane Mitchell.

---

tivity 11.3, one student asks another whether he is from Mexico. The teacher reported that the groups went to great lengths to make certain the rest of the class understood how the picture represented their assigned conversation. In a usually rowdy class, every student was dutiful, drawing or spouting ideas to the others.

ACTIVITY 11.2 Post Graphic Organizer: Rules of Volleyball

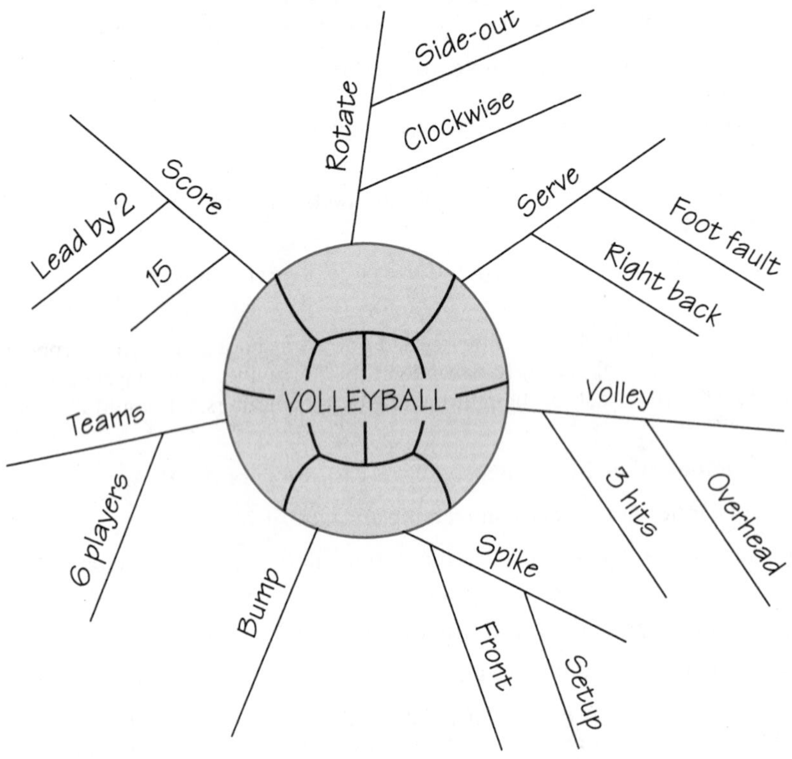

Why Cooperative Study Is Effective

Weinstein (1987) suggests that cooperative study and learning strategies are successful in aiding comprehension and retention because they fall into one or more of what she calls "categories of learning strategies"—processes and methods useful in acquiring and retrieving information. Weinstein proposes five categories of learning strategies:

1. *Rehearsal strategies*. Techniques discussed in this chapter include cooperative reading activity and think-alouds.
2. *Elaboration strategies*. Techniques discussed in this chapter include jigsaw, group retelling, cybernetic sessions, paired reading, student-generated questions, and listening strategies.
3. *Organizational strategies*. Techniques discussed in this chapter include summarizing, narrative story guides, about/point, mapping, and cooperative graphing.

ACTIVITY 11.3 Post Graphic Organizer: A Conversation in Spanish

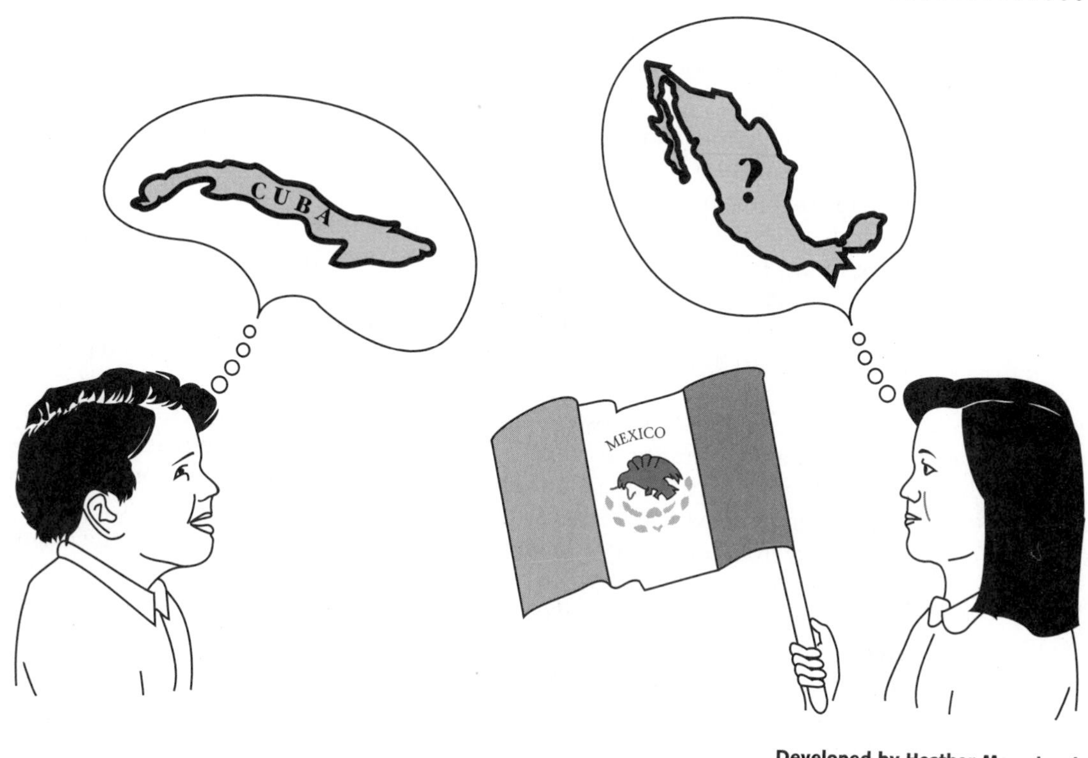

Developed by Heather Memstreet.

4. *Comprehension-monitoring strategies*. Techniques discussed in this chapter include extended anticipation guides, reciprocal teaching, and think-alouds.
5. *Affective strategies*. Techniques discussed in this chapter include paired reading, positive rewards for learning in groups, and the buddy system.

In underscoring the importance of cooperative study, we wish to reemphasize a point made frequently throughout this book: Learning is difficult in a hurried, pressured classroom environment. A first-grader recently complained, "The teacher never lets me finish. I never have enough time to finish." This is a lament that holds true in all too many classrooms. Jeremy Rifkin, in his book *Time Wars* (1987), argues that we appear to be trapped in our own technology. Rifkin maintains that the constant pressure to become more efficient causes Americans to feel that they do not have enough time to get things done. This pressure, which permeates today's classroom, is detrimental because all types of classroom effort succeed best in a calm, unhurried atmosphere in which students have freedom to explore ideas, develop creativity, solve problems, and be thoughtful and reflective.

Managing Time as the Key to Cooperative Study

Incorporating **time management**—the effective use of one's time—into the content curriculum is an important way to teach students to work cooperatively. One of the most important predeterminers of how well students do in cooperative study groups is how carefully they manage their time while studying with the group. Vaughan and Estes (1986) described two negative factors that are present with many students: compulsiveness and distractibility. Students will attend to tasks better if they are taught to concentrate and think about what they are learning, to be responsible for their own learning, and to listen carefully to directions.

Responsibility can be fostered through daily work routines, especially in the early-elementary grades. For example, after students complete assigned seatwork, they can be offered a choice of activities. In elementary school, students whose names are written on a card in green can be allowed to choose a follow-up activity from four choices that the teacher has labeled on charts in the room. Students whose names are written in yellow can select from three choices. Figure 11.1 illustrates this method of allowing students to monitor their own learning and free time. Of course the activities would be numbered and explained on a sheet given to middle and high school students.

Another effective technique for teaching time management is to get students to monitor themselves on self-evaluation logs. Ross, Rolheiser, and Hoaboam-Grey (1998) found that self-evaluation training of fifth- and sixth-grade mathematics students helped greatly in clarifying students' understanding of curricular expectations. Activity 11.4 presents a student self-evaluation log for elementary grades. Activity 11.5 presents a student self-evaluation sheet for a middle or high school class.

By the time students enter the workforce or college, they often feel short-changed in knowing how to manage their time (Britton & Tesser, 1991; Weissberg, Berentsen, Cote, Cravey, & Heath, 1982). An activity that can be modified for different grade levels is "How I Spend My Time." First, students estimate how they think they spend their time. The teacher keeps these estimates. Next, students record how they use their time for a given period. For first- or second-graders, one day is enough, from waking up until bedtime. Recording can be completed with teacher supervision during the school day. For upper-elementary and middle-school students, a week is an appropriate block of time. Students should keep records outside of school hours, but the teacher might provide some class time for "catching up." For high school and beyond, the block of time should be at least a week, with recording of all hours—even sleep—done outside of class. Next, students study their records and compare the activities on which they spent their time with their estimates of how they thought they

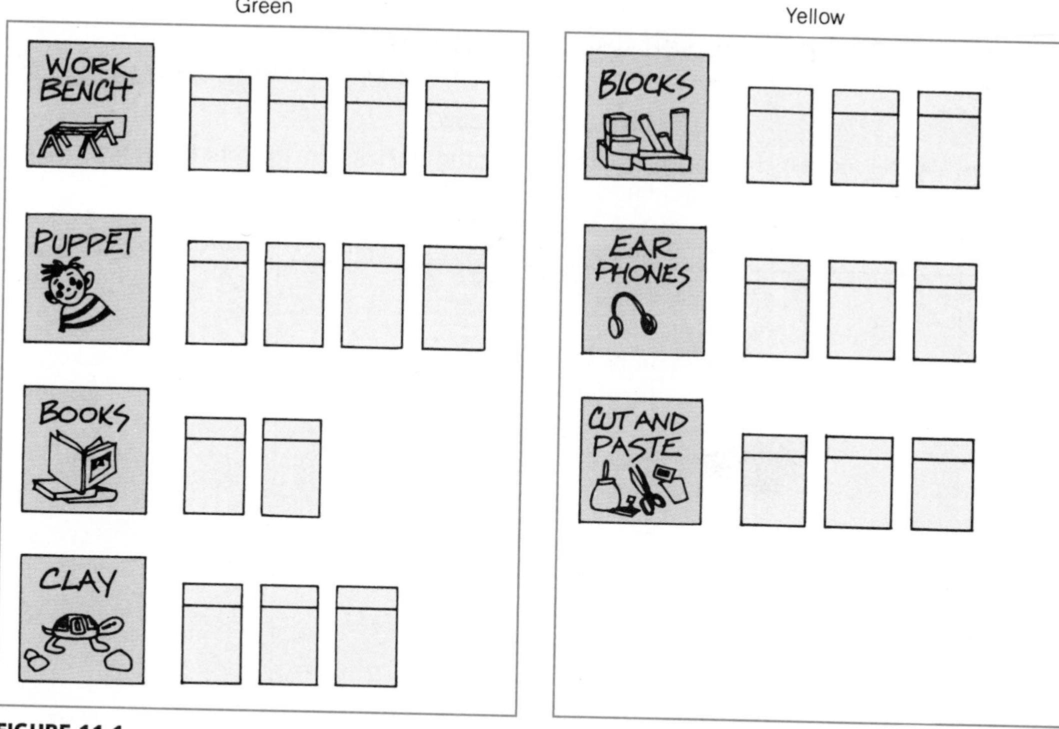

FIGURE 11.1

Room chart for student activities

would spend it. Results are often revealing and help students see where they can make changes.

Eleventh-graders who participated in such a time management study in their English class were asked to indicate

1. How much time they spent on study and recreation
2. How much more study time was needed
3. Where time could be found in the schedule for more study

The students wrote study goals such as "I will study ten more minutes each evening for English class." They also wrote rewards that they might receive if they achieved the goal, such as "Because I studied wisely, I will probably get a better grade." A classmate had to sign the contract; a parent's signature was optional. Students were to consistently practice achieving their goals for a month. Below are some responses that they recorded in their journals:

1. What was your time management goal?

   K: My time management goal was to spend more of my time studying—more quality time, that is—and thus achieve a better understanding of the material.

ACTIVITY 11.4 Student Self-Evaluation Log

Life in the Ocean

Directions: At the end of each lesson, rate yourself using the number from the code below that best describes how you think you did on that lesson.

Date	Skill	Student Evaluation	Student Comment	Teacher Comment

#5 S.O.S

#3 storm brewing

#2 calm seas

#1 smooth sailing

#4 rough seas

ACTIVITY 11.5 Daily Log Sheet for Middle and High School Classes

Day and Date	*Activities Planned*	*Activities Completed*	*Self-Evaluation of Amount Learned*	*Self-Evaluation of Enjoyment of Activity*	*Teacher or Student Comments*

(*continued*) ➤

continued

Evaluation Scale:

Ugh! I learned little or nothing		I learned some		I learned a great deal
1	2	3	4	5
I disliked doing this		It was all right		Wow! I liked it a lot
1	2	3	4	5

J: My time management goal was to increase preparation—for instance, for tests, quizzes, and essays.

E: My goal was to spend time studying and preparing for class.

2. Did you achieve this goal? Why or why not?

   K: I achieved my goal because I studied the material more extensively instead of just reading over it.

   J: I did not achieve my goal because of my lack of will and lack of time for preparation.

   E: Sort of. I did spend some more time, but not enough.

3. What did you discover about managing your time for study in English?

   K: I need to spend more time preparing for class instead of talking to friends on the phone. Also, I need to understand the material more fully.

   J: I found out that I spend most of my time working. I spent at least 7 hours a day on school days and 16–19 hours on weekends working. The rest of my time went to being at school and some time—very little—sleeping.

   E: I found that my priorities were not entirely in order. I previously would watch TV, eat dinner, and lie around before doing my homework. I now do my homework as soon as I get home, shower, and eat dinner and then I take my leisure time. I sometimes study just before going to sleep as well.

4. Was this assignment helpful? Why or why not?

   K: The assignment was helpful to me because the chart helped me to budget my time more wisely.

   J: The assignment was helpful because it made me realize what I was doing and should be doing. I should spend more time on schoolwork, but at this time it is not possible.

   E: This assignment was helpful because it allowed me to get somewhat of a schedule together in order to get things done. I seem to work much more efficiently now and my grades have improved.

The teacher observed progress in grades and attitudes. She attributes the success to students' involvement and control of their own progress. Students provided their own data about specific uses of time and then decided what they wanted to improve and how. The assignment did not take much class time, and responsibility improved.

Activities That Promote Cooperative Study

In the remainder of the chapter we explain reading, writing, and listening activities that involve sharing, collaboration, and cooperative study. They all work best in a relaxed classroom atmosphere where teachers can guide students in their efforts to work cooperatively.

Extended Anticipation Guides

A technique that can be adapted to cooperative learning is the extended anticipation guide (Duffelmeyer, Baum, & Merkley, 1987; Duffelmeyer & Baum, 1992). As noted in Chapter 5, anticipation guides can aid students in predicting outcomes. The extended guides can spark discussion and reinforce or verify information that students have learned and can enable them to modify predictions to take into account new insights and information. Activity 11.6 includes both an anticipation guide for high school students to complete individually before reading Upton Sinclair's muckraking novel *The Jungle* and an extended guide to be completed by students working in groups after reading *The Jungle*.

ABOUT/POINT

ABOUT/POINT is a versatile strategy for cooperative study (Morgan, Meeks, & Schollaert, 1986). In kindergarten and first grade, teachers can use it as a listening and speaking aid after reading a story aloud to students. An example of its use in first grade is shown as Activity 11.7. The student is identifying the sun as the source of light and heat. In upper-elementary and junior high school, students can work in groups to recall information from content material. To use the about/point strategy, teachers ask students to reread a passage, then to decide in groups what the passage is "about" and what "points"—details—support their response. Teachers can provide study sheets such as the one in Activity 11.8 on high school consumer mathematics.

Paired Reading

Another strategy that works with middle and secondary students is paired reading, developed by Larson and Dansereau (1986). Students begin by reading a short assignment and then divide into pairs. One partner is designated a "recaller" and the other a "listener." The recaller retells the passage from memory; the listener interrupts only to ask for clarification. Then the listener corrects ideas summarized incorrectly and adds important ideas from the text material that the recaller did not mention. During the time the listener is clarifying, the

ACTIVITY 11.6 Anticipation Guide and Extended Anticipation Guide for *The Jungle*

Part I: Anticipation Guide

Instructions: Before you begin reading *The Jungle*, read the statements below. If you agree with a statement, place a check in the Agree column. If you disagree with the statement, place a check in the Disagree column. Be ready to explain or defend your choices in class discussion.

Agree	*Disagree*	*Statement*
		1. Anyone who works hard can get ahead.
		2. An employer has a responsibility for his employees' safety and welfare.
		3. Companies that process packaged food should be responsible for policing themselves for health violations.
		4. Immigrants were readily accepted into the American system at the turn of the twentieth century.
		5. Unions can remedy all labor grievances.

Part II: Extended Anticipation Guide

Instructions: Now that you have read *The Jungle* and information related to the statements in Part I, get into groups to complete this section. If you feel that what you read supports your choices in Part I, place a check in the Support column below. If the information read does *not* support your choice in Part I, check the No Support column and write a reason why the statement cannot be supported in the third column. Keep your reasons brief and in your own words.

Support	*No Support*	*Reason for No Support (in your own words)*
1.		
2.		
3.		
4.		
5.		

recaller also can add clarification. In this manner, the two work together to reconstruct as much as possible of what they read. The pair can use drawings, pictures, and diagrams to facilitate understanding of the material. Students alternate the roles of reteller and listener after each reading segment, which may number four or five over the course of one class period. Wood notes that paired reading is successful because it is "based on recent research in metacognition, which suggests that without sufficient reinforcement and practice, some students have difficulty monitoring their own comprehension" (1987, p. 13). Paired reading is also based on elaboration strategy, which, according to Weinstein (1987), helps students learn new concepts by drawing on their prior experiences.

ACTIVITY 11.7 First-Grade About-Point

NAME Porche v.

Directions: Read the paragraph. Then ask yourself, "What was this selection about and the main idea?"

The sun is a very big star. It heats the earth and moon. The sun lights the earth and moon, too. We play in the sunlight.

This paragraph is ABOUT Sun
and the main idea is Sun heats
and lights the earth.

Developed by Dana S. Jubilee.

ACTIVITY 11.8 About/Point Study Sheet: Consumer Mathematics

This reading is ABOUT:

The high cost, including hidden costs, of automobile ownership.

And the POINTS are:

Few people have cash enough to buy a car outright.

Therefore, they borrow from banks, auto dealers, or small loan agencies.

Costs are affected by the state and region in which the borrower lives.

Few institutions will lend money unless the borrower purchases life insurance.

Self-Generated Questions for Cooperative Study

Recent studies center on **student-generated questions**. Davey and McBride (1986) found that children who were trained to develop probing questions after the reading, either individually or in small groups, scored better on a test of comprehension of the material. In a similar study MacDonald (1986) found that groups instructed in methods for asking questions had comprehension scores higher than the scores of groups without this training. Activity 11.9 presents questions generated by students in an elementary-science class and the answers they found after reading the textbook.

Summarizing in Groups

A number of researchers address the importance of **summarization** to the study and retention of reading material (Scardamalia & Bereiter, 1984; Garner, 1985b). Garner notes that summarization involves (1) judging ideas deemed important, (2) applying rules for condensing text, and (3) producing a shortened text in

ACTIVITY 11.9 Student-Generated Questions in Elementary Science

STUDENT-GENERATED QUESTIONS

1. What does the sun do for plants?
2. Do all plants have seeds, leaves, and flowers?
3. Can the sun harm some plants?
4. Which plants grow best in deserts?
5. What do you call plants that come back every year?
6. Which part of the plant makes the food?
7. Do all plants need the same things to grow?
8. What are the 4 things that all plants need?
9. Do people need the same 4 things?
10. Can we eat some plants?

ANSWERS

1. The sun helps the plant make food.
2. Yes, all plants have seeds, leaves, and flowers.
3. Yes, some plants only like shade and filtered sun (filtered sun is sun that has something blocking some of its rays).
4. Cactus grow best in deserts. They need very little water.
5. Perennials are plants that come back every year.
6. The leaves make the food by taking in the oxygen and sun.
7. No, some plants need more sunlight than others. Some need a lot of shade.
8. All plants need air, water, sunlight, and soil.
9. No, people do not need soil because we move around freely.
10. Yes, we can eat a lot of vegetables such as beans, tomatoes, and corn.

Developed by Susan W. Hamlin.

---

oral or written form. Studies consistently show that skilled readers have the ability to summarize, whereas unskilled readers almost always lack this ability (Scardamalia & Bereiter, 1984; Garner, 1985b; Brown & Smiley, 1977).

To learn to write effective summaries, students can be asked to work in groups and use the following six rules, suggested by Brown and Day (1983):

1. Delete all unnecessary material.
2. Delete redundancies.
3. Substitute a superordinate term for a list of items.
4. Use a superordinate term for a list of actions.
5. Select topic sentences from ones provided in the text.

6. Construct topic sentences when they are not provided explicitly in the text.

One way to have students summarize in groups is for group members to develop a concept map around the ideas they believe to be important in a chapter or a portion of a chapter. Groups can share their mapping exercises on the board, and discussion can center on why groups chose different concepts to be mapped. An example of a group-made concept map for vocational students is shown in Activity 11.10. Mapping can be an excellent cooperatively generated activity for small-group interaction. Davidson (1982) suggests that such concept maps are "low-risk" activities for even the most limited students and can be an unobtrusive way for students to summarize what they learned in the reading.

Jigsaw

Aronson (1978) describes a cooperative learning strategy called **jigsaw**, named for the jigsaw puzzle. In this strategy, each student in a five- or six-member

ACTIVITY 11.10 Concept Map: Office Technology

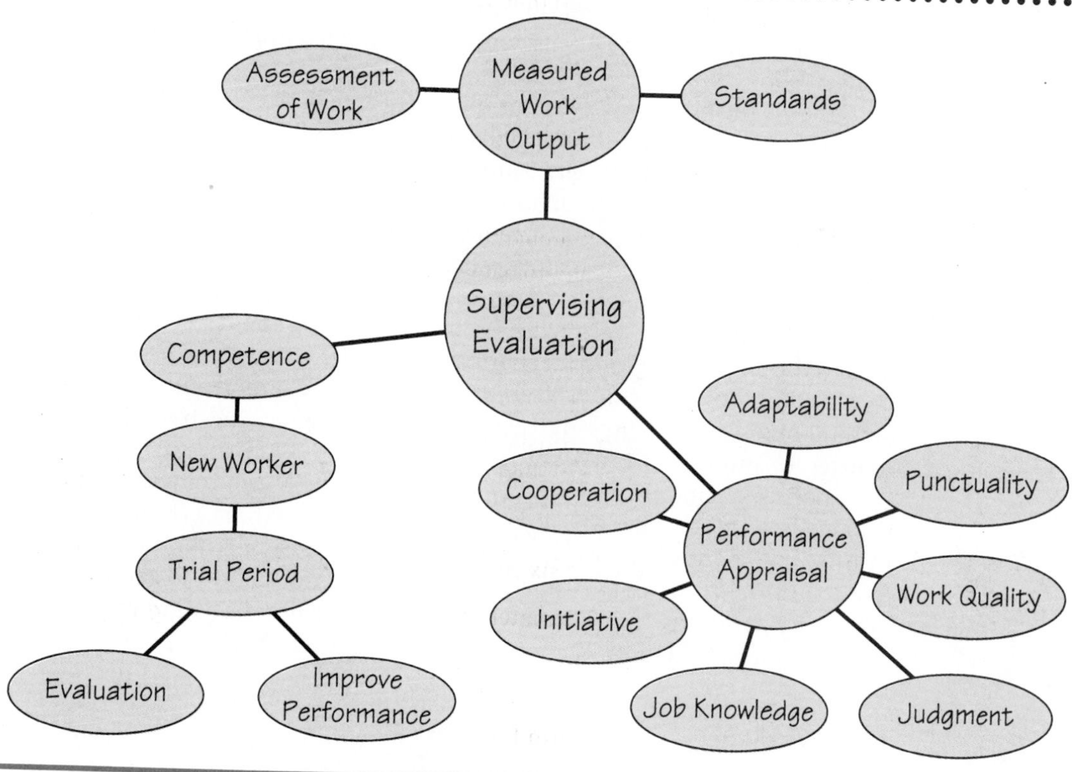

group is given unique information on a topic that the group is studying. After reading their material, the students meet in "expert groups" with their counterparts from other groups to discuss and master the information. In a variation called jigsaw II (Slavin, 1980), all students are first given common information. Then student "experts" teach more specific topics to the group. Students take tests individually, and team scores are publicized in a class newsletter.

Jigsaw uses two distinct grouping patterns: heterogeneous study groups and homogeneous discussion groups. Study groups are arranged heterogeneously by ability or age level to learn about subtopics of the main topic. The purpose of the study group is to allow each member to become expert in a particular topic in common with other group members. Discussion groups are arranged homogeneously by ability or age level to discuss the different subtopics that members studied in their study groups. The purpose of the discussion group is to allow each member to share his or her expertise with others who share a common perspective.

The number of members in each discussion group must equal or exceed the number of study groups. This is to ensure that at least one discussion group member is in each study group. For example, a class of 22 students might be divided into three groups by reading ability—say, one group of group of 7 grade-level readers, a group of 6 low-level readers, and a group of 9 average ability readers. These could be the homogeneous discussion groups of jigsaw. Discussion groups would then count off by fours to establish the heterogeneous study groups, thus ensuring equal representation of the reading groups in each study group.

Suppose the topic under discussion is "The Life of the Native American" and the subtopics are "Traditional Myths and Legends," "Occupations and Products," "Lifestyles," and "Origin and History." Each study group is assigned one of the subtopics to research, dividing the available materials and informational resources among its members. After each member completes his or her assignment, the study group meets for a sharing session. Each member teaches the other members what he or she learned about the subtopic, so that all members become experts on the assigned subtopic. They bring the results of their study back to the discussion group for sharing with students who have become experts on other subtopics. In this way, all students have the opportunity to do a small amount of research, to present their findings about what they have learned, and to listen to and learn from other students.

Another technique very similar to jigsaw is called group investigation, developed as a small-group activity for critical thinking (Sharan & Sharan, 1976). In this strategy, students work in small groups, but each group takes on a different task. Within groups, students decide what information to gather, how to organize it, and how to present what they have learned as a group project to classmates. In evaluation, higher-level thinking is emphasized.

Think-Aloud

Think-aloud, developed by Davey (1983), uses a modeling technique to help students improve their comprehension. Teachers verbalize their thoughts as they read aloud—modeling the kinds of strategies a skilled reader uses during reading and pointing out specifically how they are coping with a particular comprehension problem. The teacher models five reading comprehension techniques:

1. Forming hypotheses about text's meaning before beginning to read
2. Producing mental images (spontaneously organizing information)
3. Linking prior knowledge with a new topic
4. Monitoring comprehension
5. Identifying active ways to "fix" comprehension problems

Using a difficult text, the teacher "talks" it through out loud while students follow the text silently. This training helps poor students realize that text should make sense and that readers use both information from the text and prior knowledge to construct meaning. To demonstrate the five techniques, teachers can make predictions and show how to develop a hypothesis, describe the visual images that come to mind, share analogies and otherwise link new knowledge to prior knowledge, verbalize a confusing point or problem, and demonstrate fix-up strategies such as rereading, reading ahead to clarify a confusing point, and figuring out word meanings from context.

After the teacher models think-alouds a few times, students can work with partners to practice the strategy, taking turns in reading orally and sharing thoughts. This strategy can become an excellent cooperative study technique. Teachers also can provide students in the twosomes with a checklist to self-evaluate their progress (see Activity 11.11).

A study by Baumann, Seifert-Kessell, and Jones (1992) found that think-alouds were as effective as Directed Reading/Thinking Activities in teaching the skill of comprehension monitoring. In addition, students who performed the think-aloud strategy demonstrated more depth of comprehension-monitoring abilities. This research suggests that think-alouds are an important cooperative study strategy for teaching metacognition.

ACTIVITY 11.11 Think-Aloud Checklist

How Am I Doing on Think-Alouds?

	Not Often	*Sometimes*	*Often*	*Always*
Made predictions				
Formed mind pictures				
Used comparisons (*this* is like *that*)				
Found problems				
Used fix-ups				

Cooperative Reading Activity

Opitz (1992) describes a strategy for emphasizing cooperative study called cooperative reading activity (CRA), which he offers as an alternative to ability grouping. It entails locating a reading selection and breaking it into sections, having students individually read and identify important points of a particular section, and forming groups in which students who have read the same section come to an agreement on essential points. Each group, in turn, is expected to share its findings with the rest of the class. Opitz suggests the following steps for constructing a CRA:

1. Choose selections that are already divided by headings into sections roughly equal in length. A selection with an interesting introduction is helpful.
2. Count the sections of the selection and determine the number of students in each group. Generally, groups of four are ideal.
3. Prepare copies of the text you will use for the CRA. Prepare enough copies so that each group member will have a cut-and-paste version of the proper section and a card with the section heading, which will be used to assign students to groups.
4. Design a form that readers can use to record important information learned from the reading (see Activity 11.12 for an example from high school statistics).

To carry out a CRA, the research suggests that students first read their section and record important concepts. When students finish reading and completing their record sheets, they get into groups and each person reads the important points out loud from his or her record sheet. After everyone has a turn, each group makes a list of important details, using a marker on a piece of chart paper. If details are similar, students still write them on the group list. Then other details that students feel are important are added. Students must come to an agreement before a detail goes on the list.

When the work is completed, each group in turn reads its list to the class. Students are held accountable for all the information presented. Lists are then posted for all to see. In this manner, the groups construct cooperatively the essential meanings of the textbook.

Interactive Guide

Wood (Wood, Lapp, & Flood, 1992; Wood, 1992) offers the interactive guide as an effective solution for teachers who find that groups of students within a class need additional help with a difficult reading passage. The interactive reading guide allows for a combination of individual, paired, and small-group activity throughout a learning task. According to Wood, such a guide is based on two assumptions: (1) Students need differing amounts of time to complete a task. (2) Sometimes the best way for students to learn a subject is through interacting with other students.

ACTIVITY 11.12 Individual Record Sheet for a Cooperative Reading Activity in High School Statistics

NAME Susan

SECTION Numerical measures of variability

Important Information:

The variability is the spread of the data set.

Knowing variability can help us visualize the shape of a data set. Also we can know its extreme values.

You need a measure of variability as well as a measure of central tendency to describe a data set.

After teachers "walk step by step" through the use of the guide, students are given group assignments and are asked to work portions of the guide individually, in pairs, in small groups, and with the class as a whole. The teacher may use the guide with the whole class or with a portion of the class that needs a slower pace on a particular phase of the lesson. Activity 11.13 provides an example of an interactive reading guide used in mathematics.

Cooperative Graphing

Another excellent activity for teaching cooperative study can be termed cooperative graphing. Students work in groups to rate the importance of concepts in a chapter; the ratings appear in the form of a graph. In the second part of the lesson, students work cooperatively to justify their ratings.

Teachers can construct study guides for this cooperative graphing exercise such as the one shown in Activity 11.14. The activity can be modified for English classes or whenever story structure is being studied by changing the "most important–least important" continuum of the graph to "most liked–least liked" to enable students to rate how they empathized with characters in the story. This is an excellent activity for teaching both cooperative study and graphing.

ACTIVITY 11.13 Interactive Reading Guide: Mathematics

Work individually

Work in groups

Work in pairs

Work as a whole class

Factoring

1. Discuss instructions for each set of problems pp. 179–180.
2. Review important vocabulary; check for inclusion in notes.
3. Work problems 9 & 10, p. 179.
4. Work problems 21 & 22, p. 180.
5. Complete problems 1–4. Discuss which factor is needed.
6. Complete problems 5–8. Compare with group and discuss results.
7. Continue working problems 11–20. Check with other group members for accuracy.
8. Work even problems 24–42. If disagreement occurs, first check g.c.f., then verify by distribution.
9. Question-and-answer time for general concerns. Time for extension problems.

Developed by Cheryl Keeton; adapted from Wood (1992).

Other Activities That Involve Cooperation

In Chapter 7 we introduced the activity TRIP (Think/Reflect in Pairs) as a way to help students think reflectively and review before a test. Activity 11.15 shows a TRIP card developed for the study of Shakespeare's *Othello*; students must work cooperatively in pairs to think reflectively, work together, practice writing, and hear each other's views about the play.

In Chapter 10 we described note-taking procedures. Cooperative group work is very helpful for teaching two-column note taking. After students record and reduce their notes, the teacher has students form pairs or small groups to compare their reductions. By discussing cooperatively what reduction terms each person in a group decided on, all group members learn from each other not only about the process of reducing notes but also about the material in the notes.

A physics teacher who wished to engage his students in discovery through group work devised an activity he calls "The Shover and the Shovee" (see Activity 11.16). The activity begins with students organizing themselves into groups of three; two people are "shovers" and one is the "shovee." One of the shovers gently pushes the shovee toward a wall. The students are then asked in which way the shovee went, which is toward the wall. The vector (arrow) represents this motion as drawn on the chalkboard. The second shover now pushes the shovee toward a different wall. Again, direction is established and the vector drawn. Now both shovers gently push the shovee toward their respective walls, and this additional information is added to the chalkboard drawing. Now, students are asked what the effect of the shovers pushing with different relative

ACTIVITY 11.14 Cooperative Graphing Guide: Accounting

Cost Factors That Influence Decisions

Part I. Make a graph of how important the following concepts are, from most important to least important. An example is done for you.

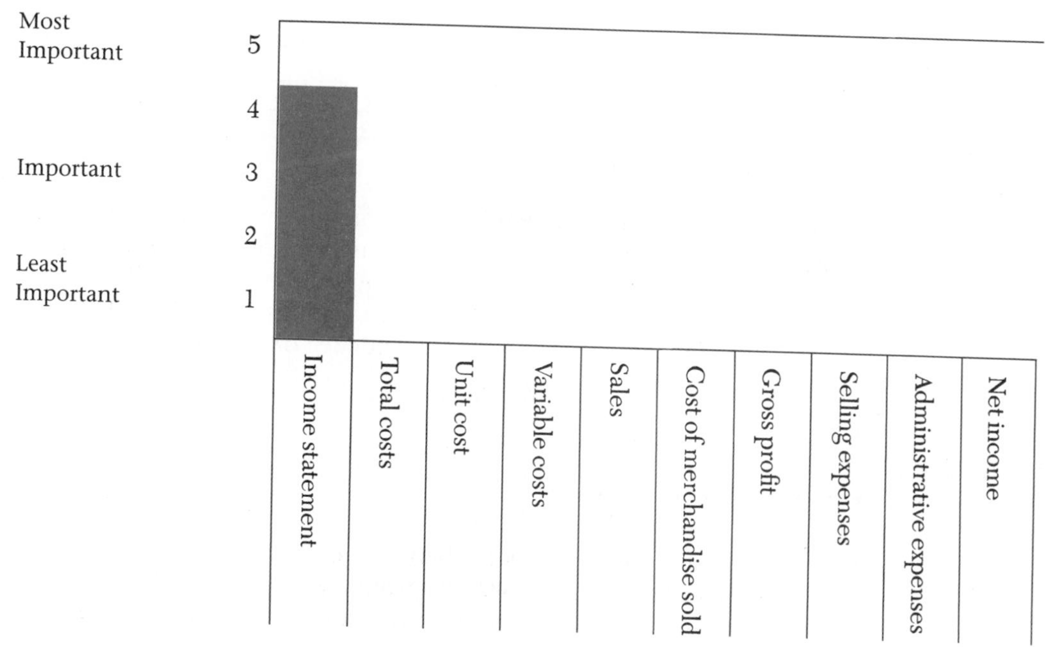

(continued) ➤

continued

Part II. Please work in small groups to justify your answers.

I gave ______________________________ an importance of 5 (most important) because ______________________________
____
______________________________.

I gave ______________________________ an importance of ____________ because ______________________________
____
______________________________.

I gave ______________________________ an importance of ____________ because ______________________________
____
______________________________.

I gave ______________________________ an importance of ____________ because ______________________________
____
______________________________.

I gave ______________________________ an importance of ____________ because ______________________________
____
______________________________.

I gave ______________________________ an importance of ____________ because ______________________________
____
______________________________.

I gave ______________________________ an importance of ____________ because ______________________________
____
______________________________.

I gave ______________________________ an importance of ____________ because ______________________________
____
______________________________.

I gave ______________________________ an importance of ____________ because ______________________________
____
______________________________.

I gave ______________________________ an importance of ____________ because ______________________________
____
______________________________.

velocities would be. Various combinations are illustrated. Last, shovers experiment with the time it takes to go from a particular point to one wall while gently shoving the shovee at different speeds toward the second wall. They can see by doing that the time to go from the starting point to the wall will be the same in each case, thus illustrating the independence of perpendicular vectors. Activity 11.16 shows what would be drawn on the chalkboard.

Listening

Listening is a study skill that can enhance learning in any classroom. Listening is a prerequisite for taking good notes from an oral presentation. Gold (1981) describes the directed listening technique as a strategy for motivating and guiding students to improve listening. Teachers motivate students before the lesson

ACTIVITY 11.15 TRIP Cards for *Othello*

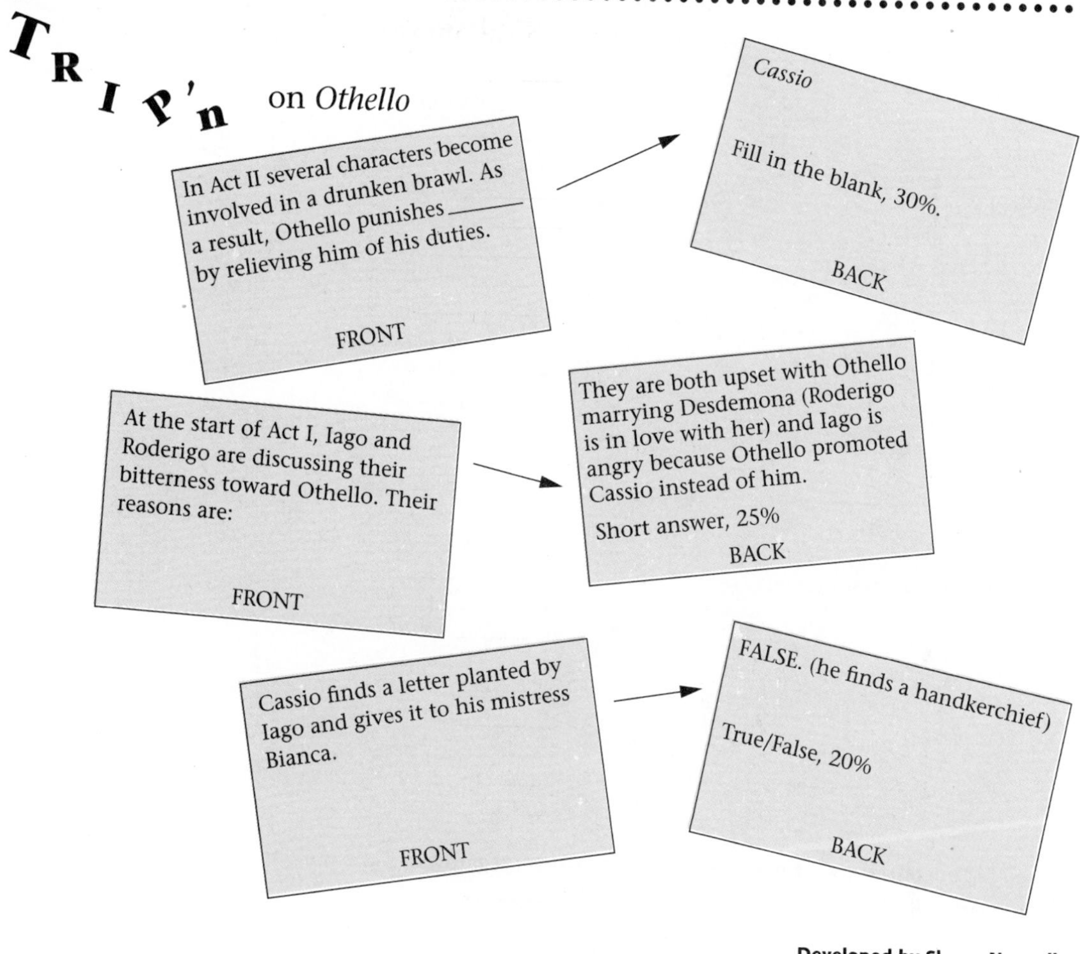
TRIP'n on Othello
In Act II several characters become involved in a drunken brawl. As a result, Othello punishes ______ by relieving him of his duties.
FRONT
Cassio
Fill in the blank, 30%.
BACK
At the start of Act I, Iago and Roderigo are discussing their bitterness toward Othello. Their reasons are:
FRONT
They are both upset with Othello marrying Desdemona (Roderigo is in love with her) and Iago is angry because Othello promoted Cassio instead of him.
Short answer, 25%
BACK
Cassio finds a letter planted by Iago and gives it to his mistress Bianca.
FRONT
FALSE. (he finds a handkerchief)
True/False, 20%
BACK

Developed by Shawn Nunnally.

by asking them to listen for certain information in the lecture or in the oral reading. In this prelecture discussion phase, students brainstorm areas of interest and questions to be answered. Teachers then deliver a lecture or read to the students portions of a chapter from a textbook. In this way, students are trained to know what they must listen for and what they are expected to learn from listening.

As a variation, listening guides, similar to the extended anticipation guides explained earlier in this chapter, can be constructed to point to parts of the lecture or oral reading that need to be emphasized. In this manner, students are taught to listen more carefully for details and key points. Through such an active listening strategy, even primary students can be trained to be better listeners.

Alvermann (1987a) developed a strategy called listen-read-discuss (LRD). With this technique, the teacher first lectures on a selected portion of material.

ACTIVITY 11.16 Discovery Through Group Work in Physics

The Shover and the Shovee

[Step 1] Shover #1

[Step 2] Shover #2

[Step 3]

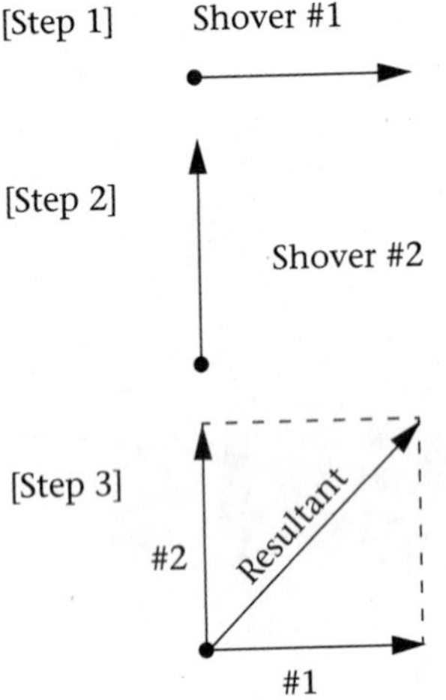

[Step 4] Various combinations

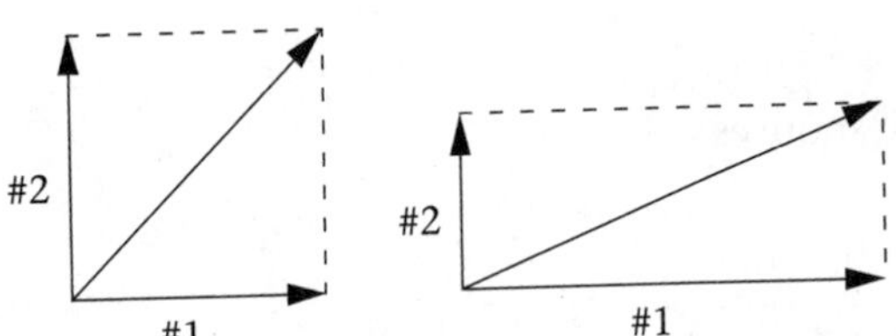

[Step 5] For constant #2, time to wall doesn't change, regardless of the magnitude of #1

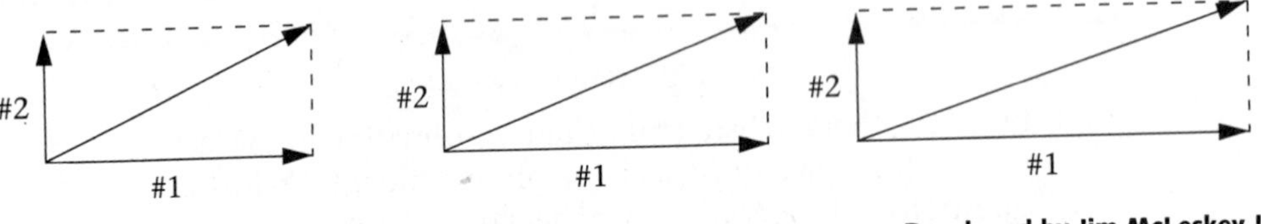

Developed by Jim McLeskey Jr.

Students then read that portion with the purpose of comparing lecture and written content. Afterward, students and teacher discuss the lecture and reading. LRD works best to promote discussion if the material is well organized.

The student listening activity (SLA) (Choate & Rakes, 1987) is another technique for improving listening skills. In using this strategy, the teacher first discusses concepts in the material and sets a clear purpose for listening, then reads aloud, interspersing several prediction cues with the reading. Finally, the teacher questions students about what they heard, using three levels of questions: factual, inferential, and applied.

Another technique, "First Step to Note Taking," also promotes listening and purpose setting. One result of this technique is that it offers practice in group note-taking strategies. Thus "First Step to Note Taking" is a listening activity, a note-taking activity, and a cooperative grouping activity. The activity can be modified for teacher-based instruction or for an independent student learning experience, depending on the ages of students. The activity consists of five steps:

1. Either the teacher or a student defines a listening purpose. If, for instance, the student is completing the activity for independent practice, perhaps he or she will listen to the evening news for the purpose of identifying the major stories and two significant details of each story.
2. Listening with a purpose commences. Students might listen to the teacher read, listen to the news on television, or listen to a tape recording, for example. No writing is allowed during the listening.
3. The students react by listing what they heard in relationship to the stated purpose. Responses are now recorded, but no modifications are made.
4. Students listen to the material again, with the list in sight. No writing is allowed during the listening. (If students listened to the evening news, then either a recording of that news broadcast or a late-evening news show would provide an appropriate second listening.)
5. Individually or in small groups, students edit the list—adding, deleting, or modifying information—and organize it into information—a logical pattern. They have now generated notes for study.

Activity 11.17 shows a list generated by students after listening a first and a second time to *All upon a Stone*, by Jean Craighead George (1971).

One-Minute Summary

In this chapter we describe cooperative study strategies that will help students to think and learn. We maintain that by explaining and modeling strategies

ACTIVITY 11.17 Listening Activity: *All upon a Stone*

Listening purpose: Listen to identify all of the creatures you hear about.

Directions: Listen once; then list as many creatures as you can in column 1. Listen a second time, and list any additional creatures in column 2.

Column 1	Column 2
shrimp	*fairy* shrimp
salamander	wood beetle
mole cricket	*other* mole crickets
sow bug	spider
lizard	sponge
ants	lichens
fireflies	
centipede	
snail	
mosquito	
butterfly	
jellyfish	

After you edit these lists, creatures can be grouped by similar characteristics, or put into sequence as they are mentioned in the story.

that foster cooperative study, teachers can show students how to obtain the most from their learning experiences. Cooperative study can enhance retention of content by providing an opportunity for students to practice, under a teacher's guidance, five important categories of learning: rehearsal, elaboration, organizational thinking, comprehension monitoring, and affective thinking. Cooperative study requires an atmosphere of seriousness of purpose, confidence, assistance, and, above all, commitment to disciplined inquiry and study. Cooperative study includes oral cooperative study, written cooperative study, and visual cooperative study. We also stress the importance of listening as an aid to study. Table 11.1 summarizes specific techniques and indicates when each can be introduced.

End-of-Chapter Activities

Assisting Comprehension

1. Think about and list ways in which you might change the daily operations of your class to incorporate some or all of the techniques described in this chapter.
2. Try specific cooperative study activities in your classes, and evaluate how well they were received by students.

TABLE 11.1 Introducing and Teaching Cooperative Study Skills: A Kindergarten Through Grade 12 Timetable

	K	*1*	*2*	*3*	*4*	*5*	*6*	*7*	*8*	*9*	*10*	*11*	*12*
Grouping	■	■	■	■	■	■	■	■	■	■	■	■	■
Extended anticipation guides				■	■	■	■	■	■	■	■	■	■
About/Point						■	■	■	■	■	■	■	■
Paired readings					■	■	■	■	■	■	■	■	■
Student-generated questions	■	■	■	■	■	■	■	■	■	■	■	■	■
Summarizations			■	■	■	■	■	■	■	■	■	■	■
Jigsaw						■	■	■	■	■	■	■	■
Think-aloud					■	■	■	■	■	■	■	■	■
Cooperative reading activity					■	■	■	■	■	■	■	■	■
Interactive guide				■	■	■	■	■	■	■	■	■	■
Cooperative graphing					■	■	■	■	■	■	■	■	■
Listening	■	■	■	■	■	■	■	■	■	■	■	■	■

Reflecting on Your Reading

1. Ask students to take the "How I Spend My Time" test described in the section on time management. Have students reflect on whether their self-analysis shows that they spend study time wisely both in and out of school. You try taking the test also.
2. Study the graphic organizer shown on the next page, and see whether you can fill in the blanks.

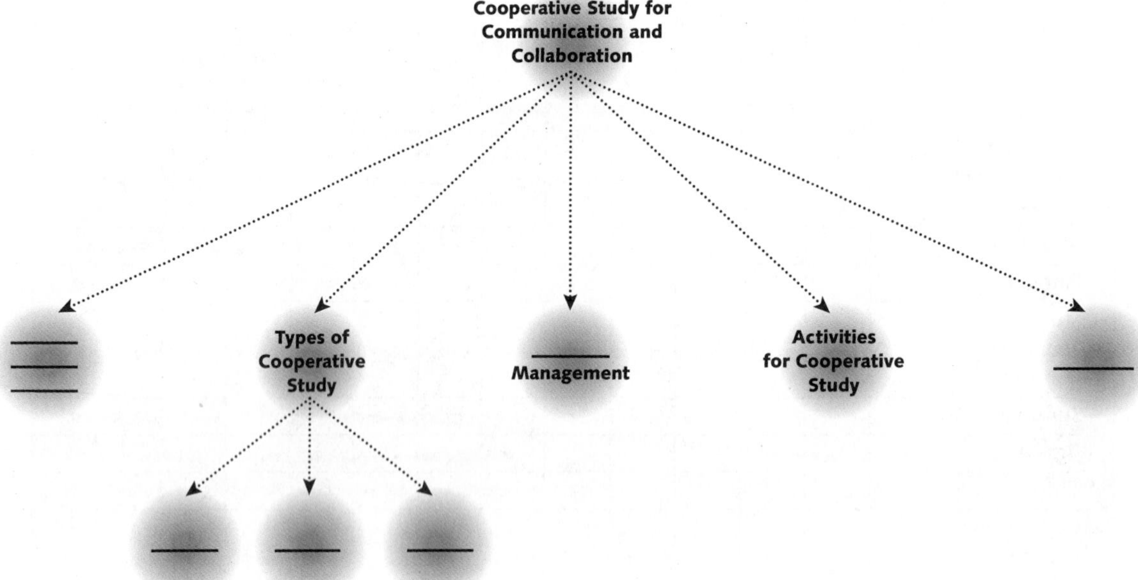
Cooperative Study for Communication and Collaboration
Types of Cooperative Study
Management
Activities for Cooperative Study

CHAPTER 12

Supporting Diverse Learners in Content Classrooms

This is not to pretend that reading is a passive act. On the contrary, it is highly creative, or recreative; itself an art. It must be so. For all the reader has before him is a lot of crooked marks on a piece of paper. From those marks he constructs the work of art.

—Joyce Cary

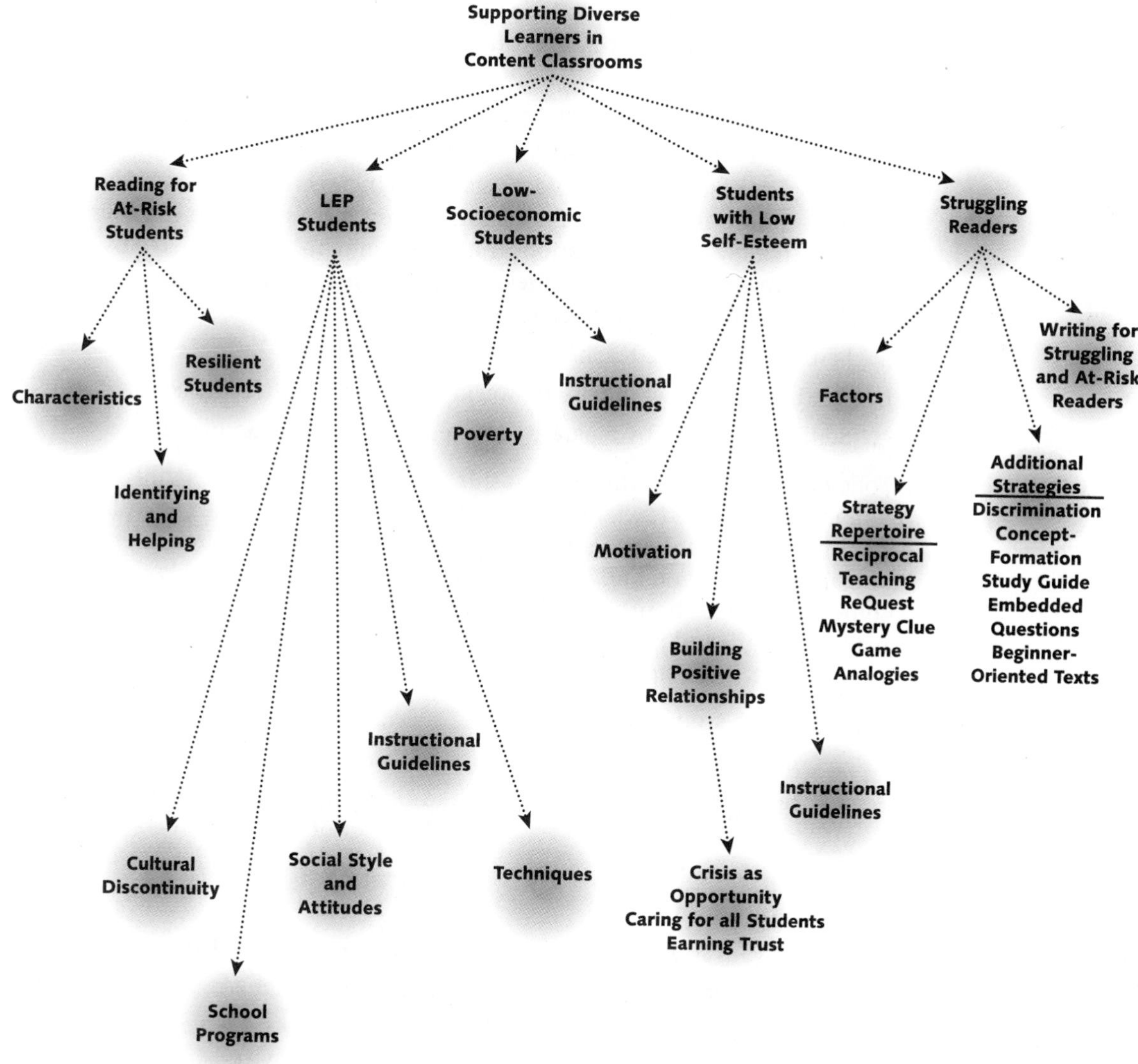

Preparing to Read

1. Here are some thoughts that at-risk students have expressed:

   "I was in line at Hardee's today with my friend Jim, and he yelled that he deserved to go first because he was five levels higher in reading than I was. Everybody heard it."

   "The teacher talked to the whole class on 'present participles'—I'm still not sure what they mean."

   "I gave the teacher a poem I made up just for her, and she told me it was nice but I needed to work harder on my handwriting. My printing wasn't neat enough."

   "I'm never going to get anywhere in school. I'm a failure. I know I'll never be what my parents want me to be. Maybe I should just give up."

   Referring to these examples, practice an imaging exercise in which you try to think as a poor reader or failing student might think. Try to experience in some small way the frustrations that children who are bewildered by constant failure and lack of respect feel every day. Imagine how these students would feel in the following circumstances:

   a. Being berated by a teacher

   b. Getting a failing grade on the weekly quiz for the fifth consecutive week

   c. Being threatened by a parent after receiving a poor report card

2. Following is a list of terms used in this chapter. Some may be familiar to you in a general context, but in this chapter they may be used in unfamiliar ways. Rate your knowledge by placing a plus sign (+) in front of those you are sure that you know, a check mark (✓) in front of those you have some knowledge about, and a zero (0) in front of those you don't know. Be ready to locate and pay special attention to their meanings when they are presented in the chapter.

   ______ at-risk students
   ______ hard-to-reach/hard-to-teach
   ______ resilient students
   ______ immigrants
   ______ refugees
   ______ culture shock
   ______ survivor guilt
   ______ cultural discontinuity
   ______ SLEP
   ______ ESL
   ______ TESOL
   ______ bilingual education
   ______ sheltered content instruction
   ______ group frame
   ______ self-efficacy
   ______ attribution theory
   ______ comprehension monitoring
   ______ fix-up strategies
   ______ reciprocal teaching
   ______ ReQuest

Shoe. Reprinted with permission of Tribune Media Services.

_____ auditory discrimination
_____ visual discrimination
_____ concept-formation study guides

Objectives

As you read this chapter, focus your attention on the following objectives. You will:

1. understand and identify characteristics of at-risk students.
2. understand why teachers have to discourage passive approaches to reading.
3. identify teacher-directed reading strategies for aiding at-risk, low socioeconomic, and low self-esteem learners.
4. identify teacher-directed reading strategies for aiding limited-English-proficiency learners.
5. identify teacher-directed reading strategies for aiding struggling readers.

Reading for At-Risk Students

Within every classroom are students who are diverse in intellectual ability, social and emotional background, language proficiency, racial background, cultural background, and physical attributes. Teachers must be prepared to deal effectively with these individual differences (Au, 1992; Heilman, Blair, & Rupley, 1994; Wassermann, 1999). Some learners are considered to be at-risk in the classroom. Some are new to the English-speaking world. Some who come from low socioeconomic backgrounds find learning more difficult; others have low self-esteem. Some learners struggle with reading; they are not able to keep up with the majority in a content classroom. And some learners may have a combination of these characteristics. In this chapter we explore some of the characteristics of each of these groups of diverse learners and some strategies that can help content teachers to teach them effectively.

The National Assessment of Educational Progress's (NAEP) *The Reading Report Card* (1998) indicates that 40 percent of fourth graders are reading at a basic level or below. When we consider high-poverty schools, 68 percent achieve below the basic level. Current statistics should give us pause: Real wages are down, the incidence of poverty is up, the youthful population is declining, and the proportion of minorities and those for whom English is not the first language is growing. In addition, minorities and those with limited English proficiency are disproportionately represented among the poor and among those who are failed by our school system. Many of these students, failed in many ways by society, will face a lifetime of debilitating poverty unless we, as educators, generate the imagination, will, and resources necessary to educate these at-risk students for independent, productive, and effective lives (Hornbeck, 1988).

At-risk students are students who are in danger of dropping out of school, usually because of educational disadvantages, low socioeconomic status, or underachievement. Although poor minority children may be at greatest risk, many other students in our classrooms also are at risk of school failure. The reasons are varied—among them, poverty, drug and alcohol abuse, crime, teen pregnancy, low self-esteem, ill health, poor school attendance, and welfare dependence.

In 1987, David W. Hornbeck, as president of the Council of Chief State School Officers, declared that the focus of the council would be on the "children and youth of the nation with whom we have historically failed." As a result of the council's work, an important volume was published that drew national attention to the plight of at-risk youth: *School Success for At-Risk Youth*. In the introduction to this volume, Hornbeck writes:

> In our grand experiment in universal free public education in America, we have fashioned a system that works relatively well, especially for those who are white, well-motivated, and from stable middle- to upper-middle-class families. But as students have deviated more and more from that norm, the system has served them less and less well. We sometimes seem to say to them, "We've provided the system. It's not our fault if you don't succeed." Whether that attitude is right or wrong, the critical mass of at-risk youth has grown proportionately so large that we are in some danger of being toppled by our sense of rightness and righteousness. Instead of blaming the students for failing to fit the system, we must design and implement a new structure that provides appropriate educational and related services to those most at risk. (Hornbeck, 1988, p. 5)

Characteristics of At-Risk Students

In Chapter 2 we discussed the four psychological needs—for power, love, freedom, and fun—described by Glasser (1986) in *Control Theory in the Classroom*. At-risk learners are desperate yet unfulfilled, trying to meet these four important affective needs. Often their lives are governed by fear, threat, and negative thinking. They feel helpless and powerless and exhibit an external locus of control (discussed in Chapter 2), feeling that they lack control of their own destiny.

Pellicano (1987) defines at-risk students as "uncommitted to deferred gratification and to school training that correlates with competition, and its reward, achieved status" (p. 47). Pellicano sees at-risk students as "becoming unproductive, underdeveloped, and noncompetitive" (p. 47) in our technological and complex world. He sees at-risk youngsters as not so much "socially disadvantaged" (the label of the 1960s) but rather as economically disadvantaged. Pellicano cites a litany of dropouts, school failures, alcohol and drug abusers, handicapped and poverty-stricken children—all putting the United States "at risk" of becoming a third-rate world power unable to respond to economic world-market forces. He calls for a national policy agenda that "legitimates the school as a mediating structure for those who are powerless to develop their own potential" (p. 49).

Zaragoza (1987) describes at-risk first-graders as children from a low socioeconomic background who often do not speak English, have poor standardized test scores, and perform unsatisfactorily on reading and writing exercises. Many of these students come from the inner city. The students that Pellicano and Zaragoza allude to manifest the poorest reading behaviors and are so fearful and negative that they often cannot be motivated, especially by threats (see Chapter 2). Psychologists tell us that when an organism is threatened, its perception narrows to the source of the threat. This may be why so many poor students "take it out" on the teacher. Feeling threatened, they don't pay attention to coursework, to commands, to anything but how to repay the teacher for all the failure and frustration they feel. Like children who have not matured, at-risk students tend to focus entirely too much on the teacher, thus developing an external locus of control. Therefore, a teacher's attitude toward students and learning can be powerful; in fact, it appears to be a major factor in promoting interested readers (Wigfield & Asher, 1984).

Identifying and Helping At-Risk Students

The current attention on at-risk students can serve a useful purpose by helping educators focus on the importance of identifying and helping these students so that they become successful learners. Care must be taken, however, that the epithet "at risk" is not used as a prediction of failure, resulting in a negative label that perpetuates a self-fulfilling prophecy (Gambrell, 1990). Another term used to describe this population is **hard-to-reach/hard-to-teach**, which also seems to place responsibility on the students. The designation "students who present special challenges" may come closer to expressing the challenge to teachers rather than the deficiencies of students; for the present, the term "at risk" seems to be accepted as the popular terminology.

How do we develop the potential of this type of student? First and foremost, teachers need to be positive and caring enough to realize that behaviors that put these students at risk cannot be changed quickly. At-risk students have acquired bad study habits and negative thinking over an entire lifetime. As Mark Twain once said, "A habit cannot be tossed out the window. It must be coaxed down the stairs a step at a time." Bad behavior and poor reading habits are difficult to break. However, through modeling and guided practice in using techniques such as those listed for good readers in Table 12.1, even the poorest students can change their reading patterns.

We know that virtually all students can learn to read. We also know a great deal about how to succeed with students who are at risk of reading failure. To succeed with these students is not always easy; in some cases, it is extremely difficult. The routes to success for at-risk students, however, are not mysterious (Allington, 1991; Au, 1992; Gambrell, 1990). The work of Allington (1991) and Pal-

TABLE 12.1 Contrasting Good and Poor Readers

Good Readers	*Poor Readers*
Before Reading	
Build up their background knowledge on the subject.	Start reading without thinking about the subject.
Know their purpose for reading.	Do not know why they are reading.
Focus their complete attention on reading.	
During Reading	
Give their complete attention to the reading task.	Do not know whether they understand or do not understand.
Keep a constant check on their own understanding.	Do not monitor their own comprehension.
Monitor their reading comprehension and do it so often that it becomes automatic.	Seldom use any of the fix-up strategies.
Stop only to use a fix-up strategy when they do not understand.	
After Reading	
Decide if they have achieved their goal for reading.	Do not know what they have read.
Evaluate comprehension of what was read.	Do not follow reading with comprehension self-check.
Summarize the major ideas in a graphic organizer.	
Seek additional information from outside sources.	

A dramatic improvement for poor readers results when they are taught to apply intervention strategies to content text.

Orange County, California, Public Schools, 1986. Used with permission.

las, Natriello, and McDill (1989) suggests that improvement in the teaching and learning of at-risk students does not lie in special remedial programs. Rather, we need to make changes in the approaches we use with these students in the regular classroom (Au, 1992).

Hilliard (1988) contends that we already have the knowledge we need to help at-risk students. Hilliard draws the following conclusions from research on programs for these students:

- At-risk students can be taught to perform successfully at demanding academic levels.
- Dramatic positive changes in the academic achievement of at-risk students are possible within a short period of time.
- There is no one way to achieve success with at-risk students.
- There are no absolute critical periods with human beings; it is never too late to learn.
- At-risk students thrive on intellectual challenge, not on low-level remedial work.
- There is no special pedagogy for at-risk students; the pedagogy that works for them is good for all students.

Resilient Students

A study by McMillan and Reed (1994) supports that hypothesis. These authors, after an exhaustive analysis of the literature concerning at-risk students, interviewed 62 students (27 elementary, 16 middle, 19 high school) who had been identified as at-risk but "resilient." **Resilient students** are those who, despite hardships and at-risk factors, bounce back and succeed in school. The research findings indicate six characteristics of resilient students:

1. They use their time well.
2. They have clear, long-term goals.
3. They possess an internal locus of control.
4. They have been positively influenced by teachers or by school expectations, believing they can succeed.
5. They came from dysfunctional homes but did not attribute failure to them.
6. Some one person, usually a teacher or a mother, was significant in helping them.

Figure 12.1 depicts a model of these factors and their influence on resilient at-risk students. In a related article, Reed, McMillan, and McBee (1995), recommend the following:

- using instructional strategies that promote an internal locus of control.
- helping students set long-term goals so they can focus forward rather than on immediate gratification.

FIGURE 12.1

A conceptual model of factors influencing resilient students at risk

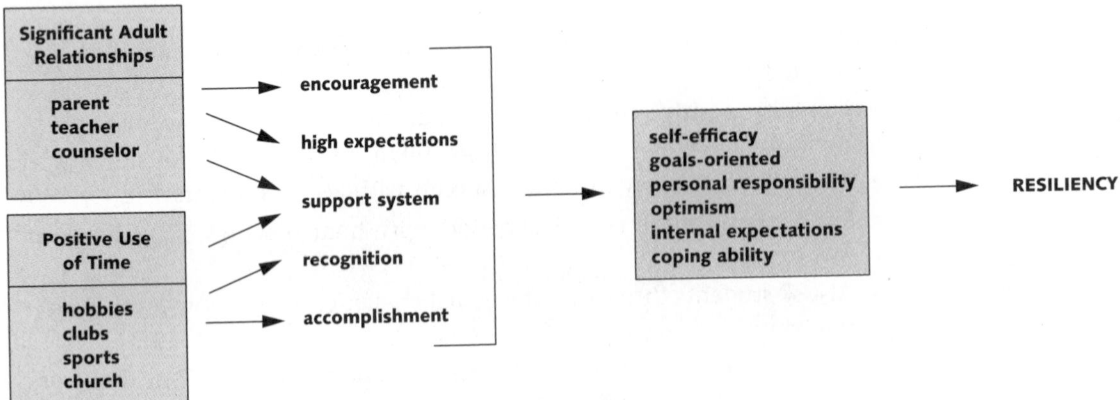

Used with permission of *The Journal of At-Risk Learners*.

- ensuring a positive, supportive school environment with high expectations but not impossible standards.
- encouraging extracurricular activities and required helpfulness, such as volunteer work.
- using cooperative grouping.
- developing strong, positive relationships with these students.

All of the characteristics and problems associated with at-risk youth cannot be adequately dealt with in a chapter such as this one. Physical and mental disabilities, substance abuse, and many other issues are beyond the scope of this chapter. What we cover in this chapter are some of the characteristics associated with at-risk youth and school failure that are critically linked to reading achievement: limited English proficiency (LEP), low socioeconomic environments, low self-esteem, and struggles with reading. These characteristics are not independent of one another. An at-risk student with limited English proficiency may come from a low-socioeconomic environment or suffer from low self-esteem. Rarely is a student at risk of school failure as a result of only one of these characteristics.

We do not claim that simply using the techniques and strategies described in this chapter will solve our nation's problem with at-risk students. The task is arduous and often frustrating for teachers, and no one set of strategies will solve such an overwhelming problem. We do suggest, however, that using the PAR Lesson Framework and the techniques explained in this text, along with much attention to the affective domain of teaching, will be taking a step in the right direction. Certainly, studies such as McMillan and Reed's indicate this is true.

We must begin now to enable this sizable group of failing students to become successful participants in the educational process.

Students with Limited English Proficiency

Public Law 93-380 (enacted in 1974) stipulates that there be provisions for bilingual education in virtually every aspect of the educational process. This law recognizes that students with limited English proficiency have special educational needs and that teachers must take into account the cultural heritage into which the student was born (Harris & Smith, 1986). Persons for whom English is a second language are sometimes designated as non-native speakers of English, or by the abbreviation L2 for second-language speakers (Leki, 1992).

Cultural Discontinuity

Teachers are being called on to work with increasing numbers of students whose first language is not English. Students who left their home countries with families who purposefully chose to move, seeking a different way of life, are **immigrants**. Other families fled their home countries because of unstable and dangerous conditions in their homeland; they might not have wanted to move but left because they were no longer safe in their own countries. They are **refugees**. Both immigrants and refugees may experience a language and cultural environment in the home that differs significantly from the language and culture of the school. The differences may be so pronounced that, for some students, there is serious conflict. A student may be placed in the position of having to choose between the school or home language and culture. According to Reyhner and Garcia (1989), such a choice is counterproductive to the educational development of the student. Rejection of the home background may result in a serious loss of self-esteem, while rejection of the language and culture of the school may result in a serious loss of educational opportunities. This dilemma is called **culture shock**. When learners are refugees, the rejection is compounded by a deep sense of loss and guilt about fleeing, often called **survivor guilt**.

One of our colleagues recounted her experience with culture shock with an example about her writing style. She found changing her writing style from the wordy discourse her Latin American colleagues expected to the concise language expected in the United States extremely confusing and difficult. She resolved this problem by writing two versions of everything she published in both places. However, those not fluent in English would find such a solution impossible. With demographers continuing to predict increasing numbers of immigrant and refugee students from Central and South America, western Europe, and Asia in our classrooms, teachers must consider how their instruction can be modified to meet the special needs of those with limited English proficiency.

Cultural discontinuity is the term that Reyhner and Garcia (1989) use to describe the serious internal conflict brought about by a disparity between the language and culture of the home and the language and culture of the school. Unfortunately, students for whom English is a second language may feel that they have to choose between the language and culture of the home and that of the school. It is important that teachers learn about the different cultures represented in their classrooms and provide instruction that encourages acceptance of the native language and culture while facilitating the learning of English. Equally important is enlisting support from the home. When the total family is involved, cultural discontinuity will not be a severe problem. Shanahan, Mulhern, and Rodriguez-Brown (1995) describe project FLAME, which helps Latino parents support their children's school learning. In fact, if a student must struggle with functioning in two disparate cultures, that of the home and that of the school, the child's literacy learning may actually be impeded (Schmidt, 1995).

School Programs

Currently, two types of programs are prevalent in American schools for **students with limited English proficiency** (**SLEP**)—pupils for whom English is not the first language but who have some degree of proficiency in spoken English so that they can receive reading and writing instruction in English. These programs are usually conducted by a specialist in teaching **English as a Second Language** (**ESL**), or **Teaching English to Speakers of Other Languages** (**TESOL**). When students receive language instruction in special programs, it is important that classroom teachers monitor student progress and make sure that students receive adequate classroom opportunities to develop English, reading, and writing skills (Mason & Au, 1990).

ESL, or TESOL, emphasizes the learning of English exclusively. In this approach, instruction in English progresses from oral skills (listening and speaking) to written skills (reading and writing). The methodology emphasizes "whole-language skills and learner-centered activities stressing the communication of meaning" (Chamot & McKeon, 1984). The ESL/TESOL approach is somewhat similar to that of secondary-school programs for teaching students a second language, although the emphasis is on basic communication. The main goal is to help students attain the language skills needed for success in school as quickly as possible. Most ESL approaches now include not only oral but also reading and writing skills (see the Technology Box). Chamot & O'Malley (1994) describe the cognitive academic language learning approach (CALLA) as a "method of reading instruction for second language learners which provides students with authentic texts that include both content area material and literature to integrate oral- and written-language skills so that students can develop all aspects of academic language and to develop strategic reading and writing through explicit instruction in learning strategies" (p. 94). The goal of ESL classes is to move students to the regular classroom as soon as possible. Many ESL classrooms have learners from 10 or more different countries, and the only common language is English.

Bilingual education provides instruction in both English and the native language in the same classroom. Separate instructional periods are provided,

TECHNOLOGY BOX

Using Computer Programs for Repeated Reading Practice

The use of a computer program for listening, reading, and speaking is far superior to the old Language Masters, which were very limited in amount of material recorded and tape-life—or tape recorders—because locating a specific place on a tape is difficult and constant rewinding causes breakdown of equipment. Instead, consider the following technological options:

The **Rosetta Stone Language Library** is a program that presents basic vocabulary and phrases in English, Russian, German, Spanish, and French. It can be useful in helping English-as-a-second-language speakers from Spanish-speaking, French, Russian, or German countries to hear and see representations of a word or phrase in their native language and in English. The program is interactive, so students can hear and respond to a speaker, then hear themselves and practice as much as they want.

With **Power Point**, teachers can use the audio option to record a selection. Students can then listen numerous times and practice the selection themselves.

With **SoundForge** (PC version) or **SoundEdit** (Mac version), teachers can record and edit a selection. Students can then listen numerous times and practice the selection themselves.

Rosetta Stone Language Library
Fairfield Language Technologies
122 South Main Street, Suite 400
Harrisonburg, VA 22801

Power Point
Microsoft
One Microsoft Way
Redmond, WA 98052

SoundEdit
Macromedia
600 Townsend Street
San Francisco, CA 94103

SoundForge
Sonic Foundry
754 Williamson Street
Madison, WI 53703

one in English and one in the students' native language. In a variation of this approach—transitional bilingual education—bilingual teachers begin instruction in the students' native language and gradually introduce English. A review of the history of bilingual education indicates that it can be very effective (Rothstein, 1998). Of course, it works only where all learners speak a common language and need to learn English as their second language.

Instructional programs for students with limited English proficiency may emphasize English, may emphasize the students' first language, or may give equal attention to both languages. Mason and Au (1990) caution that teachers should realize that bilingual education is a controversial topic. Teachers must be aware of the view of the community and school system concerning bilingual education. In some communities, parents may feel strongly that their children's education should emphasize bilingual competence; in other communities, parents want their children to speak and read only in English.

Teachers of content subjects may find themselves instructing students with limited English proficiency, when the students are included in regular classrooms as well as special classes. These students certainly can learn the same curriculum in language arts, science, and math as native English speakers (Minicucci et al., 1995). By studying eight schools with exemplary programs for language-minority students, Minicucci and her colleagues identified several characteristics of successful instruction:

1. Innovative approaches encouraging students to become independent learners
2. Use of cooperative learning
3. Making parents feel comfortable at the school
4. Intercommunication with teachers, parents, and community
5. "Families" within the school to create strong attachments
6. Innovative uses of time, particularly so students have more learning time
7. Concentrated focus on the goal of learning English

Russell (1995) describes a program called **sheltered content instruction**, which focuses on "teaching subject matter through the principles of second language acquisition" (p. 30). First, the teacher activates students' prior knowledge and introduces new experiences. Second, new concepts and ideas are added. Third, students are encouraged to apply the new knowledge. This method is very similar to the PAR system. Russell explains that sheltered language instruction calls for a balance of top-down (emphasis on prior knowledge, context, and cognition) and bottom-up (emphasis on text and language features) because the needs of the ESL learner are different from those of a proficient user of English. But the focus is on subject matter. Sheltered language instruction might best occur in an ESL classroom rather than in a regular content classroom, but knowing about it may help regular classroom teachers accommodate ESL learners in their classes. Immersion in English without any sheltered instruction is effective only by the third generation of English-as-a-second-language speakers (Rothstein, 1998).

Social Style and Attitudes

From the research of the past decade we know that culture shapes a student's view of the world, behavior, and interpretation of events. More specifically, culture shapes students' assumptions about the reading process and the value of reading (Field & Aebersold, 1990). Culture also influences a student's approach to cognitive tasks, social style, and attitudes. Fillmore (1981) identified and described five categories of cognitive activities that appear to vary substantially in different cultures:

1. *Task attention*—students' willingness to attend to a task over a period of time and their attitude toward the activity
2. *Verbal memory*—students' ability to memorize, recite, or repeat text or narration

3. *Analytical ability*—students' ability to recognize patterns and use them to generate new material
4. *Playfulness*—students' willingness to experiment with and manipulate ideas and materials
5. *Mental flexibility*—students' ability to generate guesses and predictions, consider alternatives, and hypothesize

Teachers need to be aware of cultural differences that may affect a student's approach to cognitive tasks and, in particular, may influence second-language acquisition. Purohit (1998), a teacher of Chinese immigrants, described how her students used science to learn English. They wrote letters expressing their knowledge, used the classroom as a community in which to learn, and started always from their own experiences.

Teachers need to help students use literacy as a way to bridge the culture of the first and second languages. Cook and Gonzales (1995) suggest that ESL students be encouraged to visualize and manipulate literature they read because "second language learners need a social context for both understanding and producing English." Although such activities are not new—visualization through drawing is much like post graphic organizers—they encourage students to use what they already know in making connections to this new language and culture. Chi (1995) comments that second-language learners who regard text as "only a tool to learn that language" (p. 639) rather than as a way to learn about a new culture do not learn as effectively and efficiently. When languages are contrasted, as in contrastive rhetoric studies, they demonstrate that one's culture influences how a language is used (Leki, 1992).

Differences among cultures with respect to social style and attitudes also have implications for reading instruction. A number of studies (Downing, 1973; Downing, Ollila, & Oliver, 1975; Heath, 1986; Schieffelin & Cochran-Smith, 1984) confirm that students from non-school-oriented cultures do not have the same literacy skills as students from school-oriented cultures. The value and utility of literacy in the culture, and particularly in the home environment, influence the development of literacy skills. A study by Lee, Stigler, and Stevenson (1986) found that the superior reading performance of Chinese students in Taiwan, as compared to their American counterparts, was related to social/cultural variables such as time spent in class, amount of homework, and parental attitudes. This study suggests that the Chinese students were better readers because they worked harder and were encouraged and supervised more frequently by parents and teachers. High motivation is the most powerful factor in successful learning of a second language (Leki, 1992).

Instructional Guidelines for Working with Students with Limited English Proficiency

Verplaeste (1998) found that teachers issued more directives and asked fewer and lower-level cognitive questions of ESL students in their content classes. Teachers seemed to underestimate ESL learners' competencies. They were protective but also impatient about waiting for ESL students' responses. To avoid such instructional traps when working with LEP students, teachers should keep the following guidelines in mind:

1. ESL students should be assessed and placed in appropriate programs. Specialists should be available in school districts to perform this kind of assessment.
2. Teachers need to learn as much as possible about the students' language and culture. There is ample evidence that background knowledge is a significant factor in reading comprehension (see Chapters 4 and 5). Teachers should become as knowledgeable as possible about the native cultures of students from other cultures. Field and Aebersold (1990) suggest that the teacher determine answers to the following questions: Is their native culture literate? What is the common method of instruction in their native culture? Are the relatives living in the present home literate in English? Is English spoken in the home? Is reading (in any language) a part of their home activities? It is relatively easy for a teacher to determine answers to these questions by interviewing the student, parents, relatives, or other members of the culture. Using local reference sources such as community groups, libraries, and knowledgeable professionals can also provide insights about other cultures. Culturegrams—brief descriptions of a culture—can be obtained by writing embassies or searching on the Internet.
3. Teaching practices should reflect the knowledge that oral-language ability precedes reading. Students can read what they can say and understand. Accordingly, students should begin reading instruction in their native language, or they should receive instruction that focuses on language development prior to formal reading instruction. Snow, Burns, and Griffin (1998) recommend that "an adequate level of proficiency in spoken English" (p. 10) is necessary before reading instruction begins.
4. Whenever possible, reading materials used for instruction should reflect the background and culture of the student. Teachers can supplement the existing reading materials with literature representative of the native cultures represented in the classroom. Teachers can implement daily teacher read-aloud sessions using trade books that feature minority cultures. Students can be encouraged to contribute proverbs, recipes, and stories from parents and grandparents that can be used as the basis for experience stories (Reyhner & Garcia, 1989).
5. Create learning situations in which students with limited English proficiency can develop a sense of security and acceptance. Language proficiency is developed through oral and written activities that direct the students' attention to significant features of English. Students can gain fluency in English through working with proficient English-speaking peers, learning key phrases for school tasks, and reading predictable texts.

6. Determine the students' concepts related to reading and the reading process. Johns (1986) suggests the following activities to help determine cultural differences in cognitive, social, and attitudinal factors related to reading:

   - Provide opportunities for students to share their perceptions about reading. Interview the students to determine what they think about reading and what they view as relevant and useful.
   - Think about and list the assumptions you make while teaching that students from different cultures might not share or understand.
   - Think about and list specific terminology you use during teaching that students from different cultures might not understand.
   - Audiotape or videotape several of your lessons. Note terms or assumptions that were not on your original lists.
   - Plan instructional strategies to help students from different cultures develop or refine their perceptions of reading and your instructional language.

7. Be conscious of the issues related to working successfully with students from other cultures, without feeling restricted by them. Teachers are in a unique position to positively affect the attitudes of children from differing cultures by adopting methods, materials, and ideas that are linguistically and culturally sympathetic to the students' backgrounds (Cooter, 1990). Field and Aebersold (1990) suggest, "What is most important is that we remain aware of how culture functions as a cognitive filter for all of us, shaping our values and assumptions, the ways we think about reading, and the ways we teach reading" (p. 410).

8. Time is the single greatest factor influencing success for ESL learners (Leki, 1992; Peregoy & Boyle, 1997); they need time to acculturate, to learn language, and to apply that learning to the act of reading. Teachers need to be willing to provide L2 students enough time, get to know them, consult with them often, and adapt their curriculum.

Techniques That Work Well with Limited-English-Proficiency Students

Since 1989 several approaches targeted mainly for use with limited-English-proficiency students have been published. These approaches make use of some of the strategies that we stress in this text, such as cooperative learning, response journals, higher-level thinking skills, use of visuals to teach vocabulary and concepts, directed readings, and use of predictions in reading. Ashworth (1992) concisely presents how listening and speaking, reading, and writing activities can be tailored to the needs of ESL students. By studying second-language readers at the college level, Kamhi-Stein (1998) found that most know about reading strategies but need help to build and use them efficiently.

The **group frame** from the Guided Language Experience model is recommended for reading and writing and is directly applicable to content-area material (Brechtel, 1992). Using this strategy, the teacher takes dictation (pertaining to the content area) from the class and records the information on a chart. This information is used to model revising and editing for the group. The revised dictation is reproduced and used for the reading lesson. Activity 12.1 shows a group frame from an elementary-mathematics lesson on flowcharts and algorithms. In this example, the teacher can begin with the child's native language (in this case, Spanish) or start with English and dictate later in the second language.

A modified anticipation guide (introduced in Chapter 5) can net very positive results. A group of 10 adult ESL students, 7 men and 3 women, from Vietnam, Egypt, Bangladesh, China, El Salvador, Colombia, and Hong Kong, reacted to the statements shown in Activity 12.2. First, the teacher wrote the statements on the chalkboard, to encourage reading in English. Class discussion about the students' opinions, based on their experiences in the United States, was conducted. After discussion, a passage about an American family was read. The students were eager to volunteer information and were interested in finding out about family life in each other's cultures as well as in the United States. The teacher noted that she had fewer requests during the reading time for explanation of vocabulary, and she speculated that coming to the passage with a good idea of the concepts helped the students to use context clues to make

ACTIVITY 12.1 Group Frame: Elementary Mathematics

Dictation from Students	**Dictation from Students**
We use a series of steps to solve a problem.	Usamos una serie de pasos para resolver un problema.
We can make a chart showing how we solved the problem.	Podemos hacer un esquema que nos muestra cómo resoldimos el problema.
The answer to the problem should be at the end of the chart.	La solución del problema debería estar al final del esquema.
Revised Dictation	**Revised Dictation**
A series of steps to solve a problem is called an *algorithm*.	Una serie de pasos para resolver un problema se llama un "algorithm."
The picture of this is called a *flowchart*.	El diagrama se llama un "flowchart."
Shapes of things in the flowchart tell you something.	Las formas de los pasos en el esquema te indican algo.

ACTIVITY 12.2 Modified Anticipation Guide for ESL Adults

________________ **Most marriages last a long time.**

Most students felt that marriages in the United States do not last a long time. Discussion turned to the question "What is a long time?" The students decided it meant a lifetime. We talked about divorce in the United States and how divorce is viewed in other cultures.

________________ **Television is bad for children.**

Although the class generally disagreed with the statement, several students commented that television can be both good and bad for children. We talked about the need for parents to be selective and to monitor programs. Watching TV is one way to learn English.

________________ **Women in America are equal to men in the United States.**

Most students agreed that women in the United States are equal to men. After much laughter, the Vietnamese men commented that American women seem to be superior to American men because they always get to go first!

________________ **Working mothers neglect their children.**

This statement generated the most controversy and debate among the students. The student from Egypt felt that mothers needed to be with children for long times; other students brought up the idea of quality time.

Developed by Karen Curling.

---

sense of unfamiliar vocabulary. This activity engaged ESL students in listening, speaking, and reading in English, and it respected their various cultures.

A vocabulary activity that requires ESL students to work in pairs to write sentences about new words is similar to Capsule Vocabulary. For an ESL example see Chapter 8.

Multitext activities are especially important for ESL learners. When books at many levels and on many topics are provided, ESL learners have opportunities to select, read, reread, and practice (Koskinen et al., 1999; Gee, 1999). Hadaway & Mundy (1999) share how they used picture books about science topics to create compare/contrast maps, poetry, semantic maps, and jot charts with secondary ESL students. Watching videos and movies and then discussing the content and American culture depicted in them is a good way to combine oral and written mediums (Pally, 1998). Sadly, books representing children from other countries are not as available as teachers and students would prefer. Barry's (1998) review indicates that Hispanic representation in literature is sparse.

Although such techniques help content teachers, attitudes and acceptance are absolutely necessary to achieve the results needed. Rosada (1995) muses that

> As we would say in my "south," which is after all north of Patagonia, there remains much more yet to be done. The search for understanding is essential. There, in my world, we also have stereotypes. There we also have mutual responsibility of understanding you. Not all Americans wear happy shirts and Bermuda shorts, nor do all of them walk around with a camera and innocent

eyes, taking pictures of everything. Not everyone thinks that time is money and the decisions in Washington in regard to our politics are not shared by every single North American. Do you know that we call everyone "Yankee," even my beloved friends from Virginia? After all, stereotypes are not only made in the U.S.A. (p. 7)

Students from Low-Socioeconomic Environments

Here are some descriptions of students found in low-socioeconomic, inner-city environments:

> These students are learning-disabled, slow readers who are labeled "at risk." They come from impoverished neighborhoods and score in the low range on standardized tests.
>
> These second-graders range from those unable to read to those reading fluently. Some are at primer level. One child is Attention Deficit Disordered and on medication; two receive counseling from outside sources; another is hyperactive and has many problems stemming from his homelife. There is not much extra money for anything beyond food and basic clothing. The majority are interested in school and eager to learn. They try hard and love to be hugged!
>
> My students are of low socioeconomic status. They are African-Americans ranging in age from 9 to 11 years. They fall in the mid to high range in reading and math on standardized tests. The weak ones are struggling in decoding skills, writing, comprehension, and vocabulary. A high percentage are visual and tactile learners. Their oral language skills are outstanding. They are motivated and positive about learning. The sad thing is that most of them do not get the necessary educational or cultural exposure outside of the classroom.
>
> The majority of these middle-school students are bussed to the school from a high-crime, low-income neighborhood. Ninety-two percent of them receive a free lunch. Forty percent have not passed the state literacy test by the end of sixth grade, the expected pass date. If they do not pass by the end of eighth grade, they will not receive credit for classes taken in high school.

By all accounts far too many students in classrooms today suffer from the effects of living in poverty. The impact of poverty on students' lives is profound, and the consequences are complex. Hornbeck (1988) contends that schools have persistently failed to serve students of poverty adequately.

Poverty and School Achievement

The conditions that exist in the environment of these students puts them at serious risk of school failure. Poverty is particularly associated with low achievement and dropping out of school, for reasons that include the following (Neckerman & Wilson, 1988):

- Poorly educated parents spend less time reading to their children.

- Class or ethnic differences in patterns of language acquisition contribute to difficulties in the early years of schooling.
- As poor children get older, they are much more likely to become teenage parents.
- As poor children get older, they are much more likely to get into trouble with the law or have disciplinary problems in school.

Also, the preconceived notions that some teachers hold about poor students' capacity to learn may result in less effective instruction for them.

Low-Literacy Home Environment

Adams (1990) notes that children raised in high-literacy homes may have experienced more than 1,000 hours of reading and writing activities before they even arrive at school. Many students from low-socioeconomic families come from homes characterized by oral literacy rather than books, magazines, and adults who read. In an oral environment, children are socialized through the use of stories, parables, proverbs, and legends that are committed to memory (Egan, 1987). Although these are rich language experiences, they are not the ones many teachers assume children will possess. According to Reyhner and Garcia (1989), schools often fail to recognize the cultural and linguistic strengths of students from an oral-literacy environment.

Goal Orientation and Low-Socioeconomic Environments

Many students come to school with a future orientation—able to set goals, and to set smaller subgoals in order to reach the larger goals. Some students from low-socioeconomic environments, however, have not been exposed to and have not developed the traditional goal orientation associated with school achievement. These students have had little experience with the type of success in which most teachers believe. According to May (1990), it is important for teachers to be aware that lack of goal orientation does not necessarily mean that these students are lazy. It may simply mean that the teacher must try a variety of means for motivating them. Behavior management techniques that require the teacher and student to establish short-range goals may help these students develop the skills necessary for successful school learning.

Instructional Guidelines for Working with Students from Low-Socioeconomic Environments

Surveys show that even those at the poverty level in American society see education as the key to a better life (Orfield, 1988). The teacher should keep in mind the following guidelines for working with students from low-socioeconomic environments:

1. Teachers must be sensitive to the environmental conditions of the home and community that may influence the students' behavior and achievement. Students from deprived environments tend to have a

poor self-concept and low aspirational levels, to be tardy and absent frequently, to be poorly oriented to school tasks, to display hostility toward school and authorities, and to resist or reject values that are foreign to them (Heilman, Blair, & Rupley, 1986).

2. Teachers should be aware of the impact of poor nutrition and health on learning. The capacity to learn is obviously influenced by nutrition and health. Students without sound diets and with health problems are not likely to be able to concentrate and will lack the feeling of well-being that is essential to learning. Teachers must work with families and social service agencies in the community to diagnose and address the diet and health-care needs of students to improve their capacity to learn (Levin, 1988).
3. Teachers should take action to change students' lives for the better. Rhodes's (1990) admonition, "Don't be a bystander," should be taken to heart by every teacher who works with students who live in a culture of poverty. Richard Rhodes, recipient of the Pulitzer Prize and the National Book Award for his 1987 book *The Making of the Atomic Bomb*, suffered the effects of physical abuse and poverty during early adolescence. In contemplating why he survived with his capacity to love intact, Rhodes comes to the conclusion that he did so because others not only cared but acted. He cites several teachers who took action to help him—in particular, one teacher who saw that he was undernourished and managed to supplement his meager lunch and another who saw that he was poorly clothed and provided clothing.

Teachers should not be bystanders when they see students who suffer from the consequences of poverty. Many resources are available to the teacher to help these students: social service agencies that can address the basic needs of families, including health care, shelter, nutrition, and counseling; youth agencies, such as Big Brothers and Big Sisters, that can offer enrichment programs after school, on weekends, and during summers; adult tutors, particularly senior citizens, who can work with individual students. Teachers should not be passive bystanders in the lives of children of poverty; timely intervention can make a decisive difference in the lives of these students.

Students with Low Self-Esteem

The relationship between self-esteem and learning is stressed continually throughout the current literature on at-risk students. According to Coopersmith (1967), the four basic components of self-esteem are significance, competence, power, and virtue.

Significance is found in the acceptance, attention, and affection of others, particularly significant others. At-risk students may feel rejected and ignored and believe that they do not belong.

Competence is developed as one masters his or her environment. For the student, the school environment is of particular concern. Success in school tasks generates feelings of competence. The at-risk student may experience failure in school tasks, which in turn stifles motivation and promotes feelings of incompetence.

Power resides in the ability to control one's behavior and gain the respect of others. At-risk students may feel helpless and powerless, particularly with respect to school learning, and may feel that their failure cannot be overcome (Dweck, 1975).

Virtue is worthiness, as judged by the values of one's culture and of significant others. Feelings of being worthy and valued are necessary in order for life to be fulfilling. The at-risk student may feel worthless and valueless as a result of school failure. Appearing and behaving somewhat differently from their peers may also make some students feel less worthy or acceptable (Harris & Smith, 1986).

Lack of self-esteem manifests itself most obviously during adolescence, when students are in a state of flux, constantly searching, focusing, and reevaluating themselves. During adolescence students are trying to find a stable image of themselves (Kerr, Nelson, & Lambert, 1987). Unfortunately, by the time some students enter middle school, they have a negative self-image, viewing themselves as helpless and without control over their level of achievement. They behave in ways that cause teachers to label them as unmotivated, immature, uncooperative, and even hostile. Although the behavior of these students may be inappropriate, it is most likely a reflection of their distress at facing failure in the classroom day after day.

Motivation and Self-Esteem

Motivation has been defined as the process of initiating, directing, and sustaining behavior. Motivation is viewed as a drive toward competence that is sustained and augmented by the feelings of efficacy that accompany competent interaction with the environment (Connell & Ryan, 1984). Bandura (1977) popularized the term **self-efficacy**—an individual's belief in her or his own effectiveness to cope with given situations. Self-efficacy determines the degree and quality of effort and the limits of persistence of which an individual is capable.

Self-efficacy is related to a more specific form of motivation: achievement motivation. Achievement motivation is the need to try to reach a goal that is determined by expecting and valuing the successful completion of a task (Wigfield & Asher, 1986). According to Dweck (1985), two kinds of goals are important to achievement motivation: learning goals and performance goals. Learning goals help students strive toward increased competence; performance goals lead students to gain positive and avoid negative judgment.

Attribution theory posits that motivation results from an individual's beliefs regarding the cause or reasons for success and failure. Weiner (1979) identified four categories of attributions: ability, effort, luck, and task difficulty. The principal hypothesis of attribution theorists is that students will be motivated when they attribute their successes and failures to effort rather than ability. With an effort attribution, the student is in control (internal locus of control). If students attribute failure to ability or luck, factors over which they have no control (external locus of control), motivation decreases over time.

Struggling students need a great deal of support as they work toward becoming self-regulated learners. Attribution retraining programs have been developed (McCombs, 1986) that focus on increasing the learner's self-control and competence in learning situations. These training programs focus on the selection of appropriate strategies, knowledge of when and how to use them, monitoring of comprehension, and time and stress management.

Building Positive Relationships

The importance of teachers' building positive relationships with at-risk students cannot be stressed too strongly. Brendtro, Brokenleg, and Bockern (1990) offer guidelines for building relationships that promote self-esteem; the guidelines below are adapted from their work (pp. 62–63).

Building a positive relationship is a process of giving that is typified by caring, knowledge, respect, and responsibility (Fromm, 1956). Caring is real concern for the life and growth of the student. Knowledge is genuine understanding of the students' feelings, even if they are not readily apparent. Respect is the ability to see and appreciate students as they are. Responsibility means being ready to act to meet the needs of the student.

Tracy Kidder (1989) writes in *Among Schoolchildren* about a boy who typifies low self-esteem and an impoverished environment. This fifth-grader attempted to create a science project after much encouragement from his teacher. On the day the projects were due, he "forgot" his, and Chris, his teacher, was furious. She sent him home for it and when he returned, she started to scold him. When she saw that his project was an utter failure, she realized that he had tried but failed because of his lack of resources and low self-image. The teacher then demonstrated respect and responsibility for this troubled student.

Crisis as Opportunity

The struggling students who are most difficult to work with are those who create trouble rather than friendships. These students are often labeled "hard to reach": If one were to wait for them to warm up to the adult, it might never happen. Many effective teachers have long recognized the great hidden potential of turning crisis into opportunity, as in the following story shared by a high school teacher:

> Rob entered first period class ten minutes after the bell, looking disheveled and agitated. I asked for his late pass and he swore and stormed from the room. I stepped into the hall to confront him about his behavior but recalled our discussion of "crisis as opportunity." I called him back and asked simply, "What's wrong, Rob?" "What's wrong!" he exclaimed. "I'm driving to school and my car gets hit. After I get through with the police, I'm late into the building and get stopped by the principal. When I tell him what happened he tells me to get to

> class. Now you send me out of class!" He whirled around starting down to the office. "Where are you going?" I asked. "To get a pass!" he replied. "That's OK, Rob, enough has gone wrong for one day; you're welcome in class." His hostility melted in tears. After a moment he regained his composure, thanked me and we went back in the room. (Brendtro, Brokenleg, & Bockern, 1990, p. 62)

The teacher in this example could easily have responded in a manner that would have alienated this student. Instead, the teacher used this crisis situation as an opportunity for relationship building. When a teacher manages a crisis with sensitivity, the relationship bonds become more secure.

Caring for All Students

Struggling students—students who suffer from low self-esteem, those who are withdrawn, or those from a different economic or cultural background—may not find others lining up to build relationships with them. These are the students who are sometimes ignored or rejected. These students often believe that teachers are uncaring, unfair, and ineffective (Wehlange & Rutter, 1986). Teachers need to take affirmative action to enhance the standing of these students with their peers. Doing this will require that teachers actively focus on identifying the strengths of these at-risk students (Gambrell & Wilson, 1973).

Lipsitz (1995) points out that "we are not being respectful or caring when we fail to teach children to read, compute, and write; nor are we respectful or caring when we hold different expectations for children because of their race, gender, or economic status" (p. 666). Bosworth's (1996) observations indicate that teachers tend to engage in neutral rather than caring interactions with students. Yet, "for many nonwhite students, caring is more concrete and is translated through such activities as 'spending time with someone,' 'sharing,' and 'listening when someone has a problem'" (p. 689).

Earning Trust

Perhaps the central ingredient in building positive and effective relationships is trust. According to Brendtro, Brokenleg, and Bockern (1990), trust between the student and the teacher develops over a period of time in three predictable stages.

Casing In this stage, the student has a need to "check out" the teacher. The student is involved in observing how the teacher behaves, how much power the teacher wields, and how others respond to this adult. All these observations are crucial data to students who may view virtually all teachers and adults as threatening.

Limit Testing During this stage, the student will "test out" interactions with the teacher. A student who is distrustful of the teacher's friendly manner may misbehave or provoke the teacher in order to determine whether this person is really different. In this situation, it is important for the teacher to take a calm but firm approach in order to avoid either "giving in" or confirming the student's view that this adult is really just like all the others and not to be trusted.

Predictability The previous two stages, casing and limit testing, provide a foundation for developing a more secure relationship between the student and the teacher. Consistency is important to building a trusting relationship. In such a relationship, each party—the student and the teacher—knows what to expect from the other. In some situations where trust building is difficult, it may be better for the teacher to simply acknowledge "I know you don't feel you can trust me yet, and that's all right." It takes patience and persistence to build trust, and it is important to remember that trust begets trust.

Guidelines for Working with Students with Low Self-Esteem

Intuition tells us that when students feel better about themselves, they do better in school. Improving the self-esteem of students is a major concern of most teachers, but especially for teachers of at-risk students.

1. Focus on the strengths of students with low self-esteem.
At-risk students typically have low self-esteem because they have not been successful in school. These students, however, may have had many successful experiences outside the classroom. With some discussion and probing, students often identify successful aspects of their lives that they have not recognized before. Spend time having students recall, write about, draw, and share their past achievements. Teachers must plan instruction that allows students with low self-esteem to demonstrate their strengths.

2. Make sure these students are given opportunities to read from materials that are within their reading proficiency level.
Students need to be successful in their reading in order to build positive self-concepts as readers. This means that the material should be familiar enough so that the student can use sense-making strategies. When readers continually have to deal with text that is too difficult, they expend their energy constructing a hazy model of meaning and do not have the opportunity to elaborate on the content or strategies needed to enhance comprehension (Walker, 1990).

3. Provide opportunities for students to engage in cooperative learning.
Research conducted by Johnson and Johnson (1987) and Slavin (1983) and his associates provides evidence that cooperative learning promotes higher self-esteem, greater social acceptance, more friendships, and higher achievement than competitive or individual learning activities. For instance, Forget and Morgan (1995) found that when reading to learn was emphasized in a school-within-a-school setting in working with at-risk youngsters in cooperative situations, attitudes and school attendance improved significantly. Cooperative learning experiences such as those that we described in Chapter 11 are beneficial for all students, but especially for those with low self-esteem. Students can be organized into small groups that are monitored and rewarded for both individual and group accomplishments. Cooperative learning can be used in any content area, as well as for reading and writing lessons and activities. The major principle of cooperative learning is that members of a team can succeed only if all members of the group are successful. Students have a vested interest in ensuring that the other group members learn.

Reading Instruction for Struggling Students

Proficiency in reading stands at the center of academic learning. The student who is struggling in reading avoids reading at all costs. Such students read when instructed to do so, but only to "get through" the assignment. Their view of themselves as helpless and unable to overcome failure results in lack of participation and passive reading at best. In short, these students do not learn how to read to learn.

Hurley (1995) interviewed five sixth-graders identified as low achievers in reading. They expressed anxiety, a perception that teachers are uncaring, and a fear of reading tasks, particularly reading aloud. Hurley suggests that teachers reconsider the purposes they convey for reading, especially for oral versus silent reading. A direct result might be students who become more interested in and exhibit a better attitude toward reading for information. "Educators need a heightened awareness of the possible debilitating and long-term effects that can result from forcing frightened children to perform a difficult and feared task publicly" (p. 11).

Factors to Consider

Vacca and Padak (1990) identified four factors associated with the learned helplessness that typifies many struggling students:

1. At-risk students may lack knowledge of the reading process and, as a result, may have trouble identifying appropriate purposes for reading and resolving comprehension failure. Struggling readers who experience reading difficulty must learn to be aware of the demands of the reading task and learn how to handle these demands. This awareness is important in order for readers to make decisions about the strategies needed either to meet their purposes or to resolve their comprehension difficulties.
2. At-risk readers typically view themselves as poor, ineffective readers. They do not see themselves as competent, proficient readers. This self-view may manifest itself in avoidance behaviors related to reading. These students don't read because they don't believe they will be successful.
3. When students fail to value reading as a source of information and enjoyment, they are at risk of reading failure. Motivation is a central component of the reading comprehension process (Mathewson, 1976). When students are motivated, they will want to pick up materials to read. Encouraging students to choose reading as an activity should be a primary goal of reading instruction. The teacher plays a critical role in motivating students to read. One of the keys to motivating a student to read is a teacher who values reading and is enthusiastic about

sharing a love of reading with the students. If a teacher associates reading with enjoyment, pleasure, and learning, students will be more likely to become voluntary lifelong readers (Wilson & Gambrell, 1988).

4. At-risk readers may lack the ability to monitor their own comprehension. Because they lack experience in constructing meaning, they read words passively instead of actively questioning their understanding (Walker, 1990). **Comprehension monitoring** is the conscious control of one's own level of reading comprehension (Brown, 1980). Comprehension monitoring occurs when readers begin to scrutinize their comprehension processes and actively evaluate and regulate them. In short, comprehension monitoring occurs when readers think about their own comprehension. This awareness of processing allows the reader to take remedial action to rectify comprehension failure. Before readers can independently employ specific strategies to enhance comprehension, they must be aware that their comprehension is less than adequate.

Forgan and Mangrum (1997) remind content teachers that there are many possible causes of reading failure. They use the acronym PLEASE to remind teachers what to consider:

1. **P**hysical factors that might have caused difficulties, such as poor vision, hearing, or health at an early age.
2. **L**anguage problems or delays that cause a child to be behind in development.
3. **E**nvironment—the home or community may not stress literacy or may distract from learning.
4. **A**ptitude may be over- or underestimated, causing lower or higher expectations than are fair.
5. **S**ocioeconomic status may influence the will to learn; interests and attitudes may conflict with learning.
6. **E**ducational factors such as poor educational facilities, teachers without the proper background, or lack of materials.

Strategy Repertoire

Struggling readers have access to a limited number of strategies for enhancing their comprehension of text (Olshavsky, 1975; Paris, 1986). Proficient readers use such strategies deliberately and flexibly, adapting them to fit a variety of reading situations (Duffy & Roehler, 1987). When used for resolving comprehension difficulties, these are often referred to as **fix-up strategies**. When struggling readers encounter difficulty with text, their response may be to "shut down," to stop, to give up because the text is too difficult. The proficient reader, in contrast, is aware of specific strategies—such as visual imagery, self-questioning, and rereading—that can be used to fix up or resolve the comprehension difficulty (see Activity 12.3).

ACTIVITY 12.3 Fix-Up Strategies: Elementary Mathematics

VISUALIZATION

Visualize a tree house that you and your friends would like to build in your backyard or in a nearby woods.
How would you measure it? In yards? In feet? In inches?
Visualize how big it would be and your measuring of it.
Visualize some objects that are one inch long.
Visualize some objects that are one foot long.
Visualize some objects that are one yard long.
Visualize something that is one mile long.

SELF-QUESTIONING

What are the standard units of length?
Why do I need to know them?
Why do we measure in fractions?
What if we couldn't measure in fractions?

The research suggests that proficient readers spontaneously use fix-up strategies, whereas struggling readers do not—even though they can and do use fix-up strategies under teacher direction (Gambrell & Bales, 1986). Kletzein (1991) investigated students' self-reports of strategies when reading different kinds of materials. He found little difference in the strategies used by good and poor readers, but he found that good readers were more flexible and persistent. Poor readers did not seem to know when to use appropriate strategies. In fact, the most important goal of reading instruction for the struggling reader may be to develop the ability to use strategies to enhance comprehension (Winograd & Paris, 1988).

Reciprocal Teaching

Palincsar and Brown (1986) describe a strategy to promote independent learning from a text. In this strategy, called **reciprocal teaching**, students and teachers establish a dialogue and work together in comprehending text. At the heart of reciprocal teaching are four shared goals: prediction, summarization, questioning, and clarification. First, the teacher assigns a paragraph. Next, the teacher summarizes the paragraph and asks students several questions about it. The teacher then clarifies any misconceptions or difficult concepts. Finally, the students predict in writing what will be discussed in the next paragraph or segment. When the next cycle begins, roles are reversed and students become the modelers.

We recommend this strategy because reciprocal teaching uses small segments of reading; thus the struggling reader is not overwhelmed by too much reading. It is a highly structured method that incorporates all of the language arts—listening, writing, reading, and speaking. According to Palincsar and

Brown (1986), this technique succeeds with small and large groups, in peer tutoring, in science instruction, and in teaching listening comprehension.

ReQuest

Manzo (1969) describes a questioning strategy called **ReQuest** that encourages students to ask informed questions. This procedure seems to work especially well in a remedial situation or with very poor readers. The key to this technique is that it requires students to "open up" their thinking, to question and think critically. Also, a very short selection is involved, usually a paragraph, which doesn't overwhelm the slow reader.

With this technique, the teacher and students first read silently a selected portion of the text (usually one or two paragraphs). The students then ask the teacher questions about what they read. The teacher must keep the book closed during this phase. When the students exhaust their questions, the teacher begins asking questions. During this phase, the students must also keep their books closed. The activity can be repeated with other paragraphs, as time allows. The teacher then sets purposes for reading the remainder of the lesson, referring to the questions asked and information received during the ReQuest.

Since Manzo had remedial readers and small groups in mind when designing ReQuest, some modifications for the content class are in order. The teacher probably should select a small but representative portion of text and not try to use ReQuest for a long period of time. The teacher also might want to limit the questioning time. It is likely that students' questions will be mainly literal; the teacher can then concentrate on inferences and applications. If ReQuest is used often, students will readily adapt to asking more sophisticated questions. After focusing on listening, speaking, and reading in this activity, teachers can follow the same steps using written rather than oral questions. Written questions tend to be more intricate than oral questions and will thus enhance students' levels of sophistication with writing as well. A sixth-grade mathematics teacher used ReQuest; her results are reported in Activity 12.4.

Ciardiello (1998) added a training model to ReQuest that encourages formal questioning. In stage one, divergent questions are identified; in stage two, divergent questions are classified; in stage three, divergent questions are generated. The model enhances ReQuest by enabling struggling readers to comprehend at higher levels.

Mystery Clue Game

The mystery clue game, described in Chapter 6, is useful for helping students understand the sequential-listing organizational pattern. The example provided in Activity 12.5 is adapted for first-graders in an inner-city school. The teacher used this activity to help students recognize the sequence of steps in a science experiment about fire and air. The question they were to answer was "Can fire burn without air?" The teacher wrote each step on a different card. When she presented the cards to the students, she said that she had "dropped them and needed to get the cards back in order." She had "found" the first card and placed it at the top of the pile. Their job was to put the rest of the cards in order. She

ACTIVITY 12.4 ReQuest: Middle-School Mathematics

ReQuest was used to introduce the chapter on integers. Students read the first two pages of the chapter, then asked the teacher questions directly pertaining to those pages. The students referred to their pages, but the teacher could not. After two minutes, the teacher had students close their books and she asked questions. The teacher, Ms. Marshall, comments:

> This activity was enjoyed by all—teacher and students. I noticed that even students who don't participate orally did so with "stump the teacher." Students were better able to answer the questions I asked them because they had already listened to the answers I had given to their questions. Overall, comprehension was greatly increased over past reading.

STUDENTS' SAMPLE QUESTIONS

What was the coldest temperature recorded in the United States? (80 below)
What was the name of the weather station? (Prospect Creek Camp)
In what state was the weather station located? (Alaska)
How do you write a negative integer? (-4)

TEACHER'S SAMPLE QUESTIONS

What are some examples other than those on these pages where integers are used? (profit/loss; elevation . . .)
Which number is larger, 0 or -5? (0—it is farther to the right on the number line)
Describe the location of 2 and -2 on the number line. (Positive 2 is two units to the right of 0, and negative 2 is two units to the left of 0.)

Developed by Beverly Marshall.

---

read each card aloud, pointing to the picture and word clues. After the students sequenced the cards, they completed the experiment. For follow-up, students received an ordered copy of the clues, which they cut apart and then pasted in correct sequence again. The teacher found that her students, often distracted, paid attention and participated enthusiastically. She thought that their understanding was greatly enhanced.

Analogies

Analogies (see Chapter 5) are especially helpful to struggling readers, who often require relational (concrete, gestalt, example-oriented, relevant) rather than analytical (abstract, detail and lecture-oriented, definitional) learning experiences (Anderson & Adams, 1992). At-risk readers might be better equipped to understand what they read after hearing analogies such as these:

> When I begin a new year of teaching mathematics, I always draw a little house on the board, starting with a foundation of bricks, and I explain that the foundation in math is being able to do the four basic operations—first with whole numbers, then with decimals, then with fractions. As we get into time, measurement, money, percents, and geometry, having a good foundation is absolutely

ACTIVITY 12.5 Mystery Clue Game for First-Graders

Can a Fire Burn Without Air?

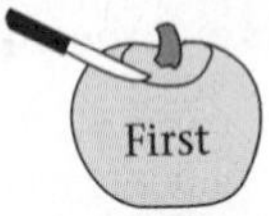

First — Use a knife to cut off the top of the pumpkin.

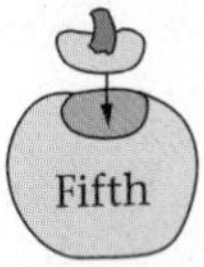

Fifth — Put the top back on the pumpkin.

Third — Put a candle inside the pumpkin.

Then

Relight the candle.

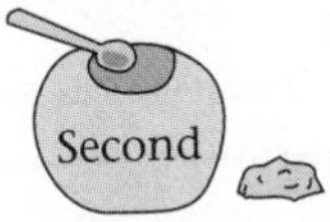

Second — Clean the inside of the pumpkin with a spoon.

Next

Cut eyes, nose, and a mouth in the pumpkin.

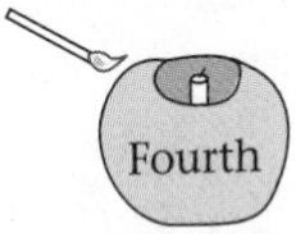

Fourth — Light the candle.

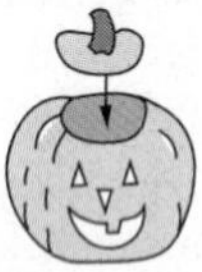

Last

Put the lid back on.

Developed by Megan K. Houston.

necessary in order to do the work. So I tell my students that we cannot have any "loose bricks" or else doing multistep problems, story problems, solving for one or more unknowns, and graphing will be impossible. Students seem to appreciate the foundation analogy and can accept that doing calculations well is as important as grasping the new concept. The teaching of the new concepts must be "laid down" on a solid understanding of old concepts and the ability to apply them.

—Kerry Blum, middle-school mathematics teacher

When a student does not understand new words or does not have any prior knowledge to link with new content, the student is likely to reject the new information. Deoxyribonucleic acid is a very complex molecule made up of different nucleotides linked together and is very difficult to understand. However, Watson and Crick's double helix model of DNA can be taught easily by taking the very basic approach of comparing it to something the students already know. By drawing a picture in students' minds of a circular staircase, and by describing the links of nucleotides as building blocks that can only match up in specific pairs (cytosine to guanine and adenine to thymine), the mystery of the DNA molecule dissolves.

—Diana Freeman, high school biology teacher

Additional Strategies for Struggling Readers and Nonreaders

What can the content-area teacher do with the student who can barely read or who is a nonreader? The teacher can (1) pretend such a student is really not that bad a reader and do nothing, (2) get help from a reading specialist, or (3) assign extra work to help a student in this situation. Ideally, content-area teachers do both (2) and (3). The reading specialist can help with basic skills while aiding the content teacher in adapting assignments for this type of student. Most of the techniques that we describe in this book will help the very poor reader or nonreader. But here we present some techniques that are especially important for the success of such students.

Auditory and Visual Discrimination Guides

Auditory discrimination can be defined as a student's ability to differentiate between sounds, including differences in rhythm, volume, and tone. **Visual discrimination** is a student's ability to perceive similarities and differences in letterlike forms, letters, and words. As children mature and develop, they usually acquire basic auditory and visual discrimination abilities. However, auditory and visual discrimination problems may continue for many children into middle school and even high school. Weaknesses in these two important areas may mean that students will be severely hindered in learning to read.

We suggest that content-area teachers ask reading specialists to evaluate nonreaders on these two important factors. Nonreaders weak in these areas can be helped through auditory and visual discrimination games and activities. For instance, the teacher or another student can call out to the nonreader words similar or alike in beginning, middle, and ending sounds to selected words in the unit. This activity can be done in this manner:

Are the beginning (middle, ending) sounds of these two words alike or different?

zygoma [word in unit], xylophone

Concept-Formation Study Guides

The ability to create superordinate generalizations is a skill often completely lacking in reluctant readers and at-risk learners. **Concept-formation study guides** (Thompson & Morgan, 1976) are excellent motivational tools for such readers. Such guides make use of a fundamental learning operation: the categorization of facts (subordinate concepts) under more inclusive, superordinate concepts. Thompson and Morgan note that "once a key concept has been acquired, we use it at different levels of abstraction, complexity, and generality, depending upon our stage of motivation" (p. 132). The function of this type of study guide is to teach the key concepts of a passage and to provide practice in applying those concepts to more complex and more general situations.

Activities 12.6 and 12.7 present two examples of concept-formation study guides. The first is for elementary students, the second for high school social studies.

Embedded Questions

Weir (1998) encourages the use of questions embedded in reading material to engage struggling readers. When they are confronted with questions during reading, they will be more likely to practice metacognitive strategies. She actually cut up reading material and inserted questions and response slots to keep students' attention while reading. Students began to make more and more elaborate responses as they answered embedded questions. Their test scores

ACTIVITY 12.6 Concept-Formation Study Guide for Elementary Students

I. Read the story. Put an X before each statement you think is true.

____ 1. A person should find out how the neighborhood feels about pets.

____ 2. Some small pets grow into large pets.

____ 3. Someone must care for your pet if you are sick.

____ 4. A kangaroo will not make a good pet.

____ 5. Do not read about a pet before you buy it.

____ 6. It is hard to keep a pet in a small apartment in the city.

II. Put true statements from Part I where they fit below.

Choosing a pet depends on:

Size   Care   Space

III. When you are finished, get together with a classmate and discuss your answers.

ACTIVITY 12.7 Concept-Formation Study Guide: High School Social Studies

The Move to Winter Grasslands

Key Concept: Social transience

Main Idea: Interaction between a people and the physical and social environment that surrounds them influences the way the basic needs of life are met.

Part I

Directions: Think of a family that you know who recently moved. What reasons did this family have for moving? In the chart below, complete a listing of reasons American families and Al'Azab families have for moving from one place to another.

Reasons for Moving

American Families	Bedouin Al'Azab Clan
1. Dad's new job	1. Good grasslands
2.	2.
3.	3.
4.	4.
5.	5.
6.	6.
7.	7.
8.	8.
9.	9.
10.	10.

Part II

From your list in Part I, answer the following questions:

1. Select those items under the "American" list that are related to making a living. Do the same thing for the Al'Azabs. How are the reasons different? Alike?
2. Based on the information you have organized above, make a list of the Al'Azab basic needs of life. Are they different from the American family's basic needs?
3. Based on the information you have organized above, define in your own words what you think *social transience* is.

---

reflected increased comprehension. Embedded questions must be carefully considered to maintain balance and variety. Selections will actually be cut up and pasted back together with questions and response slots—unless a teacher uses a computer and word processing program to create the activity. This is a fix-up activity that is best reserved for struggling readers, but the investment of time does lead to students becoming active, more proficient readers.

Beginner-Oriented Texts

The texts used in content classes are too difficult for many struggling readers. Texts that contain fewer words per sentence and page, simpler words, less metaphoric language, fewer complex sentences, and illustrations that provide context will be more successful (Cole, 1998). Media specialists can help content teachers locate such texts. High-interest/low-readability content-oriented books are also available from a few publishers. They are a good choice because they enable practice with material at the readers' instructional level (Ivey, 1999). Activity 12.8 lists some of these books and publishers.

An alternative to beginner-oriented text is rewriting (see Chapter 4). This requires an investment of time by the teacher, but it tailors the text to the specific content to be taught.

Writing for At-Risk and Struggling Readers

Motivating poor readers and students at risk of failure requires techniques to engage them in both practical and creative writing. First of all, students need to be given adequate time to write. A homework assignment in writing is usually not successful with at-risk students. In the primary and intermediate grades, students will be motivated by pictures that the class can discuss and then use as a

ACTIVITY 12.8 Resources for High-Interest/Low-Readability Content Books

From The Globe Readers' Collection (Globe Fearon, 4350 Equity Drive, Columbus, OH 43216):

Myths and Stories from the Americas
Stories of Adventure and Survival
Eight Plays of U.S. History

From The Reading Success Series (Curriculum Associates, Inc., P.O. Box 2001, North Billerica, MA 01862):

The Inside Story
Sneakers
Burgers
Jeans
Bikes
Skateboards

From Dominie Press, Inc. (1949 Kellogg Avenue, Carlsbad, CA 92008):

Global Views
American Voices
Knowing About Places

The Horn Book Guide, interactive database, reviews more than 29,000 books, searchable by level and topic (Heinemann, 88 Post Road West, P.O. Box 5007, Westport, CT 06881).

basis for a story. The class can discuss characters in a picture, and students can be asked what is happening in the picture, what may be about to happen, and what may have happened in the past. To accompany the picture, the teacher may construct partial sentences for the students to complete, such as these for a picture showing the signing of the Declaration of Independence:

1. The man in the picture is . . .
2. He is signing . . .
3. If I were at the signing, I would . . .
4. The men in the picture look . . .
5. There are no women in the picture because . . .
6. The men will soon be . . .

In addition to practicing with closure, students can be motivated to write by being given a beginning to a story, such as the following:

> The man knew it was not wise to refuse the "mugger," who was young and strong and mean looking. But he wanted to save his pocket watch. That watch is so special; it has a long history in his family. Should he refuse to give it to the thief?

By explaining why they would or would not surrender the pocket watch, students practice composing their own paragraphs.

The purpose of using writing as a means of learning is to help struggling students read and think better through awareness of their own ability to write. Research suggests that semiliterate students may have a writing vocabulary not exceeding 500 words (Tonjes & Zintz, 1981). From an emphasis on paragraphs, teachers eventually can move to research and writing about bigger amounts of information.

Perhaps the most important factor in motivating the writing of slow learners is making certain not to emphasize mechanics too soon. Many failing students have poor handwriting and often are weak in spelling and grammar. Such students get discouraged when teachers find fault and dwell on their inadequacies. Teachers should tell these students that they will be graded on the sincerity and fluency of their efforts. Later, teachers can ask for more clarity in student writing. Patience is the key when teaching students with these limitations.

The goal is to produce students who write correctly and with some style. Remember that motivation comes from following this progression when grading student writing:

Fluency → Clarity → Correctness → Eloquence & Style

At-risk students are generally characterized as passive learners who lack the ability to produce and monitor adequate reading behaviors (Harris & Graham, 1985; Torgensen & Licht, 1983). Yet, as Adler (1982) points out, "genuine learning is active, not passive. It involves the use of mind, not just the memory. It is a process of discovery, in which the student is the main agent, not the teacher" (p. 50). Writing that stresses discovery and active learning represents an excellent way for passive students to become active learners who are responsible for creating their own concepts as they write. Such techniques can aid even children with severely limited capacity to learn.

More than five decades ago, Strauss and Lehtinen (1947) successfully used writing in helping to teach brain-injured children to read. They saw writing as valuable in developing the visual-motor perception and the kinesthetic abilities of these children. Researchers since that time, including Myklebust (1965), Chomsky (1971), Moffett (1979), and Graves (1983), have advocated that writing programs be adopted in the schools. Research also has documented the benefits of teaching the writing process to learning-disabled students and other students with special needs (Barenbaum, 1983; Douglass, 1984; Kerchner & Kistinger, 1984; Radencich, 1985; Roit & McKenzie, 1985).

Zaragoza (1987) lists several fundamental elements of writing that, if followed, can help learning-disabled and at-risk children gain control and become more active and involved in their learning. She says that students need a 30-minute block of "time to write" each day—a period devoted expressly to writing so that they acquire the habit of writing. Zaragoza also calls for children to have considerable freedom in choosing the topic, in order to build self-confidence that what they say is important. The aim of process writing is to foster a feeling of control in the students so that they "learn that the influence of their choices extends beyond their work to the larger classroom environment" (p. 292). She also recommends that a revision be done after the first draft and that teachers edit this revised version. Later, children "publish" their work in the form of student-made books.

According to Zaragoza, the critical element in the writing process is the teacher-student conference. These conferences, which can take place during any phase of the program, allow for one-on-one advising, editing, and sharing. The researcher believes that emphasizing the writing process can help develop in children traits that may keep them from being tagged with an unflattering educational label.

Research shows that poor readers have trouble identifying important ideas in a passage and have trouble using the rules for summarizing (Winograd, 1984). Summary writing can help students by allowing them to reduce their thinking about the reading passage. The teacher can get these students to concentrate on the "big picture," or central theme, instead of getting caught up in minutiae. Zakaluk and Klassen (1992) report that Dan, a remedial ninth-grader labeled as learning disabled, was taught to use check marks while reading so he could identify important points. Then he used the check marks to write headings for an outline. By going back to the text, he found supporting details. Then he was able to write summary paragraphs about what he had learned.

Another practical way to get students to concentrate on the gist of the reading is to start them with the ABOUT/POINT technique, discussed in Chapter 11: "This article on cumulus clouds is about ______ and the points are ______ and ______."

A number of reading professionals and researchers have formulated rules for condensing major ideas in a text (Kintch & Van Dijk, 1978; Brown, Campione, & Day, 1981). Here are six rules that students generally should follow:

1. *Delete unnecessary detail.* With practice, students will become adept at separating important text information from minor facts and trivial statements.
2. *Delete redundant information.* Students make lists and collapse information into broader categories of information as they notice redundancies.
3. *Use blanket terms.* Students should replace lists of smaller items of information with more encompassing terms.
4. *Select topic sentences; summarize paragraphs.* Often paragraphs have easily identifiable topic sentences. Sometimes there is no discernible topic sentence, however, and students have to create their own topic sentence for the summary. Doing this can be very difficult for poor readers. Much practice is needed for these students to feel successful at this difficult step.
5. *Write first draft of summary.* Students need to integrate information by making more general certain topic sentences, key words, and phrases already compiled in steps 1 through 4. The first four steps prepare students to write the first draft of the summary.
6. *Revise summary.* With the help of other students or the teacher, students rework the summary to make it more readable. By doing so, students will get a clearer idea of the major points covered in the material.

Hare and Borchardt (1984) used similar rules in an experimental study with minority high school students. Compared to a control group, which made little progress, the experimental group improved in summary-writing ability as well as in the ability to use the rules to write summaries. It would appear from the results of this study and from our observation in the classroom that summary writing can be used to help all students.

One-Minute Summary

In this chapter we consider several groups of diverse learners: students at risk, students with limited English proficiency, students from low socioeconomic environments, students with low self-esteem, and struggling readers. We suggest that at-risk learners can become successful, as studies of resilient students indicate. The types of intervention suggested for all diverse learners include cooperative grouping, teacher interaction and high expectations, boosting students' confidence and encouraging an internal locus of control, and interesting, systematic, and strategy-based learning. Most of the techniques already presented in this textbook are appropriate with some modifications. Some additional strategies are also suggested.

There is an old saying in education that teachers must work with the haves, the "halves," and the have-nots. You probably agree that one does not have to be a great teacher to teach the haves—students with the motivation to learn and the skills to do work above their grade level. The true art of teaching is in relating to the "halves" and the have-nots. The "halves" are those who have marginal skills to learn a subject but are not motivated to do so. The have-nots usually are not motivated to learn and do not have the necessary thinking, reading, and study skills to be successful. This chapter presents unique strategies for unique individuals—at-risk students who, more than ever in our nation's history, need teacher assistance and empathy to help them become productive citizens in a technological society. The challenge that such students pose for teachers is great, and the rewards may be few. But these special students can and must be reached if our society is to prosper.

End-of-Chapter Activities

Assisting Comprehension

Browse through this textbook, and locate an activity that you think would work well with diverse learners. Describe how you would modify it.

Reflecting on Your Reading

1. Read *Among Schoolchildren* by Tracy Kidder, particularly the chapter entitled "The Science Fair," in which Chris, the teacher, confronts Robert about his failed science project. *Supporting Struggling Readers* by Barbara Walker (1992) gives many practical instructional suggestions. Also, Mary Ashworth's (1992) *First Step on the Longer Path: Becoming an ESL Teacher* will help you understand the ESL learner.
2. Study the post graphic organizer. Can you fill in the blanks?

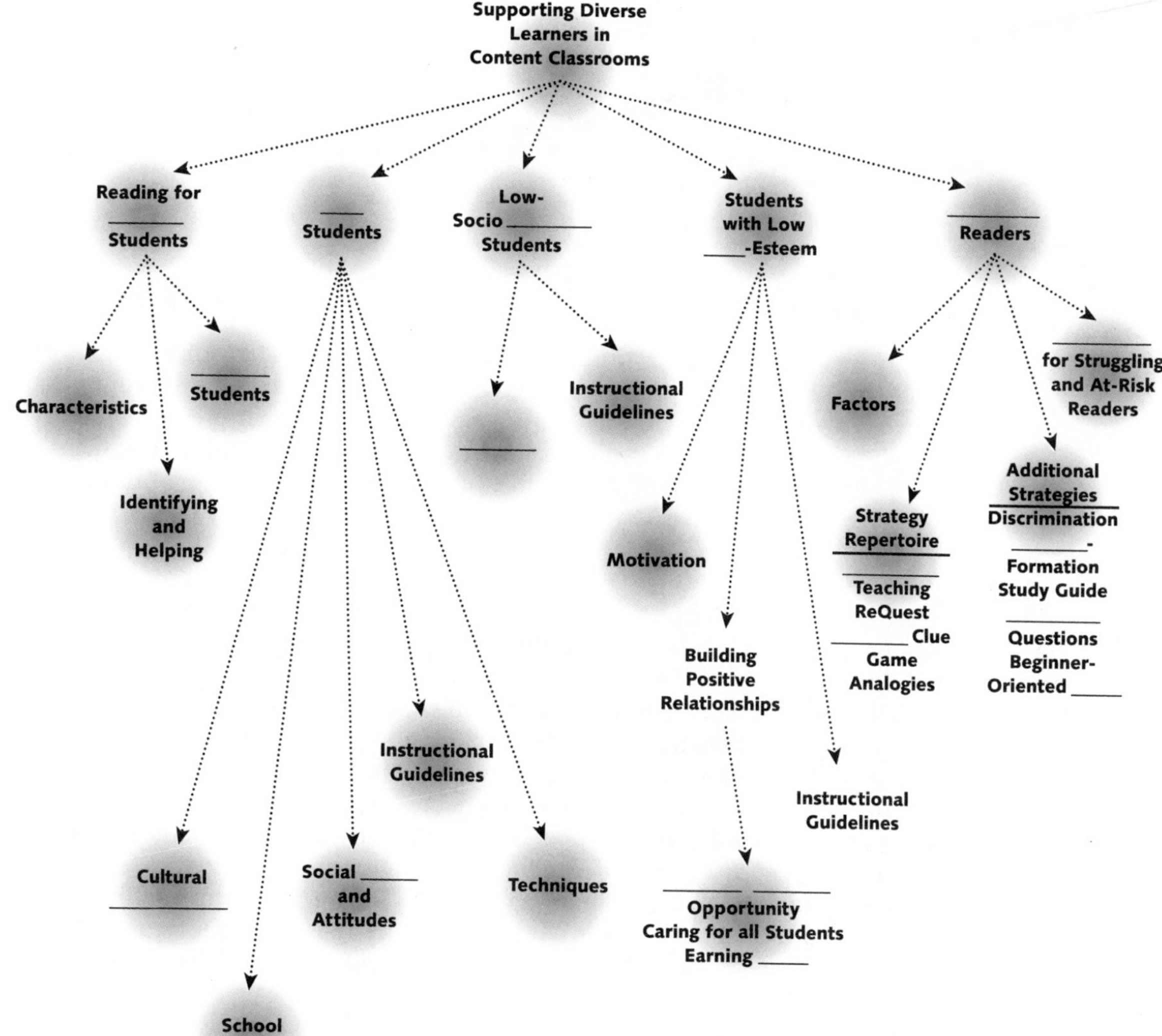
Supporting Diverse Learners in Content Classrooms
Reading for ______ Students
Characteristics
______ Students
Identifying and Helping
____ Students
Cultural ______
School Programs
Social ______ and Attitudes
Instructional Guidelines
Techniques
Low-Socio ______ Students
______
Instructional Guidelines
Students with Low ____-Esteem
Motivation
Building Positive Relationships
______ ______ Opportunity
Caring for all Students
Earning ____
Instructional Guidelines
______ Readers
Factors
Strategy Repertoire
______ Teaching
ReQuest
______ Clue Game
Analogies
______ for Struggling and At-Risk Readers
Additional Strategies
Discrimination
______-Formation Study Guide
______ Questions
Beginner-Oriented ____

APPENDIX A

Assessing Attitudes Toward Reading

Elementary Reading Attitude Survey

Directions for Use

The Elementary Reading Attitude Survey (ERAS) provides a quick indication of student attitudes toward reading. It consists of 20 items and can be administered to an entire classroom in about ten minutes. Each item presents a brief, simply worded statement about reading, followed by four pictures of Garfield. Each pose is designed to depict a different emotional state, ranging from very positive to very negative.

Administration

Begin by telling students that you wish to find out how they feel about reading. Emphasize that this is *not* a test and that there are no "right" answers. Encourage sincerity.

Distribute the survey forms. If you wish to monitor the attitudes of specific students, ask all students to write their names in the space at the top. Hold up a copy of the survey so that the students can see the first page. Point to the picture of Garfield at the far left of the first item. Ask the students to look at this picture on their own survey form. Discuss with them the mood Garfield seems to be in (very happy). Then move to the next picture and again discuss Garfield's mood (this time, a *little* happy). In the same way, move to the third and fourth pictures and talk about Garfield's moods—a little upset and very upset. It is helpful to point out the position of Garfield's *mouth*, especially in the middle two figures.

Explain that together you will read some statements about reading and the students should think about how they feel about each statement. They should then circle the picture of Garfield that is closest to their own feelings. (Emphasize that the students should respond according to their own feelings, not as Garfield might respond!) Read each item aloud slowly and distinctly; then read it a second time while students are thinking. Be sure to read the item *number* and to remind students of page numbers when new pages are reached.

Scoring

To score the survey, count four points for each leftmost (happiest) Garfield circled, three for each slightly smiling Garfield, two for each mildly upset Garfield, and one point for each very upset (rightmost) Garfield. Three scores for each student can be obtained: the total for the first ten items, the total for the second ten, and a composite total. The first half of the survey relates to attitude toward recreational reading; the second half relates to attitude toward academic aspects of reading.

Interpretation

You can interpret scores in two ways. One is to note informally where the score falls in relation to the four nodes of the scale. A total score of 50, for example, would fall about midway on the scale, between the slightly happy and slightly upset figures, therefore indicating a relatively indifferent overall attitude toward reading. The other approach is more formal. It involves converting the raw scores into percentile ranks by means of Table A.1. Be sure to use the norms for the right grade level and to note the column headings (*Rec* = recreational reading; *Aca* = academic reading; *Tot* = total score). If you wish to determine the average percentile rank for your class, average the raw scores first; then use the table to locate the percentile rank corresponding to the raw score mean. Percentile ranks cannot be averaged directly.

Technical Aspects

The Norming Project

To create norms for the interpretation of scores, a large-scale study was conducted in late January, 1989, at which time the survey was administered to 18,138 students in grades 1 through 6. A number of steps were taken to achieve a sample that was sufficiently stratified (that is, reflective of the American population) to allow confident generalizations. Children were drawn from 95 school districts in 38 U.S. states. The number of girls exceeded by only 5 the number of boys. Ethnic distribution of the sample was also close to that of the U.S. population (*Statistical Abstract of the United States*, 1989). The proportion of blacks (9.5%) was within 3 percent of the national proportion, while the proportion of Hispanics (6.2%) was within 2 percent.

Percentile ranks at each grade for both subscales and the full scale are presented in Table A.1. These data can be used to compare individual students' scores with the national sample, and they can be interpreted like achievement-test percentile ranks.

Reliability

Cronbach's alpha, a statistic developed primarily to measure the internal consistency of attitude scales (Cronbach, 1957), was calculated at each grade level for both subscales and for the composite score. These coefficients ranged from .74 to .89 and are presented in Table A.2.

It is interesting that with only two exceptions, coefficients were .80 or higher. These were for the recreational subscale at grades 1 and 2. It is possible that the stability of young children's attitudes toward leisure reading grows with their decoding ability and familiarity with reading as a pastime.

Scoring Sheet

Student name ______________________________

Teacher ______________________________

Grade ______________ Administration date ______________

Scoring guide

4 points	Happiest Garfield
3 points	Slightly smiling Garfield
2 points	Mildly upset Garfield
1 point	Very upset Garfield

Recreational reading	Academic reading
1. _____	11. _____
2. _____	12. _____
3. _____	13. _____
4. _____	14. _____
5. _____	15. _____
6. _____	16. _____
7. _____	17. _____
8. _____	18. _____
9. _____	19. _____
10. _____	20. _____
Raw score: _____	Raw score: _____

Full scale raw score (Recreational + Academic): __________

Percentile ranks		
	Recreational	
	Academic	
	Full scale	

Validity

Evidence of construct validity was gathered by several means. For the recreational subscale, students in the national norming group were asked (a) whether a public library was available to them and (b) whether they currently had a library card. Those to whom libraries were available were separated into two groups (those with and without cards), and their recreational scores were compared. Cardholders had significantly higher ($p < .001$) recreational scores ($M = 30.0$) than noncardholders ($M = 28.9$), evidence of the subscale's validity in that scores varied predictably with an outside criterion.

A second test compared students who presently had books checked out from their school library with students who did not. The comparison was limited to children whose teachers reported not requiring them to check out books. The means of the two groups varied significantly ($p < .001$), and children with books checked out scored higher ($M = 29.2$) than those who had no books checked out ($M = 27.3$).

A further test of the recreational subscale compared students who reported watching an average of less than one hour of television per night with students who reported watching more than two hours per night. The recreational mean for the low televiewing group (31.5) significantly exceeded ($p < .001$) the mean of the heavy televiewing group (28.6). Thus the amount of television watched varied inversely with children's attitudes toward recreational reading.

The validity of the academic subscale was tested by examining the relationship of scores to reading ability. Teachers categorized norm-group children as having low, average, or high overall reading ability. Mean subscale scores of the high-ability readers ($M = 27.7$) significantly exceeded the mean of low-ability readers ($M = 27.0$, $p < .001$), evidence that scores were reflective of how the students truly felt about reading for academic purposes.

The relationship between the subscales was also investigated. It was hypothesized that children's attitudes toward recreational and academic reading would be moderately but not highly correlated. Facility with reading is likely to affect these two areas similarly, resulting in similar attitude scores. Nevertheless, it is easy to imagine children inclined to read for pleasure but disenchanted with assigned reading and children academically engaged but without interest in reading outside school. The intersubscale correlation coefficient was .64, which meant that just 41 percent of the variance in one set of scores could be accounted for by the other. It is reasonable to suggest that the two subscales, while related, also reflect dissimilar factors—a desired outcome.

To tell more precisely whether the traits measured by the survey corresponded to the two subscales, factor analyses were conducted. Both used the unweighted least squares method of extraction and a varimax rotation. The first analysis permitted factors to be identified liberally (using a limit equal to the smallest eigenvalue greater than 1). Three factors were identified. Of the ten items composing the academic subscale, nine loaded predominantly on a single factor while the tenth (item 13) loaded nearly equally on all three factors. A second factor was dominated by seven items of the recreational subscale, while

TABLE A.1 Midyear Percentile Ranks by Grade and Scale

Raw Scr	*Grade 1 Rec Aca Tot*	*Grade 2 Rec Aca Tot*	*Grade 3 Rec Aca Tot*	*Grade 4 Rec Aca Tot*	*Grade 5 Rec Aca Tot*	*Grade 6 Rec Aca Tot*
80	99	99	99	99	99	99
79	95	96	98	99	99	99
78	93	95	97	98	99	99
77	92	94	97	98	99	99
76	90	93	96	97	98	99
75	88	92	95	96	98	99
74	86	90	94	95	97	99
73	84	88	92	94	97	98
72	82	86	91	93	96	98
71	80	84	89	91	95	97
70	78	82	86	89	94	96
69	75	79	84	88	92	95
68	72	77	81	86	91	93
67	69	74	79	83	89	92
66	66	71	76	80	87	90
65	62	69	73	78	84	88
64	59	66	70	75	82	86
63	55	63	67	72	79	84
62	52	60	64	69	76	82
61	49	57	61	66	73	79
60	46	54	58	62	70	76
59	43	51	55	59	67	73
58	40	47	51	56	64	69
57	37	45	48	53	61	66
56	34	41	44	48	57	62
55	31	38	41	45	53	58
54	28	35	38	41	50	55
53	25	32	34	38	46	52
52	22	29	31	35	42	48
51	20	26	28	32	39	44
50	18	23	25	28	36	40
49	15	20	23	26	33	37
48	13	18	20	23	29	33
47	12	15	17	20	26	30
46	10	13	15	18	23	27
45	8	11	13	16	20	25

Raw	*Grade 1*			*Grade 2*			*Grade 3*			*Grade 4*			*Grade 5*			*Grade 6*		
Scr	*Rec*	*Aca*	*Tot*	*Rec*	*Aca*	*Tot*	*Rec*	*Aca*	*Tot*	*Rec*	*Aca*	*Tot*	*Rec*	*Aca*	*Tot*	*Rec*	*Aca*	*Tot*
44			7			9			11			13			17			22
43			6			8			9			12			15			20
42			5			7			8			10			13			17
41			5			6			7			9			12			15
40	99	99	4	99	99	5	99	99	6	99	99	7	99	99	10	99	99	13
39	92	91	3	94	94	4	96	97	5	97	98	6	98	99	9	99	99	13
38	89	88	3	92	92	3	94	95	4	95	97	5	96	98	8	97	99	10
37	86	85	2	88	89	2	90	93	3	92	95	4	94	98	7	95	99	8
36	81	79	2	84	85	2	87	91	2	88	93	3	91	96	6	92	98	7
35	77	75	1	79	81	1	81	88	2	84	90	3	87	95	4	88	97	6
34	72	69	1	74	78	1	75	83	2	78	87	2	82	93	4	83	95	5
33	65	63	1	68	73	1	69	79	1	72	83	2	77	90	3	79	93	4
32	58	58	1	62	67	1	63	74	1	66	79	1	71	86	3	74	91	3
31	52	53	1	56	62	1	57	69	0	60	75	1	65	82	2	69	87	2
30	44	49	1	50	57	0	51	63	0	54	70	1	59	77	1	63	82	2
29	38	44	0	44	51	0	45	58	0	47	64	1	53	71	1	58	78	1
28	32	39	0	37	46	0	38	52	0	41	58	1	48	66	1	51	73	1
27	26	34	0	31	41	0	33	47	0	35	52	1	42	60	1	46	67	1
26	21	30	0	25	37	0	26	41	0	29	46	0	36	54	0	39	60	1
25	17	25	0	20	32	0	21	36	0	23	40	0	30	49	0	34	54	0
24	12	21	0	15	27	0	17	31	0	19	35	0	25	42	0	29	49	0
23	9	18	0	11	23	0	13	26	0	14	29	0	20	37	0	24	42	0
22	7	14	0	8	18	0	9	22	0	11	25	0	16	31	0	19	36	0
21	5	11	0	6	15	0	6	18	0	9	20	0	13	26	0	15	30	0
20	4	9	0	4	11	0	5	14	0	6	16	0	10	21	0	12	24	0
19	2	7		2	8		3	11		5	13		7	17		10	20	
18	2	5		2	6		2	8		3	9		6	13		8	15	
17	1	4		1	5		1	5		2	7		4	9		6	11	
16	1	3		1	3		1	4		2	5		3	6		4	8	
15	0	2		0	2		0	3		1	3		2	4		3	8	
14	0	2		0	1		0	1		1	2		1	2		1	3	
13	0	1		0	1		0	1		0	1		1	2		1	2	
12	0	1		0	0		0	0		0	1		0	1		0	1	
11	0	0		0	0		0	0		0	0		0	0		0	0	
10	0	0		0	0		0	0		0	0		0	0		0	0	

TABLE A.2 Descriptive Statistics and Internal Consistency Measures

		Recreational Subscale				*Academic Subscale*				*Full Scale (Total)*			
Grade	*N*	*M*	*SD*	S_eM	*Alpha*[a]	*M*	*SD*	S_eM	*Alpha*	*M*	*SD*	S_eM	*Alpha*
1	2,518	31.0	5.7	2.9	.74	30.1	6.8	3.0	.81	61.0	11.4	4.1	.87
2	2,974	30.3	5.7	2.7	.78	28.8	6.7	2.9	.81	59.1	11.4	3.9	.88
3	3,151	30.0	5.6	2.5	.80	27.8	6.4	2.8	.81	57.8	10.9	3.8	.88
4	3,679	29.5	5.8	2.4	.83	26.9	6.3	2.6	.83	56.5	11.0	3.6	.89
5	3,374	28.5	6.1	2.3	.86	25.6	6.0	2.5	.82	54.1	10.8	3.6	.89
6	2,442	27.9	6.2	2.2	.87	24.7	5.8	2.5	.81	52.5	10.6	3.5	.89
All	18,138	29.5	5.9	2.5	.82	27.3	6.6	2.7	.83	56.8	11.3	3.7	.89

[a]Cronbach's alpha (Cronbach, 1951).

three of the recreational items (6, 9, and 10) loaded principally on a third factor. These items, however, did load more heavily on the second (recreational) factor than on the first (academic). A second analysis constrained the identification of factors to two. This time, with one exception, all items loaded cleanly on factors associated with the two subscales. The exception was item 13, which could have been interpreted as a recreational item and thus apparently involved a slight ambiguity. Taken together, the factor analyses produced evidence extremely supportive of the claim that the survey's two subscales reflect discrete aspects of reading attitude.

Garfield Revisited: Permission to Use the ERAS

Michael C. McKenna / Georgia Southern University
Dennis J. Kear / Wichita State University

Educators wishing to use the scale should copy and paste the legend on each page of the scale.

Since its appearance, the ERAS has grounded a number of research studies of reading attitudes, and each of these studies has contributed to an understanding of the instrument. The following sources may be useful to educators who have used the ERAS:

Allen, L., Cipielewski, J., & Stanovich, K. E. (1992). Multiple indicators of children's reading habits and attitudes: Construct validity and cognitive correlates. *Journal of Educational Psychology, 84*, 489–503.

Bromley, K., Winters, D., & Schlimmer, K. (1994). Book buddies: Creating enthusiasm for literacy learning. *The Reading Teacher, 47*, 392–399.

Grisham, D. L. (1993, December). *The integrated language arts: Curriculum enactments in whole language and traditional fourth grade classrooms.* Paper presented at the meeting of the National Reading Conference, Charleston, SC.

Kush, J. C., Watkins, M. W., McAleer, M. T., & Edwards, V. A. (1995). One-year stability of the elementary reading attitude survey. *Mid-Western Educational Researcher, 8*, 11–14.

McKenna, M. C., & Kear, D. J. (1990). Measuring attitude towards reading: A new tool for teachers. *The Reading Teacher, 43*, 626–639.

McKenna, M. C., Kear, D. J., & Ellsworth, R. A. (1995). Children's attitudes toward reading: A national survey. *Reading Research Quarterly, 30*:4, 934–956.

McKenna, M. C., Stratton, B. D., & Grindler, M. C. (1992, November). *Social desirability of children's responses to a reading attitude survey.* Paper presented at the meeting of the College Reading Association, St. Louis, MO.

McKenna, M. C., Stratton, B. D., Grindler, M. C., & Jenkins, S. (1995). Differential effects of whole language and traditional instruction on reading attitudes. *Journal of Reading Behavior, 27*, 19–44.

Payne, D. A. (1994, April). *Two-year evaluation of a continuous progress K–3 program.* Paper presented at the meeting of the American Educational Research Association, New Orleans.

Rasinski, T. V., & Linek, W. (1993, November). *Do students in whole language classrooms like reading more than students in traditional classrooms?* Paper presented at the meeting of the College Reading Association, Richmond, VA.

Reinking, D., & Watkins, J. H. (1996). *A formative experiment investigating the use of multimedia book reviews to increase elementary students' independent reading* (Technical Report). Athens, GA: National Reading Research Center.

Stanovich, K. E. (1993). Does reading make you smarter? Literacy and the development of verbal intelligence. In H. Reese (Ed.), *Advances in child development and behavior* (Vol. 24, pp. 133–180). Gilsum, NH: Academic Press.

Whitney, P. (1994). *Influences on grade-five students' decisions to read: An exploratory study of leisure reading behavior.* Unpublished doctoral dissertation, University of British Columbia, Vancouver.

Mikulecky Behavioral Reading Attitude Measure

Norming and Validation Information*

The *Mikulecky Behavioral Reading Attitude Measure* (MBRAM) was developed to be a sound reading-attitudes measure appropriate for use with mature readers. To establish the instrument on sound theoretical foundations, all items were written

*Mikulecky, L. J. *The developing, field testing, and initial norming of a secondary/adult level reading attitude measure that is behaviorally oriented and based on Krathwohl's Taxonomy of the Affective Domain.* Unpublished doctoral dissertation, University of Wisconsin–Madison, 1976.

Mikulecky Behavioral Reading Attitude Measure

Name ______________________ Instructor's Name ______________________

Age __________ Sex __________ School ______________________

Example

You receive a book for a Christmas present. You start the book, but decide to stop halfway through.

VERY UNLIKE ME 1 2 3 (4) 5 VERY LIKE ME

1. You walk into the office of a doctor or dentist and notice that there are magazines set out.

   VERY UNLIKE ME 1 2 3 4 5 VERY LIKE ME

2. People have made jokes about your reading in unusual circumstances or situations.

   VERY UNLIKE ME 1 2 3 4 5 VERY LIKE ME

3. You are in a shopping center you've been to several times when someone asks where books and magazines are sold. You are able to tell the person.

   VERY UNLIKE ME 1 2 3 4 5 VERY LIKE ME

4. You feel very uncomfortable because emergencies have kept you away from reading for a couple of days.

   VERY UNLIKE ME 1 2 3 4 5 VERY LIKE ME

5. You are waiting for a friend in an airport or supermarket and find yourself leafing through the magazines and paperback books.

   VERY UNLIKE ME 1 2 3 4 5 VERY LIKE ME

6. If a group of acquaintances would laugh at you for always being buried in a book, you'd know it's true and wouldn't mind much at all.

   VERY UNLIKE ME 1 2 3 4 5 VERY LIKE ME

7. You are tired of waiting for the dentist, so you start to page through a magazine.

   VERY UNLIKE ME 1 2 3 4 5 VERY LIKE ME

8. People who are regular readers often ask your opinion about new books.

   VERY UNLIKE ME 1 2 3 4 5 VERY LIKE ME

9. One of your first impulses is to "look it up" whenever there is something you don't know or whenever you are going to start something new.

   VERY UNLIKE ME 1 2 3 4 5 VERY LIKE ME

10. Even though you are a very busy person, there is somehow always time for reading.

    VERY UNLIKE ME 1 2 3 4 5 VERY LIKE ME

11. You've finally got some time alone in your favorite chair on a Sunday afternoon. You see something to read and decide to spend a few minutes reading just because you feel like it.

    VERY UNLIKE ME 1 2 3 4 5 VERY LIKE ME

12. You tend to disbelieve and be a little disgusted by people who repeatedly say they don't have time to read.

    VERY UNLIKE ME 1 2 3 4 5 VERY LIKE ME

13. You find yourself giving special books to friends or relatives as gifts.

    VERY UNLIKE ME 1 2 3 4 5 VERY LIKE ME

14. At Christmas time, you look in the display window of a bookstore and find yourself interested in some books and uninterested in others.
VERY UNLIKE ME 1 2 3 4 5 VERY LIKE ME
15. Sometimes you find yourself so excited by a book you try to get friends to read it.
VERY UNLIKE ME 1 2 3 4 5 VERY LIKE ME
16. You've just finished reading a story and settle back for a moment to enjoy and remember what you've just read.
VERY UNLIKE ME 1 2 3 4 5 VERY LIKE ME
17. You *choose* to read nonrequired books and articles fairly regularly (a few times a week).
VERY UNLIKE ME 1 2 3 4 5 VERY LIKE ME
18. Your friends would not be at all surprised to see you buying or borrowing a book.
VERY UNLIKE ME 1 2 3 4 5 VERY LIKE ME
19. You have just gotten comfortably settled in a new city. Among the things you plan to do is check out the library and book stores.
VERY UNLIKE ME 1 2 3 4 5 VERY LIKE ME
20. You've just heard about a good book but haven't been able to find it. Even though you're tired, you look for it in one more book store.
VERY UNLIKE ME 1 2 3 4 5 VERY LIKE ME

with direct reference to the Hovland-Rosenberg tricomponent model of attitude and to the stages of Krathwohl's *Taxonomy of the Affective Domain.* A pool of 40 items, each of which was designed to reflect a specific Krathwohl substage, was reduced to 20 items after considering the evaluations of a panel of judges familiar with Krathwohl's taxonomy and after an item analysis that eliminated all items that correlated at r = .600 or less with the sum of items reflecting the Krathwohl stage appropriate to each item. The hierarchical framework hypothesized by Krathwohl was supported by an analysis of subjects' item responses using a method for Scaling a Simplex developed by Henry Kaiser (*Psychometrika,* 1962). The MBRAM hierarchy gave evidence of a .933 out of a possible 1.000 goodness-of-fit to an ideal hierarchy. This was interpreted as empirical support for the Krathwohl theoretical foundation of the MBRAM.

A graduate-level seminar on Affective Domain Measurement helped survey and refine all items to reflect everyday reading-related behaviors, thereby establishing *face validity*. Correlations of *concurrent validity* ranging from .446 to .770 were established with such formal reading-attitude measures as the Estes Scale, the Dulin-Chester Scale, and the Kennedy-Halinski Reading Attitude Measure. The MBRAM correlated more highly with the Estes Scale and the Dulin-Chester Scale than either of those measures did with the other.

To establish *construct validity,* five informal criteria for reading-attitude (self-reported Liking and Amount of reading, Teacher and Classmate judgment of reading attitude, and Number of books read in six months) were administered along with the MBRAM. All MBRAM correlations with these informal criteria were significant to the $p < .001$ level, and the majority of correlations ranged from .500 to .791. The MBRAM correlated significantly more highly with these informal measures than did the other, formal reading-attitude measures used in the study. Analysis of variance statistically demonstrated the ability of the MBRAM to discriminate subjects of high, average, and low reading-attitude as measured by the informal criteria.

The MBRAM demonstrated a test-retest reliability of .9116.

The MBRAM was administered to 1,750 subjects ranging from seventh grade through college-adult. 1,343 of the subjects were public school students selected from urban, suburban, and rural populations. These subjects were randomly sampled to create a composite, stratified Wisconsin Population Model. Norms for the MBRAM are reported for each grade level in terms of this model and also in terms of urban, suburban, and rural populations. For ease of interpretation of scores, attitude-level scoring bands are provided. No significant differences in scores of urban, suburban, or rural subjects were found from seventh to tenth grade, but rural subjects exhibited slightly higher MBRAM mean scores in the upper grades. Reading-attitude scores decreased slightly in all locations with each year in school. (See Tables A.3 and A.4.)

Stages of Krathwohl's Taxonomy as Reflected by Mikulecky Behavioral Reading Attitude Measure Items

Stage 1 (Attending) of Krathwohl's taxonomy is reflected by items 1, 3, 5, and 7 (see Table A.5). Each item provides from 1 to 5 points. A perfect score at this stage would be 4 items $\times$ 5 points, or 20 points. A student can be said to have attained a stage if he or she has 75 percent of the possible points at that stage. By interpreting items and stages, a deeper understanding of a student's reading attitude is possible.

TABLE A.3 Summary Statistics: Junior High School (Grades 7–9) and Senior High School (Grades 10–12); Urban, Suburban, and Rural Subjects, MBRAM Scores

	Urban				*Suburban*				*Rural*			
Level	*N*	Mean	Range	S.D.	*N*	Mean	Range	S.D.	*N*	Mean	Range	S.D.
Jr	127	55.93	27–90(63)	12.11	276	59.60	25–98(73)	14.33	182	60.81	22–92(70)	13.91
Sr	332	55.24	20–90(70)	12.51	144	58.29	24–95(71)	15.55	190	59.28	29–97(68)	15.17

Attitude Bands for Junior and Senior High School by Location

	Urban		*Suburban*		*Rural*	
Attitude Level	*Jr. High*	*Sr. High*	*Jr. High*	*Sr. High*	*Jr. High*	*Sr. High*
Above average	66–100	62–100	68–100	67–100	69–100	68–100
Average	53–65	49–61	52–67	59–66	54–68	52–67
Below average	20–52	20–48	20–51	20–49	20–53	20–51

TABLE A.4 Adult Norms: Results of Analyses of Variance and Post Hoc Scheffe Tests of Attitude Toward Reading (MBRAM Score) by Each Demographic Variable

All Cases	*N*	*Mean*	*S.D.*	*F-Ratio*	Post Hoc *Test of Significance*
Sex					
M	118	65.02	14.15	33.58	***
F	166	74.47	13.10		
Race					
W	262	70.78	14.36	.43	Not Significant
B	20	67.90	14.22		
O	2	65.50	0		
Education					
Less Than High School	40	66.87	12.13	2.48	*
High School	88	68.69	15.79		
Post High School	93	71.07	14.19		
College	42	73.71	13.34		
Graduate Work	22	77.09	11.13		
Family Income					
Less Than 3,000	13	69.38	12.72	2.79	*
3 – 5,000	17	70.12	13.37		
5 – 10,000	39	71.69	10.76		
10 – 20,000	112	69.26	15.23		
Greater Than 20,000	86	73.85	12.89		
No Response	17	60.94	19.46		
Employment					
Full Time	141	68.38	15.75	3.008	**
Part Time	20	75.45	11.80		
Housewife	49	74.96	11.45		
Unemployed	9	78.67	17.33		
Student	36	67.81	11.57		
Retired	29	71.10	12.26		

*p<.05
**p<.01
***p<.001

From Mikulecky, Shanklin, & Caverly (1979).

TABLE A.5 Stages of Krathwohl's Taxonomy as Reflected by Mikulecky Behavioral Attitude Measure Items

Krathwohl Stages	*Items (1–5 Points Possible Each Item)*	*Criterion Score (75 Percent of Possible Points)*
I. *Attending*: The individual is generally aware of reading and tolerant of it.	1,3,5,7	15 pts.
II. *Responding*: The individual is willing to read under certain circumstances. He or she begins to choose and occasionally enjoy reading.	11,14,16	11 pts.
III. *Valuing*: The individual begins to accept the worth of reading as a value to be preferred and even to extend to others.	13,15,17 18,19,20	23 pts.
IV. *Organization*: For the individual, reading is part of an organized value system and is so habitual that it is almost "instinctive."	9,10,12	11 pts.
V. *Characterization*: For the individual, reading is so much a part of life that both the reader and others see reading as crucial to this person.	2,4,6,8	15 pts.

APPENDIX B

Readability Information

Using the Fry Graph for Short Selections

The Procedure

The Fry graph can be used with selections of less than 100 words if some conversions are made (Forgan & Mangrum, 1985). This technique will be useful to teachers of primary grades, where material is partly visual and partly verbal, or for teachers using newspaper or magazine articles to supplement instruction. It also can help teachers measure the difficulty of word problems in math or of essay questions on tests. The material should contain fewer than 100 words; if the material contains at least 100 words, then the Fry graph can be applied. To use this short-selection version, a teacher should do the following:

1. Count the total number of words.
2. Round *down* to the nearest ten.
3. Refer to the conversion chart (Figure B.1), and identify the conversion number corresponding to the rounded number.
4. Count the number of syllables and sentences in the rounded-down number of words (see steps 1 and 2).

FIGURE B.1

Conversion chart for Fry's graph for selections with fewer than 100 words (From *Teaching Content Area Reading Skills*, 3rd ed., by Harry W. Forgan and Charles T. Mangrum II, copyright © 1985. Merrill Publishing Co., Columbus, OH. Used with permission.)

If the number of words in the selection is:	*Multiply the number of syllables and sentences by:*
30	*3.3*
40	*2.5*
50	*2.0*
60	*1.67*
70	*1.43*
80	*1.25*
90	*1.1*

5. Multiply the number of syllables by the number on the conversion chart; multiply the number of sentences by the number on the conversion chart.
6. Plot the final numbers on the regular Fry graph.

An Example

The following two essay questions have been assessed using this procedure.

	Syllables
1. To what extent do you believe it is possible for people of	17
different races, religions, or political beliefs to live together	21
in harmony? What suggestions can you make to help people	16
become more tolerant?	6
2. It is often said that communism develops fastest in those	16
countries where people do not have the basic necessities	16
of life. Why do you think this/might be possible?	6
60 words *Total*	98

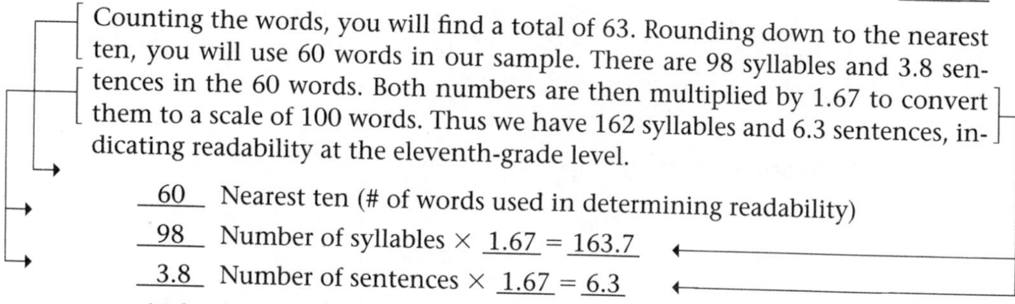

Counting the words, you will find a total of 63. Rounding down to the nearest ten, you will use 60 words in our sample. There are 98 syllables and 3.8 sentences in the 60 words. Both numbers are then multiplied by 1.67 to convert them to a scale of 100 words. Thus we have 162 syllables and 6.3 sentences, indicating readability at the eleventh-grade level.

60 Nearest ten (# of words used in determining readability)
98 Number of syllables × 1.67 = 163.7
3.8 Number of sentences × 1.67 = 6.3
11th Estimate of readability

Using the SMOG Formula

McLaughlin (1969) named his readability formula SMOG as a tribute to another formula—the FOG—and after his birthplace, London, where "smog first appeared" (p. 641). Some have said that SMOG stands for the Simple Measure of Gobbledygook! Although its name is very lighthearted, this formula is a serious solution to the problem of measuring the readability of material that students may have to read on their own.

The SMOG formula is very easy to compute. However, the teacher needs to use a calculator that computes square roots or have a table of square roots handy. To use the SMOG formula, follow these steps:

1. Count three sets of 10 sentences (a total of 30 sentences).
2. Count all words of three or more syllables.
3. Take this number, and determine the nearest perfect square root.

4. Add 3 to this square root.
5. The final number is the readability level.

Differences Between the Fry Graph and the SMOG Formula

The differences between the Fry graph and the SMOG formula are important to note. Each formula is based on a different premise, so the readability scores must be read differently. The Fry formula measures the readability of material used in an instructional setting. Because the teacher will explain the difficult words and sentences, the score is based on students' understanding 65 to 75 percent of the material at a given grade level. The SMOG formula is intended to measure the readability of material that a teacher will not be teaching. Perhaps it is material that the teacher has suggested a student use independently. Because the teacher will not be explaining the difficult words and sentences, the score is based on students' understanding 90 to 100 percent of the material. If a Fry and a SMOG were calculated on the same material, the Fry score would probably be lower. Table B.1 illustrates the basic differences between these two popular measures of readability.

TABLE B.1 A Comparison of the Fry Graph and the SMOG Readability Formula

Readability Measure	*Provides Readability Score for*	*Teacher Will Be Assisting Instruction?*	*Student is Expected to Comprehend*	*Readability Score May be*	*Apply This Formula When*
Fry	Instructional reading settings	Yes	65–75% of material	Lower*	Teacher will instruct the group using the material being measured
SMOG	Independent reading settings	No	90–100% of material	Higher*	Student will be reading the measured material on her or his own, as in report-writing, homework, etc.

*As measured on the same passage.

APPENDIX C

Vocabulary Building: Prefixes, Suffixes, and Roots

Common Prefixes

Prefix	*Example*	*Meaning*
a-, an-	amoral, anaerobic	not, without, lacking
ab-, a-, abs-	abhor, abscond	away from
ad-, ac-, af-, ag-, al-, an-, ap-, ar-, as-, at-	adhere, approach	toward
ambi-	ambivalence	both
amphi-	amphitheater	on both sides, around
ante-	antebellum	before
anti-	antibiotic	against
auto-	automatic	self
bi-	bisect	two
centi-	century	hundred
circum-	circumstance	around
con-, com-, co-, col-, cor-	correlate, cooperate, collect	with, in association, together
contra-	contradiction	against
de-	descend	away from, out of, separation
dec-, deca-	decade	ten
di-	dicotyledon	two, twice, double
dia-	diameter	through, between, across
dis-	dissatisfied	not
ex-, e-, ef-	evict	out of, from
fore-	foreground	before, front, superior
hemi-	hemisphere	half
hepta-	heptagon	seven
hexa-	hexagon	six
hyper-	hypersensitive	over, above
in-, il-, ir-, im-	invisible, illegal, irregular	not; also means "in" and is used as an intensifier
inter-	interact	between, among
intra-, intro-	introvert	within
kilo-	kilocycle	thousand
milli-	millennium	thousand
mis-	misspell	wrong, not
mono-	monopoly	one
multi-	multitude	many

Prefix	*Example*	*Meaning*
non-	nonsense	not
nona-	nonagon	nine
ob, oc-, of-	obstruct	toward, to, on, over, against
oct-	octagon	eight
omni-	omnipotent	all
pan-	pantheist	all
per-	perceive	through, thoroughly, very
pro-	promote	in favor of, advancing
quadr-	quadrupled	four
quin-	quintuplet	five
re-	reorganize	backward, again
retro-	retrograde	backward
se-	select	apart
semi-	semiannual	half
sept-	septuplet	seven
sex-	sextant	six
sub-, suc, suf-, sur-, sug-, sus-	supplant	under, below, slightly
super-	supersede	above, beyond
syn-, sym-	synchronize	with, together
tele-	telegraph	distance
tetra-	tetrameter	four
trans-, tra-	traverse	across, beyond, through
tri-	triple	three
ultra-	ultramodern	beyond, farther
un-	unnatural	not
uni-	unilateral	one

Common Suffixes

Suffix	*Example*	*Meaning*
-able, -ible	durable, visible	able
-acy	piracy, privacy	quality, state, office
-age	breakage, orphanage	pertaining to; also a noun-forming suffix
-al	rental, abdominal	adjective- or noun-forming suffix
-ance, -ence	insurance, competence	adjective- or noun-forming suffix
-ant	reliant, servant	adjective- or noun-forming suffix

Suffix	*Example*	*Meaning*
-arium, -orium	aquarium, auditorium	place, instrument
-ary	dictionary, elementary	pertaining to, connected with
-ate	activate, animate	verb-forming suffix
-ation, -ition	creation, condition	combination of *-ate* and *-ion* used for forming nouns
-cle, -icle	corpuscle, denticle	small, diminutive
-esque	picturesque	style, manner, distinctive character
-ferous	coniferous	bearing
-ful	colorful	full of
-fy, -ify	fortify, magnify	to make, to cause to be
-hood	childhood, statehood	station, condition, nature
-ic	democratic, phonic	suffix forming adjectives from nouns
-ism	conservatism, Marxism	used to form nouns denoting action, practice, principles, doctrines
-itis	appendicitis	inflammation, abnormal state or condition
-ity	acidity, familiarity	used to form nouns expressing state or condition
-ive	creative, suggestive	suffix of adjectives expressing tendency, disposition, function
-ize	memorize, modernize	verb suffix
-ment	statement	denotes an action, resulting state, product
-mony	testimony, parsimony	result or condition, denotes action or condition
-oid	ellipsoid	resembling, like
-or	conqueror, generator	one who does something
-ose, -ous	verbose, porous	full of
-osis	hypnosis	denotes action, state, process, or condition
-tude	solitude, altitude	indicates nouns formed from adjectives

Common Roots

Root	*Example*	*Meaning*
ag, act	activate, enact, agile, agency	to do
anthrop	anthropology, anthropomorphic, misanthrope	man
aqua	aquifer, aquatic, aqueous	water
aud	audible, audition, auditorium, audience	to hear
auto	automatic, automation, automaton	self
bene	benefit, benevolent, benign	good
cap, capt, chap	decapitate, capture, captain, chapter	head
ceed, cede, cess	proceed, precedent, cease	to go, yield
chrom	chromatic, chromosome	color
chron	synchronize, chronology, chronic	time
cogn	cognition, recognize, cognitive	to know
corp	corporate, corpulent, corporation	body
cred	credit, incredible, credulous	to believe
dent, dont	orthodontist, dental, dentifrice	tooth
derm	dermatology, epidermis, dermatitis	skin
dic, dict	dictionary, dictate, predict, indict	to say
don, donat	donate, donor, condone, pardon	to give
dox	doxology, paradox	belief
duc	duct, reduce, produce, conduct	to lead in
fac, fic, fy	manufacture, factory, verify	to make, do
fer	transfer, ferry, confer, defer, suffer	to bear

Root	*Example*	*Meaning*
fie	confident, infidel, confide	faith
fluc, flux	fluctuate, fluxion	to flow
graph	graphite, telegraph, phonograph	to write
gress	transgress, congress, egress	to step
ject	deject, rejection, conjecture, trajectory	to throw
loc	local, locate, location, dislocate	place
loq, loc	eloquent, elocution, interlocutor	to speak
mal	malevolent, malapropism, malefactor	bad
manu	manufacture, manuscript, manacle, manual	hand
miso, misa	misanthrope, misogamy	bad
mit, mis	emit, permit, dismissal, omit, missile	to send
morph	morphology, endomorph, metamorphosis	shape
mort	mortician, mortuary, mortify	dead
mov, mot, mob	motivate, motion, motile, remove	to move
neb	nebulous, nebula	cloudy
omni	omnipresent, omniscient, omnipotent	all
path	sympathy, empathic, pathetic	suffering, disease, feeling
ped	pedestrian, pedometer, pedicure	foot
phil	philosophy, philanthropy, philharmonic	love
pod	podiatrist, pseudopod	foot
scrib, script	transcript, prescribe, description	to write

APPENDIX D

Sample PAR Activities

Preparation Activity in Primary Science

Activity developed by Deborah Pendleton.

Activity D.1 Anticipation Guide

Directions: Put a check beside every sentence you think is true.

______ **1.** Cold-blooded animals have cold blood and warm-blooded animals have warm blood.

__✓__ **2.** An amphibian lives part of its life in water and part on land.

__✓__ **3.** All mammals have backbones.

__✓__ **4.** Birds, reptiles, and fish all lay eggs.

__✓__ **5.** All mammals have hair or fur.

__✓__ **6.** Mammals feed their young with mother's milk.

Bibliographic Data: This activity is based on Michael R. Cohen, *Discover Science*, Scott, Foresman, 1989, pp. 32–36.

Audience: The students are a group of 24 third-graders ranging in ages from 7½ to 10 years old at an urban at-risk elementary school. The majority of the students are reading at grade level. After working with the students for the past 10½ weeks, I'm finding that many of my students are "word" readers and comprehending very little of what they are reading. After realizing this, I have begun to work with the students on strategies to increase reading comprehension. Many of the students state that they enjoy reading to "find out" new things. However, very few of the students choose reading as an activity when classroom assignments have been completed.

The majority of the students are well behaved and seem to have a keen desire for learning. They are a very active, hands-on group of students who enjoy talking and sharing ideas. Many of the students have parents who are actively involved in their education and are often in the classroom.

Activity purpose: This activity is designed to prepare the students by building their background for the selected reading with the use of an anticipation guide.

Objectives

1. Students will understand the meanings of the words *anticipate*, *guess*, and *predict*.

2. Students will be able to link their prior knowledge of the subject (what they already know) with new information encountered in the reading selection.

3. By the end of the activity, students will be able to state three facts about animals with backbones.

Procedures

A. Introduction

The activity was introduced by having students refer to their What-I-Know-Activities sheets (which had been completed in a previous activity). The students were directed to read what they had listed under the heading "What I Already Know." A class discussion took place about how reading the science book would help us to increase our knowledge of animals. The class discussed how even if we think we know all there is to know, there's always something else that can be learned, and this is a reason for reading.

B. Development

1. The teacher introduced to students the following words: *anticipate, guess,* and *predict.*
2. Students wrote the words on index cards.
3. Students used dictionaries in cooperative groups to find the meanings of the words.
4. Students and teacher discussed meanings of the words: How are the words alike? How are they different? Do they all mean the same thing?

Today statement: Today we are going to use an anticipation guide to help us predict what we will find in the reading selection, and to find out if what we think we know is true or false about animals with backbones.

C. The teacher passed out the anticipation guide.

1. The teacher explained what an anticipation guide is and how it is used.
2. The teacher created a gamelike atmosphere by encouraging students to be "statement detectives" and see if they could find all the statements on the anticipation guide and to find out if what they think they know is true or false.

D. The teacher read directions and statements with students.

E. Students were encouraged to work independently and answer statements on the anticipation guide.

F. Before the reading, a simple class-graph was made of the responses to the statements.

G. While reading, students were encouraged to refer to the anticipation guide. When they encountered a statement in the reading selection that was similar to a statement on the anticipation guide, they wrote down the page number.

H. After reading the selection, the students referred to their anticipation guide and checked to see if what they thought was true or false changed.

   1. Students and teacher discussed reading selection content and change of statements, if any.

   2. Students and teacher compiled an after-reading graph to evaluate why statements changed after reading.

I. A chart was made with students entitled "What I Thought I Knew Before Reading/What I Found Out After Reading." The chart was a comparison/contrast activity.

J. Students were asked to list three facts on their "Facts About Animals" sheets in their science notebooks.

K. Students responded to end-of-chapter questions using their anticipation guide and QAR strategies.

Summary: The activity was successful. The students put a lot of thought and effort into the activity. By using the anticipation guide, the students were eager to read to find out if their responses to the statements were actually true or false as they had thought. Thus, they eagerly read the material. Throughout the reading selection, students were exclaiming, "I knew that was true!" This indicated to me that the students were actively involved.

I personally felt that the anticipation guide was not a very good one (practice is needed!). When I use an anticipation guide again (and I will!), I will try to make the statements more thought provoking so as to extend the students' thinking prior to reading.

By the end of the lesson, all of the objectives were accomplished. The students were able to use the new vocabulary, and they were able to look at what they thought they knew and what they found out new in the reading selection. The students also were able to add to their animal fact knowledge.

Overall, the anticipation guide proved to be a successful strategy. I also feel the strategy was successful because of the comments the students offered on the activity rating. Much to my surprise, they really zeroed in on why we were using the anticipation guide.

Assistance Activity in Elementary Language Arts

Activity developed by Margaret Brulatour.

Activity D.2 QAR for Fifth-Grade English Classes

Our unit topic is "Making and Meeting Personal Challenges." The time of year is not critical although I would not have students work on a QAR in pairs before we had developed a comfortable atmosphere for collaborative study. The unit topic, which invites the use of other books such as *Roll of Thunder, Hear My Cry* and *The Giver,* would likely be most appropriate in the spring as we begin to build a bridge for the leap from elementary to middle school.

Bibliography: Barry Lopez, *Crow and Weasel,* illustrated by Tom Pohrt (Toronto: Random House, 1990).

Background about book: Pertinent reading material is *Crow and Weasel* in its entirety. The students have read some of the text on their own. However, the material tests at the upper edge of the fifth-grade level (according to the Fry readability formula: 5.9 is the average number of sentences per 100 words, 116.33 the average number of syllables). The language is somewhat formal. Also, it is unlikely I could get a copy of this rather expensive book for each child. Thus I have done many read-alouds, followed by class discussion.

According to the dust jacket (as beautifully and carefully designed as the rest of the book), this story takes place long ago "in the distant era of myth time, when people and animals still spoke the same language." While the themes presented are universal, the customs delineated within the pages are an amalgamation of Native American traditions. Crow and Weasel are precisely the creatures their names imply—all the "people" in the book are featured in gorgeous illustrations as their animal namesakes; clothing and equipment have been modeled after artifacts in Smithsonian collections—the pictures are beautiful and a tremendous aid to visualization. They are also two youngsters—almost "typical" teenagers, but for wings and fur!—on the verge of adulthood. They long for an adventure to assert their independence, but so far, we are told as the story begins, none of their grand plans have met with parental approval. However, when the tribal medicine man, "Mountain Lion," has a dream about Crow and Weasel traveling to the unexplored Northern lands, the two receive reluctant permission to go.

Audience: My class consisted of two fifth-graders, one fourth-grader, and one third-grader. All four children are in a public school SPACE (Special Program for Academic and Creative Excellence). However, the variation of levels in this "class" probably reflects more accurately that found in a true classroom situation.

Activity purpose: The purpose of this QAR activity is to assist students in learning from the reading material. It allows them to develop greater comprehension even as they demonstrate that they do already comprehend the material at a satisfactory level. The questions' focus is divided between the literal, the thematic, and inferential levels of comprehension.

Objectives (attained by the QAR activity and the discussion that follows it):

Answer the journalistic questions (*who, what, where, when,* and *how*).

Identify the main idea of the story.

Connect/compare/contrast the characters' problems and triumphs to problems and triumphs in their own lives.

Suggest alternatives to the decisions and actions of the characters, and predict the possible outcomes of those different choices.

Explain the author's purpose.

Use and punctuate quotations from text.

Background about Activity:

As our reading progressed, we have looked at (and drawn our own) maps, picking out the possible routes for the journey north.

Children with camping or hiking experiences to share are invited to do so.

Representatives from the Mattaponi tribe have come to class to display traditional dress and share tribal stories.

Procedures for Developing the Activity

Teacher's directions: QAR is a question/answer relationship taxonomy with four levels: Level 1 = "right there," 2 = "think and search," 3 = "the author and you," and 4 = "on your own."

1. Create a model to use as a visual aid when explaining the QAR process to the class.
2. Divide a piece of paper into four sections, one for each level.
3. For Level 1, create a question based on literal facts, the answer to which can be found right in the text.
4. For Level 2, create a question that is answered by the text but not spelled out in such a way that one direct quotation will suffice for the answer.
5. For Level 3, create a question that relies on the student's ability to interpret what the author is saying.
6. For Level 4, create a question that relies on the student's own interpretation of the text as it relates to him or her personally. The answer will be the student's opinion, but the student ought to be able to support her or his opinion with text.
7. Review your questions to double-check their appropriateness and clarity.

8. Make an answer key. Although only the first two levels have narrowly defined "right" answers—Level 3 allows for interpretation, and 4 requires an opinion—students still need to see sample answers to all four levels.
9. Make a list of at least some of the pages where possible answers can be found. This will be useful for stimulating discussion and will allow the teacher to immediately direct a child who gets stuck. You don't want to waste class time flipping pages, hunting for a passage you know is in there *somewhere*! For this activity I would not include page numbers on the students' copies. It's a fairly short book with many pictures, and at least half the story has been read aloud in class. But I would certainly add numbers to a preparation QAR. I'd also be inclined to include page numbers for a QAR that had several questions at each level or a QAR meant to cover a lengthy text. After all, my "good" readers will get through the text anyway; as my lower-level or resistant readers skip around with their teacher-made cheat sheet, they *might* just get involved enough with the story to actually read it! Page numbers included on a homework QAR reflection activity worksheet would help students create a great study guide.
10. Create another QAR, based on the same text, with an answer key. This will be your demonstration model.

Below is the written handout with activity attached.

On the Road with Crow and Weasel
A QAR Activity

Question 1: *Right there!* Why do Crow and Weasel want to go on a journey so far from home?	Answer:
Question 2: *Think and search!* Why are the Inuit people so terrified when they first see Crow and Weasel?	Answer:
Question 3: *You and the author!* As they traveled, Crow and Weasel were often afraid. How did they handle their fears?	Answer:
Question 4: *On your own!* Do you wish you could go on a journey like Crow and Weasel? Why? How would your travels be different from theirs?	Answer:

Answer Key

Question 1: "They wanted to travel farther north than anyone had ever gone, farther north than their people's stories went" (8), or, they "wanted to do something no one had ever done" (32).

Question 2: The Inuit had never seen horses before. They thought that Weasel and Crow were gigantic, four-legged, two-headed creatures. When Weasel and Crow dismounted, the Inuit thought these horrible creatures had the ability to split themselves into pieces—the better to attack! (37–38, 40).

Question 3: They talked to each other and learned to trust and love each other more than ever before (16, 19, 27, 29, 33, 39, 45, 49, 57, 60). They studied their surroundings to try to understand the things that seemed strange and frightening (12–15, 22–23, 24, 29). They paid close attention to the ideas and customs of the few people they met on their journey (14–16, 36–43, 44–48, 55–56). They prayed and acknowledged the gifts of nature (14, 20, 24, 42, 51, 53).

Question 4: Yes, I would love to travel like Crow and Weasel. My mother, my daughters, and I take a long trip every summer. We have some definite destinations in mind, but we always allow plenty of time for detours and exploration. Mostly I just want to find out more about this country of mine. It is so big and beautiful, and I know I will never get to see all of it. Of course, my travels are quite different: I go in a car, usually on good roads. I have maps, water, plenty to eat, and a comfortable place to rest (although one late Saturday night we discovered there was not a single available hotel room between Eureka, California and Seattle, Washington—but that's another story!). Still, like Crow and Weasel, I try to pay attention to all that is different and strange to my eyes. I keep journals and souvenirs to remember the stories other people and places tell me, because I know it's likely I will never pass that way again.

Students' directions

1. First, I explained to the whole class what QAR stands for and what the exercise looks like. To clarify the concept of the exercise, I created a handout modeled after the QAR figure in our textbook. As each child looked at his or her own copy, I explained the four sections of questions.
2. Because my class was so small and I could give each unlimited attention, I gave an oral demonstration of the kinds of questions and answers rather than a completed written QAR activity. Depending on the learning styles of individuals, an oral presentation may be more helpful than yet another piece of paper.
3. Then I gave them each a copy of our QAR reflection activity worksheet and divided them into two groups of two each, arranging it so that the most academically advanced fifth-grader was paired with the third-grader. Because I wanted the exercise to be collaborative rather than competitive, I told them that some consultation between groups was allowed.
4. I set a 30-minute time limit for answering the questions. I asked them to form their answers in complete sentences and made sure they understood how to punctuate the quotations they might use.
5. At the end of the allotted time we shared the answers and discussed similarities and differences. I encouraged the children to support their views with portions of the text.

6. Assessment is credit/no credit based on the accuracy of answers to questions 1 and 2, the thought and detail displayed in 3 and 4, and overall mechanics. If I had set up this QAR as a test resulting in a numerical grade, I would have given each student a copy of the accompanying rubric.
7. In a large classroom, my follow-up activity would have each student design his or her own QAR with one question for each level and an answer key (opinion key, actually, for the last two levels). I'd divide the class into pairs, have them exchange and work through the QARs. After 30 minutes, each student would make a short (5 minutes) presentation to the class, reading aloud his or her partner's questions and the answers the partner supplied. This could work very well as an assistance activity as we read the next book in our unit.

Summary: Reaction to the QAR exercise was very positive. There was an unexpected bonus at the end of the exercise. My students realized that, because of differences in interpretation stemming from personal experiences and feelings, two answers that *seem* contradictory could actually both be "right." Next time I will include "Take another's perspective" as an objective for this activity.

Example rubric: Although I did not use my QAR as a graded test, once students were familiar with the concept, it would make a good test format. Obviously this rubric is for an open-book test—how silly to expect students to memorize page numbers! A QAR test will let me assess whether students

a. Have completed the assigned reading
b. Understand the assigned reading
   - literally
   - thematically
   - critically
c. Understand the mechanics of writing

Students get a copy of the rubric when the test date is announced. The point system rewards careful reading, expressive writing, and creative thinking. Mechanics are important but not as highly ranked.

Rubric for a QAR Formatted Test

Level 1 questions:

Answer with correct phrase(s) or sentence(s) taken directly from the book (10)
Use correct punctuation (5)
Include page number of supporting text (5)

Level 2 question(s):

Answer correctly, according to words in the text and author's meaning (10)
Use complete sentences (5)
Use correct punctuation (5)
Include page number(s) of supporting text (5)

Level 3 question(s):

Give three examples of the characters' actions (10)
Use complete sentences (5)
Use correct punctuation (5)
Include page number(s) of supporting text (5)

Level 4 questions(s):

Use at least four complete sentences in your answer (10)
Use colorful imagery and strong words (10)
Compare yourself to the characters (10)

Total possible points = 100; 100–90 = A; 89–80 = B; 79–70 = C; 69–60 = D. Unless I know the student simply had a *very* bad day, a score below 65 = a conference with me to determine steps to ensure the student's future success in class.

Reflection Activity in Middle-School Math

Activity developed by Jeannette S. Rosenberg.

Activity D.3 Anyone for a Round of Golf?

Bibliographic data: Topic of the UCSMP geometry textbook.

Audience: This activity is to be used in a geometry class at any grade level. The class I have designed the project for is filled with eighth-grade students. My geometry class has no gifted students and only one student has a Student Education Plan (SEP). On the whole this is a very enthusiastic group of students. They very much enjoy working with hands-on activities. Only 2 of the 20 students are doing poorly in the class, and this is because of their failure to complete assignments.

Purpose: This activity is designed to have students reflect on what we have learned about reflections and transformations as they are related to miniature golf.

Objectives:

1. The students will design their own miniature golf hole by creating a scale drawing and then a physical model. The hole should be designed so that a hole-in-one is possible but is not obvious.
2. The students will describe the hole-in-one possibility using geometric terms.

Procedures: This activity is used as a reflection activity. Students design a miniature golf hole. After having spent approximately two weeks covering the topic of reflections and other transformations, each student would have been provided with the information needed to design his or her own hole.

This project is designed to be completed at home and returned two weeks after it is assigned. The pertinent material would have already been discussed and students prepared for an evaluation of what they have learned through reading, practice, and class discussions. Each student would receive a copy of the attached rubric. As a class, we would read the rubric and discuss the specifics. I would provide the students with examples of what is expected.

The students are to be given approximately 30 minutes of class time in which they are to design and sketch a model of their hole on graph paper. If time allows, the students should decide the path they wish the ball to take in order to get a hole-in-one. They can begin to write this description in geometric terms. The model is to be designed at home, using any available materials, and returned with all pieces of the project within the next two weeks. The entire project will be evaluated and count as a test grade.

Summary: The students had a good time getting to create a miniature golf hole that is not easily conquered. They were given a different opportunity for testing. Rather than completing a 20-problem test, they were applying all skills learned in a chapter to one particular project. As we all know, some students do not perform well on traditional tests. This opportunity provided for a relaxed atmosphere in which the students could demonstrate their knowledge of the material through pure application.

My students worked in groups of four and were provided with two-by-fours and any other objects in the classroom to use as each group designed one hole of a miniature golf course. After each group had finished with its design, students rotated through the "course" and attempted to get a hole-in-one at each station. Each group had to sketch the hole on a piece of notebook paper and construct the path of the ball.

The projects counted as a test grade in their class. The criteria are listed on the rubric. (The students have previously completed a tessellation project for me and are familiar with rubrics.) The written report is the best presentation of their knowledge of reflections and transformations as they are related to miniature golf. The students had to be very specific in their write-ups. They had to use correct vocabulary and good writing skills.

Miniature Golf Project Rubric

The purpose of this project is to design a difficult miniature golf hole and to explain the geometry of the hole-in-one possibility. A model is required.
This project is worth 50 points as follows:

______ **1.** (15 pts.) *Physical Model*: Design a physical model in which a hole-in-one is possible but is not obvious. The class will try to determine the correct path. Be sure a path actually works on your model.

_____ **2.** (15 pts.) *Scale Drawing*: Use graph paper to draw a floor plan and indicate the scale of this drawing to your model. Also indicate the scale of this drawing to a life-size miniature golf hole. Be precise so that the reflections needed to get a hole-in-one work.

_____ **3.** (10 pts.) *Written Report*: Give an explanation in geometric terms to determine where one must aim to get a hole-in-one. Refer to your floor plan as you explain.

_____ **4.** (5 pts.) *Difficulty/Creativity*: You can earn these by designing a very difficult hole (more than three bounces) and/or a very original hole (with still at least two bounces). The class will vote on the most difficult and most creative holes. Bonus points will be given to the winners.

_____ **5.** (5 pts.) *Effort*: Teacher evaluation of your commitment to this project as reflected by your accuracy, neatness, and organization.

_____ TOTAL SCORE

Return this paper with your report.

Name ______________________________

Due date ______________________________

REFERENCES

Abrami, P. C., Chambers, B., d'Apollonia, S., Farrell, M., & DeSimone, C. (1992). Group outcome: The relationship between group learning outcome, attributional style, academic achievement, and self-concept. *Contemporary Educational Psychology, 17*, 201–210.

Abruscato, J. (1993). Early results and tentative implications from the Vermont portfolio project. *Phi Delta Kappan, 74*, 474–477.

Adams, M. J. (1990). *Beginning to read: Thinking and learning about print.* Cambridge, MA: MIT Press.

Adler, A. (1931). *What life should mean to you.* New York: Capricorn.

Adler, M. J. (1982). *The Paideia proposal.* New York: Macmillan.

Adler, M. J. (1984). *The Paideia Program: An educational syllabus.* New York: Macmillan.

Adler, M. J. (1994). *Socrates: Art, the Arts, and the great ideas.* New York: Simon & Schuster.

Adler, M. J., & Van Doren, C. (1972). *How to read a book.* New York: Simon & Schuster.

Afflerbach, P. (1987). How are main idea statements constructed? Watch the experts. *Journal of Reading, 30*, 512–518.

Aguiar, L., & Brady, S. (1991). Vocabulary acquisition and reading ability. *Reading and Writing: An Interdisciplinary Journal, 3*: 3–3, 413–425.

Alexander, D. S., & DeAlba, L. M. (1997). Groups for proofs: Collaborative learning in a mathematics reasoning course. *Primus, 7*: (3), 193–207.

Alexander, P. A., Hare, V. C., & Garner, R. (1984). The effects of time, access, and question type on response accuracy and frequency of lookbacks in older, proficient readers. *Journal of Reading Behavior, 16*, 119–130.

Allen, R., Brown, K., & Yatvin, J. (1986). *Learning language through communication: A functional approach.* Belmont, CA: Wadsworth.

Allen, V. G., Freeman, E. B., Lehman, B. A., & Scharer, P. L. (1995). Amos and Boris: A Window on teachers' thinking about the use of literature in their classrooms. *The Reading Teacher, 48*, 384–389.

Allington, R. L. (1991). How policy and regulation influence instruction for at-risk learners: Or why poor readers rarely comprehend well and probably never will. In L. Idol & B. F. Jones (Eds.), *Educational values and cognitive instruction: Implications for reform* (pp. 277–299). Hillsdale, NJ: Erlbaum.

Altea, R. (1995). *The Eagle and the rose.* New York: Warner Books.

Alvarez, M. (1998). Developing critical and imaginative thinking within electronic literacy. *Nassp Bulletin, 82*, 41–47.

Alvarez, M. C., & Rodriguez, W. J. (1995). Explorers of the universe: A pilot case study. In *Generations of Literacy: Seventeenth Yearbook of the College Reading Association* (pp. 221–236). Commerce, TX: East Texas State University.

Alvermann, D. E. (1987a). Discussion strategies for content area reading. In D. Alvermann, D. R. Dillon, & D. G. O'Brien (Eds.), *Using discussion to promote reading comprehension* (pp. 34–42). Newark, DE: International Reading Association.

Alvermann, D. (1987b). Integrating oral and written language. In Alvermann, D. (1991), The discussion web: A graphic aid for learning across the curriculum. *The Reading Teacher, 44*, 92–98.

Alvermann, D. (1991). The discussion web: A graphic aid for learning across the curriculum. *The Reading Teacher, 44*, 92–98.

Alvermann, D. (1996). Peer-led discussions: Whose interests are served? *Journal of Adolescent and Adult Literacy, 39*, 282–289.

Alvermann, D., & Swafford, J. (1989). Do content area strategies have a research base? *Journal of Reading, 32*, 388–394.

Alvermann, D. E., O Brien, D. G., & Dillon, D. R. (1990). What teachers do when they say they're having discussions of content reading assignments: A qualitative analysis. *Reading Research Quarterly, 25*, 296–321.

Alvermann, D. E., Young, J. P., Weaver, D., Hinchman, K., Moore, D., Phelps, S., Thrash, E. C., & Zalewski, P. (1996). Middle and high school students' perceptions of how they experience text-based discussions: A multicase study. *Reading Research Quarterly, 31*, (3), 244–267.

Amlund, J. T., Kardash, C. A. M., & Kulhavy, R. W. (1986). Repetitive reading and recall of expository text. *Reading Research Quarterly, 21*, 49–53.

Ammons, R. I. (1987). *Trade books in the content areas*. Tempe, AZ: Jan V.

Anderson, J. (1993). Journal writing: The promise and the reality. *Journal of Reading, 36*, 304–309.

Anderson, J., & Adams, M. (1992, Spring). Acknowledging the learning styles of diverse student populations: Implications for instructional design. In L. L. B. Border & N. Van Note Chism (Eds.), *Teaching for diversity, 49*, pp. 21–33.

Anderson, R. C. (1985). The role of the reader's schema in comprehension, learning and memory. In H. Singer & R. B. Ruddell (Eds.), *Theoretical models and processes of reading* (3rd ed., pp. 372–384). Newark, DE: International Reading Association.

Anderson, R. C., & Pearson, P. D. (1984). A schema-theoretic view of basic processes in reading comprehension. In P. D. Pearson (Ed.), *Handbook of reading research* (pp. 255–291). New York: Longman.

Anderson-Inman, L. (1998). Electronic text: Literacy medium of the future. *Journal of Adolescent and Adult Literacy, 41* (8), 678–682.

Anderson-Inman, L., & Zeitz, L. (1993). Computer-based concept mapping: Active studying for active learners. *The Computing Teacher, 21* (1), 6–10.

Angeletti, S. (1991). Encouraging students to think about what they read. *The Reading Teacher, 45*, 288–296.

Annis, L., & Davis, J. K. (1978, February). Study techniques—Comparing their effectiveness. *The American Biology Teacher*, pp. 106–110.

Annis, L., & Davis, J. K. (1982). A normative study of students' reported preferred study techniques. *Reading World, 21*, 201–207.

Apple, M. (1988). *Teachers and texts: A political economy of class and gender relations in education*. New York: Routledge & Kegan.

Applebee, A. N. (1981). *Writing in the secondary school*. Urbana, IL: National Council of Teachers of English.

Applebee, A. N., Langer, J., & Mullis, I. (1987). *Learning to be literate in America: Reading, writing and reasoning*. Princeton, NJ: Educational Testing Service.

Applebee, A., Langer, J., Mullis, I., Latham, A., & Gentile, C. (1994). *NAEP 1992 writing report card*. Washington, DC: Educational Testing Service.

Arlin, P. K. (1984). *Arlin test of formal reasoning*. East Aurora, NY: Slosson Educational Publications.

Armbruster, B. (1984). The problem of inconsiderate text. In G. Duffy, L. Roehler, & J. Mason (Eds.), *Comprehension instruction* (pp. 128–143). New York: Longman.

Armbruster, B. (1992). Content reading in RT: The last two decades. *The Reading Teacher, 46*, 166–167.

Armbruster, B., & Anderson, T. (1981). *Content area textbooks* (Reading Education Report No. 23). Urbana:. University of Illinois, Center for the Study of Reading.

Armbruster, B., & Anderson, T. (1984). *Producing "considerate" expository text: Or easy reading is damned hard writing* (Reading Education Report No. 36). Champaign: University of Illinois, Center for the Study of Reading.

Armbruster, B., Anderson, T., Armstrong, J., Wise, M., Janisch, C., & Meyer, L. (1991). Reading and questioning in content areas. *Journal of Reading Behavior, 23*, 35–59.

Aronson, E. (1978). *The jigsaw classroom*. Beverly Hills, CA: Sage.

Ashby-Davis, C. (1985). Cloze and comprehension: A qualitative analysis and critique. *Journal of Reading, 28*, 585–593.

Ashworth, M. (1992). *First step on the longer path: Becoming an ESL teacher*. Markham, Ontario: Pippin.

Atwell, N. (1987). *In the middle: Writing, reading, and learning with adolescents*. Portsmouth, NH: Heinemann.

Au, K. H. (1992). *Literary instruction in multicultural settings*. Fort Worth, TX: Harcourt Brace Jovanovich.

Aurandt, P. (1983). *Destiny*. New York: Bantam Books.

Ausubel, D. (1960). The use of advance organizers in learning and retention of meaningful verbal material. *Journal of Educational Psychology, 51*, 267–272.

Ausubel, D. (1963). *The psychology of meaningful verbal learning*. New York: Grune and Stratton.

Ausubel, D. (1968). *Educational psychology: A cognitive view*. New York: Holt, Rinehart and Winston.

Babbs, P., & Moe, A. (1983). Metacognition: A key for independent learning from text. *The Reading Teacher, 36*, 422–426.

Bader, L. (1987). *Textbook analysis chart: Reading, writing, speaking, listening and critical thinking in content area subjects*. Unpublished manuscript, Michigan State University.

Bader, L., & Pearce, D. (1983). Writing across the curriculum, 7–12. *English Education, 15*, 97–106.

Baerwoald & Fraser (1992). *World Geography*. Englewood Cliffs, NJ: Prentice-Hall.

Baines, L. (1996). From page to screen: When a novel is interpreted from film, what gets lost in the translation? *Journal of Adolescent and Adult Literacy, 39* (8), 612–622.

Baldwin, R. S., Ford, J. C., & Readance, J. E. (1981). Teaching word connotations: An alternative strategy. *Reading World, 21*, 103–108.

Bandura, A. (1977). Self-efficacy: Toward a unifying theory of behavioral change. *Psychological Review, 84*, 191–215.

Banks, Lynne Reid. (1990). *The Indian in the cupboard*. Garden City, NY: Doubleday.

Bardovi-Harlig, K., & Dornyei, Z. (1998). Do language learners recognize pragmatic variations? *TESOL Quarterly, 32* (2), 233–259.

Barenbaum, E. (1983). Writing in the special class. *Topics in learning and learning disabilities, 3*, 12–20.

Barnes, D. (1976). Applebee, A., Langer, J., Mullis, I., Latham, A., & Gentile, C. (1994). *NAEP 1992 writing report card*. Washington, DC: Educational Testing Service. New York: Penguin Books.

Barrett, T. (1972). *A taxonomy of reading comprehension*. Reading 360 Monograph. Lexington, MA: Ginn.

Barry, A. L. (1998). Hispanic representation in literature for children and young adults. *Journal of Adolescent and Adult Literacy, 41* (8), 630–637.

Bartlett, F. C. (1932). *Remembering*. Cambridge: Cambridge University Press.

Barton, J. (1995). Conducting effective classroom discussions. *Journal of Reading, 38*, 346–350.

Baumann, J. F., & Johnson, D. D. (1984). *Reading instruction and the beginning teacher: A practical guide*. Minneapolis: Burgess.

Baumann, J. F., Seifert-Kessell, N., & Jones, L. A. (1992). Effect of think-aloud instruction on elementary students' comprehension monitoring abilities. *Journal of Reading Behavior, 24,* pp. 143–172.

Baxter, J. (1985). *Designing a test.* Unpublished paper, submitted in partial fulfillment of course requirements for Reading in the Content Areas. Virginia Commonwealth University, Richmond.

Bealor, S. (1992). Minority literature book groups for teachers. *Reading in Virginia, 17*(1), 17–22.

Bean, T. W. (1988). Organizing and retaining information by thinking like an author. In S. Glazer, L. Searfoss, & L. Gentile (Eds.), *Reexamining reading diagnosis* (pp. 103–127). Newark, DE: International Reading Association.

Bean, T. W., Bean, S. K., & Bean, K. F. (1999). Intergenerational conversations and two adolescents' multiple literacies: Implications for redefining content area literacy. *Journal of Adolescent and Adult Literacy, 42:6,* 438–448.

Bean, T. W., Singer, H., Sorter, J., & Frazee, C. (1986). The effect of metacognitive instruction in outlining and graphic organizer construction on students' comprehension in a tenth-grade world history class. *Journal of Reading Behavior, 18,* 153–169.

Bean, T. W., & Steenwyk, F. L. (1984). The effect of three forms of summarization instruction on sixth graders' summary writing and comprehension. *Journal of Reading Behavior, 16,* 297–306.

Beck, I. L., McKeown, M. G., Sinatra, G. M., & Loxterman, J. A. (1991). Revising social studies text from a text-processing perspective: Evidence of improved comprehensibility. *Reading Research Quarterly, 26,* 251–276.

Bellow, S. (1987). Foreword. In Allan Bloom, *The closing of the American mind* (pp. 11–18). New York: Simon & Schuster.

Bergenske, M. D. (1987). The missing link in narrative story mapping. *The Reading Teacher, 41,* 333–335.

Berlak, H. (1992). The need for a new science of assessment. In H. Berlak, et al. (Eds). *Toward a new science of educational testing and assessment.* New York: State University of New York Press.

Berliner, D., & Biddle, B. (1995). *The manufactured crisis: myths, fraud, and the attack on America's public schools.* Reading, MA: Addison-Wesley.

Berry, M. (1969). *Language disorders of children: The bases and diagnoses.* New York: Appleton-Century-Crofts.

Beyer, B. K. (1983). Common sense about teaching thinking skills. *Educational Leadership, 41,* 44–49.

Beyer, B. K. (1984). Improving thinking skills: Defining the problem. *Phi Delta Kappan, 65,* 486–490.

Bieger, E. M. (1995). Promoting multicultural education through a literature-based approach. *The Reading Teacher, 49,* 308–311.

Biggs, S. A. (1992). Building on strengths: Closing the literacy gap for African-American students. *Journal of Reading, 35,* 624–628.

Bintz, W. P. (1993). Resistant readers in secondary education: Some insights and implications. *Journal of Reading, 36,* 604–615.

Bloom, A. (1987). *The closing of the American mind.* New York: Simon & Schuster.

Bloom, B. C. (1956). *Taxonomy of educational objectives: Cognitive domain.* New York: David McKay.

Bohan, H., & Bass, J. (1991, Fall). Teaching thinking in elementary mathematics and science. *Educator's Forum,* pp. 1, 4–5, 10.

Booth, J. R., & Hall, W. S. (1994). *Relationship of reading comprehension to the cognitive internal state lexicon.* (Reading Research Report No. 14). Athens: University of Georgia National Reading Research Center.

Borkowski, J. G., Carr, M., Rellinger, E., & Pressley, M. (1990). Self-regulated cognition: Interdependence of metacognition, attributions, and self-esteem. In B. F. Jones & L. Idol (Eds.), *Dimensions of thinking and cognitive instruction* (pp. 53–92). Hillsdale, NJ: Erlbaum.

Borkowski, J. G., Estrada, M. T., Milstead, M., & Hale, C. A. (1989). General problem-solving skills: Relations between metacognition and strategic processing. *Learning Disability Quarterly, 12*, 57–70.

Borkowski, J. G., Johnston, M. B., & Reid, M. K. (1987). Metacognition, motivation, and controlled performance. In S. J. Ceci (Ed.), *Handbook of cognitive, social, and neuropsychological aspects of learning disabilities* (Vol. *2*, pp. 147–173). Hillsdale, NJ: Erlbaum.

Borkowski, J. G., Weyhing, R. S., & Carr, M. (1988). Effects of attributional retraining on strategy-based reading comprehension in learning-disabled students. *Journal of Educational Psychology, 80*, 46–53.

Bormouth, J. R. (1969). *Development of a readability analysis.* (Final Report, Project No. 7–0052, Contract No. OEC-3-7-070052-0326). Washington, DC: USOE, Bureau of Research, U.S. Department of Health, Education and Welfare.

Bormouth, J. R. (1975). Literacy in the classroom. In W. D. Page (Ed.), *Help for the reading teacher: New directions in research* (pp. 60–90). Urbana, IL: National Conference on Research in English and ERIC/RCS Clearinghouse.

Bos, C. S., & Anders, P. L. (1990). Effects of interactive vocabulary instruction on the vocabulary learning and reading comprehension of junior-high learning disabilities students. *Learning Disabilities Quarterly, 13*: 1, 31–42.

Bosworth, K. (1996). Caring for others and being cared for: Students talk about caring in school. *Phi Delta Kappan, 76*, 686–693.

Bottomley, D. M., Truscott, D. M., Marimak, B. A., Henk, W. A., and Melnick, S. A. (1999). An affective comparison of whole language, literature-based, and basal reader literacy instruction. *Journal of Research and Instruction, 38*: 2, 115–130.

Bowen, B. A. (1999). Four puzzles in adult literacy: Reflections on the National Adult Literacy Survey. *Journal of Adolescent and Adult Literacy, 42*, 314–323.

Bracey, G. (1991). Why can't they be like we were? *Phi Delta Kappan, 73*, 104–120.

Bracey, G. (1992). The condition of public education. *Phi Delta Kappan, 74*, 104–117.

Bracey, G. (1997). *Setting the record straight: Responses to misconceptions about public education in the United States.* Alexandria, VA: Association for Supervision and Curriculum Development.

Bradbury, R. (1983, July). Goodbye Grandma. *Reader's Digest, 23*, 139–142.

Brady, M. (1993). Critical issues that will determine the future of alternative assessment. *Phi Delta Kappan, 74*, 444–456.

Brandt, R. (1988). On teaching thinking: A conversation with Art Costa. *Educational Leadership, 45*, 10–13.

Branscomb, L. et al. (1986). *A nation prepared.* New York: Carnegie Forum on Education and the Economy.

Brechtel, M. (1992). *Bringing the whole together: An integrated whole-language approach for the multilingual classroom.* San Diego: Dominie Press.

Brendtro, L. K., Brokenleg, M., & Bockern, S. V. (1990). *Reclaiming youth at risk: Our hope for the future.* Bloomington, IN: National Educational Service.

Britton, B. K., & Tesser, A. (1991). Effects of time-management practices on college grades. *Journal of Educational Psychology, 83*, 405–410.

Britton, B. K., Van Dusen, L., Gulgog, S., Glynn, S. M., & Sharp, L. (1991). Accuracy of learnability judgments for instructional texts. *Journal of Educational Psychology, 83*, 43–47.

Britton, J. et al. (1975). *The development of writing abilities*. London: Methuen/School Council.

Brophy, J. (1982). *Classroom organization and management*. Washington, DC: National Institute of Education.

Brown, A. L. (1980). Metacognitive development and reading. In R. J. Spiro, B. Bruce, & W. F. Brewer (Eds.), *Theoretical issues in reading comprehension* (pp. 453–481). Hillsdale, NJ: Erlbaum.

Brown, A. L., Campione, J. C., & Day, J. D. (1981). Learning to learn: On training students to learn from texts. *Educational Researcher, 10*, 14–21.

Brown, A. L., & Day, J. D. (1983). Macrorules for summarizing texts: The development of expertise. *Journal of Verbal Learning and Verbal Behavior, 22*, 1–5.

Brown, A. L., & Smiley, S. S. (1977). Rating the importance of structural units of prose passages: A problem of metacognitive development. *Child Development, 48*, 1–8.

Brown, J. S., Collins, A., & Duguid, P. (1989). Situated cognition and the culture of learning. *Educational Researcher, 18*, 32–42.

Brown, J., Phillips, L., & Stephens, E. (1992). *Toward literacy: Theory and applications for teaching writing in the content areas*. Belmont, CA: Wadsworth.

Brown, J., & Stephens, E. (1995). *Teaching young adult literature*. Belmont, CA: Wadsworth.

Brown, R. (1987). Who is accountable for thoughtfulness? *Phi Delta Kappan, 69*, 49–52.

Brown, S. B., & Peterson, T. T. (1969). The rebellious school dropout. *School and Society, 97*, 437–439.

Brunwin, B. (Ed.). (1989). *The Bucktrout swamp*. Written by first- to sixth-grade students at Greenbriar Elementary School, Chesapeake, VA.

Bryant, J. A. R. (1984). Textbook treasure hunt. *Journal of Reading, 27*, 547–548.

Burns, M. (1975). *The I hate mathematics! book*. New York: Little Brown & Co.

Cadenhead, K. (1987). Reading level: A metaphor that shapes practice. *Phi Delta Kappan, 68*, 436–441.

Caine, R. N., & Caine, G. (1991). *Teaching and the human brain*. Alexandria, VA: Association for Supervision and Curriculum Development.

Calfee, R. C. (1987). *The role of text structure in acquiring knowledge: Final report to the U.S. Department of Education* (Federal Program No. 122B). Palo Alto, CA: Stanford University, Text Analysis Project.

Calkins, L. (1986). *The art of teaching writing*. Portsmouth, NH: Heineman.

Calkins, L., Montgomery, K., & Santman, D. (1998). *A Teacher's guide to standardized reading tests*. Portsmouth, NH: Heinemann.

Campbell, D. (1995). The Socrates syndrome: Questions that should never be asked. *Phi Delta Kappan, 76*, 467–469.

Campbell, J., Donahue, P., Reese, C., & Phillips, G. (1996). *NAEP 1998 reading report card for the nation and states*. Washington, DC: Educational Testing Service.

Carmen, R., & Adams, W. (1972). *Study skills: A student's guide to survival*. New York: Wiley.

Carr, E., & Ogle, D. (1987). KWL plus: A strategy for comprehension and summarization. *Journal of Reading, 30*, 626–631.

Carr, E., & Wixson, K. K. (1986). Guidelines for evaluating vocabulary instruction. *Journal of Reading, 29*, 588–595.

Carson, J., Chase, N., Gibson, S., & Hargrove, M. (1992). Literacy demands of the undergraduate curriculum. *Reading Research and Instruction, 31*, 25–50.

Carter, K. (1986). Test-wiseness for teachers and students. *Educational Measurement: Issues and Practices, 5*, 20–23.

Carver, R. P. (1983). Is reading rate constant or flexible? *Reading Research Quarterly, 18*, 190–215.

Carver, R. P. (1985). How good are some of the world's best readers? *Reading Research Quarterly, 20*, 389–419.

Carver, R. P. (1990). *Reading rate: A review of research and theory*. New York: Academic Press.

Carver, R. P. (1992). Reading rate: Theory, research, and practical applications. *Journal of Reading, 36*(2), 84–95.

Carver, R. P. (1994). Percentage of unknown vocabulary words in text as a function of the relative difficulty of the text: implications for instruction. *Journal of Reading Behavior, 25* (4), 413–437.

Cashen, V. J., & Leicht, K. L. (1970). Role of the isolation effect in a formal educational setting. *Journal of Educational Psychology, 61*, 900–904.

Casteel, C. (1990). Effects of chunked text-material on reading comprehension of high and low ability readers. *Reading Improvement, 27*, 269–275.

Celano, D., & Neuman, S. (1995). Channel One: Time for a TV break. *Phi Delta Kappan, 76*, 444–446.

Chall, J. (1947). The influence of previous knowledge on reading ability. *Educational Research Bulletin, 26*, 225–230.

Chall, J. (1958). *Readability: An appraisal of research and application*. Columbus: Ohio State University, Bureau of Educational Research.

Chall, J. (1983). *Stages of reading development*. New York: McGraw-Hill.

Chamot, A. U., & McKeon, D. (1984). ESL teaching methodologies. In A. U. Chamot & D. McKeon (Eds.), *Educating the minority student: Classroom and administrative issues* (pp. 1–5). Rosslyn, VA: National Clearinghouse for Bilingual Education. (ERIC Document No. ED 260 600)

Chamot, A. U., & O'Malley, J. M. (1989). The cognitive academic language learning approach. In P. Rigg (Ed.), *When they don't all speak English: Integrating the ESL student into the regular classroom* (pp. 108–125). Urbana, IL: National Council of Teachers of English.

Chamot, A. U., & O'Malley, J. M. (1994). Instructional approaches and teaching procedures. In K. Spangenberg-Urbschat & R. Pritchard (Eds.), *Kids come in all languages: Reading instruction for ESL students* (pp. 82–107). Newark, DE: International Reading Association.

Chan, L. K. S. (1996). Motivational orientations and metacognitive abilities of intellectually gifted students. *Gifted Child Quarterly, 40*: 4, 184–193.

Chandler, T. A. (1975). Locus of control: A proposal for change. *Psychology in Schools, 12*, 334–339.

Chang, I. (1991). *A separate battle: Women and the Civil War*. New York: Lodestar Books/Dutton.

Chi, F. (1995). EFL readers and a focus on intertextuality. *Journal of Reading, 38*, 638–644.

Choate, J. S., & Rakes, T. A. (1987). The structured listening activity: A model for improving listening comprehension. *The Reading Teacher, 41*, 194–200.

Chomsky, C. (1971). Write first, read later. *Childhood Education, 47*, 296–299.

Chu, M. L. (1995). Reader response to interactive computer books: Examining literacy responses in a non-traditional reading setting. *Reading Research and Instruction, 43*, 352–366.

Ciardello, A. V. (1998). Did you ask a good question today? Alternative cognitive and metacognitive strategies. *Journal of Adolescent and Adult Literacy, 42* (3), 210–219.

Cioffi, G. (1992). Perspective and experience: Developing critical reading abilities. *Journal of Reading, 36*, 48–52.

Clark, B. (1983). *Growing up gifted: Developing the potential of children at home and at school* (2nd ed.). Columbus, OH: Merrill.

Cleary, B. (1982). *Ralph S. Mouse*. New York: William Morrow.

Cleland, J. V. (1999). We can charts: Building blocks for student-led conferences. *The Reading Teacher, 52* (6), 588–595.

Cohen, A. D. (1987). The use of verbal and imagery mnemonics in second-language vocabulary learning. *Studies in Second Language Acquisition, 9*, 43–61.

Cohen, M. R., Cooney, T. M., Hawthorne, C., McCormack, A. J., Pasachoff, J. M., Pasachoff, N., Rhines, K. L., & Siesnick, I. L. (1991). *Discover science*. Glenview, IL: Scott, Foresman.

Cole, A. D. (1998). Beginner-oriented texts in literature-based classrooms: The segue for a few struggling readers. *The Reading Teacher, 51* (6), 488–501.

Cole, R., Raffier, L. M., Rogan, P., & Schleicher, L. (1998). Interactive group journals: Learning as a dialogue among learners. *TESOL Quarterly, 32* (3), 556–568.

Coleman, J. C. (1969). *Equality of educational opportunity*. Washington, DC: Superintendent of Documents.

Coleman, M. W. (1994). *Using a collaborative learning project to teach information literacy skills to twelfth grade regular English students*. M.S. Practicum, Nova Southeastern University, Ft. Lauderdale, FL. (ERIC document Reproduction Service No. ED 371 398).

College Board, Touchtone Applied Science Associates. (1986). *Degrees of reading power*. New York: College Board.

Collins, C. (1979). Speedway: The action way to speed read to increase reading rate for adults. *Reading Improvement, 16*, 225–229.

Collins, M. L. (1977). *The effects of training for enthusiasm on the enthusiasm displayed by preservice elementary teachers*. Unpublished doctoral dissertation, Syracuse University, Syracuse, NY.

Colwell, C. G., Mangano, N. G., Childs, D., & Case, D. (1986). Cognitive, affective, and behavioral differences between students receiving instruction using alternative lesson formats. *Proceedings of the National Reading and Language Arts Conference.*

Combs, A. W., & Snygg, D. (1959). *Individual behavior*. New York: Harper & Row.

Conley, M. (1985). Promoting cross-cultural understanding through content area reading strategies. *Journal of Reading, 28*, 600–605.

Connell, J. P., & Ryan, R. M. (1984). A developmental theory of motivation in the classroom. *Teacher Education Quarterly, 11*, 64–77.

Cook, L., & Gonzales, P. (1995). Zones of contact: Using literature with second language learners. *Reading Today, 12*, 27.

Coopersmith, S. (1967). *The antecedents of self-esteem*. San Francisco: Freeman.

Cooter, R. B. (1990, October/November). Learners with special needs. *Reading Today*, p. 28.

Cooter, R. B., Jr. (1994). Assessing affective and conative factors in reading. *Reading Psychology, 15*, (2), 77–90.

Cooter, R. B., & Chilcoat, G. W. (1991). Content-focused melodrama: Dramatic renderings of historical text. *Journal of Reading, 34*, 274–277.

Cooter, R. B., Joseph, D., & Flynt, E. (1986). Eliminating the literal pursuit in reading comprehension. *Journal of Clinical Reading, 2*, 9–11.

Cosby, Bill. (1986). *How to read faster*. New York: International Paper Company in conjunction with Scholastic Press.

Cowan, G., & Cowan, E. (1980). *Writing*. New York: Wiley.

Cox, J., & Wiebe, J. (1984). Measuring reading vocabulary and concepts in mathematics in the primary grades. *Reading Teacher, 37*, 402–410.

Crapse, L. (1995). Helping students construct meaning through their own questions. *Journal of Reading, 38* (5), 389–390.

Creek, R. J., McDonald, W. C., & Ganley, M. A. (1991). *Internality and achievement in the intermediate grades*. (ERIC Document No. ED 330 656)

Crist, J. (1975). One capsule a week—painless remedy for vocabulary ills. *Journal of Reading, 31*, 147–149.

Cronin, H., Meadows, D., & Sinatra, R. (1990). Integrating computers, reading, and writing across the curriculum. *Educational Leadership, 48*, 57–62.

Cullinan, B. E., Karrer, M. K., & Pillar, A. M. (1981). *Literature and the child*. New York: Harcourt Brace Jovanovich.

Culver, V. I., & Morgan, R. F. (1977). *The relationship of locus of control to reading achievement*. Unpublished manuscript, Old Dominion University, Norfolk, VA.

Cunningham, J. W. (1982). Generating interactions between schemata and text. In J. A. Niles & L. A. Harris (Eds.). *New inquiries in reading research and instruction*. Thirty-first Yearbook of the National Reading Conference, pp. 42–47. Rochester, NY: National Reading Conference.

Cunningham, P. (1995). *Phonics They Use*. New York: Harper Collins.

Cunningham, R., & Shablak, S. (1975). Selective reading guide-o-rama: The content teacher's best friend. *Journal of Reading, 18*, 380–382.

Currie, H. (1990). Making texts more readable. *British Journal of Special Education, 17*, 137–139.

Curry, B. A. (1990). *The impact of the Nicholls State Youth Opportunities Unlimited Program as related to academic achievement, self-esteem, and locus of control*. Master's thesis, Nicholls State University, Thibodaux, LA.

Daily, G. (1995, September). A glimpse of the real world. *Learning*, 62–63.

Dale, E. (1965). Vocabulary measurement: Techniques and major findings. *Elementary English, 42*, 895–901.

Dale, E., & Chall, J. (1948). A formula for predicting readability. *Educational Research Bulletin, 27*, 11–20, 37–54.

Dale, E., & O'Rourke, J. (1976). *The living word vocabulary*. Elgin, IL: Dome.

Dale, E., O'Rourke, J., & Bamman, H. (1971). *Techniques of teaching vocabulary*. Palo Alto, CA: Field Educational Publications.

Damon, W. (1995). *Greater expectations: Overcoming the culture of indulgence in America's homes and schools*. New York: Free Press.

Dana, C., & Rodriguez, M. (1992). "TOAST: A system to study vocabulary." *Reading Research and Instruction, 31* (4), 78–84.

Danielson, K. E. (1987). Readability formulas: A necessary evil? *Reading Horizons, 27*, 178–188.

Darling-Hammond, L. (1993). Reforming the school reform agenda. *Phi Delta Kappan, 74*, 752–761.

Davey, B. (1983). Think aloud: Modeling the cognitive processes of reading comprehension. *Journal of Reading, 27*, 44–47.

Davey, B. (1987). Team for success: Guided practice in study skills through cooperative research reports. *Journal of Reading, 30*, 701–705.

Davey, B. (1988). How do classroom teachers use their textbooks? *Journal of Reading, 31*, 340–345.

Davey, B., & McBride, S. (1986). Effects of question-generation training on reading comprehension. *Journal of Educational Psychology, 78*, 256–262.

Davidson, J. L. (1982). The group mapping activity for instruction in reading and thinking. *Journal of Reading, 26*, 52–56.

Davis, B. (1985). *The long surrender*. New York: Random House.

Davis, F. B. (1944). Fundamental factors of comprehension in reading. *Psychometrika, 9*, 185–197.

Davis, M. (1998). The Amish teachers' supper. *The Reading Professor, 21* (1), 158–164.

Davis, S. J. (1990). Applying content study skills in co-listed reading classrooms. *Journal of Reading, 33*, 277–281.

Davis, S., & Winek, J. (1989). Improving expository writing by increasing background knowledge. *Journal of Reading, 33*, 178–181.

Davis, W. C. (1985). *Touched by fire: A Photographic portrait of the Civil War.* Boston: Little, Brown & Co.

Davis, W. C. (1990). *Diary of a Confederate soldier.* Columbia, SC: University of South Carolina Press.

Davison, A. (1984). Readability formulas and comprehension. In G. Duffy, L. Roehler, & J. Mason (Eds.), *Comprehension instruction* (pp. 128–143). New York: Longman.

Davison, D., & Pearce, D. (1988a). Using writing activities to reinforce mathematics instruction. *Arithmetic Teacher, 35*, 42–45.

Davison, D., & Pearce, D. (1988b). Writing activities in junior high mathematics texts. *School Science and Mathematics, 88*, 493–499.

Day, B., & Anderson, J. (1992). Assessing the challenges ahead. *Delta Kappa Gamma Bulletin, 58* (4), 5–10.

de Bono, E. (1976). *Teaching thinking.* London: Temple Smith.

Deal, D. (1998). Portfolios, learning logs, and eulogies: Using expressive writing in a science methods course. In Sturtevant, E. G., Dugan, J. A., Linder, P., & Linek, W. M. (Eds.). *Literacy and Community: Twentieth Yearbook of the College Reading Association.* Commerce, TX: Texas A & M Press, 243–256.

Dechant, E. (1970). *Improving the teaching of reading.* Englewood Cliffs, NJ: Prentice-Hall.

Dempster, F. N. (1993). Exposing our students to less should help them learn more. *Phi Delta Kappan, 74*, 433–437.

Derby, T. (1987). Reading instruction and course-related materials for vocational high school students. *Journal of Reading, 30*, 308–316.

DeSanti, R. J., & Alexander, D. H. (1986). Locus of control and reading achievement: Increasing the responsibility and performance of remedial readers. *Journal of Clinical Reading, 2*, 12–14.

Dewey, J. (1933). *How we think.* Boston: Heath.

Diamond, M., & Hopson, J. (1998). *Magic tress of the mind: How to motivate your child's intelligence, creativity, and health emotions from birth through adolescence.* New York: Penguin Putnam.

Dillon, J. T. (1983). *Teaching and the art of questioning.* Bloomington, IN: Phi Beta Kappa Educational Foundation. Fastback No. 194.

Dole, J. A., Valencia, S. W., Greer, E. A., & Wardrop, J. L. (1991). Effects of two types of prereading instruction on the comprehension of narrative and expository text. *Reading Research Quarterly, 26*, 142–159.

Douglass, B. (1984). Variations on a theme: Writing with the LD adolescent. *Academic Therapy, 19*, 361–362.

Dove, M. K. (1998). The textbook in education. *Delta Kappa Gamma Bulletin, 64* (3), 24–30.

Downing, J. (1973). *Comparative reading.* New York: Macmillan.

Downing, J., Ollila, L., & Oliver, P. (1975). Cultural differences in children's concepts of reading and writing. *British Journal of Educational Psychology, 45*, 312–316.

Dreyer, L. G. (1984). Readability and responsibility. *Journal of Reading, 27*, 334–338.

Drum, P. (1985). Retention of text information by grade, ability, and study. *Discourse Processes, 8*, 21–51.

Drum, P., Calfee, R., & Cook, L. (1981). The effects of surface structure variables on reading comprehension tests. *Reading Research Quarterly, 16*, 486–514.

Drummond, R. J., Smith, R. K., & Pinette, C. A. (1975). Internal-external control construct and performance in an individualized community college reading course. *Reading Improvement, 12*, 34–38.

Duffelmeyer, F. A. (1994). Effective anticipation guide statements for learning from expository prose. *Journal of Reading, 37* (6), 452–457.

Duffelmeyer, F. A., & Baum, D. D. (1992). The extended anticipation guide revisited. *Journal of Reading, 35*, 654–656.

Duffelmeyer, F. A., Baum, D. D., & Merkley, D. J. (1987). Maximizing reader-text confrontation with an extended anticipation guide. *Journal of Reading, 31*, 146–149.

Duffy, G. G., & Roehler, L. R. (1987). Teaching reading skills as strategies. *The Reading Teacher, 40*, 414–418.

Dunston, P. J. (1992). A critique of graphic organizer research. *Reading Research and Instruction, 31*, 57–65.

Durkin, D. (1979). What classroom observations reveal about reading comprehension. *Reading Research Quarterly, 14*, 481–533.

Durkin, D. (1981). Reading comprehension instruction in five basal reading series. *Reading Research Quarterly, 16*, 515–544.

Durkin, D. (1984). Is there a match between what elementary teachers do and what basal reader manuals recommend? *The Reading Teacher, 37*, 734–744.

Dweck, C. S. (1975). The role of expectations and attribution in the alleviation of learned helplessness. *Journal of Personality and Social Psychology, 41*, 1041–1048.

Dweck, C. S. (1985). Intrinsic motivation, perceived control, and self-evaluation maintenance: An achievement goal analysis. In C. Ames & R. Ames (Eds.), *Research on motivation in education* (Vol. 2, pp. 289–305). Orlando, FL: Academic Press.

Eanet, M., & Manzo, A. V. (1976). REAP—A strategy for improving reading/writing/study skills. *Journal of Reading, 19*, 647–652.

Earle, R., & Barron, R. F. (1973). An approach for teaching vocabulary in content subjects. In H. L. Herber & R. F. Barron (Eds.), *Research in reading in the content areas: Second year report* (84–100). Syracuse, NY: Syracuse University, Reading and Language Arts Center.

Ebbinghaus, H. (1908). *Abriss der Psychologie* (M. Meyer, Trans. and Ed.). New York: Arno Press, 1973.

Egan, K. (1987). Literacy and the oral foundations of education. *Harvard Educational Review, 57*, 445–472.

Ehlinger, J., & Pritchard, R. (1994). Using think-alongs in secondary content areas. *Reading Research and Instruction, 33* (3), 187–206.

Elley, W. B. (1992). *How in the world do students read?* The Hague, The Netherlands: International Association for the Evaluation of Educational Achievement.

Elliott, D., & Wendling, A. (1966). Capable dropouts and the social milieu of the high school. *Journal of Educational Research, 60*, 180–186.

Erickson, B. (1996). Read-alouds reluctant readers relish. *Journal of Adolescent and Adult Literacy, 40* (3), 217–221.

Erickson, B., Huber, M., Bea, T., Smith, C., & McKenzie, V. (1987). Increasing critical reading in junior high classes. *Journal of Reading, 30*, 430–439.

Ezell, H. K. (1996). Maintenance and generalization of QAR reading comprehension strategies. *Reading Research and Instruction, 36*: (1), 64–81.

Ezell, H. K., Hunsicker, S. A., Quinque, M. M., & Randolph, E. (1996). Maintenance and generalization of QAR reading comprehension strategies. *Reading Research and Instruction, 36*, (1), 64–81.

Facione, P. A. (1984). Toward a theory of critical thinking. *Liberal Education, 30*, 253–261.

Fader, D. (1966). *Hooked on books*. New York: Berkley.

Farley, W. *The black stallion*. New York: Random House.

Fader, D. (1976). *The new hooked on books*. New York: Berkley.

Feathers, K., & Smith, F. (1987). Meeting the reading demands of the real world: Literacy-based content instruction. *Journal of Reading, 30*, 506–511.

Field, M. L., & Aebersold, J. A. (1990). Cultural attitudes toward reading: Implications for teachers of ESL/bilingual readers. *Journal of Reading, 33*, 406–410.

Fielding, L. G., & Pearson, P. D. (1994). Reading comprehension: What works? *Educational Leadership, 51*, 62–68.

Fillmore, L. W. (1981). Cultural perspectives on second language learning. *TESL Reporter, 14*, 23–31.

Fink, R. P. (1996). Successful dyslexics: A constructivist study of passionate interest reading. *Journal of Adolescent and Adult Literacy, 39*, 268–280.

Fisher, C. W., & Berliner, D. (Eds.) (1985). *Perspectives on instructional time*. New York: Longman.

Fleisher, L. S., Jenkins, J. R., & Pany, D. (1979). Effects on poor readers' comprehension of training in rapid decoding. *Reading Research Quarterly, 15*, 30–48.

Flesch, R. (1949). *The art of readable writing*. New York: Harper & Row.

Flippo, R. F. (1997). *Reading Assessment and Instruction*. New York: Holt, Rinehart & Winston.

Fogarty, R. (1998). The intelligence-friendly classroom: It just makes sense. *Phi Delta Kappan, 79*: (9), 655–657.

Forgan, H. W., & Mangrum, C. T. (1985; 1997). *Teaching content area reading skills*. Columbus, OH: Merrill.

Forget, M. A., & Morgan, R. F. (1995). *An embedded curriculum approach to teaching metacognitive strategies*. Paper presented at the College Reading Association, November, 1995, Clearwater Beach, FL.

Fosnot, C. (1996). *Constructivism: Theory, perspectives, and practice*. New York: Teachers College Press.

Fowler, R. L., & Baker, A. S. (1974). Effectiveness of highlighting for retention of text material. *Journal of Applied Psychology, 59*, 358–364.

Frager, A. (Ed.). (1991). *Teaching adult beginning readers: To reach them my hand*. Syracuse, NY: College Reading Association and Literacy Volunteers of America.

Fredericks, A. (1992). Magic bullets or empty blanks? *Reading Today, 9*(4), 30.

Fromm, E. (1956). *The art of loving*. New York: Harper & Row.

Fry, E. (1968). The readability graph validated at primary levels. *The Reading Teacher, 3*, 534–538.

Fry, E. (1977). Fry's readability graph: Clarifications, validity, and extension to level 17. *Journal of Reading, 21*, 242–252.

Fry, E. (1987). The varied uses of readability measurement today. *Journal of Reading, 30*, 338–343.

Fry, E. (1989). Reading formulas—maligned but valid. *Journal of Reading, 32*, 292–297.

Fry, E. (1990). A readability formula for short passages. *Journal of Reading, 33*, 594–597.

Frymier, A. B., & Schulman, G. (1995). "What's in it for me": Increasing content relevance to enhance students' motivation. *Communication Education, 44*, 40–50.

Gagne, R. (1974). Educational technology and the learning process. *Educational Researcher, 3*, 3–8.

Galeman, D. (1995). *Emotional intelligence: Why it can matter more than IQ*. New York: Bantam.

Gallagher, J. M. (1995). Pairing adolescent fiction with books from the canon. *Journal of Adolescent and Adult Literacy, 39*, 8–14.

Gambrell, L. B. (1990). Introduction: A themed issue on reading instruction for at-risk students. *Journal of Reading, 33*, 485–488.

Gambrell, L. B. (1995). Motivation matters. In *Generations of Literacy, Seventeenth Yearbook of the College Reading Association* (pp. 2–24). Commerce, TX: East Texas State University.

Gambrell, L. B., & Bales, R. J. (1986). Mental imagery and the comprehension-monitoring performance of fourth- and fifth-grade poor readers. *Reading Research Quarterly, 21*, 454–464.

Gambrell, L. B., & Wilson, R. M. (1973). *Focusing on the strengths of children*. Belmont, CA: Fearon.

Gardner, M. K., & Smith, M. M. (1987). Does perspective-taking ability contribute to reading comprehension? *Journal of Reading, 30*, 333–336.

Garner, R. (1985a). *Strategies for reading and studying expository text*. Unpublished paper, University of Maryland.

Garner, R. (1985b). Text summarization deficiencies among older students: Awareness or production ability? *American Educational Research Journal, 22*, 549–560.

Garner, R., Alexander, P., Slater, W., Hare, V. C., Smith, J., & Reis, R. (1986, April). *Children's knowledge of structural properties of text*. Paper presented at the meeting of the American Educational Research Association, San Francisco.

Garner, R., Hare, V. C., Alexander, P., Haynes, J., & Winograd, P. (1984). Inducing use of a text lookback strategy among unsuccessful readers. *American Educational Research Journal, 21*, 789–798.

Garner, R., Macready, G. B., & Wagoner, S. (1985). Reader's acquisition of the components of the text-lookback strategy. *Journal of Educational Psychology, 76*, 300–309.

Garrison, W. B. (1992). *Civil War trivia and fact book*. Nashville, TN: Rutledge Hill Press.

Gavelek, J. R. (1986). The social contexts of literacy and schooling: A developmental perspective. In T. Raphael (Ed.), *The contexts of school-based literacy* (pp. 3–26). New York: Random House.

Gebhard, A. (1983). Teaching writing in reading and the content areas. *Journal of Reading, 27*, 207–211.

Gee, R. W. (1999). Encouraging ESL students to read. *TESOL Journal, 8* (1), 3–7.

Gentile, L., & McMillan, M. (1987). Stress and reading difficulties: Teaching students self-regulating skills. *The Reading Teacher, 41*, 170–178.

George, J. C. (1971). *All upon a stone*. New York: Crowell.

Georgia Department of Education. (1975). *Reading mathematics*. Atlanta.

Gere, A. (1985). *Roots in the sawdust: Writing to learn across the disciplines*. Urbana, IL: National Council of Teachers of English.

Gill, S., & Dupree, K. (1998). Constructivism in reading education. *The Reading Professor, 21*: (1), 91–108.

Gillespie, C. (1993). Reading graphic displays: What teachers should know. *Journal of Reading, 36*, 350–354.

Gillett, J. W., & Temple, C. (1983). *Understanding reading problems: Assessment and instruction*. Boston: Little, Brown.

Glasser, W. (1986). *Control theory in the classroom*. New York: Harper & Row.

Glatthaar, J. T. (1990). *Forged in battle: The Civil War alliance of black soldiers and white officers*. New York: Free Press.

Gold, P. C. (1981). The directed listening-language experience approach. *Journal of Reading, 25*, 138–141.

Goodlad, J. (1984). *A place called school*. New York: McGraw-Hill.

Goodman, Y. M., & Burke, C. L. (1972). *Reading miscue inventory kit: Procedure for diagnosis and correction*. New York: Macmillan.

Gordon, C. (1990). Changes in readers' and writers' metacognitive knowledge: Some observations. *Reading Research and Instruction, 30,* 1–14.

Gough, P. B. (1987, May). The key to improving schools: An interview with William Glasser. *Phi Delta Kappan,* 656–662.

Grabe, M., & Grabe, C. (1998). *Integrating technology for meaningful learning.* Boston: Houghton Mifflin.

Grady, M. P. (1990). *Whole brain education.* Bloomington, IN: Phi Delta Kappa Educational Foundation.

Graves, D. (1983). *Writing: Teachers and children at work.* Portsmouth, NH: Heinemann.

Graves, D. (1994). *A fresh look at writing.* Portsmouth, NH: Heinemann.

Graves, D., Prenn, M., & Cooke, C. (1985). The coming attraction: Previewing short stories. *Journal of Reading, 28,* 594–598.

Graves, M. F. (1985). *A word is a word . . . or is it?* New York: Scholastic.

Gray, W. (1925). *Summary of investigations related to reading* (Supplementary Educational Monographs No. 28). Chicago: University of Chicago Press.

Gray, W. (1960). The major aspects of reading. In H. Robinson (Ed.), *Development of reading abilities* (Supplementary Educational Monographs No. 90). Chicago: University of Chicago Press.

Gray, W. (1941; 1984). *Reading.* Newark, DE: International Reading Association. (Originally published 1941)

Greenlee-Moore, M., & Smith, L. (1996). Interactive computer software: The effects on young children's reading achievement. *Reading Psychology: An International Quarterly, 17,* 43–64.

Greenough, W. T., Withers, G. S., & Anderson, B. J. (1992). Experience-dependent synaptogenesis as a plausible memory mechanism. In I. Gormezano & E. A. Wasserman (Eds.), *Learning and memory: The behavioral and biological substrates* (pp. 209–299). Hillsdale, NJ: Erlbaum.

Groff, P. (1981). Direct instruction versus incidental learning of reading vocabulary. *Reading Horizons, 21* (4), 262–265.

Guillaume, A. M. (1998). Learning with text in the primary grades. *The Reading Teacher, 51* (6), 476–486.

Gusak, F. J. (1967). Teacher questioning and reading. *The Reading Teacher, 21,* 227–234.

Guthrie, J. T., Burnam, N., Caplan, R. I., & Seifert, M. (1974). The maze technique to assess and monitor reading comprehension. *The Reading Teacher, 28,* 161–168.

Guzzetti, B. (1990). Enhancing comprehension through trade books in high school English classes. *Journal of Reading, 33,* 411–413.

Guzzetti, B., Hynd, C. R., Skeels, S. A., and Williams, W. O. (1995). Improving physics texts: Students speak out. *Journal of Reading, 38,* 656–663.

Guzzetti, B., Kowalinski, B. J., & McGowan, T. (1992). Using a literature-based approach to teaching social studies. *Journal of Reading, 36,* 114–122.

Guzzetti, B., Snyder, T., & Glass, G. (1992). Promoting conceptual change in science: Can texts be used effectively? *Journal of Reading, 35,* 642–649.

Hadaway, N., & Mundy, J. (1999). Children's informational picture books visit a secondary ESL classroom. *Journal of Adolescent and Adult Literacy, 42* (6), 464–475.

Hafner, L. (1967). Using context to determine meanings in high school and college. *Journal of Reading, 10,* 491–498.

Hager, J. M., & Gable, R. A. (1993). Content reading assessment: A rethinking of methodology. *The Clearing House, 66,* 269–272.

Haggard, M. R. (1986). The vocabulary self-collection strategy: Using student interest and world knowledge to enhance vocabulary growth. *Journal of Reading, 29,* 634–642.

Halladay, M. A. K. (1994). *An introduction to functional grammar* (2nd ed). London: Edward Arnold.

Hamachek, D. E. (1975). *Behavior dynamics in teaching, learning, and growth*. Boston: Allyn & Bacon.

Hansen, J. (1981). The effects of inference training and practice on young children's comprehension. *Reading Research Quarterly, 16*, 391–417.

Hansen, J., & Pearson, D. (1983). An instructional study: Improving the inferential comprehension of fourth grade good and poor readers. *Journal of Educational Psychology, 75*, 821–829.

Hare, V. C., & Borchardt, K. M. (1984). Direct instruction of summarization skills. *Reading Research Quarterly, 20*, 62–78.

Harris, K., & Graham, S. (1985). Improving learning disabled students' composition skills: Self-control strategy training. *Learning Disability Quarterly, 8*, 27–36.

Harris, L. A., & Smith, C. B. (1986). *Reading instruction: Diagnostic teaching in the classroom*. New York: Macmillan.

Harris, T. L., & Hodges, R. E. (1995). *The literacy dictionary: The vocabulary of reading and writing*. Newark, DE: International Reading Association.

Hart, L. (1975). *How the brain works*. New York: Basic Books.

Hart, L. (1983). Programs, patterns and downshifting in learning to read. *The Reading Teacher, 37*, 5–11.

Hart, L. (1983). *Human brain and human learning*. New York: Longman.

Hartman, M., & Kretschner, R. E. (1992). Talking and writing: Deaf teenagers reading Sarah, Plain and Tall. *Journal of Reading, 36*, 174–180.

Hathaway, W. (Ed.). (1983). *Testing in the schools*. San Francisco: Jossey-Bass.

Haussamen, B. (1995). The passive-reading fallacy. *Journal of Reading, 38*, 378–381.

Hawkes, K. S., & Schell, L. M. (1987). Teacher-set prereading purposes and comprehension. *Reading Horizons, 27*, 164–169.

Hayes, H., Stahl, N., & Simpson, M. (1991). Language, meaning, and knowledge: Empowering developmental students to participate in the academic community. *Reading Research and Instruction, 30*(3), 89–100.

Healey, J. (1990). *Endangered minds*. New York: Simon & Schuster.

Heath, S. B. (1986). Critical factors in literacy development. In S. de Castell, A. Luke, & K. Egan (Eds.), *Literacy, society and schooling: A reader* (pp. 209–229). New York: Cambridge University Press.

Heathington, B., & Alexander, J. (1984). Do classroom teachers emphasize attitudes toward reading? *The Reading Teacher, 37*, 484–488.

Heilman, A. W., Blair, T. R., & Rupley, W. H. (1986; 1994). *Principles and practices of teaching reading*. Columbus, OH: Merrill.

Heimlich, J. E., & Pittleman, S. D. (1985). *Semantic mapping: Classroom applications*. Newark, DE: International Reading Association.

Heller, M. (1986). How do you know what you know? Metacognitive modeling in the content areas. *Journal of Reading, 29*, 415–422.

Henk, W. A., & Helfeldt, J. P. (1987). How to develop independence in following written directions. *Journal of Reading, 30*, 602–607.

Henry, G. H. (1974). *Teaching reading as concept development: Emphasis on affective thinking*. Newark, DE: International Reading Association.

Herber, H. (1978). *Teaching reading in the content areas* (2nd ed.). Englewood Cliffs, NJ: Prentice-Hall.

Herber, H. (1987). Foreword. In D. Alvermann, D. Moore, & M. Conley (Eds.), *Research within reach: Secondary school reading*. Newark, DE: International Reading Association.

Hiebert, E. H. (1999). Text matters in learning to read. *The Reading Teacher, 52* (6), 552–566.

Hill, W., & Erwin, R. (1984). The readability of content textbooks used in middle and junior high schools. *Reading Psychology, 5*, 105–117.

Hillerich, R. L. (1979). Reading comprehension. *Reporting on Reading, 5*, 1–3.

Hilliard, A. G. (1988). Public support for successful instructional practices for at-risk students. In D. W. Hornbeck (Ed.), *School success for at-risk youth: Analysis and recommendations of the Council of Chief State School Officers* (pp. 195–208). Orlando, FL: Harcourt Brace Jovanovich.

Hinchman, R. (1987). The textbook and three content area teachers. *Reading Research and Instruction, 26*, 247–263.

Hirsch, E. D. (1987). *Cultural literacy*. Boston: Houghton Mifflin.

Hittleman, D. R. (1978). Readability, readability formulas, and cloze: Selecting instructional materials. *Journal of Reading, 22*, 117–122.

Hoffman, J. (1992). Critical reading/thinking across the curriculum: Using I-charts to support learning. *Language Arts, 69*, 121–127.

Hoffman, S. (1983). Using student journals to teach study skills. *Journal of Reading, 26*, 344–347.

Holiday, W. G. (1983). Overprompting science students using adjunct study questions. *Journal of Research in Science Teaching, 20*, 195–201.

Holmes, B., & Roser, N. (1987). Five ways to assess readers' prior knowledge. *The Reading Teacher, 40*, 646–649.

Hornbeck, D. W. (1988). All our children: An introduction. In D. W. Hornbeck (Ed.), *School success for at-risk youth: Analysis and recommendations of the Council of Chief State School Officers* (pp. 3–9). Orlando, FL: Harcourt Brace Jovanovich.

Hornberger, T. R., & Whitford, E. V. (1983). Students' suggestions: Teach us study skills! *Journal of Reading, 27*, 71.

Howland, J. (1995). Attentive reading in the age of canon clamor. *English Journal, 84*, 35–38.

Huck, C. (1979). *Children's literature in the elementary school*. New York: Holt, Rinehart & Winston.

Huck, C., Hepler, S., & Hickman, J. (1987). *Children's literature in the elementary school*. Fort Worth, TX: Holt, Rinehart & Winston.

Huey, E. (1968). *The psychology and pedagogy of reading*. Cambridge, MA: MIT Press. (Originally published 1908)

Hunt, E. B. (1971). What kind of computer is man? *Cognitive Psychology, 2*, 57–98.

Hurd, P. (1970). *New directions in teaching secondary school science*. Chicago: Rand-McNally.

Hurley, S. R. (1995). You want to just stop reading forever. *Affective Reading Education, 14*, 8–12.

Hynd, C. (1999). Teaching students to think critically using multiple texts in history. *Journal of Adolescent and Adult Literacy, 42* (6), 428–436.

Hynd, C., McNish, M., Lay, K., & Fowler, P. (1995). *High school physics: The role of text in learning counterintuitive information*. Reading Research Report No. 16. University of Georgia: National Reading Research Center.

Iannone, P. (1998). Just beyond the horizon: Writing-centered literacy activities for traditional and electronic texts. *The Reading Teacher, 51* (5), 438–443.

International Reading Association. (1988). *New directions in reading instruction*. Newark, DE.

Ivey, G. (1999). Reflections on teaching struggling middle school readers. *Journal of Adolescent and Adult Literacy, 42* (5), 372–381.

Iwicki, A. L. (1992). Vocabulary connections. *The Reading Teacher, 45*, 736.

Jackson, F. R., & Cunningham, J. (1994). Investigating secondary content teachers and preservice teachers' conceptions of study strategy instruction. *Reading Research and Instruction, 34,* 11–135.

Jacobs, L. (1987). Reading, writing, remembering. *Teaching Pre K–8, 18,* 38.

Jacobson, J. M. (1998). *Content area reading: Integration with the language arts.* Albany, NY: Doman.

Jenkins, C., & Lawler, D. (1990). Questioning strategies in content area reading: One teacher's example. *Reading Improvement, 27,* 133–138.

Jensen, E. (1998). *Teaching with the brain in mind.* Alexandria, VA: Association for Supervision and Curriculum Development.

Johns, J. L. (1986). Students' perceptions of reading: Thirty years of inquiry. In D. B. Yaden, Jr., & S. Templeton (Eds.), *Metalinguistic awareness and beginning literacy* (pp. 31–40). Portsmouth, NH: Heinemann.

Johnson, D. W., & Johnson, R. T. (1987). *Learning together and alone: Cooperative, conjunctive, and individualistic learning.* Englewood Cliffs, NJ: Prentice-Hall.

Johnson, D., & Pearson, P. D. (1984). *Teaching reading vocabulary* (2nd ed.). New York: Holt, Rinehart & Winston.

Johnston, J. (1995). Channel One: The dilemma of teaching and selling. *Phi Delta Kappan, 76,* 437–442.

Jone, H. J., Coombs, W. T., & McKinney, C. W. (1994). A Themed literature unit versus a textbook: A comparison of the effects on content acquisition and attitudes in elementary social studies. *Reading Research and Instruction, 34,* 85–96.

Jones, F. R., Morgan, R. F., & Tonelson, S. W. (1992). *The psychology of human development* (3rd ed). Dubuque, IA: Kendall-Hunt.

Jongsma, E. (1980). *Cloze instruction research: A second look.* Newark, DE: International Reading Association.

Just, M. A., Carpenter, P. A., & Masson, M. E. J. (1982). *What eye fixations tell us about speed reading and skimming* (Technical Report). Pittsburgh: Carnegie-Mellon University.

Juster, N. (1961). *The phantom tollbooth.* New York: Random House.

Kaestle, C. F., Damon-Moore, H., Stedman, K. T., Tinsley, K., & Tollinger, W. V. (1991). *Literacy in the United States: Readers and reading since 1880.* New Haven, CT: Yale University Press.

Kahmi-Stein, L. (1998). Profiles of underprepared second language learners. *Journal of Adolescent and Adult Literacy, 41* (8), 610–619.

Kane, B. (1984). *Remarks made at the regional meeting on reading across the curriculum.* Reading to Learn in Virginia, Capital Consortium.

Kapinus, B. (1986). *Ready reading readiness.* Baltimore: Maryland State Department of Education.

Kauchak, D. P., & Eggen, P. D. (1998). *Learning and teaching: Research-based methods* (3rd ed.). Boston: Allyn & Bacon.

Kellogg, R. (1972). Listening. In P. Lamb (Ed.), *Guiding children's language learning* (pp. 141–170). Dubuque, IA: William C. Brown.

Kerchner, L., & Kistinger, B. (1984). Language processing/word processing: Written expression, computers and learning disabled students. *Learning Disability Quarterly, 7,* 329–335.

Kerr, M. M., Nelson, C. M., & Lambert, D. L. (1987). *Helping adolescents with learning and behavior problems.* Columbus, OH: Merrill.

Kibby, M. W. (1995). The organization and teaching of things and the words that signify them. *Journal of Adolescent and Adult Literacy, 39,* 208–223.

Kidder, T. (1989). *Among school children.* Boston: Houghton Mifflin.

Kinder, D., Bursuck, B., & Epstein, M. (1992). An evaluation of history textbooks. *Journal of Special Education, 25,* 472–491.

Kintch, W., & Van Dijk, T. (1978). Toward a model of text comprehension and production. *Psychological Review, 85*, 363–394.

Kirkland, N. C. (1993). *Developing a sequential relevant approach to research writing for high school juniors and seniors*. Ed.D Practicum, Nova University, Fort Lauderdale, FL. (ERIC Document Reproduction Service).

Kirsch, I. S., & Jungeblut, A. (1986). *Literacy: Profiles of America's young adults*. Princeton, NJ: National Assessment of Educational Progress.

Klare, G. (1974/75). Assessing readability. *Reading Research Quarterly, 10*, 62–102.

Kletzein, S. B. (1991). Strategy use by good and poor comprehenders reading expository text of differing reading levels. *Reading Research Quarterly, 26*, 67–86.

Kolozow, L. V., & Lehmann, J. (1982). *College reading strategies for success*. Englewood Cliffs, NJ: Prentice-Hall.

Konopak, B. C. (1988). Using contextual information for word learning. *Journal of Reading, 31*, 334–338.

Koskinen, P. et al. (1999). Shared reading, books, and audiotapes: Supporting diverse students in school and at home. *The Reading Teacher, 52* (5), 430–444.

Kotulak, R. (1996). *Inside the brain: Revolutionary discoveries of how the mind works*. Kansas City, MO: Andrews & McNally.

Kowalski, T. (1995). Chasing the wolves from the schoolhouse door. *Phi Delta Kappan, 76*, 486–489.

Laffey, J., & Morgan, R. (1983). *Successful interactions in reading and language: A practical handbook for subject matter teachers*. Harrisonburg, VA: Feygan.

Langer, J. (1981). From theory to practice: A prereading plan. *Journal of Reading, 25*, 152–156.

Larson, C., & Danserau, D. (1986). Cooperative learning in dyads. *Journal of Reading, 29*, 516–520.

Lederer, R. (1987). *Anguished english*. New York: Dell/Bantam Doubleday.

Lee, P., & Allen, G. (1981). *Training junior high LD students to use a test-taking strategy*. (Eric Document No. ED 217 649)

Lee, S., Stigler, J. W., & Stevenson, H. W. (1986). Beginning reading in Chinese and English. In B. Foorman & A. W. Siegel (Eds.), *Acquisition of reading skills* (pp. 123–149). Hillsdale, NJ: Erlbaum.

Lee, V. E., & Smith, J. B. (1994). *Effects of high school restructuring and size on gains in achievement and engagement for early secondary school students*. Madison, WI: Document Service, Wisconsin Center for Education Research.

Leinhardt, G., Stainton, C., & Bausmith, J. M. (1998). Constructing maps cooperatively. *Journal of Geography, 97*, (1), 19–30.

Leki, I. (1992). *Understanding ESL writers: A guide for teachers*. Portsmouth, NH: Heinemann.

LeNoir, W. D. (1993). Teacher questions and schema activation. *Clearing House, 66*: (6), 349–352.

Lester, J. H. (1998). The "real" experts address the textbook issues. *Journal of Adolescent and Adult Literacy, 41* (4), 282–291.

Leu, D. J., Jr. (1997). Caity's question: Literacy as deixis on the internet. *The Reading Teacher, 51* (1), 62–67.

Leu, D. J., Jr., Karchmer, R., & Leu, D.D. (1999). Exploring literacy on the internet. *The Reading Teacher, 52* (6), 636–642.

Leu, D. J., Jr. & Leu, D. D. (1999). *Teaching with the internet: Lesson from the classroom*. Norwood, MA: Christopher Gordon.

Levin, H. M. (1988). Accelerating elementary education for disadvantaged students. In D. W. Hornbeck (Ed.), *School success for at-risk youth: Analysis and recommendations of the Council of Chief State School Officers* (pp. 209–226). Orlando, FL: Harcourt Brace Jovanovich.

Levin, J. R., Levin, M. E., Glassman, L. D., & Nordwall, M. B. (1992). Mnemonic vocabulary instruction: Additional effectiveness evidence. *Contemporary Educational Psychology, 17*, 156–174.

Levin, J. R., Morrison, C. R., & McGivern, J. E. (1986). Mnemonic facilitation of text-embedded science facts. *American Educational Research Journal, 23*, 489–506.

Lin, Lin-Mao, Zabrucky, K., & Moore, D. (1997). The relations among interest, self-assessment comprehension, and comprehension performance in young adults. *Reading Research and Instruction, 36*: (2), 127–139.

Lindfors, J. W. (1980). *Children's language and learning*. Englewood Cliffs, NJ: Prentice-Hall.

Lipsitz, J. (1995). Why we should care about caring. *Phi Delta Kappan, 76*, 665–666.

Lovitt, T. C., Horton, S. V., & Bergerud, D. (1987). Matching students with textbooks: An alternative to readability formulas and standard tests. *British Columbia Journal of Special Education, 11*, 49–55.

Lowery, L. F. (1998). *The biological basis for thinking and learning* (monograph). Berkeley, CA: Lawrence Hall of Science.

Lowry, L. (1989). *Number the stars*. Boston: Houghton Mifflin.

Lynch-Brown, C., & Tomlinson, C. M. (1993). *Essentials of children's literature*. Boston: Allyn & Bacon.

MacDonald, J. (1986). Self-generated questions and reading recall: Does training help? *Contemporary Educational Psychology, 11*, 290–304.

MacLean, P. (1978). A mind of three minds: Educating the triune brain. In J. Chall & A. Mirsley (Eds.), *Education and the brain* (pp. 308–342). Chicago: University of Chicago Press.

Mahler, W. R. (1995). Practice what you preach. *The Reading Teacher, 48*, 414–415.

Manzo, A. V. (1969). The ReQuest procedure. *Journal of Reading, 11*, 123–126.

Manzo, A. V. (1975). The guided reading procedure. *Journal of Reading, 18*, 287–291.

Marashio, P. (1995). Designing questions to help students peel back the layers of a text. *Interdisciplinary Humanities, 12* (1), 27–31.

Maria, K., & Junge, K. (1993). *A comparison of fifth graders' comprehension and retention of scientific information using a science textbook and an informal storybook*. Paper presented at the annual meeting of the National Reading Conference, Charleston, SC.

Maria, K., & MacGinitie, W. (1987). Learning from texts that refute the readers' prior knowledge. *Reading Research and Instruction, 26*, 222–238.

Mason, J. M., & Au, K. H. (1990). *Reading instruction for today*. Glenview, IL: Scott, Foresman.

Masztal, N. B. (1986). Cybernetic sessions: A high involvement teaching technique. *Reading Research and Instruction, 25*, 131–138.

Mathewson, G. (1976). The function of attitudes in the reading process. In H. Singer & R. Ruddell (Eds.), *Theoretical models and processes of reading* (pp. 908–919). Newark, DE: International Reading Association.

Maurer, M. M., & Davidson, G. (1999). Technology, children, and the power of the heart. *Phi Delta Kappan, 80* (6), 458–461.

May, F. B. (1990). *Reading as communication: An interactive approach*. Columbus, OH: Merrill.

McAndrew, D. A. (1983). Underlining and note taking: Some suggestions from research. *Journal of Reading, 27*, 103–108.

McCombs, B. L. (1986). The role of the self-system in self-regulated learning. *Contemporary Educational Psychology, 11*, 314–332.

McConkie, G. W., & Rayner, K. (1976). Asymmetry of the perceptual span in reading. *Bulletin of the Psychometric Society, 8*, 365–368.

McDermott, R. P. (1978). Some reasons for focusing on classrooms in reading research. *Reading: Disciplined inquiry in process and practice.* Clemson, SC: Twenty-seventh Yearbook of the National Reading Conference.

McKenna, M. C., & Kear, D. J. (1990). Measuring attitude toward reading: A new tool for teachers. *The Reading Teacher, 43,* 626–639.

McKeown, M. G., Bede, I. L., & Worthy, J. (1992). *Engaging students with text.* Paper presented at the annual meeting of the National Reading Association Conference, San Antonio, TX.

McLaughlin, H. (1969). SMOG grading—a new readability formula. *Journal of Reading, 12,* 639–646.

McMillan, J. H., & Reed, D. F. (1994). Resilient at-risk students: Students' views about why they succeed. *Journal of At-Risk Issues, 1,* 27–33.

McMurray, M., Laffey, J., & Morgan, R. (1979). *College students' word identification strategies.* Clemson, SC: Twenty-eighth Yearbook of the National Reading Conference.

McPeck, J. (1981). *Critical thinking and education.* New York: St. Martin's Press.

McQuillian, J. (1998). *The literacy crisis: False claims, real solutions.* Portsmouth, NH: Heinemann.

McWilliams, L., & Rakes, T. (1979). *The content inventories.* Dubuque, IA: Kendall/Hunt.

Mealey, D., & Konopak, B. (1990). Content area vocabulary instruction: is preteaching worth the effort? *Reading: Exploration and Discovery, 13:* (1), 39–42.

Medo, M. A., & Ryder, R. J. (1993). The effects of vocabulary instruction on readers' ability to make causal connections. *Reading Research and Instruction, 33* (2), 119–134.

Meeks, J. W. (1991). Prior knowledge and metacognitive processes of reading comprehension: Applications to mildly retarded readers. *Advances in Mental Retardation and Developmental Disabilities, 4,* 121–142.

Meeks, J., & Morgan, R. (1978). New use for the cloze procedure: Interaction in imagery. *Reading Horizons, 18,* 261–264.

Meloth, M. S., & Deering, P. D. (1992). Effects of two cooperative conditions on peer-group discussions, reading comprehension, and metacognition. *Contemporary Educational Psychology, 17,* 175–193.

Memory, D. M. (1990). Teaching technical vocabulary: Before, during, or after reading assignment? *Journal of Reading Behavior, 22,* 39–53.

Menke, D. J., & Pressley, M. (1994). Elaborative interrogation: Using "why" questions to enhance the learning from text. *Journal of Reading, 37* (8), 642–645.

Metzger, M. (1989). *Voices from the Civil War.* New York: Crowell.

Meyer, B. J. F., Brandt, D. M., & Bluth, G. J. (1980). Use of top-level structure in text: Key for reading comprehension of ninth grade students. *Reading Research Quarterly, 16,* 72–103.

Miklos, J. (1982). A look at reading achievement in the United States. *Journal of Reading, 25,* 760–762.

Mikulecky, L., Shanklin, N., & Caverly, D. (1979). Mikulecky behavioral reading attitude measure. In *Adult reading habits, attitudes and motivations: A cross-sectional study.* Bloomington: Indiana University, School of Education.

Miller, G. (1956). The magical number seven, plus or minus two. *Psychological Review, 63,* 81–97.

Miller, G. R., & Coleman, E. B. (1971). The measurement of reading speed and the obligation to generalize to a population of reading materials. *Journal of Reading Behavior, 4* (3), 48–56.

Minicucci, C., Berman, P., McLaughlin, B., McLeod, B., Nelson, B., & Woodworth, K. (1995). School reform and school diversity. *Phi Delta Kappan, 77,* 77–80.

Moffett, J. (1979). Integrity in the teaching of writing. *Phi Delta Kappan, 61,* 276–279.

Moore, D., & Arthur, S. V. (1981). Possible sentences. In E. K. Dishner, T. W. Bean, & J. E. Readance (Eds.), *Reading in the content areas: Improving classroom instruction*. Dubuque, IA: Kendall/Hunt.

Moore, D., Moore, S. A., Cunningham, P., & Cunningham, J. (1998). *Developing readers and writers in the content areas k-12*. New York: Longman.

Moore, D., & Murphy, A. (1987). Selection of materials. In D. Alvermann, D. Moore, & M. Conley (Eds.), *Research within reach: Secondary school reading* (pp. 94–108). Newark, DE: International Reading Association.

Moore, J. C., & Surber, J. R. (1992). Effects of context and keyword methods on second language vocabulary acquisition. *Contemporary Educational Psychology, 17*, 286–292.

Moore, W. E., McCann, H., & McCann, J. (1981). *Creative and critical thinking* (2nd ed.). Boston: Houghton Mifflin.

Morgan, R., & Culver, V. (1978). Locus of control and reading achievement: Applications for the classroom. *Journal of Reading, 21*, 403–408.

Morgan, R. F., Forget, M. A. , and Antinarella, J. C. (1996). *Reading for success: A school to work approach*. Cincinnati, OH: South-Western.

Morgan, R. F., Meeks, J. W., Schollaert, A., & Paul, J. (1986). *Critical reading/thinking skills for the college student*. Dubuque, IA: Kendall/Hunt.

Morgan, R., Otto, A., & Thompson, G. (1976). A study of the readability and comprehension of selected eighth grade social studies textbooks. *Perceptual and Motor Skills, 43*, 594.

Morrison, J. L. (1999). The Role of technology in education today and tomorrow: An Interview with Kenneth Green. *On The Horizon, 7* (1), 1–4.

Morrison, T. G., Jacobs, J. S., & Swinyard, W. R. (1999). Do teachers who read personally use recommended literacy practices in their classrooms? *Reading Research and Instruction, 38* (2), 81–100.

Mosenthal, P. B., & Kirsch, I. S. (1998). A new measure for assessing document complexity: The PMOSE/IKIRSCH document readability formula. *Journal of Adolescent and Adult Literacy, 41* (8), 638–657.

Moss, J. (1990). *Focus units in literature: A handbook for elementary school teachers* (2nd ed.). Urbana, IL: National Council of Teachers of English.

Muth, K. D. (1987). Structure strategies for comprehending expository text. *Reading Research and Instruction, 27*, 66–72.

Myers, J. W. (1984). *Writing to learn across the curriculum*. Bloomington, IN: Phi Delta Kappa.

Myers, P. (1998). Passion for poetry. *Journal of Adolescent and Adult Literacy, 41* (4), 262–271.

Myklebust, H. (1965). *Development and disorders of written language*. New York: Grune & Stratton.

National Assessment of Educational Progress (1998). Education Commission of the States, Denver, CO.

National Center for Education Statistics (1996). *Reading literacy in the United States: Findings from the IEA reading literacy study*. Washington, DC: Department of Education.

National Center for Educational Statistics (1991). Washington, DC: Report No. 21-T-01.

National Commission on Excellence in Education (1983). *A nation at risk: The imperative report to the nation and the secretary of education*. Washington, DC: U.S. Government Printing Office.

Neckerman, K. M., & Wilson, W. J. (1988). In D. W. Hornbeck (Ed.), *School success for at-risk youth: Analysis and recommendations of the Council of Chief State School Officers* (pp. 25–44). Orlando, FL: Harcourt Brace Jovanovich.

Neisser, V. (1967). *Cognitive psychology*. New York: Appleton-Century-Crofts.

Nessel, D. (1987). Reading comprehension: Asking the right questions. *Phi Delta Kappan, 68*, 442–445.

Neuman, S. (1991). *Literacy in the television age: The myth of the TV effect.* Norwood, NJ: Ablex.

Newell, A., & Simon, H. A. (1972). *Human problem solving.* Englewood Cliffs, NJ: Prentice-Hall.

Novak, J. D., & Gowin, D. B. (1984). Learning how to learn. Cambridge: Cambridge University Press.

Noddings, N. (1995). Teaching themes of caring. *Phi Delta Kappan, 76* (9), 675–679.

O'Brien, R. (1971). *Mrs. Frisby and the rats of NIMH.* New York: Atheneum.

O'Dell, Scott. (1987). *The serpent never sleeps.* New York: Ballantine.

Ogle, D. (1986). KWL: A teaching model that develops active reading of expository text. *The Reading Teacher, 39,* 564–570.

Ogle, D. (1992). KWL in action: Secondary teachers find applications that work. In E. K. Dishner, T. W. Bean, J. E. Readance, & D. W. Moore (Eds.), *Reading in the content areas: Improving classroom instruction* (3rd ed., pp. 270–281). Dubuque, IA: Kendall/Hunt.

Olshavsky, J. (1975). Reading as problem solving: An investigation of strategies. *Reading Research Quarterly, 12,* 654–674.

Olson, M. W., & Gee, T. (1991). Content reading instruction in the primary grades: Perceptions and strategies. *The Reading Teacher, 45,* 298–307.

Opitz, M. (1992). The cooperative reading activity: An alternative to ability grouping. *The Reading Teacher, 45,* 736–738.

Orfield, A. (1988). Race, income, and educational inequity. In *School success for at-risk youth: Analysis and recommendations of the Council of Chief State School Officers* (pp. 45–71). Orlando, FL: Harcourt Brace Jovanovich.

Page, B. (1987). From passive receivers to active learners in English. In J. Self (Ed.), *Plain talk about learning and writing across the curriculum* (pp. 37–50). Richmond: Virginia Department of Education.

Palincsar, A. S., & Brown, A. L. (1986). Interactive teaching to promote independent learning from text. *The Reading Teacher, 39,* 771–777.

Pallas, A. M., Natriello, G., & McDill, E. L. (1989). Changing nature of the disadvantaged population: Current dimensions and future trends. *Educational Researcher, 18,* 16–22.

Pally, M. (1998). Film studies drive literacy development for ESL university students. *Journal of Adolescent and Adult Literacy, 41* (8), 620–628.

Pang, V. O., Colvin, C., Tran, M. Y., & Barba, R. H. (1992). Beyond chopsticks and dragons: Selecting Asian-American literature for children. *Journal of Reading, 46,* 216–223.

Paris, S. G. (1986). Teaching children to guide their reading and learning. In T. E. Raphael & R. Reynolds (Eds.), *Context of literacy* (pp. 115–130). New York: Longman.

Paris, S. G., Cross, D. R., & Lipson, M. Y. (1984). Informal strategies for learning: A program to improve children's reading awareness and comprehension. *Journal of Educational Psychology, 76,* 1239–1252.

Paris, S. G., Lipson, M. Y., & Wixson, K. K. (1983). Becoming a strategic reader. *Contemporary Educational Psychology, 8,* 393–396.

Paris, S. G., & Winograd, P. (1990). How metacognition can promote academic learning and instruction. In B. Jones & L. Idol (Eds.), *Dimensions of thinking and cognitive instruction* (pp. 15–52). Hillsdale, NJ: Erlbaum.

Parnes, S. J., & Noller, R. B. (1973). *Toward supersanity: Channeled freedom.* East Aurora, NY: D.O.K.

Pauk, W. (1974). *How to study in college.* Boston: Houghton Mifflin.

Paulsen, G. (1990). *Canyons.* New York: Delacorte Press.

Pearce, D. (1983). Guidelines for the use and evaluation of writing in content classrooms. *Journal of Reading, 17,* 212–218.

Pearce, D. (1987). Group writing activities: A useful strategy for content teachers. *Middle School Journal, 18,* 24–25.

Pearce, D., & Bader, L. (1984). Writing in content area classrooms. *Reading World, 23,* 234–241.

Pearce, D., & Davison, D. (1988). Teacher use of writing in the junior high mathematics classroom. *School Science and Mathematics, 88,* 6–15.

Pearson, P. D. (1985). Changing the face of reading comprehension. *The Reading Teacher, 38,* 724–738.

Pearson, P. D., & Johnson, D. (1978). *Teaching reading comprehension.* New York: Holt, Rinehart & Winston.

Pearson, P. D., & Santa, C. M. (1995). Students as researchers of their own learning. *Journal of Reading, 38,* 462–469.

Pearson, P. D., & Stephens, D. (1994). Learning about literacy: A 30-year journey. In R. Ruddell, M. Ruddell, & H. Singer (Eds.), *Theoretical models and processes of reading,* pp. 22–43, Newark, DE: International Reading Association.

Pearson, P. D., & Tierney, R. (1983). In search of a model of instructional research in reading. In S. Paris, G. Okon, & H. Stevenson (Eds.), *Learning and motivation in the classroom.* Hillsdale, NJ: Erlbaum.

Pellicano, R. (1987). At-risk: A view of "social advantage." *Educational Leadership, 44,* 47–50.

Penfield, W. (1975). *The mystery of the mind: A critical study of consciousness and the human brain.* Princeton, NJ: Princeton University Press.

Peregoy, S., & Boyle, O. (1997). *Reading, writing, and learning in ESL: A resource book for K-12 teachers.* White Plains, NY: Longman.

Perez, S. A., & Strickland, D. (1987). Teaching children how to discuss what they read. *Reading Horizons, 27,* 89–94.

Peters, E. E., & Levin, J. R. (1986). Effects of a mnemonic imagery strategy on good and poor readers' prose recall. *Reading Research Quarterly, 21,* 179–192.

Piaget, J. (1952). *The language and thought of the child.* London: Routledge and Kegan Paul.

Piaget, J. (1963). *The origin of intelligence in children.* New York: Norton.

Piaget, J., & Inhelder, B. (1969). *The psychology of the child.* New York: Basic Books.

Pope, C., & Praeter, D. L. (1990). Writing proficiency and student use of prewriting/invention strategies. *Reading Research and Instruction, 29,* 4, 64–70.

Purohit, K. D. (1998). What matters most in my science class. *Voices from the Middle, 6* (1), 26–29.

Purves, A. C., & Bech, R. (1972). *Literature and the reader: Research in response to literature, reading interests, and the teaching of literature.* Urbana, IL: National Council of Teachers of English.

Radencich, M. (1985). Writing a class novel: A strategy for LD students? *Academic Therapy, 20,* 599–603.

Rakes, G. C., Rakes, T. A., & Smith, L. J. (1995). Using visuals to enhance secondary students' reading comprehension of expository texts. *Journal of Adolescent and Adult Literacy, 39,* 46–54.

Rakes, T., & Chance, L. (1990). A survey of how subjects remember what they read. *Reading Improvement, 27,* 122–128.

Ralph, J., Keller, D., & Crouse, J. (1994). How effective are American schools? *Phi Delta Kappan, 76,* 144–150.

Raphael, T. (1984). Teaching learners about sources of information for answering comprehension questions. *Journal of Reading, 27,* 303–311.

Raphael, T. (1986). Teaching question/answer relationships, revisited. *The Reading Teacher, 39*, 516–522.

Rasinski, T., & Nathenson-Mejia, S. (1987). Learning to read, learning community: Consideration of the social contexts for literacy instruction. *The Reading Teacher, 41*, 260–265.

Rasinski, T. V., & Padak, N. D. (1993). *Inquiries in literacy learning and instruction: Fifteenth yearbook of the College Reading Association.* Kent, OH: Kent State University.

Raths, L., Wassermann, S., Jones, A., & Rothstein, A. (1986). *Teaching for thinking: Theories, strategies and activities for the classroom.* New York: Teachers College Press.

Raven, J. (1992). A model of competence, motivation, and behavior, and a paradigm for assessment. In H. Berlak et al. (Eds.), *Toward a new science of educational testing and assessment.* New York: State University of New York Press.

Rayner, K. (1978). Eye movements in reading and information processing. *Psychological Bulletin, 85*, 616–660.

Readance, J. E., Bean, T. W., & Baldwin, R. S. (1981). *Content area reading: An integrated approach.* Dubuque, IA: Kendall/Hunt.

The Reading report card: Progress toward excellence in our schools: Trends in reading instruction over four national assessments, 1971–1984. (Report No. 15-R-01) (1985). Princeton, NJ: National Assessment of Educational Progress and Educational Testing Service.

Reed, D. F., McMillan, J. H., & McBee, R. H. (1995). Defying the odds: Middle schoolers in high risk circumstances who succeed. *Middle School Journal, 27*, 3–10.

Reinking, D. (1997). Me and my hypertext☺ A multiple regression analysis of technology and literacy (sic). *The Reading Teacher, 50* (8), 626–643.

Reinking, D., & Pardon, D. (1995). Television and literacy. In T.V. Rasinski (Ed.), *Parents and teachers helping children learn to read and write* (pp. 137–145). Ft. Worth, TX: Harcourt Brace.

Reinking, D., & Wu, J. H. (1990). Reexamining the research on television and reading. *Reading Research and Instruction, 29*, 30–43.

Rekrut, M. D. (1997). Collaborative research. *Journal of Adolescent and Adult Literacy, 41*: (1), 26–34.

Rekrut, M. D. (1999). Using the internet in classroom instruction: A primer for teachers. *Journal of Adolescent and Adult Literacy, 42* (7), 546–557.

Restak, R. (1979). *The brain: The last frontier.* Garden City, NY: Doubleday.

Restak, R. (1982). The brain. *Wilson Quarterly, 6*, 89–115.

Restak, R. (1984). *The brain.* New York: Bantam Books.

Reutzel, D. R., & Daines, D. (1987). The text-relatedness of reading lessons in seven basal reading series. *Reading Research and Instruction, 27*, 26–35.

Reyes, D. J. (1986). Critical thinking in elementary social studies text series. *Social Studies, 77*, 151–157.

Reyhner, J., & Garcia, R. L. (1989). Helping minorities read better: Problems and promises. *Reading Research and Instruction, 28*, 84–91.

Rhodes, L. K., & Shanklin, N. (1991). *Windows into literacy: Assessing Learners K–8.* Portsmouth, NH: Heinemann.

Rhodes, R. (1990, October 14). Don't be a bystander. *Parade*, pp. 4–7.

Rice, G. E. (1992, April). *The need for explanations in graphic organizer research.* Paper presented at the annual meeting of the American Educational Research Association, San Francisco.

Richardson, J. (1975). *A study of the syntactic competence of adult beginning readers.* Unpublished doctoral dissertation, University of North Carolina at Chapel Hill.

Richardson, J. (1991). Developing responsibility in English classes: Three activities. *Journal of the Virginia College Reading Educators, 11*, 8–19.

Richardson, J. (1992a). Generating inquiry-oriented projects from teachers. In A. Frager & J. Miller (Eds.), *Using inquiry in reading teacher education* (pp. 24–29). Kent, OH: Kent State University, College Reading Association.

Richardson, J. (1992b). Taking responsibility for taking tests. In N. Padak & T. Rasinski (Eds.), *Literacy research and practice: Foundations for the year 2000* (pp. 209–215). Kent, OH: Kent State University, College Reading Association.

Richardson, J. S. (1994). Great read-alouds for prospective teachers and secondary students. *Journal of Reading, 38,* 98–103.

Richardson, J. (1995). Three ways to keep a middle school student in the "reading habit." *Affective Reading Education, 14,* 5–7.

Richardson, J. S. (1995). A read-aloud for cultural diversity. *Journal of Adolescent and Adult Literacy, 39,* 160–162.

Richardson, J. S. (1996). *The survival guide: Reading to learn in the english class.* Toronto, Canada: Pippin.

Richardson, J. S. (1999a). No Somali! Only English!: A case study of an adult refugee's use of appropriate materials when learning english and reading skills. *The Twenty-first yearbook of the College Reading Association.* Commerce, TX: College Reading Association yearbook.

Richardson, J. S. (1999b). *Reading is drudgery; reading is deeper meaning.* Paper presented at the 43rd conference of the College Reading Association conference, Hilton Head, SC.

Richardson, J. S. (2000). *Read it aloud! Using literature in secondary content classrooms.* Newark, DE: International Reading Association.

Richardson, J. S., & Forget, M. A. (1995). A read-aloud for algebra and geography classrooms. *Journal of Adolescent and Adult Literacy, 39,* 322–326.

Richardson, J. S., & Morgan, R. F. (1997). *Reading to learn in the content areas.* Belmont, CA: Wadsworth ITP.

Richardson, J. S., & Morgan, R.F. (1991). Crossing bridges by connecting meaning. *Texas Affect In Reading Journal, 34* (1).

Rickards, J. P., & August, G. J. (1975). Generative underlining strategies in prose recall. *Journal of Educational Psychology, 67,* 860–865.

Rifkin, J. (1987). *Time wars.* New York: Henry Holt.

Ritter, S., & Idol-Mastas, L. (1986). Teaching middle school students to use a test-taking strategy. *Journal of Educational Research, 79,* 350–357.

Robertson, J. I. (1992). *Civil War: America becomes one nation.* New York: Alfred Knopf.

Robinson, D. H. (1998). Graphic organizers as aids to text learning. *Reading Research and Instruction, 37* (2), 85–105.

Robinson, F. P. (1961). *Effective study* (rev. ed.). New York: Harper & Row.

Rogers, D. B. (1984). Assessing study skills. *Journal of Reading, 27,* 346–354.

Roit, M., & McKenzie, R. (1985). Disorders of written communication: An instructional priority for LD students. *Journal of Learning Disabilities, 18,* 258–260.

Rosada, B. (1995). The sentiments of a nation can be understood only from the heart. *Multiculturalism, 5,* 6–8.

Rosenblatt, L. (1991). Literature-S.O.S.!, *Language Arts, 68,* 444–448.

Ross, J. A., Rolheiser, C., & Hoaboam-Gray, A. (1998). *Impact of self-evaluation training on mathematics achievement in a cooperative learning environment.* Paper presented at the annual meeting of the American Educational Research Association, San Diego, CA, April 1998.

Rothstein, R. (1998). Bilingual education: The controversy. *Phi Delta Kappan, 79* (9), 672–678.

Rotter, J. B. (1966). Generalized expectancies for internal versus external control of reinforcement. *Psychological Monographs: General and Applied, 80* (1), 1–28.

Rumelhart, D. E. (1980). Schemata: The building blocks of cognition. In R. J. Spiro, B. C. Bruce, & W. F. Brewer (Eds.), *Theoretical issues in reading comprehension* (pp. 33–58). Hillsdale, NJ: Erlbaum.

Russell, S. (1995). Sheltered content instruction for second language learners. *Reading Today, 13*, 30.

Ryder, R. J., & Graves, M. F. (1994). Vocabulary instruction presented prior to reading in two basal readers. *Elementary School Journal, 95*: (2), 139–153.

Sagan, C. (1977). *The dragons of Eden.* New York: Random House.

Sakta, C. G. (1999). SQCR: A Strategy for guiding reading and higher level thinking. *Journal of Adolescent and Adult Literacy, 42*: (4), 265–269.

Salembier, G. B. (1999). SCAN and RUN: A reading comprehension strategy that works. *Journal of Adolescent and Adult Literacy, 42* (5), 386–401.

Samples, B. (1994). Instructional diversity. *The Science Teacher, 61*, 14–17.

Samuels, S. J. (1979). The method of repeated readings. *The Reading Teacher, 32*, 403–408.

Sanacore, J. (1998). Promoting the lifelong love of reading. *Journal of Adolescent and Adult Literacy, 41*, (5), 392–396.

Santeusanio, R. (1983). *A practical approach to content area reading.* Reading, MA: Addison-Wesley.

Scardamalia, M., & Bereiter, C. (1984). Development of strategies in text processing. In H. Mandl, N. L. Stein, & T. Trabasson (Eds.), *Learning and comprehension of text* (pp. 379–406). Hillsdale, NJ: Erlbaum.

Schadt, W. (1989). Literary gift exchange. *Journal of Reading, 33*, 223–224.

Schallert, D. L., & Kleiman, G. M. (1979). *Why the teacher is easier to understand than the textbook.* (Reading Education Report No. 9). Urbana: University of Illinois, Center for the Study of Reading.

Schatz, E. K. (1984). *The influence of context clues on determining the meaning of low frequency words in naturally occurring prose.* Unpublished doctoral dissertation, University of Miami.

Schieffelin, B. B., & Cochran-Smith, M. (1984). Learning to read culturally: Literacy before schooling. In H. Goelman, A. Oberg, & F. Smith (Eds.), *Awakening to literacy* (pp. 3–23). Portsmouth, NH: Heinemann.

Schmidt, P. R. (1995). Working and playing with others: Cultural conflict in a kindergarten literacy program. *The Reading Teacher, 48*, 404–412.

Schumm, J. (1992). Content area textbooks: How tough are they? *Journal of Reading, 36*, 47.

Schumm, J., Mangrum, C., Gordon, J., & Doucette, M. (1992). The effect of topic knowledge on the predicted test questions of developmental college readers. *Reading Research and Instruction, 31*, 11–23.

Schunk, D. H., & Rice, J. M. (1992). Influence of reading comprehension strategy information on children's achievement outcomes. *Learning Disabilities Quarterly, 15* (1), 51–64.

Schwartz, R. M., & Raphael, T. E. (1985). Concept of definition: A key to improving students' vocabulary. *Journal of Reading, 39*, 198–205.

Scruggs, T., Mastropier, M. A., Brigham, F. J., & Sullivan, G. S. (1992). Effects of mnemonic reconstructions on the spatial learning of adolescents with learning disabilities. *Learning Disability Quarterly, 15* (3), 154–167.

Scruggs, T., White, K., & Bennion, K. (1986). Teaching test-taking skills to elementary students: A meta-analysis. *Elementary School Journal, 87*, 69–82.

Self, J. (1987). The picture of writing to learn. In J. Self (Ed.), *Plain talk about learning and writing across the curriculum* (pp. 9–20). Richmond: Virginia State Department of Education.

Seuss, Dr. (Theodor Seus Geisel) (1960). *Green eggs and ham.* New York: Random House.

Shanahan, T. (1997). Reading-writing relationships, thematic units, inquiry learning . . . in pursuit of effective integrated literacy instruction. *The Reading Teacher, 51* (1), 12–19.

Shanahan, T., Mulhern, M., and Rodriguez-Brown, F. (1995). Project FLAME: Lessons learned from a family literacy program for linguistic minority families. *The Reading Teacher, 48,* 586–593.

Shanahan, T., Robinson, B., & Schneider, M. (1995). Avoiding some of the pitfalls of thematic units. *The Reading Teacher, 48,* 718–719.

Shanker, A. (1984, September 5). Where we stand: Who should evaluate the textbooks? *Education Week,* p. 69.

Sharan, S., & Sharan, Y. (1976). *Small-group teaching.* Englewood Cliffs, NJ: Educational Technology Publications.

Sherer, P. (1975). Skimming and scanning: De-mything the process with a college student. *Journal of Reading, 19,* 24–27.

Shyer, M. F. (1988). *Welcome home, jelly bean.* New York: Macmillan.

Siedow, M. D., & Hasselbring, T. S. (1984). Adaptability of text readability to increase comprehension of reading disability students. *Reading Improvement, 21,* 276–279.

Silva, P. U., Meagher, M. E., Valenzuela, M., & Crenshaw, S. W. (1996). E-mail: Real-life classroom experiences with foreign languages. *Learning and Leading with Technology, 23,* 5, 10–12.

Simon, K. (1993). Alternative assessment: Can real-world skills be tested? *The Link, 12,* 1–7.

Simpson, M. L. (1987). Alternative formats for evaluating content area vocabulary understanding. *Journal of Reading, 30,* 20–27.

Sinatra, R. (1986). *Visual literacy connections to thinking, reading and writing.* Springfield, IL: Thomas.

Singer, H., & Bean, T. (1988). Three models for helping teachers to help students learn from text. In S. J. Samuels & P. D. Pearson (Eds.), *Changing school reading programs* (pp. 161–183). Newark, DE: International Reading Association.

Singer, H., & Donlan, D. (1985). *Reading and learning from text.* Hillsdale, NJ: Erlbaum.

Singh, J. (1995). *Development of an alternative methodology for determining the readability of text.* Unpublished doctoral dissertation, Virginia Commonwealth University, Richmond.

Slavin, R. E. (1980). Cooperative learning. *Review of Educational Research, 50,* 315–342.

Slavin, R. E. (1983). *Cooperative learning.* New York: Longman.

Slavin, R. E. (1991). Synthesis of research on cooperative learning. *Educational Leadership, 48,* 71–82.

Sloan, G. D. (1984). *The child as critic: Teaching literature in elementary and middle schools* (2nd ed.). New York: Teachers College Press.

Smith, D. (1992). Common ground: The connection between reader-response and textbook reading. *Journal of Reading, 35,* 630–635.

Smith, F. (1971). *Understanding reading.* New York: Holt, Rinehart & Winston.

Smith, F. (1973). *Psycholinguistics and reading.* New York: Holt, Rinehart & Winston.

Smith, F. (1986). *Insult to intelligence: The bureaucratic invasion of our classrooms.* New York: Arbor House.

Smith, F. (1988). *Understanding reading: A psycholinguistic analysis of reading and learning to read* (4th ed.). Hillsdale, NJ: Erlbaum.

Smith, F. (1989). Overselling literacy. *Phi Delta Kappan, 70,* 352–359.

Smith, F. (1994). *Understanding Reading: A psycholinguistic analysis of reading and learning to read.* (5th ed). Hillsdale, NJ: Erlbaum.

Smith, M. C. (1990). A longitudinal investigation of reading attitude development from childhood to adulthood. *Journal of Educational Research, 83,* 215–219.

Smith, N. B. (1965). *American reading instruction.* Newark, DE: International Reading Association.

Smith, S., & Bean, R. (1980). The guided writing procedure: Integrating content reading and writing improvement. *Reading World, 19*, 290–294.

Smuin, S. (1978). *Turn-ons*. Belmont, CA: Fearon Pitman.

Snow, C. E., Burns, M. S., & Griffin, P. (Eds.) (1998). *Preventing reading difficulties in young children*. Washington, DC: National Academy Press.

Sosniak, L. A., & Perlman, C. L. (1990). Secondary education by the book. *Journal of Curriculum Studies, 22*, 427–442.

Spache, G. (1953). A new readability formula for primary grade reading materials. *Elementary School Journal, 53*, 410–413.

Spache, G. (1976). *Investigating the issues of reading disabilities*. Boston: Allyn & Bacon.

Sparks, D. (1995). A paradigm shift in staff development. *The ERIC Review, 3*: (3), 5–7.

Speigel, D. L., & Wright, J. (1983). Biology teachers' use of readability concepts when selecting texts for students. *Journal of Reading, 27*, 28–34.

Spor, M. W., & Schneider, B. K. (1999). Content reading strategies: What teachers know, use, and want to learn. *Reading Research and Instruction, 38* (3), 221–231.

Stahl, S. (1983). Differential word knowledge and reading comprehension. *Journal of Reading Behavior, 15*, 33–50.

Stahl, S. (1986). Three principles of effective vocabulary instruction. *Journal of Reading, 29*, 662–668.

Stauffer, R. G. (1969a). *Directing reading maturity as a cognitive process*. New York: Harper & Row.

Stauffer, R. G. (1969b). *Teaching reading as a thinking process*. New York: Harper & Row.

Steen, P. (1991). Book diaries: Connecting free reading with instruction, home and school, and kids with books. *The Reading Teacher, 45*, 330–333.

Stefl-Mabry, J. (1998). Designing a web-based reading course. *Journal of Adolescent and Adult Education, 41* (7), 556–571.

Sternberg, R. J. (1985, November). Teaching critical thinking: 1. Are we making critical mistakes? *Phi Delta Kappan, 66*, 194–198.

Sternberg, R. J. (1991). Are we reading too much into reading comprehension tests? *Journal of Reading, 34*, 540–545.

Sternberg, R. J. (1994). Answering questions and questioning answers. *Phi Delta Kappan, 76*, 136–138.

Sternberg, R. J., & Baron, J. B. (1985). A statewide approach to measuring critical thinking skills. *Educational Leadership, 43*, 40–43.

Stevenson, H. W. (1992). A conversation with Harold Stevenson. *Humanities, 13*, 4–9.

Strahan, D. B. (1983). The emergence of formal reasoning during adolescence. *Transescence, 11*, 7–14.

Strauss, A. A., & Lehtinen, L. (1947). *Psychopathology and education in the brain-injured child* (Vol. 1). New York: Grune & Stratton.

Streeter, B. (1986). The effects of training experienced teachers in enthusiasm on students' attitudes toward reading. *Reading Psychology, 7* (4), 249–259.

Strong, M. (1995). Socratic practice as an organizing principle. *Paideia Next Century, 4*, 5–6.

Sturtevant, E. (1992). *Content literacy in high school social studies: Two case studies in a multicultural setting*. Unpublished doctoral dissertation, Kent State University, Kent, Ohio.

Swafford, J. (1995). "I wish all my groups were like this one": Facilitating peer interaction during group work. *Journal of Reading, 38*, 626–631.

Swafford, J., & Alvermann, D. E. (1989). Postsecondary research base for content strategies. *Journal of Reading, 33*, 164–169.

Sylwester, R. (1995). *A celebration of neurons: An educator's guide to the human brain.* Alexandria, VA: Association for Supervision and Curriculum Development.

Tadlock, D. R. (1978). SQ3R—Why it works, based on an information processing theory of learning. *Journal of Reading, 22,* 110–112.

Tan, A. (1993). Two kinds. *Contemporary West Coast stories.* Old Saybrook, CT: The Globe Pequot Press.

Taylor, B. M., Frye, B. J., & Maruyama, G. M. (1990). Time spent reading and reading growth. *American Educational Research Journal, 72,* 351–362.

Taylor, W. (1953). Cloze procedure: A new tool for measuring readability. *Journalism Quarterly, 30,* 415–433.

Teale, W., & Sulzby, E. (1986). *Emergent literacy: Writing and reading.* Norwood, NJ: Ablex.

Templeton, S. (1991). *Teaching integrated language arts.* Boston, MA: Houghton Mifflin.

Thompson, G., & Morgan, R. (1976). The use of concept-formation study guides for social studies reading materials. *Reading Horizons, 7,* 132–136.

Thorndike, E. L. (1917). Reading and reasoning. *Journal of Educational Psychology, 8,* 323–332.

Thorndike, E. L. (1932). *Educational psychology.* New York: Columbia University, Teachers College Press.

Thurstone, L. L. (1946). A note on a re-analysis of Davis' reading tests. *Psychometrika, 11,* 185–188.

Tierney, R. J. (1998). Literacy assessment reform: Shifting beliefs, principled possibilities, and emerging practice. *The Reading Teacher, 51* (5), 374–390.

Toch, T. (1984, March 7). Bell calls on education to push publishers for better materials. *Education Week,* p. 11.

Todd, C. J. (1995). The semester project: The power and pleasures of independent study. *English Journal, 84,* 73–76.

Tonjes, M. J., & Zintz, M. V. (1981). *Teaching reading/thinking study skills in content classrooms.* Dubuque, IA: William Brown Co.

Torgensen, J., & Licht, B. (1983). The learning disabled child as an inactive learner: Retrospect and prospects. In J. McKinney & L. Feagans (Eds.), *Current topics in learning disabilities* (Vol. 1, pp. 3–31). Norwood, NJ: Ablex.

Tredway, L. (1995). Socratic seminars: Engaging students in intellectual discourse. *Educational Leadership, 53* (1), 26–29.

Turner, J., & Paris, S. G. (1995). How literacy tasks influence children's motivation for literacy. *The Reading Teacher, 48,* 662–673.

Twenty-fourth yearbook of the national society for the study of education. (1925). Bloomington, IN: Public School Publishing Company.

Unks, G. (1985). Critical thinking in the social studies classroom. *Social Education, 44,* 240–246.

Unsworth, L. (1999). Developing critical understanding of the specialised language of school science and history texts: A functional grammatical perspective. *Journal of Adolescent and Adult Education, 42* (7), 508–521.

U.S. Department of Education (1993). *The condition of Education 1993.* Washington, DC.

U.S. Study shows achievement at level of 1970 (1991, October 1). *New York Times,* A-1.

Vacca, R., & Vacca, J. (1999). *Content area reading.* New York: Longman.

Vacca, R. T., & Padak, N. (1990). Who's at risk in reading? *Journal of Reading, 33,* 486–488.

Valeri-Gold, M. (1987). Previewing: A directed reading-thinking activity. *Reading Horizons, 27,* 123–126.

Van der Heuvel, G. (1988). *Crowns of thorns and glory: Mary Todd Lincoln and Varina Howell Davis, the two first ladies of the Civil War*. New York: Dutton.

Vanderventer, N. (1979, Winter). RAFT: A process to structure prewriting. Highway One: A Canadian *Journal of Language Experience*, p. 26.

Vandiver, F. E. (1992). *Blood brothers: A short history of the Civil War*. College Station, TX: Texas A & M Press.

Van Horn, R. (1999). The Electronic classroom and video conferencing. *Phi Delta Kappan, 80* (5), 411–412.

Van Sertima, T. (1976). *The African presence in ancient America: They came before Columbus*. New York: Random House.

Vaughan, C. L. (1990). Knitting writing: The double-entry journal. In N. Atwell (Ed.), *Coming to know: Writing to learn in the intermediate grades* (pp. 69–75). Portsmouth, NH: Heinemann.

Vaughan, J., & Estes, T. (1986). *Reading and reasoning beyond the primary grades*. Boston: Allyn & Bacon.

Veatch, J. (1968). *How to teach reading with children's books*. New York: Citation Press.

Verplaeste, L. S. (1998). How content teachers interact with English language learners. *TESOL Journal, 7* (5), 24–28.

Vermette, P. (1994). The right start for cooperative learning. *High School Journal, 77*, 255–260.

Villaune, S. K., & Hopkins, L. (1995). A Transactional and sociocultural view of response in a fourth-grade literature discussion group. *Reading Research and Instruction, 34*, 190–203.

Viorst, J. (1978). *Alexander who used to be rich last Sunday*. New York: Atheneum.

Vygotsky, L. (1978a). Interaction between learning and development. In M. Cole, V. John-Steiner, S. Scribner, & E. Souberman (Eds.), *Mind in society: The development of higher psychological process* (pp. 79–91). Cambridge, MA: Harvard University Press.

Vygotsky, L. (1978b). The prehistory of written language. In M. Cole, V. John-Steiner, S. Scribner, & E. Souberman (Eds.), *Mind in society: The development of higher psychological process* (pp. 105–119). Cambridge, MA: Harvard University Press.

Wade, S. E., & Adams, R. B. (1990). Effects of importance and interest on recall of biographical text. *Journal of Reading Behavior, 22*, 331–353.

Wagner, C. L., Brock, D. R., & Agnew, A. T. (1994). Developing literacy portfolios in teacher education courses. *Journal of Reading, 37* (8), 668–674.

Wagner, J. O. (1995). Using the Internet in vocational education. *ERIC Digest No. 160* (ERIC Document Reproduction Service No. ED. 385-777).

Walberg, H. J., & Tsai, S. (1985). Correlates of reading achievement and attitude: A national assessment study. *Journal of Educational Research, 78*, 159–167.

Walker, B. J. (1990). *Remedial reading*. Washington, DC: National Education Association.

Walker, B. (1992). *Supporting struggling readers*. Markham, Ontario: Pippin.

Walpole, P. (1987). Yes, writing in math. In J. Self (Ed.), *Plain talk about learning and writing across the curriculum* (pp. 51–59). Richmond: Virginia State Department of Education.

Walpole, S. (1999). Changing texts, changing thinking: Comprehension demands of new science textbooks. *The Reading Teacher, 52* (4), 358–369.

Wassermann, S. (1987). Teaching for thinking: Louis E. Raths revisited. *Phi Delta Kappan, 68*, 460–466.

Wassermann, S. (1999). Shazam! You're a teacher. *Phi Delta Kappan, 80* (6), 464–468.

Weaver, C. (1994). *Reading processes and practice*. Portsmouth, NH: Heinemann.

Wehlange, G. G., & Rutter, R. A. (1986). Dropping out: How much do schools contribute to the problem? *Teachers College Record, 87*, 374–392.

Weiner, B. (1979). A theory of motivation for some classroom experiences. *Journal of Educational Psychology, 71*, 3–25.

Weinstein, C. E. (1987). Fostering learning autonomy through the use of learning strategies. *Journal of Reading, 30*, 590–595.

Weinstein, C. E., & Mayer, R. E. (1986). The teaching of learning strategies. In M. C. Wittrock (Ed.), *Handbook of research on teaching* (3rd ed., pp. 315–327). New York: Macmillan.

Weissberg, M., Berentsen, M., Cote, A., Cravey, B., & Heath, K. (1982). An assessment of the personal, career, and academic needs of undergraduate students. *Journal of College Student Personnel, 23*, 115–122.

Wells, H. G. (1987). *The complete short stories of H. G. Wells*. New York: St. Martin's Press.

Weir, C. (1998). Using embedded questions to jump-start metacognition in middle school readers. *Journal of Adolescent and Adult Literacy, 41* (6), 458–467.

Wepner, S. B. (1995). Using technology for literacy instruction. In S. B. Wepner, J. T. Feeley, and D. S. Strickland (Eds.), *The Administration and Supervision of Reading Programs*. New York: Teachers College Press.

Wepner, S. B., Seminoff, N. E., & Blanchard, J. (1995). Navigating learning with electronic encyclopedias. *Reading Today, 12*, 28.

Wertsch, J. V. (1978). Adult-child interaction and the roots of metacognition. *Quarterly Newsletter of the Institute of Comparative Human Development, 2*, 15–18.

Westbury, I. (1992). Comparing American and Japanese achievement: Is the United States really a low achiever? *Educational Researcher, 21*, 18–24.

White, E. B. (1951). Calculating machine. In *The second tree from the corner* (pp. 165–167). New York: Harper & Row.

White, E. E. (1886). *The elements of pedagogy*. New York: American Book Company.

Whitehead, D. (1994). Teaching literacy and learning strategies through a modified guided silent reading procedure. *Journal of Reading, 38*, 24–30.

Wiegel, H. G. (1998). Kindergarten students' organization of counting in joint counting tasks and the emergence of cooperation. *Journal for Research in Mathematics Education, 29* (2), 202.

Wigfield, A., & Asher, S. R. (1984). Social and motivational influences on reading. In P. D. Pearson (Ed.), *Handbook of reading research*. New York: Longman.

Wigfield, A., & Asher, S. R. (1986). Students' thought processes. In M. C. Wittrock (Ed.), *Handbook of research on teaching*. New York: Macmillan.

Wiggins, G. (1990, August). A conversation with Grant Wiggins. *Instructor*, p. 51.

Wigginton, E. (1986). *Sometimes as shining moment: the Foxfire experiences*. New York: Anchor/Doubleday.

Williams, J., Taylor, M. B., & Ganger, B. (1981). Text variations at the level of the individual sentence and the comprehension of simple expository paragraphs. *Journal of Educational Psychology, 73*, 851–865.

Willis, J., Stephens, E., & Matthew, K. (1996). *Technology, reading and language arts*. Boston: Allyn & Bacon.

Wilson, M. (1988). How can we teach reading in the content areas? In C. Weaver (Ed.), *Reading process and practice: From sociopsycholinguistics to whole language*. Portsmouth, NH: Heinemann.

Wilson, R. M., & Gambrell, L. B. (1988). *Reading comprehension in the elementary school*. Boston: Allyn & Bacon.

Window on the classroom: A look at teachers' tests (1984). *Captrends, 10*, 1–3.

Winograd, P. (1984). Strategic difficulties in summarizing texts. *Reading Research Quarterly, 19*, 404–425.

Winograd, P., & Paris, S. (1988). A cognitive and motivational agenda for reading instruction. *Educational Leadership, 46*, 30–36.

Wolfe, D., & Antinarella, J. (1997). *Deciding to lead: The English teacher as reformer*. Portsmouth, NH: Heinemann.

Wolfe, D., & Reising, R. (1983). *Writing for learning in the content areas*. Portland, ME: J. Weston Walch.

Wolfe, P., & Brandt, R. (1998). What do we know from brain research? *Educational Leadership, 56* (3), 8–13.

Wood, K. D. (1987). Fostering cooperative learning in middle and secondary level classrooms. *Journal of Reading, 31*, 10–18.

Wood, K. D. (1992). Fostering collaborative reading and writing experiences in mathematics. *Journal of Reading, 36*, 96–103.

Wood, K. D., Lapp, D., & Flood, J. (1992). *Guiding readers through text: A review of study guides*. Newark, DE: International Reading Association.

Woodward, A., Elliott, D. L., & Nagel, K. C. (1986). Beyond textbooks in elementary social studies. *Social Education, 50*, 50–53.

Woolf, V. (1967; c 1966). *Collected essays*. New York: Harcourt, Brace & World.

Worthen, B. (1993). Critical decisions that will determine the future of alternative assessment. *Phi Delta Kappan, 74*, 444–456.

Wray, D. (1994). Text and authorship. *The Reading Teacher 48* (1), 52–57.

The writing report card: Writing achievement in American schools. (1987). Princeton, NJ: National Assessment of Educational Progress and the Educational Testing Center.

Yeager, D. (1991). *The whole language companion*. Glenview, IL: Goodyear.

Yochum, N. (1991). Children's learning from informational text: The relationship between prior knowledge and text structure. *Journal of Reading Behavior, 23*, 87–108.

Young, T. A., & Daines, D. (1992). Student's predictive questions and teachers' prequestions about expository text in grades K-5. *Reading Psychology, 13* (4), 291–308.

Zakaluk, B., & Klassen, M. (1992). Enhancing the performance of a high school student labeled learning disabled. *Journal of Reading, 36*, 4–9.

Zaragoza, N. (1987). Process writing for high-risk learning disabled students. *Reading Research and Instruction, 26*, 290–301.

Zuber, B. L., & Wetzel, P. A. (1981). Eye movement determinants of reading rate. In B. L. Zuber (Ed.), *Models of oculomotor behavior and control* (pp. 193–208). Boca Raton, FL: CRC Press.

Activity Contributors

Special thanks to Mark A. Forget, who developed several activities and offered many suggestions for text improvements.

Dawn Watson and Walter Richards: PAR Diagram, p. 7.

Maureen Moynihan, Chesapeake, VA: Examples for Primary Language Arts and Social Studies, Activities 1.2 and 1.3, pp. 9 and 11.

Mark A. Forget, Yolanda Hightower Booth, and James J. DiNardo Jr.: Activity 1.4, p. 12.

Ann Woolford Singh: Activity 1.5 and 1.6, pp. 15 and 16.

Chris Birdsong White: Activity 2.5, p. 53.

Kelly Taylor: Activity 3.2, pp. 68–69.

Beth Pallister: Activity 3.5, p. 80.

Teachers at Norview High School, Norfolk, VA: Activity 3.6, pp. 82–83.

Marvette Darby: Activity 4.4, p. 114.

Stephen Rudlin: Activity 4.5, p. 116.

Sherry Gott: Activity 4.6, p. 117.

Kathy Feltus: Activity 4.7, p. 117; Activity 5.11, p. 147.

Mary L. Seward: Activity 4.11, p. 122.

Jeannette Rosenberg: Activity 5.1, p. 130.

Grace Hamlin: Prior Knowledge Telegram, p. 133.

Etta Malcolm: Activity 5.3, p. 138.

Kathryn Davis: Activity 5.5, p. 141; Activity 9.1, p. 293.

Laurie A. Schofield: Activity 5.6, p. 142.

Todd Barnes: Activity 5.7, p. 143.

Mark A. Forget: Activity 5.9, p. 145; Activity 6.7, p. 171; Activity 6.16, p. 183; Activity 9.2, p. 295; Activity 9.4, p. 299; Activity 9.16, p. 318.

Jacqueline T. McDonnough: Activity 6.3, p. 161.

Faye Freeman: Activity 6.4, p. 164.

Brian Alexander: Activity 6.5, p. 166.

Laura Clevinger: Activity 6.6, p. 170.

Vicki Douglas: Activity 6.8, p. 172.

Mendy Mathena: Activity 6.9, p. 173.

Candace Wyngaard: Activity 6.10, p. 174.

Serena Marshall: Activity 6.11, p. 175.

Heather Brown: Activity 6.12, p. 176.

Margaret Brulatour: Activity 6.14, p. 178.

Suzanna Hintz: Activity 6.18, p. 188.

Nancy S. Smith: Activity 6.19, p. 189.

Gail Perrer: Activity 7.4, p. 204.

Laura Allin: Activity 7.6, p. 207.

Sue Meador: Activity 7.7, p. 208.

Ronda Clancy: Activity 7.9, p. 212.

Scot M. Paterson: Activity 7.10, p. 213.

Diana Yesbeck: Activity 7.11, p. 214.

Mary Broussard: The Role of Pop Quizzes, p. 218.

Jane Baxter: Redesigning a Test, p. 220.

Charles Carroll: Activity 7.12, p. 219.

Bessie Haskins: Activity 7.13, p. 221; Activity 8.24, p. 278.

Sandra Zeller and Brenda Winston: Activity 7.15, p. 227.

Terry Bryce: Activity 8.2, p. 248.

Brian Littman: Activity 8.4, p. 251.

Tara Furges: Activity 8.5, p. 252.

Suzan McDaniel: Activity 8.8, p. 254.

Heather Hemstreet: Activity 8.10, p. 261; Activity 11.3, p. 377.

Wendy Barcroft: Activity 8.12, p. 264.

Laurie Smith: Activity 8.13, p. 265.

Jackie Meccariello and Rachel Curry: Activity 8.14, p. 266.

Kim Blowe: Activity 8.15, p. 267.

Colleen Kean: Activity 8.16, p. 270.

William Cathrell: Activity 8.17, p. 271.

Laurie Smith: Activity 8.20, p. 274.

Joe Antinarella: Activity 8.22, p. 276.

Mary Fagerland: Activity 8.23, p. 277.

Andrew Pettit: Figure 9.1, p. 288.

Dave N. Aznar: Activity 9.3, p. 298.

Chris Morgan: Activity 9.5, p. 300.

Jon Morgan: Activity 9.9, p. 307.

M. J. Weatherford: Activity 9.10, p. 308.

Terry Bryce: Activity 9.11, p. 308.

Anne Forrester: Activity 9.12, p. 309.

Sharon Gray: Activity 9.13, p. 309.

Frances Lively: Activity 9.14, p. 313.

Dianne Duncan: Activity 9.18, p. 320.

Polly Gilbert: Activity 9.19, p. 321.

Cornelia Hill: Activity 10.2, p. 332.

Roberto Lianez: Activity 10.4, p. 336.

Patricia Mays Mulherin: Activity 10.7, p. 352.

Brenda Hamilton: Activity 10.9, p. 357.

Jane Mitchell: Activity 11.1, p. 375.

Dana S. Jubilee: Activity 11.7, p. 385.

Cheryl Keeton: Activity 11.13, p. 392.

Shawn Nunnally: Activity 11.15, p. 395.

Jim McLeskey Jr.: Activity 11.16, p. 396.

Karen Curling: Activity 12.2, p. 417.

Beverly Marshall: Activity 12.4, p. 429.

Megan K. Houston: Activity 12.5, p. 430.

Author Index

Subject Index

PAR Cross-Reference Guide

GRADE LEVEL	SCIENCE	MATH
Primary	Activity 4.4, p. 114 Activity 5.5, p. 141 Activity 5.8, p. 144 Activity 8.13, p. 265 Activity 9.1, p. 293 Activity 11.7, p. 385 Activity 11.17, p. 398	Activity 6.17, p. 187 Activity 7.13, p. 221 Activity 8.24, p. 278 Activity 12.5, p. 430
Intermediate	Activity 4.8, p. 118 Activity 6.3, p. 161 Activity 6.9, p. 173 Activity 7.6, p. 207 Activity 7.16, p. 234 Activity 8.8, p. 254 Activity 10.3, p. 334 Activity 11.4, p. 380 Activity 11.9, p. 386	Activity 2.5, p. 53 Activity 3.4, p. 79 Activity 8.20, p. 274 Activity 12.1, p. 416 Activity 12.3, p. 427
Middle	Activity 5.6, p. 142 Activity 6.2, p. 161 Activity 8.9, p. 260 Activity 8.12, p. 264 Activity 8.15, p. 267 Activity 9.9, p. 307 Activity 10.5, p. 337	Activity 4.6, p. 117 Activity 5.1, p. 130 Activity 7.11, p. 214 Activity 8.23, p. 277 Activity 11.8, p. 385 Activity 12.4, p. 429
Secondary	Activity 4.3, p. 113 Activity 6.5, p. 166 Activity 6.19, p. 189 Activity 7.10, p. 213 Activity 9.5, p. 300 Activity 9.7, p. 303 Activity 9.13, p. 309 Activity 10.9, p. 357	Activity 4.9, p. 119 Activity 6.11, p. 175 Activity 6.15, p. 179 Activity 6.18, p. 188 Activity 7.3, p. 203 Activity 7.9, p. 212 Activity 9.2, p. 295 Activity 11.13, p. 392 Activity 11.12, p. 391 Activity 11.16, p. 396

GRADE LEVEL	SOCIAL STUDIES	ENGLISH/ LANGUAGE ARTS	OTHER
Primary	Activity 1.2, p. 9 Activity 1.3, p. 11 Activity 7.4, p. 204	Activity 1.2, p. 9 Activity 1.3, p. 11 Activity 3.2, p. 68 Activity 9.11, p. 308	**Health:** Activity 4.7, p. 117 **Study Skills:** Activity 10.2, p. 332
Intermediate	Activity 4.1, p. 111 Activity 6.8, p. 172 Activity 6.12, p. 176 Activity 7.7, p. 208 Activity 7.15, p. 227 Activity 7.17, p. 235 Activity 12.6, p. 432	Activity 8.2, p. 248 Activity 8.3, p. 250 Activity 8.16, p. 270 Activity 8.21, p. 275 Figure 9.1, p. 288 Activity 9.19, p. 321	**Health:** Activity 5.11, p. 147 **Music:** Activity 5.7, p. 143 **Physical Ed:** Activity 11.2, p. 376
Middle	Activity 6.4, p. 164 Activity 6.7, p. 171 Activity 7.12, p. 219 Activity 8.7, p. 253 Activity 9.10, p. 308 Activity 9.12, p. 309 Activity 10.7, p. 352	Activity 3.5, p. 80 Activity 6.10, p. 174 Activity 8.11, p. 262 Activity 8.22, p. 276 Activity 9.14, p. 313 Activity 9.18, p. 320	**Vocational Ed:** Activity 10.6, p. 342
Secondary	Activity 5.9, p. 145 Activity 8.1, p. 245 Activity 9.4, p. 299 Activity 9.16, p. 318 Activity 9.17, p. 319 Activity 10.4, p. 336 Activity 12.7, p. 433	Activity 3.3, p. 77 Activity 4.5, p. 116 Activity 5.3, p. 138 Activity 6.14, p. 178 Activity 7.18, p. 237 Activity 8.5, p. 252 Activity 9.3, p. 298 Activity 9.6, p. 300 Activity 11.1, p. 375 Activity 11.6, p. 384 Activity 11.15, p. 395 **Community College:** Activity 1.5, p. 15 Activity 1.6, p. 16 Activity 1.7, p. 17	**Art History:** Activity 10.8, p. 355 **Health:** Activity 1.4, p. 12 **Vocational Ed:** Activity 4.2, p. 112 Activity 5.4, p. 139 Activity 5.10, p. 146 Activity 6.13, p. 177 Activity 8.6, p. 253 Activity 11.10, p. 387 Activity 11.14, p. 393 **Computer Class:** Activity 4.11, p. 122 Activity 6.1, p. 159 **Foreign Language:** Activity 6.6, p. 170 Activity 8.4, p. 251 Activity 8.10, p. 261 Activity 8.17, p. 271 Activity 11.3, p. 377 **Cross-discipline:** Activity 3.1, p. 67; Activity 3.6, pp. 82–83 **Adult ESL:** Activity 12.2, p. 417